The Law of
Fraternities and Sororities

The Law of Fraternities and Sororities

Edited by

Gregory S. Parks
Professor of Law
Wake Forest University

CAROLINA ACADEMIC PRESS
Durham, North Carolina

Copyright © 2024
Gregory S. Parks
All Rights Reserved

LIBRARY OF CONGRESS CATALOGING-IN-PUBLICATION DATA

Names: Parks, Gregory, 1974- editor.
Title: The law of fraternities and sororities / edited by Gregory S. Parks.
Description: Durham, North Carolina : Carolina Academic Press, 2024. | Includes bibliographical references and index.
Identifiers: LCCN 2024002335 | ISBN 9781531026257 (paperback) | ISBN 9781531026264 (ebook)
Subjects: LCSH: Fraternal organizations--Law and legislation--United States. | Greek letter societies--United States--History.. | College students--Societies, etc.--History.
Classification: LCC KF289 .L39 2024 | DDC 344.73/079--dc23/eng/20240129
LC record available at https://lccn.loc.gov/2024002335

CAROLINA ACADEMIC PRESS
700 Kent Street
Durham, North Carolina 27701
(919) 489-7486
www.cap-press.com
Printed in the United States of America

Contents

Introduction ... xv

Contributing Authors ... xxi

PART ONE • GOVERNANCE ISSUES

CHAPTER 1 The Role of Fraternity and Sorority Legal Counsel
Gregory S. Parks ... 3

I. History of Organizational Counsel ... 4
II. Basic Models of Organizational Counsel ... 9
III. Distinctions ... 11
   a. Chief Legal Officer ... 12
   b. General Counsel ... 13
   c. Outside Counsel ... 13
IV. Strategic Thinking of the General Counsel ... 15
V. Legal Departments ... 18
   a. Structuring the Legal Department ... 19
   b. Compensation ... 21
   c. Legal Departments as Part of the Corporate Team ... 22
   d. Institutionalizing Compliance ... 22
VI. Ethics and Ethical Dilemmas ... 24
   a. First: Identification of the Client ... 25
   b. Second: When In-House Counsel Wear Too Many Hats ... 26
   c. Third: In-House Counsel's Independence, or Lack Thereof ... 27
   d. Fourth: Divergent Interests ... 28

VII.	Insurance Coverage	29
	a. An Alternative: Employed Lawyers Professional (ELP) Liability Insurance Coverage	31
VIII.	Broader Issues in the New Age of Corporate Counsel	32
IX.	Conclusion	35

CHAPTER 2 The Duty of Oversight and Director Liability
Michael R. Siebecker **37**

I.	The Fiduciary Framework for Nonprofit Directors	39
II.	The Duty of Oversight and the Business Judgment Rule	41
III.	The Yates Memo and Federal Enforcement of Corporate Criminality	45
IV.	The Incongruity Between Federal Law and State Common Law	48
V.	Implications for Oversight in Fraternal Organizations	49

CHAPTER 3 Fraternity and Sorority Governance *Alina Ball* **53**

I.	Governance Overview	53
II.	National Organization	54
III.	National Board of Directors	55
IV.	Housing Corporations	55
V.	Fraternity Foundation	56
VI.	Chapter Organization	56
VII.	National Governing Documents	57
VIII.	Interplay between National and Chapter Bylaws	60
IX.	Defining Roles and Responsibilities	62
X.	Voting Rights	63
XI.	Amendments	63
XII.	Conclusion	63

CHAPTER 4 Tax-Exempt Law: Internal Revenue Code §§501(c)(7), (3), (2), (4) *Jaclyn Cherry* **65**

I.	National and Local Chapters Organized as Section 501(c)(7) Organizations	67
II.	Taxation of Section 501(c)(7) Fraternal Organizations	70
	a. Set-Asides	71
	1. The "No Commingling" Test	72
	2. The "Negligible Possibility that the Funds Will Not Be Used for the Exempt Purpose" Test	72

b. Unrelated Business Income		74
c. Special Situation for Social Clubs		75
d. Regularly Carried On		78
e. Filing Requirements for Taxes Due		79
III. Charitable Contributions to Fraternal Organizations		80
IV. Fraternity Foundations		81
V. IRC Section 501(c)(2) Holding Company Organizations		85
VI. Property Tax Exemption		86
VII. Dormant Chapter Houses		88
VIII. IRC § 501(c)(4)		89
IX. State Law		90

CHAPTER 5 Formalizing Compliance to Reduce Board Exposure to Civil and Criminal Liability *Cheryl L. Wade* 93

I. Comparing Fiduciary Duties of For-Profit and Nonprofit Directors 96
II. Compliance 99
III. Derivative Litigation as a Mechanism for GLO Members to Influence Board Conduct 103
IV. Conclusion 110

PART TWO • RISK AND LIABILITY ISSUES

CHAPTER 6 The Mandatory Arbitration of Hazing Lawsuits *Etienne C. Toussaint* 113

I. The Rise of Hazing and Hazing-Related Lawsuits in Greek Life 117
II. Arbitration as an Alternative Dispute Resolution Mechanism 123
III. Unconscionability in Contract Law 128
IV. The Case of *Jean v. Bucknell* 133
V. When Arbitration Is Denied 141
VI. Conclusion: Lessons for Fraternities and Sororities 142

CHAPTER 7 Greek Organizations and Sexual Assault *Dara E. Purvis* 145

I. Sexual Assault at Universities 147
II. Sexual Assault and Title IX 149
III. Civil Lawsuits Against Fraternities 155

CONTENTS

CHAPTER 8   Social Host Liability   *Gregory S. Parks & Victoria Grieshammer*   169

   I. The Early Case Law   170
   II. Modern Case Law and Findings of Liability   179
   III. Modern Case Law and No Findings of Liability   184
   IV. Conclusion   193

CHAPTER 9   Liability Insurance Issues for Fraternal Organizations   *Maria C. O'Brien*   197

   I. Introduction to Fraternal Organization Insurance Liability Issues   197
   II. The Conventional Rules of Insurance Contract Interpretation   202
   III. Agency Theory—Actual Versus Apparent Authority and the Torts Lens   207
   IV. The Fraternal Organization Insurance Contract as a Tool of Social Policy—Moral Hazard   210
   V. Other Sources of Insurance Coverage—University Liability and Parents' Homeowners policies   214
      a. University/College Liability   214
      b. Homeowners' Liability   217
   VI. A Word on Criminal Liability   220
   VII. Conclusion   222

PART THREE · CONSTITUTIONAL ISSUES

CHAPTER 10   First Amendment Law: Freedom of Speech   *Glenn Harlan Reynolds*   227

   I. Some History   228
   II. The Rules   233
   III. Legal Actions over Free Speech   237
   IV. Some Specific Issues   239
      a. Prohibition of Wearing Greek Letters/Fraternity or Sorority Symbols   239
      b. Prohibition on Off-Campus Fraternity/Sorority Activities   240
      c. Depriving a Fraternity/Sorority Chapter of Due Process   240
      d. Future Legislation   241
   V. Beyond the Law   242

CHAPTER 11 The Fourth Amendment and Greeks on Campus:
Right of Privacy and Unreasonable Searches and Seizures
Aman McLeod   245

   I. The Fourth Amendment and University Student Housing   247
  II. The Fourth Amendment and Greek Housing: From
      In Loco Parentis to Full Protection   248
 III. The Fourth Amendment and Greek Housing: Important
      Fourth Amendment Doctrines   251
     a. Public/Private Actor Distinction   252
     b. Consent   252
     c. Exigent Circumstances   254
     d. Administrative Searches   255
 IV. Conclusion   258

CHAPTER 12 Equal Protection and Fraternal Organizations:
Potential Protections and Restraints *Jenny-Brooke Condon*   261

   I. Equal Protection Challenges to Differential Treatment of
     Fraternal Organizations   263
     a. Standard of Review   263
     b. Laws That Differentiate Between Fraternal Organizations
       and Other Groups   266
  II. University Decisions Denying Recognition to Fraternal
     Organizations   268
 III. Equal Protection and University Responses to Hazing   272
 IV. University Policies Requiring Nondiscrimination   274
     a. Deference to University Policy   274
     b. Harvard's Failed Effort to Eliminate Single-Sex
       Social Groups   278
  V. When Do the Activities of Fraternal Organizations
     Constitute State Action Implicating the Requirements
     of Equal Protection?   281
 VI. Conclusion   283

CHAPTER 13 Fair Housing Issues for Fraternities and
Sororities *Jade A. Craig*   285

   I. The Fair Housing Act in the Fraternity and Sorority House   288
     a. Fair Housing Act's Private Club Exemption   291
     b. Claims of Discrimination by Members Residing
       on Organization Houses   291

	c. Disability Rights	293
	1. Service Animals	294
	2. Emotional Support Animals	296
	3. Addressing Requests for Accommodations	297
	4. Conflicts Among Members Regarding Service/Assistance Animals	302
	5. Physical Access for Students with Disabilities	303
	d. LGBTQ+ Residents	306
	e. Risks of Discrimination in the Expulsion of Members	310
II.	Local Government Land Use Regulation	314
	a. Application of the Fair Housing Act	314
	b. Bias and Gender Stereotyping in the Regulation of Fraternity and Sorority Residences	315
III.	Housing Policy in Acquiring and Maintaining Organization Residences	319
	a. Hate Crimes Against Fraternity and Sorority Residences	319
	b. Disparities in Access to Greek Houses	323
	c. University Financing of Greek Residences	324
	d. The Private Real Estate Market for Greek Housing	327
IV.	Conclusion	329

PART FOUR · BROADER ISSUES

CHAPTER 14 Antitrust and Consumer Protection Law
Susan Navarro Smelcer — 333

I.	Introduction	333
II.	Antitrust Law and the University	335
III.	Fraternities' Use of Antitrust Claims Against Universities	345
IV.	Overview of Consumer Protection and Unfair Trade Practices Laws	352
	a. Limiting "Unfair" and "Deceptive" Practices Under FTC Act, Section 5	353
	b. Limiting "Unfair" and "Deceptive" Practices Under State UDAP Laws	357
V.	Recent Attempts by Fraternal Organizations to Allege Violations of State Consumer Protection and UTP Laws	359
VI.	Conclusion	365

CHAPTER 15	**Employment Law Issues for Fraternities and Sororities** *Ann C. Juliano*	**367**
I.	The Basics	368
	a. Employment at Will	368
	b. Definition of Employee	368
II.	Overview of Federal Antidiscrimination Laws	371
	a. Immigration	371
	b. Discrimination	371
III.	Terms and Conditions of Employment	376
	a. Wages and Hours	377
	b. Workplace Safety	377
	c. Worker's Compensation	378
	d. Unemployment Compensation	378
IV.	A Few Thoughts on Other State Law Issues	379
V.	Fraternal-Organization-Specific Issues	380
	a. Hiring High-Level Employees	380
	b. Wage and Hour Issues	382
	c. Worker's Compensation	384
	d. Terminating the Employment Relationship	385
	e. Employment Issues and COVID-19	386
VI.	Conclusion	387

CHAPTER 16	**Intellectual Property Rights** *Ashley R. Dobbs*	**389**
I.	Introduction to Intellectual Property	390
	a. Patent	390
	1. Limitations to Patents	392
	b. Trade Secret	392
	1. Definitions	392
	2. Acquiring Rights	393
	3. Examples	393
	c. Copyright	395
	1. Definitions	395
	2. What Is NOT Protected by Copyright?	395
	3. Acquiring Rights	396
	4. Benefits of Federal Registration	397
	5. Examples	398
	d. Right of Publicity/Right of Privacy	399
	e. Trademark	399

II. Trademarks—Common Law and Federal Law	400
a. US Trademark Rights Are Initially Acquired Under Common Law by the First to Use the Mark in Commerce	401
1. Use Can Be Through Authorized Licenses	402
b. A Mark Must Be **Both** Distinctive and Not Likely to Cause Confusion with Other Marks in the Marketplace	403
1. Distinctiveness	403
2. No Likelihood of Confusion with an Existing Mark Used with Similar Goods/Services	405
c. Federal Law Expands upon These Rights	408
1. Expanded Geographic Rights to the Entire US (and Territories)	408
2. Collective Marks	408
3. Intent to Use Applications	409
4. "Famous" Marks—Expansive Protection but High Bar to Prove	410
i. Expanded Protection	410
ii. Pleading and Evidentiary Requirements	410
d. Benefits and Limits of Federal Trademark Registration	412
e. USPTO Application Process	413
1. Use-Based and Intent-to-Use Applications	413
2. Evidence of Use	414
3. International Classes and Filing Fees	414
4. Substantive Review	415
5. Reconsideration/Appeal	415
6. Impact of Final Rejection	415
f. Trademark Licensing	416
III. Best Practices for Fraternal Organizations—Trademark	418
a. Trademark Registration and Maintenance	419
b. Control and Enforcement of Rights Required	420
1. Collective Membership—Internal Controls	421
i. Limitations of This Approach	423
ii. Best Practices Checklist	424
2. Third Party Licensing—Internal and External Controls	425
3. Licensing Internal Controls—Best Practices Checklist	426
4. Licensing—External Controls—Best Practices Checklist	427

IV.	Avoiding IP Liability by Members and Chapters	429
	a. Trademark Infringement of Third Parties	429
	1. Trademark Infringement Defined	429
	2. Burden of Proof	430
	3. Defenses	430
	4. Application to Fraternal Organizations	433
	5. Best Practices	434
	b. Copyright Infringement of Third Parties	435
	1. Copyright Infringement Defined	435
	2. Burden of Proof	435
	3. Defenses	436
	4. Best Practices	437
V.	Conclusion	437

CHAPTER 17 Property and Zoning Law *Shelley Ross Saxer* 439

I.	Zoning	440
	a. Single-Family Residential	440
	b. Historic Landmarks and Districts	443
	c. Institutional Zoning	444
	d. Variances and Special-Use Permits	447
	e. Nonconforming Uses	455
	f. Eminent Domain and Takings	458
	g. State Preemption	460
II.	Neighbors and Private Land-Use Controls	461
	a. Restrictive Covenants	461
	b. Nuisance	462
	c. Other Neighborhood Challenges	463
III.	Property Issues Within the Fraternal Organization and the College or University	464
IV.	Conclusion	467

Index   469

Introduction

In my 2011 co-edited book, *Black Greek-Letter Organizations 2.0: New Directions in the Study of African American Fraternities and Sororities*, Craig Torbenson offered an excellent overview of the early history of collegiate Greek-letter fraternities and sororities. He highlighted that college fraternities and sororities were made to meet the intellectual and social needs of students. The early American attempts to replicate physical and social features of English college provided the framework for student college life in US colleges. Due to the dispersed population in the colonies, the education system was both diffused and decentralized. Using memorization and recitation as methods of classroom learning, courses were taken by all, allowing for little flexibility in curriculum. Colonial colleges also modeled the English system by dividing the student body into classes, which formed as the first form of student associations, as each class designation had its own rituals, customs, clothes, and social activities. However, within the early collegiate world, the individual student had little freedom, as there were consistent tensions between faculty and students. Students aimed to take control of their own college life through the establishment of organizations, clubs, and eventual sororities and fraternities.

The earliest British North American student organization on record was established in 1703 at Harvard. While this organization was rooted in religious context, by 1719 several more secular organizations had been established. Student organizations often emerged out of a few individuals' thoughts and interests. By 1760, literary societies became the paramount form of student organization, providing students with the intellectual opportunity and spirit often lacking in the recitation structure of the classroom. The competition for entry, along with the resources of these literary societies resulted in its membership and activities often taking priority over the college curriculum.

The decline of literary societies is closely associated with the rise of fraternities and sororities. A given fraternity or sorority was created by a few individuals sharing similar ideals, with goals of prompting brotherhood or sisterhood. Fraternities and sororities shared similar characteristics as literary societies, with initiation rites, pins, and mottos. However, while literary societies filled an intellectual vacuum, the fraternity system was social, providing an escape from class work and training.

Phi Beta Kappa was the first prototype of a college fraternity, established at William and Mary College in 1776, functioning originally as a literary society. However, this organization departed from the norm by also providing an avenue for social activities. Phi Beta Kappa first spread through Southern states, establishing chapters at around twenty colleges. Though the records from this time have been lost, it is known that communication among early chapters was infrequent, meaning each chapter developed as an autonomous unit with its own traditions and practices. The next recorded appearance of Greek-letter organizations occurred in 1812 at University of North Carolina, with the establishment of Kappa Alpha. With further expansion, by the late 1820s, the fraternity movement had been fully established.

The origins of sororities are associated with coeducational colleges of the Midwest and South, as an imitation of the established men's fraternities. The first women's organizations were established at Wesleyan in 1851, with these secret literary societies remaining local organizations until the early 1900s. The first sorority was established in 1874 at Syracuse, as the term sorority became more frequently used to specify female fraternities.

Fraternities and sororities initially expanded in several ways, including via personal contact and recruitment over summer vacations. An additional process involved local organizations building up their qualifications, soliciting from well-established organizations, and applying for membership in a national fraternity or sorority. The modern method of expansion is called colonization. Colonization entails a national organization identifying a college and determining that it wishes to establish a chapter, then sending representatives to recruit members.

Fraternities expanded during the 1800s. However, their growth was periodic and interspersed between inactive periods. Growth was stagnated during such inactive periods because the fraternity system was greatly affected by a host of factors. Some factors included the Civil War and faculty opposition. It also included anti-fraternity state regulations stemming from populist attacks on their perceived exclusive, undemocratic, and unsavory behavior.

A great expansion of fraternities and sororities was then seen from 1900 to 1930. Growth was not only spurred by the economic prosperity of the 1920s, which resulted in increased college enrollment, but also by sororities and fraternities filling the housing vacuum left by discontinued student dormitories on college campuses. Amid this growth, umbrella organizations, including the National Interfraternity Conference, National Panhellenic Conference, and eventual National Panhellenic Council, were formed by 1929.

The 1930s showed a continued spread of organizations, yet the establishment of new organizations slowed. The Great Depression of the 1930s, World War II in the 1940s, and anti-fraternity legislation in the 1950s saw many national organizations becoming defunct, merging with other organizations, or going inactive. Ultimately, this process of consolidation was likely healthy for these organizations as a social institution, as the number of total fraternities and sororities had become otherwise unwieldy.

From the 1960s onward, the Greek system continued to grow. The 1970s showed more than 2000 new chapters established at 545 schools, predominantly in the South. Despite the internal problems which plagued the institutions in the 1980s—including sexual abuse, hazing, and racism charges—fraternity and sorority membership reached an all-time high by the 1990s. By 2000, the proliferation of new organizations and chapters throughout the country changed the fraternity landscape, with a variety of other organizations, such as Latino, multicultural, religious, black, and LGBTQ, providing other organization options as well.

The overall growth of fraternities and sororities is reflected by the composition of the student body throughout time. By 1928, more than half of the national fraternities had membership exclusivity based on rules or religion, resulting in non-secret and nonsectarian fraternities being organized to counter these ideals. Many college students believed actual brotherhood was best enacted through integrating different religious and races, resulting in the eventual formation of interracial fraternities. Similarly, as enrollments of students from different backgrounds increased, many of these individuals banded together to form a fraternity. The establishment of the first black fraternity did not occur until 1906, at Cornell; however, the emergence of these organizations largely occurred at Howard University between 1908 and 1920. This process of proliferation of organizations based on specific religions, races, and nationalities allowed fraternities to include all types of students, expanding to new campuses in the process.

Despite the prevalence of collegiate Greek-letter fraternities and sororities, research into the law as it relates to them is limited. In fact, there has never been a comprehensive work on the role of fraternity and sorority law. However, research into the broader organizational field has developed, giving rise to the 1970s theory of the organizational internalization of the law.

The internalization of the law theory posits the notion that large bureaucratic organizations have increasingly internalized necessary components of the legal system. As detailed by Lauren Edelman and Mark Suchman in their 1999 article, "When the Haves Hold Court: Speculations on the Organizational Internalization of Law," in *Law and Society Review*, internalization has likely occurred in four ways: legal rulemaking has internalized through the "'legalization'" of individual firms and or larger organizational fields, legal dispute processing through the increasing employment of alternative dispute resolution, legal expertise through the growing importance and changing role of inside counsel, and legal enforcement through the reemergence of private organizational security staff.

These internalizations are significant because they could allow organizations to "hold court" by blending many of the public legal system's roles. Internalized adjudication may additionally bestow advantages upon organizations. For example, the organization is usually benefited by turning organizational decisionmakers into private law makers, by enabling organizations to manage a larger range of problems through informal dispute resolution rather than through traditional litigation, and by expanding the role of private security within organizations while simultaneously reducing public accountability. On the other hand, a drawback of internalized adjudication is that organizations continue to have bureaucratic hierarchical structures and mixed motivations, which can result in bias, and can possibly be forced to turn to outside forums of the public legal system if the internal system is deemed unsuccessful or illegitimate.

The advantages arising out of organizational internalization of the law become exaggerated under the light of Marc Galanter's "repeat player" theory. In his 1974 article, "Why the 'Haves' Come Out Ahead: Speculations on the Limits of Legal Change," in *Law and Society Review*, Galanter details the differences between litigants who go to court once versus those that are "repeat players." He argues that "repeat players" have multiple advantages within the legal system, such as the initial knowledge and the ability to plan transactions, continuous access to specialists as well as reduced startup costs, and relationships with institutional members. Galanter's argument highlights that repeat litigants enjoy such advantages that they are able to significantly obstruct one-time litigants from attaining social reforms through alternatives to the legal system.

The internalization of law may be changing large organizations from "well-endowed players in the legal game (Galanter's repeat players) to being nothing less than the playing field itself." This trend of internalization of the law has had a great impact on the legal landscape as a whole. Internalization has allowed organizations to simultaneously become legislators, judges, counsels, and cops. These roles allow organizations to control and change external rules. Galanter's "repeat players" experienced benefits in gaining legal representation, promoting rule changes, and influencing courts, while, more recently, large bureaucratic organizations assume the roles throughout the entire legal process. To internalize law, however, organizations likely must alter their own structures. Instead of viewing this trend as replacing the public legal system, it can be viewed as bringing components of the public process into the decision-making of businesses in the private realm.

By combining the legislator, judge, counsel, and cop roles, the internalization of law has given organizations greater control and power than in previous years. The question is thus raised: what could the internalization of the law look like in collegiate Greek-letter fraternities and sororities? This book seeks to offer an overview of the legal landscape of the critical issues that collegiate Greek-letter fraternities and sororities should understand and integrate into their day-to-day work. In the first section of the book, we explore the range of issues that deal with processes, standards, rules, and practices that fraternities and sororities must follow. Among the governance issues we explore are the role of organizational legal counsel (Chapter 1); the duty of oversight and director liability (Chapter 2); the role of organizational governing documents (Chapter 3); the strictures around Internal Revenue Code 501(c)(2), (3), (4), and (7) entities (Chapter 4); and board conduct that may give rise to organizational civil and criminal liability (Chapter 5). In the second section, we explore risk and liability issues such as arbitration in hazing cases (Chapter 6), sexual assault (Chapter 7), social host liability (Chapter 8), and liability insurance (Chapter 9). In the third section, we explore United States Constitutional issues like freedom of speech (Chapter 10), right to privacy and unreasonable searches and seizures (Chapter 11), equal protection law (Chapter 12), and fair housing (Chapter 13). In the final section, we explore broader issues like antitrust and consumer protection (Chapter 14), employment law (Chapter 15), intellectual property (Chapter 16), and property and zoning issues (Chapter 17).

In conclusion, thank you to my colleagues at Wake Forest University School of Law for supporting this project. Also, thank you to Ronald Stovall—a past Regional Vice President on the Board of Directors of our fraternity, Alpha Phi Alpha Fraternity, Incorporated—for letting me serve as an Associate Legal Counsel under his leadership. It gave me a more practical perspective on many of the issues covered in this book. Thank you to Sean Callan and John Christopher at Fraternal Law Partners for providing feedback and critique on many of the chapters in this book. They were critical in helping guide the research of the contributing authors—leaders in their areas of scholarship but who, mostly, had never studied fraternities and sororities. I also thank my Wake Forest University School of Law colleagues—Wilson Parker, Keith Robinson, Audra Savage, and Steve Virgil—for offering their critical eyes and feedback on chapters. Also, thank you to the judge I clerked for on the United States Court of Appeals, Andre M. Davis, for sharing his critiques on one chapter. Lastly, but most importantly, thank you to my research assistants—Tamara Allen, Clare Magee, Samantha Mondello, Victoria Riddle, and Lane Wilson-Powell—for their tremendous copy-editing and Bluebooking work.

Contributing Authors

Alina Ball	Professor of Law, University of California College of the Law, San Francisco
Jaclyn Cherry	Professor of Law, University of South Carolina School of Law
Jenny-Brooke Condon	Professor of Law, Seton Hall University School of Law
Jade A. Craig	Assistant Professor of Law, Nova Southeastern University Shepard Broad College of Law
Ashley R. Dobbs	Professor of Law, Legal Practice and Director, Intellectual Property and Transactional Law Clinic, University of Richmond School of Law
Victoria Grieshammer	Associate Attorney, Shaw Bransford & Roth
Ann C. Juliano	Professor of Law, Villanova University School of Law
Aman McLeod	Associate Professor of Law, University of Detroit Mercy School of Law
Stephen Miller	Professor of Law, University of Idaho College of Law

Maria O'Brien	Professor of Law, Boston University School of Law
Gregory S. Parks	Professor of Law, Wake Forest University School of Law
Dara E. Purvis	Professor of Law, Temple University Beasley School of Law
Glenn Harlan Reynolds	Professor of Law, University of Tennessee School of Law
Shelley Ross Saxer	Laure Sudreau Chair in Law, Professor of Law, Pepperdine University Caruso School of Law
Michael R. Siebecker	Maxine Kurtz Faculty Research Scholar and Professor of Law
Susan Navorro Smelcer	Assistant Professor of Law, Georgia State University College of Law
Etienne C. Toussaint	Assistant Professor of Law, University of South Carolina School of Law
Cheryl L. Wade	Harold F. McNiece Professor of Law, St. John's University School of Law

PART ONE:
GOVERNANCE ISSUES

CHAPTER 1

The Role of Fraternity and Sorority Legal Counsel

Gregory S. Parks

The topic of fraternity and sorority inside counsel is one that has never been explored. This chapter takes an initial look at the topic by way of the role of inside counsel in corporate settings. Inside counsel to major corporations have had to constantly alter their roles and priorities to successfully position the legal departments within the greater organizations. In recent years, inside counsel have gained more power and status compared to attorneys in outside firms. They make more decisions than in the past, and they are generally the first lawyers to examine potential legal issues.[1] The evolution has had a significant impact on the roles that inside counsel have within corporations.[2] Ultimately, legal officers play, or should play, a central role in the corporate governance of companies where they work. However, to do so, they must grapple with a range of challenges and dynamics.

---

1. Robert L. Nelson & Laura Beth Nielsen, *Cops, Counsel, or Entrepreneurs: The Shifting Role of Lawyers in Large Business Corporations*, in THE LEGAL LIVES OF PRIVATE ORGANIZATIONS, 394-30, 394 (Lauren B. Edelman & Mark C. Suchman eds., 2000) (discussing the roles of inside counsel in large corporations).
2. *Id.* at 423.

I. History of Organizational Counsel

During the last 30 years, the stardom of corporate general counsel has risen.[3] Taking a position as general counsel of a corporation was once considered a respectable exit strategy for lawyers who had been passed over for partnership.[4] Today, the office attracts well-known partners from elite corporate law firms, typically carries a senior title within the corporate hierarchy, and is associated with significant prestige within the legal profession.[5] This "Inside Counsel Movement" means that in-house counsel are now "the dominant providers of legal services to corporate America."[6]

In the last 20 years, demands on general counsel have increased and shifted focus.[7] After the Organizational Sentencing Guidelines were enacted in 1991, corporations were incentivized to attach greater import to compliance functions such as promulgating codes of behavior, instituting training programs, and creating company-wide compliance controls and procedures.[8]

In some ways, the present authority of in-house counsel reflects their status in the 1930s.[9] After the Civil War, judges were lured from federal and state courts to serve as general counsel to railroads.[10] Then, during the 1920s and '30s, corporate counsel became an even more esteemed position. They were both business and legal advisors, highly regarded by senior management for their wisdom.[11] Lawyers comprised 75% of the CEOs of major companies in this era, compared to 5% today.[12] Corporate counsel often arranged solutions to financing challenges that con-

---

3. Tanina Rostain, *General Counsel in the Age of Compliance: ...*, 21 GEO. J. LEGAL ETHICS 465, 465 (2008).

4. *Id.*

5. *Id.*

6. Pam Jenoff, *Going Native: Incentive, Identity, and the Inherent Ethical Problem of In-House Counsel*, 114 W. VA. L. REV. 725, 730 (2012).

7. Rostain, *supra* note 3, at 466.

8. *Id.* at 467.

9. Deborah DeMott, *The Discrete Roles of General Counsel*, FORDHAM L. REV. 955, 958 (2005).

10. *Id.* at 958–59.

11. *Id.* at 958.

12. Carl D. Liggio, Sr., *A Look at the Role of Corporate Counsel: Back to the Future—Or Is It the Past?*, 44 ARIZ. L. REV. 621, 621 (2002).

fronted businesses in this era of smaller, less developed capital markets.[13] Attorneys in these roles were highly sought after by corporate management and paid 65% of CEO salaries on average.[14]

In the 1940s, there was a decline in esteem due to the rise of business school "wunderkinds" that led to different hiring practices and compensation structures.[15] The general counsel's role became one of a "relatively minor management figure, stereotypically, a lawyer from the corporation's principal outside law firm who had not quite made the grade as partner."[16] General counsel were limited to handling routine corporate housekeeping and serving as liaisons between management and private law firms.[17] Corporate counsel's average salary fell to 30% of the CEO's. The most skilled lawyers were incentivized to turn down corporate counsel roles in favor of private law firms.[18] In the 1950s and '60s, only four government agencies existed that could pose a credible challenge to global financial institutions—the Federal Trade Commission, the Department of Justice, the Internal Revenue Service, and the Securities and Exchange Commission.[19] Corporations simply could not justify the expense of maintaining a full legal department when regulatory and legal issues could typically be avoided through good business practices.[20]

The power shifted away from private law firms and toward the corporate sector again in the 1960s and '70s, and the number of in-house corporate lawyers increased dramatically.[21] The late 1960s saw a significant rise in the regulation of business and thus in the corporate demand for legal services. Class actions, derivative shareholder suits, products liability, and discrimination suits also grew in the '60s, requiring legal departments to adopt more proactive policies and aggressive litigation defense.[22] Numerous federal agencies came into existence in the '70s,

---

13. DeMott, *supra* note 9, at 958.
14. *Id.*
15. *Id.*
16. *Id.* at 959.
17. *Id.*
18. Carl D. Liggio, *The Changing Role of Corporate Counsel.* Emory L.J. 1201 (1997).
19. John B. McNeece IV, *The Ethical Conflicts of the Hybrid General Counsel and Chief Compliance Officer*, 25 GEO. J. LEGAL ETHICS 677, 679 (2012).
20. *Id.* at 679.
21. DeMott, *supra* note 9, at 960.
22. McNeece, *supra* note 19, at 680.

creating more work for general counsel to help corporations avoid the penalties that could be imposed and the increasing number of enforcers of those penalties.[23] The increased regulation led corporations to use both in-house lawyers and outside counsel as on-call legal experts of the company's business, but they often relied more on outside law firms for important services for several reasons.

First, corporate managers lacked sophisticated information concerning the types of legal services the firm needed and discernment about the quality of advice it was receiving. In-house lawyers could not fully analyze the capabilities of all the available lawyers and monitor their performance over time. Companies could, however, trust large law firms to render this service.[24] Second, big law firms were able to acquire significant knowledge about the client's business, which was a requirement to deal with the complexity of regulation.[25] As a result, the general counsel (GC) role was perceived as a pre-retirement or secondary track for attorneys, acting only as a liaison between the corporation and an elite law firm. The prestige of the GC reached its lowest point in the 1970s. Very few companies had internal legal departments, and the organized bar made no effort to accommodate corporate counsel.[26]

Since the late '70s, there has been a resurgence of in-house corporate counsel due to *increased volume of lawsuits* (corporations began to use lawsuits against each other as regular business practice in the '60s and '70s), *greater government regulation* (beyond just the SEC, IRS, FTC, and DOJ to include the "alphabet soup" agencies, Title VII, ADA, environmental regulations, etc.), and *skyrocketing cost of outside legal services* (salaries in the legal profession grew substantially, and many corporations felt they were being overcharged).[27] More attorneys became corporate counsel, and recruiting was more often conducted through raids of other corporate counsels than from private firms. As a result of these

---

23. *Id.*

24. Larry E. Ribstein, *Delawyering the Corporation*, 2012 Wis. L. Rev. 305, 309 (2012).

25. *Id.*

26. Liggio, *supra* note 18, at 622–23.

27. Mary C. Daly, *The Cultural, Ethical, and Legal Challenges in Lawyering for a Global Organization: The Role of the General Counsel*, 46 Emory L.J. 1057, 1060 (1997).

and other factors, there was a 40% increase in the number of in-house lawyers between 1970 and 1980.[28]

In the 1980s, in-house counsel became significant players in provision of legal services,[29] leading to an additional 33% increase in in-house lawyers between 1980 and 1991.[30] Corporate legal departments grew significantly in size and general counsel became responsible for several foundational functions including (1) managing and reviewing the legal services provided to corporate clients by outside counsel, (2) supplying routine legal services (and occasionally handling transactions and litigation), (3) counseling clients on regulatory requirements, and (4) creating compliance programs.[31]

As the popularity of corporate counsel revivified, the death of Big Law was expedited by the erosion of firm-building incentives. Vicarious liability became untenable when law firms became subject to regulatory liabilities in the late 1980s. The demand for legal expertise increased the demand for standout lawyers. However, this forced firms to hire more associates per partner, abandoning the "out" part of the up-out associate promotion ladder in the company. This made it harder for firms to deliver on their promise to screen, mentor, and monitor associates, which, in turn, caused Big Law's reputational "bond" to decline. It forced clients to find other ways to close the gap in information between themselves and their lawyers. Furthermore, rising legal fees, global competition, and financial restructuring motivated corporate clients to build up their in-house legal departments.[32]

Additionally, lawyers would be judged in the corporate culture on their merits and abilities rather than their "rainmaker" status in Big Law.[33] This work style and culture attracted women and minorities, who may have been rainmakers but whose lifestyles or interests did not fit with Big Law, to seek in-house positions.[34] This started a trend that continues today. Significantly, the number of women who hold senior legal officer positions in-house is decidedly greater than the number of

---

28. *Id.* at 1059.
29. Rostain, *supra* note 3, at 470.
30. Daly, *supra* note 27, at 1059.
31. *Id.*
32. *Id.*
33. Liggio, *supra* note 18, at 628.
34. Liggio, *supra* note 18, at 628.

women who hold comparable roles in law firms.[35] According to an American Corporate Counsel Association (ACCA) study of the corporate legal profession, 20% of chief legal officers, 20% of deputy general counsel, and 30% of assistant general counsel are women.[36]

From the late '90s onward, increasing dominance of employed counsel was predicted, despite retained private counsel's efforts to remain competitive (through price competition and alternative billing). Private firms were still being employed by smaller corporations, but there was less of this work, and it was mostly transactional.[37] Today, in-house counsel have a distinct professional identity as legal service providers, enjoying substantial stature and responsibility within the organization.[38] Formal roles include providing legal advice to corporate officers and members of the board, representing the organization before judiciary and regulatory bodies, serving as an educator of corporate constituents regarding legal rules, performing deal-maker functions in transactions, and acting as a powerful intermediary between law firms and executive leadership.[39] Informal roles include compliance monitoring, ethics education and promotion, managing the legal department, participating in strategic planning, and planning for and managing crises.[40]

Finally, the historical evolution and development of in-house counsel authority can notably be seen in the birth of the ACCA, which has grown to approximately 10,000 members since it was founded in 1982.[41] Importantly, the growth of the ACCA is a symbolic legitimization of in-house lawyering as a viable career option.[42]

---

35. Id.

36. Id.

37. Id.

38. Robert C. Bird & Stephen Kim Park, *The Domains of Corporate Counsel in an Era of Compliance*, 53 AM. BUS. L.J. 203, 209 (2016).

39. Id.

40. Id.

41. Jenoff, *supra* note 6.

42. Daly, *supra* note 27, at 1063.

II. Basic Models of Organizational Counsel

There are several models for an in-house legal department, which are described by one expert as follows:

> In most cases, their authority was formalized in the reporting relations of their organizations: The large majority of respondents reported directly to the Chief Executive Officer or Chair of the Board. Even in the minority of instances when General Counsel reported directly to the Chief Financial Officer, they insisted that they had easy access to the highest officials of the company and often brought disagreements with their direct superiors to them. The GC's occupied positions of power within the managerial hierarchy and were expected to play a significant role in monitoring compliance within the organization. Formal reporting lines, however, did not define the parameters of their authority. The majority of GC's, who reported to the CEO or Chair, used their direct access as a venue to raise issues of concern. Those who did not report directly to the CEO or Chair insisted that informality at the top levels of their companies facilitated communication with the CEO and Board on such matters.[43]

In a "Full-Service Organization," the legal department is extensively involved with every aspect of the corporation, including litigation.[44] In an "Integrated Corporate Law Department," the legal department provides in-house services to the corporation that outside counsel cannot but serves merely as a liaison between the firm and outside counsel when outside counsel is needed.[45] Under "The Monitor" model, the law department plays a monitoring and liaison role between the corporation and outside counsel.[46] Finally, in the "Traffic Officer" model, the legal department directs work to outside counsel and pays the bills when they come in, a currently much less prevalent model than in the 1970s.[47]

---

43. Rostain, *supra* note 3, at 473.
44. Liggio, Sr., *supra* note 12, at 629.
45. *Id.*
46. *Id.* at 630.
47. *Id.*

General counsel's role as legal advisor can put them at odds with its role in promoting compliance. Their unique position in the corporate structure also means that they may be excluded from important informational loops within the corporation, such as in the case of *Smith v. Van Gorkom,* when the CEO/chairman pushed through a merger without ever informing the existing general counsel.[48]

As a corporate officer and member of senior management team, the general counsel is typically appointed to an office by the board of directors but reports directly to the CEO. They are responsible for many non-legal functions, including in HR, corporate secretarial, and governmental affairs. General counsel may find themselves being asked to give fiduciary advice in this role as well. As one general counsel stated, "I think that weaving the concepts behind an officer's fiduciary duty into regular work conversations (even if not explicitly referred to as a 'fiduciary duty') can be easily and gently accomplished and is a good reminder."[49] This reflection on their fiduciary responsibilities as a corporate officer and member of the senior management team "may sensitize them to the importance of advising other officers about their duties."[50]

General counsel also engage in corporate strategy along with the other senior management. General counsel are essential in "implementing major strategic and operational objectives" to form a competitive advantage.[51] Additionally, the general counsel is the top administrator of the corporation's internal legal department, responsible for managing the department's budget, setting policies for the department, and hiring and supervising the lawyers within it. General counsel must choose the size of hierarchy—the number of reporting levels with different compensation structures—within the department, as well as its degree of centralization.

As an agent of the corporation in dealings with third parties, the general counsel represents the corporation in dealings both with junior members of the department and with those outside of the corporation. As a board member, it is recommended that the GC report to the CEO

---

48. DeMott, *supra* note 9.

49. Lyman Johnson & Dennis Garvis, *Are Corporate Officers Advised About Fiduciary Duties?*, 64 BUS. LAW. 1105, 1119 (2009).

50. *Id.* at 1120.

51. Ben W. Heineman, Jr., *Resolving the Partner-Guardian Tension: The Key to General Counsel Independence*, 42 DEL. J. CORP. L. 149 (2017).

and the board to ensure that the GC can go over the CEO's head if needed, so it is important for the GC to have a relationship with the board and the chair. Additionally, the GC is the "guardian" who implements protective measures to maintain the business integrity and manage their risks.[52] The GC's reputation outside of the company will further their ability to function as a good partner-guardian within the cooperation.[53]

Ultimately, there are numerous options for the organizational structures of both the general counsel's office and the counsel's office in relation to the greater company.

III. Distinctions

Due to their unique "positioning" in the client-company entity, in-house counsel face extreme pressures that require them to choose between the professional rules meant to guide their practices and the very separate and different practical requirements of their work. In-house counsel have a large roster of constituents (hundreds, thousands), but in-house counsel seem to be more aware of their need for independence and use this independence. Most outside counsel are illustrated by their belief that they are "owned" by none and are more intent on securing their paycheck than examining and judging the potential misuse of what they have been retained to do. In-house counsel work in an ambiguously defined environment, employed by one company, but with many clients. Their client is an entity, and they are obligated to serve the entity's best interests as an organizational client.

In-house counsel must provide whatever services their clients need, while most outside counsel can easily define the parameters of their practice. In-house counsel are seen as generalists, often assembling and retaining the talent needed to address a legal matter under the guise that they rarely supervise them, and they are increasingly likely to retain a team of talent that is not made up of lawyers who carry their own professional responsibility. Moreover, distinctions exist between the chief legal officer, general counsel, corporate counsel, and in-house counsel.

---

52. Id.
53. Id.

a. Chief Legal Officer

The chief legal officer (CLO) does and should have a significant role over corporate governance and the culture of integrity and is necessary for the effectiveness of compliance.[54] The CLO in the general counsel analyzes the "ethical, legal, policy, political, and risk considerations" for each business strategy and decision.[55] Additionally, since the economic crisis of 2008–2011, the CLO faces new challenges, spurred by several changes in legislation.[56]

The CEO usually hires the CLO, who is a part of the senior management team and should work closely with the CEO and CFO on advising business decisions, as the CLO serves as the main legal advisor. The general counsel must maintain the integrity of the company.[57] The Sarbanes-Oxley (SOX) Act in 2002 changed the role and power of the directors, the catalyst for the new reality which the CLO must recognize. The SOX Act required that certain internal financial controls be instituted in companies that are publicly traded, in addition to establishing compliance practices and whistleblower provisions.[58] This was followed by the Dodd-Frank Act in 2010, which further heightened standards and requirements of corporations.[59] The Dodd-Frank Act altered corporate regulation and therefore changed corporate governance and the roles of each member of the company.

The CLO is in charge of managing the legal department. The CLO must ensure that there are adequate staff (lawyers, paralegals, and assistants) and technology. In addition, the company's legal budget should have funding for outside counsel.[60] The lawyers of the outside counsel should report to the general counsel, and the general counsel must defend those lawyers. Some companies assign lawyers to different business groups so that they are available when needed.

---

54. Bird & Park, *supra* note 39.

55. E. Norman Veasey & Christine T. Di Guglielmo, *Indispensable Counsel: The Chief Legal Officer in the New Reality* 25 (2012).

56. E. Norman Veasey & Christine T. Di Guglielmo, *The Tensions, Stresses, and Professional Responsibilities of the Lawyer for the Corporation*, 62 Bus. Law. 1, 1 (2006).

57. *Id.* at 3–4.

58. Bryan E. Hopkins, Legal Risk Management For In-House Counsel And Managers. 7 (2014).

59. *Id.* at 14–15.

60. *Id.* at 159.

b. General Counsel

The general counsel, led by the CLO, is responsible for "ensuring compliance with regulations and maintaining an ethical culture," two roles that are fiercely debated. Compliance professionals have challenged this view of general counsel, preferring non-legal officers to be acting as the corporation's moral conscience in a way that is less legalistic and amoral. The general counsel provides legal service to the corporation, represents it before judiciary and regulatory bodies, serves as an educator of constituents about legal rules, investigates misconduct, prepares litigation and regulator requests, performs deal-making functions for corporate transactions, advances mergers and acquisitions, serves as intermediary with outside law firms, and so on. Their responsibilities have increased with its prestige and are not likely to shrink any time soon.[61]

General counsel serve three roles in their organizations: exert personal influence to ensure the organization operates with integrity, position the legal department as an integral part of the organization, and determine work priorities of the legal team.[62] General counsel must have strong independence and have connections to senior leadership other than the CEO. Additionally, they must have the courage to speak out and be courageous and confident in disagreeing without being disagreeable.[63] Finally, the greatest tension in the role of the general counsel is the double duty of being both a partner to the business leaders and a guardian of the integrity of the corporation.

c. Outside Counsel

Organizations retain outside counsel for a variety of reasons. At many organizations, outside counsel must sign a retainer agreement, accepting corporate cost controls to minimize the fees they charge.[64] Outside counsel is different from in-house counsel in a variety of ways. While outside counsel may be asked to supervise provision of legal services on behalf of a corporate client, this scenario is unlikely to survive long term

---

61. Bird & Park, *supra* note 39.
62. *Id.*
63. Heineman, *supra* note 52.
64. Robert Eli Rosen, *The Inside Counsel Movement, Professional Judgement and Organizational Representation*, 64 Ind. L.J. 479, 511 (1989).

because it can lead to conflicts of interest and relationship issues with external law firms.[65] An initial, and perhaps obvious distinction, is that an attorney at a firm generally works for a number of clients where an in-house attorney has a single client.[66] Second, outside counsel are expected to be rainmakers or bring in revenue in ways that make them indispensable to the firm, while in-house counsel are arguably more expendable as "back office expenses."[67]

Additionally, outside counsel may specialize in discrete areas of the law, generating value to clients based on their specialization. In contrast, in-house counsel are often known as the "Swiss Army Knife" of the legal profession, performing organizational responsibilities well beyond their outside counterparts.[68] Outside counsel primarily play a tactical role for their clients, while in-house counsel play a strategic role for their organization, sitting at the intersection of law and business.[69] Outside counsel often lack executive authority, whereas in-house counsel have power to promote action within their organization.[70] Outside counsel are also less likely to possess institutional and historical industry knowledge that is valuable for an organizations.[71] Thus, organizations may be reluctant to hire outside counsel for preventive and preemptive work that in-house counsel regularly complete because they prefer to work with attorneys who are known, trusted, and easily accessible.[72]

However, there are some areas in which outside counsel are most useful to organizations. Litigation is the largest legal service that organizations outsource to outside counsel,[73] even though outside counsel are not privy to the informal, "watercooler" information when outside counsel learns facts that have been distilled by the organization in advance of litigation.[74] Outside counsel have a role to play when an orga-

---

65. Omari Scott Simmons & James D. Dinnage, *Innkeepers: A Unifying Theory of the In-House Counsel Role*, 41 Seton Hall L. Rev. 77, 114 (2011).
66. Jenoff, *supra* note 6, at 733.
67. *Id.*
68. Simmons & Dinnage, *supra* note 66, at 112.
69. *Id.* at 113.
70. *Id.* at 114.
71. *Id.* at 139.
72. *Id.* at 115.
73. *Id.* at 126.
74. Daly, *supra* note 27, at 966.

nization conducts an internal investigation and needs an independent third party outside the legal department who can provide the directors with unvarnished, objective advice.[75]

Outside counsel can play a transitional role for organizations while new in-house attorneys undergo training and onboarding processes.[76] Outside counsel are helpful for quick consultations, and to bounce ideas off of as well.[77] Additionally, outside counsel often work with other organizations and can provide general insight into what practices are becoming "industry standard."[78] Further, outside counsel can call the IRS and other regulators to discuss issues on a no-name basis, which may be more difficult for an in-house attorney calling on behalf of his or her organization client.[79] Finally, outside counsel provide an important network of professional colleagues for in-house attorneys.[80]

IV. Strategic Thinking of the General Counsel

The responsibilities of general counsel have expanded in the face of new challenges for public and private organizations, which has led them to employ particular strategies in the workplace. The position is being reshaped by powerful political and economic headwinds produced by globalization, technological innovation, and the convergence of lawyers possessing starkly different skillsets.[81] The abilities to communicate, inspire, identify risk, execute strategy, control costs, ensure efficiency, and nurture talent are rapidly becoming the premium skills necessary in successful GCs.[82] To surmount these challenges, general counsel must as-

---

75. Veasy & Gugliemo, *supra* note 56, at 10.

76. Cynthia Lewin, *The General Counsel's Role: Similarities and Differences from a Nonprofit Perspective, in* BEST PRACTICES FOR GENERAL COUNSEL at *8 (Aspatore 2014), WL 3773047.

77. *Id.*

78. *Id.*

79. *Id.*

80. *Id.*

81. BJARNE P. TELLMAN, BUILDING AN OUTSTANDING LEGAL TEAM: BATTLE TESTED STRATEGIES FROM A GENERAL COUNSEL 25 (2017).

82. *Id.* at 25.

semble legal teams that are able to operate with the greatest efficacy and provide a high level of support to their organization.

A general counsel's quest to acquire the hard, operational capabilities to succeed is to develop a strong organizational design. In order to organize the team while making the best use of available resources and skills, the general counsel must (1) assess their existing team and (2) identify the core risks facing their company.[83] By proceeding methodically from that point forward, a general counsel can move toward building an effective legal team.

Once a team has been divided between specialists and generalists, the general counsel ought to appoint the legal leadership team within the first 100 days of entering the position.[84] While there are no ironclad rules as to team size and composition, maintaining leadership positions are essential for the general counsel to operate effectively. First, leaders within the legal team can provide the general counsel with input that will allow for the organizational structure of the team to morph and meet new challenges or overcome previously unidentified deficiencies.[85] Second, appointing a leadership team early in the process will allow the general counsel to persuade them of his or her view on certain matters.[86] This persuasion, in turn, will improve communication between the general counsel and team leaders as well as produce advocates for the general counsel's point of view within the organization. Third, by including the leadership in the decision-making process, those decisions that are reached will be legitimized, more moderate outcomes will occur, and members of the leadership team will be encouraged to advocate for the decision as something that reflects their own input.[87]

Even after the creation of a leadership stratum within each specialty area of the legal team, the general counsel must organize how these disparate groupings will interact with one another. A common organizational archetype for large companies is referred to as a matrix structure.[88] A matrix structure consists of vertical geographic groupings of a

---

83. *Id.* at 56.
84. *Id.* at 91.
85. *Id.*
86. *Id.*
87. *Id.*
88. *Id.* at 99.

company (i.e., North America, Asia, etc.) and horizontal functional groupings (i.e., marketing, R&D, etc.).[89] In addition to structuring the legal team as discussed above, the general counsel must also develop work distribution processes. Depending on the size of the team, work can be distributed by specialty or by designating specific contact people for different departments.[90] In smaller legal departments, the latter may be the best approach.[91] This method simplifies the process of contacting the general counsel's office for people outside the legal team—all they need is a single phone number.[92] That legal team lawyer can then navigate the back end of the general counsel's office to find answers and provide advice.[93]

Similar to the way in which a legal team is built to be responsive to the general counsel, the general counsel must ensure that resource allocation for the legal team—in the form of budgeting—is responsive to the general counsel's office. If the financing of the legal team is under the control of someone other than the GC, or if sources of funding are segmented between various actors and offices within the company, then the legal team will become subject to the agenda of other actors and offices.[94] Another necessary operational component is a formal performance evaluation procedure. Measuring the quality of legal advice can be difficult, and it can be "even harder to measure [the quantity of advice] in a way that provides meaningful results, except in a few highly routinized areas."[95]

Further evidence of the general counsel's evolving role in modern organizations is its newfound responsibility of acquiring technology. General counsel can be prone to making the conceptual mistake of seeking out new technology first and then attempting to apply that technology to problems subsequently identified.[96] Reflecting the new expectation of general counsel as managers and procurers, they must first conduct a process analysis to determine what underlying inefficiencies

---

89. *Id.*
90. Lewin, *supra* note 77, at *9.
91. TELLMAN, *supra* note 82, at 99.
92. *Id.*
93. *Id.*
94. *Id.* at 107.
95. Lewin, *supra* note 77, at *9.
96. TELLMAN, *supra* note 82, at 182.

exist, and then seek out those technologies which correct those inefficiencies.[97] Such inefficiencies consist of how tasks are received, handled, and allocated.[98] Additional procedural inefficiencies include the prioritization, delegation, and completion of the myriad consultative and litigative responsibilities of the legal team.[99] Technologies of use to general counsel might include cloud computing, telecommunication tools, and e-billing services.[100] Technology not only improves team effectiveness, but it also reduces risk by allowing for transparency and standardization across all legal operations.[101] By using these tools, the general counsel is able to focus the efforts of their legal team on high-priority tasks and routinize administrative procedures in ways that boost productivity.

Ultimately, it is the strategic thinking and priorities of the general counsel that position them, and the legal department, in a successful position within the organization.

V. Legal Departments

A general counsel is not just a lawyer but manager of the legal team, responsible for organizing that team's work, setting goals, and measuring success.[102] The emergence of in-house legal departments is a multifaceted phenomenon. The growth of in-house legal departments may be explained by the same transaction-cost economizing that has led to the greater divisionalization in the modern corporation.[103]

This framing of the legal department as a service department can lead to legal departments having a reactive role.[104] General counsel must be diligent to demonstrate that the legal department is a proactive part of the organization, key to its success.[105] Developing a culture of proactivity can be achieved through setting out a work plan, in which different tasks

---

97. *Id.*
98. *Id.* at 183.
99. *Id.*
100. *Id.* at 188, 192, 197.
101. *Id.* at 202.
102. Lewin, *supra* note 77, at *5.
103. Simmons & Dinnage, *supra* note 66, at 96.
104. Lewin, *supra* note 77, at *6.
105. *Id.*

and initiatives are assigned to members of the legal department.[106] Examples of categories within a work plan include (1) preparing for the organization's trajectory, (2) education and training efforts, (3) improving organizational efficiency and effectiveness, and (4) improving the legal department's efficiency and effectiveness.[107]

To prepare for the organization's trajectory, the legal department can ask what kind of legal support is needed in light of the organization's strategic plan.[108] This might involve a review of emerging technologies, key Supreme Court decisions or pending legislation, and other changes to the legal environment on any given topic of interest to the organization.[109] Education and training may involve teaching employees about the legal department, conduct that is and is not permissible, and when and how to raise legal questions.[110] This can be accomplished through standard annual training as well as though ad hoc training driven by the types of questions and problems that appear to be facing the legal department more regularly.[111] Improving the organization's efficiency and effectiveness may involve exempting low-risk activities from legal review, preparing template contracts, or building processes that allow employees to quickly reproduce materials.[112] Similarly, improvements to the legal department's efficiency and effectiveness can be obtained through technology training, cross-training in specialty areas of the law, developing written guidance for the department, and finding ways to make collaboration more effective.[113]

a. Structuring the Legal Department

The general counsel is responsible for structuring the legal department and must do so in a way that optimizes the department's ability to serve the organization's needs.[114] "Over-compartmentalization of legal

---

106. *Id.* at *7.
107. *Id.*
108. *Id.*
109. *Id.*
110. *Id.*
111. *Id.*
112. *Id.*
113. *Id.*
114. Veasey & Guglielmo, *supra* note 56, at *33.

tasks and decentralization and dissipation of legal staff" may create problems.¹¹⁵ In determining how to spread out work within the legal department, general counsel should focus on the extent to which organizational structures may inhibit the lawyers' abilities to identify and solve issues.¹¹⁶ If an individual lawyer or team of lawyers is assigned only to a single piece of a larger, more complex deal, they may not have the knowledge or context needed to recognize problems.¹¹⁷ General counsel must build structures that help individual lawyers consider how much they need to know about a matter as a whole in order to perform their discrete tasks.¹¹⁸ General counsel should monitor legal departments for compartmentalization and whether it raises any flags that indicate misfeasance or the possibility of future problems.¹¹⁹ This gatekeeper or "watchdog" role inevitably may strain the relationship between the general counsel and members of the legal department.¹²⁰

One option for legal departments is a partially centralized, partially decentralized structure.¹²¹ Here, different business units may have their own "in-house" counsel that reports to the business heads of those units on legal matters and reports administratively to the general counsel.¹²² The general counsel can support the independence of these assigned "in-house" counsel, but must emphasize that the counsel should first report to them if they experience pressure from the business heads to do something ethically or legally inappropriate.¹²³ The general counsel may then assess the situation and step in as necessary.¹²⁴

However, excessive decentralization can create risks. General counsel cannot be involved in everything, but "there may be times when the fact that the general counsel is not aware of an issue can result in damage to the corporation."¹²⁵ In decentralized legal departments, reporting from

---

115. *Id.*
116. *Id.*
117. *Id.*
118. *Id.* at 34.
119. *Id.*
120. *Id.*
121. *Id.*
122. *Id.*
123. *Id.*
124. *Id.*
125. *Id.* at 35.

the lawyers working within business units becomes vitally important in ensuring the general counsel is apprised of important operations.[126] Additionally, the general counsel should maintain an active role in managing relationships with outside counsel and the selection of in-house counsel for different projects.[127] Finding the balance between centralization and decentralization is a challenge in legal departments. There are inherent difficulties in balancing the "'concentrated expertise' of centralized attorneys and the 'superior operating contacts' of field attorneys."[128] The best solution for an individual legal department may only be identified after experimentation with different strategies.[129]

Finally, general counsel must keep budget considerations in mind when structuring the legal department. General counsel may often face pressures from budget constraints that limit "their ability to staff the legal department or to retain outside counsel in a manner they believe to be optimal in the best interests of the corporation."[130] Thus, the general counsel may find themselves in a "lobbying" position to persuade the CFO and CEO that legal resources are needed.[131] It may also be necessary to inform the board of directors "that some needed legal advice has not been provided because of budget constraints."[132]

b. Compensation

Across the United States, general counsel compensation is typically on par with that of outside counsel,[133] although this may not be the case in cities like New York, where law firms pay increasingly unrealistic salaries.[134] However, inflated pay scales in those locations may eventually create problems for law firms who are unable to retain senior attorneys who do not become partners.[135] Legal departments should compensate

---

126. *Id.* at 35.
127. *Id.* at 34.
128. *Id.* at 35.
129. *Id.*
130. *Id.*
131. *Id.*
132. *Id.*
133. Daly, *supra* note 27, at 1221.
134. *Id.*
135. *Id.*

their attorneys in a way that reflects their value and assures availability and retention of top attorneys, including those considering a move from a large firm.[136] This may require developing innovative compensation structures so that senior lawyers in the legal department are compensated competitively.[137]

c. Legal Departments as Part of the Corporate Team

The general counsel must be able to hold firm to decisions about appropriate legal conduct for the corporation while also preventing the legal department from becoming "the place where ideas go to die."[138] Practically, a legal department can demonstrate its role as part of the corporate team by attending different departments' staff meetings.[139] Legal departments can also provide training videos, background memos, and written guidance on a variety of topics.[140] The more employees understand different issues, the lower the risk for the organization as a whole.[141] Importantly, a legal department should endeavor to always make time to explain their decisions. Whenever a legal department provides an answer to an employee, it should explain the law and reasoning that form the basis of that conclusion.[142] Taking the mystery out of legal advice will encourage more people to make use of a legal department and support the message that the department is not the enemy; it is part of the same corporate team working toward the same goals.[143]

d. Institutionalizing Compliance

General counsel play a significant role in institutionalizing compliance.[144] Since the Organizational Sentencing Guidelines were enacted in 1991, "the incentives for corporations to create internal compliance

---

136. *Id.* at 1222.
137. *Id.*
138. Lewin, *supra* note 77, at *4.
139. *Id.*
140. *Id.*
141. *Id.*
142. *Id.*
143. *Id.*
144. Rostain, *supra* note 3, at 483.

mechanisms in every sphere of corporate activity has grown."[145] Corporations are expected to organizationally minimize risk of unethical and unlawful activity through controls like ethics codes, self-audits, compliance training, whistleblower protections, and designation of compliance personnel.[146] This regulatory approach to institutional compliance raises questions about the general counsel's authority to execute compliance functions across the organization via the legal department.[147]

One option is for general counsel to expand the legal advice they provide to include an assertion of responsibility over and proliferation of compliance mechanisms throughout the organization.[148] In this model, general counsel must develop hybrid expertise by marrying their legal knowledge with managerial techniques.[149] Another option is to diffuse compliance functions throughout the entire legal department and into the organization's non-legal business units.[150] General counsel would cede authority over compliance to other managers, reflecting a recent trend towards emergence of non-attorney, multidisciplinary compliance professionals within corporations.[151] A third, perhaps most likely, option is to create a legal department that maintains control over some key compliance functions while delegating others outside the department.[152]

General counsel may see value in retaining control over compliance issues like ethics, while leaving human resources, occupational health and safety, and financial compliance to other specialists within the organization.[153] In many organizations, there may be a chief compliance officer who may be an attorney, but who reports to the general counsel.[154] One general counsel explained the importance of centralizing compliance within a legal department, noting that "If people care about it, it's

---

145. *Id.* at 480.
146. *Id.*
147. *Id.*
148. *Id.*
149. *Id.*
150. *Id.* at 481.
151. *Id.*
152. *Id.*
153. *Id.*
154. *Id.*

in legal."[155] Another general counsel suggested splitting compliance functions between the general counsel and the CFO, with "the CFP having responsibility for all financial compliance and the general counsel overseeing all other compliance, including environmental and safety audits."[156] Still other general counsel may situate ethics and other compliance outside the legal department, believing accountants or business people better at setting up compliance systems in different organizational contexts.[157] Additionally, pushing compliance functions outside the legal department may help cut costs for an otherwise high-cost legal department.[158]

Regardless of the organizational form they take, internal compliance mechanisms are important to sensitizing employees about ethical issues that may arise in their jobs.[159]

VI. Ethics and Ethical Dilemmas

General counsel are often faced with unique ethical situations that other lawyers would not be presented with. In order to understand the challenges of ethical decision-making among in-house counsel, one must first understand the work of in-house counsel and what roles they serve in an organization.[160] There are five defining characteristics of in-house corporate counsel that distinguish them from their colleagues in private practice and may shed light on the unique ethical dilemmas facing internal legal departments. First, the fate of in-house counsel is economically dependent on a single client, their employer.[161] Second, in-house counsel tend to assume responsibilities in the organization that far exceed those of a typical attorney-client relationship.[162] Third, in-

---

155. *Id.* at 482.
156. *Id.*
157. *Id.*
158. *Id.*
159. *Id.* at 483.
160. Hugh Gunz & Sally Gunz, *Ethical Challenges in the Role of In-House Counsel*, 69 Case W. Res. L. Rev. 953, 960 (2019).
161. Sally R. Weaver, *Ethical Dilemmas of Corporate Counsel: A Structural and Contextual Analysis*, 46 Emory L.J. 1023, 1027 (1997).
162. *Id.* at 1027.

house counsel have access to informal sources of information through physical proximity to their clients and its non-legal employees.[163] Fourth, the close working relationship between management and in-house counsel can create confusion and uncertainty about the in-house counsel's role in representing the organization.[164] Fifth, because in-house counsel are also employees of their client, there are myriad opportunities for employment-related disputes to arise that otherwise might not arise in a traditional attorney-client relationship.[165] These characteristics can lead to four situations that implicate ethical issues for in-house counsel.

a. First: Identification of the Client

Under Model Rule 1.13, an attorney "represents the organization acting through its duly authorized constituents."[166] The rule does not distinguish a relationship between an in-house lawyer and its organizational client from the relationship of an outside lawyer and its relationship with an organizational client.[167] When an organization client behaves in a manner discordant with established law, Rule 1.13 admonishes a lawyer to "proceed as is reasonably necessary in the best interest of the organization," but in a way that "minimizes disruption of the organization and the risk of revealing information relating to the representation to persons outside the organization."[168] In other words, the rule does not create a safe harbor for attorneys who choose to become whistleblowers.[169] Instead, attorneys may suggest a separate legal opinion be considered on the issue or refer the matter to a "higher authority in the organization," among other non-enumerated options.[170] Notably, each of the suggestions in Rule 1.13 are permissive, meaning the attorney has the responsibility to determine the appropriate course of action under the circum-

---

163. *Id.*
164. *Id.* at 1028.
165. *Id.*
166. *Id.* at 1032.
167. *Id.*
168. *Id.* at 1033.
169. *Id.*
170. *Id.*

stances.[171] The potential costs of in-house counsel are high, especially given the close working relationship between in-house counsel and senior management.[172]

However, in-house counsel can take steps to mitigate and prepare for these risks by clearly defining their role as counsel for the organization, rather than counsel for any one individual at the organization;[173] proactively identifying specific circumstances in which confusion about their role could arise; and providing Miranda-like warnings to organization employees "when it is apparent that the organizations' interests are adverse to those" of the employee.[174] Finally, in-house counsel should discuss the ethical obligations of attorneys under Rule 1.13 with senior management before, rather than after, a situation arises, and establish written policies for resolving internal conflicts.[175]

b. Second: When In-House Counsel Wear Too Many Hats

Many in-house counsel are officers of the corporation, serve on the board of directors and management committees, maintain compliance roles, and have equity interest in an organization through employee stock option plans.[176] The Model Rules offer no guidance about ethical issues implicated by these various roles.[177] Rule 1.7 provides general rules governing conflicts of interest, and the comments to the rule suggest that the lawyer "should determine whether the responsibilities [of multiple roles] may conflict."[178] In *Simms v. Exeter Architectural Products, Inc.*, the United States District Court for the Middle District of Pennsylvania considered whether an attorney's ownership of stock created a conflict of interest that precluded the attorney from representing the corporation.[179] The court found that when an attorney is both an advo-

---

171. *Id.* at 1034.
172. *Id.*
173. *Id.*
174. *Id.*
175. *Id.* at 1035.
176. *Id.*
177. *Id.*
178. *Id.* at 1036.
179. *Id.*

cate for and an owner of an entity, "it appears to be extremely difficult if not impossible for the attorney to give advice as a non-interested party," and thus an attorney's ownership of stock precluded the attorney from representing the organization.[180]

In-house counsel should limit their role in an organization to serving as legal advisor, avoiding non-legal functions for the entity when the counsel's ability to render legal advice would diminish as a result.[181] Furthermore, in-house counsel should consider the extent to which they participate in internal investigations involving highly sensitive matters, opting instead to secure outside counsel to avoid implicating conflicts of interest.[182] Finally, in-house counsel should bring a second attorney with them to conversations in which the advice they render could be characterized as business rather than legal advice.[183]

c. Third: In-House Counsel's Independence, or Lack Thereof

In-house counsel may face ethical dilemmas when faced with their own independence, or lack thereof.[184] Model Rule 2.1 provides in part that "in representing a client, a lawyer shall exercise independent professional judgment and render candid advice," even if that advice may be unpleasant or contrary to what the client wants to hear.[185] Rule 1.7 highlights situations in which an attorney's independence may be compromised, and Rule 1.16 provides that an attorney may withdraw where representation would result in a violation of the Model Rules of Professional Conduct or the law.[186] The United States District Court for the Northern District of Ohio addressed the question of whether inside or outside counsel is more likely to have independence to tell senior management what they may not want to hear in a shareholder class and derivative action.[187] The court concluded that retaining outside counsel to

---

180. *Id.* at 1036–37.
181. *Id.* at 1039–40.
182. *Id.* at 1040.
183. *Id.*
184. *Id.*
185. Jenoff, *supra* note 6, at 734.
186. *Id.* at 736.
187. Weaver, *supra* note 162, at 1041.

advise directors is "one of the few safeguards to ensure the legitimacy of their acts and to aid the court in assessing the reasonableness of a derivative settlement or termination."[188] The court also held that representation of an organization by in-house counsel does not resolve the conflict that would arise in the case of dual representation because "in-house attorneys are inevitably subservient to the interests of the defendant directors and officers whom they serve."[189]

d. Fourth: Divergent Interests

Divergent interests between in-house counsel and their employer-clients on employment-related disputes implicate a number of ethical issues, including the duty of loyalty and obligation to maintain their clients' confidences.[190] The ACCA has suggested a theory that in-house counsel should be treated exactly the same as their colleagues in private practice on matters of this nature, but courts do not always agree.[191] In *General Dynamics Corp. v. Superior Court*, the court concluded that failing to allow in-house lawyers a remedy that is not available to their outside counterparts would "almost certainly foster a degradation of in-house counsel's professional stature."[192] In other words, failing to afford corporate counsel certain rights may lead to the very diminution in professional status that in-house counsel fear when they continue to maintain that equal status means equal treatment.[193] This situation is perhaps the most difficult to address, given that in a competitive corporate market, in-house counsel who sue their employing organizations may unfortunately find it difficult to find subsequent employment.[194] However, in-house counsel could develop internal dispute resolution policies and procedures, or negotiate employment agreements that increase the possibility that future disputes are resolved without litigation.[195]

---

188. *Id.* at 1042.
189. *Id.*
190. *Id.* at 1046.
191. *Id.* at 1049.
192. *Id.*
193. *Id.*
194. *Id.* at 1050.
195. *Id.*

Confidentiality and privilege issues also arise for general counsel. Attorney-client privilege is necessary for effective legal representation, even when the only client is a corporation. The rationale of this privilege is that it encourages complete and candid communication between attorneys and their clients.[196] But the blurring of attorney-client privilege is a problem, and it is a no-win scenario in which the lawyer needs all the facts to provide the best representation but is simultaneously required not to divulge information or break privilege.

The automatic protection of attorney-client privilege disappears when officers discuss related personal legal matters with counsel when counsel only formally represents the organization.[197] In addressing whether officers have a personal privilege with respect to conversations with in-house counsel, the federal circuits apply a test that makes it difficult to invoke such a privilege.[198] Officers must demonstrate that they (1) approached counsel for the purpose of seeking legal advice; (2) made it clear they were seeking legal advice in their individual rather than representative capacity; (3) counsel saw fit to communicate with them, knowing a conflict of interest could arise; (4) conversations were confidential; and (5) the substance of the conversations did not concern matters within the organization or general affairs of the organization.[199]

VII. Insurance Coverage

General counsel often mistakenly assume they are protected under their organization's Directors and Officers (D&O) liability insurance.[200] However, general counsel may not have full coverage or be protected at all.[201]

There are seven steps to understand if your in-house legal team needs malpractice insurance, including (1) assess liability exposures, including

---

196. Scott W. Williams, *Keeping Secrets "In-House": Different Approaches to Client Confidentiality for General Counsel*, 1 J. LEGAL ADVOC. & PRAC. 78, 82 (1999).
197. *Id.* at 83.
198. *Id.*
199. *Id.* at 83–84.
200. Kara Altenbaumer-Price, *Claims Against In-House Counsel: Will the Insurance Be There?*, 44 BRIEF 10, 13 (2014).
201. *Id.*

malpractice claims, government/regulatory exposure, securities litigation exposure/third-party claims, etc.; (2) determine the scope of your company's indemnification/advancement obligations to in-house lawyers, which would include reviewing applicable state statutes governing corporate indemnification, the company's indemnification grant, and any written indemnification agreements or policies; (3) determine the extent to which indemnification is extended to non-officer in-house lawyers and employees; (4) consider whether any such indemnification is mandatory or permissive; (5) consider scenarios where the company may be legally or financially unable to fund a defense, such as financial insolvency, derivative claims, or a change in control; (6) review your existing corporate insurance policies to determine the scope of coverage already afforded to your in-house attorneys; and (7) identify potential gaps in coverage.[202]

An indemnification agreement gives counsel a contract upon which to sue if all else fails and the company denies an indemnification at point of claim. Since both D&O and employed lawyers' insurance contain some sort of exclusion for claims brought by one insured against another, indemnification may be the surest form of protection.[203] Indemnification can also address coverage for losses that fall outside of insurance settlements, such as increased consideration in mergers and acquisition deals, fines, penalties, disgorgement in regulatory actions, or breach of contract damages.[204]

A threshold issue for in-house counsel is whether the organization is obligated to indemnify and advance defense costs in the event a claim is made against an attorney in the legal department.[205] Indemnification is generally governed by the law of the state in which the organization is incorporated, so the first step is reviewing the state's indemnification statute.[206]

Malpractice insurance is an additional measure for which in-house counsel can negotiate in surveying their insurance protection.[207] Orga-

---

202. John C. Tanner, et al., *Does the Gatekeeper Lawyer Need Insurance?*, ACC Docket (September 2008).
203. Altenbaumer-Price, *supra* note 201.
204. *Id.*
205. Tanner, et al., *supra* note 203.
206. *Id.*
207. *Id.*

nizations are unlikely to offer indemnification for counsel if they have decided to sue.[208] Additionally, counsel's personal financial resources may be at risk if the organization files for bankruptcy, so it can be beneficial to shift a portion of the risk to an insurer.[209]

It is unlikely that Errors & Omissions (E&O) Coverage covers the legal department.[210] Additionally, D&O Coverage is designed to protect officers, executives, outside directors, and the companies they serve, specifically protecting against the legal expenses of fighting litigation and liability exposure.[211] Officers are usually protected by D&O insurance, but lower-level in-house attorneys are generally not covered.

a. An Alternative: Employed Lawyers Professional (ELP) Liability Insurance Coverage

Employed Lawyers Professional (ELP) Liability Insurance Coverage is a type of "legal malpractice policy" specifically designed to cover the in-house counsel activities as the company's lawyer.[212] ELP policies can cover in-house attorneys who are not the general counsel, paralegals, and contract attorneys.[213] The claims it can protect against include, but are not limited to, ethics and licensing hearings, moonlighting, pro bono work, service on not-for-profit boards, claims by employees, SEC and regulatory claims, third party claims, legal advice given to executives, and personal injury.[214] Additional claims carriers may protect against negligent misrepresentation in a contract, conflict of interest (contract negotiations and dual representation), misrepresentation, malpractice, and wrongful termination/negligent advice.[215] Most will also cover claims made against counsel by related entities such as holding companies.[216]

---

208. *Id.*
209. *Id.*
210. *Id.*
211. Altenbaumer-Price, *supra* note 201.
212. *Id.*
213. *Id.*
214. *Id.*
215. *Id.*
216. *Id.*

This is a relatively inexpensive coverage—less than $10,000 per million dollars of policy limits. The issue with this policy is that rarely are the general counsel in a position to be sued. Rather, they are immediately fired.[217] The need for coverage thus typically arises when general counsel work on matters that involve reliance on third parties, who may be more likely to sue if they believe the lawyer has exercised poor judgment or acted improperly.[218] Coverage can vary widely depending on the carrier, so counsel should pay close attention to specific terms and conditions about which support staff are covered, modification requirements to include professionals beyond general counsel, and limits on defense costs.[219]

It may be prudent to purchase both D&O insurance and ELP insurance from the same carrier, if possible, to avoid scenarios where carriers point fingers at each other as bearing sole responsibility for coverage.[220] This may take the form of two standalone policies or by adding an ELP addendum to the organization's D&O policy.[221]

VIII. Broader Issues in the New Age of Corporate Counsel

Now is the "platinum age" for corporate counsel.[222] However, there are an array of new challenges that they must navigate—e.g., high cost of legal services, technology, globalization, and conducting internal investigations, just to name a few.

The "spiraling cost of legal services" has redefined the corporate legal department.[223] Due to increasing business and legal costs, corporations are deciding to hire their own in-house counsel in order to lower the costs of seeking outside counsel.[224] "Both for fear of malpractice and

---

217. Id.
218. Id.
219. Id.
220. Id.
221. Id.
222. Liggio, Sr., *supra* note 12, at 631.
223. Id.
224. Omari Scott Simmons, *The Under-Examination of In-House Counsel*, 11 TRANS. TENN J. BUS. L. 145 (2009).

injuring an important client relationship, outside counsel would typically leave no stone unturned, no case unread, and no possible issue unsearched."[225] Conversely, in-house counsel can make affordability judgments in assuming certain risks.[226] "Thus, costs will continue to be a dominant factor in extending the breadth of inside counsel's responsibilities and the depth of their power."[227]

New technology has perhaps most impacted the corporate structure, and in-house legal departments along with it.[228] There will likely be "continued erosion of the 'information gatekeeper' function of outside counsel for the corporate legal community."[229] "Until the advent and growth of Lexis in the late 1970s, the outside law firm was the principal gatekeeper to legal knowledge for the corporate law department. There were few places—such as law school law libraries, bar libraries, and large corporate law firm libraries—which had either the resources on hand, or the ready access to arcane legal knowledge. Until Lexis, if an inside corporate lawyer wanted access to legal information, the most readily available source was the corporate law firm. As such, the law firm was the gatekeeper of the corporate law department's information and knowledge base."[230] But the advent of the internet, including vast amounts of legal resources, along with the increasing number of computer-literate attorneys, has altered the balance of power between outside and in-house counsel.[231]

Additionally, technology has changed the ways attorneys and their clients communicate and interact.[232] Corporate legal departments are at the forefront of using technology to increase efficiency and effectiveness in their communications and instantaneous responses to legal problems.[233] However, "this in turn requires the use of massive databases that accumulate the institutional knowledge of the entity so as to permit the lawyers to provide answers to common types of legal problems without

---

225. Liggio, Sr., *supra* note 12, at 631.
226. *Id.*
227. *Id.*
228. *Id.* at 633.
229. *Id.*
230. *Id.*
231. *Id.*
232. *Id.*
233. *Id.*

having to reinvent the wheel."[234] The new technology may have additional effects on how lawyers think and must be trained. While lawyers within corporations are becoming businesspeople, other legally trained people will be creating new ways to automate contracts, learning to value litigation, developing new metrics for evaluating lawyers, and inventing new ways for compliance mechanisms to anticipate and prevent problems. These law-trained individuals will evolve from mechanics to architects, forcing law schools to integrate certain types of theories with legal skills.[235]

An additional challenge has been the evolution in the role and prestige of corporate counsel amidst the globalization of the economy. Corporate counsel must now develop management structures to deliver legal services abroad, include lawyers from different countries with different legal systems into the same organizations, and navigate between legal systems and regulations.[236] The globalization of business and capital markets has posed new and distinct challenges for the corporate counsel of multinational organizations. There is concern that the changes in corporate counsel's role may cause them to lose their professional identity associated with the rule of law, as it represents increasingly powerful global business entities.

On top of these dynamics, after enactment of the organizational sentencing guidelines in 1991, a new era of corporate criminal responsibility began.[237] "The guidelines provide that the court will look to acceptance of responsibility, cooperation, and the level of tolerance by higher-ups in the organization in determining the 'culpability' level of the organization."[238] But for general counsel, prevention is key to keeping an organization out of trouble.[239] General counsel will likely "be most interested in the guideline that permits the court to include 'the steps taken by the organization prior to the offense to prevent and deter criminal conduct' in the 'culpability score,' the figure used in determining

---

234. *Id.* at 633–34.
235. *Id.*
236. Daly, *supra* note 27.
237. Harry S. Hardin, III & Andrew R. Lee, *Pitfalls for In-House Counsel*, 25 BRIEF 33, 34 (1995).
238. *Id.*
239. *Id.*

criminal penalties after a corporate conviction."[240] High-quality internal compliance programs can help an organization receive a reduced "culpability score" in the event of prosecution, which requires general counsel to devote significant time and effort into developing these programs.[241] This is especially true for organizations that deal in public securities.[242] The first step in preparing a prevention plan is examining substantive areas of the law such as antitrust, whistleblower laws, and other relevant statutes that an internal investigator may not have time to comprehensively evaluate.[243] This means the legal department may need a few generalists or specialists with investigative abilities who can monitor and enforce both the organization's policies and federal and state statutes.[244] If prevention fails, a swift internal investigation is vital.[245]

IX. Conclusion

There has never been an analysis of the role of fraternity or sorority legal counsel. This chapter seeks to import the most consequential ideas from the corporate sector to the nonprofit, membership-based, Greek-letter organization sector. Among the major points of consideration in the fraternity and sorority space should be what model of legal representation fraternities and sororities should seek. Should it be outside counsel for discrete issues or ongoing counsel? Should it be in-house that does the bulk of the work or serves as a liaison with outside counsel? Should there be an in-house legal team, led by a general counsel? What kind of lawyers should comprise such a team if there is one—contracts, tax, higher education, litigation, constitutional issues, property, intellectual property, et cetera? Another critical question is whether legal counsel should have narrow or broad responsibilities? Are they to focus simply on legal issues, or are they a chief legal officer focused on an array of issues the organization faces or must face? Yet an-

---

240. *Id.*
241. *Id.*
242. *Id.*
243. *Id.*
244. *Id.*
245. *Id.*

other question is whether inside legal counsel should be paid, and how much? Even if they are a member of the fraternity or sorority they are representing, are there resources, and does it make sense, to compensate in-house counsel? On top of all of that, what role should they play in the compliance process around internal issues like hazing prevention and external issues like compliance with Internal Revenue Service policies? In an effort to protect legal counsel, how should they navigate ethical dilemmas that put their law licenses in jeopardy? And how will they be provided with liability insurance? These are just some of the issues that fraternity and sorority legal counsel should be thinking about as they represent their Greek-letter organization clients.

CHAPTER 2

The Duty of Oversight and Director Liability

Michael R. Siebecker

Could the directors of a fraternity's national office be liable for failing to detect and prevent criminal or other nefarious activity occurring within the organization? This question seems particularly important considering recent national scandals involving fraternal hazing, sexual misconduct, forced consumption of alcohol and drugs, embezzlement, and other financial misdeeds. Answering the question, however, requires looking not only at the fiduciary framework governing the relationship between directors and the fraternal organizations they serve, but also at the heightened scrutiny federal prosecutors now employ regarding corporate misconduct.

Regarding fiduciary obligations, directors of nonprofit corporations owe essentially the same fiduciary duties as directors of for-profit corporations. Those duties include the duty of care and the duty of loyalty, as well as the component duty of oversight. Despite the existence of the oversight duty, the common law presumption embodied in the "Business Judgment Rule" (BJR) has generally shielded directors from liability for lax oversight practices, even with criminal activity running rampant throughout the corporation. Except in cases involving fraud, illegality, conflicts of interest, or gross negligence, courts have presumed the decisions of corporate managers comported with their fiduciary duties. Specifically with respect to the duty of corporate managers to implement effective monitoring mechanisms to identify and stave off corporate wrongdoing, the common law sets an incredibly low hurdle for directors to overcome liability. Only an utter failure to attempt to ensure a reasonable information gathering and reporting system exists will establish the lack of good faith that is necessary for director liability. Some recent cases suggest courts might be willing to impose a slightly more stringent standard on directors for failed oversight, but the prevailing framework still greatly insulates directors for all but the most egregious decisions.

In contrast to the rather lax oversight obligations imposed under the common law, the Department of Justice (DOJ) has recently redoubled its prior dedication to aggressive prosecution of individual directors and officers ultimately responsible for corporate misconduct. In September 2015, former Deputy Attorney General Sally Yates disseminated an official policy memorandum entitled *Individual Accountability for Corporate Wrongdoing* ("Yates Memo").[1] According to the Yates Memo, in the process of investigating corporate malfeasance, prosecutors should seek to identify and punish individual executives, officers, and board members ultimately responsible for corporate crimes. The indictment of several Volkswagen executives at the center of the auto emissions defeat device scandal represents a prominent example of this new prosecutorial focus.[2] The recent federal sentencing of a former national fraternity treasurer to two and a half years in prison for embezzlement arguably represents another.[3]

The aggressive refocusing of DOJ prosecution of corporate criminality under the Yates Memo creates a significant disparity between federal

---

1. Memorandum from Sally Q. Yates, Deputy Attorney General, Individual Accountability for Corporate Wrongdoing (Sept. 9, 2015), https://www.justice.gov/dag/file/769036/download. *See also Individual Accountability*, U.S. Just. Dep't, https://www.justice.gov/dag/individual-accountability (detailing the six steps discussed in the Yates Memo to strengthen pursuit of individuals in corporate wrongdoing cases).

2. *See* Hiroko Tabuchi, et al., *6 Volkswagen Executives Charged as Company Pleads Guilty in Emissions Case*, N.Y. Times (Jan. 11, 2017), https://www.NYTimes.com/2017/01/11/business/volkswagen-diesel-vw-settlement-charges-criminal.html (reporting criminal charges announced by federal prosecutors in the Volkswagen emissions cheating scandal); Jack Ewing, et al., *Volkswagen Executive's Trip to U.S. Allowed F.B.I. to Pounce*, N.Y. Times (Jan. 9, 2017), https://www.NYTimes.com/2017/01/09/business/volkswagen-emissions-scandal-oliver-schmidt.html (reporting the arrest of Oliver Schmidt in connection with Volkswagen's emission cheating).

3. Press Release, U.S. Att'ys' Off., E. Dist. of Pa., Former National Fraternity Treasurer Sentenced to 2½ Years in Prison for Embezzling $2.9 Million (Feb. 22, 2022), https://www.justice.gov/usao-edpa/pr/former-national-fraternity-treasurer-sentenced-2-years-prison-embezzling-29-million.

standards for criminal prosecution of individual corporate actors and common-law standards governing the fiduciary duties of officers and directors. Pursuant to the Yates Memo, directors and officers arguably face greater oversight responsibilities than the common law requires. The persistence of this rift between federal prosecutorial and common law fiduciary standards creates incredibly important implications for corporate officers and directors. Perhaps most important, common-law standards surrounding the BJR no longer provide clear guidance for avoiding civil or criminal liability. After all, the imposition of any criminal sanctions for failed oversight would result in an exception to the BJR's application and expose officers and directors to civil liability. With this aggressive federal focus on the potential culpability of individual corporate actors, minimally compliant oversight under the common law could become criminally actionable.

Thus, directors of fraternal nonprofit corporations must consider not only the common law fiduciary framework generally governing the propriety of their decisions, but also the aggressive federal prosecution of corporate directors for failed oversight. To provide a sufficient background for understanding the need for robust oversight, this chapter explores (1) the fiduciary framework for nonprofit directors, (2) the duty of oversight and the Business Judgment Rule, (3) the Yates Memo and federal enforcement of corporate criminality, (4) the incongruity between federal law and common law, and (5) the implications for oversight in fraternal organizations.

I. The Fiduciary Framework for Nonprofit Directors

As a general matter, nonprofit entities are governed by an amalgam of state and federal law. Every state has a nonprofit entity statute and, through the tax regulations promulgated by the Internal Revenue Service (IRS), the federal government regulates permissible activities to maintain a nonprofit's qualification for tax-exempt status.[4] With respect to state law, the content of the nonprofit organizational statutes might

---

4. Thomas Lee Hazen & Lisa Love Hazen, *Punctilios and Nonprofit Corporate Governance — A Comprehensive Look at Nonprofit Directors' Fiduciary Duties*, 14 U. PA. J. BUS. L. 347 (2012).

differ from one jurisdiction to the next. A majority of states, however, base their nonprofit statutes on the Model Nonprofit Corporations Act (MNCA), the fourth edition of which was recently adopted by the Business Law Section of the American Bar Association in 2021.[5] Moreover, despite the potential for fragmentation in nonprofit entity law, the fiduciary framework embraced among the various state jurisdictions remains substantially similar.[6] As a result, describing the general fiduciary framework governing directors of a national fraternal organization becomes possible.

Based largely on the governance structure of for-profit corporations, directors of nonprofit organizations owe fiduciary duties to the entities they serve.[7] The duties of care and loyalty, along with the component duty of good faith, provide the backbone of that fiduciary structure.[8] Some jurisdictions also impose on directors a duty of obedience.[9] In general, the duty of care requires directors to act with the same care an ordinarily prudent person would exercise under similar circumstances. The duty of loyalty mandates that directors act in the best interests of the organization, without conflicts or privileging of personal gain. The duty of good faith, often considered a subsidiary duty within the duties of loyalty and care,[10] targets the need for adequate attention to compliance, candor, and transparency.[11] The duty of obedience simply requires that directors advance the stated purpose of the nonprofit entity.[12]

Despite strong fiduciary obligations imposed on directors of nonprofit entities, holding directors accountable remains more difficult than

---

5. Model Nonprofit Corporations Act (Am. Bar Ass'n, 4th ed. 2021).

6. Hazen & Hazen, *supra* note 4, at 361.

7. Gary W. Jenkins, *Incorporation Choice, Uniformity, and the Reform of Nonprofit State Law*, 41 Ga. L. Rev. 1113, 1124–25 (2007).

8. Model Nonprofit Corporations Act §830 (Am. Bar Ass'n, 4th ed. 2021) ("Section 830(a) establishes the basic standards of conduct for all directors and its mandate governs all aspects of directors' conduct, including the requirements in other provisions of Section 830 and the duties often referred to as 'care' and 'loyalty.'").

9. Weil, Gotschall & Manges LLP, Guide to Nonprofit Governance 2 (2019).

10. Hazen & Hazen, *supra* note 4, at 385 ("[T]he obligation of good faith is subsumed in the duties of care and loyalty.").

11. Leo E. Strine, Jr., et al., *Loyalty's Core Demand: The Defining Role of Good Faith in Corporation Law*, 98 Geo. L.J. 629, 673–88 (2010).

12. Thomas Lee Hazen & Lisa Love Hazen, *Duties of Nonprofit Corporate Directors—Emphasizing Oversight Responsibilities*, 90 N.C. L. Rev. 1845, 1863–64 (2012).

in the for-profit context. Unlike for-profit corporations, nonprofit organizations do not have shareholders who can advance derivative claims on behalf of the corporation.[13] Enforcement of the fiduciary duties, therefore, largely falls within the purview of state and federal governments.[14] The differing enforcement power and proclivities of state attorneys general across the United States, however, have raised persistent concerns about unchecked nonprofit board abuses.[15]

II. The Duty of Oversight and the Business Judgment Rule

A nonprofit director's duty of oversight stems from the general duty of good faith. Just like directors in for-profit corporations, nonprofit directors must exercise responsibility for ensuring the organization complies with relevant laws and does not engage in widespread wrongdoing.[16] The official comments to the MNCA state the following:

> Where conduct has not been found deficient on other grounds, decision-making outside the bounds of reasonable judgment can give rise to an inference of bad faith. That form of conduct, sometimes characterized as 'reckless indifference' or 'deliberate disregard,' giving rise to an inference of bad faith also can raise a question regarding whether the director could have reasonably believed that the best interests of the corporation would be served.[17]

---

13. Peter Molk & D. Daniel Sokol, *The Challenges of Nonprofit Governance*, 62 B.C. L. Rev. 1497, 1513 (2021); George W. Dent, Jr., *Corporate Governance Without Shareholders: A Cautionary Lesson From Non-Profit Organizations*, 39 Del. J. Corp. L. 93 (2014).

14. Molk & Sokol, *supra* note 14, at 1515–27.

15. Hazen & Hazen, *supra* note 4, at 357; Lloyd Hitoshi Mayer, *Fragmented Oversight of Nonprofits in the United States: Does it Work? Can It Work?*, 91 Chi.-Kent L. Rev. 937 (2016).

16. Stephen M. Bainbridge, *Enhanced Accountability: The Catholic Church's Unfinished Business*, 53 U.S.F. L. Rev. 165 (2019); Simone van Ommeren-Akelman, *Closing the Side-Door: An Argument for Imposing a Duty of Oversight on University Boards of Trustees*, 32 Hastings Women's L.J. 79, 87 (2021).

17. Model Nonprofit Corporations Act §831, cmt. B (Am. Bar Ass'n, 4th ed. 2021).

Instead of directors blithely ignoring potential instances of misconduct, the duty of oversight essentially requires some good-faith attempt at effective information gathering and monitoring.

The application of the BJR to the duty of oversight, however, creates a particularly slippery fiduciary standard.[18] The BJR operates as a legal presumption that in the absence of fraud, illegality, conflicts of interest, or gross negligence, officers and directors comported with their fiduciary duties, even with criminal activity running rampant throughout the organization.[19] Although some courts have found nonprofit directors liable for egregious fiduciary breaches,[20] establishing gross negligence or one of the other exceptions to the BJR remains quite difficult.[21]

With respect to the duty of nonprofit directors to implement effective monitoring mechanisms to identify and stave off corporate wrongdoing, Delaware common law—which governs the vast majority of for-profit corporations in the United States—sets an incredibly low hurdle for directors and officers to overcome liability. Although cases involving oversight breaches in the contexts of nonprofits remain rather spare, existing law and scholarship support the notion that the fiduciary oversight duty applies equally to for-profit and nonprofit corporations.[22] The Delaware Court of Chancery's decision in *In re Caremark International*[23] in 1996 and the Delaware Supreme Court's decision in *Stone v. Ritter*[24] in 2006 exemplify the BJR's benefits for directors and officers in relation to busi-

---

18. Id. cmt. D; Atinuke O. Adediran, *Nonprofit Board Composition*, 83 Ohio St. L.J. 357 (2022).

19. Michael R. Siebecker & Andrew M. Brandes, *Corporate Compliance and Criminality: Does the Common Law Promote Culpable Blindness?*, 50 Conn. L. Rev. 387, 393 (2018); Michael R. Siebecker, *Bridging Troubled Waters: Linking Corporate Efficiency and Political Legitimacy Through a New Discourse Theory of the Firm*, 75 Ohio St. L.J. 103, 132 (2014); Michael R. Siebecker, *The Duty of Care and Data Control Systems in the Wake of Sarbanes-Oxley*, 84 Chi.-Kent L. Rev. 821, 825–26 (2010).

20. Hazen & Hazen, *supra* note 12, at 1852; *see, e.g.*, NCUA v. Siravo, No. CV 10-1597-GW (MANx), 2011 WL 8332969 (C.D. Cal. Jul. 7, 2011); Susan F. Zinder, *Legal Ethics: The Health Lawyer's Ritual: Striving for Good Governance with Wise, Wicked, Simple, and Unable to Ask Board Members*, 20160208 AHLA Seminar Papers 31, 26 (2016).

21. Joseph Mead & Michael Pollack, *Courts, Constituencies, and the Enforcement of Fiduciary Duties in the Nonprofit Sector*, 77 U. Pitt. L. Rev. 281, 297–316 (2016).

22. Bainbridge, *supra* note 16, at 165; van Ommeren-Akelman, *supra* note 16, at 87; Hazen & Hazen, *supra* note 4, at 357.

23. *In re* Caremark Int'l, 698 A.2d 959 (Del. Ch. 1996).

24. Stone v. Ritter, 911 A.2d 362 (Del. 2006).

ness oversight. *Caremark* and *Stone* also represent an extremely low threshold for directors and officers[25] to achieve in order to avail themselves of the protections from liability under the BJR for violations of state law. This standard permits those individuals to mount only minimal efforts in order to qualify for immunity from liability.

In *Caremark*, shareholders of a healthcare company brought a derivative suit alleging directors violated their fiduciary duties in failing to uncover an illegal kickback scheme used by company employees that eventually led the company to plead guilty to felony criminal charges.[26] In its determination that the board did not breach its fiduciary duties despite failing to detect and prevent the criminal misconduct, the Court held "only a sustained or systematic failure of the board to exercise oversight—such as an *utter failure to attempt* to assure a reasonable information and reporting system exits—will establish the lack of good faith that is a necessary condition to liability."[27] In *Stone,* where shareholders of AmSouth bank claimed its directors failed to identify and prevent corporate employees from violating federal anti-money-laundering laws, the Delaware Supreme Court affirmed the *Caremark* standard.[28] Articulating a willful ignorance of the "red flags" exception, the Court added that liability could also arise when, after implementing a minimally compliant information-gathering system, a board "consciously failed to

---

25. It is important to note that the holdings in *Caremark* and *Stone* are not explicitly applicable to both directors and officers. *See Stone*, 911 A.2d at 373 (applying standards of oversight to director conduct); *Caremark*, 698 A.2d at 970 (articulating only the directors' duty of care standard without specific reference to officers). However, the Delaware Supreme Court held in 2009 that the *Caremark* standards of oversight apply not only to directors, but to officers as well. Gantler v. Stephens, 965 A.2d 695, 708–09 (Del. 2008); *see also* Darren Guttenberg, Note, *Waiving Farewell Without Saying Goodbye: The Waiver of Fiduciary Duties in Limited Liability Companies in Delaware, and the Call for Mandatory Disclosure*, 86 S. CAL. L. REV. 869, 877 n.31 (2013) (reviewing case law suggesting directors and officers are afforded the same presumption of competence under the BJR); Verity Winship, *Jurisdiction Over Corporate Officers and the Incoherence of Implied Consent*, 2013 U. ILL. L. REV. 1171, 1173 n.6 (2013) (citing *Gantler*, 965 A.2d at 708–09) (explaining that *Gantler* was the first case in which the equivalence of director and officer duty was explicitly stated by a court); Lawrence A. Hamermesh & A. Gilchrist Sparks III, *Corporate Officers and the Business Judgment Rule: A Reply to Professor Johnson*, 60 BUS. LAW 865, 876 (2005) (arguing that the policies underlying the BJR apply with "equal force" to both directors and officers).
26. *Caremark*, 698 A.2d at 961–62.
27. *Id.* at 971 (emphasis added).
28. *Stone*, 911 A.2d at 370.

monitor or oversee its operations thus disabling themselves from being informed of risks or problems requiring their attention."[29]

The "utter failure to attempt" threshold in *Caremark* and the "red flags" exception in *Stone* offer great insulation to nonprofit directors in the face of criminal activity occurring in the organization. At least as the contours of common law fiduciary duties are articulated in Delaware—by far the most important and influential corporate jurisdiction in the United States—nonprofit directors rarely face personal civil, let alone criminal, liability for corporate misdeeds.[30] Quite to the contrary, potentially liable directors and officers have generally enjoyed a cozy relationship with government prosecutors.[31] While individual executives certainly face intense media scrutiny in the midst of corporate scandals,[32] those same high-ranking corporate agents receive significant incentives for identifying institutional corporate wrongdoing in exchange for leniency regarding their individual complicity in the corporate crime.[33]

---

29. *Id.*

30. *See* OFFICE OF SEN. ELIZABETH WARREN, 1ST ANN. REP., RIGGED JUSTICE: 2016 HOW WEAK ENFORCEMENT LETS CORPORATE OFFENDERS OFF EASY 4 (Jan. 2016), https://www.warren.senate.gov/files/documents/Rigged_Justice_2016.pdf ("Despite this rhetoric, DOJ civil and criminal settlements—and enforcement actions by other federal agencies—continually fail to impose any serious threat of punishment on corporate offenders.").

31. *Id.*

32. *Id.*

33. *Id.*

III. The Yates Memo and Federal Enforcement of Corporate Criminality[34]

The Yates Memo instructs federal prosecutors to ferret out and punish individual executives, officers, and board members who commit crimes on behalf of the corporation.[35] The Memo arose in the aftermath of several major banking scandals where the failure to hold corporate executives responsible rocked public confidence in the capital markets and justice system.[36] The prosecutorial policy shift embraced in the Yates Memo stemmed from the basic realization:

> Corporations can only commit crimes through flesh-and-blood people. It's only fair that the people who are responsible for committing those crimes be held accountable. The public needs to have confidence that there is one system of justice and it applies equally regardless of whether that crime occurs on a street corner or in a boardroom.[37]

---

34. In prior work, I provided a similar explication of the prevailing standards under the Yates Memo. As a result, some of this section is an edited excerpt from Michael R. Siebecker & Andrew Brandes, *Corporate Compliance and Criminality, Does the Common Law Promote Culpable Blindness?*, 50 CONN. L. REV. 387, 393 (2018).

35. *See* Sally Q. Yates, Remarks at the New York City Bar Association White Collar Crime Conference (May 10, 2016), https://www.justice.gov/opa/speech/deputy-attorney-general-sally-q-yates-delivers-remarks-new-york-city-bar-association ("[H]olding accountable the people who committed the wrongdoing is essential if we are truly going to deter corporate misdeeds, have a real impact on corporate culture and ensure that the public has confidence in our justice system. We cannot have a different system of justice — or the perception of a different system of justice — for corporate executives than we do for everyone else.").

36. *See* Opinion, *No Crime, No Punishment*, N.Y. TIMES, (Aug. 25, 2012), http://www.NYTimes.com/2012/08/26/opinion/sunday/no-crime-no-punishment.html (reporting that no banks or executives would face criminal charges for the financial crisis and public confidence in the law eroding); *see also* Sarah White, *Not One Top Wall Street Executive Has Been Convicted of Criminal Charges Related to 2008 Crisis*, HUFF. POST (Sept. 13, 2013, 7:50 AM), http://www.huffingtonpost.com/2013/09/13/wall-street-prosecution_n_3919792.html (comparing various countries' handling of criminal charges after the crisis and what regulations led to the difference); Aruna Viswanatha, *Elizabeth Warren Says DOJ and SEC Are Lousy at Enforcement*, WALL ST. J., (Jan. 29, 2016, 3:15 PM), https://www.wsj.com/articles/BL-WB-60687 (detailing Elizabeth Warren's comments on weak enforcement by the SEC).

37. William D. Cohan, *Justice Dept. Shift on White-Collar Crime is Long Overdue*, N.Y. TIMES, (Sept. 11, 2015), https://www.NYTimes.com/2015/09/12/business/dealbook/justice-dept-shift-on-white-collar-crime-is-long-overdue.html.

By attempting to hold individual corporate actors responsible for corporate crimes, the DOJ hoped to restore a crumbling public trust.[38]

Despite early skepticism regarding the impact of the Yates Memo on criminal prosecutions of individual corporate actors,[39] little doubt remained following the arrests of several Volkswagen executives connected with the auto emissions defeat device scandal.[40] In January 2017, Volkswagen pled guilty on three criminal felony counts and paid $4.3 billion in fines resulting from its emissions cheating device installed in thousands of diesel vehicles[41] and from obstructing justice in lying about the scheme.[42] But in addition to simply securing the corporation's confession of guilt, the DOJ announced criminal charges against six Volkswagen executives for

---

38. Devlin Barrett, *Justice Department Renews Focus on White-Collar Cases*, WALL ST. J., (Sept. 9, 2015, 9:43 PM), https://www.wsj.com/articles/justice-department-renews-focus-on-white-collar-cases-1441849429.

39. *See* OFFICE OF SEN. ELIZABETH WARREN, *supra* note 30, at 4 ("Despite this rhetoric, DOJ civil and criminal settlements—and enforcement actions by other federal agencies—continually fail to impose any serious threat of punishment on corporate offenders."); U.S. CHAMBER, INSTITUTE FOR LEGAL REFORM, DOJ'S NEW THRESHOLD FOR 'COOPERATION' 4–5 (May 2016), https://instituteforlegalreform.com/wp-content/uploads/2020/10/YatesMemoPaper_Web.pdf; David Woodcock & John T. Sullivan, Commentary, *Individuals in the Cross Hairs? What This Means for Directors*, JONES DAY (March 2016), http://www.jonesday.com/individuals-in-the-cross-hairs-what-this-means-for-directors-03-10-2016/ ("The Yates Memo has the potential to affect many aspects of corporate investigations and prosecutions, but it does not change the standards for proving criminal conduct beyond a reasonable doubt, which is a serious hurdle to proving individual liability. Nevertheless, the government's focus on individual liability creates additional risks."); Rena Steinzor, *White-Collar Reset: The DOJ's Yates Memo and its Potential to Protect Health, Safety, and the Environment*, 7 WAKE FOREST J.L. & POL'Y 39, 66–67 (2017).

40. *See* Tabuchi et al., *supra* note 2 (reporting criminal charges announced by federal prosecutors in the Volkswagen emissions cheating scandal); Ewing, et al., *supra* note 2 (reporting the arrest of Oliver Schmidt in connection with Volkswagen's emission cheating).

41. *See* Tabuchi et al., *supra* note 2 (reporting criminal charges announced by federal prosecutors in the Volkswagen emissions cheating scandal); For a detailed discussion of the Defeat Device Scandal, see Guilbert Gates, et al., *How Volkswagen's 'Defeat Devices' Worked*, N.Y. TIMES, (Mar. 16, 2017), https://www.nytimes.com/interactive/2015/business/international/vw-diesel-emissions-scandal-explained.html?mcubz=0.

42. Press Release, Off. of Pub. Affs., U.S. Dep't of Just., Volkswagen AG Agrees to Plead Guilty and Pay $4.3 Billion in Criminal and Civil Penalties; Six Volkswagen Executives and Employees are Indicted in Connection with Conspiracy to Cheat U.S. Emissions Tests (Jan. 11, 2017), https://www.justice.gov/opa/pr/volkswagen-ag-agrees-plead-guilty-and-pay-43-billion-criminal-and-civil-penalties-six.

their instrumental roles in perpetuating the fraud.[43] Publicly emphasizing the new focus on individual culpability, Deputy Attorney General Yates stated, "[t]his wasn't simply the action of some faceless, multinational corporation.... This conspiracy involved flesh-and-blood individuals.... We've followed the evidence—from the showroom to the boardroom—and it brought us to the people whose indictments we announce today."[44] Prior to this new zealous prosecution program, the common-law presumption embodied in the BJR regularly shielded directors and officers from liability for lax oversight practices. By targeting individual wrongdoers responsible for perpetrating—or casting a blind eye to—Volkswagen's fraudulent scheme, the DOJ ushered in a new era of stringent scrutiny of directors and officers regarding corporate oversight practices.

Moreover, the prosecution of corporate wrongdoing by the federal government under the Yates Memo extends to nonprofit organizations as well as for-profit corporations. Around the time of the Volkswagen scandal in 2017, a Minnesota nonprofit and two of its principals agreed to pay over $4.5 million to settle claims that the entity violated the False Claims Act by hiring unlicensed healthcare providers and fraudulently submitting thousands of claims.[45] The following year, the DOJ announced a three-year prison sentence for the deputy chairman and secretary general of a Chinese non-governmental organization for bribery and money laundering.[46] The focus remains on prosecuting the individuals responsible for corporate criminality. As recently as October 2021, in a memo from current Deputy Attorney General, Lisa Monaco, the DOJ announced that zealous prosecution of corporate wrongdoing would continue under the guidelines of the original Yates Memo.[47]

---

43. Tabuchi et al., *supra* note 2.
44. Press Release, *supra* note 43.
45. Jones Day, Comment., *Yates Memo's Influence Felt in DOJ Health Care Enforcement* (Aug. 2017), https://www.jonesday.com/en/insights/2017/08/yates-memos-influence-felt-in-doj-health-care-enforcement.
46. *See* Press Release, S. Dist. N.Y., U.S. Dep't of Just., Patrick Ho, Former Head of Organization Backed by Chinese Energy Conglomerate, Sentenced to 3 Years in Prison for International Bribery and Money Laundering Offenses (Mar. 25, 2019), https://www.justice.gov/usao-sdny/pr/patrick-ho-former-head-organization-backed-chinese-energy-conglomerate-sentenced-3.
47. Memorandum from Lisa Monaco, Deputy Att'y Gen., U.S. Dep't of Just., Corporate Crime Advisory Group and Initial Revisions to Corporate Criminal Enforcement Policies (Oct. 28, 2021), https://www.justice.gov/dag/page/file/1445106/download.

IV. The Incongruity Between Federal Law and State Common Law

The shift in prosecutorial focus by the DOJ pursuant to the Yates Memo has substantially disrupted the lazy coziness between the government and ostensibly complicit corporate actors. With the government now holding directors and officers to higher standards of oversight than the common law requires, leniency for individual transgressions no longer comes with simple cooperation in securing criminal sanctions against the corporate entity. Instead, the DOJ requires a complete confession from individual corporate actors and compatriot implication. For instance, pursuant to the US Attorney's Manual that guides DOJ prosecutions:

> [Compliance programs must be] established by corporate management to prevent and detect misconduct and to ensure that corporate activities are conducted in accordance with applicable criminal and civil laws, regulations, and rules.... However, the existence of a compliance program is not sufficient, in and of itself, to justify not charging a corporation for criminal misconduct undertaken by its officers, directors, employees, or agents.[48]

Moreover, the Yates Memo eliminates or severely restricts former officer and director safe havens such as corporate cooperation credits, individual plea-bargaining agreements, and the prioritization of prosecutions of companies over those that target individuals.[49]

In light of the focus on individual culpability for corporate malfeasance, the common law fiduciary standards for oversight announced in *Caremark* and *Stone* do not provide reliable guidance for avoiding civil or criminal liability. Those cases articulate the contours of corporate fiduciary duties far out of line with what federal prosecutors demand. As a result, counsel for for-profit and nonprofit directors suggest imple-

---

48. US Dep't of Just., US Att'y's Manual § 9-28.800 (2015), https://www.justice.gov/usam/usam-9-28000-principles-federal-prosecution-business-organizations#9-28.800.

49. *Id.*

menting corporate compliance systems far more stringent than required under prevailing common law.[50] As one legal advisor commented:

> [T]he increase in the number of enforcement actions against non-profit boards and their officers and directors and the Yates Memo sends the message that the government is taking an increased interest in compliance oversight and that those individuals who fail to satisfy their duties will be held accountable for misconduct arising within the organization.[51]

Information-gathering and reporting systems that might minimally comport with common-law fiduciary duties can no longer fully insulate corporate officers and directors from liability. To the extent government prosecutors uncover some individual complicity in corporate criminality, the broad protection afforded by the BJR will simply not apply. As a result of the Yates Memo, what might have been a minimally compliant oversight system under the common law now becomes actionable.

V. Implications for Oversight in Fraternal Organizations

In light of the rather lax oversight duty embedded in existing corporate fiduciary principles and the renewed dedication by the federal government to zealous prosecution of corporate wrongdoing, what practical implications arise for directors of fraternal organizations regarding their oversight obligations? As stated at the outset of this chapter, answering this question seems especially important considering a spate of recent national scandals involving fraternal hazing, sexual misconduct, forced consumption of alcohol and drugs, embezzlement, and other financial misdeeds. At least three important practical considerations arise

---

50. *See, e.g.*, Michael W. Peregrine, *Beyond Caremark: Individual and Corporate Liability Considerations*, N.Y.L. Sch. Compliance & Enf't Blog (Dec. 7, 2016), https://wp.nyu.edu/compliance_enforcement/2016/12/07/beyond-caremark-individual-and-corporate-liability-considerations/; Woodcock & Sullivan, *supra* note39; Michael Volkov, *Corporate Directors in the Enforcement Cross-Hairs*, Corruption, Crime & Compliance Blog (March 23, 2016), http://blog.volkovlaw.com/2016/03/corporate-directors-enforcement-cross-hairs/.

51. Zinder, *supra* note 20, at 26.

from this growing tension between state and federal standards for nonprofit director conduct.

First, nonprofit directors should not expect that compliance with existing common-law fiduciary standards will insulate them from liability or prosecution. Although the duty of good faith and the component duty of oversight remain essential to effective operation of a fraternal organization, the common law sets an incredibly low bar for what represents actionable director misconduct.[52] The "utter failure to attempt" threshold in *Caremark* and the "red flags" exception in *Stone* make it seem as if even with criminal activity infecting the fraternal organization, directors remain comfortably immune from liability or responsibility.

Although the common law might cast a blind eye to oversight failures, the federal government and other regulatory bodies now pursue those lapses with dedicated fervor. When criminal activity occurs within the fraternal organization, directors get scrutinized well beyond whether they utterly failed to implement an effective information-gathering and monitoring system that could have rooted out the nefarious activity occurring under their watch. An ethic of holding individuals at the highest rungs of management responsible for what occurs within an organization provides the new beacon for enforcement.[53] So even when criminal

---

52. *See* Stephen M. Bainbridge et al., *The Convergence of Good Faith and Oversight*, 55 UCLA L. Rev. 559, 560–61 (2008) (citing Bayless Manning, *The Business Judgment Rule and the Director's Duty of Attention: Time for Reality*, 39 Bus. Law. 1477, 1494 (1984), (noting that "most of what boards do 'does not consist of taking affirmative action on individual matters' but rather consists of a 'continuing flow of supervisory process'")); *id.* (citing Jonathan L. Johnson, et. al., *Boards of Directors: A Review and Research Agenda*, 22 J. Mgmt. 409, 411 (1996), finding that "[m]onitoring the performance of corporate management is not just one of the board's three principal functions, it is, arguably, *prima inter pares*.").

53. Zinder, *supra* note 20, at 14 ("[T]he risks associated with failures of board members to fulfill their role fall not only upon the organizations, but on the board members themselves. While such exposure is not unprecedented, with the September 9, 2015 issuance of the Yates Memorandum the government has signaled that it is shifting its focus to individuals so that, unlike after the financial crisis where individuals were not held accountable for the failures of their corporations, individuals at all levels of the organization (including the board) will increasingly be the specific focus of government regulatory and enforcement expectations and actions.").

hazing occurs at a local chapter, the national fraternity may be the target for culpability.[54]

Second, fraternal directors must look to other regulatory regimes for guidance regarding what risks of liability might arise for failed oversight. Surveying the full panoply of those statutes, rules, and regulations lies far outside the scope of this short chapter. Nonetheless, whether with respect to state consumer fraud statutes, the False Claims Act, federal civil rights laws, anti-money-laundering regulations, or a host of other financial or moral regulations, directors will more likely be held to account for the organization's failure to comply with the law than in the past. In light of the 2015 Yates Memo and the recent rededication to its principles by the current DOJ, asserting that directors comported with common law fiduciary duties will fall on deaf ears. Those fiduciary guardrails remain in place to guide nonprofit directors, but how they get embraced on the ground requires a deeper understanding of a wider web of laws and regulations that affect the organization's actual practices.

Third, to insulate themselves more fully from prosecution or liability, directors of fraternal organizations should implement a robust information-gathering and monitoring system to ferret out any persistent wrongdoing within the organization. Whether with respect to conflicting financial transactions involving directors and officers, malfeasance in soliciting contributions, ensuring safe practices at local chapters, or myriad other activities that the fraternal organization might pursue, directors need to keep abreast of what transpires under their watch.[55] Rather than adopt an oversight process that remains minimally compliant with lax common law standards, nonprofit directors should pursue best practices.[56]

But what are those best practices for oversight that nonprofit directors should pursue? Scholars and practitioners offer a wide swath of suggestions. Among some of the most important, directors should consider (1) requiring annual disclosures for directors and officers regarding fi-

---

54. David W. Bianchi & Michael E. Levine, *Hazing Horrors: Who's Accountable*, 55 TRIAL 52 (2019).

55. WEIL, GOTSCHALL & MANGES LLP, GUIDE TO NONPROFIT GOVERNANCE 2 (May 2019), https://www.weil.com/~/media/guide-to-nonprofit-governance-2019.pdf.

56. Hazen & Hazen, *supra* note 4, at 395–403.

nancial relationships with the organization, other directors and officers, or members; (2) adopting a robust conflicts of interest policy covering directors, officers, and key employees; (3) embracing a fair and transparent system for executive compensation and retention; (4) publishing a code of conduct and ethics to guide all who inhabit the organization; (5) implementing a whistleblower policy that incentivizes the flow of information regarding transgressions at any level within the organization; (6) engaging in annual self-evaluations to identify potential shortcomings and matters requiring special attention; and (7) employing a robust system to monitor financial transactions, whether related to investments, solicitations, or general operations.[57] Although some ambiguity obviously exists regarding what best practices actually entail, the aspirational focus better insulates directors from liability than an approach targeting minimal compliance.

In the end, the content of the duty of oversight for nonprofit directors remains in a state of some flux. The fiduciary framework governing the duties of nonprofit directors seems to require a low level of oversight. But in recent years, nonprofit directors have come under fire from the federal government and other regulatory bodies when criminal activity infects the organization. In order to lessen the likelihood of liability—both for directors and the nonprofit organizations they serve—directors of fraternal organizations should embrace a robust system for information gathering and monitoring that best enables the board to ensure compliance with the mission of the enterprise and compliance with the law.

---

57. *Id.*; WEIL, GOTSCHALL & MANGES LLP, *supra* note 55, at 2.

CHAPTER 3

Fraternity and Sorority Governance

Alina Ball

I. Governance Overview

There are six subgroups of collegiate-based fraternities and sororities: (1) National Asian, Pacific Islander, and Desi American Panhellenic Association; (2) National Multicultural Greek Council; (3) National Panhellenic Conference; (4) National Pan-Hellenic Council; (5) North American Interfraternity Conference; and (6) independent or local fraternities. All groups are governed under similar structures, but each possesses different histories and approaches that explain their distinctions. This chapter explores the corporate law commonalities among these subgroups regarding governance issues.

Corporate governance is a generic term that refers broadly to the rules, structures, processes, customs, or laws by which organizations are operated, regulated, and controlled. Moreover, corporate governance encompasses the ways in which rights and responsibilities are distributed between the various constituencies of an organization. In the context of fraternities and sororities, the constituencies that comprise their governance models include the national organization, chapter organization, housing corporation, national directors,[1] alumni members, undergradu-

---

1. While sororities and fraternities use different names internally, the law recognizes the individuals who make up the legislative body of the corporation as the directors.

ate or collegiate members, chapter and national officers, and national and chapter committee members. When one speaks of sorority or fraternity governance, they may mean any one of, all of, or the intersection between multiple of these constituencies. Moreover, an individual may serve multiple roles and functions within the fraternal organizational structure, making it difficult to discern in which capacity they may be acting.

As an individual's governance duties are context-dependent, it is necessary first to understand the various entities within the fraternity and sorority structure and then isolate specific governance issues for analysis. The following briefly describes the various entities and relationships within the sorority and fraternity structure to provide the rudiments of fraternity and sorority governance.

II. National Organization

The national organization of the sorority or fraternity ("National")[2] is the administration hub and provides educational resources to the chapters. Even for a fraternity with a national arm, there is substantial autonomy at the chapter level.[3] Generally, the National is incorporated as a nonprofit[4] in the state of its national headquarters.

Acknowledging that some fraternities may refer to volunteer alums who help educate chapters as "directors," this essay does not use the term directors in that context.

2. Although this essay uses the term "National," it acknowledges that several fraternal organizations are indeed international in scope. Moreover, not every sorority or fraternity has a national or international counterparty. Indeed, the term "local" can be used to describe fraternities and sororities that are independently established at a single campus or location, with no national presence. However, single chapter sororities and fraternities are considered the exception and not the rule. National organizations are ubiquitous within fraternal structures and their influence on the industry necessitates their inclusion in a conversation on sorority and fraternity governance and corporate structure.

3. *See* Smith v. Delta Tau Delta, Inc., 9 N.E.3d 154, 161–63 (Ind. 2014) (describing the chapter as "self-governing" and finding "no evidence that the national fraternity assumed any duty of preventative, direct supervision and control of the behaviors of its local chapter members"); *see also* Bogenberger v. Pi Kappa Alpha Corp., 104 N.E.3d 1110, 1120 (Ill. 2018) (finding the national organization lacked control over the chapter because, even though the national organization promulgated rules for the chapter, the facts did not establish it dictated how the chapter implemented those rules).

4. Usha Rodrigues, *Entity and Identity*, 60 EMORY L.J. 1257, 1304 (2011) ("Fraternities and sororities are exempt organizations classified as social clubs under § 501(c)(7).").

III. National Board of Directors

State corporation codes endow the board of directors (or council)[5] of the National with the central role of managing the affairs of the National. Thus, the board of directors has the inherent authority to legally bind the National. However, directors only have this authority when acting as a collective body, not in their capacity as individual directors.

Directors are often elected by delegates from the chapters and are responsible for supervising the operations of the National. The board of directors does not run the day-to-day operations. Instead, the officers—often appointed by the directors—are delegated authority from the board of directors to manage the day-to-day operations of the chapter, under the oversight of the board. Both directors and officers have fiduciary duties to the National. Chief among them are the duty of care, the duty of loyalty, and the duty of good faith.

IV. Housing Corporations

Sorority and fraternity housing is conservatively estimated at the collective value of approximately three billion dollars. It is estimated that one in eight American students at four-year colleges lives in a fraternity or sorority house. Thus, in recent years, Nationals have recognized the goodwill connected to sorority and fraternity real estate, causing separate entities to be formed to own, operate, and maintain the real estate. These housing corporations are often organized as tax-exempt nonprofits. A trend is for there to be a tax-exempt national housing corporation with subsidiary LLCs or subordinate nonprofits for each held real property. For the subordinate nonprofits, the national housing corporation could be the solo voting member. Separating each property into its own subsidiary or subordinate entity limits liability for the national housing corporation.

The housing corporation will own the property where the collegiate chapter members live and engage in social activities and rituals. As a

---

5. While the internal name can vary and may be unique to the sorority or fraternity, the governing body (regardless of its name) is recognized by the state as the board of directors.

corporation, the housing corporation must maintain a board of directors and officers. Typically, the housing corporation directors and officers are chapter alumni.

V. Fraternity Foundation

The National may form a foundation to assist and fund the charitable and educational activities and projects that benefit the alumni and undergraduate members[6] or otherwise exemplify the values of the sorority or fraternity. Fraternity foundations are nonprofit corporations with public charity tax-exempt status.[7] As corporations, these foundations must maintain a board of directors and officers. Typically, the foundation directors are the alumni members.

VI. Chapter Organization

Unlike the National, housing corporations, or foundations, most sorority and fraternity chapters are undergraduate groups organized as nonprofit, unincorporated associations.[8] This means that, although chapters are recognized by the college or university, they do not file for state incorporation and are not organized as legal entities that provide limited liability.[9] Chapters are also recognized by the National, and are often comprised of either collegiate, graduate, or alumni members.

---

6. Ted Lieder & Marvin Friedlander, *Fraternity Foundation Grants*, EXEMPT ORGANIZATIONS-TECHNICAL INSTRUCTION PROGRAM, I.R.S., N-1 (2003) https://www.irs.gov/pub/irs-tege/eotopicn03.pdf ("Financial support provided by fraternity foundations to fraternity or sorority members typically includes scholarships and funding for leadership classes.").

7. *See* Daley v. Alpha Kappa Alpha Sorority, Inc., 26 A.3d 723, 726 (D.C. 2011) ("Separate from AKA is the Foundation, which is a private nonprofit entity incorporated in Illinois that provides scholarships and other community-oriented programs. The Foundation was created in 1980 by leaders of AKA but is a separate legal entity.").

8. Howard L. Oleck, *Nonprofit Unincorporated Associations*, 21 CLEVE. ST. L. REV. 44, 45 (1972).

9. Short v. Ross, Nos. X10UWYCV126023797, X10UWYCV136023885, X10UWYCV146023606, X10UWYCV146023607, 2015 WL 5981142, at *2 (Conn. Super. Ct. Sept. 16, 2015) 2 (describing an unincorporated fraternity chapter as "a legally recognized entity insofar as it can sue and be sued in its own name").

Chapters can be organized to be specific to a college or university and, in limited circumstances, geographic region. Although often unincorporated, chapters are still tax-exempt associations under § 501(c)(7).[10]

VII. National Governing Documents

As a general matter, fraternities and sororities are social clubs pursuant to Internal Revenue Code § 501(c)(7).[11] A social club or voluntary organization's constitution, bylaws, and other rules are a contract between the organization and members unless they are against public policy.[12] Organizations are, therefore, contractually obligated to follow their own rules.[13]

---

10. *See* Rodrigues, *supra* note 4; *see also* sources cited *infra* note 11.

11. *See* I.R.C. § 501(c)(7) (2022) (listing as a category of exempt organizations: "[c]lubs organized for pleasure, recreation, and other nonprofitable purposes, substantially all of the activities of which are for such purposes and no part of the net earnings of which inures to the benefit of any private shareholder"); 26 C.F.R. § 1.501(c)(10)(a)(2) (providing "a national college fraternity" as an example for "[a]ny organization described in section 501(c)(7)"); *see also* Zeta Beta Tau Fraternity, Inc. v. Comm'r., 87 T.C. 421, 434 (1986) (concluding that the petitioner, a fraternity, is a "social club described in section 501(c)(7)" and "that national college fraternities are intended by Congress to be treated as exempt under section 501(c)(7) ...").

12. *See* Daley v. Alpha Kappa Alpha Sorority, Inc., 26 A.3d 723, 731 (D.C. 2011) ("'[T]he formal bylaws of an organization are to be construed as a contractual agreement between the organization and its members....'" (quoting Meshel v. Ohev Sholom Talmud Torah, 869 A.2d 343, 361 (D.C. 2005))); Grand Chapter, Order of Eastern Star v. Klutch, 125 A. 72, 74 (Md. App. Ct. 1924) (maintaining that organizational policies regarding membership should not be questioned "unless some principle of public policy is involved"); *see also* 24th Senatorial Dist. Republican Comm. v. Alcorn, 820 F.3d 624 (4th Cir. 2016) ("The constitution and by-laws adopted by a voluntary association constitutes a contract between the members, which, if not immoral or contrary to public policy, or the law, will be enforced by the courts." (quoting Gottlieb v. Econ. Stores, Inc., 102 S.E.2d 345, 351 (1958))).

13. *See* N.A.A.C.P. v. Golding, 679 A.2d 554, 561 (Md. App. Ct. 1996) ("While we ordinarily refrain from reviewing decisions of unincorporated private associations, we note that if an organization acts inconsistently with its own rules, its action may be sufficiently arbitrary to invite judicial review."); Grempler v. Multiple Listing Bureau of Harford Cnty., Inc., 266 A.2d 1, 4–5 (Md. App. Ct. 1970) (expressing that a private voluntary organization's authority over membership is "subject only to its own constitution, charter and by-laws.").

Endowing the national board of directors with binding authority does not resolve a variety of governance issues that are likely to arise for fraternities and sororities. It does not explain, for example, the mechanisms for resolution when these constituencies disagree, nor how to determine which specific matters are decided by which constituencies. Thus, judicial decisions[14] and, primarily, the bylaws[15] of the National fill these gaps to create the sorority and fraternity governance structure.

Like all corporations, the National is governed by the internal affairs doctrine,[16] which requires that it must abide by the default rules of corporate governance of its state of incorporation.[17] If the National adopts bylaws, those bylaws must also be consistent with their state's corporate code.[18] Adopting bylaws allows the sorority or fraternity to—within reason—customize its governance and internal processes to meet its par-

---

14. *See e.g.*, Sigma Chi Fraternity v. Regents of Univ. of Colo., 258 F. Supp. 515 (D. Colo. 1966) (upholding campus ban on racially restricted membership selection as reasonable); *but see* Cynthia Estlund, *Are Unions A Constitutional Anomaly?*, 114 MICH. L. REV. 169, 203 n.182 (2015) (explaining that there are few cases "reviewing significant legal intrusions into the internal affairs of voluntary associations."); *Short, supra* note 9, at *2 ("Further compounding the confusion [of the fraternity chapter] is a dearth of case law which discusses, defines or otherwise clarifies the relationships, rights, and responsibilities of [chapter] members, either to each other, the association, or third parties.").

15. *See* Josephine R. Potuto, *The NCAA Rules Adoption, Interpretation, Enforcement, and Infractions Prcesses: The Laws that Regulate Them and the Nature of Court Review*, 12 VAND. J. ENT. & TECH. L. 257, 267–68 (2010) (discussing formal associations as "fundamentally big contracts," where NCAA bylaws outline the "shared normative and cultural understandings [regarding] a wide range of subject areas with multi-varied and complex interrelationships," such as recruitment, academic eligibility, boards, councils, cabinets, committee, and sanction violations). Often referred to as constitutions, bylaws are called different names by different sororities and fraternities. But the law recognizes the governing entity document as the bylaws of the corporate entity regardless of the internal name.

16. Edgar v. MITE Corp., 457 U.S. 624, 645 (1982) ("The internal affairs doctrine is a conflict of laws principle which recognizes that only one State should have the authority to regulate a corporation's internal affairs—matters peculiar to the relationships among or between the corporation and its current officers, directors, and shareholders—because otherwise a corporation could be faced with conflicting demands.").

17. As voluntary associations, fraternities and sororities enjoy freedom from intrusive regulation of their internal affairs. *See, e.g.*, Roberts v. U.S. Jaycees, 468 U.S. 609, 622–23 (1984) (holding government action unconstitutional if there is "intrusion into the internal structure or affairs of an association" like a "regulation that forces the group to accept members it does not desire").

18. MODEL NONPROFIT CORP. ACT § 8.01(b) (AM. BAR ASS'N 3d ed. 2008).

ticular circumstances.[19] Bylaws also signal to directors, officers, chapter members, and outside parties that the fraternity or sorority has devoted time and attention to understanding its governance, meaning that its leadership takes the responsibilities of operating a sorority or fraternity chapter seriously. Thus, bylaws are a staple charter document for fraternities and sororities.

Once adopted, the bylaws are the legally binding rules[20] for both the internal governance and external dealings of the sorority or fraternity. Officers, directors, and members regularly consult the bylaws for issues on voting processes, actions that legally bind the National, and understanding fiduciary duties. Although primarily an internal document, individuals outside the National will also consult and review the bylaws. For example, the bylaws must be submitted to the Internal Revenue Service or filed with the state attorney general if the National is a charitable organization.[21] Financial institutions such as banks may also review of the bylaws before engaging with the sorority or fraternity. In the event of a litigation dispute, judges will also review and interpret the bylaws.[22] For these reasons, bylaws need to be thoughtfully drafted and regularly consulted by the National and its various constituencies to avoid confusion, provide direction and consistency, and inspire confidence, accountability, and transparency in the operations of the sorority or fraternity.

Considered proprietary, National bylaws are not readily available outside of fraternity or sorority membership. Although distinct to each sorority or fraternity, generally, the bylaws address requirements of the board of directors—specifically around notice to directors, meeting re-

---

19. Jill E. Fisch, *Governance by Contract: The Implications for Corporate Bylaws*, 106 Cal. L. Rev. 373, 378 (2018) (describing firm constituents' engagement with bylaws as an example of private ordering); Airgas, Inc. v. Air Prods. & Chem., Inc., 8 A.3d 1182, 1188 (Del. 2010) (describing charters and bylaws as contracts to which contract interpretation applies).

20. George S. Geis, *Ex-Ante Corporate Governance*, 41 J. Corp. L. 609, 611 (2016) (discussing bylaws as ex-ante "vehicle for expanding, constraining, or channeling power in the corporate ecosystem").

21. Lloyd Hitoshi Mayer, *Fragmented Oversight of Nonprofits in the United States: Does it Work? Can it Work?*, 91 Chi.-Kent L. Rev. 937, 951 (2016).

22. *See e.g.*, Stark v. Zeta Phi Beta Sorority, Inc., 587 F. Supp. 2d. 170, 177 (D.D.C. 2008) (referencing sorority bylaws in suit where member was expelled from sorority); Shaheen v. Yonts, No. 5:06–CV–00173, 2009 WL 87458, at *3 (Jan. 13, 2009) (referencing fraternity constitution and statutory code to determine if alumni advisor must monitor or control the activities of the fraternity members).

quirements, voting procedures, and processes conformance which will show fulfillment of the fiduciary duties; membership classification, eligibility, and voting authority; indemnification of the directors and officers; and amendment procedures.

VIII. Interplay between National and Chapter Bylaws

A chapter applies to the National to be recognized (often designated by Greek-letters), because the chartering and revocation of a charter are governed exclusively through the National. The majority of the chapter's governance model is influenced by the National, but the specifics of how the chapter governs itself are left for the chapter leadership to determine.

Although unincorporated, chapters also often have bylaws. These bylaws must be consistent with university and college policies, especially regarding alcohol and safety,[23] and are substantially informed by on the National bylaws. Chapters are often required to include or incorporate by reference in their bylaws required provisions from the National.[24] The provisions determined by the National are used to create uniformity and cohesion among the various chapters of the sorority or fraternity.[25] This practice also ensures that practical matters, such as membership dues, are consistently remitted by chapters to the National. Chapters are often required in their bylaws to collect national dues and fees from its members and remit the correct amounts to the National. Chapters may be required to obtain the National's approval to participate in certain pro-

---

23. Furek v. Univ. of Del., 594 A.2d 506, 520 (Del. 1991) (finding "the university cannot abandon its residual duty of control" over fraternities); *but see* Univ. of Denver v. Whitlock, 744 P.2d 54, 60 (Colo. 1987) ("[F]raternity and sorority self-governance with minimal supervision appears to have been fostered by the University.").

24. *See e.g.*, Brown v. Delta Tau Delta, 118 A.3d 789, 794 (Me. 2015) (finding local chapter bylaws were required to adopt national organization's constitution).

25. Jeanette Norris, Paula S. Nurius & Linda A. Dimeff, *Through Her Eyes: Factors Affecting Women's Perception of and Resistance to Acquaintance Sexual Aggression Threat*, 20 Psych. Women Q. 123, 125 (1996) ("The Greek [fraternity] system constitutes a historically stable social system with many aspects that increase feelings of comfort and conformity among its members: established charters and bylaws, longstanding traditions involving highly scripted events and family-like referents ...").

gramming or to use the National's intellectual property to ensure that it is used within the correct guidelines and monitored.[26]

As a self-governing organization, the chapter is solely responsibility for executing the bylaw provisions and policies, including enforcing the National's standards and code of conduct. In the event the chapter does not adhere to the National's bylaws or standing rules, the bylaws may provide the National with various avenues of recourse. For example, the bylaws may state that if the chapter is out of compliance with national procedures, the National may revoke contractual rights—withdraw insurance coverage or intellectual property rights of the chapter—which would deactivate the chapter and effectively cause the chapter to stop functioning.[27] Additionally, chapter revocation by the National would constitute a material default of the former chapter's lease with the housing corporation or its subsidiary entity, terminating the lease, and immediately ending the former chapter's access to the sorority or fraternity house. In these ways, adherence to the chapter bylaws,[28] several portions of which are determined by the National to have primacy in the event of conflicting provisions in other documents, are a matter of survival for sorority and fraternity chapters.

---

26. Smith v. Delta Tau Delta, 9 N.E.3d 154, 164 (Ind. 2014) ("The relationship between the national fraternity and the local fraternity involves the national fraternity offering informational resources, organizational guidance, common traditions, and its brand to the local fraternity.").

27. Jared S. Sunshine, *The Fraternity as Franchise: A Conceptual Framework*, 42 J.C. & U.L. 375, 403 (2016) ("Invariably, the national [fraternity] organization reserves the power to revoke the charter of chapters that become delinquent in their fees, or violate the terms of that charter and its associated bylaws and risk management policies.... And like the dispossessed franchisee, the members of the dissolved university [fraternity] chapter are not then free to set up a rival fraternity on campus: fraternity constitutions specify that members, once admitted, are not permitted to affiliate with any other fraternity.").

28. In addition to bylaw provisions required by the National, the chapter may also execute intellectual property agreements with the National that can be revoked if the chapter is not in compliance with national standards of conduct.

IX. Defining Roles and Responsibilities

It often requires substantial human capital to effectively operate a chapter. Instead of reinventing the wheel with every new board of directors, fraternities and sororities incorporate into their bylaws the officer position titles and responsibilities necessary for effective operation. In addition to the president, secretary, and treasurer positions that state statutes contemplate or require, chapter bylaws regularly include additional officer positions such as Vice President of Communications, Vice President of Membership, Vice President of Recruitment, Vice President of Intellectual Development, Social Chair, or Philanthropy Chair. Chapter bylaws may also permit the establishment of committees such as the Nominating Committee, Program Committee, Membership Committee, Finance Committee, and Standards Committee. In this way, the bylaws also serve an archival function to memorialize the chapter's best practices for operationalizing its work. This is particularly helpful because, as an unincorporated association, the chapter does not have a default governance structure under the state statute.

The chapter bylaws provide the eligibility requirements for various positions. The board of directors of the chapter often consists of the elected officers. Thus, eligibility for officers and directors is the same. Eligibility may include chapter membership in good standing with a minimum GPA requirement to hold an office. Membership eligibility may specify enrollment, with good standing, in a specific college or university, and require a minimum number of course credits completed. Although members are selected by the chapter, individual members are often approved by the National as well. The bylaws also explain what actions members must take to remain in good standing, such as attending all required chapter meetings, ceremonies, orientations, and maintaining a minimum GPA. Members may also have to attend and participate in various conferences to be eligible for office nomination. Moreover, members are required to pay dues and fees, the majority of which are remitted back to the National.

Although officers and committees may be delegated authority to implement programs and responsibilities of the chapter, the board of directors cannot delegate all of its authority or any authority inconsistent with the bylaws. For example, the ability to amend the bylaws cannot be delegated to a committee of a chapter. The committee may be tasked with reviewing the bylaws and recommending revisions, but revising the bylaws is often reserved for a supermajority vote of the chapter members. In this way, the bylaws explain the distribution of power among the various constituencies of the chapter.

X. Voting Rights

Sorority and fraternity members often possess voting rights at the chapter level and elect delegates to vote on the chapter's behalf at national conventions. At the chapter level, chapter bylaws provide the procedures for both member and director voting. Given their importance in the corporate governance of a chapter, voting procedures are often mandated by the National. Generally, all members in good standing are eligible and encouraged to vote on chapter matters. Common matters that members must vote on include the recruitment and selection of new members, chapter policies, and amendments to the bylaws. Chapter members also vote to elect delegates to attend, represent, and vote for them at the national convention. General members may be defined as those who can attend national meetings but are not eligible to vote because sometimes members must be affiliated with a collegiate or alumni chapter to have voting rights at the national level.

XI. Amendments

Chapter bylaws can be revised by the members after proper notice at any membership meeting. However, national bylaws are amended, after proper notice to voting delegates, often on a semiannual basis and voted on at the national conventions.

XII. Conclusion

Although necessary for good governance, chapter bylaws are not likely to address every governance matter that may arise during the lifecycle of the sorority or fraternity. For this reason, chapters need to amend their bylaws over time and adopt board resolutions and membership policies to supplement the bylaws. Thus, thoughtfulness in drafting bylaws and adherence to these internal procedures and protocol is key to fraternity or sorority success.

CHAPTER 4

Tax-Exempt Law: Internal Revenue Code §§ 501(c)(7), (3), (2), (4)

Jaclyn Cherry

Most fraternal organizations[1] operate in coordination with several entities with similar missions, but choose these organizational relationships carefully to meet their own unique purposes. They take on different entity structures that often include a national fraternity operating as an Internal Revenue Code (IRC) § 501(c)(7) parent organization with several autonomous local chapters, also operating as § 501(c)(7) organizations; a national house corporation operating as either a § 501(c)(7) or (c)(2) organization; a local house corporation operating as a § 501(c)(7); a § 501(c)(3) national or local foundation; or a § 501(c)(2) holding company, which can address specific property issues. While not common, if an organization wanted to participate in political or advocacy activities, a § 501(c)(4) could be created. What varies most in the structural choices that are made by organizations is the unique mission each entity wishes to carry out. For instance, if it is important for an entity to receive funding for charitable or educational efforts, it can create or align itself with a § 501(c)(3) foundation. If in fact the entity will only be involved in social fellowship activity, formation as a standalone § 501(c)(7) usually suffices.

---

1. "Fraternal organization" as used in this chapter is shorthand for both fraternities and sororities.

Operating under any complex and layered structure requires knowledge of tax-exempt law, often lacking among fraternal leaders and members. Therefore, this chapter sets out and clarifies the differences between IRC status as §§ 501(c)(7), (3), (2) or (4) organizations as they pertain to fraternal entities. Further, it lays out the benefits and possible concerns for becoming and maintaining each IRS-designated type of organization, citing IRS code and regulation sections, applicable Private Letter Rulings (PLRs), Revenue Rulings (RRs), and case law. The particular tax-exempt issues fraternal organizations may face is also addressed.

The IRC governs the law of §§ 501(c)(7), (3), (2) and (4) organizations, except for in the area of property tax exemption, which is governed by state law. This chapter will not only address the applicable federal laws but will also canvass the case law and trends regarding charitable property tax exemption for tax and planning purposes. As set forth above, fraternal organizations choose a mixture of these structures to operate, each having significant operational and tax consequences.

For the most part, fraternal foundations are the only organizations of this group that qualify for § 501(c)(3) status. They generally operate as nonprofit organizations that have been granted IRC § 501(c)(3) status by the Internal Revenue Service (IRS). This status permits the foundation to gift funds to another organization for its charitable purpose and receive tax-deductible donations from donors. This section of the IRC exempts qualifying organizations from federal income taxation as follows:

> Corporations, and any community chest, fund, or foundation, organized and operated exclusively for religious, charitable, scientific, testing for public safety, literary, or educational purposes, or to foster national or international amateur sports competition (but only if no part of its activities involve the provision of athletic facilities or equipment), or for the prevention of cruelty to children or animals, no part of the net earnings of which inures to the benefit of any private shareholder or individual, no substantial part of the activities of which is carrying on propaganda, or otherwise attempting, to influence legislation (except as otherwise provided in subsection (h)), and which does not participate in, or intervene in (including the publishing or distributing of statements), any

political campaign on behalf of (or in opposition to) any candidate for public office.[2]

According to this section of the IRC, 501(c)(3) organizations must be organized and operated for charitable, educational, or other listed purposes and meet two additional tests: that no part of the organizations' net earnings inure to the benefit of any private shareholder or individual;[3] and that there be no substantial lobbying or any political electioneering. The political activities limitations do not seem to be an issue for fraternal organizations but will be discussed briefly later in the chapter. How all these tests play out in practical terms as fraternal chapters and national house organizations interact with foundations will be discussed as well.

I. National and Local Chapters Organized as Section 501(c)(7) Organizations

Most national and local fraternal chapters are organized as nonprofit organizations or unincorporated associations that have been granted IRC § 501(c)(7) exempt status governed by federal law. IRC Section 501(c)(7) creates the "social club" exemption. It provides income tax exemption to clubs organized for pleasure, recreation, and other nonprofit purposes, so long as substantially all of its activities are for exempt purposes and no part of its earnings inures to the benefit of any private shareholder. The purpose of a social club is to permit individuals to join together, to provide recreational or social facilities, and to furnish goods and services to its members. To qualify for exemption, personal interaction must exist among members. In general, this exemption extends to social and recreational clubs that are supported solely by membership fees, dues, and assessments.[4] The basis for the exemption from federal income taxes lies in the theory that the income for these entities is more correctly described as the pooled income of its members, and therefore, should not be taxed twice.[5]

---

2. IRC. § 501(c)(3).

3. Id.

4. 26 C.F.R. § 1.501(c)(7)-1.

5. McGlotten v. Connally, 338 F. Supp. 448 (D.D.C. 1972); see also S. Rep. No. 91-552, at 71 (1969).

To be tax exempt, a social club must establish that: (1) it is a club both organized and operated exclusively for pleasure, recreation, and other nonprofit purposes and (2) that no part of its net earnings inures to the benefit of any private individual. To meet the first requirement there must be "personal contacts," "fellowship," or a "commingling" among the club's members.[6] "Fellowship" does not need to be present among every member as long as commingling is a material part of the organization.[7] Members of the organization must be tied together by some common objective directed toward pleasure, recreation, and other nonprofit purposes. The organization's primary objective should not be to provide a service to its members or to save money for its members,[8] and the membership of the club must be limited, and not extend to the general public. Membership restrictions based on race, color, or religion are not permitted.[9]

A social club that is engaged in business is considered to not be operating for pleasure, recreation, or any other nonprofit purpose. Solicitation by advertisement or otherwise for public patronage of its facilities will be considered prima facie evidence that the club is engaged in business and is not operating for tax exempt purposes.[10]

If a group provides services and recreational facilities that are open to the general public or sells products, it is not organized and operated exclusively for exempt purposes.[11] This does not mean that a social club will lose its exemption if it has dealings with the general public. A social club may gain a minimal portion of its gross receipts from the general public's participation in the club's affairs, provided that the participation is incidental to and in furtherance of the organization's purpose and that the outside income does not inure to the members' benefit.[12] This allow-

---

6. Rev. Rul. 58-589, 1958-2 C.B. 266.

7. IRS Gen. Couns. Mem. 23,688 (month day, 1943); Rev. Rul. 58-589, 1958-2 C.B. 266. Statewide and nationwide organizations that are made up of local groups and chapters satisfy the fellowship requirement, as long as "fellowship" constitutes a material part of the local groups and chapters.

8. *See* Rev. Rul. 70-32, 1970-1 C.B. 132; see also I.R.S. Priv. Ltr. Rul. 2010-43-042 (Oct. 29, 2010), where an organization in which the only personal contact among the members consisted of an online forum failed to meet the "commingling" requirement.

9. IRS Priv. Ltr. Rul. 2010-43-042 (Oct. 29, 2010).

10. 26 C.F.R. § 1.501(c)(7)-1(b).

11. "General public" does not include a member's family or dependents.

12. An organization may receive 35% of its gross receipts from something other than membership fees, dues, and assessments. Of that 35%, not more than 15% may be derived

ance of outside income applies when the receipts from the general public are to pay for their share of the expense, or when the transactions are incidental, trivial, non-recurrent activities.[13]

When a substantial part of a Section 501(c)(7) organization's income is from the general public, however, it will not qualify for exemption because this means it has a substantial nonexempt purpose, namely serving the general public. A social club may receive up to 35% of its gross receipts from nonmember sources, including investment income. Within the 35% amount, no more than 15% of gross receipts may be derived from nonmember use of club facilities and services. Where the permitted levels of nonmember income are exceeded, all facts and circumstances will be considered in determining whether the club continues to qualify for exemption. To police nonmember usage of social clubs, the IRS issued Revenue Procedure 71-17,[14] which establishes record-keeping requirements for general public usage. A significant factor reflecting a nonexempt purpose is gross receipts from the general public.[15] When 75% or more of a group using club facilities are members who pay for club services, it is presumed that the entire group are guests of the members, and not the general public. Adequate records must always be kept, and most especially where nonmembers are involved. With respect to all other situations involving use by nonmembers, the club must maintain detailed records of the date, the total number in the party, the total number of nonmembers, the total charges, the charges attributable to nonmembers, and the charges paid by members.[16] If a member pays for nonmembers, a statement signed by the member is required, indicating whether and how much the member will be reimbursed. These provisions ensure that the business use of the social club reflects "personal

---

from the general public's use of the club's facilities or services or from other activities not furthering the organization's purpose. IRS Tech. Adv. Mem. 199912033 (June 25, 1998). This other income (clubs' investment income and net revenue from nonmembers) is not extended tax exemption under § 501(c)(7) of the IRC. *See* I.R.C. § 512(a)(3).

13. Rev. Rul. 66-149, 1966-1 C.B. 146. However, the IRS allowed an exception where income is derived from investment of the proceeds of the organization's former clubhouse, pending the acquisition of new premises.

14. Rev. Proc. 71-17, 1971-1 C.B. 683.

15. *Id.*

16. *Id.*

contacts," "fellowship," or a "commingling" among the business entity or its employees or guests and the other members.

A § 501(c)(7) organization must also meet the private inurement test.[17] While individual members of social clubs obviously derive benefits from their membership, these benefits are a permissible result of the dues and assessments that they have paid to the club. Private inurement occurs when non-dues-generated benefits accrue to members, as when, for example, a social club engages in a business activity for profit (such as the provision of goods and services to nonmembers) that is designed to benefit the members through lower dues or enhanced facilities. The only way the club's net earnings may inure to members of the organization is in the form of additional services offered by the club, without an increase in dues or fees. The pro rata distribution of assets to members upon dissolution of a social club is not considered private inurement, although it may be a taxable event to the recipient.[18]

II. Taxation of Section 501(c)(7) Fraternal Organizations

The only income on which social clubs do not pay federal taxes is their member-generated income and investment income that is set aside. Member-generated income is income from dues, fees, charges, or similar amounts paid by members as consideration for providing them, their dependents or guests, goods, facilities, or services in furtherance of the organization's exempt purposes.[19] All other income is taxed — as for example, investment income (that is not set aside) or income for goods and services paid for by nonmembers.

Since the rationale for the exemption of social clubs is the double-taxation rationale, it makes sense that a social club is only exempt from tax on receipts by its members, because exemption is provided to permit individuals to come together to provide social and recreational facilities and services on a pooled income basis, without tax consequences. In other words, the tax exemption is granted to place members in the same

---

17. IRC § 501(c)(7); *see also* IRC § 501(c)(3).
18. Rev. Rul. 58-501, 1958-2 C.B. 262.
19. IRC. § 512(a)(3)(B).

position as if the member had purchased the goods or services themself. If nonmember income were not taxed, the organization could reduce costs and increase services, which would create an untaxed benefit for the members of the organization. As a result, all outside income, including investment income and receipts from the general public, is taxed, but for one exception set out in the Tax Reform Act of 1969, which added a provision to the IRC that exempted from taxation the investment income of social clubs that was "set aside" for charitable or educational purposes.

a. Set-Asides

The investment income of Section 501(c)(7) fraternal organizations is oftentimes found to be taxable under Section 512(a)(3)(A),[20] though in a House report[21] accompanying the Tax Reform Act of 1969, Congress recognized that investment income could be used by fraternal (and other membership organizations) to further the tax-exempt purposes of the organization and that taxing this would be inappropriate. Therefore, statutory exceptions were enacted as IRC § 512(a)(3)(B)(i) and (ii). These sections state that amounts "set aside" by fraternities and sororities for exempt purposes such as scholarships, student loans, loans on local chapter housing, leadership and citizenship schools, and similar services and activities could be considered educational or charitable purposes.[22] Therefore, such transactions allow for funding opportunities between organizations. If a foundation misuses or otherwise awards a grant that is not an appropriate charitable or educational purpose, it can lose its § 501(c)(3) status, so a fraternal chapter should be advised to not use "set aside" funds for questionable projects. Any mistake in this area could result in taxation (though it would not cost the foundation its exempt status).

In *Zeta Beta Tau Fraternity v. Commissioner*,[23] the court set out two tests for determining whether money was properly "set aside" for income tax purposes. It stated that with regard to Section 501(c)(7) orga-

---

20. Zeta Beta Tau Fraternity, Inc. v. Comm'r, 87 T.C. 421 (1986); *See also* BRUCE R. HOPKINS, THE LAW OF TAX EXEMPT ORGANIZATIONS, § 18.1, at 303 (4th ed. 1983).
21. H. R. Rept. No. 91-413 (1969).
22. *See* S. Rep. No. 91-552 (1969).
23. *Zeta Beta Tau Fraternity, Inc.*, 87 T.C. 421.

nizations, unrelated business taxable income includes all income generated by the organization other than "exempt function income" less expenses related to exempt function income,[24] and allowed for "set asides." It continued that the IRC allows deductions for moneys which are "permanently set aside during the taxable year for a purpose specified in section 170(c)."[25] The two tests are:

1. THE "NO COMMINGLING" TEST

A fund is properly "set aside" if "the organization [does not] commingle it with any amount which is not to be set aside. However, adequate records describing the amount set aside and indicating that it is to be used for the designated purpose are sufficient."[26]

2. THE "NEGLIGIBLE POSSIBILITY THAT THE FUNDS WILL NOT BE USED FOR THE EXEMPT PURPOSE" TEST

Under 26 C.F.R. § 1.642(c)–2(d), funds are properly set aside if "under ... the circumstances of the particular case the possibility that the amount set aside, or to be used, will not be devoted to such purpose or use is so remote as to be negligible."

Fraternal organizations have long followed safe harbor rules set out in the closing agreements from the settlement between the IRS and Phi Gamma Delta[27] for implementing funding from set-aside funds or fraternity foundations. In this settlement agreement, the IRS made it clear that all investment income that is to be set aside should first be deposited in a separate bank account. As qualifying expenditures are incurred, appropriate documentation must be presented to the set-aside account so that funds can be used for qualifying expenditures. While it is permissible for a fraternal foundation to fund educational programs in advance, there can be no reimbursement of general funds to set-aside funding until the

---

24. IRC. § 512(a)(3)(A).

25. 26 C.F.R. § 1.642(c)-2; *see Zeta Beta Tau Fraternity, Inc.*, 87 T.C. 421.

26. 26 C.F.R. § 1.512(a)-4(b)(5).

27. Phi Gamma Delta Club v. United States, 5 F. Supp. 140 (1933); *see* Barbra S. Bromberg, *Revisiting the Phi Gamma Delta IRS Settlement: Part I*, FRATERNAL L. PARTNERS NEWSL. (Fraternal L. Partners, Cincinnati, Ohio),Jan. 1999.

qualifying expenditure is incurred.²⁸ Further, with regard to educational allocations, meal events are not considered qualifying expenditures. A fraternity can set out the details of an educational event so that the educational content percentage can go through set aside funds or be covered by a related fraternity foundation through careful documentation.

Historical materials such as photographs and documents that fraternities wish to display are generally believed to be fundable by a fraternity's set-asides or by a fraternity foundation. The key question is always whether the archives or museum has placed the fraternity in historical context that extends beyond the fraternity experience. It is advisable to open these displays to the public and relate the archives to the fraternity and its role in societal history.²⁹ Often fraternal organizations wish to assist needy alumni or issue awards. To accomplish these goals, the fraternity should establish procedures for granting awards and set out follow-up procedures. Guidelines should be clear and nondiscriminatory, with no indicia of private inurement or private benefit. With careful attention to detail, these types of programs with individuals and family members can be maintained.

Regarding affinity card income and other similar types of income, the current belief is that such income for Section 501(c)(7) organizations is royalty income subject to the "set-aside" rules.³⁰

Nonmember income can be nontaxable and "set aside" when a fraternity fundraises for charitable purposes,³¹ and when the funds are used for social and fraternal purposes. If a fraternal organization rents chapter house rooms to nonmembers or serves meals to them, then it will incur taxable income. As noted earlier, nonmember gross receipts cannot exceed 15% of gross receipts and if they do, the fraternity risks losing its § 501(c)(3) tax-exempt status even though it paid taxes on the profits.³² Passive income used for charitable purposes has a ceiling of 35% for nonmember income but similar to the rule above, the fraternal organization can lose tax-exempt status³³ if not careful.

---

28. Bromberg, *supra* note 27.
29. *Id.*
30. *See* Sierra Club, Inc. v. Comm'r, 86 F.3d 1526 (9th Cir. 1996).
31. *Id.*
32. *See* IRC § 512(a)(3); *see also* Rev. Proc. 71-17, 1971-1 C.B. 683.
33. IRC § 501(c)(7). *See* Sierra Club, Inc. v. Comm'r, 77 T.C.M. (CCH) 1569 (1999); *Sierra Club, Inc.*, 86 F.3d 1526.

Another area of focus for social clubs regards their sales of property.[34] Normally, income from the sale of property will qualify as passive, untaxed income to an exempt organization. But because the unrelated business income tax falls differently on social clubs, such sales income, because it does not come from members, is unrelated business taxable income. Congress, in IRC Section 512(3)(D), allowed social clubs to sell property used directly in the performance of exempt functions, and not pay any tax on the sales income, if in a period beginning one year before the sale and ending three years after it, the organization had used the proceeds to purchase other property used directly in performance of its exempt functions.[35]

b. Unrelated Business Income

While fraternal organizations do not generally engage in business activities, if they do, the unrelated business income tax (UBIT) rules, which tax the unrelated business taxable income of an otherwise exempt organization, apply.[36] Generally, unrelated business taxable income is defined as the gross income derived by any organization from any unrelated trade or business regularly carried on by it, less allowable deductions.[37]

There are three elements that must be met for determining whether there is unrelated business income tax payable in accordance with the IRC and applicable regulations. UBIT is payable by tax-exempt organizations on their net income when the income is:

- from a trade or business,
- regularly carried on, and
- substantially unrelated to the organization's exempt purposes.[38]

---

34. *See* Atlanta Athletic Club v. Comm'r, 980 F.2d 1409 (11th Cir. 1993).
35. IRC § 512(3)(D).
36. *Id.* § 511(a).
37. *Id.* § 512(a)(1).
38. 26 C.F.R. § 1.513-1 *et seq.*

c. Special Situation for Social Clubs

The unrelated taxable income of Section 501(c)(7) social clubs is defined as gross income except exempt function income.[39] In other words, income need not be generated by a trade or business regularly carried on, substantially unrelated to its exempt purposes, for a social club to incur the unrelated business income tax. It simply has to be nonexempt function income, and it is taxed as unrelated business income. Exempt function income is income from dues, fees, charges, or similar amounts paid by the organization's members in consideration for goods, facilities, or services provided to them, their dependents, or their guests, in furtherance of the organization's exempt purposes.[40] Everything else is nonexempt function income and is taxable.

Congress imposed the unrelated business income tax on all the non-membership income of social clubs because of a perceived unfairness:

> [W]here the organization receives income from sources outside the membership ... upon which no tax is paid, the membership receives a benefit not contemplated by the exemption in that untaxed dollars can be used by the organization to provide pleasure or recreation (or other benefits) to its membership.... In such a case, the exemption is no longer simply allowing individuals to join together for recreation or pleasure without tax consequences. Rather, it is bestowing a substantial additional advantage to the members of the club by allowing tax-free dollars to be used for their personal recreational or pleasure purposes.[41]

As an example, applying the statutory definition of Section 501(c)(7) to a golf club would mean that the dues and assessments paid by members of the club generate nontaxable exempt function income. It also means that greens fees paid by members for themselves, their family members, or their guests are nontaxable exempt function income. If the golf course is open to members of the public, however, the greens fees paid by nonmembers would be unrelated taxable income. Also, if there

---

39. IRC § 512(a)(3)(A).
40. IRC § 512(a)(3)(B).
41. S. Rep. No. 91-552, at 71 (1969).

were a clubhouse on the golf course that served both members and nonmembers, the income from the food and drink sold to members would be nontaxable exempt function income, but the income from the food and drink served to nonmembers would be unrelated taxable income. When it provides goods or services to nonmembers, thereby generating taxable income, the social club may deduct the expenses connected with the generation of that income as long as the activity is run with a profit motive.[42]

The passive income of Section 501(c)(7) organizations is not exempt function income. This means that its interest and investment income is taxed as unrelated business income under IRC Section 512(a). Though, as stated above, a Section 501(c)(7) organization can deduct expenses related to income-producing activities. This then poses an interesting issue: whether losses incurred in an income-producing activity can be used as deductions against passive income.[43] For example, can the social club that serves nonmembers in its clubhouse, but loses money on the activity, deduct these losses against its investment income?

The IRS's position is that these losses can be used to offset passive income as long as the activity that generated the losses is carried on in an attempt to make a profit. Thus, where a social club provides food and drink to nonmembers at prices that do not cover costs, there is no profit motive and no deduction for losses allowable against other income.[44]

Because Section 501(c)(7) organizations are taxed on their outside income, a significant amount of litigation has occurred to determine how this tax is computed. In *Ye Mystic Krewe of Gasparilla v. Commissioner*,[45] a social club staged an annual "pirate invasion" of Tampa, Florida, and a parade, from which it derived concession and souvenir income. The issue was whether the expenses of the "invasion" and parade could be deducted against this income, and this in turn depended on whether these expenses were directly connected with the production of

---

42. IRC § 512(a)(3)(A).

43. *Id.*

44. Rev. Rul. 81-69, 1981-1 C.B. 351; Brook, Inc. v. Comm'r, 799 F.2d 833 (2d Cir. 1986); N. Ridge Country Club v. Comm'r, 877 F.2d 750 (9th Cir. 1989). But see Cleveland Athletic Club, Inc. v. United States, 779 F.2d 1160 (6th Cir. 1985), which did not require proof of a profit motive, but only a "basic purpose of economic gain" for losses to be deductible.

45. Ye Mystic Krewe of Gasparilla v. Comm'r, 80 T.C. 755 (T.C. 1983).

the income. In a fact-specific holding, the court said that expenses for providing seating, refreshments, and an event logbook were related to the production of concession income and could be deducted, but the expenses of the invasion and parade itself were not related to the concession income and could not be deducted. On a side issue involving the taxation of investment income from a special fund used to maintain the organization's pirate ship during the year, which was on public view, but not accessible to the public, the court did not accept the Krewe's position that viewing the ship was an educational activity that would have exempted fund income from taxation. As an observation, it might have been prudent for the social club to have held educational tours and lectures, open to the public, aboard the pirate ship, thereby creating a charitable, educational activity that may have been considered exempt function income by the IRS.

In *Portland Golf Club v. Commissioner*,[46] a Section 501(c)(7) golf club had taxable investment income against which it tried to take as a deduction the losses it had suffered in its other taxable activity, the sale of food and drink to nonmembers. These losses would have completely offset the investment income. The United States Supreme Court held that losses from these sales could be taken as a deduction against investment income only if those sales were motivated by an intent to profit. Because of its method of cost allocation of fixed club expenses to its sales to nonmembers, the club was found not to be operating on a profit motive, and the deduction was not allowed.[47]

The United States Supreme Court[48] had taken up this issue because of an apparent split in the Circuits. The Portland Golf Club had reported the investment income on its Form 990 but took as a deduction against its interest income losses that it said it suffered in selling food and drink to nonmembers. The United States Supreme Court upheld the IRS's position, saying that "petitioner may use losses incurred in sales to non-members to offset investment income only if those sales were motivated by an intent to profit."[49] The problem was with the methods that

---

46. Portland Golf Club v. Comm'r, 497 U.S. 154 (1990).
47. *Id.*
48. *Id.*
49. *Id.* at 163–64.

the golf club had used to determine losses on one hand and demonstrate a profit motive on the other.[50]

The golf club had used a gross-to-gross formula in allocating fixed expenses to the nonmember sales in order to determine net income (or losses) from the sales. Under this formula, the deduction of fixed expenses resulted in the sales showing a loss, which was then a deduction against the club's investment income. But then the club attempted to show that it had a profit motive in these sales, not by using the gross-to-gross formula in allocating expenses, which would have shown a consistent loss and lack of a profit motive, but by looking at the actual economic cost of the activity.[51]

The United States Supreme Court said that they could not have it both ways. They had to use the same formula in demonstrating a profit motive as they did in computing losses. Having used the gross-to-gross formula in computing losses, they were stuck with it in demonstrating a profit motive. It thus followed, under the gross-to-gross expense formula, nonmember sales activity consistently lost money, thus there was no profit motive, and therefore losses from this activity could not be used as a deduction against investment income.[52]

d. Regularly Carried On

Fraternal organizations are subject to the normal UBIT rules if they engage in a business that is regularly carried on, which is generally not common practice. If this occurs, though, they must pay taxes on the net profits of the unrelated business that is regularly carried on. According to the IRS, insurance activity, merchandise marketing and travel tours fall within this rule. A fraternal organization can lose its tax-exempt status if it engages in any of these "nontraditional" activities substantially, regardless if it has paid tax on the proceeds or whether the activity is profitable.[53]

---

50. *Id.* at 168.
51. *Id.* at 169.
52. *Id.* at 171.
53. *Id.*

In *Atlanta Athletic Club*,[54] the issue was whether the property that was sold had been used directly in performance of the club's exempt functions. If the property did not qualify as having been used directly in the performance of the club's exempt functions, tax was due on the sale proceeds. The Tax Court determined that the tax was due because the club's use of the property, which was vacant land across the road from club facilities, was too sporadic to qualify the land as "directly used" for the club's exempt purposes. In what was basically a rereading of the facts, the Eleventh Circuit found that holding "Turkey Trots," kite flying contests, pasture parties, hot air balloon rides, fishing contests, and operating jogging trails on the property qualified it as directly used for the club's exempt recreational purposes. Because the sale proceeds were used to construct a new tennis facility and renovate the clubhouse (which passed unremarked, even though such use appears not to meet the terms of the statute, which speaks in terms of a subsequent purchase), the court found the terms of Section 512(a)(3)(D) were met and no tax was due.[55]

e. Filing Requirements for Taxes Due

If a fraternal organization has over $1,000 of gross UBIT or set-asides, it must file a Form 990-T for that fiscal year. Such tax returns are due on the fifteenth day of the fifth month following the close of the organization's fiscal year, unless extended. There is a separate extension form required for this return.[56]

---

54. *Atlanta Athletic Club*, 980 F.2d 1409.
55. *Id.*
56. *Extension of Time to File Exempt Organization Returns*, IRS, https://www.irs.gov/charities-non-profits/extension-of-time-to-file-exempt-organization-returns (last visited on July 28, 2022).

III. Charitable Contributions to Fraternal Organizations

An important component to the fraternal organizational structure is the fraternity- or sorority-created Section 501(c)(3) foundation. If set up correctly, the organizations can not only attract tax-deductible donations, but can also grant designated funds to a Section 501(c)(7) fraternal chapter for charitable or educational use. The funds must be carefully dispersed, and all transactions documented since questions can arise as to the use of such funds.

The granting of a tax deduction for charitable contributions and gifts is governed by Section 170, which states:

> (a) Allowance of deduction.
> > (1) General Rule. There shall be allowed as a deduction any charitable contribution (as defined in subsection (c)) payment of which is made within the taxable year. A charitable contribution shall be allowable as a deduction only if verified under regulations prescribed by the Secretary.[57]

Not all donations to all tax-exempt organizations are deductible. While contributions to § 501(c)(3) organizations are generally deductible (which is why organizations seek (c)(3) status), contributions to other § 501 organizations are usually not deductible or there are limitations imposed on what does qualify for a deduction.

For purposes of Section 170, a gift will qualify as a "charitable contribution" if it is donated to or for the use of the following types of organizations:[58]

> (1) a state or possession of the United States, or a political subdivision of any of the foregoing, or the United States or the District of Columbia, but only if the contribution or gift is made for exclusively public purposes.

---

57. IRC § 170(a)(1).
58. *See* IRC § 170(c).

(2) a corporation, trust, or community chest, fund, or foundation;[59] (3) organizations organized and operated exclusively for religious, charitable, scientific, or literary purposes, or to foster national or international amateur sports competition or for preventing cruelty to children or animals; (4) organizations where no part of their net earnings inures to the benefit of any private shareholder or individual; and (5) organizations not disqualified for tax exemption under Section 501(c)(3) by reason of attempting to influence legislation and that does not participate in, or intervene in, any political campaign on behalf of or in opposition to any candidate for public office.[60]

The tax laws governing tax-exempt charitable organizations and deductible gifts are closely intertwined. The IRC frequently cross-references many of the sections on organizations that are considered charitable with the income tax charitable contribution deduction rules.[61]

IV. Fraternity Foundations

Most fraternities and sororities create separate fraternal foundations (though a few are created as trusts), organized as publicly supported IRC § 501(c)(3) entities under Section 170(b)(1)(A)(vi),[62] to receive tax-deductible contributions designated for the fraternal organization. The foundations may use these contributions to support the fraternities and sororities in their charitable and educational endeavors.[63] They must be

---

59. The corporation, trust, or community chest, fund or foundation must be created or organized in the U.S. or in any possession thereof (but not in a foreign country), or under the laws of the United States, any state, the District of Columbia, or any possession of the U.S. *See* IRC § 170(c)(2)(A).

60. IRC § 170(c); *see* NICHOLAS P. CAFARDI & JACLYN FABEAN CHERRY, UNDERSTANDING NONPROFIT AND TAX EXEMPT ORGANIZATIONS (3d ed. 2022).

61. *See* IRC §§ 501(c), 170.

62. Organizing under this IRC section is preferable, as organizing as a 509(a)(2) exempt organization can create investment issues.

63. IRC § 501 (c)(3) organizations can only gift to other Section 501(c)(3) organizations or other 501(c) organizations if the gift is being used for the exempt purposes for which the Foundation is organized. *See* 26 C.F.R. § 1.501(c)(3)-1(d)(3)(i), which defines educational as (a) The instruction or training of the individual for the purpose of improv-

separate autonomous organizations with their own charitable missions, boards of directors, and separate financial accountability.

For example, in Revenue Rule 56-403,[64] the IRS stated that a foundation could award scholarships solely to university undergraduate members of a designated fraternity and still qualify for Section 501(c)(3) exemption, because the foundation was deemed to be fulfilling its public purpose by providing for a large enough class or group of individuals. The foundation limited its scholarships to members of all chapters of the designated fraternity who were in their senior year and met scholarship, character, and service to the institution criteria. The IRS stated that no specific persons were ever designated, and the foundation's purposes were not personal in nature but were of a nature to benefit the public.[65]

There are numerous IRS Private Letter Rulings (PLRs) in this area, where individual groups have written to the IRS to ask for its opinion with regard to a specific set of facts. Though they are not considered binding, they do allow individuals and courts to understand how the IRS is interpreting certain code sections and regulations.

Specifically, in a 2005 PLR,[66] the IRS determined that a Section 501(c)(7) national fraternity and a Section 501(c)(3) charity that supported the charitable activities of the fraternity, could enter a joint venture being proposed without jeopardizing the charity's Section 501(c)(3) status. The joint venture that the organizations entered into to acquire land, develop it, and build a building that each would use, was entered into through several subsidiary organizations.[67] After ensuring that each organization was continuing to meet their missions as Section 501(c)(7) and 501(c)(3) organizations, the IRS stated that "public charities may engage in financial transactions, even with related parties (such as the fraternity), as long as the terms are for FMV (or better) and no private inurement or private benefit results."[68]

---

ing or developing his capabilities; or (b) The instruction of the public on subjects useful to the individual and beneficial to the community.

64. Rev. Rul. 56-403, 1956-2 C.B. 307.

65. Id.

66. IRS PLR 2005-38-052 (Aug. 12, 2005).

67. Id.

68. David L. Forst et al., *Joint Venture with Non-501(c)(3) Affiliated Entity did not Affect Charity's Tax-Exempt Status*, 103 J. TAX'N 315 (2005).

In PLR 8823088,[69] the IRS allowed a private foundation grant that would be used to finance a portion of a fraternity house which would be used for educational purposes. The IRS stated that since the use was charitable and educational, the grant would not be a taxable expenditure under IRC § 4945(d)(4).[70] The IRS cited Rev. Rul. 75-195,[71] noting that a sufficient public purpose must be shown in order for a grant of this type to be acceptable.

Fraternal organizations must carefully request grants from their affiliated § 501(c)(3) foundations and the foundations must, in turn, follow the IRC rules for issuing such support.[72] One way for a fraternal organization to comply is to become very familiar with the IRC rules that govern this area and make sure that all the necessary documentation is prepared, and records maintained. Grant requests are generally signed by a representative of the fraternity's board of directors and follow-up documentation and reports kept by the secretary of the board or another appropriate individual.

A fraternal foundation may fund chapter or graduate consultants and other leadership trainers, as an educational award, so long as these individuals document their hours.[73] Foundations may fund sponsored conventions and leadership conferences and the like but generally only a percentage. It is rare that the IRS would consider all that occurs at these conferences as educational, so a fraternal organization should carefully document what it expects to seek funding for. Foundations can fund the "net" in fraternal educational programs, not the "gross."[74] The *Phi Delta*

---

69. IRS PLR 88-23-088 (June 10, 1988).

70. IRC § 4945(d)(4)(B) provides that the term "taxable expenditure" means any amount paid or incurred by a private foundation as a grant to an organization unless the private foundation exercises expenditure responsibility with respect to such grant.

71. Rev. Rul. 75-195, 1975-1 C.B. 78.

72. IRC § 501(c)(3) requires that organizations that operate under this code section only award grants to other Section 501(c)(3) organizations or other exempt organizations, like a 501(c)(7), if used for charitable or educational purposes.

73. Barbra Schwartz Bromberg, *Educational Grants from Foundation to Fraternity*, FRATERNAL L. PARTNERS NEWSL. (Fraternal L. Partners, Cincinnati, Ohio), Jan. 2005.

74. *Id.* For example, if a fraternity sponsors a conference that is 60% educational by IRS standards with the expenses being $120,000 and attendees paying $60,000 as an admission fee, the most a Foundation can fund is $30,000. There may be no doubling up of Foundation funds and fraternity set aside funds.

Theta[75] case, decided in 1989, allowed for the funding of written materials and publications being used by a fraternal organization so long as the publications are 100% educational. Therefore, publications regarding alcoholism, other health and safety issues, and new member materials are not considered educational. A foundation may grant funds for the administrative expenses of a fraternal organization that relates to educational functions, though this must be documented through time sheets and other materials.[76] Allocation of funding between educational and noneducational materials is not permitted.

In PLR 201219026,[77] the IRS made clear that charities cannot own chapter houses when it revoked the tax-exempt status of a fraternal house corporation that owned and operated a fraternal chapter house. The IRS stated that this was not a charitable activity, even though the house corporation did not use the house for social or fraternal purposes and the chapter house was required to abide by university standards for fraternity houses, giving the university authority over the house corporation, in order to meet its educational mission. The house corporation argued that because the university could not meet its needs in this area and the house corporation could, that the IRS generally permitted another charity to step into such a role. The IRS did not agree.[78] The IRS did state that an organization providing housing for students where no other housing was available through the college or community may qualify as a charitable organization under Section 501(c)(3).[79] In this case, it seems that the IRS did not like the chapter house ownership by the house corporation, perhaps questioning the true usage of the property.

A bill to amend the IRC of 1986 to provide for collegiate housing and infrastructure grants[80] was introduced in April 2021. If the amendment is adopted, grants by fraternal foundations for these purposes would not

---

75. Phi Delta Theta Fraternity v. Comm'r, 887 F.2d 1302 (1989).
76. *Id.*
77. IRS PLR 2012-19-026 (May 11, 2012).
78. *See also* Rev. Rul. 64-118, 1964-1 C.B. 182, where organization assisting in educating students, affiliated with fraternity at a university, whose primary activity is operating and maintaining a chapter house, on a rental basis, for use and benefit of members of a local chapter of the fraternity, does not qualify for exemption as an educational organization within Section 501(c)(3).
79. Rev. Rul. 76-336, 1976-2 C.B. 143.
80. H.R. 2421, 117th Cong. (2021).

jeopardize their § 501(c)(3) status. This bill has sat idly for many years so there is no indication that it will move quickly.

V. IRC Section 501(c)(2) Holding Company Organizations

Occasionally, a fraternal organization will create a holding company to meet its needs. The IRC section for holding companies is Section 501(c)(2), which states that the following organizations qualify: "Corporations organized for the exclusive purpose of holding title to property, collecting income there from, and turning over the entire amount thereof, less expenses, to an organization which itself is exempt under this section."[81] These organizations are formed to collect income, pay expenses, distribute earnings to the exempt organization, overcome state laws that prevent exempt organizations from holding property, protect the nonprofit from liability, enhance the organization's ability to borrow against property, and simplify management and accounting. Congress limited the benefit of these companies by permitting title-holding companies to receive only up to 10% of gross income from unrelated business activities.[82] These entities are often used when property is purchased or held for future uses.[83] If a § 501(c)(2) organization is formed for these purposes, it must be organized to be responsive to the other exempt entity. That is, there must be a measure of control by the other exempt entity, and this is often difficult when local house corporations are involved.

---

81. 26 IRC § 501(c)(2).
82. Id.
83. IRC § 501(c)(2).

VI. Property Tax Exemption

As a matter of state law, tax-exempt organizations may escape the obligation to pay state and local taxes on real estate they own and that they use for their exempt activities. This tends to be a narrower exemption than the state income tax exemption, in that it applies primarily to Section 501(c)(3) organizations, and not to the other types of federally tax-exempt organizations. Often, Section 501(c)(2) holding companies qualify for property tax exemption when they are holding property for § 501(c)(3) organizations. This can be useful for Section 501(c)(3) fraternal organizations. For instance, a § 501(c)(2) organization holding property for a § 501(c)(3) fraternal foundation or house corporation might qualify for property tax exemption, allowing for a large savings for these organizations. Each state has its own criteria for whether the real estate of an exempt organization qualifies for this exemption. For example, in Pennsylvania, which has had a good deal of activity in this area, the exemption from local real estate taxes of "purely public charities" is written into the state constitution.[84] In New York, the tax exemption of church property has been the subject of unsuccessful constitutional challenges.[85]

At a time when many state and local governments are strapped for income, many questions have been raised about the continuing need for the local property tax exemption for charitable organizations,[86] and devices such as "PILOTs" (payments in lieu of taxes) by which a charity reimburses the local municipality for the police, fire, and other municipal services it receives have been used.[87]

---

84. PA. CONST. art. VIII, § 2(a)(v); *see* THE PENNSYLVANIA CONSTITUTION: A TREATISE ON RIGHTS AND LIBERTIES (Ken Gormley & Joy McNally eds., 2020).

85. Walz v. Tax Comm'n of City of N.Y., 397 U.S. 664 (1970).

86. PROPERTY TAX EXEMPTION FOR CHARITIES: MAPPING THE BATTLEFIELD (Evelyn Brody ed., 2002); Robert T. Bennett, *Real Property Tax Exemptions of Non-Profit Organizations*, 16 CLEV.-MAR. L. REV. 150 (1967); Janne Gallagher, *Sales Tax Exemptions for Charitable, Educational, and Religious Nonprofit Organizations*, 7 EXEMPT ORG. TAX REV. 429 (1993); William R. Ginsberg, *The Real Property Tax Exemption of Nonprofit Organizations: A Perspective*, 53 TEMPLE L.Q. 291 (1980); Margaret A. Potter & Beaufort B. Longest, Jr., *The Divergence of Federal and State Policies on the Charitable Tax Exemption of Nonprofit Hospitals*, 19 J. HEALTH POL., POL'Y & L. 393 (1994); Rebecca S. Rudnick, *State and Local Taxes on Nonprofit Organizations*, 22 CAP. U.L. REV. 321 (1993).

87. Jaclyn Fabean Cherry, *Property Tax Exemption of Charitable Nonprofit Organizations: A Uniform Possibility*, 18 WAKE FOREST J. BUS. & INTELL. PROP. L. 1 (2017).

In *Illinois Beta House Fund Corp.*,[88] the house fund corporation appealed a finding by the Illinois Department of Revenue that property owned by the corporation was not exempt from property tax for the year 2000. The property in question was used by the University of Chicago to house student members of the Illinois Beta Chapter of the Phi Delta Theta Fraternity. The corporation argued that it was exempt from property tax under the state's Property Tax Code because the property was being used for "university or other educational purposes,"[89] although rooms were occasionally rented to nonmembers of the chapter. During 2000, one nonmember person resided in the house. The Illinois statute exempted property used for school purposes, and the corporation argued that the test for exemption under the statute was strictly how the property was used, and that its "use" qualified it for tax exemption.[90] The court did not agree, and in fact found no similarities with the corporation's interpretation of several cases it presented.[91] In all of the referenced cases, the organizations had close connections or were functioning on behalf of an educational entity. Here, the court stated that there was little interaction. The only evidence of a connection in this case was that a fraternity alumnus met with a Greek advisor to discuss alumni events. The court determined that this "limited contact"[92] did not demonstrate a close connection or affiliation with the university and therefore did not meet the requirements of the statute. It stated that the corporation was not entitled to property tax exemption.

In *Case Western Reserve University v. Wilkins*,[93] the university appealed the denial of its application for property tax exemption for a residential facility known as Magnolia House. The university had entered into an agreement with the Zeta Pi Chapter of Alpha Phi fraternity house corporation for use for ten years to house members of the Alpha Phi

---

88. Ill. Beta House Fund Corp. v. Il. Dep't of Revenue, 887 N.E.2d 847 (Ill. App. Ct. 2008).

89. *Id.* at 427.

90. *Id.* at 434.

91. *Id.* at 436. *See also* Ass'n of Am. Med. Colls. v. Lorenz, 17 Ill. 2d 125, 160 N.E. 763 (1959); Big Ten Conference, 312 Ill. App. 3d 88, 244 Ill. Dec. 518, 726 N.E.2d 114 (2000); Illini Media Co. v. Dep't of Rev., 279 Ill. App. 3d 432, 216 Ill. Dec. 69, 664 N.E.2d 706 (1996); People *ex rel.* Goodman v. Univ. of Ill. Found., 388 Ill. 363, 58 N.E.2d 33 (1944).

92. *Illinois Beta House Fund Corp.*, 382 Ill. App. 3d at 435.

93. Case W. Res. Univ. v. Wilkins, 105 Ohio St.3d 276, 825 N.E.2d 146 (2005).

sorority. The court strictly construed the applicable state statute and determined that the decision denying property tax exemption was correct. The court stated that the use by the corporation was not educational and that it was not an educational institute itself, as required by the statute. Also, use of the house was limited to sorority members, and not open to the entire student population to carry out the educational mission.[94]

VII. Dormant Chapter Houses

When collegiate chapters or national fraternities or sororities lose a chapter house or the house becomes dormant, special attention must be paid to the operation and management of that house since, without planning, there can be significant tax and other consequences.[95] Since these § 501(c)(7) organizations must carry out activities in keeping with their exempt status, namely social activities, engaging in any nontraditional activities could jeopardize their tax-exempt status. If the percentage of gross receipts from nontraditional activities is less than 5%, the nontraditional activities are considered insubstantial and do not affect an organization's tax-exempt status. But if gross receipts from general public usage of facilities or services permitted are more than the 15%,[96] then it is possible that the house corporation could lose its tax-exempt status. When these houses become dormant, it is natural for organizations to want to seek sources for funding them immediately to pay the mortgages and other expenses. Seeking funding from outside, "nontraditional" sources, however, until a chapter is reinstated, is something that should be planned for at the beginning of these relationships to be prepared for this type of event. Several options can be considered. If ownership is by a national housing corporation, which owns multiple properties, it may cause no issues if the dormant house is rented to nonmembers of the fraternal entity since the income would not exceed the 15% cap. The national house would not lose tax-exempt status but could

---

94. *Id.* at 280. See also Sherwood Forest Country Club v. Litchfield, 2008-0194 (La. 12/19/08), 998 So. 2d 56, which held that this club organized and operated for pleasure did not meet the definition of fraternal organization as designated in the state statute.

95. Dianne C. Bailey & Seth M. Huffstetler, *Dormant Chapter Houses*, FRATERNAL L. PARTNERS NEWSL. (Fraternal L. Partners, Cincinnati, Ohio), Jan. 2011.

96. IRC § 501(c)(7); I.R.C. § 512(a)(3); Rev. Proc. 71-17, 1971-1 C.B. 683.

pay taxes on this income. If there is not enough cushion for a national house corporation to absorb this dormant house income, then the house corporation could create a § 501(c)(2) organization to hold the property. The § 501(c)(2) organization could only break even in this scenario, paying the parent house corporation only what it collects from the non-members, and each entity would file a separate tax return.[97]

A chapter house that is owned locally could be in a different situation. It might be able to leave the house dormant for a while if it believes it will be active again within a short time. If there are no prospects of the house returning to active status, the IRS could revoke the organization's tax-exempt status. Other options for the locally owned dormant house might include revising the articles of incorporation, and redefining the membership, though this could be a difficult approach. A board of directors would have to agree that this was a proper approach for the organization and ensure that no other legal requirements would be violated should this action be taken. The local house could create a § 501(c)(2) organization and move forward as a national group would, or it could allow the § 501(c)(7) organization to begin operating as a for-profit, which would naturally end the tax-exempt organization. This course of action would not be the one to choose if there were any chance of the fraternal organization operating again within the chapter house, because once the tax-exempt status is revoked or the organization dissolved, the process would need to begin all over again for becoming tax exempt. There are no guarantees that once lost, tax-exempt status can be regained.

VIII. IRC § 501(c)(4)

While fraternal organizations may not generally create a separate § 501(c)(4) organization, they may do so if interested in participating in political activity or substantial advocacy. The political activities test for Section 501(c)(4) organizations only prohibits substantial electioneering. Lobbying and insubstantial electioneering are permissible.[98] This section allows exemption for:

---

97. Bailey & Huffstetler, *supra* note 95.
98. Rev. Rul. 68-656, 1968-2 C.B. 216; 26 C.F.R. § 1.501(c)(4)-1(a)(2)(ii); Rev. Rul. 2004-6, 2004-1 C.B. 328.

Civic leagues or organizations not organized for profit but operated exclusively for the promotion of social welfare, or local associations of employees, the membership of which is limited to the employees of a designated person or persons in a particular municipality, and the net earnings of which are devoted exclusively to charitable, educational, or recreational purposes.[99]

While there is no organizational test, per se, for Section 501(c)(4) entities, the statute requires that they be organized as nonprofit organizations, subject to the nondistribution constraint.[100] The operational test for Section 501(c)(4) organizations requires that they be operated exclusively for § 501(c)(4) purposes, but the IRS interprets "exclusively" to mean "primarily," which means that non-§ 501(c)(4) activities are permissible as long as they are not substantial.[101] The private inurement test for Section 501(c)(4) organizations requires that no part of the net earnings of such entities inure to the benefit of any private shareholder or individual.[102] It prohibits "excess benefit" transactions as well.[103]

IX. State Law

Becoming familiar with the nonprofit or unincorporated association statutory law of the state of incorporation must be a part of all decisions made by or for nonprofit organizations and unincorporated associations. This may include a review of the Model Nonprofit Corporate Act[104] as well as a review of the state statute itself.

---

99. I.R.C. § 501(c)(4).

100. *Id.* ("Civic leagues and organizations organized not for profit ..."). The nondistribution constraint requires a 501(c)(3) organization to direct all profit back into the entity to be used for purposes set out in its mission.

101. 26 C.F.R. § 1.501(c)(4)-1(a)(2)(i).

102. I.R.C. § 501(c)(4)(B).

103. I.R.C. § 4958(e)(1). See also 26 C.F.R. § 1.501(c)(4)-1(a)(2)(ii), which states no § 501(c)(4) organization can have as its primary activity "operating a social club for the benefit, pleasure, or recreation of its members" or "carrying on a business with the general public in a manner similar to organizations which are operated for profit."

104. MODEL NONPROFIT CORPORATION ACT (AM. BAR ASS'N 4th ed. 2022). While there seem to be no significant changes effecting fraternal organizations in the Model Nonprofit Corporation Act, 4th ed., a quick review is always advisable. In the 2008, third

As discussed previously, property tax is governed by state law. Other taxes, such as sales and use tax, employment and charitable solicitation laws are all governed by the state of incorporation, or in some cases, where there is physical presence. Charitable solicitation laws of several states may apply if an organization actively seeks funding in several jurisdictions. A majority of states have developed elaborate registration and filing systems requiring charities and fundraising solicitors to register, file annual reports, and notify the state of any change in status.[105] Solicitation of donors provides a charity with an opportunity to not only raise funds, but also to communicate a message or provide education.

State regulatory schemes usually have three common elements: (1) they require mandatory disclosure through state and local registration and licensing, making financial and operational information available to the public; (2) they make it unlawful for any fraudulent solicitation activities to be carried on by professional solicitors or anyone raising money on the organization's behalf; and (3) they require contractual provisions that control the cost of solicitation and administration so that the amount available for the charitable purpose is increased.[106] It is imperative that fraternal organizations become familiar with and abide by these charitable solicitation laws. While there are often heavy fees attached for noncompliance, the more important component for abiding by these rules is to instill confidence in the general public and the donors of the charitable activity of the fraternal organization.

---

edition of the Act "a fundamental transaction properly held in trust or otherwise dedicated to a charitable purpose may not be diverted from that purpose without an appropriate order" and "in transactions such as mergers" private inurement is prohibited. MODEL NONPROFIT CORPORATION ACT (AM. BAR ASS'N 3d ed. 2008).

105. *See* Ellen Harris et al., N.Y.U. Program on Philanthropy and the Law, *Fundraising into the 1990s: State Regulation of Charitable Solicitation After* Riley, 24 U.S.F. L. REV. 571, 572 (1990); *see also* Loren Prescott Jr., *Pennsylvania Charities, Tax Exemption, and the Institutions of Purely Public Charity Act*, 73 TEMP. L. REV. 951 (2000); Am. Charities for Reasonable Fundraising Reg. v. Pinellas Cnty., 189 F. Supp. 2d 1319 (M.D. Fla. 2001); Am. Target Advert., Inc. v. Giani, 199 F.3d 1241 (10th Cir. 2000); RESTATEMENT OF CHARITABLE NONPROFIT ORGS. § 4.05. (AM. L. INST., Tentative Draft No. 3, 2019); OHIO REV. CODE ANN. § 1716.08 (LexisNexis 2023); VA. CODE ANN. § 57-54 (2023); N.Y. EXEC. LAW § 173-a (Consol. 2023); S.C. CODE ANN. § 33-56-140 (2021).

106. Karen S. Quandt, Comment, *The Regulation of Charitable Fundraising and Spending Activities*, 1975 WIS. L. REV. 1158, 1160 (1975).

CHAPTER 5

Formalizing Compliance to Reduce Board Exposure to Civil and Criminal Liability

Cheryl L. Wade

Fraternities and sororities (Greek-letter organizations or "GLOs" as used herein) are nonprofit organizations that present uniquely complex issues when considering the GLO directors' ability to oversee and manage the organizations' potential exposure to criminal and civil liability. Legal analysis of the fiduciary obligations of nonprofit directors borrows from, and analogizes to, the law of directorial fiduciary duty in the for-profit context. There are, however, important structural differences between for-profit and nonprofit firms that require consideration when thinking about how GLO boards operate. The potentiality of criminal and civil liability for a GLO is uniquely driven by the misconduct of its members. GLOs may be held liable for their members' misconduct.[1] Even when a GLO successfully defends itself and avoids liability, there are serious costs for GLO defendants, such as attorneys' fees and harm

---

1. In 2017, a national fraternity was convicted on several counts relating to a hazing incident that caused a pledge's death. *See GUILTY! A National Fraternity Criminally Convicted*, FRATERNAL L. NEWSL. (Fraternal L. Partners, Cincinnati, Ohio) Nov., 2017, https://fraternallaw.com/newsletter2/guilty-a-national-fraternity-criminally-convicted. Another fraternity was prosecuted for selling drinks to an individual who was too young to legally consume alcohol. *See* State v. Zeta Chi Fraternity, 696 A.2d 530 (N.H. 1997). And a national fraternity faced civil liability in a defamation suit. *See* Blalock v. Alpha Phi Alpha Fraternity, Inc., 1:22-CV-01085 (Fulton Cnty. Sup. Ct., Ga. filed March 17, 2022) (Westlaw).

to the organization's reputation due to negative publicity that may accompany litigation. The potential liability of GLOs is also exacerbated by the idiosyncratic characteristics of some of its members. Because GLO undergraduate members are young, they are not always cognizant of the conceivable consequences of their conduct.

GLO members and investors in for-profit firms are analogous constituencies. For-profit firms depend on their shareholders and creditors for capital. GLOs look to the dues, fundraising, and service provided by members for the funds to operate. There is, however, no analogue in for-profit corporations to the liability problems potentially presented by the wrongdoing of hundreds or thousands of GLO members, or large numbers of relatively immature collegiate members.[2] A GLO's exposure to civil or criminal liability for the negligent, reckless, or intentional acts of members (particularly its collegiate members who may be likely to engage in hazing and underage drinking) is significant.

In the for-profit setting, however, shareholder misconduct is largely irrelevant to the potential legal liability of a corporation, unless a misbehaving shareholder owns a controlling block of shares, or also serves as an officer or director of the firm in which they have invested. Officers and directors who own shares in the corporations they govern may cause their firms to incur civil or criminal penalties and fees *only* when the individual acts on the corporation's behalf in their role as a corporate agent.

In this chapter, I explore the role of GLO boards in reducing organizational exposure to civil and criminal liability. What can GLO boards do to reduce the possibility of fines, penalties, and settlements? What can GLO directors do to prevent the filing of litigation that may harm the GLO's reputation and drain precious resources when mounting a defense? The task of GLO boards seems monumental in light of the large number of members and the relatively small number of individuals who serve on GLO boards.[3]

---

2. For example, Tau Kappa Epsilon has had almost 300,000 initiated members and approximately 12,000 current collegiate members. *See* ABOUT TAU KAPPA EPSILON INTERNATIONAL FRATERNITY, https://www.tke.org/about. Alpha Phi Alpha Fraternity, Inc., the first Black GLO in the United States, has approximately 70,000 members in the third decade of the twenty-first century. *See,* ALPHA PHI ALPHA FRATERNITY, INC., https://apa1906.net.

3. For example, the International Board of Directors of Tau Kappa Epsilon "consists of eight elected officers, two at-large members, and the chairman of the Collegiate Advi-

The boards of nonprofit organizations such as GLOs owe a fiduciary duty of obedience that includes an obligation to monitor compliance with applicable law.[4] This obligation includes a duty to monitor compliance with laws that prohibit assault, battery, hazing, and underage drinking. The requirement under fiduciary duty law for GLO boards to monitor compliance is clear. The practical implications and the steps required to fulfill a board's monitoring obligation, however, are not. How can GLO boards with only a dozen or so directors get the information they need to monitor their organization's compliance with civil and criminal law?

For-profit boards owe a similar monitoring obligation that is subsumed within their fiduciary duty of loyalty.[5] Most for-profit corporate boards require the firm's officers to install compliance programs that, at least ostensibly, provide senior officers with the information they need to uncover pervasive, systemic compliance failures on the part of corporate employees. These compliance programs include mandates from corporate directors to establish information and reporting systems designed to prevent sustained compliance failures.

Senior officers at for-profit firms must establish programs that aim to monitor managers' and employees' compliance with the law when their boards mandate them to do so. GLO boards may also establish systems aimed to monitor their officers' and employees' compliance with applicable law. It is at this point that the structural differences between for-profits and nonprofits become most relevant with respect to GLO board conduct and organizational civil and criminal liability. GLO boards, unlike for-profit boards, must concern themselves with the thousands of members who may purport to act on the GLO's behalf while failing to comply with laws that, for example, prohibit hazing or underage drinking. Corporate shareholders, however, cannot easily and credibly act on behalf of a corporation because they have no authority to do so under state corporate laws. For-profit boards have no need to concern themselves with the misconduct of shareholders (the constituency that is the for-profit analogue to nonprofit or GLO members).

---

sory Committee" which has nine collegiate members. *See* ABOUT TAU KAPPA EPSILON INTERNATIONAL FRATERNITY, https://www.tke.org/about.

4. *See id.*
5. *See id.*

Because much of the risk of civil and criminal liability is generated by the activities of collegiate members, alumni and graduate chapter members can play a potentially powerful monitoring role that reduces the risk of their organization's liability. Alumni members can insist that GLO boards fulfill their obligation to exercise oversight of their organization's compliance obligations by encouraging GLO boards to require information and reporting systems aimed at revealing misconduct. Later in this chapter, I discuss the way compliance programs are structured in the for-profit context. These programs may serve as models for GLO boards attempting to reduce their organization's exposure to civil and criminal liability.

I. Comparing Fiduciary Duties of For-Profit and Nonprofit Directors

Corporate directors owe two fundamental fiduciary duties to their shareholders and their firms. Directors owe a duty of care that is breached only when their decision-making processes are grossly negligent.[6] Corporate boards also owe a duty of loyalty that is breached when directors make decisions in a way that elevate their personal interests over the interests of the corporation and its shareholders.[7] One type of duty of loyalty breach involves conflicts of interest. Conflicted directors breach their duty of loyalty when their conflicted transactions are not ratified by disinterested shareholders or directors who received full disclosure about the conflict, or when the transaction is not fair to the corporation.[8] A second subcategory of loyalty breaches involves the corporate opportu-

---

6. *See generally* Kamin v. Am. Express Co., 387 N.Y.S.2d 993 (App. Div. 1st Dept. 1976); Smith v. Van Gorkom, 488 A.2d 858 (Del. 1985). In duty of care cases, courts focus on a board's decision-making process rather than the substance of the decision. Unwise decisions do not breach the directorial duty of care. Only decisions resulting from a grossly negligent process breaches a board's duty of care. *Id.*

7. *See* Bayer v. Beran, 49 N.Y.S.2d 2 (Sup. Ct. 1944).

8. *See* Fliegler v, Lawrence, 361 A.2d 218 (Del. 1976). A subcategory of conflicted director cases involves board members who take business opportunities that belong to the corporation for themselves. In these cases, courts apply the corporate opportunity doctrine. *See, e.g.,* Broz v. Cellular Info. Syss., Inc., 673 A.2d 148 (Del. 1996); *In re* eBay, Inc. S'holders Litig., 2004 WL 253521 (Del. Ch. Jan. 23, 2004).

nity doctrine. In these cases, corporate officers and directors are liable if they take for themselves a business opportunity that belongs to the corporation.[9] Finally, subsumed within the duty of loyalty is the for-profit directors' obligation of good faith, which includes the requirement that boards monitor compliance with all applicable laws and regulations.[10]

Nonprofit directors owe fiduciary duties that are akin to those owed by for-profit board members:

> Under corporate law, both nonprofits and for-profits are governed by boards of directors who are responsible for selecting management, ensuring financial integrity, and otherwise guiding the organization. These directors must comply with fiduciary duties of care, loyalty, and obedience. When it comes to the enforcement of these duties, the law does little to distinguish between for-profit and nonprofit organizations—an approach criticized by many commentators ...[11]

Nonprofit directors must use reasonable judgment to fulfill their duty of care,[12] and refrain from acting in their own self-interest, rather than the organization's best interests, to avoid breaching their duty of loyalty.[13] Nonprofit directors also owe a duty of obedience that requires them to make decisions that "substantively further their organization's mission."[14] In this respect, fiduciary duties owed by for-profit and nonprofit direc-

---

9. *See e.g.*, *Broz*, 673 A.2d 148; and *In re* eBay, Inc. S'holders Litigation, 2004 WL 253521. In these cases, corporate directors and officers breach their fiduciary duty of loyalty when they take a corporate opportunity. Under the corporate opportunity doctrine, courts determine whether a business opportunity is a corporate opportunity by asking four things: is the opportunity in the corporation's line of business; is the corporation financially capable of developing the opportunity; is the opportunity one that the corporation is interested in or does the firm reasonably expect to take the opportunity; and will the director or officer who takes the opportunity herself be in conflict with the interests of the corporation. *Id.*

10. *See* Stone v. Ritter, 911 A.2d 362 (Del. 2006).

11. Joseph Mead & Michael Pollack, *Courts, Constituencies, and the Enforcement of Fiduciary Duties in the Nonprofit Sector*, 77 U. PITT. L. REV. 281, 293 (2016) [hereinafter Mead & Pollack].

12. *Id.* at 303.

13. *Id.* at 305.

14. *Id.* at 307.

tors begin to diverge. "The conventional wisdom is that, in the for-profit world, the duty of obedience is almost a dead letter."[15]

Another point of divergence of nonprofit and for-profit directorial duties occurs with respect to monitoring obligations:

> Nonprofit directors go well beyond the boardroom and are often called to wear many hats, functioning as unpaid staff, as fundraisers, as lobbyists, as well as governors. There is also a common expectation that nonprofit directors contribute financially to their organization—quite the opposite of the custom in the for-profit board. Insofar as nonprofit board members are asked to wear other hats, their oversight obligations tend to be de-emphasized.[16]

The locus of *for-profit* directors' monitoring duties is in the obligation of good faith that courts analyze under the fiduciary duty of loyalty.[17] The source of *nonprofit* directors' monitoring obligations is analyzed as part of their duty of obedience. One information resource for nonprofit organizers describes the monitoring obligation under the duty of obedience. "Board members must ensure that the organization complies with all applicable federal, state, and local laws and regulations, and that it remains committed to its established mission."[18] A law firm in the business of advising nonprofit organizations helpfully elaborates on the monitoring duties of nonprofit boards:

> In addition to the nonprofit board members' duties of care and loyalty, directors also have a duty of compliance with laws and legal standards. The duty of compliance has often been referred to as the duty of obedience, but 'compliance' is the more common term in modern governance discussions. Obviously, the duty to comply with legal standards requires the board to

---

15. *Id.*
16. *Id.* at 334.
17. *Stone*, 911 A. 2d 362.
18. *Candid Learning, Where Can I Find Information on a Board's Legal Duties?*, CANDID LEARNING https://learning.candid.org/resources/knowledge-base/legal-duties-of-the-nonprofit-board/ (last visited Dec. 13, 2023).

ensure the organization is acting within the scope of relevant law when operating its programs.[19]

In the next section, I discuss what compliance can look like for GLOs and what GLO directors can learn from for-profit compliance programs.

II. Compliance

How can GLO boards get information about sustained compliance failures when there are thousands of members who may break the law or behave negligently or recklessly? GLO boards and officers have not made the installment of compliance programs an integral and well-developed part of organizational governance, unlike corporate directors and officers.[20] There are, however, university compliance programs that are ap-

---

19. Nancy Griffith, *Duties of Non-Profit Board Members—Duty of Compliance*, BAUERGRIFFITH LAW FIRM (July 15, 2013), https://bauergriffith.com/duties-of-non-profit-board-members-duty-of-compliance/.

20. In this statement describing the obligations of a GLO board, there is no discussion of a duty to monitor compliance with law:

"The Board of Directors sets the strategic vision for the Fraternity and traditionally addresses "big picture" type matters. The strategic vision is then implemented by the Chief Executive Officer, undergraduate members, and volunteers. The Board of Directors is not involved in the day-to-day operations of the Fraternity and does not manage the tactics used to achieve the strategic vision. Implicit in this philosophy is the importance of sound governance. It is the duty of the Board of Directors to set governance policy, as well as reasonable limitations of the CEO, and monitor the performance of the organization." http://sigtau.org/wp-content/uploads/2018/01/Responsibilities-Duties-and-Expectations.pdf.

There is no discussion of monitoring obligations in this statement describing the role of GLO officers:

"If you become an officer in a fraternity, you have additional leadership duties and responsibilities. The house president oversees all activities and meetings and represents the fraternity at Greek life meetings. The vice president assists the president and helps coordinate activities. The treasurer collects member dues, keeps financial records and oversees spending budgets. The fraternity marshal leads new member initiation, and the chaplain is in charge of monitoring brotherhood and fraternity rituals. Other positions and duties vary. Many fraternities have officers that lead programs in social, community service, networking, intramurals, professional development and academic areas." https://education.seattlepi.com/fraternities-sororities-make-money-2629.html.

plicable to GLOs. For example, Pennsylvania State University established an Office of Fraternity and Sorority Compliance as part of its Student Affairs department.[21] Compliance coordinators who work for the university review and approve the activities of GLOs and "implement risk management plans" in order to monitor hazing, alcohol abuse, and sexual misconduct.[22] Ohio State has implemented oversight and risk management approaches to address GLO member misconduct.[23] Eastern Illinois University requires GLO chapter leaders to sign an "anti-hazing compliance agreement," and requires chapters to create a syllabus designed to educate new members about hazing risks.[24] Eastern Illinois University provides written guidance that defines and describes hazing, and also established "a confidential hazing reporting process for anyone who becomes aware of suspected hazing activity on campus."[25] The university's Fraternity & Sorority Programs office reviews the reports.[26] These examples of compliance programs are part of university governance and are not part of the internal governance processes of GLOs.

The fiduciary duty of obedience, which includes the requirement that the boards of fraternal and nonprofit organizations monitor compliance with law, may remain merely rhetorical without a well-developed structure for compliance within GLOs. Compliance departments, compliance officers, compliance training, and guidance are integral parts of for-profit corporate governance. But GLO boards do not typically require GLO officers or employees to install and implement compliance programs. Well-developed compliance programs are not typically part of the internal processes of GLOs, even though these programs would help GLO boards reduce the risks of organizational liability.

---

21. Regis Becker & Gates Garrity-Rokous, *Compliance and Greek Life: Tools for Oversight and Collaboration*, PA. STATE UNIV. & OHIO STATE UNIV. (2018), https://assets.corporatecompliance.org/Portals/1/PDF/Resources/past_handouts/Higher_Ed/2018/GS4_garrity-rokous-becker_3.pdf.

22. Id.

23. Id.

24. Memorandum from Nathan Wehr, Interim Dir. of Fraternity & Sorority Programs, E. Ill. Univ., to Chapter Presidents and Chapter Advisors (Jan. 31, 2017), https://www.eiu.edu/grklife/Hazing%20Compliance%20SP18.pdf.

25. Id.

26. Id.

As a normative matter, BoardEffect, a firm that advises nonprofits on organizational governance matters, counsels nonprofit boards to create structured measures to monitor compliance with applicable law and regulations:

> There is no legal requirement for nonprofit organizations to have a legal and compliance department; nonetheless, all nonprofit organizations are required to know and follow all state and federal laws that govern them. Not all nonprofits will have sufficient funds or staff to establish a formal legal and compliance department, especially if they're just starting up. In this case, the board should designate someone to be accountable for legal and compliance matters, such as the board president or the executive committee. Alternatively, boards may appoint a lawyer to their advisory committee or hire one as needed.[27]

BoardEffect warns nonprofit managers about the costs of compliance failures. It suggests a more formalized approach to compliance, and notes that a more structured method to monitoring compliance may potentially help nonprofits that must defend against alleged misconduct.[28] Specifically, and most relevant for GLO boards, is BoardEffect's recommendation to include a policy that protects whistleblowers who disclose misconduct that could expose organizations to civil and criminal liability, and its suggestion that the board adopt an organizational code of conduct.[29]

Whistleblower protections and codes of conduct are essential elements of for-profit corporate compliance programs. Whistleblower Sherron Watkins precipitated the eventual uncovering of egregious wrongdo-

---

27. Lena Eisenstein, *Should Nonprofits Have a Legal and Compliance Department?*, BOARDEFFECT BLOG (Nov. 22, 2019, https://www.boardeffect.com/blog/should-nonprofits-have-legal-compliance-department/.

28. "The lack of compliance can lead to violations and penalties and can quickly damage a nonprofit's reputation. Nonprofits have much to benefit by setting up a Corporate Compliance Plan. A formalized compliance plan gives nonprofits the benefit of being transparent and accountable, which will help in the event that they're being investigated over allegations of illegal or unethical actions." *Id.*

29. *Id.*

ing at Enron in the early 2000s.[30] Watkins has said that "being labeled a whistleblower has been a challenge to her career ever since."[31] Watkins's career challenges occurred after Enron collapsed. Her story, however, demonstrates the importance of whistleblowers and the need for compliance programs that provide whistleblower protections for employees who report wrongdoing from retaliation that may take place within the firm, as opposed to the kinds of external challenges Watkins faced.

Compliance programs are created and installed at for-profit firms to help for-profit corporate boards fulfill the fiduciary duties they owe the corporation and its shareholders.[32] These programs are integral components of internal governance processes, designed to enhance corporate employees' adherence to applicable law and regulations created by sources that are external to the firm. Compliance processes also monitor and enhance adherence to a for-profit firm's internal norms, policies,

---

30. *See* Mengqi Sun, *Former Enron Executive: SEC Whistleblower Program Is a Game Changer,* WALL ST. J. (July 7, 2021, 9:00 AM), https://www.wsj.com/articles/former-enron-executive-sec-whistleblower-program-is-a-game-changer-11625662801.

Ms. Watkins first wrote her one-page fraud complaint anonymously and placed it in an employee dropbox in August 2001, but she decided to identify herself the next day and meet with Kenneth Lay, Enron's chief executive at the time. She didn't report what she knew directly to the government in hopes Enron executives would report it themselves, but later she was interviewed by the SEC and the Justice Department for their investigations into Enron and testified at congressional hearings.

… She said she felt shunned after her name became attached to the Enron collapse. "It's a toxic label, where you won't work in your chosen career ever again, and you lose friendships. People are hesitant to really join in a venture with you or move forward, just because there's too much noise around that label 'whistleblower,'" she said.

31. *Id.*

32. A bad faith failure to monitor compliance with law is established when fiduciaries consciously disregard their duties or engage in an intentional dereliction of their obligations, thereby violating the duty of loyalty. This means that a conscious disregard of a board's obligation to install a compliance program may be construed as a duty of loyalty breach. *See Stone* , 911 A. 2d 362. Compliance programs include several practical features that are designed to gather, report, and assess information about corporate employees' adherence to applicable law. Typically, compliance programs have an education and training component to ensure that employees fully understand the laws with which they must comply and the measures that are required to achieve compliance. Other program features may include a compliance department, compliance managers and officers, and mechanisms and procedures for reporting compliance failures. *Id.*

and practices.[33] Compliance programs in the GLO context can provide a similar benefit. For example, a national fraternity convicted for the hazing death of a pledge had an anti-hazing policy. A more formalized and well-structured compliance system would focus not only on laws and regulations that are external to the GLO, but also provide mechanisms to monitor compliance with the GLO's internal policies.

Compliance programs developed by for-profit corporations would serve as good models for more formal GLO compliance structures. GLO boards may educate themselves about the architecture of for-profit corporate compliance programs by hiring legal counsel. Counsel can also advise GLO officers as they fulfill their directors' mandate to create and implement a more formalized approach to compliance for the GLO.

III. Derivative Litigation as a Mechanism for GLO Members to Influence Board Conduct

What can inspire directors to do all they can to lower the organization's risk of exposure to civil and criminal liability? Creating and structuring more formal compliance mechanisms is costly and time consuming. What incentives do GLO directors have to require GLO officers or managers to formalize organizational compliance? In this regard, understanding the practical implications of applying the principles of derivative litigation to impact the relationship between GLO boards and members is an imperative. The possibility of filing a derivative suit against directors and the GLO itself when the organization faces potential liabil-

---

33. Compliance involves "the processes by which an organization seeks to ensure that employees and other constituents conform to applicable norms—which can include either the requirements of laws or regulations or the internal rules of the organization." GEOFFREY P. MILLER, THE LAW OF GOVERNANCE, RISK MANAGEMENT AND COMPLIANCE 3 (1st ed. 2014). "The contemporary compliance function serves a core governance function.... But, unlike other governance structures, its origins are exogenous to the firm." Sean J. Griffith, *Corporate Governance in an Era of Compliance*, 57 WM. & MARY L. REV. 2075, 2078 (2016). Effective compliance programs require information flow from employees who are deep "in the interior of the organization" to senior managers and executives who are charged with monitoring law compliance. Senior managers must communicate with mid-level managers and even low-level employees about the firm's compliance goals and requirements. This information is conveyed in employee training programs.

ity for compliance failures is a powerful incentive for boards and managers to formalize their GLO's compliance monitoring function.

Derivative litigation, and the procedural prerequisites to bringing this type of litigation in the for-profit context, have fostered communication between shareholders and their boards. The same is possible for GLO members and GLO boards. When a GLO's board engages in an extreme and sustained failure to monitor law compliance, members may consider derivative litigation. One commentator defined derivative actions in the nonprofit context:

> A 'derivative action' is subject to at least two definitions. The first is that it is an action brought in the name and for the benefit of a business entity, other than by the business entity, to enforce its rights. The second, that it is an action brought in the name and for the benefit of a business entity against the wishes of those otherwise in control of the entity, in the name and for the benefit of the entity to enforce its rights.[34]

In both the for-profit and nonprofit settings, derivative litigation is a mechanism for holding boards of directors accountable when they breach their fiduciary duties. There is, however, a fundamental difference between the way board-monitoring obligations are articulated for nonprofits and for-profits. For-profit boards owe fiduciary duties to the corporation *and* to the firm's shareholders.[35] Nonprofit boards owe duties (including the duty to monitor compliance with all applicable federal and state law) to the organization.[36] There is, in the nonprofit con-

---

34. Thomas E. Rutledge, *Who Will Watch the Watchers?: Derivative Actions in Nonprofit Corporations*, 103 Ky. L.J. Online 31 (Apr. 22, 2015), perma.cc/BG7B-T9WQ.
While some may lament that such an open policy to bringing derivative actions invites ill-conceived and even abusive suits, the protections of the demand rule will remain in place, as does the ability of the court to determine that a constituent seeking to initiate a suit does not adequately represent the corporation's interests. Simply put, the absence of a significant number of nonprofit derivative actions even in those states where they are expressly recognized by statute evidence that fears of abuse are unjustified. *Id.* at 53.

35. *See generally* Cleaveland D. Miller, *The Fiduciary Duties of a Corporate Director*, 4 U. Balt. L. Rev. 259 (1975).

36. *See e.g.*, Pamela A. Mann, *Nonprofit Governance*, (Carter Ledyard & Milburn LLP, N.Y.C, NY), 2020, https://www.clm.com/wp-content/uploads/2020/11/Nonprofit-Governance.pdf; Ellis Carter, *Fiduciary Responsibility of Nonprofit Boards*, CharityLawyer

text, no clearly articulated directorial duty that corresponds to the for-profit context where directors owe duties to shareholders. This difference in the identity of the beneficiaries of board fiduciary duties may make a difference in the internal governance of GLO/nonprofit organizations when compared to for-profit corporations.

There is room for disagreement in the nonprofit setting about whether members have standing to bring derivative suits, but a significant number of commentators agree that members should be able to file derivative litigation on behalf of their organizations:

> Directors of nonprofit organizations owe fiduciary duties to their organizations, but the content of these duties—and how and when courts should enforce these duties—has long been debated among scholars and courts. This debate emerges in several areas, including ... who should be allowed to sue to enforce duties (standing) ...[37]

Furthermore, "[n]onprofits do not have shareholders, but there may still be constituencies who arguably should be able to bring derivative suits. For example, in a membership nonprofit, the ability to bring a derivative suit could be conferred on members."[38]

When for-profit boards breach fiduciary obligations in a way that causes harm to the corporation or indirect harm to investors, shareholders may hold boards accountable by filing (or threatening) derivative litigation against the board.[39] Shareholders' pecuniary interests suffer

---

Blog (Apr. 8, 2019), https://charitylawyerblog.com/2019/04/08/fiduciary-responsibility-nonprofit-boards/.

37. Mead & Pollack, *supra* note 11.

38. Thomas Lee Hazen & Lisa Love Hazen, *Punctilios and Nonprofit Corporate Governance—A Comprehensive Look at Nonprofit Directors' Fiduciary Duties*, 14 U. PA. J. BUS. L. 347, 411 (2012). *See also* Rutledge, *supra* note 34, at 52:
> In light of the many ways in which a nonprofit corporation may be structured, courts should be afforded significant leeway in determining that particular actors have a sufficient interest in the venture to initiate the court's investigation of management's discharge of its obligations. Clearly, *ab initio* members of a membership corporation should be afforded the capacity to initiate a derivative action.

39. When shareholders' interests are harmed, they may file direct suits against directors or officers. When, however, shareholders' harm is derivative of harm to the corporation, shareholders lack standing to file a claim. Because the corporation is an entity that is separate from its shareholders, officers, or directors, only the corporation has standing

indirectly when the firms in which they invest are harmed. Harm to the corporation causes indirect harm to shareholders when the corporations in which they invest must pay criminal or civil fines and penalties. Furthermore, scandals that harm a for-profit firm's reputation may also reduce shareholder profits if consumers stop doing business with the firm. When this happens, shareholders can resort to derivative litigation—an equitable remedy that allows shareholders to sue boards when directors breach fiduciary duties and the corporation is harmed. Members' interests in GLOs and other nonprofit organizations, however, typically do not involve pecuniary interests that are similar to shareholders' wealth-maximization goals. This means that in the nonprofit context, the ability of members to hold boards accountable for harm to the organization through derivative litigation is not as clear as it is in the for-profit context.

What should happen when GLO boards fail to monitor law compliance and cause their fraternity or sorority to incur civil or criminal penalties, fines, and related costs? The harm to members when a nonprofit fails to monitor compliance is significantly and qualitatively different from harm to shareholders when for-profit boards breach monitoring obligations. The pecuniary harm a GLO suffers does not impact the financial interests of GLO members. The harm to members is disappointment and regret concerning the reputational harm to the GLO that may negatively impact its social and charitable missions. The nature of the GLO member's harm is more emotional than pecuniary. Because of the type of harm GLO members suffer when GLO boards fail to monitor compliance with law, some may conclude that members lack standing to

---

to file litigation seeking recovery for the harm inflicted. *See, In re* Medtronic, Inc. S'holder Litig., 900 N.W.2d 401 (Minn. 2017). "... [A]n individual shareholder may not assert a cause of action that belongs to the corporation ..." *Id* at 406. For example, if a corporate officer embezzles funds from a corporation, any litigation filed against the officer must be brought as a derivative suit. The shareholders of the corporation in this instance are harmed, but the harm is indirect. Shareholders' harm is derivative of the harm to the corporation and shareholders who want to pursue a claim under these facts must adhere to the procedural requirements for derivative claims. Demand is one example of the procedural prerequisites to bringing derivative litigation. If, however, corporate officers structure a transaction that impairs shareholders' voting rights, the affected shareholders may bring a direct claim against the officers and need not make a demand that the boards sue the officers. The shareholders harm in this instance does not derive from harm to the corporation. It is a direct claim.

bring a derivative suit. This conclusion, however, is not inevitable. Some courts and commentators would disagree and recognize the right of members to file derivative claims, even though members have no expectation of profits or financial gain when they join GLOs. For this reason, nonprofit firms, particularly GLOs, would benefit from a clearer understanding of the ways in which members can bring derivative suits when boards fail to monitor compliance with law.

One of the procedural prerequisites for bringing derivative litigation is the mandate that plaintiffs must first approach the board and demand that it takes action. In the for-profit context, the shareholders would sue on behalf of the corporation.[40] In the GLO context, the plaintiffs would be the organization's members. The substance of the demand requirement would be to demand that the board file a complaint against the individuals who harmed the organization. A derivative litigation plaintiff may also demand that the board take some corrective action to stop or prevent harm to the organization. A board's corrective action taken in response to a GLO member's demand may eliminate board oversight failures that harm the organization. This strategic use of the demand requirement would open the lines of communication between GLO members and their boards. It can be a process that is focused on communication and a mechanism to persuade boards to do all that is reasonably possible to avoid criminal and civil liability.

In some instances, GLO and other nonprofit members may not have to make a demand of their boards before filing a derivative claim on behalf of their organizations.[41] But nonprofit firms like GLOs generally function under laws that are similar to those applied to for-profit corpo-

---

40. In the for-profit context, derivative litigation is similarly described as an equitable remedy created by courts to protect shareholders from directorial and managerial conflicts of interest and misconduct that harms the corporation. Without this equitable remedy, shareholders lack standing to hold officers and directors accountable for harm to the corporation. The power of corporate shareholders, however, to hold boards and managers accountable must be balanced against the need to protect managerial decision making and the corporation itself. So, courts require derivative litigation plaintiffs to overcome procedural hurdles to bringing suits. Procedural prerequisites such as the demand requirement protect corporation boards from shareholders who want to infringe upon board discretion for personal gain, or to harass directors. The demand requirement gives corporate directors the chance to take corrective action and keeps courts out of internal corporate governance matters. *See* Marx v. Akers, 666 N.E.2d 1034 (N.Y. 1996).

41. *See e.g.,* Model Nonprofit Corporation Act (AM. BAR ASS'N, 4th ed. 2021); N.C. Nonprofit Corporation Act, N.C. GEN. STAT. § 55A (2023).

rations. The procedural prerequisites to filing derivative litigation in the nonprofit context may not be as thoroughly analyzed as the requirements for bringing derivative suits on behalf of for-profit firms, but it is not clear that nonprofit derivative plaintiffs can skip the demand requirement:

> In a derivative action brought on behalf of a nonprofit corporation, the plaintiff must be expected to either make a demand or plead futility. If it is a membership organization, the plaintiff must also plead that they are a member and are able to represent the interests of similarity situated members in representing the interests of the corporation.[42]

Shareholders of for-profit corporations expend a great deal of time and resources litigating whether demand must be made under a particular set of facts. In the for-profit setting, if demand is required it must be made, unless the board of directors cannot be expected to do the right thing because the directors have an interest in the matter that shareholder plaintiffs are challenging. When shareholders establish that board members are conflicted and will not likely pursue litigation against wrongdoers who have harmed the corporation, demand is excused and is not required.[43] Shareholders may file the litigation themselves when demand is excused. Demand-excusal tests, however, should *not* apply to nonprofits or GLOs. Rather than attempting to avoid demand, GLO members can embrace the demand requirement in order to foster communication with GLO directors and provide them with notice about compliance failures.

GLO members who know something about compliance and monitoring failures within their organization can demand that the board do something about it. Members who suspect ongoing and pervasive non-

---

42. Rutledge, *supra* note 34, at 45.

43. *See Marx*, 666 N.E.2d 1034. In New York, demand is excused if derivative suit plaintiffs allege particularized facts that, if established, would show that most of the board is interested in the transaction about which plaintiffs complain. Demand will also be excused if plaintiffs allege specific facts that establish that directors did not attempt to get the information about the challenged transaction that was reasonably necessary for them to make an informed decision, or that the board did not exercise its business judgment when it approved the transaction plaintiffs challenge. *Id.* at 1218–19. Delaware courts have established a similar test for demand excusal. Grimes v. Donald, 673 A.2d 1207 (Del. 1996), *overruled* by Brehm v. Eisner, 746 A.2d 244 (Del. 2000).

compliance with civil and criminal law should request that boards, in satisfaction of their good faith obligation under the duty of obedience, look into the suspected noncompliance. Members need not file litigation. Instead, they can make demand on the GLO board to take corrective action that requires them to fulfill their obligation to engage in good faith compliance monitoring. Members can ask their boards to take the kind of remedial action that would satisfy their duties to monitor and oversee compliance with law.

At least one Texas attorney has successfully represented corporate shareholders who demanded that boards monitor and inquire about allegations of noncompliance. Boards responded favorably, honoring the attorney's requests on behalf of his clients that directors oversee and inquire about claims of employee noncompliance. Shareholders have achieved modest success in eliminating directorial fiduciary breaches by simply asking the board to fulfill its obligation of good faith. Boards have responded favorably to shareholders' demands that directors take corrective action.[44]

More specifically, shareholders have made demands that requested that directors fortify corporate codes of conduct. The companies that received such requests had compliance programs, but the programs had "no muscle."[45] For example, even though monitoring and reporting systems were in place, at some companies they were merely cosmetic. Employees' complaints or reports of corporate noncompliance were implicitly discouraged. Shareholders demanded that boards revise codes of conduct or compliance codes to include clauses with strong language that clearly prohibited retaliation against whistleblowers.

GLO members who use the demand process put "directors on notice of a compliance failure. Without notice of deficiencies in the architecture of a compliance program," boards cannot take remedial action.[46] The pre-suit demand process is a mechanism that can provide directors with notice of potential civil and criminal liability because of the organization's compliance failures. GLO directors are not involved in the

---

44. *See* Cheryl L. Wade, *"We Are An Equal Opportunity Employer": Diversity Doublespeak*, 61 WASH. & LEE L. REV. 1541, 1572–74 (2004).

45. Telephone Interview with Steve Kardell, Partner, Kardell Law Group (Aug. 11, 2003).

46. *Id.*

day-to-day operations of their organizations. They volunteer for the GLO and are likely to be employed elsewhere, so they are also likely to be unaware of compliance failures within their organizations. GLO members who demand that boards take remedial action serve as an important source of information for directors.

IV. Conclusion

It is imperative for GLO graduate chapters to undertake an additional responsibility that may help to reduce the possibility that a GLO will incur criminal and civil liability. I suggest that GLO graduate chapters elect individuals who will monitor undergraduate chapters. This monitoring should include training and educating undergraduates about the GLO's policy and legal obligations that prohibit criminal activities such as underage drinking and conduct such as hazing that can lead to criminal and civil liability. When GLO graduate chapter leaders discover criminal or civil infractions, they must encourage their GLO's board members to implement systems that monitor compliance with law and GLO policy by providing the board information about compliance failures. More specifically, GLO graduate chapter leaders may write demand letters to GLO boards insisting that they take seriously their obligations to monitor the GLO's compliance with law and GLO policy.

GLOs help to shape the lives of their undergraduate members and help to transform and shape society. By helping GLO boards to monitor compliance, graduate chapter leaders protect their organizations from the burdens and costs of litigation and preserve the ability of their organizations to continue their important philanthropic work.

PART TWO:
RISK AND LIABILITY ISSUES

CHAPTER 6

The Mandatory Arbitration of Hazing Lawsuits

Etienne C. Toussaint

Since the late twentieth century, Greek-letter organizations have exploded in popularity on college campuses across the United States.[1] However, this expansion has been accompanied by the escalating problem of "hazing" during the member initiation process.[2] As a result, national fraternities and sororities have increasingly been embroiled in litigation resulting from the injuries and, in some instances, death suffered by prospective members during underground pledging activities.[3] For example, in 2007, two collegiate members of the Alpha Xi Chapter of Kappa Alpha Psi Fraternity, Inc. at Florida A & M University were sentenced to two years in prison after Marcus Jones, a fellow Florida A & M undergraduate student, sustained severe injuries during a pledging-related hazing incident.[4] Fraternities and sororities across the country have taken various steps to combat this ongoing problem, from anti-hazing policies to moratoriums on membership intake, and even to

---

1. Gregory E. Rutledge, *Hell Night Hath No Fury Like a Pledge Scorned ... and Injured: Hazing Litigation in U.S. Colleges and Universities*, 25 J.C. & U.L. 361, 365–66 (1998).

2. *Id.*

3. *Id.* at 362.

4. The Associated Press, *Pair sentenced to 2 years each in FAMU hazing*, GAINESVILLE SUN (Jan. 29, 2007), https://www.gainesville.com/story/news/2007/01/30/pair-sentenced-to-2-years-each-in-famu-hazing/31510687007/.

suspensions of individual chapters and their members.[5] Nevertheless, hazing persists and increasingly threatens the viability of fraternities and sororities. When hazing becomes ingrained in a Greek-letter organization's culture, the fraternity or sorority risks being shackled by a negative stigma that can ruin its positive reputation and hinder its public-oriented mission. When hazing results in costly litigation, fraternities and sororities risk bankrupting their organizations altogether.

Some fraternities and sororities have turned to mandatory arbitration to avoid lengthy and expensive litigation that may drain organizational resources. Arbitration is a private dispute resolution mechanism that exists outside of the traditional court system and relies upon a neutral arbitrator to resolve disputes after receiving evidence and hearing arguments.[6] Once the dispute has been settled, a court confirms the arbitration award. For example, in 2007, E. Martyn Griffen, a college junior and "aspirant" of the Psi Chapter of Alpha Phi Alpha Fraternity, Inc. at the University of Pennsylvania, sued two members of the collegiate chapter after he sustained injuries during pledging-related hazing activities.[7] Griffen sought damages for assault and battery, negligence, and intentional infliction of emotional distress from the individual defendants. He also sought damages for negligence from the national organization. The defendants moved to dismiss the lawsuit or, alternatively, stay litigation pending the results of arbitration based on an arbitration provision in Griffen's application for membership.[8] After considering arguments regarding the potential unconscionability of the arbitration provision, the District Court of Eastern Pennsylvania granted the fraternity's mo-

---

5. Dara Aquila Govan & Michael V. W. Gordon, *Old School Values and New School Methods: Preserving the Integrity of the Pledge Process and Defending against Hazing Liability*, in BLACK GREEK LETTER ORGANIZATIONS 2.0: NEW DIRECTIONS IN THE STUDY OF AFRICAN AMERICAN FRATERNITIES AND SORORITIES (Matthew W. Hughey et al. eds., 2011), https://academic.oup.com/mississippi-scholarship-online/book/24306/chapter-abstract/185983415?redirectedFrom=fulltext.

6. *See generally* Joseph Daly, *Arbitration: The Basics*, 5 J. AM. ARB. 1 (2006) (providing a primer on the basics of arbitration).

7. Griffen v. Alpha Phi Alpha, Inc., No. 06-1735, 2007 WL 707364 (E.D. Pa. Mar. 2, 2007).

8. Dan McCarthy & Manley Burke, *Arbitration Clause is Enforceable in Hazing* Case, FRATERNAL L. PARTNERS (Sept. 2007), https://fraternallaw.com/newsletter2/arbitration-clause-is-enforceable-in-hazing-case.

tion to stay litigation and compel arbitration.[9] Although fraught with debate on the merits of the plaintiff's unconscionability claim, the outcome opened the doorway for a faster, cheaper, and perhaps most importantly, private dispute resolution process for the fraternity.

Despite its advantages (e.g., greater efficiency, lower costs, and privacy),[10] arbitration has been challenged by fraternity and sorority members who discover that they have unknowingly agreed to mandatory arbitration in their membership agreements, thereby eliminating their ability to resolve disputes in court. In some instances, members have attempted to vacate arbitration awards by attacking the neutrality of the arbitrator and the fairness of the arbitration process itself, such as in the 2018 case of *McKinzie v. Alpha Kappa Alpha Sorority, Inc.*[11] In other cases, such as *Griffen v. Alpha Phi Alpha, Inc.* in 2007 and, more recently, in *Jean v. Bucknell University* in 2021,[12] members have sought a court ruling that the arbitration provision in the application for membership is unconscionable and therefore should not be enforced.

The concept of unconscionability in contract law describes contractual terms that are so extremely one-sided in favor of a party with superior bargaining power that the terms "shock the conscience" of the court.[13] In other words, no reasonable person would agree to an unconscionable term in a contract because it unjustly exploits the disadvantages of weaker parties, producing a grossly unfair bargain. Courts tend to distinguish procedural unconscionability, which focuses on the fairness of the bargaining process, from substantive unconscionability, which focuses on the fairness of the contractual terms.[14] Due to the theoretical "freedom of contract" that fraternity and sorority members enjoy to privately negotiate the terms of their membership agreements,

---

9. *Id.*

10. Allied-Bruce Terminix Cos. v. Dobson, 513 U.S. 265, 280 (1995); Daly, *supra* note 6, at 36 ("A primary reason parties choose arbitration is to avoid the expense and time involved in the discovery necessary to prepare a case if it went to court.").

11. McKinzie v. Alpha Kappa Alpha Sorority, Inc., No. 1-17-2337, 2018 WL 6843633 (Ill. App. Ct. Dec. 27, 2018).

12. Griffen v. Alpha Phi Alpha, Inc., No. 06-1735, 2006 WL 3302438 (E.D. Pa. Nov. 9, 2006); Jean v. Bucknell Univ., 534 F.Supp. 3d 404 (M.D. Pa. 2021).

13. Brady Williams, *Unconscionability as a Sword: The Case for an Affirmative Cause of Action*, 107 Calif. L. Rev. 2015 (2019).

14. Richard J. Hunter Jr., *Unconscionability Revisited: A Comparative Approach*, 68 N.D. L. Rev. 145 (1992).

coupled with the voluntary nature of membership in such extracurricular organizations, it is difficult to invalidate arbitration clauses by claiming unconscionability in the process or substance of the bargain.

Still, fraternities and sororities have reason to be cautious, especially as it relates to hazing cases. In *Jean v. Bucknell University*, a federal court for the Middle District of Pennsylvania denied a motion to enforce a fraternity's arbitration clause when former Bucknell University student John Jean filed a lawsuit against the university after an alleged hazing incident.[15] The court determined that several provisions in the arbitration agreement were overly broad and ambiguous, and therefore could not be relied upon to deny Jean his day in court. This case highlights the critical need for fraternities and sororities to seek the advice of counsel when they incorporate mandatory arbitration clauses in their membership agreements. Specifically, a seasoned attorney can help to reduce the ambiguity of such provisions and thereby increase the likelihood of their enforcement. This case also suggests that fraternities and sororities should explore other ways to protect themselves from liability if a court fails to enforce their arbitration agreements.

This chapter explores these issues as follows. Part I begins by briefly reviewing the rise of hazing and hazing-related lawsuits in fraternities and sororities across the United States. Then, Part II reviews the concept of arbitration, which has been included in many fraternity and sorority membership agreements to avoid some of the litigation risks associated with hazing-related lawsuits. This part clarifies several reasons why membership organizations include mandatory arbitration clauses in their membership agreements. Part III follows by discussing the doctrine of unconscionability in contract law, which has been used by litigants to challenge the enforceability of arbitration agreements. This part explains how courts determine whether an arbitration provision is unconscionable. Next, Part IV reviews the recent case of *Jean v. Bucknell University*, detailing the facts of the case and explaining why the court denied the fraternity's motion to compel arbitration, notwithstanding its inclusion in the application for membership. Then, Part V explores the impact of the court's decision to deny the fraternity's motion to compel arbitration. Finally, this chapter concludes by explaining how fraterni-

---

15. Jean v. Bucknell Univ., No. 4:20-CV-01722, 2021 WL 1521724 (M.D. Pa. Apr. 16, 2021) (memorandum decision).

ties and sororities can avoid the outcome of *Jean v. Bucknell University* by incorporating best practices in the drafting of arbitration clauses in their membership agreements. This final part also considers other ways that Greek-letter organizations can contractually protect themselves from the public exposure of hazing incidents.

I. The Rise of Hazing and Hazing-Related Lawsuits in Greek Life

Hazing has a long history in academic institutions. According to Gregory S. Parks and Tamara L. Brown, hazing existed as early as Plato's Academy in 387 BC and continued well into the Middle Ages to establish hierarchy among students.[16] As colleges and universities were established during the colonial era of the United States, hazing emerged as a common practice to distinguish students of different ranks.[17] By the nineteenth century, hazing would come to define fraternity and sorority culture in the United States as well. Greek-letter organizations incorporated Masonic rituals designed to symbolize the "murder, burial, and resurrection" of prospective members during the pledge process.[18] Physically demanding initiation activities conducted in groups called "pledge clubs" served not only to convey the pledge's individual transformation of mind, body, and spirit, but also to forge bonds of trust between current and new members.[19] After World War II, hazing evolved to incorporate military culture and became seen as a way for prospective members to prove their worthiness for membership by completing various tests designed by the fraternity or sorority.[20] It became common, especially among historically Black Greek-letter organizations (BGLOs), to witness pledge clubs dressing alike, walking together in a straight line, singing fraternity songs, reciting poetry, referring to members as "big

---

16. Gregory S. Parks & Tamara L. Brown, *In the Fell Clutch of Circumstance: Pledging and the Black Greek Experience*, in AFRICAN AMERICAN FRATERNITIES AND SORORITIES: THE LEGACY AND THE VISION 437, 437–38 (Tamara L. Brown, Gregory S. Parks, & Clarenda M. Phillips eds., 2005).

17. *Id.*
18. *Id.* at 439.
19. *Id.* at 447–48, 441.
20. Rutledge, *supra* note 1, at 369.

brother" or "big sister," and even submitting to public acts of humiliation while "pledging" on campus.[21]

Scholars argue that the modern version of pledging that includes physically demanding—and often violent—hazing activities erupted during the late 1970s and early 1980s.[22] The outlawing of traditional pledging processes by many fraternities and sororities in the late twentieth century coincided with the rapid growth of Greek-letter organizations on college and university campuses.[23] However, some critics argue that the end of formal pledging amplified dangerous hazing activities and has consequently only made matters worse.[24] As national offices of fraternities and sororities struggled to provide adequate oversight over individual chapters, the process of hazing moved "underground" and grew more physically and psychologically intense.[25] In some cases, excessive alcohol drinking became a part of the pledging process as well.[26] As a result, hazing-related deaths ballooned in number. Whereas scholars have identified evidence of approximately one hazing-related death every three years during the first 132 years of fraternity and sorority life on college campuses, more recent studies have revealed an average of three significant hazing-related injuries (many of which resulted in death) per year since 1970.[27] As to be expected, the rise in hazing-related deaths triggered an associated rise in lawsuits. These suits were not only brought against the local chapters who inflicted harm or death to pledges, but also against the national offices of fraternities and sororities that support and coordinate the collective mission of local chapters. Further, lawsuits were brought against the colleges and universities that cer-

---

21. Parks & Brown, *supra* note 16, at 443; Dara Aquila Govan, Note, *"Hazing Out" the Membership Intake Process in Sororities and Fraternities: Preserving the Integrity of the Pledge Process Versus Addressing Hazing Liability*, 53 RUTGERS L. REV. 679, 686 (2001).

22. Govan, *supra* note 21, at 687.

23. *Id.*

24. RICKY L. JONES, BLACK HAZE: VIOLENCE, SACRIFICE, AND MANHOOD IN BLACK GREEK FRATERNITIES 91 (2004); *Pledging a Brother, Not Intaking a "Paper Brother,"* BLACK ISSUES IN HIGHER EDUC., June 12, 1997, at 26.

25. Govan, *supra* note 21, at 686.

26. *See* Hank Nuwer, *U.S. Hazing Deaths Database Part 1: 1838–1999*, HANK NUWER UNOFFICIAL HAZING CLEARINGHOUSE (Oct. 6, 2022), http://www.hanknuwer.com/hazingdeaths.html; *see also, e.g.*, Davies v. Butler, 602 P.2d 605 (Nev. 1979).

27. Govan, *supra* note 21, at 681–83; Nuwer, *supra* note 26.

tify the status of local chapters of national fraternities and sororities as campus-based student organizations.[28]

In 1986, the case of *Ballou v. Sigma Nu General Fraternity* established the agency relationship between local chapters of fraternities and sororities and their national offices.[29] As Gregory Parks explains, "Agency theory is a method of determining if a relationship exists between two parties and thus one should be held responsible for the actions of the other."[30] Specifically, the relationship must be a consensual fiduciary relationship whereby the agent retains authority to act on behalf of and bind the principal with respect to third parties, and the principal retains the right to control the agent's actions with respect to third parties through interim instructions. In *Ballou*, the father of Lurie Barry Ballou (Barry), a prospective fraternity member of Sigma Nu General Fraternity (Sigma Nu) at the University of South Carolina, sued the local chapter and national office of the organization for the wrongful death of his son after a hazing incident. Barry had died from alcohol poisoning after being psychologically coerced into drinking excessive amounts of alcohol during a pledging event in the fall of 1979.[31] The national office of Sigma Nu, an unincorporated association, claimed that the hazing activities of the local chapter fell outside of their agency relationship, severing the causal chain that would trigger their liability.[32] However, the South Carolina Court of Appeals held that even though a prospective member of the national organization could only join through the local chapter, the national office retained accountability for the membership process and had set the guidelines for new fraternity member initiation.[33] Accordingly, the Court of Appeals affirmed the trial court's jury verdict against Sigma Nu, which totaled $200,000 in actual damages and $50,000 in punitive damages.[34]

---

28. *See generally* Douglas E. Fierberg, *Student Victims: Strategies and Issues For Successful Civil Litigation*, AM. TRIAL LAWYERS ASS'N (July 2007); Rutledge, *supra* note 1, at 368.

29. Ballou v. Sigma Nu Gen. Fraternity, 352 S.E.2d 488 (S.C. Ct. App. 1986).

30. Gregory S. Parks and Elizabeth Grindell, *The Litigation Landscape of Fraternity and Sorority Hazing: Criminal and Civil Liability*, 99 NEB. L. REV. 649, 669 (2020) [hereinafter *Criminal and Civil Liability*].

31. *Ballou*, 352 S.E.2d at 491–92.

32. *Id.* at 495.

33. *Id.* at 496.

34. *Id.* at 492.

To be sure, the question of agency discussed in *Ballou* is still hotly contested by fraternities and sororities. The *Ballou* court based its determination of agency primarily on the fraternity's admission. As the court declared, "Sigma Nu concedes that an agency relationship existed between it and the local chapter. As Sigma Nu's agent, the act of the local chapter in conducting hell night was binding upon Sigma Nu if performed within the scope of the agency, even though not authorized by the general fraternity."[35] Parks further explains, "the court found that the chapter exercised its apparent authority when it created 'hell night' as part of its initiation process."[36] Actual authority arises when an agent reasonably believes that they have been authorized to act on behalf of a principal based upon the express or implied communications of the principal, whether delivered orally, in writing, or by conduct. Conversely, apparent authority arises when a third party reasonably believes that an agent is authorized to act on behalf of a principal based upon certain communications or actions (either direct or indirect) of the principal. In each case, a finding of actual or apparent authority requires first the existence of an agency relationship.

Since *Ballou*, courts have been reluctant to find an agency relationship between local Greek-letter chapters and their national offices.[37] However, there has been a recent trend in hazing litigation whereby courts allow plaintiffs who are injured in hazing activities by local chapters of national fraternal organizations to recover from their national affiliates through the doctrine of respondeat superior.[38] In such instances, the national organization as a master becomes vicariously liable for the actions of the local chapter as a servant when the national fraternity authorizes and tasks the local chapter with recruitment and

---

35. *Id.* at 495–96.

36. Parks & Grindell, *Criminal and Civil Liability, supra* note 30, at 670, n.198 ("Actual authority refers to specific powers granted to a third party by a principal to act on its behalf, while apparent authority exists where a reasonable third party would understand that an agent had authority to act.")

37. *Id.* at 671 (explaining that courts "recognize that it is difficult for national fraternities to monitor the daily actions of every chapter and hold that a chapter involved in hazing is not enough to place liability on the national fraternity outright"); *see also* Prime v. Beta Gamma Chapter of Pi Kappa Alpha, 47 P.3d 402, 413 (Kan. 2002) (holding that the national fraternity was not liable for injuries stemming from a local chapter's hazing activities because the national fraternity only served as a "support organization").

38. Parks & Grindell, *Criminal and Civil Liability, supra* note 30, at 676.

membership intake responsibilities for the organization, and wrongful acts within the scope of the local chapter's authorization inflict harm on third parties.

Given the litigation risks facing national Greek-letter organizations from local chapter hazing activities after *Ballou*, fraternities and sororities devised various strategies to eliminate the risks of hazing. Across the board, Greek-letter organizations began purchasing general liability insurance to cover local chapters.[39] However, insurance policies generally do not cover intentionally inflicted injuries from hazing activities and have therefore been deemed inapplicable in many states with anti-hazing laws.[40] Many Greek-letter organizations have been explicit in communicating to their members that their general insurance policies do not apply to injuries stemming from hazing or excessive alcohol usage.[41] Additionally, some fraternities and sororities have adopted risk management policies and procedures.[42] For example, in 1987, various Greek-letter organizations formed a coalition called the Fraternity Information and Programming Group with a goal of promoting best practices for risk management and potentially reducing the cost of insurance.[43] Further still, some fraternities and sororities have banned the usage of alcohol on organizational property.[44] Others have tried to coordinate their membership intake process through their national office, effectively ending formal pledging at the local chapter level altogether.[45]

One leading strategy to avoid the potentially crippling expenses of litigation has been to incorporate arbitration clauses into fraternity and sorority applications for membership. The case of *Griffen v. Alpha Phi Alpha, Inc.* in 2007 clarified how courts might interpret such contractual

---

39. Shane Kimzey, Note, *The Role of Insurance in Fraternity Litigation*, 16 REV. LITIG. 459, 460 (1997).

40. *See* Govan, *supra* note 21, at 710.

41. Gregory S. Parks & Elizabeth Grindell, *The Litigation Landscape of Fraternity and Sorority Hazing: Defenses, Evidence, and Damages*, 79 WASH. & LEE L. REV. 335 (2022) [hereinafter *Defenses, Evidence, and Damages*].

42. *Id.*

43. *See* Andrea Starks-Corbin, *FIPG Policy No Longer Exists*, ASS'N OF FRATERNITY/ SORORITY ADVISORS (April 17, 2019), https://www.afa1976.org/news/447366/FIPG-Policy-No-Longer-Exists.htm.

44. Parks & Grindell, *Defenses, Evidence, and Damages*, *supra* note 41.

45. Parks & Brown, *supra* note 16, at 444.

provisions.[46] In that case, E. Martyn Griffen, a college junior and an "aspirant" of the Psi Chapter of Alpha Phi Alpha Fraternity, Inc. (Alpha Phi Alpha) at the University of Pennsylvania, suffered injuries during pledging-related hazing activities.[47] Griffen sued both the local chapter and the national office of the fraternity, claiming assault and battery by the local chapter members, among other claims, and also claiming negligence by the national office for failing to adequately oversee the membership intake activities of the local chapter.[48] However, unlike many earlier hazing cases, Griffen had signed an application for membership that included an arbitration agreement. The Alpha Phi Alpha arbitration agreement stated, in relevant part:

> Any grievances and disputes regarding membership intake should generally be referred to the National Director of Membership Services for investigation and resolution. Matters that cannot be resolved within the Fraternity will be referred to arbitration.... The aspirant, his heirs and assigns, and [the Fraternity], its officers, employees, agents, affiliates, chapters and members, agree that any and all disputes, conflicts, claims and/or causes of action of any kind whatsoever, [i]ncluding but not limited to: contract claims, personal injury claims, bodily injury claims, injury to character claims and property damage claims arising out of or relating in any manner whatsoever to the Intake process and application shall be subject to and resolved by compulsory and binding arbitration under the Federal Arbitration Act, 9 U.S.C. Section 1, et seq. and the commercial rules of the American Arbitration Association.[49]

The *Griffen* court upheld the enforceability of Alpha Phi Alpha's arbitration agreement, concluding that Griffen had not been subjected to fraud, duress, or any other type of coercion in the formation of the contract.[50] Further, the court held that the language of the arbitration agree-

---

46. Griffen v. Alpha Phi Alpha, Inc., No. 06-1735, 2007 WL 707364, at *3 (E.D. Pa. Mar. 2, 2007).
47. Parks & Grindell, *Defenses, Evidence, and Damages, supra* note 41.
48. Griffen v. Alpha Phi Alpha, Inc., No. 06-1735, 2007 WL 707364, at *3 (E.D. Pa. Mar. 2, 2007).
49. *Id.* at *2.
50. *Id.* at *5–6.

ment was substantively broad enough to include the types of injuries suffered by Griffen during the hazing activities.[51] However, arbitration clauses in fraternity and sorority membership agreements are not always deemed to be enforceable.

II. Arbitration as an Alternative Dispute Resolution Mechanism

The use of arbitration as a method of alternative dispute resolution predates the formation of the United States and the establishment of the federal court system under the US Constitution. For example, both Native American nations and British colonial settlers used arbitration and mediation to resolve disputes.[52] Further, arbitration was often used to resolve commercial and labor disputes in early America.[53] However, arbitration also faced opposition because it bypassed the traditional judicial system and weakened the role of the courts in the US political economy.[54] In response to staunch advocacy by New York's Wall Street business community, Congress enacted the Federal Arbitration Act (FAA) in 1925, which applies to all arbitration agreements that implicate interstate commerce.[55] Section 2 of the FAA provides:

---

51. *Id.* at *8–9.

52. Dennis R. Nolan, Labor Arbitration Law and Practice in a Nutshell 2–3 (West Publishing Co. 1979); Matt Arbaugh, *Making Peace the Old Fashioned Way: Infusing Traditional Tribal Practices into Modern ADR*, 2 Pepp. Disp. Resol. L.J. 303, 303 (2002); Robert Ackerman, *Disputing Together, Conflict Resolution and the Search for Community*, 18 Ohio St. J. Disp. Resol. 27, 46–47 (2003).

53. Lee Korland, *What an Arbitrator Should Investigate and Disclose: Proposing a New Test for Evident Partiality Under the Federal Arbitration Act*, 53 Case W. Res. L. Rev. 815, 817 (2003) (noting the usage of arbitration throughout the U.S. colonies prior to the American Revolution); Lewis L. Maltby, *Private Justice: Employment Arbitration and Civil Rights*, 30 Colum. Hum. Rts. L. Rev. 29, 30 (1998) ("For decades, private arbitration has been the vehicle of choice for unions, and it has worked well in this context.").

54. Scholars note that judicial hostility to arbitration was evident in English common law. *See* Thomas E. Carbonneau, Cases and Materials on the Law and Practice of Arbitration 49 (rev. 3d ed. 2003); Roger J. Perlstadt, *Timing of Institutional Bias Challenges to Arbitration*, 69 U. Chi. L. Rev. 1983, 1983 (2002).

55. *See* Sarah Rudolph Cole, *Incentives and Arbitration: The Case Against Enforcement of Executory Arbitration Agreements Between Employers and Employees*, 64 UMKC L. Rev. 449, 465 (1996) ("Businessmen grew to favor arbitration not only because it offered them

A written provision in any maritime transaction or a contract evidencing a transaction involving commerce to settle by arbitration a controversy thereafter arising out of such contract or transaction ... shall be valid, irrevocable, and enforceable, save upon such grounds as exist at law or in equity for the revocation of any contract.[56]

In simple terms, arbitration can be described as "a process of dispute resolution in which a neutral third party (arbitrator) renders a decision after a hearing at which both parties have an opportunity to be heard."[57] Since the early twentieth century, arbitration provisions have become a common feature of business, consumer, and employment contracts that involve interstate commerce.[58] This trend was amplified by several seminal Supreme Court cases that endorsed arbitration as a viable dispute resolution mechanism when a matter is brought in state rather than federal court,[59] when there is inequality in bargaining power,[60] and even when both parties to a transaction do not contemplate the interstate dimensions of their agreement.[61]

The establishment of arbitration as a dispute resolution mechanism occurs by (1) a contractual agreement to arbitrate disputes and (2) the existence of a conflict, which is typically a contractual dispute. Like litigation proceedings, arbitration hearings allow both parties to present documents, exhibits, and other evidence to support their claims.[62] How-

---

autonomy from governmental regulation, but also because it allowed for a faster and more reliable means of dispute resolution."); Scherk v. Alberto-Culver Co., 417 U.S. 506, 511 (1974) (explaining that the FAA was created to place arbitration on "the same footing as other contracts").

56. 9 U.S.C. 2 (1994); *see* Allied-Bruce Terminix Cos. V. Dobson, 513 U.S. 265, 273–74 (1994) (adopting a broad interpretation of the phrase "involving commerce").

57. BLACK'S LAW DICTIONARY 105 (6th ed. 1990).

58. Daly, *supra* note 6, at 8–9 ("But, in 1974, the judicial hostility toward arbitration turned to support when the Supreme Court held that an arbitral forum would be just as fair as a courtroom for parties to an international agreement who had agreed to arbitrate a securities fraud claim pursuant to U.S. law."); *see* Prima Paint Corp. v. Flood & Conklin Mfg. Co., 388 U.S. 395 (1967); Moses H. Cone Mem'l Hosp. v. Mercury Constr. Corp., 460 U.S. 1 (1983).

59. *See* Southland Corp. v. Keating, 465 U.S. 1 (1984).

60. *See* Gilmer v. Interstate/Johnson Lane Corp., 500 U.S. 20 (1991).

61. *See generally* Allied-Bruce Terminix Cos. v. Dobson, 513 U.S. 265 (1995).

62. Parks & Grindell, *Defenses, Evidence, and Damages, supra* note 41.

ever, the rules of civil procedure and evidence that govern judicial proceedings in the traditional courtroom do not apply to arbitration. Instead, the arbitrator as a neutral third party renders a decision on the merits after hearing both parties' cases. That decision must be "final, binding and without any qualification or condition as to the finality of an award whether or not agreed to by parties."[63] Arbitration is preferred by many organizations because it offers "privacy, a more efficient process, a neutral decision-maker with expertise in the field, and most importantly, it is inexpensive."[64] Further, the parties have more control over the scheduling of hearings and the confidentiality of the proceedings.[65] Administering arbitral institutions, such as the American Arbitration Association (AAA) and the International Chamber of Commers (ICC), help to simplify the process with "time tested rules ... qualified and experienced arbitrators, and ... qualified staff to assist and to answer procedural questions."[66]

Arbitration is especially relevant to Greek-letter organizations that find themselves threatened by lawsuits for hazing-related deaths or injuries because of the unpredictable nature of jury verdicts and the potentially high costs of judgments or settlements.[67] While a typical courtroom trial can extend over several years with massive lawyering fees,[68] arbitration hearings, on the other hand, can generate a dispute resolution in a year or two that balances the interests of both parties while maintaining fairness and cost efficiency.[69] Importantly, hazing-related

---

63. Schaefer v. Allstate Ins. Co., 590 N.E.2d 1242, 1245 (Ohio 1992).

64. William C. Terrell, *Pledging to Stay Viable: Why Fraternities and Sororities Should Adopt Arbitration as a Response to the Litigation Dilemma*, 43 U. MEM. L. REV. 511, 541 (2012); Theodore J. St. Antoine, *Mandatory Arbitration: Why It's Better Than It Looks*, 41 U. MICH. J.L. REFORM 783, 784 (2008).

65. L. Tyrone Holt, *Whither Arbitration? What Can Be Done to Improve Arbitration and Keep Out Litigation's Ill Effects*, 7 DEPAUL BUS. & COM. L.J. 455, 463–64 (2009); In re Teligent, Inc., 640 F.3d 53, 57–58 (2d. Cir. 2011); Samuel Estreicher & Steven C. Bennett, *The Confidentiality of Arbitration Proceedings*, N.Y. L.J., Aug. 13, 2008.

66. Daly, *supra* note 6, at 21.

67. Thomas J. Stipanowich, *Arbitration: The "New Litigation,"* 2010 U. ILL. L. REV. 1, 24 (2010).

68. Seth Lipner, *Is Arbitration Really Cheaper?*, FORBES (July 14, 2009, 2:00 PM), https://www.forbes.com/2009/07/14/lipner-arbitration-litigation-intelligent-investing-cost.html?sh=2c34c1484ed1.

69. F. Hodge O'Neal, *Resolving Disputes in Closely Held Corporations: Intra-Institutional Arbitration*, 67 HARV. L. REV. 786, 790 (1954); Daly, *supra* note 6, at 11 ("It is not

deaths and their associated lawsuits have brought intense public scrutiny upon fraternities and sororities, threatening to tarnish their public service missions with the terrible choices of a few bad actors.[70] Arbitration promises to divert negative media attention away from the national organization and toward resolving the hazing-related dispute between the member and the individual chapter in a fair and just way.

The enforceability of an arbitration agreement is premised on the concept of freedom of contract.[71] A party cannot be coerced into an arbitration agreement. Rather, they must willingly and knowingly assent to the terms of the contractual bargain, especially when it includes the removal of a right that is a common feature of business transactions—the right to sue in a court of law for a breach of contract. When private individuals mutually assent to the terms of a contractual bargain, they will generally be enforced by courts unless they are unlawful or violate public policy.[72] Courts have held that fraternal organizations have the right to determine their own member selection process because membership is a privilege, not a right.[73] As a result, an arbitration agreement between a Greek-letter organization and its members will generally be held to be unenforceable only when (1) there is evidence that the parties have not mutually assented to the arbitration agreement, (2) the dispute in question was not included in the scope of the arbitration agreement, or (3) the arbitration agreement is deemed procedurally or substantively unenforceable because it is unlawful or otherwise contradicts the fundamental premise of contractual liberty.[74]

Nonprofit organizations can include arbitration clauses in their membership applications/agreements or, alternatively, in their governing

---

uncommon for cases to be arbitrated within a few months from the origin of the conflict, not years.").

70. *See* Taylor v. Van-Catlin Constr., 30 Cal. Rptr. 3d 690, 693 (Cal. Ct. App. 2005).

71. Benyon v. Garden Med. Group, 161 Cal. Rptr. 146, 149 (Cal. Ct. App. 1980) ("[I]n order to be enforceable an agreement to arbitrate must have been openly and fairly entered into by the parties.").

72. *See, e.g.*, Hooters of Am. v. Phillips, 173 F.3d 933, 938 (4th Cir. 1999) (noting that the arbitration provisions "when taken as a whole, however, are so one-sided that their only possible purpose is to undermine the neutrality of the proceeding").

73. *See* Falcone v. Middlesex Cnty. Med. Soc'y, 162 A.2d 324, 332 (N.J. Super. Ct. Law Div. 1960); Williams v. Black Rock Yacht Club, 877 A.2d 849, 856 (Conn. App. Ct. 2005).

74. *See* Aaron-Andrew P. Bruhl, *The Unconscionability Game: Strategic Judging and the Evolution of Federal Arbitration Law*, 83 N.Y.U. L. Rev. 1420, 1422 (2008).

documents, such as their articles of incorporation, bylaws, constitutions, or policies and procedures of the organization.[75] Consequently, it is the third scenario noted above—the question of coercion on procedural or substantive grounds—that is often raised as a defense to contract enforceability. One way to raise this type of claim is through the doctrine of unconscionability.

A party to a valid and enforceable arbitration agreement can request a "stay of litigation" pending the results of arbitration or ask the court to "compel arbitration."[76] However, before compelling arbitration, a court must first determine whether a valid and enforceable arbitration agreement exists, and whether the matter in dispute falls within the scope of that agreement. Courts apply traditional contract formation principles to determine the validity of agreements to arbitrate.[77] Thus, a party can seek to avoid the enforceability of a valid arbitration agreement by raising traditional contract defenses, such as fraud, duress, and unconscionability.[78]

An important question for courts is determining who (i.e., an arbitrator or a judge) decides whether an arbitration agreement is valid, enforceable, or applicable to a specific dispute. It is generally presumed that courts will resolve such questions. However, parties can agree to resolve questions of "arbitrability" through the arbitration process itself.[79] To do so, the parties must include express contractual language (often called a "delegation provision")[80] in the arbitration agreement that "clearly and unmistakably" delegates questions of arbitrability to the arbitrator.[81] If an arbitration agreement includes a delegation provision, then the party

---

75. *See e.g.*, Radio Station KFH Co. v. Musicians Ass'n, Local No. 297, Am. Fed'n Musicians, 220 P.2d 199, 205 (Kan. 1950); Golden Seed Co., v. Funk Seeds Int'l, Inc., 315 N.E.2d 140, 141 (Ill. App. Ct. 1974); 117 AM. JUR. *Trials* § 391 (2012).

76. 9 U.S.C. §§ 3–4 (2000); Alexander v. Anthony Int'l, L.P., 341 F.3d 256, 263 (3d Cir. 2003).

77. Allied-Bruce Terminix Cos. v. Dobson, 513 U.S. 265, 281 (1995) ("States may regulate contracts, including arbitration clauses, under general contract law principles.").

78. Daly, *supra* note 6, at 43 ("Agreements not properly ratified, procured by fraud, or expired are not valid agreements and, therefore, may deprive the arbitrator of authority to hear the case.").

79. *Id.* at 42 ("U.S. courts favor assigning the duty to the courts, but allow the parties to assign determination of jurisdictional matters to the arbitrator via the arbitration clause itself."); Rent-A-Center, West, Inc. v. Jackson, 561 U.S. 63, 68–69 (2010).

80. Rent-A-Center, West, Inc. v. Jackson, 561 U.S. 63 (2010).

81. Opalinksi v. Robert Half Int'l Inc., 761 F.3d 326, 335 (3d Cir. 2014).

challenging the validity or enforceability of the arbitration agreement must also challenge the validity of the delegation provision too.[82] Otherwise, as long as the delegation provision is clear and unmistakable, claims regarding the arbitration agreement's arbitrability will be sent to arbitration for resolution.

III. Unconscionability in Contract Law

Due to the philosophical concept of "freedom of contract" that governs private ordering in the United States, courts do not generally intervene when a contractual party has mistakenly entered into a bad deal due to their poor judgment. However, an exception is made when there is extreme unfairness or coercion in a contract. The doctrine of unconscionability serves as a defense to contract enforceability by protecting weaker parties against the potential unfairness or bad faith of stronger parties in the contract bargaining process. In so doing, it seeks to avoid overreaching by parties with greater bargaining power and "the incorporation and legal enforcement of one-sided, oppressive or unfair contracts or clauses" into the deal.[83] Further, the concept of unconscionability fills the gap left by the traditional doctrines of fraud, duress, and mutual mistake.

In the eighteenth century, an unconscionable contract or contractual provision was understood to be one that "no man in his senses, not under delusion, would make, on the one hand, and which no fair and honest man would accept on the other."[84] Yet, this abstraction did not offer a clear legal framework, forcing judges to assess unconscionability on a case-by-case basis. In 1951, the New York Court of Appeals defined an unconscionable contract as one that is "so grossly unreasonable or unconscionable in the light of the mores and business practices of the time

---

82. Henry Schein, Inc. v. Archer & White Sales, Inc., 139 S. Ct. 524, 530 (2019) ("[I]f a valid agreement exists, and if the agreement delegates the arbitrability issue to an arbitrator, a court may not decide the arbitrability issue.").

83. Camilo A. Rodriguez-Yong, *The Doctrines of Unconscionability And Abusive Clauses: A Common Point Between Civil and Common Law Legal Traditions*, Oxford U. Compar. L. F. (2011), https://ouclf.law.ox.ac.uk/the-doctrines-of-unconscionability-and-abusive-clauses-a-common-point-between-civil-and-common-law-legal-traditions/.

84. Earl of Chesterfield v. Janssen, 2 Ves. Sr. 125, 28 Eng. Rep. 82, 100 (Ch. 1750).

and place as to be unenforceable according to its literal terms."[85] However, this definition still left room for ambiguity. In 1962, the legislature included the concept of unconscionability in New York's commercial law with the passage of § 2-302 of the Uniform Commercial Code. That provision states:

> (1) If the court as a matter of law finds the contract or any clause of the contract to have been unconscionable at the time it was made the court may refuse to enforce the contract, or it may enforce the remainder of the contract without the unconscionable clause, or it may so limit the application of any unconscionable clause as to avoid any unconscionable result. (2) When it is claimed or appears to the court that the contract or any clause thereof may be unconscionable the parties shall be afforded a reasonable opportunity to present evidence as to its commercial setting, purpose and effect to aid the court in making the determination.

A similar law, N.Y. Real Property Law § 235-c,[86] was passed in 1976 to govern real estate transactions. However, in both cases, the law merely provided courts with discretion to decide, on a case-by-case basis, whether a contract or a clause of a contract is unconscionable, as well as the power to render the contract or contract clause as being unenforceable. As the Restatement Second of Contracts § 208 (released in 1981) makes clear in its summary of the common law, there is no consensus on the contours of the doctrine of unconscionability. It states:

> If a contract or term thereof is unconscionable at the time the contract is made a court may refuse to enforce the contract, or may enforce the remainder of the contract without the unconscionable term, or may so limit the application of any unconscionable term as to avoid any unconscionable result.

Accordingly, case law has remained critical to defining both where to identify unconscionability in contracts and how to define unconscionable contractual terms. For example, in 1965, in *Williams v. Walker-Thomas Furniture Co.*, the United States Court of Appeals for the Dis-

---

85. Mandel v. Liebman, 303 N.Y. 88, 94 (1951).
86. N.Y. REAL PROPERTY LAW § 235-c (2014).

trict of Columbia Circuit defined unconscionability as "an absence of meaningful choice on the part of one of the parties together with contract terms which are unreasonably favorable to the other party."[87] In that case, the plaintiff Williams had signed a contract with Walker-Thomas Furniture Company that stipulated that she could not own any item purchased from the store on credit until the balance on any payment accounts had been paid off, granting the store a right to redeem all the furniture she had ever purchased in the event of a default on a single item. Alongside the existence of gross inequality of bargaining power, the court further explained:

> The manner in which the contract was entered is also relevant to this consideration. Did each party to the contract, considering his obvious education or lack of it, have a reasonable opportunity to understand the terms of the contract, or were the important terms hidden in a maze of fine print and minimized by deceptive sales practices?[88]

In 1967, Professor Arthur Allen Leff added clarity to the doctrine of unconscionability by suggesting that courts should assess both the procedural fairness and the substantive fairness of the bargain. Procedural unconscionability, Leff explained, manifests when a party lacks a meaningful choice during the contract negotiation process, thereby resulting in a grossly inequitable or oppressive outcome. On the other hand, substantive unconscionability occurs when the specific terms of a deal are so unfair or oppressive to one of the parties that it creates a grossly unjust outcome. While Leff's framework helped courts understand where to locate unconscionability in the contract formation process, the defining aspects of unconscionable contractual terms or unconscionable contract negotiation behavior remained unclear.

According to Paul Bennet Marrow, case law has revealed at least three categories of scenarios where a contract or contractual provision will be deemed unconscionable by courts: "[1] Its effect is profoundly discriminatory to one of the contracting parties. [2] It contains language that attempts to sanction abusiveness, arbitrariness or the imposition of a needlessly burdensome condition. [3] It contains language the real meaning

---

87. Williams v. Walker-Thomas Furniture Co., 350 F.2d 445 (D.C. Cir. 1965).
88. Id.

of which is intentionally obscured from one of the parties."[89] Profound discriminatory effect has been found where there is exploitation, where a party is entitled to a benefit that is unrelated to the subject matter of the bargain, where a party has unfettered power to act arbitrarily and unilaterally, where a court is denied power to exercise lawful judicial discretion, and where the bargain sanctions acts counter to public policy.[90] Contractual language that sanctions abusiveness, arbitrariness, or needlessly burdensome conditions has been found in cases where a party is granted the right to abuse the dignity of another party, where a party has taken unfair advantage of another party's position, and where the contract is one of adhesion.[91] Contractual language that intentionally obscures a party's intent has been found in cases where a party is unable to understand the terms of the agreement due to a physical or mental handicap, where a party is deprived of information that has a bearing on the meaning of contractual language, and where a party is denied recourse from defects that are discovered upon delivery of a product or service.[92]

Marrow further explains that there are four general rules that describe when courts will deny claims of unconscionability:

> [1] As a general rule, commercially reasonable agreements are not unconscionable simply because there is a disparity in bargaining power or because a given provision is exacting in nature.
>
> [2] Contracts will not be struck as unconscionable if they require the implication of a condition not agreed to by the parties.
>
> [3] If a party to a commercially reasonable bargain has completed its obligations before the claim of unconscionability is made, the contract will be upheld.
>
> [4] A covenant that has the effect of merely recognizing a condition or status otherwise permissible by law will be upheld.[93]

---

89. Paul B. Marrow, *Contractual Unconscionability: Identifying and Understanding Its Potential Elements*, N.Y. STATE BAR ASS'N J., Feb. 2000.
90. *Id.*
91. *Id.*
92. *Id.*
93. *Id.*

Courts have devised various factors in assessing procedural and substantive unconscionability that encompass these insights. For example, Kansas courts list ten factors that are illustrative of the types of concerns raised by jurisdictions across the country:

(1) The use of printed form or boilerplate contracts drawn skillfully by the party in the strongest economic position, which establish industry wide standards offered on a take it or leave it basis to the party in a weaker economic position;
(2) a significant cost-price disparity or excessive price;
(3) a denial of basic rights and remedies to a buyer of consumer goods;
(4) the inclusion of penalty clauses;
(5) the circumstances surrounding the execution of the contract, including its commercial setting, its purpose and actual effect;
(6) the hiding of clauses which are disadvantageous to one party in a mass of fine print trivia or in places which are inconspicuous to the party signing the contract;
(7) phrasing clauses in language that is incomprehensible to a layman or that divert his attention from the problems raised by them or the rights given up through them;
(8) an overall imbalance in the obligations and rights imposed by the bargain;
(9) exploitation of the underprivileged, unsophisticated, uneducated and the illiterate; and
(10) inequality of bargaining or economic power.[94]

These types of factors played an important role in the case of *Jean v. Bucknell.*

---

94. Wille v. Sw. Bell Tel. Co., 549 P.2d 903, 907 (Kan. 1976) (internal citations omitted).

IV. The Case of *Jean v. Bucknell*

John Jean was a sophomore at Bucknell University who applied to participate in the membership intake process of the Iota Chapter of Kappa Delta Rho Fraternity during the fall of 2020. In 2009, Bucknell had banned the Iota Chapter from the university for three years due to a pledging-related hazing incident. The national organization had revoked the chapter's recognition for four years due to the same incident. After returning to Bucknell, Iota Chapter was required to remain alcohol-free for one year. Jean received a bid (invitation) from the Iota Chapter to participate in the fall 2020 initiation events (pledge) with six other students (the pledge class).[95]

Jean, only 5'4 and weighing 130 pounds, claimed that on the night of September 10, 2020, his pledge class was forced to participate in an alcohol drinking game that involved consuming large amounts of vodka over the course of the evening. Jean attempted to leave the pledge event, but he was pressured to stay by the members of Iota Chapter. When Jean eventually left the fraternity house, he was confronted by one of his fellow pledge group members and punched in the face for his decision to leave. Jean fell to the ground, vomited, and lost consciousness. Jean was later taken to the hospital where he was treated for alcohol poisoning, a concussion, and extensive bodily injuries sustained during the initiation event, including cigarette burns on his feet.[96]

On September 22, 2020, Jean filed suit in the United States District Court for the Middle District of Pennsylvania against Bucknell University, Kappa Delta Rho Fraternity, the Iota Chapter, and three members of the Iota Chapter for hazing, assault and battery, negligence, and negligence per se.[97] Bucknell University subsequently filed a motion to dismiss under Federal Rule of Civil Procedure 12(b)(6), asserting that Jean had failed to state a claim upon which relief could be granted. Specifically, Bucknell argued that the university owed no duty to Jean that extended to the hazing allegations in the lawsuit. The court granted Bucknell's motion to dismiss on September 10, 2021, denying Jean's claim that a new common-law duty of care between the university and its students

---

95. Jean v. Bucknell Univ., 534 F.Supp. 3d 404 (M.D. Pa. 2021).
96. *Id.*
97. *Id.*

was warranted under *Althaus ex rel. Althaus v. Cohen*,[98] or that existing common-law duties of care applied to the hazing allegations.[99]

Iota Chapter and the members of Iota Chapter who were included in Jean's lawsuit moved separately to compel arbitration and stay discovery pending resolution of their motion to compel. The motion to compel arbitration relied upon a mandatory arbitration clause that Kappa Delta Rho Fraternity had included in the new member registration form that all pledges of the fraternity are required to complete prior to initiation. Under the Claim and Dispute Resolution Plan ("the Plan") included in the new member registration form, all new members agree to submit to arbitration "any legal or equitable Claim, Dispute, demand or controversy" between the new members and the fraternity.[100] Jean completed the new member registration form on September 8, 2020, both checking the box and typing his initials under the Plan to convey his assent to the terms of the contract.[101]

Jean contested the enforceability of the arbitration provision in the new member registration form on the grounds that (1) it was unconscionable, (2) it violated public policy, and (3) it impermissibly divided the proceedings related to the alleged hazing activities since Bucknell University was not a signatory to the arbitration agreement. As noted above, when reviewing motions to compel arbitration, courts first determine whether it is the court or an arbitrator who must determine the arbitrability of the matter in question. If the party requesting arbitration establishes the existence of a delegation provision in the arbitration agreement, then the arbitrator will decide all questions of arbitrability.[102]

In this case, the court concluded that the Plan did not convey a "clear and unmistakable intent to delegate questions of arbitrability to an arbitrator."[103] As the court explained, "Nowhere in the provision is language

---

98. Althaus ex rel. Althaus v. Cohen, 756 A.2d 1166, 1169 (Pa. 2000).

99. Jean v. Bucknell Univ., 534 F.Supp. 3d 404 (M.D. Pa. 2021).

100. Jean v. Bucknell Univ., No. 4:20-CV-01722, 2021 WL 1521724, at *6 (M.D. Pa. Apr. 16, 2021) (memorandum decision).

101. *Id.* at *2.

102. *See* Henry Schein, Inc. v. Archer & White Sales, Inc., 139 S. Ct. 524, 529 (2019).

103. Jean v. Bucknell Univ., No. 4:20-CV-01722, 2021 WL 1521724, at *6 (M.D. Pa. Apr. 16, 2021) (memorandum decision); HealthplanCRM, LLC v. AvMed, Inc., 458 F. Supp. 3d 308, 326 (W.D. Pa. 2020) ("[S]imply incorporating by reference a rule that permits an arbitrator concurrent authority with the Court, without clarifying that the arbi-

stating that the Plan applies to disputes regarding the validity and enforceability of the Plan ... [or] to disputes beyond ... substantive legal claims."[104] Thus, the court proceeded to assess Jean's substantive legal claims, focusing on the claim of unconscionability. In the court's final opinion on the matter, US Chief Middle District Judge Matthew W. Brann began the analysis by clarifying how Pennsylvania state law views the doctrine of unconscionability.

Under Pennsylvania law, a party challenging an arbitration agreement bears the burden of proving that it is "both procedurally and substantively unconscionable."[105] According to Judge Brann, substantively unconscionable agreements are those that unreasonably favor the party with superior bargaining power. Conversely, procedurally unconscionable agreements are those where one party lacks any meaningful choice in the bargaining process for accepting a particular provision. Judge Brann also clarified that Pennsylvania has adopted a sliding-scale approach to assess unconscionability. Under this approach, a finding of a high degree of procedural unconscionability can lead to a contract or contractual provision being deemed unenforceable, even if the agreement has a low degree of substantive unconscionability, and vice versa.[106] Finally, Judge Brann noted that the court may hold an entire contract unenforceable under the doctrine of unconscionability, or merely deem certain provisions to be unconscionable and thereafter sever them from the contract.[107]

Judge Brann began the court's analysis by considering substantive unconscionability. He first noted several examples of arbitration provisions that have been deemed substantively unconscionable, such as "severe restrictions on discovery, high arbitration costs borne by one party, limitations on remedies ... curtailed judicial review ... [and] where it allows

---

trator's authority is exclusive, may be insufficient to show the required 'clear and unmistakable' intent.").

104. Jean v. Bucknell Univ., No. 4:20-CV-01722, 2021 WL 1521724, at *7 (M.D. Pa. Apr. 16, 2021) (memorandum decision).

105. Ostroff v. Alterra Healthcare Corp., 433 F. Supp. 2d 538, 543 (E.D. Pa. 2006); Zimmer v. CooperNeff Advisors, Inc., 523 F.3d 224, 230 (3d Cir. 2008).

106. Quilloin v. Tenet HealthSystem Phila., Inc., 673 F.3d 221, 230 (3d Cir. 2012).

107. Jean v. Bucknell Univ., No. 4:20-CV-01722, 2021 WL 1521724 (M.D. Pa. Apr. 16, 2021) (memorandum decision); Nino v. Jewelry Exch., Inc., 609 F.3d 191, 206 (3d Cir. 2010).

one party to unilaterally select an arbitrator, or to unilaterally amend the arbitration agreement."[108] However, as Judge Brann explained, the ultimate decision is in the court's discretion. Plaintiff Jean had claimed that several aspects of the Plan's arbitration agreement were substantively unconscionable and that they collectively put him at a gross disadvantage. Specifically, Jean emphasized the Plan's "[1] provisions limiting discovery and [2] judicial review, [3] unfairly imposing costs upon Jean, [4] allowing Kappa Delta Rho to unilaterally amend or terminate the Plan, and [5] permitting Kappa Delta Rho to unilaterally select the arbitral forum and [6] two members of a panel of arbitrators."[109] The court responded to each of these substantive unconscionability claims in turn.

First, while Judge Brann agreed that denying a party access to *any* form of judicial review could be deemed unconscionable, the Plan's limitation of judicial review to that which is permitted under the FAA was not enough to make the agreement unreasonably unfair on those grounds.[110] Second, Judge Brann reviewed the Plan's requirement that each party bears their own costs of arbitration, including the expenses of producing witnesses and attorneys' fees. According to the court, "[a]n arbitration provision that makes the arbitral forum prohibitively expensive for a weaker party is unconscionable."[111] However, when a party makes this claim, Judge Brann explained, they also bear the burden of proving their inability to pay the cost of arbitration. Here, since Jean had not presented any evidence regarding an inability to pay arbitration-related costs, the court concluded that it was unable to determine that the Plan's cost-shifting provision was unconscionable.[112]

Third, Judge Brann analyzed whether Kappa Delta Rho's contractual right to unilaterally amend and terminate the Plan was substantively

---

108. Jean v. Bucknell Univ., No. 4:20-CV-01722, 2021 WL 1521724, at *9 (M.D. Pa. Apr. 16, 2021) (memorandum decision); *Ostroff*, 433 F. Supp. 2d at 543.

109. Jean v. Bucknell Univ., No. 4:20-CV-01722, 2021 WL 1521724, at *9 (M.D. Pa. Apr. 16, 2021) (memorandum decision).

110. Jean v. Bucknell Univ., No. 4:20-CV-01722, 2021 WL 1521724 (M.D. Pa. Apr. 16, 2021) (memorandum decision); Hall St. Assocs., LLC v. Mattel, Inc., 552 U.S. 576, 586 (2008).

111. Jean v. Bucknell Univ., No. 4:20-CV-01722, 2021 WL 1521724, at *11 (M.D. Pa. Apr. 16, 2021) (memorandum decision); Clymer v. Jetro Cash & Carry Enters., Inc., 334 F. Supp. 3d 683, 692 (E.D. Pa. 2018).

112. Jean v. Bucknell Univ., No. 4:20-CV-01722, 2021 WL 1521724 (M.D. Pa. Apr. 16, 2021) (memorandum decision).

unconscionable. As the court explained, "an arbitration agreement allowing one party the unfettered right to alter the arbitration agreement's existence or its scope is illusory."[113] However, as *Crump v. MetaSource Acquisitions, LLC* made clear,[114] courts in the Third Circuit have found unilateral-modification provisions *not* to be illusory when they require: "(1) modifications be made in writing; (2) all parties be provided notice; (3) all parties consent to any modifications; and (4) modifications be effective 'only prospectively.'"[115] Here, since Kappa Delta Rho's Plan only satisfied two of the four factors elaborated in *Crump*, Judge Brann concluded that this section of the arbitration agreement gave the fraternity unfettered discretion to modify its obligations, rendering it unconscionable.

Fourth, Judge Brann considered whether the Plan's arbitrator-selection process was substantively unconscionable. Under the Plan, after the parties have jointly selected an arbitrator, Kappa Delta Rho retained sole discretion to select two additional arbitrators forming a three-member panel to decide on the merits of the dispute. Judge Brann concluded that the language effectuating this selection process was unconscionable because "its ambiguity opens the door for an unconscionable result."[116] As Judge Brann further explained, "it is not impossible for Kappa Delta Rho to simply select two arbitrators to serve on a panel which will then retroactively bless Kappa Delta Rho's interpretation of [this] section."[117] The court also noted the contract rule of contra proferentem, which construes ambiguities in vague contract provisions against the drafter. Notwithstanding the assumption that parties will act in good faith in selecting an arbitrator, scholars note that "[a]rbitrators have great latitude when rendering a decision and can decide cases based on their own

---

113. Jean v. Bucknell Univ., No. 4:20-CV-01722, 2021 WL 1521724, at *13 (M.D. Pa. Apr. 16, 2021) (memorandum decision); Crump v. MetaSource Acquisitions, LLC, 373 F. Supp. 3d 540, 545 (E.D. Pa. 2019).

114. *Crump*, 373 F. Supp. 3d at 545.

115. Jean v. Bucknell Univ., No. 4:20-CV-01722, 2021 WL 1521724, at *13 (M.D. Pa. Apr. 16, 2021) (memorandum decision) (emphasis omitted) (citations omitted).

116. *Id.* at *15.

117. *Id.*; Daly, *supra* note 6, at 65 ("The manner in which arbitrators are chosen, the potential for bias on the part of a party-appointed arbitrator, institutional bias, the "repeat player effect," and the potential for bias of arbitrators who sit on permanent panels are all situations which can affect the neutrality of an arbitrator.").

subjective notions of justice and equity, disregarding substantive law."[118] Judge Brann expressed a desire to disincentivize parties from drafting ambiguous contractual provisions, especially in the arbitration context.

Fifth, Judge Brann considered whether Kappa Delta Rho's unilateral right to select the arbitral forum was substantively unconscionable. While the selected forum is limited to "any federal or state-recognized Arbitration Association, or a similar, local group of arbitrators," the Plan did not grant members any right to voice an opinion on the arbitral forum selected, which would determine the pool of potential arbitrators.[119] As Judge Brann explained, "Just as courts have found the unilateral selection of an arbitrator unconscionable, so too have they found that provisions allowing one party to control the creation of the pool of potential arbitrators are unconscionable or fundamentally unfair."[120] Judge Brann concluded that it would be unconscionable to allow one party to select the arbitral forum "with unfettered discretion" and subject to no meaningful limitation.[121] Judge Brann emphasized that the Plan's usage of the phrase "or a similar, local group of arbitrators" was vague and therefore too broad.[122] Judge Brann further expressed concern that the Plan "does not require the arbitral forum selected to be independent or impartial," leaving open the possibility that Kappa Delta Rho could select a biased arbitral forum.[123] As a result, the court concluded that this provision was unconscionable.

Sixth, and finally, Judge Brann explored whether the Plan's limitations on the scope of discovery were substantively unconscionable. Under the

---

118. Daly, *supra* note 6, at 57; *but see* Gilmer v. Interstate/Johnson Lane Corp., 500 U.S. 20, 26 (1991) (quoting Mitsubishi Motors Corp. v. Soler Chrysler-Plymouth, Inc. 473 U.S. 614, 628 (1985)) (clarifying that, "[b]y agreeing to arbitrate a statutory claim, a party does not forgo the substantive rights afforded by the statute; it only submits to their resolution in an arbitral, rather than a judicial forum").

119. Jean v. Bucknell Univ., No. 4:20-CV-01722, 2021 WL 1521724, at *16 (M.D. Pa. Apr. 16, 2021) (memorandum decision).

120. *Id.*; Daly, *supra* note 6, at 65 ("The choice of an arbitrator from a pool is meaningless if the system of choosing arbitrators for the pool is biased.").

121. Jean v. Bucknell Univ., No. 4:20-CV-01722, 2021 WL 1521724, at *16 (M.D. Pa. Apr. 16, 2021) (memorandum decision).

122. *Id.*

123. *Id. See e.g.*, Floss v. Ryan's Fam. Steak Houses, Inc., 211 F.3d 306, 314 (6th Cir. 2000) ("In light of [the arbitral forum's] role in determining the pool of potential arbitrators, any such bias would render the arbitral forum fundamentally unfair.").

Plan, "The arbitrator shall be the sole judge of the relevance, materiality and admissibility of evidence offered. Conformity to legal rules shall not be necessary."[124] The Plan also "prohibits the arbitrator from allowing more than twenty hours of depositions, or twenty interrogatories, requests for production, or requests for admission per side, absent a showing of good cause."[125] Plaintiff Jean contended that this provision would lead to an unconscionable result because of the power granted to Kappa Delta Rho to select the arbitral panel and shape the selection of the arbitral panel. However, the Supreme Court has held that limitations on discovery do not render an arbitration provision invalid if parties have a "fair opportunity to present their claims."[126] Although the Plan places limitations on discovery, Judge Brann concluded that Jean had not been deprived of a fair opportunity to present his claims, and thus determined that the discovery limitations were not unconscionable.

Next, Judge Brann considered procedural unconscionability, which occurs when one of the parties experiences a lack of meaningful choice. According to the court, a lack of meaningful choice may arise when there is an "unfair surprise" in the contractual terms,[127] often relating to boilerplate contracts (traditionally classified as "contracts of adhesion") that are difficult for one of the parties to understand,[128] or when there is "apparent but not genuine assent."[129] While contracts of adhesion are often viewed as unfair, more is required for such agreements to be deemed procedurally unconscionable. As Judge Brann explained, courts generally consider "the take-it-or-leave-it nature of the standardized form of the document, the parties [sic] relative bargaining positions, and the degree of economic compulsion motivating the adhering party."[130] Plaintiff Jean argued that Kappa Delta Rho's arbitration agreement was procedurally unconscionable because he had no power to negotiate the terms,

---

124. Jean v. Bucknell Univ., No. 4:20-CV-01722, 2021 WL 1521724, at *17 (M.D. Pa. Apr. 16, 2021) (memorandum decision).
125. Id.
126. Gilmer v. Interstate/Johnson Lane Corp., 500 U.S. 20, 31 (1991).
127. Germantown Mfg. Co. v. Rawlinson, 491 A.2d 138, 145 (Pa. Super. Ct. 1985).
128. Id.
129. Id. at 147.
130. Jean v. Bucknell Univ., No. 4:20-CV-01722, 2021 WL 1521724, at *19 (M.D. Pa. Apr. 16, 2021) (memorandum decision); Golden Gate Nat'l Senior Care, LLC v. Beavens, 123 F. Supp 3d 619, 632 (E.D. Pa. 2015).

which were presented to him on a take-it-or-leave-it basis. Kappa Delta Rho countered by noting that joining a fraternal organization is a voluntary endeavor and prospective members are therefore under no pressure to join. Further, that defendant argued that Jean had failed to show that he could not join another fraternity if he disagreed with their terms.

The court agreed with Kappa Delta Rho that the Plan was not a contract of adhesion. Judge Brann explained that joining a fraternal organization is akin to participating in a voluntary athletic or recreational activity. Accordingly, "The signer is under no compulsion, economic or otherwise, to participate, much less to sign the exculpatory agreement, because it does not relate to essential services."[131] Nevertheless, Judge Brann concluded that the arbitration agreement could still be deemed procedurally unconscionable because it amounted to an unfair surprise, especially to a 20-year-old college student without legal training. On this point, the court emphasized the complexity and confusing nature of the Plan, which spanned 33 sections across 12 pages, filled with several "inconsistent and overly vague terms," and failed to provide "the core components of the arbitration process."[132] Ultimately, Judge Brann concluded that the agreement is procedurally unconscionable because "it is so confusing that Jean could not have meaningfully agreed to the terms of the Plan as they were actually presented to him."[133]

Finding the arbitration agreement to be substantively unconscionable on three out of six of Jean's claims, and to be procedurally unconscionable when viewed in its totality, the court considered whether to sever the unconscionable provisions from the Plan or to deem the entire arbitration agreement unenforceable. A court can remove an unconscionable provision from a contract if it is not an essential part of the agreement. But, where "the sickness has infected the trunk, [the court] must cut down the entire tree."[134] Judge Brann concluded, "[w]hile none of the unconscionable provisions in the Plan appear to be an "essential aspect of the arbitration agreement," the Court finds that the number and nature of these provisions demonstrates an effort to sys-

---

131. Toro v. Fitness Int'l, LLC, 150 A.3d 968, 975 (Pa. Super. Ct. 2016).
132. Jean v. Bucknell Univ., No. 4:20-CV-01722, 2021 WL 1521724, at *20 (M.D. Pa. Apr. 16, 2021) (memorandum decision).
133. Id.
134. Alexander v. Anthony Int'l, L.P., 341 F.3d 256, 271(3d Cir. 2003).

tematically disadvantage fraternity members who seek to arbitrate against Kappa Delta Rho under the Plan."[135] By allowing the fraternity to "select the arbitral forum, unilaterally alter the terms of the Plan without members' consent, and elect for the selection of an arbitral panel," the Plan gave "an inordinate amount of power" to the fraternity at the expense of members.[136]

Judge Brann declined to sever the unconscionable terms. As a result, on April 16, 2021, the court denied the motion to compel arbitration as well as the motion to stay discovery pending resolution of the motions to compel.

V. When Arbitration Is Denied

After Judge Brann denied Kappa Delta Rho's motion to compel arbitration on the grounds that the fraternity's arbitration agreement was unconscionable, John Jean's lawsuit proceeded through the traditional court system. On September 16, 2022, Judge Brann filed an order to dismiss the case of *Jean v. Bucknell*.[137] No details have been released as of the date of this writing explaining why the case was dismissed. In the interim, John Jean has transferred to Boston University.[138]

Bucknell University did take immediate steps to respond to the risks posed by the Iota Chapter's hazing culture for other students on campus. On November 15, 2020, the chapter was officially terminated from the university following an administrative hearing for violating the Bucknell University Student Code of Conduct and the Bucknell Anti-Hazing Policy.[139] Bucknell's Anti-Hazing Report noted that the termination was based on "underage provision/consumption of alcohol" that "subjects

---

135. Jean v. Bucknell Univ., No. 4:20-CV-01722, 2021 WL 1521724, at *22 (M.D. Pa. Apr. 16, 2021) (memorandum decision).

136. *Id.*

137. Melissa Farenish, *Lawsuit Regarding Alleged Brutal Hazing at Bucknell Fraternity Dismissed*, NORTHCENTRALPA.COM (Sep. 19, 2022), https://www.northcentralpa.com/news/crime/lawsuit-regarding-alleged-brutal-hazing-at-bucknell-fraternity-dismissed/article_beddbb5a-375e-11ed-b2ae-e78e48f762e4.html

138. Nick DeMarchis, *University Chapter of Kappa Delta Rho Suspended After Alleged Hazing*, BUCKNELLIAN (Feb. 24, 2021), https://bucknellian.net/102888/news/university-chapter-of-kappa-delta-rho-suspended-after-alleged-hazing/

139. *Id.*

the student[s] to a risk of emotional or physical harm."[140] According to *The Bucknellian*, the Iota Chapter of Kappa Delta Rho is the sixth fraternity or sorority to be suspended, either temporarily or permanently, from Bucknell University since 2011.[141] All of the remaining members of Kappa Delta Rho at Bucknell University were moved to alumni status.

Finally, the national office of Kappa Delta Rho revoked the charter and recognition of the chapter from the national organization. According to the Executive Director of Kappa Delta Rho, the national fraternity's decision "was guided by a deep commitment to [its] values, among which is respect for all persons at all times."[142]

VI. Conclusion: Lessons for Fraternities and Sororities

The case of *Jean v. Bucknell* demonstrates that arbitration is not a simple solution to the problem of hazing in Greek-letter organizations. As *Jean* makes clear, when language in an arbitration agreement is overly broad or ambiguous, or when it grants too much discretionary authority to one of the parties, it may be found unconscionable and deemed unenforceable by courts. As a result, it is critical that fraternities and sororities who desire to incorporate mandatory arbitration clauses in their membership agreements seek the advice of counsel. A few specific lessons can be gleaned from the case of *Jean v. Bucknell*.

First, courts are unlikely to find that boilerplate fraternity and sorority membership agreements are contracts of adhesion because joining a Greek-letter organization is a voluntary activity and, therefore, not compulsory or related to an essential service. Nevertheless, a court may still find such an agreement to be *procedurally* unconscionable, especially when it includes arbitration provisions that are filled with complex and vague legal jargon. Such contractual language may amount to an "unfair surprise" to college students who are untrained in legal mat-

---

140. *Id.*

141. Nick DeMarchis, *Jean Lawsuit Against University Dismissed*, Bucknellian (Sept. 15, 2021), https://bucknellian.net/105834/news/jean-lawsuit-against-university-dismissed/.

142. DeMarchis, *supra* note 138.

ters.[143] Accordingly, it may be wise for fraternities and sororities to write their arbitration agreements in simple language that is easy for the layperson to understand. Further, college chapters of national Greek-letter organizations, perhaps in collaboration with graduate chapter advisors or their national offices, may consider offering workshops for prospective members to review the provisions of their membership agreement prior to submission.

Second, *Jean* reveals that courts may find arbitration agreements to be *substantively* unconscionable when they grant the fraternity or sorority unilateral discretion to (1) amend and terminate the arbitration agreement, (2) select the arbitrator or significantly control the selection of the arbitral panel, or (3) select the arbitral forum. By maintaining sole discretion in such matters without any meaningful limitation on the Greek-letter organization's decision-making power, the court in *Jean* revealed that the agreement can amount to an illusory promise that puts the members at a grossly unfair disadvantage. The limitation of discretion does not mean that the fraternity or sorority must relinquish their leadership role in the decision-making process. For example, as the *Jean* court explained, unilateral-modification provisions have been found not to be illusory when they require that such modifications only apply prospectively and are made in writing with proper notice to and consent of all relevant parties.[144]

Third, the language in the arbitration agreement must not leave the door open for the possibility of bias on the part of the fraternity or sorority in the arbitration process. For example, the *Jean* court noted that limiting the arbitral forum to "any federal or state-recognized Arbitration Association, *or a similar, local group of arbitrators*" was unconscionable because it did not clarify how to identify the "local group of arbitrators," nor did it require that they be independent and impartial.[145] Such ambiguities open the door for "institutional bias," whereby the arbitration tends to favor one class of participants over another.[146] Alternatively, they open the door for a challenge to the partiality of the arbitra-

---

143. *Supra* note 127 and accompanying text.
144. *Supra* note 113–115 and accompanying text.
145. *Supra* note 119–122 and accompanying text.
146. Daly, *supra* note 6, at 66; Perlstadt, *supra* note 54, at 1986–87.

tor.[147] If an arbitrator has substantial past dealings with one of the parties, and fails to disclose such conflicts of interest, there may be grounds for a court to vacate the award.[148] Further, if an arbitrator lacks legal knowledge on important socially sensitive matters, such as civil rights or racial or sexual discrimination, the process may be subject to more rigorous scrutiny. Indeed, some scholars have argued that arbitration involving socially sensitive topics should be open to the public to influence future social behavior.[149] These are key issues that must not be overlooked by attorneys in the drafting process.

Finally, the *Jean* case reveals that the existence of only a few unconscionable provisions in an arbitration agreement can render the entire agreement unenforceable, notwithstanding the inclusion of a severability clause. As the court explained, where "the sickness has infected the trunk, [the court] must cut down the entire tree."[150] Courts will ultimately assess whether all of the provisions in the arbitration agreement, taken together as a whole, can be viewed as systematically disadvantaging fraternity or sorority members and thereby denying them access to a fair and impartial dispute resolution forum. This risk suggests that arbitration agreements are not foolproof. Fraternities and sororities must consider alternative ways to protect themselves from liability if a court fails to grant their motion to compel arbitration.

---

147. Korland, *supra* note 53, at 822 (discussing the American Bar Association's Code of Ethics for Arbitrators in Commercial Disputes, which calls for arbitrators to reveal certain conflicts of interest that might impugn their impartiality).

148. Daly, *supra* note 6, at 67.

149. Daly, *supra* note 6, at 74–75.

150. *Supra* note 134.

CHAPTER 7

Greek Organizations and Sexual Assault

Dara E. Purvis

When the intersection of sexual assault and Greek life at universities is raised, the typical problem in mind is higher rates of sexual assault perpetrated by fraternity members against women at the university. This stereotype is not entirely inaccurate—studies show that members of fraternities do commit a disproportionate number of sexual assaults compared to male students who are not affiliated with a fraternity[1]—but it also oversimplifies the picture. For example, even as members of fraternities are disproportionately perpetrators of sexual assault, they are also disproportionately victims of sexual assault. Members of both sororities *and* fraternities are more likely than unaffiliated students to experience unwanted sexual contact and sexual harassment.

---

1. Notably, however, fraternity houses are not the most common location of sexual assaults committed against college students. Rather, the most common location for sexual assaults is university dorms. *See* Andrea A. Curcio, *What Schools Don't Tell You About Campus Sexual Assault*, SALON (Aug. 26, 2017, 9:59 AM), https://www.salon.com/2017/08/26/what-schools-do-not-tell-you-about-campus-sexual-assault_partner/.

As a result, the legal issues arising out of claims of sexual assault are complicated and multilayered. First, how universities investigate and punish claims of sexual assault brought by a student continues to be a moving target, as the Department of Education has issued different guidance under different presidential administrations. Second, as universities attempt to combat sexual assault through broader programmatic action, Greek-letter organizations have challenged policies that they perceive as punishing or imposing a presumption of guilt upon fraternity members. Third, the relationship between individual chapters of Greek organizations and the university may change as universities limit or condition the existence of fraternities and sororities based on their agreement to specific preventative efforts such as mandatory counseling and increased enforcement of alcohol policies.

Finally, victims of sexual assault have brought a variety of civil claims against both fraternity chapters and national fraternal organizations under several theories of negligence. Both the chapters and national organizations face conflicting pressures regarding their role in investigating and punishing individual members or chapters that face allegations of sexual assault. Although court treatment of such claims has varied, a court is more likely to find liability on the part of the chapter or national organization where it has been informed of such allegations and not acted by investigating the allegations and taking ameliorative action. At the same time, however, other national organizations have been criticized for conducting internal investigations rather than leaving all response to the university and law enforcement, and universities have demanded that national organizations turn over the records of their investigations for the university to review.

Although the legal ground continues to shift, a few takeaways are clear. First, sexual assault continues to be a major problem on college campuses, with members of Greek organizations disproportionately involved as both victims and perpetrators. Second, Greek organizations, and particularly fraternities, ignore the problem at their peril. Some courts have shown increased willingness to find negligence on the part of fraternities based on the widespread knowledge of sexual assault on college campuses, and if a chapter knows of recent allegations against its members and fails to act, the chapter exposes itself to further liability. Greek organizations should view themselves as becoming part of the solution to sexual assault by instituting preventive measures and responding promptly to allegations of sexual assault by taking steps to minimize further risk.

I. Sexual Assault at Universities

Although estimates of the numbers vary greatly, there is little question that sexual assault is a major problem on college campuses across the country. Many general estimates say that one in five women is sexually assaulted during her time in college.[2] A 2015 survey of the students at nearly 30 college campuses reported 23% of female students and 5% of male students reported that they had been sexually assaulted.[3] Another survey the following year with responses from 23,000 students had very similar numbers.[4]

Studies have further found that women in sororities are even more at risk of sexual assault than non-affiliated college women.[5] One study of 1,000 women at a single university found that sorority members were over four times as likely to have been sexually assaulted.[6] One researcher's work asking why attributed the greater risk to a correlation between sorority membership and "vulnerability-enhancing attitudes and behaviors," including "contact with fraternity men."[7] She found that frequent interactions with students in fraternities was "significantly related" to the likelihood that a sorority member was subjected to sexual assault.[8]

Researchers in the 1990s famously determined that a majority of gang rapes on campus were committed by fraternity members.[9] Studies have found that fraternity members are three times as likely as non-fraternity members to perpetrate sexually aggressive behaviors, including sexual

---

2. *See* Karen M. Tani, *An Administrative Right to Be Free from Sexual Violence? Title IX Enforcement in Historical and Institutional Perspective*, 66 Duke L.J. 1847, 1850 (2017); Lavinia M. Weizel, Note, *The Process That Is Due: Preponderance of the Evidence As the Standard of Proof for University Adjudications of Student-on-Student Sexual Assault Complaints*, 53 B.C. L. Rev. 1613, 1613 (2012).

3. Michelle J. Anderson, *Campus Sexual Assault Adjudication and Resistance to Reform*, 125 Yale L.J. 1940, 1970 (2016).

4. *Id.*

5. Tanya Asim Cooper, *#SororityToo*, 2020 Mich. St. L. Rev. 355, 362 (2020).

6. Jacqueline C. Minow & Christopher J. Einolf, *Sorority Participation and Sexual Assault Risk*, 15 Violence Against Women 835, 844 (2009).

7. Cortney A. Franklin, *Sorority Affiliation and Sexual Assault Victimization: Assessing Vulnerability Using Path Analysis*, 22 Violence Against Women 895, 902 (2016).

8. *Id.* at 913.

9. John D. Foubert & Bradford C. Perry, *Creating Lasting Attitude and Behavior Changes in Fraternity Members and Male Student Athletes: The Qualitative Impact of an Empathy-Based Rape Prevention Program*, 13 Violence Against Women 71 (2007).

assault.[10] Another study found that if a woman college student attended one party at a fraternity per month, the risk of her experiencing sexual assault increased significantly.[11] Even when asked whether they themselves have committed sexual assault, fraternity members answer yes at a higher rate than other men college students.[12] Additionally, national media coverage of sexual assault on college campuses often focuses on fraternities, which have not helped their image by chanting messages supporting or promoting sexual assault.[13]

One aspect of this phenomenon that receives less popular attention is the greater risk that fraternity members also have in being the *victims* of sexual assault.[14] Studies have found that about 6% of men college students are sexually assaulted,[15] and that the risk for fraternity members is "dramatically higher" than for non-Greek men.[16] One study found that the risk of nonconsensual "sexualized touching" was primarily responsible for the increased risk.[17] Some of this difference may be attributed to hazing by other fraternity members,[18] but the numbers cannot be explained by sexualized hazing practices alone.

Whatever the reason, the rate of sexual assault and the effect it has on members of fraternities and sororities is not going away any time soon. The legal response to allegations of sexual assault, however, has been changing in recent years. The next section discusses the primary regula-

---

10. Alexandra Willingham, Note, *Opening the Door: Expanding Civil Redress for Sexual Assault Through Fraternity Insurance*, 72 Stan. L. Rev. 1717, 1720 (2020).

11. Michele Landis Dauber & Meghan O. Warner, *Legal and Political Responses to Campus Sexual Assault*, 15 Ann. Rev. L. & Soc. Sci. 311, 316–17 (2019).

12. Cortney A. Franklin et al., *Sexual Assault on the College Campus: Fraternity Affiliation, Male Peer Support, and Low Self-Control*, 39 Crim. Just. & Behav. 1457, 1467 (2012); *see also* Gregory S. Parks & Sabrina Parisi, *White Boy Wasted: Race, Sex, and Alcohol Use in Fraternity Hazing*, 34 Wis. J.L. Gender & Soc'y 1, 34 (2019).

13. *See e.g.*, Lisa W. Foderaro, *At Yale, Sharper Look at Treatment of Women*, N.Y. Times (Apr. 7, 2011), http://www.nytimes.com/2011/04/08/nyregion/08yale.html.

14. Bennett Capers, *Real Rape Too*, 99 Cal. L. Rev. 1259, 1273 (2011).

15. Willingham, *supra* note 10, at 1720.

16. Maya Luetke et al., *High Prevalence of Sexual Assault Victimization Experiences Among University Fraternity Men*, 36 J. Interpersonal Violence 11755, 11759 (2021).

17. C.A. Mellins et al., *Sexual Assault Incidents Among College Undergraduates: Prevalence and Factors Associated with Risk*, PLOS ONE 12(11): e0186471 at 15 (2017), https://doi.org/10.1371/journal.pone.0186471.

18. Bennett Capers, *On "Violence Against Women,"* 13 Ohio St. J. Crim. L. 347, 354 n.58 (2016).

tions of how universities respond to sexual assault and how those changing regulations affect students and Greek organizations.

II. Sexual Assault and Title IX

Over the last 10 years, federal directives to universities regarding how they respond to allegations of sexual assault have significantly changed, as different presidential administrations prioritized very different principles. The federal law in question, Title IX of the Education Amendments Act of 1972, forbids discrimination on the basis of sex in education programs that receive federal funding.[19] Even private universities typically receive federal funding in the form of federal student loans or research grants, so Title IX applies to almost all colleges and universities. It is also well established through regulation and caselaw that if schools fail to adequately prevent and respond to sexual assaults committed by and against members of the school community, the schools have violated Title IX.[20]

Title IX's prohibition of sex discrimination is obviously very general and does not provide specific recommendations of policies, procedures, or rules, so further direction from the Department of Education is extremely important. In 2011, the Department's Office for Civil Rights issued a Dear Colleague Letter giving guidance about a variety of policies schools should implement.[21] The letter came after significant protests pointing out ways that schools failed to respond to survivors of sexual assault.[22] Seeking to correct many of the shortcomings brought to light, the 2011 letter required that schools have a Title IX coordinator to supervise and coordinate all policies and proceedings related to Title

---

19. 20 U.S.C. § 1681(a) (2018).

20. Sarah L. Swan, *Discriminatory Dualism in Process: Title IX, Reverse Title IX, and Campus Sexual Assault*, 73 OKLA. L. REV. 69, 70–71 (2020); *see also* Alexandra Brodsky, *Against Taking Rape "Seriously": The Case Against Mandatory Referral Laws for Campus Gender Violence*, 53 HARV. C.R.-C.L. L. REV. 131, 132 (2018).

21. Dear Colleague Letter from Assistant Secretary for Civil Rights Russlynn Ali, Office for Civil Rights, U.S. Dep't of Educ. (Apr. 4, 2011), http://www2.ed.gov/about/offices/list/ocr/letters/colleague-201104.pdf (formally rescinded by the Department in 2017).

22. Naomi Mann, *Classrooms into Courtrooms*, 59 HOUS. L. REV. 363, 375–76 (2021).

IX.[23] The letter also spent considerable time discussing what the procedural structure of sexual assault claims should look like. For example, the letter states that a student bringing a claim of sexual assault should be offered support services such as medical and academic support while the claim is being processed, that the student bringing a claim and the accused student cannot cross-examine each other at a hearing, and that both students should have an opportunity to present witnesses.[24] The letter also states that the school's proceeding should use the legal standard of preponderance of the evidence, the typical civil standard often explained as more likely than not.[25] Following the 2011 Dear Colleague Letter, the Department of Education also increased its enforcement efforts, making public the names of schools that were being investigated for potential violations of Title IX.[26] Along similar lines, the other major statute that applies to allegations of sexual assault at universities—the Jeanne Clery Disclosure of Campus Security Policy and Campus Crime Statistics Act (Clery Act)—was also amended in 2013 to strengthen reporting requirements.[27]

In 2014, the Department issued more specifics in the form of a document titled "Questions and Answers on Title IX and Sexual Violence,"[28] issued the same day that the White House released the first report from President Obama's Task Force to Protect Students from Sexual Assault.[29] The Q&A supplemented the procedural requirements from the 2011 Dear Colleague Letter, further explaining things that schools should include in the complaint process.[30]

---

23. Anderson, *supra* note 3, at 1973.

24. *Id.*

25. *Id.*

26. Naomi M. Mann, *Taming Title IX Tensions*, 20 U. PA. J. CONST. L. 631, 643–44 (2018).

27. 20 U.S.C. § 1092(f) (2012).

28. Questions and Answers on Title IX and Sexual Violence, Office for Civil Rights, U.S. Dep't of Educ. (Apr. 29, 2014), http://www2.ed.gov/about/offices/list/ocr/docs/qa-201404-title-ix.pdf (formally rescinded by the Department in 2017).

29. Haley C. Carter, *Under the Guise of "Due Process": Sexual Harassment and the Impact of Trump's Title IX Regulations on Women Students of Color*, 36 BERKELEY J. GENDER L. & JUST. 180, 190 (2021).

30. Anderson, *supra* note 3, at 1975.

After President Trump's election in 2016, however, the Department of Education, under the leadership of Betsy DeVos, took a sharp turn. In the fall of 2017, the Department withdrew both the 2011 Dear Colleague Letter and the 2014 Q & A. Where the Obama administration had a perspective focusing on the harm of sexual assault and a desire to better support survivors of sexual assault, the Trump administration focused on the harm of false accusations of sexual assault. For example, the Acting Assistant Secretary of the Department of Education's Office of Civil Rights argued that 90% of sexual assault accusations "fall into the category of 'we were both drunk,' 'we broke up, and six months later I found myself under a Title IX investigation because she just decided that our last sleeping together was not quite right.'"[31]

The Department of Education accordingly promulgated new regulations that took effect in August 2020.[32] The new regulations also focus on procedural requirements, but from the position that school hearings related to allegations of sexual assault should more closely resemble criminal proceedings, with more protection of the rights of the accused. Most notably, the regulations effectively require schools to use the clear and convincing standard rather than preponderance of the evidence, making it harder to prove allegations of sexual assault.[33] Schools must also now presume the innocence of an accused student, rather than beginning from a position of neutrality. Schools are further required to provide accused students with specific notices of allegations and the evidence against them.[34] One attorney practicing at a Boston law firm specializing in representing accused students reported that the result has been a significant increase in the number of students bringing complaints who

---

31. Mann, *supra* note 22, at 380–81.

32. Nondiscrimination on the Basis of Sex in Education Programs or Activities Receiving Federal Financial Assistance, 34 C.F.R. § 106.44(a) (2020); *see also* Carter, *supra* note 29, at 194.

33. Swan, *supra* note 20, at 95.

34. *See id.* at 93–94. The 2020 regulations also required holding live hearings and directed decisionmakers not to rely on statements of witnesses who refused cross-examination at the hearings, but those portions of the regulations were vacated by a Massachusetts court hearing broad challenges to the regulations. See Letter from the Office for Civil Rights, U.S. Dep't of Educ., to Students, Educators, and other Stakeholders re *Victim Rights Law Center et al. v. Cardona*, (Aug. 24, 2021), https://www2.ed.gov/about/offices/list/ocr/docs/202108-titleix-VRLC.pdf.

hire lawyers to supervise the university-level case.[35] Proposed revisions to these regulations continue under the Biden administration.[36]

As public attention has continued to focus on sexual assault at universities, both formal and informal action has often focused on fraternities. In recent years, allegations of sexual assault committed by fraternity members have sparked student protests outside of fraternity houses and other public criticism of fraternities as facilitating and concealing sexual assault committed by their members.[37] Some of the actions in response have focused on education and peer support. For example, San Diego State University offers a class called FratMANers: Fraternity Men Against Negative Environments and Rape Situations, encouraging discussion among fraternity members about how to prevent sexual assault.[38] Other universities that run broad prevention and intervention programs target fraternity and sorority members to participate.[39]

Very recently, two universities in Utah have responded to allegations of sexual assault by suspending and closely supervising Greek organizations. After two allegations of sexual assault committed at fraternity houses were raised in quick succession, the University of Utah suspended *all* fraternity and sorority activities, not just the fraternities in which the sexual assaults allegedly took place.[40] A more formalized pro-

---

35. Letter from Naomi Shatz, Partner, Zalkind Duncan & Bernstein Law Firm, to OCR Re: Title IX Public Hearing (June 11, 2021), https://www.bostonlawyerblog.com/files/2021/06/Shatz-OCR-Testimony-6-11-21-1.pdf.

36. *See* Press Release, U.S. Dep't of Educ., The U.S. Department of Education Releases Proposed Changes to Title IX Regulations, Invites Public Comment, (June 23, 2022), https://www.ed.gov/news/press-releases/us-department-education-releases-proposed-changes-title-ix-regulations-invites-public-comment.

37. Anemona Hartocollis & Giulia Heyward, *After Rape Accusations, Fraternities Face Protests and Growing Anger*, N.Y. TIMES, https://www.nytimes.com/2021/10/01/education/fraternities-rape-sexual-assault.html (last updated Oct. 12, 2021).

38. Angela Carone, *Fraternity Culture Linked to College Sexual Assault Problem*, KPBS.ORG (Oct. 21, 2014, 3:00 AM), https://www.kpbs.org/news/education/2014/10/21/fraternities-and-campus-sexual-assault-problem.

39. Heather M. Karjane et al., Research for Practice, *Sexual Assault on Campus: What Colleges and Universities Are Doing about It, 12* (US Dep't of Just., 2005), http://www.ncjrs.gov/pdffiles1/nij/205521.pdf; Heather M. Karjane et al., Research for Practice, *Campus Sexual Assault: How America's Institutions of Higher Education Respond*, 128 (US Dep't of Just., 2002) https://www.ncjrs.gov/pdffiles1/nij/grants/196676.pdf.

40. Courtney Tanner, *University of Utah Suspends Fraternity and Sorority Activities After 2nd Sexual Assault Report*, SALT LAKE TRIBUNE (Feb. 1, 2022, 3:53 PM), https://www.sltrib.com/news/education/2022/02/01/university-utah-suspends/.

gram was adopted by Utah State University in Logan as part of a settlement agreement. Several students reported sexual assaults committed by the same student, who was a fraternity member. One of the later victims sued the university, arguing that by failing to act in response to earlier reports, the university was responsible for the later assaults by the same student.[41] The university ultimately settled the lawsuit, and as part of the settlement agreement, created a new structure of supervision for fraternities and sororities. First, the university required any Greek organization that wanted to formally affiliate with the school to sign relationship agreements.[42] Although such agreements were entirely voluntary, the university would refuse to officially recognize groups that did not sign—those groups would not be listed on the university website, be able to use university marketing and communication tools, receive discounted rates for rental of university facilities, and so on.[43] Second, all officially recognized fraternities and sororities would operate under more formal oversight of Greek organizations, including a new advisory committee, a full-time staff member charged with supervising Greek organizations, and substantive requirements such as holding annual trainings about how to prevent sexual assault.[44] Most, but not all, Greek organizations signed relationship agreements and have subsequently operated under the increased supervision.[45]

Such actions may be encouraged by a current circuit split as to the circumstances in which universities may be liable under Title IX for failing to respond to allegations of Title IX violations. The question turns on how to interpret deliberate indifference.[46] In 1999, the Supreme Court

---

41. Courtney Tanner, *She Was Raped at a Utah State University Fraternity. Now the School will Pay Her $250k and She'll Help Improve Its Response to Sexual Assault*, SALT LAKE TRIBUNE , https://www.sltrib.com/news/education/2018/07/05/utah-state-university/ (last updated July 5, 2018, 8:13 PM).

42. Amanda DeRito, *Fraternities and Sororities Sign Relationship Agreements with USU*, UTAH STATE TODAY (Aug. 10, 2020), https://www.usu.edu/today/story/fraternities-and-sororities-sign-relationship-agreements-with-usu.

43. *Id.*

44. *Id.*

45. *Fraternity and Sorority Status Reports*, UTAH STATE UNIV., https://www.usu.edu/involvement/fsl/status/index (listing recognized and unrecognized groups).

46. Lauren E. Groth et al., *Giving* Davis *Its Due: Why the Tenth Circuit Has the Winning Approach in Title IX's Deliberate Indifference Controversy*, 98 DENV. L. REV. 307, 309 (2021).

held that a school is only liable for damages under Title IX if its deliberate indifference subjected students to harassment: "the deliberate indifference must, at a minimum, 'cause [students] to undergo' harassment or 'make them liable or vulnerable' to it."[47] In recent years, different appellate courts have applied this language quite differently. The Sixth Circuit focused on the idea that the school caused students to undergo further harassment. The case was brought by several Michigan State students who alleged that they had been sexually assaulted and reported their sexual assaults to the school, but the school had not taken adequate action to protect them from further contact with their alleged assailants.[48] The Sixth Circuit held that the students would have only had viable claims if they could point to specific incidents of harassment that the school had failed to protect them from after reporting their assaults—Title IX liability was only triggered if they could show that later harassment would not have happened but for the deliberate indifference of their school.[49]

By contrast, the Tenth Circuit read the Supreme Court's language more broadly. In a case involving allegations of sexual assault committed by fraternity members, the court focused on the word vulnerable. It held that by failing to investigate or otherwise discipline the alleged assailants and by allowing them to attend class alongside their alleged victims, the university had made the victims vulnerable to sexual harassment.[50] This increased vulnerability—even without specific incidents of harassment—was sufficient to trigger liability under Title IX.[51]

This circuit split has yet to be addressed by the Supreme Court, so unless and until it is, universities face a lack of clarity regarding their liability. As a result of this varied treatment, as well as the changing policies of the Department of Education, it seems likely that universities will continue to have myriad responses to sexual assault. In addition to university action, moreover, fraternities face potential civil lawsuits, the subject of the next section.

---

47. Davis, Next Friend of LaShonda D. v. Monroe Cnty. Bd. of Educ., 526 U.S. 629, 644–45 (1999).

48. *See* Kollaritsch v. Mich. State Univ. Bd. of Trustees, 298 F. Supp. 3d 1089, 1098–1100 (W.D. Mich. 2017), *rev'd* and *remanded*, 944 F.3d 613 (6th Cir. 2019).

49. *See* Kollaritsch v. Mich. State Univ. Bd. of Trustees, 944 F.3d 613, 624 (6th Cir. 2019).

50. Farmer v. Kan. State Univ., 918 F.3d 1094, 1097 (10th Cir. 2019).

51. *Id.* at 1103.

III. Civil Lawsuits Against Fraternities

In addition to the university's procedures, victims of sexual assault may bring separate legal actions against parties they believe are responsible for their assault. This may include criminal charges, which only affect Greek organizations tangentially, such as situations in which sorority or fraternity members are called as witnesses. Civil claims may also arise, however, and in recent years, civil claims have been brought against fraternity chapters and national fraternity organizations, as well as the individual assailants.

Such civil lawsuits claim a form of negligence. Most broadly, this means that the defendant organization owed the plaintiff some kind of duty, breached the duty, and the plaintiff suffered an injury because of the breach. In the context of sexual assault claims, the plaintiff typically argues that the fraternity chapter or national organization owed the plaintiff a duty of care to prevent fraternity members from committing sexual assault; failed to take adequate measures to ensure prevention; and, as a result, a fraternity member sexually assaulted the plaintiff. In such claims, one of the largest hurdles is establishing why the fraternity chapter or national organization owed a duty of care to the plaintiff. There is no general duty to prevent people around you from being harmed by another person—a more specific justification is needed to create such a duty (for example, a parent has a duty of care to their child and is liable if they stand by while someone else hurts their child).[52]

As an example of framing this duty of care, consider the case *Doe v. Andrews*. The plaintiff, a college student from Alabama, attended a party at the Pi Kappa Alpha fraternity house at the University of Tennessee-Chattanooga. The fraternity had a risk management team that instituted a variety of policies intended to restrict underage drinking: checking the IDs of attendees, marking the hands of attendees who were too young to legally drink alcohol, stationing "Sober Monitors" throughout the house, and only serving alcohol that attendees over the age of 21 brought with them and checked with Sober Monitors.[53] Despite these

---

52. *See* Whitney L. Robinson, *Hazed and Confused: Overcoming Roadblocks to Liability by Clarifying A Duty of Care Through A Special Relationship Between A National Greek Life Organization and Local Chapter Members*, 49 U. Mem. L. Rev. 485, 500 (2018–2019).

53. Doe v. Andrews, No. 3:15-CV-1127, 2017 WL 3443598, at *3–4 (M.D. Tenn. Aug. 9, 2017).

measures, an underage member of the fraternity provided the underage plaintiff with alcohol before and outside of the party until she was blackout drunk, took her inside the fraternity house to a locked bathroom, and sexually assaulted her.[54]

The plaintiff argued that both the Pi Kappa Alpha chapter and the national Pi Kappa Alpha organization had a duty to protect her against the risk of harm, such as a chapter member committing sexual assault.[55] As the court explained, in order to find a special relationship that meant either group had a duty to protect the plaintiff from a third party harming her, the court had to assess public policy considerations, whether the harm was reasonably foreseeable, and a balancing test looking at additional factors, such as the social value of the activity the defendant was engaged in.[56] In addition, liability would only attach if the organization had both the means and the ability to control the third party who harmed the plaintiff.[57]

The plaintiff argued that the national organization took on a duty by organizing chapters and requiring that they comply with national standards that included a prohibition of "sexually abusive behavior" and underage alcohol consumption.[58] Her logic was that by setting out the rules, yet not effectively enforcing them, the national organization had taken on a duty of care that it then breached. The court disagreed, reasoning that the national organization had not made any representations about how it would protect attendees at an individual party, the national standards explicitly disclaimed the national organization's ability to supervise chapters and members, and there was no evidence that the national organization could control individual members at all.[59]

By contrast, the court agreed with the plaintiff's argument as to the Pi Kappa Alpha chapter's potential supervisory abilities. As the court ex-

---

54. *Id.* at *4. As a note on vocabulary, in most of the cases discussed throughout this chapter, the court is evaluating a claim against a motion for summary judgment. As a result, the court takes all factual allegations made by the plaintiff as true, and phrases its language accordingly. I have followed a similar pattern, omitting "allegedly" while acknowledging that the court had not completed factfinding nor is final factfinding available in many cases due to a settlement.

55. *Id.* at *7.
56. *Id.* at *8.
57. *Id.*
58. *Id.* at *10.
59. *Id.* at *10–11.

plained, the chapter took several visible enforcement steps to monitor activities during the party. Additionally, the chapter clearly had ways to control individual members, and in fact had suspended the membership of the student who sexually assaulted the plaintiff after her allegations were brought to their attention.[60] This meant that the chapter was, at least in theory, in a position to prevent harm.

The court did not ultimately find that the chapter owed a duty to the plaintiff, however, because of another factor: foreseeability. In order to impose negligence liability on the Pi Kappa Alpha chapter, the harm that the chapter allegedly failed to prevent had to be reasonably foreseeable, and the court ruled that the harm in question was not.[61] Although sexual assault at a fraternity party was, as the court put it, "foreseeable, in the sense that it does not defy the rules of logic and common sense to think that it might happen," reasonable foreseeability required something more than possibility.[62]

This distinction between the possibility of generalized risk and knowledge of specific risk has been determinative in numerous lawsuits. Many plaintiffs in civil lawsuits arising out of sexual assaults committed by fraternity members have pointed to the statistics described earlier to argue that it is reasonably foreseeable for both fraternity chapters and national organizations that fraternity events—particularly parties at which alcohol is served—create a significant risk that a fraternity member will commit sexual assault.

Courts have typically rejected such arguments, but only where the foreseeability is based on a generalized risk. In some cases, the generalized risk seems high, but a court still finds it has not risen to the level of reasonable foreseeability sufficient for tort liability. For example, a series of cases arose out of the unrecognized Pi Kappa Phi chapter at Stockton University in New Jersey. Stockton University took away formal university recognition of the chapter in 2010, and advised students not to attend events organized by unrecognized groups for safety reasons on the university website.[63] The "rogue" Pi Kappa Phi chapter continued to op-

---

60. *Id.* at *12.
61. *Id.* at *13.
62. *Id.*
63. Joe Hernandez, *Did Stockton U. Do Enough to Protect Students from Members of 'Rogue Fraternity'?*, WHYY.ORG (Sept. 4, 2018), https://whyy.org/segments/did-stockton-u-do-enough-to-protect-students-from-members-of-rogue-fraternity/.

erate, however, and was known by at least some students as "Spike Kap" due to incidents involving women students' drinks being drugged.[64] Over the course of four weeks in 2018, four separate students filed lawsuits claiming they were sexually assaulted after attending a party hosted by Pi Kappa Phi.[65] Some of the plaintiffs included the national Pi Kappa Phi organization in their suits, arguing that the national organization was on "constructive notice" of the misconduct of the chapter because of a "systematic problem of bad acts and underage drinking."[66] The New Jersey court found that this was not sufficient to create reasonable foreseeability, however, because the national organization had not been informed of any specific examples of sexual assault committed by Stockton chapter members.[67] In one case, the student victim spoke with other members of Pi Kappa Phi after the incident and was told that the student who assaulted her would be banned from future events "because of his out of control conduct."[68] Even this was not enough in the eyes of the court, however, because the plaintiff did not allege that chapter members or the national organization were aware that the individual student "posed [a] specific risk to sexually assault female party guests."[69] Nor, in another case, had the national organization been specifically warned that there were prior incidents involving date rape drugs and spiked drinks.[70] The university warning students away from the house and a whisper network among students about sexual assaults committed at fraternity events, in other words, were not enough to show reasonable

---

64. Rebecca Everett & Matt Gray, *Did Fake Fraternity 'Run for the Hills' After Being Named in Stockton U. Sex Assault Lawsuits?*, NJ.COM (Aug. 4, 2018, 12:05 PM), https://www.nj.com/news/2018/08/did_fake_frat_named_in_stockton_sex_assault_suits.html.

65. Rebecca Everett, *4th Stockton Student Claims in Suit She was Drugged and Raped*, NJ.COM (July 30, 2018, 9:30 PM), https://www.nj.com/atlantic/2018/07/4th_student_sues_claiming_she_was_drugged_and_rape.html.

66. M.R. v. Stockton Univ., No. CV 18-11431, 2019 WL 3451620, at *8 (D.N.J. July 31, 2019); S.U. v. Stockton Univ., No. CV 18-12145, 2019 WL 3417324, at *6 (D.N.J. July 29, 2019); D.D. v. Stockton Univ., No. CV 18-13506, 2019 WL 3369709, at *7 (D.N.J. July 26, 2019).

67. *M.R.*, 2019 WL 3451620, at *8.

68. *Id.*

69. *Id.*

70. D.N. v. Stockton Univ., No. CV 18-11932, 2019 WL 2710500, at *7 (D.N.J. June 28, 2019).

foreseeability sufficient to impose liability upon the chapter or the national organization.

Along similar lines, another court explained that widespread general knowledge of an increased risk of sexual assault at universities was not enough to make the risk foreseeable. In that tragic case, a student died by suicide two months after being sexually assaulted at a fraternity party.[71] The student's mother brought a lawsuit on her behalf against the fraternity chapter in question, citing national press coverage and a report by the Department of Justice about the rates of sexual assault at universities as evidence that the risk of sexual assault was foreseeable.[72] The court found that "such information, standing alone," was insufficient.[73] In order to show that the chapter was aware that the individual student was a risk, the plaintiff should have shown prior misconduct by the individual student, or some conduct earlier on the night of the assault indicating danger.[74] Generalized risk—even a quantifiable and substantial risk—was not enough.

There are some examples, however, of courts willing to use recent misconduct by the chapter in question—not the individual assailant—as sufficient to create reasonable foreseeability. In one such case, a 19-year-old student was invited to a Pi Kappa Alpha party hosted at an on-campus apartment and served alcoholic drinks until she was extremely intoxicated.[75] The student was then brought to the bedroom of another student by two men, one a fraternity member, who played rock paper scissors to decide which one would sexually assault the intoxicated teenager.[76] The fraternity member committed the assault, then was discovered by other fraternity members who ejected both him and his victim from the party. He then took the intoxicated student to another location in a dorm, where he again sexually assaulted her while the assault was watched and videotaped by other students.[77]

---

71. Jackson-Locklear v. William Patterson Univ., No. CV 16-5449, 2018 WL 1942521, at *1 (D.N.J. Apr. 24, 2018).

72. *Id.* at *4.

73. *Id.*

74. *Id.*

75. Jones v. Pi Kappa Alpha Int'l Fraternity, Inc., 431 F. Supp. 3d 518, 522 (D.N.J. 2019).

76. *Id.* at 523.

77. *Id.* at 523.

The victim ultimately brought lawsuits with 20 causes of action against the multiple people involved in her assault.[78] One claim was the tort of negligent supervision, brought against the national organization of Pi Kappa Alpha for "failure to exercise reasonable care" in supervising the chapter whose members were involved in various capacities in the sexual assault.[79] Negligent supervision required showing that the supervisor had a duty to supervise the persons or entities that committed the tort, that the supervisor knew or had reason to know that the supervisee was dangerous, there was a reasonable foreseeability of harm, and the negligent supervision was the proximate cause of the harm.[80] At the pleading stage, the court found that the plaintiff had stated a viable claim involving a supervisory relationship sufficient to create a duty, given that the national fraternity organization required that chapters consent to supervision and could revoke or suspend membership for noncompliance.[81] In assessing the foreseeability of sexual assault committed by a member of the chapter, the court found that the student's citation to both general studies of the greater risk of sexual assault committed by fraternity members and past incidents involving the chapter in question, violations of alcohol policy, and allegations of sexual assault were sufficient to claim foreseeability.[82]

Similarly, another case arising out of Brown University focused on recent disciplinary charges brought against other members of the fraternity in question. A student alleged that she was drugged at a fraternity party and sexually assaulted in her dorm room.[83] The university initially found the fraternity chapter responsible for misconduct related to the incident, but reduced the penalty after problems arose relating to the reliability of the tests showing the date-rape drug GHB in the student's system.[84] The reduced penalty was compounded by the university dropping the investigation into the student who provided the laced beverages, who was coincidentally the son of a university trustee.[85] The uni-

---

78. *Id.* at 521.
79. *Id.* at 526.
80. *Id.* at 527.
81. *Id.* at 529.
82. *Id.*
83. Doe v. Brown Univ., 304 F. Supp. 3d 252, 256 (D.R.I. 2018).
84. *Id.*
85. *Id.*

versity withdrew official recognition from the fraternity, but after the investigation was dropped and the penalty reduced, the fraternity allegedly continued recruiting new members and engaged in behavior intimidating the victimized student.[86]

After the student brought suit against the national fraternity (among many other defendants), the national fraternity argued that they should be dismissed from the lawsuit because they did not owe the student any duty of care.[87] The student's logic was that the national organization exercised control over organization and discipline of the individual chapter, and that it had been informed that there had been at least five disciplinary charges brought against members of the chapter in the last three years.[88] Although the court acknowledged that the charge might not ultimately prove successful, it found that the student's argument was sufficient to state a plausible claim of negligent supervision.[89]

Another frame for a negligence claim is premises liability, focusing on fraternities (often the national fraternity organization) as the owner of a location in which the sexual assault took place. The application of premises liability is often complicated, however, because both fraternity chapters and national organizations rarely actually own the chapter house.[90] Similarly, the question of the duty of care is significant—the same issues of foreseeability exist in the premises liability frame, but the claim must also establish why the landowner owes a duty of care to the person on the premises. This often involves determining whether the plaintiff was an invitee or licensee, meaning someone who was on the premises for the benefit of the occupant (invitee), or on the premises for their own benefit (licensee). A landowner has a stronger duty to protect an invitee, so the plaintiff in such cases typically argues that they were an invitee.[91] Given that cases typically begin at a fraternity party, plaintiffs bringing such a claim must first convince a court that their presence at the party was for the benefit of the fraternity, rather than a social event they attended for their own benefit. Such arguments can be framed—most spe-

---

86. *Id.* at 257.
87. *Id.* at 262.
88. *Id.*
89. *Id.* at 264.
90. *See* Robinson, *supra* note 53, at 502; Willingham, *supra* note 10, at 1746–47.
91. *See* Willingham, *supra* note 10, at 1748–49.

cifically, plaintiffs can argue that fraternities invite women to make the fraternity seem more attractive to potential members—but are not always persuasive.

Even if that first step is successful, moreover, the same question of foreseeability from the negligent supervision framing must be answered. As in the previous cases, evidence of recent warnings of danger has been determinative. In one successful example, the victim of sexual assault committed in a student's room in the fraternity house during a party reported her assault the next day to the president of the chapter.[92] The president responded that they had "been concerned" about that student "for a while" due to his drinking problem and recent violent fights with other fraternity members.[93] The court, characterizing the plaintiff student as a social invitee, looked to "foreseeability, control, and the relationship of the parties" to determine whether the plaintiff had stated a viable premises liability claim.[94] The court used a broad interpretation of foreseeability:

> It is ... foreseeable that allowing a group of eighteen-to-twenty-year-olds control over a residence where alcohol-related parties are held presents the potential for misconduct, including sexual assault. A national fraternity knows, or should know, that social events carried on in a building that houses one of its local chapters presents the potential for sexual assault, particularly where alcohol consumption is an integral part of the event.[95]

The court ultimately concluded that the national fraternity did owe a duty of care to the plaintiff student based in premises liability.[96]

An older case referenced specific past incidents in forming a similar conclusion as to a chapter's liability. A student who attended a party at the Delta Tau Delta fraternity house at Indiana University at Bloomington was sexually assaulted by a fraternity alumnus who had offered her

---

92. Brown v. Delta Tau Delta, 2015 ME 75, ¶ 4, 118 A.3d 789, 790.

93. *Id.* at 790–91; *see also* Toby Franklin, Brown v. Delta Tau Delta: *In A Claim of Premises Liability, How Far Should the Law Court Go to Assign A Duty of Care?*, 68 ME. L. REV. 363, 365 (2016).

94. *Brown*, 118 A.3d at 793.

95. *Id.*

96. *Id.* at 795.

a ride home from the party after she was separated from the friends she arrived at the party with.[97] In evaluating foreseeability, the court considered the totality of circumstances around the event in question, which could include but was not limited to "prior similar incidents."[98] The court then cited two categories of information that the fraternity had prior to the sexual assault. First, there was statistical information provided to the fraternity chapter by the national organization about the risk of sexual assault committed on college campuses, including the higher risk that fraternity members were perpetrators of sexual assault. Second, there were two recent incidents of sexual harassment and assault committed by members of the same Delta Tau Delta chapter preceding the facts underlying the lawsuit in question. As a result, the court concluded that "to hold that a sexual assault in this situation was not foreseeable, as a matter of law, would ignore the facts and allow [Delta Tau Delta] to flaunt the warning signs at the risk of all of its guests."[99]

Although the decision was abrogated by a later case, the later decision does not undercut the Delta Tau Delta court's reasoning. The question in the latter case was whether to use the totality of the circumstances test, including fact-specific considerations as the Delta Tau Delta court did, or whether to use a general analysis that did not consider the specific facts in question. The later court concluded that a more general analysis of foreseeability was appropriate "without addressing the specific facts of the occurrence."[100] In a sad irony, that more general analysis was applied against the very same chapter in yet another sexual assault case.[101] In October 2013, a sophomore and sorority member was set up with John Enochs, a sophomore member of Delta Tau Delta, as her date to a dance.[102] While at the Delta Tau Delta chapter house, the sorority member blacked out, and a friend witnessed Enochs having sex with her while she appeared to be asleep.[103] She later realized she had likely been

---

97. Delta Tau Delta, Beta Alpha Chapter v. Johnson, 712 N.E.2d 968, 970 (Ind. 1999), *abrogated by* Rogers v. Martin, 63 N.E.3d 316 (Ind. 2016).
98. *Id.* at 971.
99. *Id.* at 973–74.
100. *Rogers*, 63 N.E.3d at 325.
101. *See* Doe v. Delta Tau Delta Beta Alpha Chapter, No. 16-CV-01480, 2018 WL 3375016 (S.D. Ind. July 11, 2018).
102. *Id.* at *2.
103. *Id.*

sexually assaulted and another friend reported it to several other members of Delta Tau Delta. Eighteen months later, another student attended a social event at the Delta Tau Delta house and reported that she was sexually assaulted by Enochs.[104] The second victim brought several claims of negligence against the Delta Tau Delta chapter, arguing that "the harm she suffered was foreseeable to DTD, first and foremost because DTD, through several of its members, was aware of allegations that Mr. Enochs had sexually assaulted another woman at a prior fraternity-sorority event."[105] By contrast, Delta Tau Delta argued that:

> (1) 'DTD did not have actual knowledge or reason to believe a criminal assault would occur on April 11, 2015'; and (2) knowledge of assault allegations made 18 months prior to the assault alleged by Ms. Doe is irrelevant, because it does not constitute contemporaneous knowledge of a current threat.[106]

The court rejected the fraternity's arguments and concluded that the relevant analysis considered the broad type of plaintiff—"an invitee to a social fraternity event"—and the broad type of harm—"sexual assault by a member previously alleged to have committed sexual assault, where the fraternity knew or should have known of the prior allegations"—and that summary judgment for Delta Tau Delta was inappropriate. (Perhaps for the best, the national Delta Tau Delta organization suspended the chapter's charter in 2017 after multiple reports of hazing.)[107]

Another case came to different results regarding liability of the chapter versus the national organization. In *Scheffel v. Phi Kappa Psi*, the plaintiff argued both the chapter and national organization were negligent and bore some responsibility for her sexual assault at a fraternity party.[108] The court agreed with the plaintiff that the fraternity had a duty to exercise reasonable care to protect her as a licensee under premises

---

104. *Id.*

105. *Id.* at *4.

106. *Id.*

107. Michael Reschke, *Delta Tau Delta Suspends IU Chapter Over Hazing*, Herald-Times, (Jan. 10, 2017, 12:15 AM), https://www.heraldtimesonline.com/story/news/2017/01/10/delta-tau-delta-suspends-iu-chapter-over-hazing/117585402/.

108. Scheffel v. Or. Beta Chapter of Phi Kappa Psi Fraternity, 359 P.3d 436, 441–42 (Or. Ct. App. 2015).

liability.[109] Her claims thus turned on the foreseeability of the sexual assault, and the court concluded that general knowledge of sexual assaults committed by fraternity members was enough that the fraternity could reasonably foresee a risk to female guests, particularly given specific education and preventative efforts around sexual assault led by the university and the national Phi Kappa Psi organization.[110]

To be clear, these examples are not the universal approach. Several Michigan State students sued the university, the school's chapter of Kappa Sigma, and the national Kappa Sigma organization after a single Kappa Sigma member was accused of two separate sexual assaults.[111] The first took place in the stands of a football game and was reported to the Michigan State police a couple of months later. A month after that report, another student was sexually assaulted by the same fraternity member at the fraternity house.[112] That second victim argued that the Kappa Sigma chapter was negligent in failing to protect her. A Michigan court rejected her claim under the logic that she was a licensee, and so the fraternity only owed her a duty to refrain from willful and wanton misconduct.[113] The court concluded that even assuming that the fraternity knew of the first allegation of sexual assault, there was no evidence that other fraternity members knew that he had invited the second victim over to the house, nor that she was there.[114] As a result, the chapter's negligence rose at best to the level of ordinary negligence, not the worst misconduct necessary to show breach to a licensee.

Other courts have rejected the use of generalized evidence of the risk of sexual assault. In 2003, the Eighth Circuit explicitly held that evidence that allegations of sexual assault committed by other members of the same fraternity in other locations were insufficient as a matter of law to establish premises liability.[115] In the absence of any individualized evidence, the decision for many courts is even easier. For example, the victim of a sexual assault committed by a member of Tau Kappa Epsilon

---

109. *Id.* at 444.
110. *Id.* at 447.
111. Kollaritsch v. Mich. State Univ. Bd. of Trustees, No. 15-CV-1191, 2016 WL 10733962 (W.D. Mich. Nov. 23, 2016).
112. *Id.* at *2.
113. *Id.* at *5.
114. *Id.*
115. Ostrander v. Duggan, 341 F.3d 745, 749 (8th Cir. 2003).

at Northwest Missouri State University sued the chapter and the house association that owned the fraternity house under a premises liability theory.[116] A Missouri court found that the general premises liability rule applied to a landlord such as the house association was that the landlord was not liable unless the landlord had knowledge of a dangerous condition that the tenant could not have discovered.[117] The court concluded that the house association did not have any specific knowledge of an increased risk of sexual assault, as the only recent allegation of sexual assault committed by a member of the fraternity had occurred a few years before and the accused student had since graduated.[118] To the extent that fraternity events or members represented an increased risk of sexual assault, the victim and house association would have had the same general knowledge, so no negligence could arise.[119]

Finally, a few lawsuits have been brought against national fraternity organizations under a theory of vicarious liability. Vicarious liability often operates in a business context as a principal/agent relationship, where the principal may be vicariously liable for the acts of their agent. The key limitation in applying this concept in the context of sexual assault claims is that it is nearly impossible, for obvious reasons, to argue that an individual fraternity member is acting as an agent of the national fraternity, particularly during the commission of a criminal act.[120] An alternative framing of vicarious liability that is at least slightly more applicable is the idea of master/servant, in which the master controls the actions of the servant.

Predictably, this introduces the question of how much control a national fraternity organization exercises over the actions of chapters and even individual members of those chapters. Proving vicarious liability thus requires showing both that the national fraternity had the ability to control the smaller entity, and knowledge that the smaller entity was

---

116. A.R.R. v. Tau Kappa Epsilon Fraternity, Inc., 649 S.W.3d 1(Mo. Ct. App. W.D. 2022), *transfer denied* (May 31, 2022), *transfer denied* (Aug. 30, 2022).

117. *Id.* at 10.

118. *Id.*

119. *Id.*

120. *See e.g.*, *Brown*, 2015 ME 75, ¶ 8, 118 A.3d at 791 ("Because there is nothing in the record suggesting that Clukey was acting as an agent of [fraternity] or [national fraternity] at the time of the assault, we reject Brown's vicarious liability claims....").

doing something wrong in a way that the national fraternity could have intervened to prevent the harm but chose not to.[121]

This is extremely difficult to do. In *Scheffel*, where a court found the fraternity chapter could in theory be found negligent under premises liability, the court rejected a vicarious liability argument about the national fraternity. The plaintiff argued that the national Phi Psi fraternity had a variety of ways of controlling the individual chapter, including withdrawing charters, disciplining individual members, providing guidance, and requiring policies minimizing the risks of alcohol and sexual assault.[122] The court found that even with all these examples of relationships and at least some control over the chapter and membership, the control was "essentially remedial" and insufficient to trigger vicarious liability.[123] This finding is consistent with unsuccessful arguments for vicarious liability of national fraternities in other contexts, including hazing, injuries from fights, and car accidents.[124]

As with Title IX regulations and procedures, civil lawsuits continue to be an unpredictable area of law where different courts have reached opposite results. But a few takeaways for Greek organizations are clear. First, national organizations continue to remain largely excluded from such lawsuits on the logic that they do not exercise sufficient control over chapters and individual members. Even the policies promulgated by national organizations forbidding sexual assault and requiring commitments from chapters to prevent and address sexual assault have generally not been viewed as taking on liability for sexual assaults committed by chapter members or at fraternity houses. To the extent that a national organization is worried that its actions to prevent sexual assault could be viewed as assuming control, the organization could state that they cannot adequately police and control individual members, lay out steps for chapters to take such as reporting allegations to their uni-

---

121. *See* Grenier v. Comm'r of Transp., 51 A.3d 367, 388 (Conn. 2012) ("Ultimately, whether a national fraternity may be held liable for the actions of one of its local chapters depends both on its ability to exercise control over the local chapter as well as its knowledge either that risk management policies are not being followed or that the local chapter is engaging in inappropriate behavior.").

122. *Scheffel*, 359 P.3d at 455.

123. *Id.*

124. *See* Cassandra Coolidge, *Fraternizing with Franchises: A Franchise Approach to Fraternities*, 66 EMORY L.J. 917, 932 n.102 (2017).

versity's Title IX coordinator, and establish other clear directives that do not centralize responses to allegations of sexual assault with the national organization.

This is particularly important because the takeaway should *not* be that acknowledging the problem of sexual assault could trigger liability. The courts that have been more willing to potentially apply liability broadly have not relied on whether a national organization or a chapter takes steps to prevent sexual assault, but rather the general national awareness of sexual assault and past allegations at that university or the fraternity chapter in question. Instituting policies around preventing sexual assault does not give rise to civil liability.

What does trigger liability, however, is not responding to existing allegations. It is in the interest of fraternities, therefore, to have both preventative efforts and swift actions responding to allegations that make clear that the fraternity is not putting later people at risk. This does not mean that a fraternity should attempt to supplement or replace the investigation performed by the university or even law enforcement—the goal should be effective prevention of any other incidents. Steps such as tighter control on alcohol at social events, closing off private areas of fraternity houses during parties, and fostering an environment that treats preventing sexual assault as part of the culture of the fraternity will likely be effective.

CHAPTER 8

Social Host Liability

Gregory S. Parks & Victoria Grieshammer

Greek life is a ubiquitous part of university culture, and fraternities and sororities are often spaces for students to bond and have fun. They are also sites of mishaps and injuries, though, which are frequently fueled by alcohol.[1] Under social host liability, fraternities and sororities—and host institutions—can be held responsible for injuries resulting from these events. Social host liability places responsibility on these organizations and institutions for the damages resulting from alcohol they provided.[2]

As a general matter, social host liability may be imposed where the event host has a legal duty of care, based on a "special relationship" with guests and third parties, to protect them from alcohol-related harm.[3] If a court determines that such a legal duty exists, social host liability adheres if it is proved that (1) the duty of care was breached, (2) the actual injury sustained by the plaintiff was a direct result of alcohol intoxication, (3) the injury that resulted was reasonably foreseeable, and (4) imposing a legal duty on the social host is fundamentally fair.[4] Social host

---
1. Spring J. Walton et al., *The High Cost of Partying: Social Host Liability for Fraternities and Colleges*, 14 WHITTIER L. REV. 659, 659 (1993).
2. *Id.* at 660–61.
3. *Id.* at 664.
4. *Id.* at 664–65.

liability is influenced by factors such as institutional knowledge that an event was occurring, the nature of the property on which the injury occurred, whether a member of the organization caused the injuries, and whether the organization provided alcohol to the individual who caused the injuries or who was injured.[5] These facts can be difficult to establish, particularly at the national level of fraternal organizations. As such, this section explores when fraternities or sororities are held liable, and why or why not.

I. The Early Case Law

During the 1970s and 1980s, courts laid the groundwork for fraternity and sorority social host liability. In *Wiener v. Gamma Phi Chapter of Alpha Tau Omega Fraternity*, the plaintiff brought an action against the Gamma Phi Chapter of Alpha Tau Omega for injuries resulting from an automobile accident.[6] He also brought an action against a fraternity member and the owners and operators of a ranch where the driver of the automobile was given alcoholic beverages during a fraternity party.[7] The plaintiff claimed negligence on the part of the fraternity for serving alcohol to an underage individual; allowing the individual to drive the car that plaintiff was in when it crashed; failing to supervise functions at the ranch; and failing to provide a safe means of transportation.[8] "The trial court entered an order allowing a motion to quash service of summons as to defendant Gamma Phi Chapter of Alpha Tau Omega Fraternity, an unincorporated association, and sustained the demurrers filed by each of the other defendants."[9]

Although the party was thrown at a ranch, rather than on fraternity property, the complaint alleged that the fraternity made arrangements for and conducted the party; that it invited students, some of whom were minors, to attend; and that it caused beer and alcoholic beverages to be

---

5. *See infra* section II.
6. Wiener v. Gamma Phi Chapter of Alpha Tau Omega Fraternity, 485 P.2d 18, 19 (Or. 1971), *superseded by statute*, Act effective July 25, 1979, ch. 30, 1979 Or. Laws 321 (limiting liability of licensees).
7. *Id.* at 20.
8. *Id.* at 20–21.
9. *Id.* at 19–20.

served to all attendees of the party, including the driver.[10] The plaintiff further alleged that the "fraternity knew or should have known that [the driver] was a minor, and that he had driven an automobile to the premises and would necessarily have to return" home.[11] The court reasoned that the fraternity's "status as host and its direct involvement in serving the liquor ... [were] sufficient to raise the duty ... to refuse to serve alcohol to a guest when it would be unreasonable under the circumstances to permit him to drink."[12] It therefore held that the trial court erred in sustaining Gamma Phi Chapter's demurrer against plaintiff's cause of action.[13] It reversed the decision of the trial court as to Gamma Phi Chapter, but "the judgments in favor of [the fraternity member] and the owners and operators of the Ranch" were affirmed.[14]

The Beta Rho Chapter of Beta Theta Phi was not held liable in *Stein v. Beta Rho Alumni Ass'n, Inc.*[15] Here, the plaintiff was a burlesque dancer hired to perform at a fraternity party.[16] The fraternity members were drinking and, during her show, they began grabbing at her.[17] After her performance, she was dragged out of a dressing room, thrown off of a bridge, and was seriously injured.[18] The plaintiff sued the Beta Rho Alumni Association on four theories: (1) that the fraternity provided too much alcohol, (2) that the alcohol was served to underage individuals, (3) that the fraternity did not provide protection to the plaintiff, and (4) that the fraternity failed to stop the assault.[19]

The court here held that the defendant could not be held liable despite its landlord-tenant relationship because the defendant did not have the right to control the actions of the officers and members of the local fraternity, and thus it could not be held vicariously liable for injuries suffered by the plaintiff.[20] Additionally, the court held that there was no

---

10. *Id.* at 23.
11. *Id.*
12. *Id.*
13. *Id.*
14. *Id.* at 23–24.
15. Stein v. Beta Rho Alumni Ass'n, 621 P.2d 632, 634 (Or. Ct. App. 1980).
16. *Id.*
17. *Id.*
18. *Id.* at 634–35.
19. *Id.* at 635.
20. *Id.* at 637.

evidence that the defendant knew that the local fraternity was going to have a party, that the defendant did not know the fraternity members were intoxicated and rowdy prior to the plaintiff's performance, and that "[t]here was no evidence of prior conduct to put the defendant on notice."[21] Specifically, the court reasoned that the plaintiff was unable to prove the requisite existence of an agency relationship such that the defendant had the right to control the physical details of the members' actions "as in the relationship of the master and servant."[22] "The mere fact that the defendant owned and furnished the house [did] not make the members of the local fraternity agents of the defendant."[23] Further, despite the landlord-tenant relationship, there was no evidence of the defendant's knowledge of the events or the risk, and the defendant had no duty to supervise parties and provide protection.[24]

In *Ballou v. Sigma Nu General Fraternity*, though, the fraternity was held responsible when the father of a deceased fraternity pledge brought a wrongful death action against the fraternity.[25] A jury decided in favor of the father, the fraternity appealed, and the appellate court affirmed.[26] In this case, the deceased participated in an event called "hell night" that required the pledges to consume alcohol at several points throughout the night.[27] At ten thirty in the evening, the pledge laid down, and several members of the fraternity checked on him, concerned by his pale color and lack of responsiveness, but ultimately left him on the couch.[28] He was found deceased the next morning.[29]

On appeal, the fraternity argued that there was no evidence of actionable negligence on its part.[30] The court disagreed, and it first established that state law "has determined that a fraternal organization owes a duty of care to its initiates not to cause them injury in the process."[31] In light

---

21. *Id.* at 638.
22. *Id.* at 637.
23. *Id.*
24. *Id.* at 638.
25. Ballou v. Sigma Nu Gen. Fraternity, 352 S.E.2d 488, 490–91 (S.C. Ct. App. 1986).
26. *Id.* at 490.
27. *Id.* at 491.
28. *Id.* at 492.
29. *Id.*
30. *Id.*
31. *Id.*

of that duty, then, the evidence allowed the jury to determine that Sigma Nu "created a hazardous condition" for the deceased by "plying [him] with dangerous quantities of alcoholic liquors and beverages over a short period of time, and pressuring [him] to consume these intoxicants to excess" and then failing to assist him when he became ill.[32]

Sigma Nu next argued that "the proximate cause of [the victim's] death was his own voluntary consumption of the alcohol."[33] The court similarly rejected this argument, stating that the evidence showed that the "primary purpose" of providing alcohol was to push the pledges to extreme intoxication through ridicule and pressure, and that alcohol played the "leading, if not the principal, role in the initiation process."[34] Therefore, the deceased may not have consumed deadly amounts of alcohol without the prompting of fraternity brothers, and the deceased may not have passed away if he had not been abandoned by the brothers after reaching acute alcohol intoxication.[35] The court was careful to point out that liability could be established here because "the action does not involve a third party," and that "the party furnishing the alcohol promoted its excessive consumption by the injured party."[36]

Lastly, Sigma Nu argued that it should not be held liable for the wrongful death because the brothers were not performing acts "within the scope of the local chapter's agency with Sigma Nu," despite acknowledging an agency relationship.[37] But Sigma Nu's bylaws prescribed an initiation ceremony and did not prohibit additional initiation activities.[38] This chapter had chosen to supplement its initiation ceremony with the hell night activity, which was a "required" component of proceeding to the initiation ceremony.[39] Because "the introduction of new members 'is the life blood of all such organizations,'" the court deter-

---

32. *Id.* at 493.
33. *Id.*
34. *Id.* at 494.
35. *Id.*
36. *Id.*
37. *Id.* at 495.
38. *Id.* at 496.
39. *Id.*

mined that the fraternity chapter was acting "within the scope of apparent authority conferred on it by Sigma Nu."[40]

In *Fassett v. Delta Kappa Epsilon*, three teenagers who had just left a Delta Kappa Epsilon fraternity party collided with another driver in an automobile accident.[41] One of the passengers, Monica Buckley, was killed, and the other passenger, Anne Fassett, was rendered a quadriplegic.[42] Fassett and the estate of Buckley both brought suit against several members of the fraternity, and the cases were consolidated.[43] "The district court concluded that, as a matter of Pennsylvania law, a defendant would have had to have physically served (i.e., directly handed) an alcoholic beverage to [the driver] in order to be civilly liable."[44] The United States Court of Appeals for the Third Circuit held that the district court's "conclusion as to the scope of Pennsylvania social host liability law is unduly restrictive" and that it therefore erred in granting summary judgment to the defendants.[45] The court examined three Pennsylvania Supreme Court cases to establish the scope of social host liability in Pennsylvania law.[46] It ultimately concluded that social host liability "does apply to those circumstances in which *minors* serve alcohol to minors."[47] In addition, the court rejected the defendant's argument that social host liability can only apply where the defendant was a "furnisher" of alcohol by physically handing alcohol to a minor.[48]

The court followed a three-step reasoning process established by the Pennsylvania Supreme Court.[49] First, it looked to the relevant criminal code to determine if the action committed constituted a criminal offense.[50] Second, it determined if the criminal code established a standard of conduct that was applicable in civil liability.[51] Third, it looked to the

---

40. *Id.* (quoting Derrick v. Sovereign Camp, W.O.W., 106 S.E. 222, 224 (S.C. 1921) (Cothran, J., concurring)).
41. Fassett v. Delta Kappa Epsilon, 807 F.2d 1150, 1152 (3d Cir. 1986).
42. *Id.* at 1153.
43. *Id.*
44. *Id.* at 1154.
45. *Id.* at 1157.
46. *Id.* at 1158.
47. *Id.* at 1160.
48. *Id.* at 1161.
49. *Id.* at 1160.
50. *Id.*
51. *Id.*

Pennsylvania accomplice statute in order to establish that "it is the minor who ... must be characterized as the 'principal' in the crime" and that any other person to whom the criteria of accomplice applies "may then be held to be the minor's accomplice."[52] In order to hold a defendant civilly liable as an accomplice under this standard, it must be clear that "(1) the alleged accomplice must have had an *intention* to promote or facilitate the consumption of alcohol by a minor ... and (2) the alleged accomplice must have *aided, agreed or attempted to aid* in the minor's consumption of alcohol."[53] In addition to intent to aid, the court determined that the aid given must be substantial to find a minor civilly liable as an accomplice.[54] "Each defendant's liability or freedom from liability must depend not on the particular label attached to him, but rather on the complex of factors which determine whether the particular defendant, in aiding, agreeing or attempting to aid a minor in consuming liquor, did so in a substantial fashion."[55]

When applying this standard to the defendants, the court reasoned that one of the defendants was the fraternity president, who planned the party and supplied some of the alcohol; another was the fraternity treasurer, who signed a blank check to purchase alcohol; and the next three defendants "all knowingly allowed their apartment to be used for the purpose of serving intoxicants to minors."[56] It held, then, that there were questions of fact as to whether the "defendants intentionally rendered substantial assistance" to the driver.[57]

In *Quinn v. Sigma Rho Chapter of Beta Theta Pi Fraternity*, a pledge brought action against the fraternity for injuries he sustained during the initiation ceremony.[58] During this ceremony, the plaintiff, a minor, was instructed to drink a 40-ounce pitcher of beer, then an eight-ounce bot-

---

52. *Id.* at 1161.
53. *Id.*
54. *Id.* at 1164.
55. *Id.*
56. *Id.*
57. *Id.*
58. Quinn v. Sigma Rho Chapter of Beta Theta Pi Fraternity, 507 N.E.2d 1193, 1195 (Ill. App. Ct. 1987).

tle of whiskey, and was left to sleep on the hardwood floor.[59] He suffered from neurological damage to his arms and hands.[60] On appeal, the

> question presented ... [was] whether the fraternity owed a duty to plaintiff with respect to requiring the commission of very dangerous acts, including the highly excessive consumption of intoxicants, as a part of the initiation ceremony. In other words, if there is a duty on the party of fraternities and sororities to refrain from requiring participation in such acts....[61]

The trial court dismissed the complaint for failure to state a cause of action, and the appellate court reversed and remanded.[62]

The defendant fraternity argued that "it had no duty to prevent plaintiff's intoxication" because its relationship with plaintiff should be characterized as a "social host-guest relationship" and pointed to cases that denied liability against social hosts for furnishing alcohol.[63] The court declined to characterize the relationship in this manner, reasoning that the situation "consist[ed] of more than the mere furnishing of alcohol" because the plaintiff was "required to drink to intoxication in order to become a member of the fraternity" and that, "[w]hen required to consume such large amounts of alcohol, it is foreseeable and likely that injuries will occur."[64] As a result, it held "that a legal duty [had been] created and the complaint state[d] a cause of action in negligence."[65] But the court "narrowly construe[d] this duty" based on "two factors."[66] The first factor was that the plaintiff was *required* to drink, which "sufficiently distinguishe[d] the instant case from the social host-guest situation."[67] The second factor was the pertinent state statute against hazing that indicated a "social policy against embarrassing or endangering our youth" and therefore established a cause of action for negligence.[68]

---

59. *Id.*
60. *Id.*
61. *Id.*
62. *Id.* at 1198.
63. *Id.* at 1197.
64. *Id.*
65. *Id.*
66. *Id.* at 1198.
67. *Id.*
68. *Id.*

In *Alumni Ass'n, Delta Zeta Zeta of Lambda Chi Alpha Fraternity v. Sullivan*, the appellant, a minor, was served alcohol at a fraternity party and set fire to another fraternity house.[69] The fraternity home destroyed by the fire brought suit against the appellant, who filed a joinder complaint against the college, national fraternity, and fraternity chapter that served him alcohol.[70] As to the national fraternity and fraternity chapter, the joinder complaint alleged that the chapter created a known foreseeable risk by serving alcohol to a minor, and that the national fraternity, as the owner of the chapter house at which the party took place, should be liable because it knew or should have known that alcohol was being served to minors.[71] The trial court dismissed the appellant's complaint with prejudice based on the defendants' preliminary objections.[72] On appeal, the court affirmed the dismissal as to the national fraternity and the college but reinstated the joinder complaint as to the fraternity chapter.[73]

The court pointed to *Congini by Congini v. Portersville Valve Co.*, a Pennsylvania Supreme Court decision that "extended the scope of liability to include social hosts, who knowingly serve or furnish alcoholic beverages to a minor" and allowed these hosts to be held liable for "harm proximately resulting from the minor's intoxication" because "minors are deemed legally incompetent to handle the effects of alcohol."[74] The appellant's allegations of negligence against the fraternity chapter were enough to sustain the joinder complaint given that the chapter did not challenge the allegations that it was the social host of the event at which the appellant was served alcohol.[75] Therefore, the court held that there was a foreseeable risk of "harm to life and property" resulting from the chapter serving alcohol to minors.[76] The appellant could not establish liability in regard to the national fraternity, though, because he did not plead that it knowingly furnished alcohol to him, and instead pleaded

---

69. Alumni Ass'n, Delta Zeta Zeta of Lambda Chi Alpha Fraternity v. Sullivan, 535 A.2d 1095, 1097 (Pa. Super. Ct. 1987).
70. *Id.*
71. *Id.*
72. *Id.*
73. *Id.*
74. *Id.* at 1099.
75. *Id.* at 1100.
76. *Id.*

that the national fraternity knew or should have known of the chapter's alcohol service to minors.[77]

In *Jefferis v. Commonwealth of Pennsylvania*, the plaintiff, a minor, was injured after drinking alcohol at a Theta Chi fraternity party and filed action arguing that the fraternity was negligent under social host liability theory for furnishing alcohol to a minor.[78] The trial court granted the fraternity's motion for summary judgment, and plaintiff appealed.[79] On appeal, the court reversed and remanded, holding that the trial court erred in its interpretation of social host liability law.[80] It established the following test to be used "to determine the extent of liability in a social host situation involving an intoxicated minor:"

(1) the defendant must have intended to act in such a way so as to furnish, agree to furnish or promote the furnishing of alcohol to the minor, and
(2) the defendant must have acted in a way which did furnish, agree to furnish, or promote the furnishing of alcohol to the minor, and
(3) the defendant's act must have been a substantial factor in the furnishing, agreement to furnish, or the promotion of alcohol to the minor.[81]

The court explained that:

[f]actors relevant to determining whether the defendant's act was a substantial factor in the commission of the tort include, but are not limited to, the nature of the act encouraged, the amount of assistance given, the defendant's presence or absence at the time of the tort, the defendant's relation to the tortfeasor and the foreseeability of the harm that occurred.[82]

Accordingly, the court remanded and instructed the trial court to answer the question of whether the national fraternity "intentionally ren-

---

77. *Id.* at 1099–1100.
78. Jefferis v. Commonwealth, 537 A.2d 355, 356 (Pa. Super. Ct. 1988).
79. *Id.*
80. *Id.* at 357, 359.
81. *Id.* at 358.
82. *Id.*

dered substantial assistance to the minor appellant in his consumption of alcohol."[83]

Throughout these fundamental cases, courts grappled with the level of involvement and knowledge on the part of fraternities and sororities that was needed to hold them responsible for alcohol-related injuries or damages. Courts have found that a fraternity that knew or should have known that a minor was consuming alcohol provided by the fraternity was enough to raise the question of liability and submit the case to the jury. Alternatively, the rule the court rejected as unduly restrictive in *Fassett* required proof that a fraternity "physically hand[ed]" alcohol to a minor. Another important element of the social host liability analysis that is reflected in these cases is the differentiation between a social host-guest relationship—in which the injured individual is an unaffiliated third party—and events that are required for membership in fraternities and sororities. Courts similarly considered the organization's status as either a local chapter or national organization. Last, the victim's status as an underage drinker proved to be particularly important, creating a greater risk of liability. In these courts' eyes, the group's status as legally incompetent to consume alcohol, despite being legal adults, resulted in foreseeability of property damage and injury. Many of these factors continued to be reflected in the fraternity and sorority social event liability cases that followed.

II. Modern Case Law and Findings of Liability

Social host liability on college campuses has its roots in the 1970s and 1980s, when courts began to impose liability on fraternities for alcohol-related risk.[84] As Peter Lake, noted higher education legal scholar, indicated, "[t]hese cases constituted a shift away from notions of exclusive student personal responsibility for high-risk drinking injuries."[85]

---

83. *Id.* at 358–59.

84. *See* Peter F. Lake & Joel C. Epstein, *Modern Liability Rules and Policies Regarding College Student Alcohol Injuries: Reducing High-Risk Alcohol Use Through Norms of Shared Responsibility and Environmental Management*, 53 OKLA. L. REV. 611, 616 (2000).

85. *Id.* at 616–17.

Starting in the 1990s, courts offered greater nuance and texture to what constitutes social host liability.

In *Gilhooly v. Zeta Psi Fraternity*, the plaintiff was walking by the fraternity house on her way elsewhere.[86] She slipped and fell on the sidewalk in front of the fraternity house, and subsequently brought action against the fraternity.[87] In considering whether to characterize the property as commercial or residential, the court emphasized the use made of the property and the nature of the ownership.[88] It stated, "[w]hile defendant argues that the fraternity house is used exclusively as a residence for its members it is evident from the statements of defense counsel that it is also used as a social club for both its residential and nonresidential members."[89]

Further, the dues "paid by both residential and nonresidential members [were] not utilized to defray cost of room and board for the residential members but instead [were] used to pay, at least in part, for social events which include parties and alumni functions."[90] Because the home was used for social functions, the court reasoned that it was likely that the invited guests would need to use the sidewalk in front of the house to enter the house.[91] "[S]afe access to defendant's fraternity house, especially at night during social events [was] a foreseeable and necessary element to be considered in defendant's function as a successful social club"[92] The fraternity was considered a hybrid organization because it was both commercial and residential, and therefore Zeta Psi was a commercial landowner and subject to liability for negligent maintenance of its sidewalk.[93]

In *Beta Beta Chapter of Beta Theta Pi Fraternity v. May*, the plaintiff attended a Beta Theta Pi fraternity party that featured a makeshift pool.[94]

---

86. Gilhooly v. Zeta Psi Fraternity, 578 A.2d 1264, 1265 (N.J. Super. Ct. Law Div. 1990).

87. *Id.*

88. *Id.* at 1266–67.

89. *Id.* at 1267.

90. *Id.*

91. *Id.*

92. *Id.*

93. *Id.* at 1267–68.

94. Beta Beta Chapter of Beta Theta Pi Fraternity v. May, 611 So. 2d 889, 890–91 (Miss. 1992).

She was pushed into the pool against her will, and she injured her foot.[95] The plaintiff brought a negligence action against the fraternity and the housing corporation, alleging that the defendants were negligent in designing and constructing a temporary pool on the premises, which created a dangerous condition she was not warned of.[96] She additionally alleged that the fraternity was negligent in providing alcohol to underage individuals, and that the housing corporation was negligent in failing to properly supervise the fraternity.[97]

The appellate court upheld the jury verdict that found for the plaintiff.[98] Additionally, the court established that the fraternity was a suable entity because, despite being an unincorporated organization, "an unincorporated association authorized by statute to contract in its own name for certain purposes, has a legal capacity to be sued on such contracts in its association name."[99] In determining this, the court emphasized that the fraternity did business with private and public entities, and that it had economic and social effects on the local community.[100]

In *Butler v. Gamma Nu Chapter of Sigma Chi*, a university student was assaulted by a member of the Gamma Nu Chapter of Sigma Chi in the portion of a residence hall that was under the jurisdiction of the fraternity.[101] The student sued the fraternity, the fraternity's local chapter, and the fraternity member for assault, battery, outrage, and civil conspiracy.[102] A jury returned a general verdict, awarding the plaintiff $25,000 in actual damages against a chapter member, the chapter, and national fraternity; it awarded $5,000 in punitive damages against the local chapter.[103] The jury found the national and local fraternity responsible based on their own negligence, rather than respondeat superior.[104] The appellants brought issues regarding relevance of evidence, hearsay, jury in-

---

95. *Id.* at 891.
96. *Id.* at 890.
97. *Id.*
98. *Id.* at 889–90.
99. *Id.* at 893–94.
100. *Id.* at 894.
101. Butler v. Gamma Nu Chapter of Sigma Chi, 445 S.E.2d 468, 469 (S.C. Ct. App. 1994).
102. *Id.*
103. *Id.*
104. *Id.* at 471.

structions, and a special verdict form.[105] The appellate court affirmed the jury's finding and denied the appellants' arguments.[106]

In *Weber v. Delta Sigma Phi Fraternity*, the fraternity cosponsored a hayride during which a vehicle hit a wagon and injured many of the people aboard.[107] A jury found the national fraternity and local chapter liable, even though the national fraternity was not named in the suit.[108] The national fraternity argued on appeal that it was not named as a defendant or served with process and, thus, the trial court erred in finding that it was a party defendant.[109] The appellate court held that the trial court properly found that local and national fraternities constitute separate entities as they have "different officers and different geographical locations."[110] Here, the national fraternity was located in Michigan, and the plaintiff never served process on the national fraternity as required by the Michigan Court Rules.[111] Therefore, while the national fraternity could not be held liable for the accident as they were never a properly made party to the suit, the local fraternity remained responsible as they were a proper party throughout the court proceedings and fully sponsored the hayride event.[112]

In *Godfrey v. Omega Psi Phi, Omicron Kappa Chapter*, the plaintiff was an unsuspecting victim of a round of the "knockout game" taking place at a party held at the fraternity house of Omega Psi Phi, Omicron Kappa Chapter.[113] This game involved the attendees of the party walking up to unknowing bystanders and hitting the victims in the head to knock them out.[114] The plaintiff lived next to the fraternity house, and when the plaintiff was walking to his car, he was attacked by the party members who hit him in the head from behind, knocking him unconscious.[115]

---

105. *Id.* at 469–71.

106. *Id.* at 470–72.

107. Weber v. Delta Sigma Phi Fraternity, No. 203736, 1999 Mich. App. LEXIS 2400, at *2, (Ct. App. Sept. 28, 1999) (per curiam).

108. *Id.* at *1, *5–6.

109. *Id.* at *5.

110. *Id.* at *6.

111. *Id.*

112. *See id.* at *11–12, *14.

113. *See* Godfrey v. Omega Psi Phi, Omicron Kappa Chapter, No. 1703220003, 2017 WL 1091235, at *2 (Mo. Cir. Ct. Feb. 15, 2017).

114. *Id.*

115. *Id.*

Plaintiff fell to the ground and began convulsing; the party members continued to physically attack him until they returned to the fraternity house.[116] The plaintiff claimed that he suffered "traumatic brain injury, a seizure, headaches, memory loss, loss of teeth, a dislocated shoulder, head and facial lacerations and bruising, and emotional distress."[117] Plaintiff brought action against the fraternity chapter, alleging that it was negligent in:

> promoting and hosting a party without proper security or supervision, allowing aggressive groups and/or individuals to attend the party, failing to monitor the aggressive groups and/or individuals, allowing intoxicated guests to attend and/or remain at the party, failing to stop the knockout game, and failing to remove guests who exhibited dangerous propensities.[118]

The defendant argued that it could not be held liable because it did not control the property, was not involved in the planning of the party, had no knowledge of any prior violent crimes on the property, did not owe a duty to the plaintiff to protect him from the criminal acts of third parties, and the plaintiff was not an invitee to the party.[119] The jury found in favor of the plaintiff and awarded him $630,000 in compensatory damages and $1,000,000 in punitive damages.[120]

Generally, establishing liability on the part of fraternities and sororities for injuries that occur at their events or on their properties can be difficult. In the instances where claims against national organizations or local chapters have succeeded, though, there are important distinctions in the facts and in the courts' analyses. For example, the social or business aspects of the organization, as well as the nature of the property where the injuries occurred influences the analysis. When a Greek-letter organization ("GLO") operates like a business or social club, it may be more likely to be found liable as a social host than a GLO that operates only as a residence. Additionally, the nature of the relationship between the national and local levels of the organizations is continuously import-

---

116. *Id.*
117. *Id.*
118. *Id.* at *2–3.
119. *See id.* at *3.
120. *Id.*

ant in the liability analysis, and a strong relationship between the two leads to a higher likelihood that both will be held liable. Lastly, when the organization has control over the perpetrator, or when organization members participate in or oversee the incident, these facts will weigh in favor of establishing a GLO's responsibility for injuries occurring on its properties or at its events.

III. Modern Case Law and No Findings of Liability

Starting in the 1990s, courts also offered greater nuance and texture to what failed to constitute social host liability. In *Millard v. Osborne*, a student died in a car accident after drinking at a party at a Lambda Chi Alpha fraternity house.[121] The estate sued Lambda Chi Alpha, the national fraternity, for providing alcohol to a minor.[122] The trial court ruled that the plaintiff produced no evidence of a disputed factual issue as to whether defendants knowingly served alcohol to minors, and that a showing that the fraternity *should have known* was not enough.[123] It reasoned that the national fraternity is a separate organization that cannot be held liable because it only has the power to discipline *after* a violation, and it does not monitor activities.[124]

On appeal, the plaintiff asserted a "substantial assistance" theory, arguing that the national fraternity aided and assisted the decedent in his consumption of alcohol by its policies and actions.[125] The appellate court upheld the trial court's decision, reasoning that the national fraternity could not be responsible because it did not encourage alcohol consumption, and it could not control the actions of its fraternity members.[126]

In *Booker v. Lehigh University*, an underage student brought suit against the university for injuries sustained in a fall after she became

---

121. Millard v. Osborne (*Millard II*), 611 A.2d 715, 715–16 (Pa. Super. Ct. 1992).
122. *See id.* at 716.
123. Millard v. Osborne (*Millard I*), 12 Pa. D. & C.4th 637, 645 (Ct. Com. Pl. 1991), *aff'd*, 611 A.2d 715 (Pa. Super. Ct. 1992).
124. *Id.* at 645–46.
125. *Millard II*, 611 A.2d at 716–17.
126. *Id.* at 719.

intoxicated at several on-campus fraternities and attempted to walk home on a steep, wooded path.[127] At these parties, she poured her own alcohol, was not asked to show identification, and did not observe any security guards from Lehigh, or anyone who was hired by the fraternities.[128] The plaintiff pointed to Lehigh's social policy, which required students to register parties with the school, but otherwise specified that the responsibility to follow its requirements, such as prohibiting underage drinking and hiring security guards, rested with the party hosts.[129]

The plaintiff argued that the social policy created a duty to protect underage students, and that Lehigh failed to implement its policy and ensure the attendance of security guards.[130] She also argued that Lehigh was responsible as the landlord of the fraternity homes at which she drank.[131] The court characterized the arguments as an in loco parentis claim and rejected them.[132] It reasoned that "[p]laintiff... was an adult.... There can be no question that she was competent, legally or otherwise, to decide, inter alia, whether to break the law."[133] It further reasoned that colleges are not insurers of student safety, and that the social policy did not create a legal duty for Lehigh to control its students, as the policy made clear that the responsibility to follow the rules rested on the hosts of the parties.[134] Additionally, the court followed Pennsylvania Supreme Court precedent in declining a "known or should have known" standard, instead holding that "Lehigh did not knowingly furnish alcohol, or knowingly aid or assist plaintiff's consumption of alcohol."[135] Lastly, the court summarily rejected landlord liability, concluding that "no potential liability could be imposed on Lehigh" on this basis.[136]

In *Sparks v. Warren*, the plaintiff brought a negligence claim against Sigma Chi fraternity to recover for injuries sustained in an assault by a

---

127. Booker v. Lehigh Univ., 800 F. Supp. 234, 235–36 (E.D. Pa. 1992), *aff'd*, 995 F.2d 215 (3d Cir. 1993).
128. *Id.* at 235.
129. *Id.* at 236–37.
130. *Id.* at 237.
131. *Id.*
132. *Id.* at 237–38, 240.
133. *Id.* at 238.
134. *Id.* at 238, 240.
135. *Id.*
136. *Id.* at 240–41.

minor fraternity member who had obtained alcohol at a local chapter house.[137] The assault did not occur on fraternity property.[138] The court held the fraternity not liable because the plaintiff presented no evidence that the fraternity knew or should have known that underage drinkers could be violent.[139] Further, he incorrectly characterized the risk of the defendant's failure to supervise members and prevent underage drinking.[140] Rather, "[t]he risk flowing from the negligence alleged here is not that a minor will drink but that someone predictably will be exposed to danger of an assault if defendants were negligent as alleged."[141]

In *Foster v. Purdue University Chapter, Beta Mu of Beta Theta Pi*, a fraternity member was rendered quadriplegic when he dove headfirst onto a makeshift "waterslide" erected by the fraternity.[142] He brought charges against the fraternity chapter, the housing association, and the national fraternity.[143] The general rule in Indiana was that, because the chapter was an unincorporated association, negligence would be imputed to all members.[144] The court denied the plaintiff's argument that the organization should have an exception to this rule because the fraternity existed independent of its members.[145] As to the housing association that owned the house the fraternity members lived in, the plaintiff proposed two theories: assumption of duty and vicarious liability as agents.[146] The plaintiff argued that there was a special relationship giving rise to a duty to control created by the association's bylaws, giving them the ability to create rules and regulations.[147] The court denied this argument, reasoning that the housing association, although it could pass resolutions, was only able to give recommendations.[148] "[I]f it contracted to control the social behavior of members of the Purdue Chapter, [the

---

137. Sparks v. Warren, 856 P.2d 337, 338 (Or. Ct. App. 1993).

138. *Id.*

139. *Id.* at 339.

140. *Id.*

141. *Id.*

142. Foster v. Purdue Univ. Chapter, Beta Mu of Beta Theta Pi, 567 N.E.2d 865, 867 (Ind. Ct. App. 1991).

143. *Id.*

144. *Id.* at 870.

145. *Id.* at 870–71.

146. *Id.* at 871.

147. *Id.*

148. *Id.*

plaintiff], as an Association member, would be contractually bound to control his own behavior."[149] As to vicarious liability, the court denied the argument that the fraternity social chairmen who purchased alcohol acted as agents because there were no facts indicating "that the association manifested an intent to create an agency relationship."[150]

Finally, the court "conclude[d] that ... [t]he [national] Fraternity did not gratuitously assume a duty to control alcohol consumption by the Purdue Chapter members."[151] The court focused on several important factors, such as the fraternity discouraging alcohol abuse in its advisory pamphlet, sanctioning at least one chapter for alcohol-related problems, and conducting an inspection of the Purdue Chapter.[152] Further, the national fraternity functioned only as a resource and support service organization, offering guidelines to local chapters with no power to implement specific procedures within the chapters.[153]

In *Brakeman v. Theta Lambda Chapter*, the plaintiff was a guest of a member of Theta Lambda Chapter of Pi Kappa Alpha at a party hosted by the chapter at a bar.[154] The plaintiff was injured when she fell out of one of the bar's windows.[155] She brought a premises liability claim against the fraternity.[156] The court held that the fraternity could not be held liable because there was no evidence to show the fraternity had the requisite control to be a possessor of the land on which the plaintiff was injured.[157]

With respect to "control," the court reasoned that "[i]n order to have the occupation or control of premises necessary to impose a legal duty with respect to the condition or use of those premises, one must ordinarily have the power and the right to admit individuals to the premises, or to exclude them from the premises."[158] Here, the bar staff was on the premises, took responsibility for determining if patrons were legally able

---

149. *Id.*
150. *Id.* at 871–72.
151. *Id.*
152. *Id.*
153. *Id.*
154. Brakeman v. Theta Lambda Chapter of Pi Kappa Alpha, No. 01–0250, 2002 Iowa App. LEXIS 1258, at *2 (Ct. App. Nov. 25, 2002).
155. *Id.* at *1–2.
156. *Id.* at *1.
157. *Id.* at *7–8.
158. *Id.* at *6.

to drink, served the alcohol, and had the right to shut down the party.[159] Further, there was no evidence indicating the fraternity was able, or expected, to enter the premises and cure defects, nor that any member of the fraternity caused the fall.[160]

In *Miller v. International Sigma Pi Fraternity*, the plaintiff, an underage individual, sustained injuries at a Sigma Pi fraternity.[161] The plaintiff sued the fraternity and the university, alleging the fraternity was liable as an accomplice because it aided and encouraged a violation of the underage drinking statute.[162] The court held that there was no liability for the fraternity.[163] The dispositive issue was that no one in the organization knew about this party specifically.[164] One element necessary to be considered an accomplice to providing alcohol to minors is that "the defendant must have acted in a way which did furnish, agree to furnish, or promote the furnishing of alcohol to the minor."[165] Here, there was no liability in providing alcohol to minors because the national fraternity and university did not act in concert with the local fraternity in furnishing alcohol to the underage plaintiff.[166]

In terms of social host liability, "[i]n order to be liable as a social host, one must have 'knowingly furnished' alcoholic beverages to a minor."[167] The plaintiff argued that, because the fraternity had tried to stop parties before, and because similar incidents of underage drinking had occurred, they must have known that alcohol was being served to minors.[168] The court denied this argument, reasoning "[u]nless defendants fraternity and university had actual knowledge of the party at which the plaintiff was injured, liability will not follow. The [p]laintiff fails to aver actual knowledge on the part of plaintiff."[169] The court also denied that

---

159. *Id.* at *6–7.

160. *Id.* at *7.

161. Miller v. Int'l Sigma Pi Fraternity, 41 Pa. D. & C.4th 282, 283, 285 (Pa. Ct. Com. Pl. 1999).

162. *Id.* at 284.

163. *Id.* at 289–90.

164. *Id.* at 287.

165. *Id.* at 285 (quoting Jefferis v. Commonwealth, 537 A.2d 355, 358 (Pa. Super. Ct. 1988)).

166. *Id.*

167. *Id.* at 285–86 (quoting Alumni Ass'n v. Sullivan, 572 A.2d 1209, 1212 (Pa. 1990)).

168. *Id.* at 286.

169. *Id.*

the fraternity should sustain liability as a vendor under a state statute because it did not know about or sponsor the party.[170]

The court also rejected arguments under business invitee, public nuisance, and imputed conduct theories. "A business invitee is a person who is invited to enter or remain on the land of another for a purpose directly or indirectly connected with business dealings,"[171] but the plaintiff failed to allege that the fraternity was the possessor of the land in question.[172] Secondly, because the fraternity was not involved in the party thrown by the local chapter, a public nuisance claim was considered invalid.[173] Finally, the court denied the imputed conduct argument by simply stating that the national fraternity should not be held responsible for any negligent conduct of the local fraternity.[174]

In *Gwin v. Phi Gamma Delta Fraternity*, a non-fraternity member fell off the roof of a fraternity house after drinking at a party there.[175] The plaintiff sued the fraternity and the college.[176] The lower court granted summary judgment to the fraternity, and the appellate court affirmed.[177] The plaintiff presented three theories for fraternity liability: social host or land occupier, violation of a statute that prohibited serving alcohol to minors, and abandoning the plaintiff in a position of peril.[178] Under the social host theory, the court reasoned that the plaintiff's voluntary intoxication led to a lower standard of care on the basis that adults should be responsible for themselves.[179] Further, the danger of going onto a roof is obvious, so the landowner had no duty to warn.[180] In regard to the state statute violation, the court held that the fraternity was not liable for injuries the plaintiff suffered due to his own intoxication.[181] Finally, the court reasoned that the duty not to abandon the plaintiff is only applica-

---

170. *Id.* at 287.
171. *Id.* at 288 (quoting Emge v. Hagosky, 712 A.2d 315, 317 (Pa. Super. Ct. 1998)).
172. *Id.*
173. *Id.* at 289.
174. *Id.*
175. Gwin v. Phi Gamma Delta Fraternity, No. 71694, 1997 Ohio App. LEXIS 4658, at *3–4 (Ct. App. Oct. 16, 1997).
176. *Id.* at *1–2.
177. *Id.* at *15.
178. *Id.* at *6.
179. *Id.* at *8–9.
180. *Id.* at *10.
181. *Id.* at *14.

ble if he was placed in danger by the defendant's negligence, which was not the case.[182]

In *Kappa Sigma International Fraternity v. Tootle*, an intoxicated driver who had attended a fraternity party struck and killed another driver.[183] The intoxicated driver was drinking before he attended the party at a Kappa Sigma International Fraternity house, and then brought and consumed his own alcohol while at the party.[184] He then drove while still intoxicated.[185] The decedent's estate brought suit against the international fraternity as well as its local chapter.[186] The trial court denied the fraternity's motion for summary judgment and the appellate court reversed this decision.[187] Importantly, even though the fraternity was serving alcohol, there was direct testimony that the driver only consumed his own alcohol.[188] Further, it was not enough that the driver was drinking at the party; the fraternity must have "knowingly sold, furnished, or served alcoholic beverages" to the driver.[189] Because the fraternity did not knowingly provide alcohol to the driver, it was not relevant whether the fraternity knew he was intoxicated or that he would be driving.[190]

In *Holiday v. Poffenbarger*, the plaintiff was stabbed after walking by a fraternity house belonging to the Mu Chapter of Sigma Pi Fraternity International.[191] The perpetrator, an underage individual, drank in his dorm room and then went to the fraternity house.[192] He got into an altercation that began at the house, continued outside, and ended when he stabbed the plaintiff.[193] The plaintiff sued both the national and local fraternity.[194] The court held that the fraternity was not negligent and that it was not liable for giving alcohol to underage individuals.[195] The court

---

182. *Id.* at *15.
183. Kappa Sigma Int'l Fraternity v. Tootle, 473 S.E.2d 213, 214 (Ga. Ct. App. 1996).
184. *Id.*
185. *Id.*
186. *Id.*
187. *Id.*
188. *Id.* at 215.
189. *Id.*
190. *Id.*
191. Holiday v. Poffenbarger, 973 N.Y.S.2d 276, 279 (App. Div. 2013).
192. *Id.* at 278.
193. *Id.* at 279.
194. *Id.*
195. *Id.* at 280.

reasoned that the national fraternity did not knowingly provide the alcohol; that the perpetrator was drunk before arriving at the party; and that, even though a fraternity member gave the perpetrator a drink at the party, one of his friends took the drink from him.[196] It was undetermined whether the perpetrator drank anything at the party.[197]

In *Whebbe v. Beta Eta Chapter of Delta Tau Delta Fraternity*, the plaintiff was severely injured by a nonfraternity member during a fight at a fraternity party.[198] Although the confrontation started verbally, the plaintiff was suddenly hit in the head by an unidentified person and fell and hit his head on the pavement.[199] He subsequently had a seizure, was hospitalized in a coma, and suffered several lasting mental and physical disabilities.[200] The plaintiff brought a negligence claim against the fraternity on the theory of landowner liability.[201] The court affirmed the lower court's ruling of no liability because a landowner does not have a duty to protect an invitee from the criminal actions of a third party.[202] It decided this in spite of the fact that police had been called to the fraternity house 14 times in 11 months.[203] Further, the university had warned the fraternity that it did not approve of the parties.[204] Importantly, though, the party was not sanctioned by the national fraternity even though it was a registered university event.[205] The plaintiff had also brought his own alcohol.[206]

Focusing on landowner liability, the court stated that a landowner's duty to an invitee is to "use reasonable care in carrying on activities ... and to maintain the property's physical condition to ensure entrants ... are not exposed to unreasonable risks of harm."[207] It further reasoned

---

196. *Id.* at 278, 280.

197. *Id.* at 278.

198. Whebbe v. Beta Eta Chapter of Delta Tau Delta Fraternity, No. A12-1675, 2013 Minn. App. Unpub. LEXIS 270, at *2–3 (Mar. 25, 2013).

199. *Id.* at *3.

200. *Id.* at *3–4.

201. *Id.* at *6.

202. *Id.* at *8–9.

203. *Id.* at *1.

204. *Id.* at *2.

205. *Id.*

206. *Id.* at *2–3.

207. *Id.* at *6 (quoting Rasivong v. Lakewood Cmty. Coll., 504 N.W.2d 778, 783 (Minn. Ct. App. 1993)).

that foreseeability is irrelevant if duty has not been established, so the previous police interactions with the fraternity were irrelevant.[208] Because there was no duty in this case—and no special relationship because the victim was not vulnerable or dependent—the fraternity had no power over him, and it did not deprive him of protection.[209]

In *Pawlowski v. Delta Sigma Phi Fraternity*, the plaintiff was illegally served alcoholic beverages at an off-campus party thrown by the Fraternity's Theta Iota Chapter.[210] At approximately one o'clock in the morning, the intoxicated plaintiff left the party and was struck and killed by a motor vehicle while crossing the street.[211] The court held that public policy made clear that the "Fraternity had no duty to control the conduct of the individual members of its Theta Iota Chapter so as to protect [the plaintiff]. Connecticut adheres to the principle... that generally there is no duty to control the conduct of a third person."[212]

In its analysis of the national fraternity's duty to control, the court observed that "[n]umerous appellate courts from other jurisdictions have concluded that, in the absence of control of the day-to-day activities of the local chapter, a national fraternity does not have a duty to supervise the activities of a local chapter in order to prevent harm to the third parties."[213] Additionally, because the national fraternity did not have a special relationship with the plaintiff, it owed him no special duty.[214] Finally, the court reasoned that there was no valid claim for respondeat superior because there was no evidence that the individual fraternity members were agents of the national fraternity.[215]

When liability does not attach to a GLO, it is often because of either interceding factors or a lack of clear connection between the injury and the organization's involvement. For example, when the incident is the result of the criminal actions of a third party, sororities and fraternities generally are not responsible for protecting the victim from that third

---

208. *Id.* at *9–10.

209. *Id.* at *11.

210. Pawlowski v. Delta Sigma Phi Fraternity, No. CV030484661, 2010 WL 3326707, at *1 (Conn. Super. Ct. July 28, 2010).

211. *Id.*

212. *Id.*

213. *Id.* at *3.

214. *Id.*

215. *Id.*

party. Additionally, organizations typically do not owe a duty to, or have a special relationship with, victims unless there are additional facts that give rise to this duty, such as a victim's special vulnerability. Most important, though, is the role that GLOs play in controlling the details leading up to the incident. In terms of the relationship between the national organization and the local chapter, when the national organization did not act in concert with the local chapter in planning the event or in supplying alcohol, for example, liability will likely not be established for the national organization. Further, it is often not enough that the organization simply supplied alcohol at the event, admitted an intoxicated person, or allowed an individual to consume his or her own alcohol on its premises. Instead, it must have "knowingly served" alcohol to the victim or to the individual or individuals who harmed the victim. The organization also will not be liable if it should have known that the individual in question was underage, already intoxicated, or would be driving; it must actually know. Additionally, when the GLO members are involved—either as victims or perpetrators—courts often take into consideration that the members are not controlled by the organization, that the organization does not encourage alcohol consumption, and that the members are not acting on behalf of the organization.

IV. Conclusion

The first step to reducing social event liability is to understand the relevant state laws.[216] Generally, though, the two major responsibilities of the host are to, first, avoid overconsumption of alcohol by guests, and second, ensure intoxicated guests get back home safely.[217] There are several methods GLOs can employ when planning an event that will help

---

216. *Social Host Liability*, INS. INFO. INST., https://www.iii.org/article/social-host-liability (last visited Aug. 25, 2022, 12:33 PM).
217. SCOTT BOWER & JOAN BILSLAND, HOST LIABILITY 7 (10th ed. 2016), https://www.google.com/url?sa=t&rct=j&q=&esrc=s&source=web&cd=&ved=2ahUKEwjE3_-D-_75AhUIL0QIHdt5CzEQFnoECAYQAQ&url=https%3A%2F%2Fwww.bennettjones.com%2F-%2Fmedia%2FFiles%2FBennettJones%2FPublications%2FBennett-Jones--Host-Liability-2016--10th-Edition-12Page.pdf&usg=AOvVaw36B6MLwKzh0kGFNUoNI-gQ.

to achieve these goals.[218] If an event includes drinking, hosts should encourage guests to establish a designated driver to drive them home after the event, and hosts should make sure to limit their own alcohol intake to be able to better judge guests' sobriety.[219] Ensure that guests are not pressured to drink, avoid serving alcohol to any guests who are visibly intoxicated, and make sure that nonalcoholic beverages and food are also being served.[220] Explicitly stating that overdrinking is not condoned and prohibiting drinking games can help attendees keep their drinking limited.[221] These tactics can help to decrease over-drinking while also making clear that the organization does not encourage drinking.

Taxi vouchers can also be provided to guests to encourage attendees to abstain from drinking and driving.[222] Hosts should ensure that any guests who do not use a cab service have designated drivers that do not drink alcoholic beverages to drive them home after the event.[223] It may be helpful to hire a professional bartender who is trained to recognize signs of intoxication and will know not to serve to guests who are visibly intoxicated.[224] Event hosts should enforce the conduct rules and be an example for all guests.[225] Additionally, hosts should structure the event so that drinking is limited.[226] For example, toward the end of the evening, hosts should stop serving liquor and switch to an alternative beverage, such as coffee, tea, or soft drinks, and encourage all of their guests to wear seatbelts as they drive home.[227]

---

218. INS. INFO. INST., *supra* note 216.

219. *Id.*

220. *Id.*

221. BOWER & BILSLAND, *supra* note 217, at 8.

222. *Id.* at 7.

223. *What is a Host's Responsibility When Having a Holiday Party?*, SPIVEY L. FIRM: BLOG (Dec. 2, 2016), https://www.spiveylaw.com/blog/what-is-a-host-s-responsibility-when-having-a-holiday-party/.

224. *Id.*

225. *See* Julia E. Judish, *Harassment at Events: Liability Concerns and Prevention Best Practices*, PILLSBURY WINTHROP SHAW PITTMAN LLP: INSIGHTS (Feb. 2, 2018), https://www.pillsburylaw.com/en/news-and-insights/harassment-at-events-liability-concerns-prevention-best-practices.html.

226. BOWER & BILSLAND, *supra* note 217, at 8.

227. INS. INFO. INST, *supra* note 216.

Even if drinking is not involved, GLOs should pay attention to equal opportunity issues and ensure that a social event is not discriminatory.[228] For example, they should opt for a gender-neutral activity instead of a "males only" football game.[229] Establishing a comprehensive, written anti-harassment policy and publicizing it prior to the event will also aid in reducing discrimination-related liability.[230] Additionally, hosts should empower GLO members to avoid harm and help stop harm through mandatory sexual harassment training as well as bystander intervention training.[231] Hosts should avoid sponsoring physical activities that are high risk, such as skiing.[232] If they sponsor an event centered around physical activities, hosts should require participants to sign a waiver and specify that the event is not mandatory.[233] To further show that an event is not mandatory or business related, hosts should schedule the event away from the official GLO premises and on a weekend.[234] Further, hosts should make it explicit whether the event is purely social or has an association with the organization.[235] If the event includes alcohol, hosts should establish a drink limit, such as handing out drink tickets to guests upon entry, and assign someone to check IDs and filter out underage drinkers.[236] Hosts are responsible for making sure that minors are not drinking.[237] Additionally, hosts should avoid naturally provocative locations, such as casinos or bars. Establishing expectations prior to the event can help decrease social event liability.[238] Finally, if any form of misconduct arises in relation to an event, hosts should immediately act upon it and investigate.[239]

---

228. *See* Jennifer Brown Shaw & Carolyn Burnette, *Potential Liability for Employer-Sponsored Social Events*, SHAW L. GROUP (Apr. 11, 2007), https://shawlawgroup.com/2007/04/potential-liability-for-employer-sponsored-social-events/.
229. *Id.*
230. Judish, *supra* note 225.
231. *Id.*
232. Shaw & Burnette, *supra* note 228.
233. *Id.*
234. *Id.*
235. Judish, *supra* note 225.
236. Shaw & Burnette, *supra* note 228.
237. SPIVEY L. FIRM, *supra* note 223.
238. Shaw & Burnette, *supra* note 228.
239. *Id.*

CHAPTER 9

Liability Insurance Issues for Fraternal Organizations

Maria C. O'Brien

I. Introduction to Fraternal Organization[1] Insurance Liability Issues

For the most part, liability insurance for fraternal organizations is subject to the same forces dominating the much larger market for general liability insurance. For fraternal organizations, these forces include a perception of increased litigiousness, rising premiums, changing societal tolerance for acceptable fraternity behavior, the decline of the in loco parentis doctrine, and ever-present concerns about moral hazard. As Tom Baker and Peter Siegelman have noted: "[T]ort cases are typically denominated in terms of a victim suing an injurer. But injurers do *not* typically pay the damages (if any) for which they are held liable, insurers do."[2]

---

1. For the sake of simplicity and to avoid repetition, references to both fraternities and/or sororities are often encompassed by the term "fraternal organizations" in this chapter. Thanks also to Marilyn Icsman and Alex Deaton for research assistance, proofreading and commonsense suggestions.

2. Tom Baker & Peter Siegelman, *The Law and Economics of Liability Insurance: A Theoretical and Empirical Review*, in RESEARCH HANDBOOK ON THE ECONOMICS OF INSURANCE LAW, 488, 488 (Daniel Schwarcz & Peter Siegelman eds., 2015).

For fraternities, the liability insurance landscape for first-party property claims is generally indistinguishable from first-party claims of other insureds.[3] Liability coverage for third-party tort claims is distinct, however, since the conventional tortfeasor/insurer relationship is often further complicated by the presence of two additional parties: the homeowner's insurer of the tortfeasor's parents, and the liability insurer of the affiliated college or university.

Additionally, insured fraternities and their insurers have encountered a steadily less forgiving public and court system, particularly with respect to claims of sexual assault. By 1985, the market for liability coverage for fraternities was in crisis.[4] Much has been written about the causes of the so-called liability insurance crisis of the mid-1980s. The crisis was characterized by steep and often unanticipated increases in premiums,[5] which triggered disruptions in the markets for myriad products and services. Commentators disagree to some extent about the precise causes of this crisis, but the expansion of tort liability which began in the 1960s,[6] combined with subsequent judicial decisions which created uncertainty for liability insurers, undoubtedly intensified the need for insurers to

---

3. *See* Shane Kimzey, *The Role of Insurance in Fraternity Litigation*, 16 Rev. Litig. 459, 462–63 (1999) (stating that 2% of fraternity claims result from fires and 6% result from property damage).

4. Not long after a resurgence in Greek life across hundreds of college campuses: a young man grievously injured in a Kappa Alpha-related accident reached a settlement with the fraternity that, over the course of his lifetime, could amount to some $21 million—a sum that caught the attention of everyone in the Greek world. Liability insurance became both ruinously expensive and increasingly difficult to obtain. The insurance industry ranked American fraternities as the sixth worst insurance risk in the country—just ahead of toxic waste removal companies. 'You guys are nuts,' an insurance representative told a fraternity CEO in 1989, just before canceling the organization's coverage; 'you can't operate like this much longer.'

See generally Caitlin Flanagan, *The Dark Power of Fraternities*, Atlantic https://www.theatlantic.com/magazine/archive/2014/03/the-dark-power-of-fraternities/357580/ (Sep. 9, 2019, 2:00 PM).

5. George L. Priest, *The Current Insurance Crisis and Modern Tort Law*, 96 Yale L.J. 1521, 1521 (1987). Priest noted that premiums increased so dramatically in some cases that certain products and services were "withdrawn from the market" as coverage was unavailable at any price. Everything from "vaccines, general aircraft, and sports equipment and [...] intrauterine devices, wine tasting and day care ..." was affected.

6. *See e.g.*, Kenneth S. Abraham, *Making Sense of the Liability Insurance Crisis*, 48 Ohio St. L.J. 399 (1987).

control costs by limiting coverage. Essentially, there was no "completely reliable way for insurers to draft around the threat of expansive interpretation of an insurance policy, for the threat itself is that policy language is subject to expansive interpretation."[7] There is no reason to believe that fraternal organizations and their insurers were immune from this phenomenon. On the contrary, changes in liability rules and social norms that reduced or eliminated defenses such as contributory negligence and assumption of the risk, and rejected victim stigma in, for example, sexual assault cases, undoubtedly increased the volume of tort claims and the corresponding cost of liability insurance.[8]

The expansion of tort liability was probably not the only source of these cost increases. There is broad consensus that American legal rules operate to encourage tort litigation: the "American rule," which frees a losing party from covering the cost of their opponent's legal expenses, and the availability of contingent fees make litigation much less risky than in other legal regimes.[9] For fraternities and sororities, the expansion of tort liability and nearly simultaneous erosion of norms that may have kept certain classes of plaintiffs from bringing suit in the past[10] forced insurers to adopt the kinds of programs that are now required by both the college or university and the national organization. Legal changes, especially those enacted at the state level but experienced by

---

7. Kenneth S. Abraham, *The Once and Future Crisis*, 4 J. RISK & UNCERTAINTY 353, 366 (1991).

8. "The expansion in the scope of legal liability during the past several decades is well known. [...] A variety of other changes in technical legal doctrines have made it easier for accident victims to recover damages for their injuries." Scott Harrington & Robert E. Litan, *Causes of the Liability Insurance Crisis*, 239 SCIENCE 737, 740 (1988).

9. Abraham, *supra* note 6, at 409 (noting that "[i]n effect [contingency fees] the plaintiff sells a portion of his claim to his attorney in return for counsel fees, and he does not risk liability for his opponent's fees.").

10. *See* Ellen M. Bublick, *Tort Suits Filed by Rape and Sexual Assault Victims in Civil Courts: Lessons for Courts, Classrooms and Constituencies*, 59 S.M.U. L. REV. 55 (2006) (attributing the rise in civil tort litigation for sexual assault to a number of factors including increased social responsibility for sexual assault prevention whereas older cases only expected the victim to report the case, increased media attention through the development of television, increased economic and political power for women, greater discussion of sexual topics, increased social acceptance of consensual sexual activity, decreased public sanctions against the women who report, the movement for rape law reform which brought attention to the issue itself, and increased social support for victims through the creation of rape crisis centers).

these organizations which typically operate in numerous states, inject an unwelcome degree of uncertainty for insurers. If an insurer is doubtful about a court's inclination to read exclusionary language expansively and a jury's willingness to assign blame to both a plaintiff and defendant, the insurer has no choice but to adopt the kinds of programs that institutions of higher education and insurers require of fraternal groups.

Settlements were becoming strikingly large; premiums were rising in response and a complete collapse of the market for fraternity coverage seemed likely. In response to these developments, insurers and fraternal national organizations took a series of steps (reflected in the insurance contracts themselves along with teaching materials and other forms of communication from the nationals to the local chapters) designed to insulate nationals from liability arising out of tortious conduct by local officers, members, and pledges. The effectiveness and utility of the contract language and ancillary tools employed to protect nationals are the primary focus of this chapter.

More than 30 years after the watershed Kappa Alpha incident,[11] which appears to have sharply focused insurer and national organization attention on the potential unwinding of the market for fraternal organizations, there is now a large enough body of caselaw to enable conclusions about every aspect of liability insurance for fraternities. National organizations have consistently taken the position that they do everything possible to push local chapters to avoid dangerous conduct (including the service of alcohol to minors) and therefore, the exclusions in their liability policies should be strictly honored as there is no agency theory or other special relationship that would justify extending liability to them. The volume of litigation suggests local chapters deviate from nominal national group behavior expectations with some regularity. Of course, this is not particularly surprising given the youth and inexperience of local chapter leadership. (Indeed, some have argued that under-

---

11. Hank Nuwer, Wrongs of Passage: Fraternities, Sororities, Hazing and Binge Drinking 173–174 (1999) (explaining the story of Rusty Combes, a member of the Kappa Alpha Fraternity, who was awarded a $21 million settlement after he was left paralyzed by an alcohol-related car crash caused by another member of the fraternity who was playing with the car's accelerator).

age drinking, unrestrained sexual conduct, and high-risk behavior *is at the core* of fraternity life.)[12]

The stated aims and apparent expectations of the national organizations may be at odds with the observed behavior of local chapters. Alcohol consumption by underage students is generally acknowledged as rampant,[13] and affiliated colleges and parents seem to be either willfully ignorant or simply unconcerned about conduct which often leads to catastrophic injury or death. When a serious incident occurs, local officers and members may be surprised to discover that it is often impossible to access insurance coverage via the national even though the local is typically required to pay premiums for that coverage to remain in good standing.[14] Colleges and universities, repeat players in these cases to be

---

12. *See* Gordon W. Maples et al., *Behaviors Viewed as Deplorable by Peers: A Different Approach to Programming to Curb Unacceptable Behaviors in Fraternities and Sororities*, 14 ORACLE: RSCH. J. OF THE ASS'N OF FRATERNITY/SORORITY ADVISORS 1, 2 (2019) ("Excessive drinking has also been shown to be a more socially acceptable behavior within these organizations than outside of them, as it is often regarded as central to the fraternity/sorority socialization process."); *see also* Anna North, *Is College Sexual Assault a Fraternity Problem?*, N.Y. TIMES (Jan. 29, 2015, 10:14 AM) (quoting John D. Foubert, professor at Oklahoma University), https://archive.nytimes.com/op-talk.blogs.nytimes.com/2015/01/29/is-college-sexual-assault-a-fraternity-problem/ ("[R]esearch ... 'has shown that fraternities are three times more likely to commit sexual assault than other college men.'"); *see also* Sydney Shupe, The Influence of Fraternity and Sorority Characteristics on Alcohol Exposure: Who is at Risk? (May 2022) (Ph.D. dissertation, East Tennessee State University) (East Tennessee State University Electronic Theses and Dissertations) (finding Greek organizations have an increased risk of overconsumption, alcohol abuse, and fraternity members living with one another leads to an increase in alcohol consumption).

13. *See* Beth Mcmurti, *Why Colleges Haven't Stopped Binge Drinking*, N.Y. TIMES (Dec. 14, 2014), https://www.nytimes.com/2014/12/15/us/why-colleges-havent-stopped-binge-drinking.html; *see also National News Briefs; Typical Binge Drinker: Under-Age College Man*, N.Y. TIMES, June 19, 2000, at A13.

14. *See* David Glovin, *Fraternities Worse than Animal House Fail to Pay for Casualties*, DAILY INDEP. (Mar. 28, 2013), (quoting Lee John Myndhart), https://www.dailyindependent.com/news/local_news/fraternities-worse-than-animal-house-fail-to-pay-for-casualties/article_52435f75-d268-581c-973b-bab3fbf68e9e.html (stating that the victim of fraternal hazing, Lee John Myndhart, felt as if he is "a casualty of the strenuous efforts by national fraternities such as Lambda Chi to avoid paying compensation for deaths and injuries at their local chapters."); *see also* John McCormick, *Should I Allow My Son to Join a Fraternity*, HUFFINGTON POST (Mar. 21, 2014, 3:27 PM), https://www.huffpost.com/entry/should-i-allow-my-son-to-join-a-fraternity_b_5004197 (writing about the shock of a parent to find out the lack of insurance, the author says, "[T]he biggest revelation in Flanagan's story is that national fraternities often leave parents stuck paying the bill. Par-

sure, have adopted several largely successful strategies to distance themselves from legal liability. This frequently leaves the third-party liability coverage of tortfeasor parents' homeowners' policies as the only source to cover damages.

It is, without a doubt, a positive for fraternity tort victims that there is a viable source of funds available to provide compensation and, at least in some cases, to cover expected future subrogation demands by the injured student's health insurer. Whether a tort victim's parents' homeowners' are the optimal place to fix liability is a separate issue and depends largely on the lens through which one considers the broad question of how to resolve the tension between the high-risk/unregulated behaviors that appear to attract students to fraternities and other (invariably more sophisticated) actors.

II. The Conventional Rules of Insurance Contract Interpretation

The interpretation of insurance contracts is one of the most common functions of state (and sometimes federal) courts. This repeat task performed by courts in all jurisdictions in the US over hundreds of years has resulted in a uniform body of rules governing the applicability of exclusionary (and other) terms in insurance contracts. Along with the doctrine of contra proferentum,[15] which aids in resolving conflicts over ambiguous contract terms, American courts consistently recognize that

---

ents have a false sense of security that in the unlikely event their son gets into legal trouble, the fraternity's insurance will pay.... In reading this, I had to put the article down and catch my breath."); *see also* Tim Evans, *National Fraternity Groups Excused from Hazing Lawsuits*, INDYSTAR, (June 17, 2014, 4:42 PM), (quoting Stephen Wagner, the attorney representing the deceased party), https://www.indystar.com/story/news/education/2014/06/17/national-fraternity-groups-excused-hazing-lawsuits/10697223/ ("They strongly believe that a national fraternity is in a better position to prevent hazing and alcohol deaths than the local chapter led by 18- and 20- year olds.").

15. The doctrine of Contra Proferentum states that "In choosing among the reasonable meanings of a promise or agreement or a term thereof, that meaning is generally preferred which operates against the party who supplies the words or from whom a writing otherwise proceeds." RESTATEMENT (SECOND) OF CONTRACTS §206 (AM. L. INST. 1981). The rationale for application of the doctrine to adhesive contracts is, of course, the absence of meaningful bargaining power on the part of the non-drafting party.

interpretation of an insurance contract is a question of law and that ordinary rules of contract interpretation apply to insurance contracts. Specifically, the Plain Meaning Rule governs the interpretation of insurance contracts in the same way it applies to other kinds of commercial contractual arrangements. As courts have noted repeatedly, "[i]f a policy provision is unambiguous, then a court must enforce the policy as it is written and cannot defeat express provisions, including exclusions from coverage."[16] (While there has been a small debate about how to understand "plain meaning" in a particular context and whether context in fact ever matters,[17] this academic issue does not appear to have overly concerned state courts as they grapple with construing the exclusions and other parts of insurance contracts for national organizations and their affiliated locals.)

For insurers of national fraternal organizations, exclusionary language that is typically directed at the national's local chapters is often critical to the disposition of cases in which a tort plaintiff seeks to impose liability on the national in addition to the local. Many colleges and universities have written policies that require affiliated fraternal groups to obtain liability insurance with minimum coverage levels and local chapters that do not heed these requirements typically risk revocation of recognition by the college or university. Rutgers University, for example, supplies its local fraternal groups with a one-page sheet that states, "it is recommended for fraternities and sororities at Rutgers, State University of New Jersey that each chapter must have liability insurance coverage with adequate limits for personal injury in place prior to hosting any chapter events."[18] National organizations also distribute handouts to local chapters and outline insurance requirements. For example, the Beta

---

16. *See* Auto-Owners Ins. Co. v. American Central Ins. Co., 739 So. 2d 1078, 1081 (1999); *see also* Admiral Ins. Co. v. Anderson, 529 F. Supp. 3d 804, 810 (N.D. Ill. 2021) ("Under Illinois law, which governs the substance of the parties' dispute, insurance policies are construed in accordance with ordinary rules of contract interpretation. [citations omitted] If the terms of the policy are clear and unambiguous, they must be given their plain and ordinary meaning unless doing so would violate public policy.").

17. *See* Daniel P. O'Gorman, *Oliver Wendell Holmes's Theory of Contract Law at the Massachusetts Supreme Judicial Court*, 13 N.E. U. L. Rev 73, 120 (2021); *see also* James Fagan, *The Legal Phoenix: The Plain Meaning Rule is Dead, Long Live the Rule!*, 29 Cal. W. L. Rev 373, 377–378 (1993).

18. Letter from Dep't of Risk Mgmt. & Ins., Rutgers Univ., Insurance Requirements for Fraternities and Sororities (on file with author).

Theta Pi Risk Management Policy asserts that its goal is to help members "live out Beta's values"—i.e., mutual assistance, intellectual growth, trust, responsible conduct, and integrity. Insurance coverage is explicitly unavailable for violations of the law (including consumption/serving alcohol to underage students) and for acts of hazing, including acts of hazing that involve "beer pong" and "sexually abusive behavior."[19]

Finally, the Association of Fraternity/Sorority Advisors and several of the large insurance brokers have developed their own informational insurance materials for local chapters.[20] A common theme among all these publications is an explicit emphasis on the absence of coverage for behavior that is inconsistent with local, state, and federal laws and/or the rules of the national organization.

The policies that are typically sold to the national and which chapters contribute premiums dollars for inclusion are, as one would expect, written in a manner consistent with the handouts/brochures student chapter leaders receive. That is, they contain explicit and generally unambiguous exclusions for hazing, underage alcohol-related claims, and sexual misconduct.

The exclusion in an insurance policy for a fraternity or sorority functions in the same way it does in any other kind of liability policy—it identifies a category of claims that do not trigger coverage. Most courts also acknowledge the ALI's admonition that exclusions are to be interpreted narrowly.[21]

Explicit policy language with equally clear exclusionary language refusing coverage for injuries sustained in connection with excessive/underage alcohol consumption, sexual abuse, consumption of illegal drugs, hazing, or any other illegal acts is a hurdle for torts plaintiffs seeking to hold a national organization liable. That is because the insurer will not cover a risk it never agreed to cover and, in fact, excluded from policy coverage. This argument is, of course, not a defense to the underlying

---

19. Memorandum from Bd. of Trs., Beta Theta Pi, Beta Theta Pi Risk Management Policy (Aug. 2020) (on file with author).

20. *See* Assoc. of Fraternity/Sorority Advisors, *Fraternity/Sorority Insurance FAQ* (2010) (citations omitted) (on file with author) ("[S]o long as you ... did not violate any laws or the risk management policy or intentionally cause harm to the other person and you were acting in good faith. An individual is protected when acting in the scope of their duties on behalf of the Fraternity/Sorority while in compliance with its policies.").

21. RESTATEMENT OF LIAB. INS. § 32 (AM. L. INST. 2018).

claim; it is a defense to coverage. The crux of cases in which locals are successfully excluded from national liability protection is a convincing claim that the plain language of the policy renders the exclusion effective. Most courts (although not all) appear unwilling to effectively rewrite policy language, even in cases of egregious harm.

In cases of serious harm or death, the divergence of interests between the national and the local are made very clear. Many nationals proscribe steps to be taken by local members following an incident. Frequently, the steps include local chapter officers providing answers to questions about what happened, when, and with whom. The students, possibly focused for the first time on the seriousness of their wayward conduct, may incorrectly believe that chapter interests are aligned with national interests during the investigation.[22] Not unlike employees who cooperate with employer lawyers on the erroneous assumption that those lawyers represent them, too, student members of the local may discover that not only do they not have access to liability coverage from the national, the national, in cooperation with the affiliated college, disclaims all responsibility for the harm.[23] This leads directly to outreach to parents and their homeowner's carrier.

The problem of asymmetry of information is particularly acute in cases involving very young adults and the representatives of nationals and insurers who can be described as repeat players. This problem is not limited to insurance for fraternities. The literature with respect to the advantages enjoyed by repeat players is voluminous.[24] It is impossible,

---

22. *See* Glovin, *supra* note 14; *see also* Transcript of Record at 141–48, Liberty Corp. Cap., Ltd. v. Cal. Tau Chapter of Sigma Alpha Epsilon Fraternity at Cal. Polytechnic State Univ., No. CV 11-2626 (C.D. Cal. Dec. 3, 2012) (arguing that the national fraternity's policies were incredibly vague and were meant to help the national fraternity evade coverage); *see also* Anderson Cooper, *How Hazing Led to the Death of Fraternity Pledge Sam Martinez*, CBS News (Nov. 28, 2021, 6:57 PM), https://www.cbsnews.com/news/sam-martinez-hazing-washington-state-university-death-60-minutes-2021-11-28/ (discussing the steps that the national fraternity told its members to take which potentially interfered with the overall investigation of the incident).

23. *See e.g.*, Gregory S. Parks & Elizabeth Grindell, *The Litigation Landscape of Fraternity and Sorority Hazing: Defenses, Evidence and Damages*, 79 Wash. & Lee L. Rev. 335, 338–39 (2022) ("Fraternity and sorority national organizations are structured to shield themselves from liability for the local chapters and their members' actions.").

24. *See e.g.*, Andrea Chandrasekh & David Horton, *Empirically Investigating the Source of the Repeat Player Effect in Consumer Arbitration* (Nov. 19, 2019), https://ssrn.com/abstract=3489596; *see also* Lisa B. Bingham, *On Repeat Players, Adhesive Contracts*

except on a case-by-case basis and by looking at anecdotal interviews and deposition testimony, to generalize about the knowledge and experience of college students as they move through the presumably unfamiliar process of insurance (and possible criminal) investigation. However, their lack of experience and familiarity with the details of the relevant insurance documents, would suggest that insurers and national representatives usually have the upper hand, as repeat players.

Local chapters buy liability insurance because they are required to do so and, at least in some cases, because they are somewhat risk averse. Often, purchasers of insurance are more risk averse because they expect higher losses. The requirement by colleges and nationals that locals purchase liability coverage is undoubtedly a positive response to what would otherwise lead to spiraling price increases brought on by adverse selection. (Adverse selection refers to a situation in which a party with information about risk that is not available to the other party, purchases insurance with that additional information in mind. Unchecked, adverse selection leads to higher prices which causes consumers with average or lower expected losses to decline insurance. As premium prices continue to rise, the number of people who can afford coverage drops until the remaining pool consists solely of high-risk insureds.)[25]

The requirement that locals join the insurance pool as a condition of recognition by the college and the national is a forceful pushback against adverse selection. However, it results in a cross subsidy of risky locals by less risky locals.

---

and the Use of Statistics in Judicial Review of Employment Arbitration Awards, 29 McGeorge L. Rev. 223 (1998); Shauhin A. Talesh, *Insurance and the Law*, in Int'l Encyclopedia of Soc. and Behav. Scis. 215 (2nd ed. 2015), noting that:
> most individuals do not have much knowledge about precisely what they are purchasing, especially because they often purchase insurance through intermediaries such as agents (who often offer minimal explanation of what the insurance policy provisions mean). On the other hand, insurance companies are often repeat players, wealthy, and the more sophisticated economic entity when dealing with a prospective insured. ... Moreover, insurance companies not only have more information, but better information concerning the meaning and value of the insurance policy....

See also Kevin T. McGuire, *Repeat Players in the Supreme Court: The Role of Experienced Lawyers in Litigation Success*, 57 J. Pol. 187 (1995); *see also* Bahaar Hamzehzadeh, *Repeat Player vs. One-Shotter: Is Victory All That Obvious?*, 6 Hastings Bus. L.J. 239 (2010).

25. For a simple and clear discussion of adverse selection and insurance, *see* Ben Chowdhury, *How Information Asymmetry Can Drive Up Insurance Rates*, Harv. Bus. School Online Bus. Insights Blog (June 30, 2017), https://online.hbs.edu/blog/post/how-information-asymmetry-can-drive-up-insurance-prices.

III. Agency Theory—Actual Versus Apparent Authority and the Torts Lens

A small number of courts, relying on agency theory or respondeat superior have found national organizations liable for local chapter conduct that resulted in serious harm. Whether this represents a growing trend[26] or not is not entirely clear. In South Carolina, for example, a 1986 decision in *Ballou* in which the court found in favor of extending liability to the national Sigma Nu, because the national admitted the agency question.[27] *Ballou* involved a pledge who died following an evening of heavy drinking at a fraternity house. Crucially, the national conceded that local members were its agents. *Ballou* clearly turned on the national admitting an agency relationship with the local. It argued that these agents acted outside of the scope of their authority and that therefore it was not responsible for the specific conduct of the agents that led to Mr. Ballou's death. The court rejected this argument, noting that liability could be imposed on the national so long as the local chapter's excessive drinking activities fell within the scope of the local's actual or apparent authority.

Other courts, although not many, have relied on *Ballou* to support an extension of liability to national entities despite assertions by the national that the conduct of a local was beyond its ability to regulate or outside the scope of the agency relationship.[28]

---

26. Gregory S. Parks & Elizabeth Grindell, *The Litigation Landscape of Fraternity and Sorority Hazing: Criminal and Civil Liability*, 99 Neb. L. Rev 649, 676 (2020) argues that "[D]espite this history of barring recovery from national fraternal organizations directly, the current trend in this litigation area is increasingly directed toward allowing plaintiffs injured in fraternal hazing incidents to recover damages from their national affiliates through respondeat superior, in addition to traditional agency theory." Particularly in cases where the national tasked the local with induction of new members and noting that new members are the "lifeblood" of these organizations, some courts have characterized the national as a kind of corporate entity with local chapters as its business agents. *See e.g.*, the line of South Carolina cases beginning with *Mitchell v. Leech*, 48 S.E. 290 (S.C. 1904).

27. *See* Ballou v. Sigma Nu Gen. Fraternity, 352 S.E.2d 488, 492, 495 (S.C. Ct. App. 1986).

28. *See e.g.*, Krueger v. Fraternity of Phi Gamma Delta Inc., 2001 WL 1334996 at *4 (Mass. Super. Ct. May 18, 2001) (finding that the national chapter owed a duty of care to its initiates not to cause harm to them during the initiation process, therefore denying Phi Gamma Delta's motion to dismiss); *see also* Smith v. Delta Tau Delta, Inc., 988 N.E.2d 325, 340 (Ind. Ct. App. 2013) (reversing trial court's summary judgment in favor of the national

The line of South Carolina cases evinces a strong concern with the compensation impulse that is so frequently observed in a range of tort/insurance cases. The construction of auto liability policies for example,[29] and the view of numerous scholarly commentators suggests that, at least in some cases, courts understand that the extension of liability is in part a response to an overarching impulse to provide compensation for injuries and loss.

Professor George Priest famously argued that:

> the expansion of tort liability since the mid-1960s has been chiefly motivated by the concern of our courts to provide insurance to victims who have suffered personal injury. The most fundamental of the conceptual foundations of our modern law is that the expansion of tort liability will lead to the provision of insurance ... expanded tort liability, thus, is a method of providing insurance to individuals ... who have not purchased or cannot purchase insurance themselves. This insurance rationale suffuses our modern civil law and must be acknowledged as one of the great humanitarian expressions of our time.[30]

The core tort impulse—to compensate for grave injury or death—is an impulse that is most likely to be satisfied when liability is extended to national organizations. Even if parents of tortfeasors and/or affiliated colleges can function as a source of compensatory (or punitive) dollars, the likelihood that serious harm will be fully redressed increases substantially when the national is jointly and severally liable. Tort theory has been focused on the conflict between an "economics" approach and a "moral" approach for some time now.[31] As Judge Posner describes the

---

fraternity because a genuine issue of material fact existed as to whether the national chapter owed a duty to the local chapter and its members), *vacated*, 9 N.E.3d 154 (Ind. 2014).

29. *See* Kenneth S. Abraham & G. Edward White, *Rethinking the Development of Modern Tort Liability*, 101 B.U. L. Rev. 1289, 1307–10 (2021); *see also* Gerhard Wagner, *Tort Law and Liability Insurance, in* 31 The Geneva Papers on Risk and Insurance 277, 281–286 (2006).

30. Priest, *supra* note 5, at 1525.

31. *See e.g.*, John Gardner, *Tort Law and Its Theory, in* The Cambridge Companion to the Philosophy of Law 352 (John Tasioulas ed. 2020); *see* Mark F. Grady, *A New Positive Economic Theory of Negligence*, 92 Yale L.J. 799, 829 (1983) (introducing an alternative economic theory to the conventional approach that compares the cost and benefits of an untaken precaution that was a "but-for" cause which is meant to be more

"conflict," an instrumental approach penalizes economically wasteful acts by raising the cost and thereby reducing future wasteful harm. The moral or "corrective justice" approach is "that tort law is about empowering people who have been wrongly injured to obtain some sort of redress against the injurers."[32] For parties to the kinds of tort claims we are concerned with here—serious injuries or death resulting from hazing, sexual assault and/or excessive alcohol consumption—the "corrective justice" approach is arguably more helpful as almost everyone seems to agree that tort law is most useful when, as Cristina Carmody Tilley has argued, it reinforces social norms and community values.[33] Social approval (or at least tolerance) for the most serious kinds of tortious conduct that arises in connection with fraternity initiations and other social events is by all accounts on the decline.

In particular, and of note here, is the unmistakable reduction in tolerance for sexual misconduct. While by no means limited to fraternity events, reports of campus-affiliated sexual assaults have been on the rise for years and show no signs of abating. How best to address this problem is ultimately left to the courts. In cases where no criminal charges are brought (possibly because the presence of alcohol has made a victim's recollection cloudy), civil liability is front and center. Alexandra Willingham has argued for a greater emphasis on civil litigation as a more effective deterrent than criminal prosecution.[34] Her claim is that national fraternities exercise significant control over their individual chapters, which should be sufficient to trigger liability on the part of nationals who have almost unlimited power to discipline locals. She calls for a change in our "legal-cultural understanding of fraternity responsibility"[35] and rigorous tracking of data to enable fraternities to monitor po-

---

consistent with the practice of courts and minimizing social cost); *see also* Richard A. Posner & William M. Landes, *The Positive Economic Theory of Tort Law*, 15 GA. L. REV. 851, 920 (1981) (introducing a new positive economic theory of tort law that makes the assumption that judges are trying to maximize efficiency).

32. Richard A. Posner, *Instrumental and Noninstrumental Theories of Tort Law*, 88 IND. L.J. 469, 470 (2013).

33. Cristina Carmody Tilley, *Tort Law Inside Out*, 126 YALE L.J. 1320 (2017); *see also* Benjamin C. Zipursky, *Substantive Standing Civil Recourse, and Corrective Justice*, 39 FLA. ST. U. L. REV. 299 (2011).

34. Alexandra Willingham, *Opening the Door: Expanding Civil Redress for Sexual Assault Through Fraternity Insurance*, 72 STAN L. REV. 1717 (2020).

35. *Id.* at 1758.

tential offending members. Given the clear and consistent desire of both colleges and nationals to distance themselves from the most egregious conduct of affiliated fraternal locals, it is hard to imagine who would elect to collect and maintain such a database and how claims about privacy and inaccurate data could be handled.

Nonetheless, Ms. Willingham argues persuasively that social mores with respect to sexual misconduct are changing (and need further change). If tort law is to reinforce social norms effectively, the relationship between nationals and locals will indeed have to be examined closely for evidence of the kind of tight control she suggests exists. Tight control implies, as courts have noted, an agency relationship. The presence of a legitimate agency relationship, in turn, forces courts to consider the effect of exclusions written in plain language, which are designed to do nothing more than insulate the principal no matter what.

For the *Ballou* court and its progeny, this would not present a serious conflict. In other, more numerous jurisdictions, the agency claim is far more problematic, and exclusions are simply to be read as an ordinary part of the contract.

IV. The Fraternal Organization Insurance Contract as a Tool of Social Policy— Moral Hazard

It is all but impossible to escape concerns about moral hazard in connection with any discussion of insurance liability. Liability allocation as between local and national fraternal organizations is no exception. Some have commented that moral hazard concerns are yet another reason to follow the plain language contract interpretation approach clearly favored by nationals—an approach clearly illustrated by that Supreme Court of Illinois in *Bogenberger v. Pi Kappa Alpha*.[36]

In the fall of 2012, David Bogenberger was a freshman pledge of the Pi Kappa Alpha fraternity affiliated with Northern Illinois University. As part of the pledging process, he was required to participate in an event which he and other pledges knew involved the consumption of copious

---

36. Bogenberger v. Pi Kappa Alpha Corp., Inc, 104 N.E.3d 1110 (Ill. 2018).

amounts of vodka. The local did not obtain permission to host this event as required by school policy. Possibly anticipating negative publicity or worse, the chapter president texted officers and members instructing them to delete photos or videos of pledges who had passed out after drinking. At some point during that night, David died. The local chapter's charter was revoked and David's father, as administrator of his son's estate, filed a complaint alleging negligence against the national organization, the local chapter, officers and pledge board members, active local members, and nonmember sorority women who assisted in hosting the event. The gist of the complaint was that David was owed a duty of reasonable care by each defendant.

The *Bogenberger* court began with a conventional analysis of the requirements to establish tort liability. The court noted that Illinois law "ha[s] long recognized that 'every person owes a duty of ordinary care to all others to guard against injuries which naturally flow as a reasonably probable and foreseeable consequence of an act, and such a duty does not depend on contract, privity of interest or the proximity of relationship, but extends to remote and unknown persons.'"[37] This inquiry requires focus on whether an agency relationship existed between the national and its local. Noting that "[a] mere allegation of agency is insufficient to establish actual agency,"[38] the court found that even though locals were supposed to adhere to the national's fraternity constitution, the national derived at least 75% of its gross income from dues and fees collected from local members, and the national had the authority to expel or suspend chapters and individual members, no agency relationship existed.[39]

The crux of this finding was the absence of control over the local by the national organization. Noting that hazing and pledging are not the same, the Illinois court concluded that all the chapter's behavior that was inconsistent with the requirements of the national constitution tended to suggest a *lack* of control on the part of the national. Bogenberger's administrator also alleged direct liability for chapter conduct and the court rejected this too on the ground that an affirmative duty to aid or protect only arises where there is a legally recognized "special relationship." Finding no special relationship between the national and local, the

---

37. *Id.* at 1118 (citations omitted).
38. *Id.* at 1119 (citations omitted).
39. *Id.* at 1120–21.

court declined to impose what would amount to an "unrealistic burden" on the national. Citing cases from Maine,[40] Louisiana,[41] Kentucky,[42] and Connecticut,[43] the court acknowledged that there is a range of views across other states, and some have extended liability to national organizations on facts very similar to those in *Bogenberger*. In Illinois, however, the law is clear that a national whose control over a local is in question cannot be liable on either an agency theory or a direct liability theory.

Bogenberger and the Illinois approach are consistent with cases in Minnesota[44] and North Carolina.[45] It is an approach that relies on a close reading of policy language—especially the exclusions—and enforces exclusions in the policy as written. Additionally, it is an approach that at least does not aggravate any tendencies toward morally hazardous behavior on the part of fraternity members. Under the impression that all manner of behavior is "covered," young and virtually always inexperienced fraternity members may mistakenly believe that their conduct, should it result in harm, is likely to be much less costly than it really is.[46] This miscalculation presumably increases the appeal of the dangerous conduct as the threat of meaningful financial consequences is viewed as extremely remote. The presence of insurance coverage, which local members are unlikely to understand in detail, may reduce the level of care. This, of course, is the essence of moral hazard. Expansion of the *Bogenberger* approach—which makes explicit the lack of coverage for

---

40. Brown v. Delta Tau Delta, 2015 ME 75, ¶ 9, 118 A.3d 789, 792.

41. Morrison v. Kappa Alpha Psi Fraternity, 31, 805, p. 14–18 (La. App.2 Cir. 5/7/99); 738 So. 2d 1105, 1118–19 (La. Ct. App.1999) (finding that the national chapter of Kappa Alpha Psi was not vicariously liable for the actions of the local chapter's president because there was no evidence that the national organization obtained control over the physical details of the president's acts of hazing, assaulting, or battering).

42. Grand Aerie Fraternal Order of Eagles v. Carneyhan, 169 S.W.3d 840 (Ky. 2005).

43. Grenier v. Comm'r of Transp., 51 A.3d 367, 389 (Conn. 2012).

44. *See* Liberty Corp. Capital Ltd. v. Phi Omega Chapter at Minn. State Univ. Moorhead, No. 06-CV-4808, 2008 WL 3911259, at *7 (D. Minn. Aug. 19, 2008) (stating that the local chapter did not qualify as an insured under the national's policy and, even if it had, the alcohol exclusion would clearly exempt them from coverage).

45. *See* Mynhardt v. Elon Univ., 725 S.E.2d 632, 633–34, 637 (N.C. Ct. App. 2012) (declining to create new law recognizing an agency relationship between Lambda Chi and the plaintiff in a suit where the plaintiff suffered permanent paralysis after being thrown to the ground by a member of the fraternity).

46. *See* Maples, *supra* note 12; *see also* North, *supra* note 12; *see also* Shupe, *supra* note 12.

locals, respect for exclusions, and the serious divergence of interests between the local and national—may help mitigate the moral hazard problem, at least at the margins.

The moral hazard issue here is important. Although there appears to be no way to verify empirically, the tendency of insureds to exercise less care when insurance is present, is a well-documented phenomenon and there is no reason that think it is inapplicable to fraternal groups. Moral hazard may be summed up as the tendency to take less care when spending someone else's funds. In the fraternity context, local members may underestimate the cost of risky behavior based on a faulty assumption the insurer will cover most or all first- or third-party losses. A review of a small sample of the literature provided to locals by nationals suggests that accurate information with respect to exclusions is readily available to local leadership. What is unclear is whether locals meaningfully absorb the material they are given. A strong argument in support of the approach in *Bogenberger* and similar cases is that a contracts approach to exclusion language discourages morally hazardous conduct by locals.

Comparing *Bogenberger* with *Ballou* puts the moral hazard problem front and center: does a torts lens which favors maximizing the funds available to compensate victims also increase the likelihood that fraternity members will, confused and unfocused, engage in even greater amounts of harmful and socially undesirable conduct believing that they have insurance coverage? Or put another way, does the *Bogenberger* approach, which is arguably rigid and narrow and places great weight on the lack of control nationals have over locals, effectively put locals on notice that they will not be able to access national liability insurance? Clear answers to these questions would require empirical work that appears not to exist. However, if the data suggested that clear, albeit harsh, signaling about the lack of insurance coverage had the effect of reducing the drinking, drug use, sexually inappropriate behavior, and hazing that gives rise to so many of these cases, that alone would justify robust support for *Bogenberger*.

The problem is that while signaling by nationals to locals is very clear on paper and, apparently, in training sessions with new officers, it is much less clear when locals discover that deviations from the rules do not in fact trigger disciplinary action. The culture of some fraternal organizations may be so steeped in illegal alcohol consumption that it is hard to imagine what sort of signaling could overcome decades of cultural messaging which seems to suggest that a primary purpose of fraternity membership is participation in alcohol-fueled events.[47]

Maybe the *Bogenberger* solution, which is deeply respectful of contract terms and sympathetic to the struggles of the adults at the nationals who cannot be always present to oversee the shenanigans of the very young adults at each local, is the best approach. What is certain though is that by protecting the interests of national organizations, courts that follow *Bogenberger* are increasing the odds that tort victims and or surviving family members will have many fewer dollars available to compensate them for their losses.[48]

V. Other Sources of Insurance Coverage — University Liability and Parents' Homeowners policies

a. University/College Liability

In situations in which courts may refuse to extend a national's liability coverage to local officers and members, there are two additional places plaintiffs frequently look for indemnity—the affiliated college's own liability insurance and the third-party liability coverage potentially available to college-age offspring who are members of their parents' household when not at school. Consider first the circumstances under which an affiliated college or university may be liable.

---

47. *See* Maples, *supra* note 12; *see also* Shupe, *supra* note 12; *see also* Ben Guarino, *Can Frat Brothers be Taught to Drink Less? Not So Easily, Study Says*, Wash. Post (May 23, 2016, 4:13 AM) https://www.washingtonpost.com/news/morning-mix/wp/2016/05/23/fraternity-brothers-resist-efforts-to-curb-alcohol-consumption-study-says/ (finding that Greek organizations are harder to reach when it comes to trying to curb drinking, fraternities often view drinking as part of achieving their social goals).

48. Insurers can:
    use exclusions and sub limits to eliminate or reduce coverage available for liability losses that pose a high degree of moral hazard, most commonly because of the more substantial control that the policyholder has over the occurrence of the loss. These contract features have the potential to decrease ex ante moral hazard.

Baker Seigelman, *supra* note 2, at 499 (ex ante moral hazard is reduction in care that would prevent liability—the essence of National and college mandated insurance materials seems to be focused on ex ante preventative measures.).

Colleges and universities with connections to Greek life are often alleged to have a sufficiently strong connection to a fraternal group to justify extending liability for harm to a pledge or other student to the school's own insurer. Plaintiffs generally rely on one or more of four theories to support a theory of school liability. These are landowner liability, custodial liability, assumption of a duty, and vicarious liability.

Landowner liability is the most straightforward of these theories. It relies on showing that the school, as owner of the premises where the harm occurred, is liable because of the property relationship. The analysis in *Davidson v. UNC at Chapel Hill*,[49] which focused on whether the university owed an injured cheerleader a duty of care, is instructive. The court, in finding a duty of care, emphasized that the injury took place "in Carmichael Auditorium, a sports venue owned by UNC and located on the UNC campus...."[50] Framing the issue as whether the school owed a duty of care to a student-athlete who was part of a school-sponsored team, the North Carolina court also noted that the school had undertaken to "advise and educate cheerleaders in regard to safety. Therefore ... [UNC] owed plaintiff a duty of care."[51]

In cases in which the injuries are sustained on premises not owned or controlled by the college, results are generally more favorable to defendant schools. In *Mynhardt v. Elon University*,[52] another North Carolina decision, the plaintiff suffered permanent paralysis following a confrontation with a fraternity member of the Delta Pi chapter of a fraternity at Elon and another student individual who was not an Elon student. Noting that the location of the fight was "located off the Elon campus and was not owned by Elon" or the local or national, the court concluded that the university's mere promulgation of rules designed to regulate Greek organizations was insufficient to trigger a duty of care to the plaintiff. Elon's regulations did not constitute a voluntary undertaking which, in North Carolina, creates a duty of care. Distinguishing *Davidson*, the North Carolina court observed:

> We want to encourage universities and Greek organizations to adopt policies to curb underage drinking and drinking-re-

---

49. Davidson v. Univ. of N.C. at Chapel Hill, 543 S.E.2d 920 (N.C. Ct. App. 2001).
50. *Id.* at 922.
51. *Id.* at 929.
52. *See Mynhardt*, 725 S.E.2d 632.

lated injuries or other incidents. Adopting such policies, however, does not make a university or Greek organization an insurer of every student, member or guest who might participate in off-campus activities. [cites omitted] We hold that [Elon and fraternity] ... assumed no duty to protect Plaintiff from drinking-related injuries at an off-campus party.[53]

In addition to the absence of a property nexus between *Elon* and the injured student, the court also rejected theories of liability premised on a special relationship or an agency relationship. "[A] university should not generally be an insurer of its students' safety ... the student-university relationship, standing alone, does not constitute a special relationship giving rise to a duty of care."[54]

The result in Elon is utterly unsurprising given the sharp decline of the in loco parentis theory which once justified robust regulation of students' personal lives by colleges. This kind of regulation—which extended to permissible hours off campus, suitability of roommates, and all manner of sexual conduct—is far more intrusive than most would consider appropriate today.[55]

Theories of custodial liability have also eroded as it has become increasingly apparent that universities do not, in fact, exercise custodial control in many cases involving student misconduct. If schools cannot (and do not wish to) regulate where, when, and with whom students spend time, then it is difficult to demonstrate that injured students were in some sense in the custody of the institution.[56]

---

53. *See id.* at 637.

54. *See id.*

55. Most schools have dropped "visiting hours" for opposite-sex friends for example and completely abandoned attempts to regulate where and with whom students spend the night. For an exception, *see* Univ. of Notre Dame, *Undergraduate Residence Hall Visitation*, https://dulac.nd.edu/community-standards/standards/ (last visited June 23, 2022) ("[V]isiting hours for guests of the opposite sex are not to begin before 9 a.m. on any day and are not to extend beyond 2 a.m. on Friday and Saturday nights and midnight on Sunday through Thursday nights."); *see also* Jon Krakauer & Laura L. Dunn, *Don't Weaken Title XI Campus Sex Assault Policies*, N.Y. TIMES, Aug. 3, 2017, https://www.nytimes.com/2017/08/03/opinion/weakening-college-sex-assault-policies.html (stating that by pursuing more criminal charges for sexual assault cases, the burden of proof on the plaintiff will increase, thus creating a lower chance of conviction for a rapist).

56. *See* Bradshaw v. Rawlings, 612 F.2d 135, 138 (3d Cir. 1979) ("[M]odern American college is not an insurer of the safety of its students. Whatever may have been its respon-

Finally, as with the defense raised by national organizations with respect to their agency relationship with locals, the landscape for claims involving schools is mixed. In *Coughlan v. Beta Theta Pi*,[57] the court noted that liability could attach if the university assumed a duty of care as evidenced by efforts to actively prevent hazing. For example, a school that sent its own employees to supervise a fraternity party at which serious injuries occurred may be found to have assumed a duty of care for those in attendance at the event. Even repeatedly communicating with fraternal locals about rules and possible sanctions for hazing infractions could give rise to a finding that the school voluntarily assumed a duty of care for those injured by hazing.[58]

Finally, as with any successful claim of vicarious liability, a plaintiff who was hazed needs to show that the student who hazed and caused harm to another was acting within the scope of plausible employment with the school.[59]

b. Homeowners' Liability

When plaintiffs pursue individual chapter officers and members, a defendant's parents' homeowners' coverage is typically implicated. Efforts to obtain defense and settlement costs via parents' coverage have

---

sibility in an earlier era, the authoritarian role of today's college administrations has been notably diluted in recent decades."); *see also* Rabel v. Ill. Wesleyan Univ., 514 N.E.2d 552, 560–61 (Ill. App. Ct. 1987) (finding no custodial relationship existed between the university and a student suing for injuries related to a fraternal prank and stating "the university's responsibility to its students, as an institution of higher education, is to properly educate them. It would be unrealistic to impose upon a university the additional role of custodian over its adult students and to charge it with the responsibility for assuring their safety").

57. Coughlan v. Beta Theta Pi Fraternity, 987 P.2d 300, 312 (Idaho 1999) (citations omitted) (finding allegations supported an inference that the university assumed a duty to exercise reasonable care because university employees knew of Beta Theta Pi serving alcohol to underage students and knew or should have known Coughlan was intoxicated).

58. *See* Furek v. Univ. of Del., 594 A.2d 506, 520 (Del. 1991) (finding that a University's hazing policy and communication of that policy to fraternities constitute an assumed duty of the safety of the University's students).

59. *See* Yost v. Wabash Coll., 3 N.E.3d 509, 519 (Ind. 2014) (rejecting a vicarious liability theory for the university because the mere contention that "Wabash benefits from the presence of fraternities on campus" is not sufficient evidence that the local fraternity is a representative of the university itself).

resulted in a range of outcomes that are not easily categorized. To understand this landscape, it is important to recall that homeowners' third-party liability coverage almost never covers intentional torts, and that coverage typically extends only to regular members of the household. A tortfeasor-student needs to show that he or she qualifies as an insured under the policy. Many policies do cover college-age offspring until they graduate even if they do not live at home.[60] If the student is covered by their parents' policy, then the remaining hurdle is the standard exclusion for intentional acts that cause harm. Often insurers will provide a defense under a reservation of rights letter but refuse to indemnify on the grounds that the conduct in question is explicitly excluded.

Consider for example, *Nationwide Gen. Ins. v. DiBileo*,[61] which involved a dispute between the homeowners' carrier of the parents of the young defendants in the notorious *Piazza* suit.[62] Nationwide insured defendant students in the *Piazza* case via policies issued to their parents. In search of a declaratory judgment that it had no duty to defend the *Piazza* defendants, Nationwide asserted that because the events leading up to Piazza's death constituted a criminal act, physical abuse, and or an intentional act, its duty to defend was foreclosed. The court disagreed, noting that some of the allegations arising out of the tragic events involved claims of negligence that Nationwide was contractually committed to defend. ("It was plausibly pleaded that [defendants] assumed a

---

60. *See* Kimzey, *supra* note 3, at 483.

61. Nationwide Gen. Ins. Co. v. DiBileo, 550 F. Supp. 3d 205, 213 (M.D. Pa. 2021).

62. Piazza v. Young, 403 F. Supp. 3d 421 (M.D. Pa. 2019). The facts in *Piazza v. Young* were widely reported in the national media and generated much discussion about whether and how to punish fraternity members who compelled others to drink to excess and how to compensate victims of hazing. In *Piazza,* one of the pledges who consumed prodigious quantities of alcohol died after hours of neglect by fraternity members. *See* Julia Jacobs, *Ex-Fraternity Member at Penn State is First to Plead Guilty in Hazing Death of Timothy Piazza*, N.Y. TIMES (June 13, 2018), https://www.nytimes.com/2018/06/13/us/fraternity-death-penn-state.html; *see also* Douglas Belkin, *Colleges Team Up for Report Card on Fraternities to Curb Bad Behavior*, WALL ST. J. (June 15, 2018, 4:40 PM), https://www.wsj.com/articles/colleges-team-up-for-report-card-on-fraternities-to-curb-bad-behavior-1529095209; *see also* Susan Svrluga, *'Hit Them in Their Heart': These Parents Lost Kids to Hazing. They're Trying to Make Sure it Doesn't Happen Again*, WASH. POST (Nov. 3, 2019, 6:58 PM), https://www.washingtonpost.com/local/education/hit-them-in-their-heart-these-parents-lost-kids-to-hazing-theyre-trying-to-make-sure-it-doesnt-happen-again/2019/11/03/1426660e-ead5-11e9-85c0-85a098e47b37_story.html.

duty of care and then breached it by failing to get professional medical aid [for Mr. Piazza].")[63]

It is well established that "mixed" complaints—i.e., those alleging a mix of excluded and covered claims—will generally trigger an insurer's duty to defend. With respect to the narrower duty to indemnify, an insurer will generally avoid liability for damages if the facts adduced at trial support a finding of criminal, intentional, or abusive conduct that is excluded by the policy.[64]

In other cases, courts have taken a rather narrow view of "intentional act" which made it virtually impossible for the homeowners' insurer to enforce its exclusion. In a particularly egregious case out of New York, David Massa, an intoxicated college student, threw a 55-gallon oil drum out of a fraternity house window which struck and injured another student below.[65] The injured student sued alleging negligence (it goes without saying that an allegation of negligence as opposed to intentional misconduct is most likely to trigger coverage and is therefore likely to be the one issue on which tort victim and tortfeasor agree). The New York court concluded that the homeowner's policy exclusion for intentional acts did not bar coverage in this case because:

> The evidence does not conclusively establish that anyone was directly below the window when plaintiff looked outside, that he saw anyone below, or that he knew there was anyone there when he pushed or threw the drum outside. Therefore, there is a possible basis for a factual determination that, from plaintiff's point of view, it was unexpected, unintended, and unforeseen that the drum would strike someone ...[66]

Similarly, in *Admiral Ins. Co. v. Anderson*,[67] an Illinois court concluded that, while a close question, the hazing alleged by the family of a young woman seeking to join a sorority (which resulted in her suicide)

---

63. *DiBileo*, 550 F. Supp. 3d at 213.

64. For a good discussion of this common problem, see, for example, Outboard Marine Corp. v. Liberty Mut. Ins. Co., 607 N.E.2d 1204, 1220 (Ill. 1992). *See generally* KENNETH S. ABRAHAM & DANIEL SCHWARCZ, INSURANCE LAW AND REGULATION 615–26 (7th ed. 2020).

65. Massa v. Nationwide Mut. Fire Ins. Co., 904 N.Y.S.2d 531 (App. Div. 2010).

66. *Id.* at 1663.

67. Admiral Ins. Co. v. Anderson, 529 F. Supp. 3d 804 (N.D. Ill. 2021).

was clearly excluded; however, because other counts in the complaint appeared to allege negligence acts, they could "potentially seek recovery for covered losses."[68]

Clearly the optimal strategy for a defendant seeking coverage under a parent's policy is to insist that the complaint, at least in part, tells a story rooted in negligence. Oddly enough, this approach is also optimal for plaintiffs hoping to force parents/insureds of tortfeasors to pay for the harm caused by their offspring. If throwing a barrel out a window onto the street below is not a clearly intentional act likely to cause harm, then the value of contract exclusions for intentional torts is hard to identify.[69]

When decisions like *Bogenberger* and *Mynhardt* effectively insulate nationals and colleges and cutoff liability for harm caused by officers and members of fraternal groups, we should expect to see defendants turn to the lone remaining source of coverage—homeowner's products. Should this trend away from hard-to-enforce conduct-based exclusions grow, categorical exclusions—e.g., for offspring over the age of 18 unless they reside at home—are likely to become more attractive to insurers.

VI. A Word on Criminal Liability

Even a casual review of the facts in hazing, sexual assault, and alcohol consumption-resulting-in-death cases suggests that criminal prosecution must sometimes be top of mind. Many states have now formally criminalized hazing by statute.[70] From time to time, perpetrators of especially vicious acts of hazing and sexual assault are charged criminally, and the facts in these cases are often horrific. For example, in the *Piazza* case, several fraternity members were charged with involuntary man-

---

68. *Id.* at 812.

69. *See* McCormick, *supra* note 14; *see also* Anderson Cooper, *How Hazing Led to the Death of Fraternity Pledge Sam Martinez*, CBS News (Nov. 18, 2021, 6:57 PM) (quoting Jolayne Holtz, mother of Sam Martinez), https://www.cbsnews.com/news/sam-martinez-hazing-washington-state-university-death-60-minutes-2021-11-28/ ("They set themselves up to ensure that if something goes wrong, that they can't be held accountable. And they'll point to the rogue fraternity members or they'll point to the university or they'll point at the young dead pledge and blame them, but it's never their fault.").

70. Parks & Grindell, *supra* note 24, at 652–53.

slaughter.[71] Recently, five men convicted in connection with the hazing death of a Bowling Green State University student were sentenced in Ohio[72]. The facts of the case are remarkably like those surrounding Timothy Piazza's death. The Ohio police investigating the case noted that "several of the fraternity members lied to investigators and destroyed both physical and electronic evidence."

Perhaps the most remarkable feature of this criminal case (a civil action against Bowling Green is pending) is the short jail sentences meted out to all defendants, who ranged in age from 20 to 22. The maximum sentence imposed by the Ohio court was a mere 28 days, although the fraternity officers and members pled to, inter alia, reckless homicide, hazing, and tampering with evidence. The sentencing guidelines in Ohio for reckless homicide (a third-degree felony) call for anywhere between nine to 36 months of incarceration.[73]

In a case that garnered significant attention in Pennsylvania, Chun Hsien Deng (known as "Michael") died while vacationing with fraternity brothers who engaged in a form of hazing known as the "glass ceiling."[74] Blindfolded and placed in freezing temperatures, Michael was beaten. Fraternity members never sought medical attention for him, and he died the next day. In a remarkable turn of events, the national organization of Pi Delta Psi was charged criminally with aggravated assault and involuntary manslaughter. Pi Delta Psi was banned from Pennsylvania for 10 years and ordered to pay more than $112,000 in fines.[75]

Criminal consequences for national organizations remain rare but are probably indicative of rising public exasperation with fraternal

---

71. Sheryl Gay Stolberg, *18 Penn State Students Charged in Fraternity Death*, N.Y. TIMES (May 5, 2017), https://www.nytimes.com/2017/05/05/us/penn-state-fraternity-death-timothy-piazza.html (eight students charged with involuntary manslaughter).

72. Livia Albeck-Ripka, *Bowling Green Fraternity Brothers Sentenced in Hazing Death of Student*, N.Y. TIMES (June 16, 2022), https://www.nytimes.com/2022/06/16/us/ohio-hazing-death-sentence.html.

73. OHIO REV. CODE ANN. §2903.041 (West 2022). Third-degree felonies ordinarily have prison terms ranging from nine to thirty-six months unless they are an explicitly listed felony, which reckless homicide and fraternal hazing are not. *See* OHIO REV. CODE ANN. §29.2914 (West 2022).

74. Jeremy Bauer-Wolf, *Statewide Ban on a Fraternity*, INSIDE HIGHER ED (Jan. 8, 2018), https://www.insidehighered.com/news/2018/01/09/after-hazing-death-fraternity-banned-pennsylvania-10-years.

75. *Id.*

conduct that causes great harm and seems to resist all serious efforts to reduce or eliminate it. Should criminal prosecutions of nationals and/or locals become more common for hazing and other harms caused by student officers and members of fraternal groups, we might expect to see less emphasis on liability coverage, at least where the state can prove intent as an element of the alleged offense. Of course, the goals of the criminal justice system are quite different from those of civil courts. The prospect of short criminal sentences, though, may further encourage surviving family members to pursue civil remedies as an additional punishment.[76]

VII. Conclusion

Insurance doctrine necessarily sits at the intersection of the social function of insurance with its powerful ability to discourage socially undesirable conduct—e.g., drunk driving, poor upkeep of property, negligent supervision of minor children, and all manner of reckless behaviors—and respect for written contract terms. Parties to a contract of insurance often consist of a sophisticated drafter who is intimately fa-

---

76. *See Brown*, 2015 ME at ¶ 30–31, 118 A.3d at 796 (reversing summary judgment for Delta Tau Delta on basis of premise liability because "[I]t is certainly foreseeable that turning a fraternity house over to college students, where parties and alcohol-related events are likely to occur, creates the potential for sexual misconduct."); *see also* Jones v. Pi Kappa Alpha Int'l Fraternity, Inc., 431 F. Supp. 3d 518, 527–30 (D.N.J. 2019) (stating that it would be plausible that an agency relationship did exist between the national, local chapter, and individual defendants to bring about a case of negligent supervision resulting in sexual assault because the national chapter had known about previous incidents of sexual assault and the lack of intervention by individual defendants was the proximate cause of the plaintiff's assault); *see also* State v. Petagine, 290 So. 3d 991, 994 (Fla. Dist. Ct. App. 2020) (holding the state provided sufficient evidence to charge the president of Pi Kappa Phi at Florida State University with felony hazing because the president attended meetings where the dangers of pledges becoming intoxicated were discussed, yet he encouraged the event to happen); *see also* State v. Brown, 630 N.E.2d 397, 400 (Ohio Ct. App. 1993) (affirming conviction of defendant for complicity to haze and complicity to assault for paddling new initiates which resulted in 210 days of jail time and a $250 fine); *see also* Doe v. Brown Univ., 304 F. Supp. 3d 252, 263–64 (D.R.I. 2018) (citing *Brown*, 2015 ME at ¶ 30–31, 118 A.3d at 796) (finding that the court should follow previous rulings which have stated that "[N]ational fraternity had duty of care where it is certainly foreseeable that turning a fraternity house over to college students, where parties and alcohol-related events are likely to occur, creates the potential for sexual misconduct—a known safety issue on college campuses.").

miliar with all its terms, and an inexperienced insured who admittedly has done little or nothing to become informed about the scope of coverage or pertinent exclusions. The enduring impulse to ensure a source of compensation for tort injuries and the desire of insurers to reduce the likelihood of injury is in permanent tension in most cases involving fraternal organizations. No one favors more underage drinking, inappropriate or criminal sexual conduct, or hazing rituals that involve a high likelihood of injury or death. At the same time, most are reluctant to see courts effectively rewrite or ignore contract language that private parties have agreed to and paid for.

This tension explains the current state of the law with respect to liability coverage for local chapters, national organizations, institutions of higher learning, and parents' homeowners' policies. On the one hand, national fraternities and sororities seem to be very cognizant of increasing societal hostility toward certain behaviors—especially with respect to sexual misconduct. Indeed, the nationals' focus on education of local chapter leaders and the structure of their insurance contracts reveals an acute awareness of the highly risky behavior of at least some local members. The risk is apparently so great that the contract exclusions and coverage definitions, together, can only be read as anticipating the kinds of tragic injuries sustained in cases like *Piazza*, *Ballou*, and *Bogenberger*.

Despite what appear to be at least nominally sincere efforts to educate chapter locals, the approach of the nationals and their insurers simultaneously suggests a degree of futility and resignation. The nationals seem to understand that the power of insurance to deter undesirable conduct on the part of college students is not as great as one might hope. Some of this failure is no doubt due to the youth and inexperience of student members. Some is also possibly a function of the disconnect between the educational materials and the unspoken "good times" promised to pledges who make it to full membership. To succeed in substantially reducing or eliminating the kinds of risky behavior that get locals into serious trouble might require changing the very nature of the fraternal experience. If drinking, hazing, and other kinds of civil and criminal misbehavior *are the point,* then nothing in an insurance contract can be expected to reduce or eliminate the behavior except possibly the eradication of the organizations themselves.

The persistent loyalty and commitment of many members to their fraternal groups makes their disappearance unlikely, and possibly even undesirable.

PART THREE:
CONSTITUTIONAL ISSUES

CHAPTER 10

First Amendment Law: Freedom of Speech

Glenn Harlan Reynolds

The issue of free speech on campus has come up often in recent years. In assessing this debate as it affects fraternities and sororities, there are several overall issues to keep in mind. First, public universities are directly subject to the Constitution, while private universities are not. Second, there are important distinctions between First Amendment rules and more general free speech rules and norms. Third, regardless of the Constitution, many universities, both public and private, are bound by free speech policies that they have individually adopted, or that are imposed by accreditors. And finally, members of fraternities and sororities enjoy the same rights as other members of the university community, as do the organizations themselves, though they may be subject to some limits in exchange for official recognition. Though these facts have generated some resistance from university students and administrators, federal courts have been quite consistent in maintaining the rights of free speech on campus over several decades. Students, of course, may still face administrative harassment that can be quite intimidating for those unwilling or unable to file suit, and they also face intense peer pressure, for which the law provides somewhat less in the way of remedies, though perhaps more than is commonly believed. These issues will be discussed further in this chapter.

I. Some History

In the early days of American colleges and universities, modern concepts of free speech on campus were unknown. Higher education, in those days, was intended largely for the indoctrination of clergymen, with a sideline in providing a degree of polish to the sons (never daughters) of the rich and the powerful.[1]

As things progressed, general American concepts of free speech began to apply on campus as well, though these were more a matter of administrative tolerance than of law. First Amendment law was in its infancy, and prior to the rise of the incorporation doctrine in the mid-20th century, the Bill of Rights, including the First Amendment, was not applicable to the states at all,[2] meaning that there was no First Amendment protection for speech on the campuses of state universities, as there was no protection from state interference with free speech anywhere. And private universities, then as now, were not subject to the First Amendment at all.

With the arrival of the 20th century, notions of academic freedom and free speech began to take hold. Professors, who in most cases had served at pleasure, started to come under a tenure system that promoted academic freedom.[3] Organizations like the American Association of University Professors and the American Civil Liberties Union took an

---

1. GLENN HARLAN REYNOLDS, THE NEW SCHOOL 9–12 (2014) (outlining history of higher education in America).

2. The Supreme Court declared in Barron v. Baltimore, 32 U.S. 243 (1833) that the Bill of Rights applies only to the federal government. In the mid-20th century, the Court began finding that certain rights protected in the Bill of Rights apply to the states because they are "incorporated" in the notion of liberty embodied in the Fourteenth Amendment's command that states not deprive citizens of liberty without due process of law. U.S. CONST. AMEND XIV. Though this process has been described as "selective incorporation," at this point the vast majority of Bill of Rights protections have been incorporated against the states via the Court's 14th Amendment jurisprudence. The First Amendment's protections of free speech, assembly, and press were among the first to be so incorporated and have been among the rights most strongly protected against state interference by the Supreme Court and lower federal courts.

3. ERWIN CHEMERINSKY & HOWARD GILLMAN, FREE SPEECH ON CAMPUS 52–62 (2017); Jonathan Turley, *Harm and Hegemony: The Decline of Free Speech in the United States*, 45 HARV. J. L. & PUB. POL'Y 571 (2022), https://www.harvard-jlpp.com/wp-content/uploads/sites/21/2022/07/TURLEY_VOL45_ISS2.pdf (both summarizing rise and decline of free speech thought in American academia).

active role in promoting freedom of speech and thought on campus.[4] Additionally, the courts began to attach importance to expressive freedoms in general, particularly to the rights of both professors and students to speak freely on matters of public importance.[5]

In the 1960s, the Civil Rights movement bolstered the case for free speech on and off campus. Segregationists like Bull Connor, George Wallace, and Lester Maddox tried to silence their opponents by using both the law and extralegal violence, violence that was then winked at by authorities who pretended to be unable to control public passions. It was obvious that the good guys were not the people trying to censor political speech.

Meanwhile on campus, the Berkeley Free Speech Movement became a rallying point for student activists across the nation. Around 1970, there was a widespread consensus that free speech was good, and that free speech for everyone could only be protected and maintained if there was free speech even for groups or individuals that many disliked or regarded as dangerous. Thus, when Nazis planned a march in Skokie, Illinois, the American Civil Liberties Union sided with their free speech rights, and so did the courts.[6]

But a backlash was already brewing. The rise of Title VII and Title IX regimes began to produce a sort of "HR culture" on campuses in which anything that might upset someone was scrutinized as possibly creating a "hostile environment."[7] Feminist theorists like Catharine MacKinnon and Andrea Dworkin treated free speech as a fundamentally oppressive male construct.[8] Critical legal studies scholars and their offshoots in Critical Race Theory took a similar line on speech and race.

---

4. *Id.* at 59–61.

5. *See, e.g.*, Keyishian v. Board of Regents, 385 U.S. 589 (1967) (invalidating anti-communist loyalty oath for state university faculty); sources cited *supra* note 3.

6. Philippa Strum, When The Nazis Came to Skokie: Freedom for Speech We Hate (1999).

7. *See* Gail Heriot, *The Roots of Wokeness: Title VII Damage Remedies as Potential Drivers of Attitudes Toward Identity Politics and Free Expression*, Tex. Rev. L. & Pol. (forthcoming), https://papers.ssrn.com/sol3/papers.cfm?abstract_id=4034768.

8. *See e.g.*, Catharine MacKinnon, *Not A Moral Issue*, 2 Yale L. & Pol'y Rev. 321 (1984) (First Amendment should not trump regulation of pornography because pornography harms women); *compare* Thomas Emerson, *Pornography and the First Amendment: A Reply to Professor MacKinnon*, 3 Yale L. & Pol'y Rev. 120 (1984) (defending traditional First Amendment doctrine).

By the 1980s, campuses were enacting "speech codes" that purported to ban speech deemed "harmful" or "offensive." These codes made no effort to fit within the traditional First Amendment and free speech doctrines. As a result, they consistently lost when challenged in court. Unpersuaded by the various forms of new scholarship, federal courts applied existing free speech doctrine and pronounced these codes inconsistent, illegal, and unconstitutional.[9]

By the turn of the 21st century, colleges and universities had largely given up on promulgating speech codes, but years later, in the 2010s, such efforts began to appear again. Worse yet, many schools did not even adopt codes, but began subjecting speakers they disliked to arbitrary administrative actions rooted in vague terms like "harm," or "our values" that could be (and were) interpreted in whatever fashion was convenient at the time. The in terrorem impact of such arbitrariness seemed to be entirely intentional.

This legal landscape regarding speech on campus continues into the present day. In many states, there are blooming legislative efforts to restrict censorship by university administrations, at least at state universities. Numerous states have passed laws banning the establishment of policies limiting campus free speech to designated "free speech zones," often under substantial restrictions.[10] Others have gone further, passing laws guaranteeing free speech in general on campus to both students and professors.[11] There have also been calls for Congress to amend the

---

9. CHEMERINSKY & GILLMAN, *supra* note 3, at 682–83.

10. *See e.g.*, FIRE, *Florida becomes ninth state to ban restrictive campus free speech zones* (Mar. 12, 2018), https://www.thefire.org/florida-becomes-ninth-state-to-ban-restrictive-campus-free-speech-zones/.

11. *See e.g.*, Heather Duncan, *Tennessee legislators craft a campus free-speech law that actually protects free speech*, KNOXVILLE MERCURY, May 24, 2017 ("The 'Campus Free Speech Protection Act,' sponsored by two Knoxville-area legislators, forbids public colleges from corralling student demonstrators into a 'free speech zone;' disinviting a controversial speaker scheduled by a student or faculty member (or charging a student group unusual security fees to host one); denying funding to student groups based on the viewpoints they promote; or firing professors for controversial statements made in class.... The law states that the campus is 'a marketplace of ideas for all students and all faculty, in which the free exchange of ideas is not to be suppressed because the ideas put forth are thought by some—or even by most—members of the institution's community to be offensive, unwise, immoral, indecent, disagreeable, conservative, liberal, traditional, radical, or wrong-headed.'"); *see also* Kimberly Hale, *Campus Free Speech in Texas*, ACCESSIBLE LAW, Dec. 4, 2019 ("The Campus Free Speech Bill affects Texas's public universities

federal Higher Education Act to provide increased protection for free speech on campus, following efforts by the Trump Administration to do so via executive order.[12]

Beyond these legislative efforts, there are growing efforts on the part of free-speech activists to use existing laws to push back against university attempts at curtailing student speech. And where—as is often the case when fraternities or sororities are involved—those efforts at curtailing speech involve gender discrimination or stereotyping, activists are increasingly using the powerful tools offered by Title IX.[13] (Even where a complaint to the Department of Education under Title IX does not result in action against a college or university, the resulting investigation

---

by increasing free speech protections for any person engaging in expressive activities on campus. "Expressive activities" include protesting, giving (and listening to) speeches, distributing flyers and pamphlets, carrying signs, and circulating petitions. The law designates the common outdoor areas of university campuses as traditional public forums, which are areas that are typically open to the public for political speech and debate, for example, a public park, street, or sidewalk. The new designation will be an adjustment because, prior to the Campus Free Speech Bill, universities were generally designated as limited public forums, which meant that universities could limit the subject matter or content of the speech (e.g., all political or religious speech), as well as the speaker (e.g., all non-university affiliated members). Now, however, the Campus Free Speech Bill permits any person—not only university-affiliated members—to freely engage in expressive activities on campus without the need to first ask the university for permission to do so. The law also aims to expand protections for student groups and faculty members who wish to invite outside guests to speak on campus.") (citations omitted).

12. Rachelle Peterson, *To Protect Free Speech On Campuses, President Trump Needs More Than An Executive Order*, THE FEDERALIST, March 28, 2019 ("The Higher Education Act is the best vehicle to protect freedom of speech. As a statute, it is more permanent than an executive order. As the gateway to federal student aid, the lifeblood of all but a handful of colleges and universities, it holds great sway over higher education. The Higher Education Act already has, in §1011a, a strong statement in support of free speech and religious freedom on campus. It declares that 'an institution of higher education should facilitate the free and open exchange of ideas' and that 'students should not be intimidated, harassed, discouraged from speaking out, or discriminated against.' Currently the law includes no enforcement mechanism. It merely declares that colleges 'should not' permit such harassment, discrimination, or other threats to free speech and intellectual freedom. It has no means to hold colleges accountable when they permit—or even sponsor—such discrimination.").

13. *See* Glenn Harlan Reynolds, *Bros Are People Too*, USA TODAY, May 23, 2017, https://www.usatoday.com/story/opinion/2017/05/23/universities-have-become-hostile-to-men-glenn-reynolds-column/102015432/ (listing examples of gender stereotypes aimed at male students and fraternities on campus).

can be tedious, stressful, and sometimes expensive. The process, as they say, is often the punishment.) In addition, federal courts, displaying a degree of impatience, are beginning to pierce the "qualified immunity" veil to find university officials personally liable for damages when they violate the free speech rights of students.[14]

Generally speaking, government officials, including public university administrators, benefit from qualified immunity when sued. Sometimes called "good faith immunity," this protects them from personal liability unless they violate a clearly established constitutional right. The problem for university administrators is that free-speech rights on campus are clearly established, meaning that they are increasingly facing potential personal liability. University of North Texas administrators, for example, punished math professor Nathaniel Hiers for criticizing the concept of "microaggressions," then pleaded qualified immunity when sued. The District Court rejected that claim, finding that "any reasonable university official would have known that it was unconstitutional to discontinue his employment because of his speech."[15] Likewise, California State University's Chancellor and CSU-San Marcos President Karen Haynes were denied qualified immunity for discriminating against a campus pro-life group because of its views. The District Court noted that there was clear precedent on hand: "The judge noted the Southworth ruling

---

14. *See* Hiers v. Bd. of Regents, 4:20-CV-321-SDJ (E.D. TX , Mar. 11, 2022) https://adflegal.org/sites/default/files/2022-03/Hiers-v-The-Board-of-Regents-of-the-University-of-North-Texas-System-2022-03-11-Opinion.pdf.

15. Hiers v. Bd. of Regents, 4:20-CV-321-SDJ (E.D. TX , Mar. 11, 2022) https://adflegal.org/sites/default/files/2022-03/Hiers-v-The-Board-of-Regents-of-the-University-of-North-Texas-System-2022-03-11-Opinion.pdf; *See also* Greg Piper, *College officials can be personally liable for firing professor in free speech case, judge rules*, JUST THE NEWS, March 16, 2022, https://justthenews.com/nation/free-speech/judge-strips-immunity-college-officials-firing-professor-critical?utm_source=daily&utm_medium=email&utm_campaign=newsletter. ("University of North Texas officials should have known that math professor Nathaniel Hiers' speech 'touched on a matter of public concern and that discontinuing his employment because of his speech violated the First Amendment,' U.S. District Judge Sean Jordan wrote in a 69-page memorandum and order Friday. He refused to grant qualified immunity to UNT officials who allegedly retaliated against Hiers in 2019 for writing 'Don't leave garbage lying around' on a faculty lounge chalkboard above a stack of flyers, not sanctioned by UNT, explaining microaggressions.... Student, faculty and community litigants have targeted qualified immunity for university and K-12 officials, from volleyball coaches to school board members, in several speech-related lawsuits in recent years.").

from 2000 concerned conduct 'identical to the challenged conduct here,' and the 9th U.S. Circuit Court of Appeals—which governs CSUSM—adopted the 'unbridled discretion' standard in 2012."[16] Twice in one year, the US Court of Appeals for the Eighth Circuit denied qualified immunity to University of Iowa officials who discriminated against Christian student groups.[17]

This chapter will discuss existing legal protections for free speech on campus, the limits thereto, and the way those tend to play off where Greek life is involved. It will also offer some suggestions for future actions and changes. It seems likely that we are in for much more action on this front.

II. The Rules

Free speech doesn't mean that campus officials have no power to regulate what is said. In fact, they have considerable powers within the limits imposed by the Constitution.

Among other things, campus officials can require that courses taught on campus reflect the subject matter intended to be taught: a course on metallurgical engineering, for example, must be taught on metallurgical engineering, not the threat posed by the Illuminati. Likewise, universi-

---

16. Greg Piper, *Pro-life students win lawsuit against public university for biased funding process*, THE COLLEGE FIX, Aug. 15, 2019.

17. Greg Piper, *Appeals court strips legal immunity from college officials—again—for anti-Christian bias*, JUST THE NEWS, July 16, 2021, https://justthenews.com/government/courts-law/appeals-court-strips-legal-immunity-college-officials-again-anti-christian ("For the second time this year, the 8th U.S. Circuit Court of Appeals has ruled against the University of Iowa for discriminating against a Christian student club. The Friday ruling upheld a district court's decision to strip legal immunity from university officials for derecognizing InterVarsity Christian Fellowship following a 2018 injunction involving another Christian group.... 'Employees of the University of Iowa targeted religious student organizations for discriminatory enforcement of its Human Rights Policy,' an action that was 'clearly unconstitutional,' Judge Jonathan Kobes wrote for the unanimous three-judge panel. They simultaneously 'carv[ed] out exemptions and ignor[ed] other violative groups with missions they presumably supported,' he wrote, either turning 'a blind eye to decades of First Amendment jurisprudence '"or proceeding 'full speed ahead knowing they were violating the law.' The panel wasn't convinced by the university's argument that officials made a good-faith error in elevating antidiscrimination principles over the First Amendment.").

ties may require that professors and students interact in a courteous and professional fashion. Although profane and abusive language in public settings is protected by the First Amendment,[18] universities may ban such language in classrooms and other academic settings. And both student and faculty work may be judged on what is said, so long as the judgment is done according to professional, rather than purely political standards.[19] As Cass Sunstein writes, "The university can impose subject-matter or other restrictions on speech only to the extent that the restrictions are closely related to its educational mission."[20]

One argument for more extensive regulation is often found in the form of statements to the effect that "hate speech isn't free speech." This statement, however, has found no support in the courts. "Hate speech" is a legally undefined term, meaning no more than speech that the term's user hates. The Supreme Court has consistently found that speech that people don't like, find offensive, or are upset by, is not thereby deprived of its First Amendment protection.[21]

As Erwin Chemerinsky and Howard Gillman wrote:

> Many prominent scholars have argued that hate speech conveys nothing useful to the marketplace of ideas, and by silencing its victims, it limits the exchange of ideas and undermines a university's obligation to provide all students with an environment conducive to learning. In the 1990s, persuaded by the powerful arguments for its regulation, over 350 colleges

---

18. *See e.g.*, Cohen v. California, 403 U.S. 15 (1971) (jacket reading "Fuck the Draft" protected by First Amendment against charges of indecency, offensiveness, etc.).

19. This summary is taken from CHEMERINSKY & GILLMAN, *supra* note 3, at 65–70.

20. CASS R. SUNSTEIN, ACADEMIC FREEDOM AND THE LAW: LIBERALISM, SPEECH CODES, AND RELATED PROBLEMS, IN THE FUTURE OF ACADEMIC FREEDOM 107 (Louis Menand, ed., 2017).

21. *See* Matal v. Tam, 582 U.S. 218 (2017) ("Those few categories of speech that the government can regulate or punish—for instance, fraud, defamation, or incitement—are well established within our constitutional tradition. *See* U.S. v. Stevens, 559 U. S. 460, 468 (2010). Aside from these and a few other narrow exceptions, it is a fundamental principle of the First Amendment that the government may not punish or suppress speech based on disapproval of the ideas or perspectives the speech conveys.... Indeed, a speech burden based on audience reactions is simply government hostility and intervention in a different guise.") (Kennedy, J., concurring). *See also* Texas v. Johnson, 491 U.S. 397 (1989) (Serious offensiveness inherent in burning a flag not a justification for criminalizing flag-burning.)

and universities adopted codes restricting hate speech. But every court to consider such a code declared it unconstitutional. In this matter we side with the courts; though the advocates of restricting hate speech are motivated by the best intentions, speech cannot and should not be prohibited for expressing hate. We strongly agree with the need to create a conducive learning environment for all students, but there is simply no way to regulate hate speech without censoring ideas. That is never permissible on college campuses.[22]

Chemerinsky and Gillman are correct, but perhaps too generous. It is possible that the advocates of restricting hate speech are indeed motivated by the "best intentions," but that assumes facts not in evidence. It is equally possible that they are driven by a desire to silence views with which they disagree and are simply using a concern for a "conducive learning environment" as an excuse. Even the term "hate" is flexibly defined. One is quite safe on campus addressing hateful language to Republicans, white cis males, pro-lifers, and other groups disfavored by the campus zeitgeist. On the other hand, exquisite sensitivity is deployed when people criticize those views, and groups, which are viewed more favorably by those in power. Without a neutral definition—and, even scarcer, a neutral application—of "hate," hate speech regulations are inevitably going to have a one-sided impact.

As the Supreme Court said in *West Virginia v. Barnette*, "If there is any fixed star in our constitutional constellation, it is that no official, high or petty, can prescribe what shall be orthodox in politics, nationalism, religion, or other matters of opinion, or force citizens to confess by word or act their faith therein."[23] This means that public universities are not free to prescribe acceptable views, whether on politics, race, religion, sex, nor may they punish views they deem unacceptable. At question in *Barnette* was a mandatory flag salute and pledge of allegiance for schoolchildren. In modern universities, it's more likely to be a mandatory pledge of allegiance to diversity doctrine or "anti-racism." In either case, public officials who attempt to mandate views, statements, or affirma-

---

22. CHEMERINSKY & GILLMAN, *supra* note 3, at 82–83.
23. W. Va. State Bd. of Educ. v. Barnette, 319 U.S. 624, 642 (1943).

tions of faith are stepping over the line. This is true whether the requirements are aimed at students in general, or at fraternities and sororities.

Even patently offensive messages are protected by the First Amendment. Periodically, fraternities are sanctioned for members who wear blackface, or hold "ugly woman" contests, and the like; such sanctions then routinely fail when challenged on First Amendment grounds.[24] Whatever message the university wants to send, and whatever environment it is attempting to establish, the First Amendment bars the use of censorship and punishment to shut down disapproved messages.

Efforts to sidestep this rule by simply declaring offensive views "violence" are popular but fail in court. The Constitution distinguishes between speech and violence, and speech is tantamount to violence in only a few circumstances. So-called "true threats"—in which a particular person is credibly threatened with imminent violence—fall outside the First Amendment.[25] But statements like the Marxist phrase, "Come the revolution, you'll be first against the wall" are not imminent enough, and the Supreme Court has recognized that "mere political hyperbole" does not constitute a true threat.[26] Advocates of the "speech as violence" trope also often cite the "fighting words" doctrine of *Chaplinsky v. New Hampshire*.[27] But the *Chaplinsky* rule applies only to what John Hart Ely called "a quite unambiguous invitation to a brawl[.]"[28] In fact, the *Chaplinsky* rule has never been used to uphold a speech regulation since *Chaplinsky* itself was decided. "Incitement" is another exception, but again, it is quite limited. In *Brandenburg v. Ohio*,[29] the Court held that to be charged

---

24. *See, e.g.*, Michele N.K. Collison, *Judge Cites First-Amendment Protection in Overturning Suspension of Fraternity*, CHRONICLE OF HIGHER EDUCATION, September 4, 1991, https://www.chronicle.com/article/judge-cites-first-amendment-protection-in-overturning-suspension-of-fraternity/; Joshua Rhett Miller, *College Won't Punish Students for Blackface Photo, Citing First Amendment*, N. Y. POST, Sept. 12, 2019, https://nypost.com/2019/09/12/college-wont-punish-students-for-blackface-photo-citing-first-amendment/.

25. *See* Virginia v. Black, 538 U.S. 343, 359–360 (2003) (describing true threats doctrine) ("'True threats' encompass those statements where the speaker means to communicate a serious expression of an intent to commit an act of unlawful violence to a particular individual or group of individuals.")

26. Watts v. U.S., 394 U.S. 705, 708 (1969).

27. 315 U.S. 568 (1942).

28. JOHN HART ELY, DEMOCRACY AND DISTRUST 114 (1980).

29. 395 U.S. 444 (1969).

with incitement, the speaker must intend to promote, and must be likely to succeed in promoting, imminent lawless action. Very few (if any) of the campus statements that are tarred as "violence" fall under any of these narrow exceptions.

III. Legal Actions over Free Speech

When people are deprived of free speech, the remedy is generally via a lawsuit. The most common sort of action growing out of campus free speech violations is a so-called "1983 action" after 42 U.S.C. § 1983. Section 1983 allows a civil lawsuit against:

> every person who, under color of any statute, ordinance, regulation, custom, or usage, of any State or Territory or the District of Columbia, subjects, or causes to be subjected, any citizen of the United States or other person within the jurisdiction thereof to the deprivation of any rights, privileges, or immunities secured by the Constitution and laws" of the United States.[30]

The "under color of" state law language has been interpreted to require state action to make out a violation. As a result, while state universities are vulnerable to suit under this statute, private universities are not. State sovereign immunity is abrogated (overridden) by this statute, though certain official immunity doctrines—most significantly "qualified immunity" for government officials, which includes state university officials—remain. However, courts seem increasingly willing to deny officials' claims of qualified immunity where the violation of rights is clear. In addition, attorney fees can be awarded to a prevailing plaintiff.

Private universities (as well as public ones) may be liable under other federal and state civil rights laws that govern private, not just state, conduct, such as the civil rights conspiracy statutes in 42 U.S.C. § 1985, 18 U.S.C. § 241 (a criminal statute) and potentially various state civil rights laws. Though, to date, those have not seen much employment. As Oberlin College recently discovered, private universities may also face sub-

---

30. 42 U.S.C. 1983.

stantial damages for libelous statements made by their employees,[31] something that may come up whenever unfounded charges are made against a fraternity or its members.

In addition, private universities may be bound by internal free-speech policies, and internal due-process policies, under principles of contract law. This may be the case even where those policies are unwritten, where there is a generally understood policy or practice on campus.[32] In addition, of course, private universities, and private university administrators, are not able to plead official immunity, as they are not government officials.

Furthermore, though these have not yet played a significant role in higher education free-speech litigation, colleges and their administrators, as well as student groups and even outside actors, may face liability under various tort theories, such as interference with contractual relations or intentional infliction of emotional distress. As with the *Oberlin* libel case, damages could conceivably mount up to significant amounts.

The law is not always friendly to student organizations, though. An organization seeking official recognition from the university (as is the case with most fraternities and sororities) may have to accept additional supervision from the university in exchange. In *Christian Legal Society v. Martinez*, the Supreme Court held that a university could condition official recognition and funding on an organization having to accept all comers, to the point that a Christian legal group might be forced to accept people who did not share its religious beliefs, or who engaged in sexual practices that it regarded as immoral and un-Christian.[33] Though this decision was actually more narrow than this description suggests, and turned to a degree on some unwise stipulations of fact agreed to by the CLS, it is generally read as granting universities a degree of autonomy in regulating organizations that are officially recognized by the school. With a 5–4 decision featuring a strong dissent by the conserva-

---

31. *See Court Won't Hear Appeal of $25 Million Judgment Against Oberlin*, CBS News, August 30, 2022, https://www.cbsnews.com/news/oberlin-court-wont-hear-appeal-in-25-million-judgment/.

32. *See* Perry v. Sindermann, 408 U.S. 593 (1972) (finding professor fired over public criticism of administration was protected by de facto tenure system created by university practice over time).

33. 561 U.S. 661 (2010).

tive justices, it is possible that this case would come out differently before today's Court, but such speculation is always risky.[34]

IV. Some Specific Issues

Following is a discussion of some particular issues related to fraternities and sororities, as an illustration of how the law tends to play out.

a. Prohibition of Wearing Greek Letters/ Fraternity or Sorority Symbols

Under the First Amendment, the prohibition of wearing Greek letters or symbols is a content-based restriction of speech. Thus, where public universities are concerned, it receives strict scrutiny, meaning that it must serve a compelling governmental interest and be the least restrictive means of achieving that goal. Restrictions on speech that are subjected to strict scrutiny almost always fail, and it is difficult to imagine any justification for this one that would constitute the requisite compelling government interest. Greek letters are far less offensive than the "Fuck the Draft" language at issue in *Cohen v. California*,[35] the armbands protesting the Vietnam War in *Tinker v. Des Moines Indep. School Dist.*[36] or the upside-down flag with a peace symbol in *Spence v. Washington*.[37] Private universities, of course, are not so constrained, though they may be limited by internal policies or by state civil rights laws.

---

34. In recent decades, courts have been very deferential to university administrators, something I attribute in part to the fact that the judiciary is the most academic branch of government. As a practical matter, one must have a graduate degree, a J.D. or equivalent, in order to be a judge or justice, and the work of appellate courts in particular is somewhat academic. Judges even wear robes reminiscent of academic garb. *See* GLENN HARLAN REYNOLDS, THE JUDICIARY'S CLASS WAR 10–33 (2018) (describing class sympathies of judiciary and effects on decisions).
35. 503 U.S. 15 (1971).
36. 393 U.S. 503 (1969).
37. 418 U.S. 405 (1974).

b. Prohibition on Off-Campus Fraternity/Sorority Activities

The area of prohibiting off-campus activities is somewhat unclear. The Supreme Court has recognized the right of purely social groups to associate,[38] and has held that the First Amendment restricts the power of the state to impose liability on an individual solely because of his association with another.[39] It has also held that the First Amendment protects "the right to associate with others in pursuit of a wide variety of political, social, economic, education, religious, and cultural ends."[40]

Set against this is the argument that fraternities and sororities, if officially recognized by the University, are subject to a degree of supervision and control by the university.[41] Although a number of lower courts have held that fraternities and sororities have expressive associational rights,[42] whether restrictions on off-campus activity would excessively burden those rights is less clear. Private universities possess more latitude here, though to the extent that they engage in more supervision of student groups, they run the risk of assuming more responsibility than they might otherwise possess.

c. Depriving a Fraternity/Sorority Chapter of Due Process

Student groups possess due-process rights against university action, whether that action concerns speech or other behavior. This means that rules that are vague, or that are arbitrarily enforced, may be held unconstitutional. A vague rule is one that "contains no clues which could assist a student, an administrator, or a reviewing judge in determining whether conduct not transgressing statutes is susceptible to punishment by the University."[43] This is often the case with catch-all terms like "misconduct." Likewise, terms like "offensive" "inappropriate," or "harmful" are likely to be too vague.

---

38. Evans v. Newton, 382 U.S. 296, 298 (1966).
39. NAACP v. Claiborne Hardware, 458 U.S. 886, 888 (1982).
40. Roberts v. U.S. Jaycees, 468 U.S. 609, 622 (1984).
41. Christian Legal Soc'y v. Martinez, 561 U.S. 661 (2010).
42. *See, e.g.*, Iota XI Chapter v. Patterson, 538 F. Supp.2d 915 (E.D. Va. 2008).
43. Soglin v. Kauffman, 418 F.2d 163, 168 (7th Cir. 1969).

The due-process requirements for disciplining a student organization are straightforward: notice, an opportunity to be heard, and a decision based on evidence in the record. The right to introduce exculpatory/rebuttal evidence and to cross-examine the university's witnesses is also crucial. If these requirements are satisfied, then so is due process.[44]

It is also the case that both private and public universities have an obligation to follow their published standards of conduct and procedure in these proceedings, and they also may be bound by customs and practices that have evolved over time.[45]

d. Future Legislation

As mentioned earlier, numerous states have passed legislation aimed at protecting free speech on campus. Such legislation is likely to spread, at least among the "red" states, as higher education increasingly takes sides in American politics, and increasingly shows tendencies toward suppressing opposition views. Representatives of Greek-letter organizations would be wise to take a role in the drafting and passage of such legislation, with an eye toward carving out strong protection for fraternities and sororities. Ideally, from the Greek perspective, such laws would not only offer strong protection for free speech and association on campus, even among organizations receiving official recognition, but would also permit personal liability on the part of university officials for violating those freedoms.

At the federal level, a future Republican administration might well produce increased interest in amending the Higher Education Act to provide additional free speech protections as well. The precatory language suggesting that higher education institutions "should" protect free speech might be replaced by mandatory language, with a loss of federal funding as a potential sanction. Personal liability for university administrators might add additional teeth as well. Given the apparent sympathies of the federal higher education bureaucracy, drafters are more likely to rely on judicial enforcement than on bureaucratic measures. I

---

44. Iota XI Chapter, 538 F. Supp.2d at 915; Sigma Chi Fraternity v. Regents of Univ. of Colo., 258 F. Supp. 515, 528 (D. Colo. 1966).

45. *See* Perry v. Sindermann, 408 U.S. 593 (1972) (finding professor fired over public criticism of administration was protected by de facto tenure system created by university practice over time).

suspect that a generous damages regime, coupled with statutory attorneys' fees, would promote the growth of a vigorous plaintiffs' bar that would facilitate enforcement by "private attorneys general." It is my experience, and I have heard similar things from other lawyers in higher education, that many higher education administrators tend to believe that ordinary law does not apply in the university setting. Such legislation would likely change that.

V. Beyond the Law

Of course, while litigation and legislation have their place, the retreat from free speech in higher education is a cultural phenomenon. A half century ago, there was a near-consensus on the importance of freedom of speech, even for "the thought we hate." Today, that consensus is no longer a consensus. While a majority of Americans probably continue to support traditional free speech doctrines, it is very doubtful that a majority of educational administrators, faculty, and even students feel that way. Even journalists seem strangely unsupportive of free speech these days, to the point where one might well find stronger and broader support for free expression among truck drivers than among reporters and editors at major publications.

Changes in the law can certainly drive culture. Title IX, and its accompanying sanctions, changed not only the role of women's sports, but the role of women on campus. Changes in sexual harassment law certainly changed corporate culture dramatically where women are involved. And, of course, the 1964 Civil Rights Act significantly changed racial practices in employment and in higher education. Likewise, legislation at the state and federal level can certainly promote changes in higher education culture. However, universities mostly welcomed the racial and sexual changes of that era; they may greet free speech legislation with less enthusiasm. That said, simple self-preservation might provide sufficient incentive.

The changes in campus culture were the result of steady pressure by, at least in the early decades, a relatively small number of faculty and staff. Counter-pressure might suffice to make a change in campus culture too. One thing that Greek organizations might do as a service activity is educate their members about the importance of free speech in a free society, and to educate other members of the campus community as well. They should also be encouraged to stand up and resist efforts at stereotyping, othering, and marginalizing members of the Greek community. Universities rightly abhor and oppose such efforts aimed at other members of the community, but if diversity and inclusion are to mean anything, then every member of the university community should be equally respected. This means that every member of the university community should have a voice, even if other members would rather that voice be silenced.

CHAPTER 11

The Fourth Amendment and Greeks on Campus: Right of Privacy and Unreasonable Searches and Seizures

Aman McLeod

This chapter will discuss how state and federal courts have interpreted the scope of the Fourth Amendment's protection for privacy and against unreasonable searches and seizures in fraternity and sorority (Greek) housing. Its main thesis will be that the courts have tended to treat Greek houses more like private homes for Fourth Amendment purposes. It will also discuss some of the problems raised by some courts' interpretations of Fourth Amendment doctrines concerning how administrative and consent searches have been applied to Greek houses.

The chapter will start with a survey of Fourth Amendment doctrine as it pertains to searches of domiciles, of which Greek houses are a type. Then, it will discuss several Fourth Amendment doctrines that have been the subject of important litigation concerning Greek housing: the doctrines concerning consent to search, exigent circumstances, and administrative searches. The chapter will conclude by discussing the implications of its findings for the privacy of residents of Greek housing, especially the problems that could be caused by expansive interpretations of university authority to conduct administrative searches, or of Greek organizations consenting to those searches as a condition of university or college recognition.

According to an article in the *Hechinger Report* in 2021, there were an estimated 750,000 members of sororities and fraternities on American college and university campuses.[1] These organizations are popular, in part, because they offer social connections, a sense of belonging, and a home away from home for students, many of whom are living apart from their families for the first time.[2] Universities and colleges bear some responsibility for the health and safety of their students and for maintenance of order on their campuses,[3] but what educational institutions do in furtherance of this responsibility has implications for their students' constitutional rights, particularly their right to privacy in their dwellings on campus. This chapter will discuss how the courts have interpreted and applied the protections of one of the Constitution's primary guarantors of privacy, the Fourth Amendment, to university student housing, especially Greek housing. Following a brief discussion of Fourth Amendment and its protections, it will discuss how those protections have been extended to Greek housing, such that these houses receive substantially the same treatment as private homes. Then, it will turn to a discussion of several Fourth Amendment doctrines that have been the subject of important litigation in the Greek housing context, including consent to search, exigent circumstances, and administrative searches. It will conclude with a summary of Fourth Amendment law regarding searches of Greek houses, and some of the potential challenges to their privacy posed by expansive readings of the consent and administrative search doctrines.

---

1. Jill Barshay, *PROOF POINTS: New Poll Points to College and Career Benefits of Greek life Despite Criticism*, HECHINGER REPORT, July 19, 2021, https://hechingerreport.org/proof-points-new-poll-points-to-college-and-career-benefits-of-greek-life-despite-criticism/(last visited June 17, 2022).

2. *Point/Counterpoint: The Future of Greek Life*, DAILY EMERALD (EUGENE, OR), Apr. 5, 2021.

3. *See e.g.*, Peter F. Lake, *The Rise of Duty and the Fall of Loco Parentis and Other Protective Tort Doctrines in Higher Education Law*, 64 Mo. L. REV. 1, 2 (1999).

I. The Fourth Amendment and University Student Housing

The Fourth Amendment states the following:

> The right of the people to be secure in their persons, houses, papers, and effects, against unreasonable searches and seizures, shall not be violated, and no Warrants shall issue, but upon probable cause, supported by Oath or affirmation, and particularly describing the place to be searched, and the persons or things to be seized.[4]

In *Katz v. United States*, the United States Supreme Court said that the Fourth Amendment protects people, not places,[5] and, in subsequent cases, made clear that the Fourth Amendment offers protection to people in any situation or place in which they have a reasonable expectation of privacy.[6] One of the places where a person's expectation of privacy is most reasonable is in their home, which is why the Court has said that the Fourth Amendment offers extensive protections for privacy in people's dwellings.[7] For example, government officials generally may not search a home for evidence of a crime without first obtaining a warrant,[8] although they are permitted to search some other locations for such evidence with probable cause, but without obtaining a warrant,[9] or even in some cases without probable cause.[10] Sometimes, searches in the home

---

4. U.S. Const. amend. IV.
5. Katz v. United States, 389 U.S. 347, 351 (1967).
6. *See e.g.*, Smith v. Maryland, 442 U.S. 735, 740 (1979) (discussing Katz v. United States, 389 U.S. 347, 361(1967)) (Harlan, J. concurring).
7. *See e.g.*, Stephanie M. Stern, *The Inviolate Home: Housing Exceptionalism in the Fourth Amendment*, 95 Cornell L. Rev. 905, 907 (2010).
8. *See e.g.*, Kentucky v. King, 563 U.S. 452, 459 (2011); Brigham City v. Stuart, 547 U.S. 398, 403 (2006); Groh v. Ramirez, 540 U.S. 551, 559 (2004); Payton v. New York, 445 U.S. 573, 586 (1980). *But see e.g.*, Mincy v. Arizona, 437 U.S. 385, 392–93 (1978) (noting that warrantless searches of homes are permitted in exigent circumstances).
9. *E.g.*, California v. Acevedo, 500 U.S. 565, 569 (1991) (automobiles searches permitted on probable cause but without a warrant).
10. *E.g.*, City of Ontario v. Quon, 560 U.S. 746, 761 (2010) (searches of government employees related to work-related misconduct); California v. Greenwood, 486 U.S. 35, 41–42 (1988) (searches of abandoned property and refuse); New Jersey v. T.L.O., 469 U.S. 325, 341–42 (1985) (searches in schools); Almeida-Sanchez v. United States, 413 U.S. 266, 272 (1973) (searches of individuals or vehicles seeking to cross an international border to enter the United States).

are also permitted without a warrant under exigent circumstances[11], but these exceptions to the warrant requirement involve situations in which the person is already in government custody,[12] or where the police have lawfully entered the home, such as when they have obtained consent to search,[13] or when the police are otherwise legally present in the home and observe items that are obviously contraband.[14] The Court has also said that government searches for administrative reasons can be performed in some situations without a warrant, but that these searches should be for health and safety and limited in their scope and authorization.[15] Evidence that is seized in the home (or elsewhere) in a manner that violates a suspect's Fourth Amendment rights, generally cannot be used against that suspect at trial,[16] and arrests that are made in a home in violation of a suspect's Fourth Amendment rights can affect the admissibility of evidence gathered pursuant to the illegal arrest.[17]

II. The Fourth Amendment and Greek Housing: From In Loco Parentis to Full Protection

The question has arisen as to whether the Fourth Amendment applies to fraternity and sorority housing in the same way that it applies to other homes. Such housing is not usually owned by its residents individually. These dwellings are usually owned by one of the following organizations: the educational institution that hosts the fraternity or sorority or the fraternity or the sorority to which the chapter belongs.[18]

---

11. Mincey v. Arizona, 437 U.S. 385, 394 (1978) (warrantless searches of homes are permitted under exigent circumstances).

12. *E.g.*, Chimel v. California, 395 U.S. 752, 762–63 (1969) (searches incident to arrest of a suspect, including the body of the suspect and the immediate area around the suspect); Griffin v. Wisconsin, 483 U.S. 868, 873–78 (1987) (searches of probationers and parolees).

13. Schneckloth v. Bustamonte, 412 U.S. 218, 219 (1973) (consent searches).

14. *E.g.*, Ker v. California, 374 U.S. 23, 36–41 (1963).

15. *See infra* Part D.3.

16. *E.g.*, Brown v. Illinois, 422 U.S. 590, 597–600 (1975); United States v. Ceccolini, 435 U.S. 268, 274–76 (1978).

17. *E.g.*, Brown, 422 U.S. at 601–605.

18. *See* HAROLD C. RIKER WITH FRANK G. LOPEZ, COLLEGE STUDENTS LIVE HERE 18–20 (1961).

The specific question of whether fraternity or sorority housing should be treated the same as a home for Fourth Amendment purposes has been considered by a few courts, and these courts have all decided that fraternity and sorority houses should be treated the same as other sorts of homes for the purpose of government searches and seizures.[19] Specifically, the courts have treated fraternity and sorority houses as living arrangements in which the tenants share many common areas, but still enjoy a reasonable expectation of privacy, even in those common areas.[20] The finding of a reasonable expectation of privacy in the common areas of Greek houses is in marked contrast to the way some courts have treated the common areas in other multi-unit dwellings (e.g., apartment buildings), where no such reasonable expectation has been found.[21] Lemons, in his discussion of the application of the Fourth Amendment more generally to student housing, concluded that whether a reasonable expectation of privacy will be found in the common areas of a Greek house or a regular student dormitory will depend on a highly fact-specific analysis which considers "the openness, security, and use of the area in question."[22] Lemons' summary suggests that the floorplan of, and access to, Greek houses have contributed to several courts finding a reasonable expectation of privacy in the common areas of these houses.

Extension of Fourth Amendment protection to Greek housing appears to be a mid-to-late 20th-century occurrence. Before the 1960s, courts often issued rulings that shielded institutions of higher education

---

19. *See e.g.*, Reardon v. Wroan, 811 F.2d 1025, 1027, n.2 (7th Cir. 1987); Farmer v. Kan. State Univ., No. 16-CV-2256-JAR-GEB, 2017 U.S. Dist. LEXIS 37100 at *28 (D. KS, Mar. 17, 2017); Milam v. Commonwealth, 438 S.W.3rd 347, 350 (Ky. 2015); City of Fargo v. Lee, 580 N.W.2d 580, 582 (ND 1998); State v. Pi Kappa Alpha Fraternity, 491 N.E.2d. 1129, 1131–32 (Ohio 1986); State v. Reining, 2011-Ohio-1545, at *20–21, (Ohio Ct. App. 2011).

20. *E.g.*, Reardon v. Wroan, 811 F.2d at 1030; Milam v. Commonwealth, 438 S.W.3rd at 349–50; State v. Reining 2011-Ohio-1545, at *22.

21. *See e.g.*, United States v. Rheault, 561 F.3d. 55, 59 (1st Cir. 2009); United States v. Paradis, 351 F.3d 20, 31 (1st Cir. 2003); United States v. Miravalles, 280 F.3d 1328, 1331 (11th Cir. 2002); United States v. Eisler, 567 F.2d 814, 816 (8th Cir. 1977); United States v. Cruz Pagan, 537 F.2d 554, 558 (1st Cir. 1976); *see also* Bryan R. Lemons, *Public education and Student Privacy: Application of the Fourth Amendment to Dormitories at Public Colleges and Universities*, 2012 BYU EDUC. & L.J. 31, 40 (2012).

22. Lemons, *supra* note 21, at 42.

from interference and liability in their interactions with their students.[23] This was often done by invoking the doctrine of *in loco parentis* and other tort immunities to protect colleges and universities from students.[24] The phrase *in loco parentis* is literally translated from Latin as "in the place of a parent," and describes a situation in which an individual or an organization assumes a parent-like role over someone else who functionally assumes the role of that parent's child.[25] Scholars[26] have cited *Gott v. Berea College*[27] as being emblematic of this approach to understanding the relationship between colleges and universities and their students. In *Gott,* a restaurateur sued Berea College claiming that the college illegally harmed his business by forbidding students from dining there. In rejecting his claim, the Court of Appeals of Kentucky stated the following:

> College authorities stand *in loco parentis* concerning the physical and moral welfare, and mental training of the pupils, and we are unable to see why to that end they may not make any rule or regulation for the government, or betterment of their pupils that a parent could for the same purpose.[28]

Emblematic of the shift away from the invocation of *in loco parentis* doctrine that occurred in the 1960s was *Dixon v. Alabama State Board of Education.*[29] In that case, the US Court of Appeals for the Fifth Circuit had to decide whether the due-process clause of the 14th Amendment prohibited the expulsion of students at Alabama State College without

---

23. *See e.g.,* People ex. rel. Pratt v. Wheaton College, 40 Ill. 186, 187 (Ill. 1866); Lake, *supra* note 4, at 3–9; Jason A. Zwara, *Student Privacy, Campus Safety, and Reconsidering the Modern Student-University Relationship,* 38 J.C. & U.L. 419, 432 (2012).

24. Kristen Peters, *Protecting the Millennial College Student,* 16 S. Cal. Rev. L. & Soc. Just. 431, 433 (2007).

25. *See* Susan Stuart, *In Loco Parentis in the Public Schools: Abused, Confused, and In Need of Change,* 78 U. Cin. L. Rev. 969, 973 (2010).

26. *E.g,* Peters, *supra* note 24 at 433; Zwara, *supra* note 23 at 433.

27. 161 S.W. 204 (Ky. 1913).

28. *Id.* at 206. *See also* John B. Stetson University v. Hunt, 102 So. 637, 640 (Fla. 1924). Other cases point to the widespread use of the *in loco parentis* doctrine and its demise, including Regents of University of California v. Superior Court, 413 P.3d 656, 665–66 (Cal. 2018); Avila v. Citrus Community College Dist., 131 P.3d 383, 389 (Cal. 2006); Helfman v. Northeastern University, 149 N.E.3d 758, 768–69 (Mass. 2020); Hartman v. Bethany College, 778 F. Supp. 286, 293 (N.D. W.Va. 1991).

29. 294 F.2d 150 (5th Cir. 1961).

notice or hearing, following participation in a protest against racial segregation.[30] By a vote of 2–1, the three-judge panel sided with the students, and rejected the argument for a less demanding interpretation of the due-process clause that would have let colleges and universities dismiss students at any time and for any reason.[31] Zwara noted that this case heralded a shift by the courts from viewing the relationship between the university and the student as one of parent to child, to one of contractual partners who owed certain agreed upon duties to each other, and a relationship in which the state could properly intervene.[32] A study by this author of cases discussing government searches of Greek residences provides some support to the supposition that through the mid-20th century, little thought was given to applying the protections of the Constitution to interactions between colleges and universities on the one hand, and their students on the other. The study, which looked at cases concerning the application of the Fourth Amendment to searches of Greek housing, revealed no cases that occurred before the 1970s, while the results also showed that no case after that period denied that the Fourth Amendment applied to searches of these dwellings.[33]

III. The Fourth Amendment and Greek Housing: Important Fourth Amendment Doctrines

Today, questions regarding the application of the Fourth Amendment to Greek housing mostly concern the application of exceptions to the amendment's warrant requirement in the context of Greek housing as a form of group housing for students enrolled at a university or college. Exceptions to the warrant requirement that often appear in the cases are the exceptions concerning consent, exigent circumstances, and admin-

---

30. *Id.* at 152–155.

31. *Id.* at 157–58.

32. Zwara at 434. *See also* New Jersey v. T. L. O., 469 U.S. 325, 336 (1985); Morale v. Grigel, 422 F. Supp. 988, 997 (D. NH 1976); Commonwealth v. Neilson, 666 N.E.2d 984, 986–87 (Mass. 1996); State v. Rodriguez, 521 S.W.3d 1, 9 (Tex. Crim. App. 2017).

33. The study was done using the following LexisNexis search term: (sorority or fraternity) and "fourth amendment" and house.

istrative searches. The treatment these exceptions have received has implications for the privacy of fraternity and sorority members that will be addressed in this section.

a. Public/Private Actor Distinction

The Court has held that the Fourth Amendment only protects individuals against unreasonable searches and seizures by people acting on behalf of a government entity.[34] This means that searches of student dwellings conducted by institutional officials at private colleges and universities are not regulated by the Fourth Amendment, and, therefore, not subject to the exclusionary rule, unless there "are clear indices of the [g]overnment's encouragement, endorsement, and participation," in the searches.[35] Although the Court's rulings that the Fourth Amendment does not apply to searches by private actors could be seen as merely emphasizing the plain language of the amendment, it is important to mention here because the question of whether a search of a student dwelling was sufficiently motivated by government authorities to implicate a student's Fourth Amendment rights has arisen in a court case.[36]

b. Consent

The Supreme Court has long made it clear that a suspect's Fourth Amendment rights are not violated when the suspect consents to a search or entry by government agents if that consent is obtained voluntarily,[37] and the person who gives consent has either actual or apparent authority over the area to be searched.[38] The Court has employed a "totality of the circumstances" test to determine the voluntariness of the consent to search, which includes consideration of all the circumstances of the situation under which consent was given.[39] Regarding authority to

---

34. *See e.g.,* United States v. Jacobson, 466 U.S. 109, 113 (1984); Walter v. United States, 477 U.S. 649, 662 (1980).

35. *E.g.,* Duarte v. Commonwealth, 407 S.E.2d 41, 42 Va. Ct. App. (1991) (quoting *Skinner v. Railway Labor Exec. Ass'n,* 489 U.S. 602, 615–16 (1989)).

36. *See* Duarte v. Commonwealth, 407 S.E.2d. at 42.43.

37. *See e.g.,* Schneckloth v. Bustamonte, 412 U.S. 218, 224–25 (1973).

38. *See e.g.,* Illinois v. Rodriguez, 497 U.S. 177, 181 (1990).

39. *See* Schneckloth at 233; *see also* Lemons, *supra* note 20, at 51–52.

consent to a search, the Court has made it clear that actual authority to authorize a search does not come from an ownership interest in the property, but from:

> [m]utual use of the property by persons generally having joint access or control for most purposes, so that it is reasonable to recognize that any of the co-inhabitants has the right to permit the inspection in his own right and that the others have assumed the risk that one of their number might permit the common area to be searched.[40]

Put differently, apparent authority to authorize a search can come from anyone who would reasonably appear, on the facts available, to have authority to authorize a search of the premises.[41] Finally, the scope of a consent search is defined by the object of the search,[42] and the scope can be limited further by the person granting consent.[43] Of relevance to Greek organizations, residents of a Greek house appear to be authorized to approve searches of common areas and their own rooms,[44] and host institutions (assuming the authority that courts have given to landlords) may authorize searches of common areas, but not students' individual rooms.[45] Note, however, that the authority of the institution to authorize any search will turn on its authority over the premises. For example, if the host institution owns or in some way manages the building that houses the Greek organization, it could be assumed that it would have more authority to authorize a search than if it does not own or manage the building. This can be surmised from the fact that most of the cases concerning landlords' authority to consent concern situations where the landlord is the owner or manager of the premises.[46]

Most of the cases concerning the consent exception have focused on whether consent to search can be voluntarily obtained by government agents who have not identified themselves as such when they sought consent. An example of such a case is *State v. Pi Kappa Alpha Fraternity*,

---

40. United States v. Matlock, 415 U.S. 164, 171 n.7 (1974).
41. *See e.g.*, Rodriguez, 497 U.S. at 185–86.
42. Florida v. Jimeno, 500 U.S. 248, 251 (1991).
43. *Id.* at 252.
44. *See* Lemons, *supra* note 20, at 55–56.
45. *Id.* at 56–57.
46. *Id.* at 56 n.160.

in which the Ohio Supreme Court considered whether the manager of a fraternity house voluntarily consented when two state liquor control agents sought to enter a fraternity house where they believed that alcohol was being illegally sold.[47] The court held that the agents' failure to identify themselves and their use of verbal misrepresentations to gain entry to the fraternity house rendered the manager's consent to enter involuntary, which meant that the ensuing search of the premises was in violation of the Fourth Amendment.[48] There is a division of authority on this point however, as the Texas Court of Appeals reached the opposite conclusion about whether undercover law enforcement officers could obtain voluntary consent to search a fraternity house.[49] Given the small number of cases on point, it is not appropriate to draw firm conclusions about the application of the consent exception to Greek houses when government officials do so undercover, and courts have reached different conclusions as to whether the Fourth Amendment is offended when government agents conceal their identities to gain consent to enter other kinds of dwellings for the purpose of conducting a search.[50]

c. Exigent Circumstances

The US Supreme Court has recognized three scenarios that qualify for the exigent circumstances exception to the Fourth Amendment's protection against warrantless searches and entries: (1) hot pursuit of a fleeing suspect,[51] (2) the need to render assistance to an injured person or to prevent imminent injury,[52] and (3) the need to prevent the imminent destruction of evidence of a crime.[53] The Court has mandated that

---

47. 491 N.E.2d 1129, 1131 (Ohio 1986).

48. *Id.* at 1132–33. *See* Czerniak v. Owens, 2006-Ohio-4436, p.17–22 (Ohio Ct. App. 2006).

49. *State v. Lofgren*, 47 S.W.3d 167, 169 (Tex App. 2001).

50. *See* Michael D. Ricciuti, *When Can the Police Lie? The Limits of Law Enforcement Officers' Use of Deception in Obtaining Consent to Search a Home*, 55 SUFFOLK U. L. REV. 1, 12–15 (2022).

51. *E.g.*, United States v. Santana, 427 U.S. 38, 42–43 (1976); *but see* Welsh v. Wisconsin, 466 U.S. 740, 753 (1984) (holding that pursuit of a fleeing misdemeanant will rarely constitute a sufficient emergency to justify warrantless entry into a dwelling).

52. *E.g.*, Brigham City v. Stuart, 547 U.S. 398, 403 (2006).

53. *E.g.*, Kentucky v. King, 563 U.S. 452, 460 (2011); *Minnesota v. Olson*, 495 U.S. 91, 100 (1990).

the government officers conducting the search have an objectively reasonable belief that the exigent circumstances exist for the warrantless search to satisfy this exception to the Fourth Amendment.[54] In the Greek housing context, *Reardon v. Wroan* is an example of an exigent circumstances case, in which the Seventh Circuit Court of Appeals determined that a warrantless entry into a fraternity house by three police officers, and their brief detention of two of the residents, was justified by a reasonable belief that a burglary was in progress.[55] *State v. Reining* is another case in which a court considered whether the exigent circumstances exception justified warrantless entry into a fraternity house by police officers when they saw two people smoking on a balcony.[56] Upon seeing the smoke, the police entered the building, smelled what they thought was marijuana, searched the house, and cited two students for several misdemeanors.[57] The Ohio Court of Appeals ruled that the search failed to fall within the exigent circumstances exception because observing two students smoking marijuana, which was a misdemeanor, would not justify entry under the exception.[58] Perhaps the most important lesson from all of the cases in which the courts applied the consent and the exigent circumstances exceptions is that the way in which the doctrines were applied in these cases does not appear to differ materially from the way that they are applied in searches of non-Greek housing. This is because the courts have not developed any special doctrines for consent or exigency for police searches of Greek houses that differs from the doctrines that are applied to searches of non-Greek housing.

d. Administrative Searches

Another major issue concerning the application of the Fourth Amendment to Greek houses is the application of the administrative search exception to the amendment's warrant requirement. Although the heyday of the *in loco parentis* view of the university-student relationship has passed, courts still adopt the view that institutions of higher

---

54. *E.g.*, Brigham City, 547 U.S. at 403.
55. *See e.g.*, Murdock v. Stout, 54 F.3d 1437, 1142 (9th Cir. 1995); *Reardon v. Wroan*, 811 F.2d 1025, 1026–27, 1029–30 (7th Cir. 1987).
56. *See* State v. Reining, 2011-Ohio-1545, at *2–14, (Ohio Ct. App. 2011).
57. *Id.* at *3.
58. *See id.* at *29–36.

learning retain the power to regulate and discipline their students,[59] but that this power must be exercised in accordance with the students' legal rights.[60] Many universities and colleges require students who live in campus housing to sign a contract permitting the institution to make random inspections of their residences for the purpose of ensuring their health and safety and that of the university community.[61] Universities and colleges sometimes also extend this policy to fraternities and sororities as a condition of maintaining their working relationship with the institution (i.e., recognition).[62] When a university or college[63] asks students to consent to inspections of their living quarters as a condition for living in university housing, or of fraternity or sorority recognition, Fourth Amendment issues can arise. The lower courts are divided on whether consent procured under such circumstances constitutes legally effective consent to search, with some treating consent to enter for health, safety, and maintenance of an "educational atmosphere" as sufficient to allow the police to conduct a warrantless entry and seizure if university officials find contraband during such a search.[64] This is what occurred in *State v. Hunter*, where a court ruled that a student's agreement to searches of his dorm room for the aforementioned reasons, justified a search of his room for contraband by a university official, and the subsequent seizure of contraband from his room outside of his presence and without a

---

59. *See e.g.,* Franklin v. Atkins, 409 F. Supp. 439,451 (D. Colo. 1976); Lemons, *supra* note 21 at 57, citing Esteban v. Cent. Mo. State Coll., 415 F2d. 1077, 1089 (8th Cir. 1969).

60. *See e.g.,* Lemons, *supra* note 21 at 57, citing Smyth v. Lubbers, 398 F. Supp. 777, 785 (W.D. Mich. 1975). *See also* Anobile v. Pelligrino, 303 F.3d 107, 119–20 (2d Cir. 2001) (also noting that a reasonable expectation of privacy is present in dormitory dwellings).

61. *See* Lemons, *supra* note 21 at 58.

62. *See e.g., Fraternity & Sorority Inspection,* Ohio University, https://www.ohio.edu/facilities/safety/fire/frat-inspection (last visited Sept. 27, 2022).

63. The Fourth Amendment and the Fourteenth Amendment, which incorporates it, only apply to state and federal higher education institutions, but Fourth Amendment claims can come into play when private colleges and universities are alleged to have violated students' constitutional rights under color of law. *See e.g.,* Wagner v. Holtzapple, 101 F. Supp. 3d 462, 469 (M.D. Pa. 2015).

64. *Compare* Medlock v. Trustees of Indiana University, 738 F.3d 867, 872 (7th Cir. 2013), *and* Wagner 101 F. Supp. at 477 *and* State v. Hunter, 831 P.2d 1033, 1036–37 (Utah Ct. App. 1992) (finding consent to be effective), *with* Piazzola v. Watkins, 442 F.2d 284, 289–90 (5th Cir. 1971), *and* Smyth v. Lubbers, 398 F. Supp. 777, 788 (W.D. Mich. 1971) and Devers v. Southern Univ., 712 So. 2d. 199, 207 (La. Ct. App. 1998) (finding consent ineffective).

warrant by a police officer.[65] In reaching its decision, the court emphasized that the investigation was not criminal in nature, but was motivated by a desire to maintain an "educational environment," as it had been commenced following reports of rowdy behavior and property damage on the floor of the dormitory building where the student lived.[66]

However, the US Supreme Court has held that administrative searches by government officials without a warrant are permitted under some circumstances, even without consent.[67] Primus's survey of the Court's administrative search jurisprudence revealed that searches of this type were often conducted in residences, and are permitted if they involve only minimally intrusive means aimed at ensuring health and safety, that requiring an individualized probable cause determination could not protect.[68] Furthermore, for such searches to be constitutional, the government was required to demonstrate that it was acting pursuant to a warrant or a statute that limited its discretion to search by requiring the government to justify the search either before or after the fact to a neutral decision-maker.[69] Many courts have applied this doctrine to searches of student dwellings, and have found the searches constitutional when they complied with the administrative search exception's requirements.[70] However, as *Devers v. Southern University* indicates, how a court interprets the wording of an institution's inspection policy can be crucial to whether searches pursuant to that policy are upheld under the administrative search provision. For example, in that case, the Louisiana Court of Appeals found that the inspection provision in Southern University's student rental agreement was too broadly worded for searches under it

---

65. *See* Hunter, 831 P.2d at 1034–35, 1038.

66. *See id.* at 1034, 1036–37.

67. *See e.g.*, Donovan v. Dewey, 452 U.S. 594, 600–06 (1980); Camera v. Municipal Court, 387 U.S. 523, 539–40 (1967); *See* v. City of Seattle, 387 U.S. 541, 546 (1967). *See also* New York v. Burger, 482 U.S. 691, 719–20 (1987) (noting that the exception from the warrant requirement for administrative searches generally applies to industries with a "long tradition of government regulation," or those involved with "an immediate danger to health or life."

68. Eve Brensike Primus, *Disentangling Administrative Searches*, 111 COLUM. L. REV. 254, 260 (2011)

69. *Id.* at 267.

70. *See e.g.*, Hunter, 831 P.2d at 1036; State v. Kappes, 550 P.2d 121, 124 (Ariz. Ct. App. 1976).

to fall under the administrative search exception, because it did not limit the grounds for inspections to health and safety.[71]

When evidence of a crime is discovered during an administrative search of a student dwelling, some have said that law enforcement must still obtain a warrant to enter a student's dwelling and seize the evidence.[72] These courts appear to have reached this conclusion because the object of the administrative searches was to ensure the health and safety of the students, and both cases involved the discovery of items that were obviously contraband, but not related to the subject of the search.[73] When the police entered the student dwellings after being alerted to the contraband, these courts held that they did so with neither the appropriate type of consent nor in the context of any exigent circumstance that would justify entry without a warrant, which made the contraband inadmissible as evidence against the defendants.[74]

IV. Conclusion

This chapter has presented an overview of the application of the Fourth Amendment to Greek housing. It presents a picture in which students in fraternity and sorority housing enjoy substantial protection under the Fourth Amendment. Courts have given student housing most of the same protections as non-student housing, and most importantly, have done away with the *in loco parentis* doctrine, under which students enjoyed less constitutional protection for their individual rights. Most Fourth Amendment doctrines appear to apply to Greek housing in the same way that they apply to non-Greek housing and other student housing.

A recent US Supreme Court decision rejecting an extension of the "community caretaker" exception to the Fourth Amendment's warrant requirement, strengthened the privacy protections afforded to residents

---

71. Devers, 712 So. 2d at 204–05. The inspection provision stated the following: "The University reserves all rights in connection with assignments of rooms, inspection of rooms with police, and the termination of room occupancy." *Id.* at 204.

72. *See e.g.,* State v. Rodriguez, 529 S.W.3d 81, 90–93 (Tex. Ct. App. 2015); Commonwealth v. Neilson, 666 N.E.2d 984, 987 (Mass. 1996).

73. *See* Neilson 666 N.E.2d at 985; Rodriguez 529 S.W.3d at 85–87.

74. Neilson 666 N.E.2d at 987; Rodriguez 529 S.W.3d at 87–93.

of Greek housing. The "community caretaker" exception allows the police to search without a warrant when they are not conducting a criminal investigation, and when they are acting to assist a person who appears to need assistance or acting to protect the public against perceived hazards.[75] One of the key cases in this area of law is *Cady v. Dombrowski*, in which the Court ruled that evidence of a crime found after a safety-motivated search of an impounded vehicle was admissible because the search was reasonable under the Fourth Amendment.[76] In *Caniglia v. Strom*, the Court considered whether this exception permitted warrantless entry into a home to search for firearms to prevent their use in a suicide or a murder, and decided that it did not permit such a search or entry, based on the notion that homes deserve more protection than vehicles under the Fourth Amendment.[77] A decision to extend the "community caretaker" exception to homes, which would have included Greek housing, could have led to a significant reduction in the Fourth Amendment protections afforded to students in such housing, given the expansion of authority that it would have given police to search when they believed that public safety demanded doing so.

However, the current state of the of the consent and administrative search doctrines presents a challenge to the privacy of Greek residences under the Fourth Amendment. As noted above, some courts seem prepared to allow universities and colleges broad authority to search based on the agreements that they require students to sign as a condition for living in university housing, or for officially recognizing a fraternity or a sorority. These agreements may contain provisions allowing the university to search student rooms or dormitory buildings for health, safety, or maintenance of discipline, but courts differ as to whether signing these provisions constitutes consent for searches aimed at finding evidence of crimes, or whether the consent includes permission for the warrantless entry of the police into the student's room. Where consent is not given, administrative searches can still be conducted for health and safety reasons in university-owned housing, and the question in these searches remains how much the courts will allow the motive of keeping students

---

75. Mary Elisabeth Naumann, *The Community Caretaker Doctrine: Yet Another Fourth Amendment Exception*, 26 Am. J. Crim. L. 325, 330–342 (1999).

76. 413 U.S. 433, 447–48 (1973).

77. *See* Caniglia v. Strom, 141 S. Ct. 1596, 1599–1600 (2021).

healthy and safe to overlap with the motive of finding evidence of a crime when conducting these searches, and whether they will allow the police to enter student dwellings without a warrant to seize the evidence discovered during the search. The question of the breadth of the consent and the administrative search exceptions will remain a serious one for Greek organizations, as at least two public universities have required Greek organizations to consent to university employees and law enforcement officers entering and searching their residences whenever there is reason to think that laws or university rules are being broken.[78] How courts respond to this development will provide an answer the question of whether a Greek house is a home away from home.

---

78. *See e.g.,* Jake New, *Search and Seizure,* INSIDE HIGHER ED, Aug. 23, 2016, https://www.insidehighered.com/news/2016/08/23/new-rules-iu-allow-officials-enter-fraternities-sororities-probable-cause.

CHAPTER 12

Equal Protection and Fraternal Organizations: Potential Protections and Restraints

Jenny-Brooke Condon

For fraternal organizations, the constitutional guarantee of equal protection is a source of both potential rights and constitutional restraints. The Fourteenth Amendment Equal Protection Clause[1] protects individuals from class-based discrimination at the hands of the government but does not constrain private entities or individuals unless they engage in "state action."[2] Accordingly, fraternal organizations may seek the Fourteenth Amendment's protections when they experience differential treatment by the state,[3] but in the case of organizations operating at public colleges and universities or private universities receiving fed-

---

1. U.S. Const. amend. XIV, § 2.

2. *See* The Civil Rights Cases, 109 U.S. 3 (1883); Moose Lodge No. 107 v. Irvis, 407 U.S. 163, 172 (1972) (noting in case challenging racial discrimination by a local branch of a national fraternal organization that "discriminatory action by the State ... is prohibited by the Equal Protection Clause" whereas "that clause 'erects no shield'" against private conduct no matter how "'discriminatory or wrongful'") (quoting Shelley v. Kraemer, 334 U.S. 1, 13 (1948)).

3. Sioux City Bridge Co. v. Dakota Cnty., 260 U.S. 441, 445 (1923) ("The purpose of the equal protection clause of the Fourteenth Amendment is to secure every person within the State's jurisdiction against intentional and arbitrary discrimination, whether occasioned by express terms of a statute or by its improper execution through duly constituted agents.") (internal citation and quotation marks omitted).

eral funding, the Fourteenth Amendment may also restrain such organizations from engaging in unequal treatment themselves.[4]

Fraternal organizations have invariably invoked the Constitution's guarantee of equal protection to challenge state laws alleged to single out fraternal organizations for unfair treatment. Take, for example, a fraternity's challenge to an Illinois anti-hazing statute.[5] They have also asserted equal protection violations when universities revoke recognition of fraternities as authorized student groups in response to student disciplinary violations.[6] Some commentators have also argued that university policies restricting fraternal organizations from recruiting new members during the early semesters of college violate equal protection because they single out fraternities for unequal barriers to membership enrollment.[7]

For reasons explained further below, these kinds of challenges are typically unsuccessful because courts evaluate state laws and policies that regulate fraternal organizations under a deferential rational basis standard. That standard is not difficult for universities to meet.

Although fraternities and sororities are private organizations, when they operate at public colleges and universities or at private universities that receive federal funding, their activities may implicate the Fourteenth Amendment and related civil rights statutes under the "state action" doctrine.[8] As the U.S. Supreme Court has stated, if the state "insinuate[s] itself into a position of interdependence with" the private organization such that the state "must be recognized as a joint participant in the challenged activity," the private club's discriminatory acts

---

4. *See generally* Moose Lodge, 407 U.S. at 172.

5. *See e.g.*, People v. Anderson, 591 N.E.2d 461, 468–69 (Ill. 1992) (rejecting vagueness and equal protection challenge to Illinois's hazing statue, which was invoked in charges against two college students involved in a deadly hazing incident).

6. *See* Pi Lambda Phi Fraternity, Inc. v. Univ. of Pittsburgh, 229 F.3d 435 (3rd Cir. 2000). Plaintiffs argue that this treatment constituted differential and unfair punishment not visited upon other groups. *Id.*

7. James Harvey, *Deferred Rush: A Violation of Equal Protection?* FRATERNAL LAW PARTNERS (Sept. 2005), https://fraternallaw.com/newsletter2/deferred-rush-a-violation-of-equal-protection.

8. *See* Danielle Hernandez, *Entwinement: Why Sororities and Fraternities Should Be Subject to the Constitution*, 6 EMORY CORP. GOVERNANCE & ACCOUNTABILITY REV. PERSPECTIVES 1043 (2019).

"cannot be considered to have been so 'purely private' as to fall without the scope of the Fourteenth Amendment."[9]

The below summary of equal protection decisions concerning fraternal organizations shows that the Equal Protection Clause is not a robust source of protection when fraternal organizations claim unfair treatment. Putting aside whether fraternal organizations might have viable claims to protection under the First Amendment right to association (addressed separately in Chapter 10), courts generally give wide latitude to colleges and universities when they regulate student groups, including fraternities and sororities. However, the Equal Protection Clause may provide a source of constitutional protection when fraternal organizations can establish that their unfair treatment constitutes discrimination on behalf of some other characteristic, such as gender, which receives heightened protection under the Equal Protection Clause. Finally, the possibility that fraternal organizations at state schools may engage in activities deemed to constitute "state action" has implications for fraternity and sorority recruitment practices and their long history of single-sex membership restrictions.

I. Equal Protection Challenges to Differential Treatment of Fraternal Organizations

a. Standard of Review

In its most simple formulation, equal protection demands that the State treat like groups alike.[10] As the Supreme Court has noted, "[w]hen those who appear similarly situated are nevertheless treated differently, the Equal Protection Clause requires at least a rational reason for the difference, to ensure that all persons subject to legislation or regulation are indeed being 'treated alike, under like circumstances and condi-

---

9. Moose Lodge, 407 U.S. at 172.
10. Engquist v. Oregon Dept. of Agr., 553 U.S. 591, 602 (2008) ("As we explained long ago, the Fourteenth Amendment 'requires that all persons subjected to ... legislation shall be treated alike, under like circumstances and conditions, both in the privileges conferred and in the liabilities imposed.'") (quoting Hayes v. Missouri, 120 U.S. 68, 71–72 (1887)).

tions."[11] Accordingly, if the government appears to single out an individual or group for differential treatment, "the specter of arbitrary classification is fairly raised, and the Equal Protection Clause requires a 'rational basis for the difference in treatment.'"[12]

That standard, however, is not a difficult hurdle for the State to meet.[13] Indeed, successful challenges to state classifications that receive rational basis review are "rare."[14] Moreover, when assessing the rationality of state laws challenged under equal protection, the Court focuses not on the legislature's actual purpose in enacting the law, but on whether the law may be supportable *by any conceivable rational justification* that the State *could have* considered.[15] Indeed, the Supreme Court has stated that "those attacking the rationality of the legislative classification have the burden to [negate] every conceivable basis which might support it."[16] Members of the Court have at times disagreed about the appropriateness of post hoc judicial theorizing as to appropriate state justifications.[17] But the settled approach to equal protection doctrine requires only a plausible justification for state classifications, the standard regularly followed by the lower federal courts.[18] This means that legislatures and govern-

---

11. *Id.*

12. *Id.* (quoting Village of Willowbrook v. Olech, 528 U.S. 562, 564 (2000)).

13. *See* Erwin Chemerinsky, *The Rational Basis Test Is Constitutional (and Desirable)*, 14 GEO. J.L. & PUB. POL'Y 401, 402, 410 (2016) (describing the test as "enormously deferential[,]" "almost empty[,]" and thus easy to meet); JEROME A. BARRON & C. THOMAS DIENES, CONSTITUTIONAL LAW 305 (9th ed. 2013) (describing challengers' burden to overcome rational basis review as "essentially insurmountable").

14. ERWIN CHEMERINSKY, CONSTITUTIONAL LAW 732 (5th ed. 2017).

15. *See e.g.*, F.C.C. v. Beach Commc'ns, Inc., 508 U.S. 307, 309 (1993) (describing the equal protection inquiry before it as "whether there is any conceivable rational basis justifying th[e] distinction").

16. *Id.* at 315.

17. *See* Neelum J. Wadhwani, Note, *Rational Reviews, Irrational Results*, 84 TEX. L. REV. 801, 806 n.32 (2006) (noting that although "the scales are tipped in favor of any conceivable purpose" several justices in dissenting and concurring opinions have disagreed with this approach) (citing *Beach Commc'ns, Inc.*, 508 U.S. at 313, 323 n.3 (1993) (Stevens, J., concurring); Schweiker v. Wilson, 450 U.S. 221, 236–37, 244–45 (1981) (Powell, J., dissenting); U.S. R.R. Ret. Bd. v. Fritz, 449 U.S. 166, 179, 186 (1980) (Brennan, J., dissenting)).

18. "The federal circuit courts of appeal generally tend to apply the 'any conceivable purposes' test to rational basis review." Wadhwani, *supra* note 17, at 806 n.32; *see e.g.*, Pi Lambda Phi, 229 F.3d at 447 n.6 (hypothesizing that if the University subjected a frater-

ment actors have considerable leeway to regulate fraternal organizations without running afoul of equal protection.[19]

There are, however, important limitations to this deferential approach to equal protection doctrine. If a law burdens a suspect class or infringes upon a fundamental right, then the government must meet the demands of heightened judicial review to justify its chosen means of classification.[20] For example, if a law classifies on the basis of race, national origin, or in some cases, immigration status—which have all been recognized as suspect classes—then the law must meet the requirements of strict scrutiny.[21] That means that the government must have a compelling reason for its classification and the law must be narrowly tailored to achieve that interest.

Laws that classify on the basis of gender are evaluated under intermediate scrutiny, which requires that the state have an important governmental reason for drawing the classification and the means chosen must substantially related to that purpose.[22] Additionally, the discrimination must be supported by an "exceedingly persuasive justification."[23]

Fraternal organizations are not recognized as a suspect class under equal protection doctrine, and in fact, do not meet the requirements for suspect class treatment. They do not constitute a discrete and insular minority that has faced a history of discrimination or lack political power.[24] Accordingly, unless a fraternal organization can show that a law burdens a fundamental right such as a First Amendment right to asso-

---

nity to a different standard than all student groups it would have had a rational reason for doing so because it was the only student group with off-campus housing).

19. Chemerinsky, *supra* note 14, at 412 ("The Court has declared that under rational basis review, the actual purpose behind a law is irrelevant and the law must be upheld 'if any state of facts reasonably may be conceived to justify' its discrimination.").

20. Beach Commc'ns, Inc., 508 U.S. at 313 (noting that deferential rational basis review only applies "to a statutory classification that neither proceeds along suspect lines nor infringes fundamental constitutional rights").

21. Chemerinsky, *supra* note 14, at 404.

22. *Id.*; United States v. Virginia, 518 U.S. 515, 531 (1996); Frontiero v. Richardson, 411 U.S. 677, 682 (1973) (plurality opinion) ("[C]lassifications based upon sex ... are inherently suspect and must therefore be subjected to close judicial scrutiny.").

23. *Id.*

24. Kenji Yoshino, *The New Equal Protection*, 124 HARV. L. REV. 747, 758–59 (2011) (observing that the canon on suspect classifications based upon political vulnerability and historic discrimination is now effectively closed and limited to the groups recognized by 1977).

ciation,[25] most laws and policies alleged to treat fraternities and sororities differently than other groups are likely to be viewed under deferential rational basis review and upheld as a result.[26] Some examples are discussed next.

b. Laws That Differentiate Between Fraternal Organizations and Other Groups

The Supreme Court adopted a deferential approach to state laws restricting fraternal organizations early in the last century and that has remained the dominant approach to fraternity and sororities' equal protection claims. Specifically, in 1915, in *Waugh v. Board of Trustees of University of Mississippi*,[27] the Supreme Court evaluated a challenge to a Mississippi statute that outright banned "Greek letter fraternities and societies in the state's educational institutions."[28] A member of the Kappa Sigma Fraternity at Millsaps College filed a suit claiming that the law denied him equal protection and due process of law.[29]

The Court rejected those claims, agreeing with the lower court that the statute was "based on an obvious and rational distinction[.]"[30] The Court also credited the legislature's "control of the colleges and universities of the state, and [its] right to legislate for their welfare" which it deemed "not subject to any control by the courts."[31] Invoking the familiar deference of rational basis review, the Court reasoned: "[i]t is not for us to entertain conjectures in opposition to the views of the state, and annul its regulations upon disputable considerations of their wisdom or necessity."[32]

---

25. Sororities and fraternities often challenge state laws and university policies by claiming an infringement of the First Amendment Right to Free Association. But a majority of courts that have addressed these claims have declined to recognize fraternal organizations' broadly defined associational interests, and thus routinely evaluate state laws and policies under rational basis scrutiny. For a discussion of cases asserting that fraternal organizations' rights to First Amendment association were violated by laws that singled them out for particular treatment, see the discussion at Chapter 11, *supra*.

26. *Pi Lambda Phi*, 229 F.3d at 447 n.6 (discussing scrutiny).

27. 237 U.S. 589 (1915).

28. *Id.* at 591.

29. *Id.* at 593.

30. *Id.* at 595.

31. *Id.* at 596.

32. *Id.* at 597.

In the decades that followed, lower federal courts have upheld similar state laws outlawing fraternities in the face of equal protection challenges. For example, in *Webb v. State University of New York*,[33] a federal district court upheld a New York statute banning college fraternities, concluding that the law was clearly constitutional. The district court similarly invoked the state's "special duty of supervision and control of its educational institutions" and reasoned that a state may adopt such measures, including the outlawing of certain social organizations, as it deems necessary to fulfill those duties.[34]

Similarly, in *Hughes v. Caddo Parish School Board*,[35] a district court upheld a Louisiana law banning fraternities and sororities in public high schools, and the Supreme Court affirmed, citing *Waugh*.[36] To be sure, decisions impacting high school students could be explained based upon the long-recognized judicial deference to the states with respect to the state mission of educating minors.[37] However, *Waugh* has never been overturned.[38]

---

33. 125 F. Supp. 910 (1954).

34. *Id.* at 912.

35. 57 F. Supp. 508 (W.D. La. 1944), *aff'd*, 323 U.S. 685 (1945).

36. 323 U.S. 685 (1945). For a similar ruling see *Satan Fraternity v. Board of Public Instruction for Dade County*, 22 So. 2d 892 (Fla. 1945) (upholding Florida law "banning the organization of fraternities, sororities, and other secret organizations in the public schools of Florida and prohibiting pupils enrolled therein from becoming members of such organization").

37. *See* Tinker v. Des Moines Indep. Cmty. Sch. Dist., 393 U.S. 503, 507 (1969) (striking down policy banning expressive political speech by students while noting that the "Court has repeatedly emphasized the need for affirming the comprehensive authority of the States and of school officials, consistent with fundamental constitutional safeguards, to prescribe and control conduct in the schools").

38. Some commentators have claimed that "[a]lthough never expressly overruled, *Waugh* relies on a rights-versus-privileges theory of higher education, no longer followed by courts[.]" Mark D. Bauer, *Freedom of Association for College Fraternities After Christian Legal Society and Citizens United*, 39 J.C. & U.L. 247, 276 (2013) (noting "*Waugh*'s analysis and conclusion" conflicts with *Healy v. James*, 408 U.S. 169 (1972), which held a university could not limit recognition of student political group based upon their expressive conduct and political views and *Tinker v. Des Moines Independent County School District*, 393 U.S. 503 (1969), which held that public school students' freedom of expression could not be restricted without a showing that it would materially and substantially interfere with the school's educational mission). Those cases, however, involved penalizing and restraining the speech of student groups for their political views, activity that receives the highest protection under the First Amendment. *See Healy*, 408 U.S. at 187 ("[M]ere disagreement of the President with the group's philosophy affords no reason to

Courts have similarly rejected other challenges to state law alleged to single out fraternal organizations for disfavored treatment. For example, in *People v. Anderson*,[39] two college students prosecuted under Illinois's hazing statute for their role in a deadly hazing incident, challenged the law as a violation of equal protection. The defendants argued that the statute singled out students in schools, colleges, universities, or other educational institutions and did not similarly regulate members of the general public.[40] The court rejected the argument, relying upon deferential reasoning similar to that in *Waugh*. Citing the legislature's broad authority to regulate for the general welfare and its legitimate interest in preventing physical injury, the court reasoned "there is a rational basis for limiting the reach of the hazing statute since it is reasonable to assume that most hazing occurs in colleges, universities and other schools."[41]

These decisions make clear that courts will defer to legislative classifications regulating fraternal organizations if the laws have a plausible rational basis. As set forth next, this approach to legislative enactments also characterizes equal protection challenges to university policies.

II. University Decisions Denying Recognition to Fraternal Organizations

The relationship between fraternal organizations and the colleges and universities that host them is one of intersecting interests and benefits. Fraternities often operate with the consent or official recognition of the host college or university where they are located.[42] This allows for closer regulation of the private, local chapters' conduct and can benefit the chapters too by granting them access to university resources and facili-

---

deny it recognition."). Whether *Healy* affords protection to fraternal organization's associational rights is a much different question and is not clear.

39. 591 N.E.2d 461, 464 (Ill. 1992). The challengers also claimed that it was unconstitutionally vague and overbroad.

40. *Id.* at 468–69.

41. *Id.* ("The legislature need not deal with all conceivable evils at once; it may proceed one step at a time.").

42. Gregory F. Hauser, *Social Fraternities at Public Institutions of Higher Education: Their Rights Under the First and Fourteenth Amendments*, 19 J.L. & EDUC. 433, 435 (1990).

ties in exchange for agreeing to comply with the university rules.[43] When local chapters lose official recognition from their host institutions, they forfeit these benefits, which can be critical to their existence, particularly if national chapters do not otherwise significantly support them.[44] Thus, when universities suspend or revoke a fraternity's or sorority's official recognition as student organizations following incidents of misconduct by their members, organizations have challenged such decisions as unequal treatment that violates equal protection.[45] Such claims have never succeeded.

For example, in *Pi Lambda Phi Fraternity, Inc. v. University of Pittsburgh*,[46] a fraternity challenged the university's decision to strip the local chapter "of its status as a recognized student organization after several of its members were arrested in a drug raid at the chapter's fraternity house."[47] Pi Lambda Phi claimed that this treatment violated equal protection because the fraternity received harsher punishment than other campus organizations.[48]

The United States Court of Appeals for the Third Circuit summarily rejected the claim, relegating its rationale to a mere footnote.[49] It reasoned that there was no showing that the university held fraternal organizations to a different standard than all other student groups and, even if it did, the university would have had a rational basis for doing so.[50] The court reasoned that because fraternities and sororities were the only "student organizations that maintain their own off-campus housing for students ... it is clearly rational for the University to subject them to certain rules that do not apply to other student organizations."[51]

---

43. *Id.*

44. *Id.*

45. Some fraternal organizations do cut ties with host universities and forfeit the privileges attendant with official recognition. *See* Bill Schackner, *Breakaway Fraternities Sidestepping Newly Heightened Oversight at WVU*, PITTSBURG POST GAZETTE, Jan. 27, 2019.

46. 229 F.3d 435 (3rd Cir. 2000).

47. *Id.* at 438.

48. *Id.* at 447 n.6.

49. *Id.* The majority of the decision was devoted to addressing the fraternity's claim that the decision violated its First Amendment right of association, which the Court also rejected. *Id.* at 446–47 (holding that "the University's action neither directly nor incidentally affected the Chapter's expressive interests").

50. *Id.* at 447 n.6.

51. *Id.*

Other courts have cited *Pi Lambda Phi* approvingly. For example, in *Phi Kappa Tau Chapter House Association of Miami University v. Miami University*,[52] the U.S. District Court for the Southern District of Ohio granted a motion to dismiss a fraternity's challenge to the university's suspension of its recognition. There, a law enforcement investigation into the shooting of fireworks from the fraternity led to the discovery of marijuana and fireworks inside the chapter house.[53] The school determined that the fraternity had "violated fire code standards and the Code of Student Conduct."[54] Although the fraternity did not raise equal protection objections to the punishment, only due process claims, the court cited the Third Circuit's decision in *Pi Lambda Phi* and granted the university's motion to dismiss, noting that "'a university has the power to withdraw recognition if an organization breaks university rules.'"[55]

Universities therefore stand on solid legal footing when they sanction fraternal organizations for misconduct by denying official recognition and likely do not run afoul of their equal protection obligations. Courts have not addressed, however, whether universities may proactively impose differential rules upon fraternal organizations that are not required of other student organizations based upon fears of future misconduct.[56]

For example, some universities have implemented so-called "deferred rush" policies whereby fraternities and sororities are prohibited from recruiting new members during the initial freshman academic term.[57] Such measures aim to encourage freshmen to adjust to campus life before committing to fraternity membership in order to prevent hazing, drug and alcohol abuse, and other threats to safety.[58] When UVA's for-

---

52. No. 1:12-cv-657, 2013 WL 427416 (S.D. Ohio Feb. 4, 2013).

53. *Id.* at *1.

54. *Id.* at *1.

55. *Id.* at *10 (quoting *Pi Lambda Phi Fraternity*, 229 F.3d at 445).

56. James Harvey, *Deferred Rush: A Violation of Equal Protection?* FRATERNAL LAW PARTNERS (Sept. 2005), https://fraternallaw.com/newsletter2/deferred-rush-a-violation-of-equal-protection.

57. *See* Ann O'Hanlon, *Fraternities at U-VA. Must Delay 'Rush'; School Leader Decries Underage Drinking*, WASH. POST, Apr. 5, 1998, 1998 WLNR 8147780 ("Postponing the annual membership drive is becoming an increasingly popular decision on campuses nationwide, partly because officials feel it gives freshmen a chance to adjust to college life before being swept into intense drinking scenes during the rush period.").

58. *Id.* (noting University of Maryland, Dartmouth, the University of Pennsylvania, and University of Mississippi all experimented with deferred rush).

mer President John T. Casteen III announced his school's policy of a deferred rush in 1998, he contended that "[t]he culture surrounding rush, including its acceptance of underage use of alcohol, poses a significant hazard to the intellectual culture that is the University's natural environment."[59]

Deferred rush policies gained attention following the University of Colorado's decision to defer rush in 2005 following the alcohol poisoning death of a student rushing one of the school's fraternities.[60] Although sororities on campus reluctantly agreed to the university's new rules, Colorado's fraternities declined to comply and chose to forego official university recognition.[61] The fraternities reportedly considered litigation challenging the policy, but in the end never filed suit.[62] Colorado's off-campus fraternities remained unsanctioned by the university for some time, but many are now officially recognized.

Some have questioned whether policies singling out fraternal organizations comport with the requirements of equal protection given that freshmen are typically free to participate in all other campus activities and student organizations without similar restrictions.[63] Fraternal organizations might argue that such policies are irrational since they are both overinclusive and underinclusive. They are underinclusive given that they do not reach all binge drinking on campus, and, in fact, some student-related alcohol deaths do not involve freshmen at all, including the one at the University of Virginia which prompted the deferred rush policy at that institution.[64] The National Panhellenic Conference has claimed, for example, that such policies are ineffective.[65] Deferred rush policies are also arguably overinclusive in that

---

59. *Id.*
60. *Fraternity Group, Colorado Clash on Reforms*, Assoc. Press, Jan. 27, 2005.
61. Dave Curtin, *Frat Group Rejects Delayed Rush at CU*, Denver Post, Jan. 26, 2005.
62. Harvey, *supra* note 56.
63. Harvey, *supra* note 56. For an argument acknowledging that colleges have "the right to impose regulations over the rush process" see Robert E. Manley, *People Problems*, Fraternal L., Sept. 1982, at 2.
64. O'Hanlon, *supra* note 57 (noting the student death at UVA, which prompted the policy, was a fourth-year student).
65. Brittany Anas, *Greeks Leery of Deferred Recruitment Sorority Group Says New Guidelines Discriminatory, Hurt Finances*, Boulder Daily Camera, Jan. 20, 2005 (noting statement from National Panhellenic Conference that "deferred rush does not 'eliminate' alcohol abuse or hazing").

they ban even those campus rush activities that are safe and healthy for members of the community.

Given that universities have long had substantial discretion regarding the terms by which they recognize fraternal organizations,[66] it is unlikely that such challenges would be successful. Once again, under rational basis review, courts will likely defer to university conclusions that a slight delay in rush periods will promote health and safety.[67] Under rational basis review, a state need not adopt the perfect solution to a problem but can regulate incrementally to address even its partial dimensions.[68] As the Supreme Court has repeatedly recognized, a policy is not unconstitutional under rational basis review simply because the state's chosen means of regulation may not work very well.[69]

III. Equal Protection and University Responses to Hazing

Equal protection principles have also been invoked in efforts to hold colleges and universities responsible for alcohol abuse and hazing within fraternities. In *Gruver v. Board of Supervisors of Louisiana State University & Agriculture & Mechanical College ex rel. Louisiana*,[70] parents of a student who died following a hazing incident sued Louisiana State University (LSU), alleging that the school discriminated on the basis of gen-

---

66. Hauser, *supra* note 42 at 435–38 ("A critical tool for the institutions has been the power to 'recognize' a chapter.").

67. Hauser, *supra* note 42, at 435–36 ("Host campuses have also long regulated membership in fraternity chapters by exercising control of the chapters' recruitment (usually known as 'rushing.')").

68. Bankers Life and Casualty Co. v. Crenshaw, 486 U.S. 71, 84–85 (1988) (upholding state measure that was merely a "partial solution" to problem of frivolous litigation and noting the long establish principle that state measure "need not be so perfectly calibrated in order to pass muster under the rational-basis test").

69. Dandridge v. Williams, 397 U.S. 471, 485 (1970) ("In the area of economics and social welfare, a State does not violate the Equal Protection Clause merely because the classifications made by its laws are imperfect. If the classification has some reasonable basis, it does not offend the Constitution simply because the classification is not made with mathematical nicety or because in practice it results in some inequality.") (internal quotation and citations omitted).

70. 401 F. Supp. 3d 742, 745 (M.D. La. 2019), *aff'd*, 959 F.3d 178 (5th Cir. 2020).

der in violation of Title IX of the Education Amendments Act of 1972,[71] by failing to adequately respond to the allegedly known dangers to men posed by fraternity hazing while the school responded more proactively to dangers with respect to sororities.[72]

Rejecting LSU's motion to dismiss, the district court ruled that the plaintiffs plausibly pled gender discrimination by alleging that LSU knew of the hazing problem for men within fraternities but showed deliberate indifference to its risks even while taking "strong corrective action" with respect to sororities.[73] The family and the university later settled.[74]

Gruver could serve as a model for using equality-based arguments to challenge universities' failures to adequately protect students from the risks of alcohol and hazing connected to fraternal organizations, even though the gender dimensions of such policies will necessarily turn on the facts. Where plaintiffs successfully make out a claim of unequal treatment based upon gender, courts will evaluate whether the challenged policy or action satisfies intermediate scrutiny, a far less deferential analysis than the rational basis review that typically applies to university policies regulating fraternal organizations.

---

71. 20 U.S.C.A. §§ 1681 et seq. Title IX bans sex discrimination by any educational institution that receives federal funding and is at least as protective as the requirements of gender nondiscrimination under the Equal Protection Clause. *See* David S. Cohen, *Title IX: Beyond Equal Protection*, 28 Harv. J. L. & Gender 217, 245 (2005) (summarizing judicial and academic analysis of whether Title IX is coextensive with the Equal Protection Clause and arguing that the statute is more protective).

72. Gruver, 401 F. Supp. 3d at 762.

73. *Id.*

74. Livia Albeck-Ripka, *Parents of L.S.U. Student Who Died After Hazing Are Awarded $6.1 Million*, N.Y. Times, Mar. 13, 2023 (describing jury award against former fraternity member after the family reached settlements with the other defendants including LSU).

IV. University Policies Requiring Nondiscrimination

Outside of disciplinary sanctions and prophylactic safety rules, equal protection concerns have also been raised in response to university rules that require fraternal organizations to abide by policies of nondiscrimination.[75] These policies have received renewed attention in recent years in light of university efforts to mandate nondiscrimination based upon gender and sexual orientation.

a. Deference to University Policy

Courts have long recognized that colleges and universities may prohibit racial and religious discrimination by student groups, including fraternal organizations.[76] Such policies are constitutionally permissible if they reasonably relate to the university's promotion of educational objectives as well as "the principle of racial and religious equality[.]"[77] Policies requiring racially inclusive student organizations are now largely accepted as the norm. The latest challenges have involved sexual orientation and gender

In 2010, the US Supreme Court recognized that universities may require nondiscrimination on the basis of sexual orientation as a condition of recognizing student groups. In *Christian Legal Society Chapter of the University of California v. Martinez*,[78] the Court upheld the nondiscrimination policy of a public university, Hastings Law School, in the face of a First Amendment challenge by a Christian student group that wished to exclude LGBTQ people.[79] Although the case did not address

---

75. Caroline S. Engelmayer & Michael E. Xie, *Social Groups Sue Harvard Over Sanctions*, THE HARVARD CRIMSON (Dec. 3, 2018) (reporting lawsuit filed by group of fraternities, sororities, and students against Harvard after it issued policy refusing to recognize student groups that exclude members on the basis of gender), at https://www.thecrimson.com/article/2018/12/3/social-groups-sue-over-sanctions/.

76. *See* Sigma Chi Fraternity v. Regents of Univ. of Colo., 258 F. Supp. 515 (D. Colo. 1966).

77. *Id.* at 527 (noting that "there is nothing in [this goal] that can be regarded as an excessive exercise of power" particularly where the Supreme Court had upheld the total banning of fraternal organizations).

78. 561 U.S. 661 (2010).

79. *Id.* at 690 (finding the policy reasonably justified).

the interests of fraternal organizations, its reasoning likely provides further support for colleges and universities that wish to impose nondiscrimination rules upon sororities and fraternities.

The Court reasoned that because private social groups have no entitlement to official university recognition, groups that refuse to abide by universities' reasonable nondiscrimination polices have no basis for claiming that nonrecognition amounts to a First Amendment violation.[80] The Court also rejected the claim that nonrecognition has constitutional significance because it effectively eliminates student groups' ability to exist.[81] In a footnote, the Court emphasized that fraternal organizations can and do exist without official university recognition and may even flourish.[82]

Martinez generally suggests that universities have wide latitude under the Constitution to impose nondiscrimination policies on student groups, including fraternal organizations. But whether this latitude includes an ability to ban single-sex student groups like fraternities and sororities is less clear.

Fraternal organizations, of course, have long been organized as single-sex institutions, a characteristic that many view as desirable and nondiscriminatory. And even in *Mississippi University for Women v. Hogan*,[83] and *United States v. Virginia*,[84] the seminal cases finding that single-sex educational institutions discriminated on the basis of gender in violation of equal protection, the Court never suggested that all single-sex educational institutions are constitutional.

In those cases, the Supreme Court ruled that the state may not exclude students from admissions to public colleges and universities on the basis of gender without demonstrating an important governmental purpose and exceedingly persuasive justification that is substantially

---

80. *Id.*

81. *Id.*

82. *Id.* at 691 n.21 (citing Baker, *Despite Lack of University Recognition, Pi Kappa Theta Continues to Grow*, THE NEW HAMPSHIRE, Sept. 28, 2009, pp. 1, 5 (unrecognized fraternity able to grow despite severed ties with the University of New Hampshire; Battey, *Final Clubs Provide Controversial Social Outlet*, YALE DAILY NEWS, Apr. 5, 2006, pp. 1, 4 (Harvard social clubs, known as "final clubs," "play a large role in the experience of ... students" even though "they became completely disassociated from the university in 1984").

83. 458 U.S. 718 (1982).

84. 518 U.S. 515 (1996).

furthered by the gender-based classification.[85] The Court held that the single-sex policies at issue in each case failed to meet that standard because they excluded willing and able students and were driven by gender stereotypes.[86] But that does not mean all single-sex institutions that expand options for members of both sexes for reasons other than stereotypes would similarly fail.

Still, following the Supreme Court's rulings in *Hogan* and *Virginia*, some commentators questioned whether single-sex fraternities and sororities should also be required to conform to the gender inclusivity mandated in these decisions.[87] Those calling for the end of single-sex fraternities have argued that state colleges and universities that sanction such organizations embrace similar gender-based stereotypes by suggesting gender is "relevant in assessing compatibility, congeniality, responsibility, loyalty, and other qualifications" for student organizations.[88] Whether states violate equal protection by sanctioning single-sex fraternal organizations, however, is a separate question from whether a university may enforce a policy *requiring* fraternal organizations to admit members regardless of their gender.

One circuit court that addressed that question concluded that universities may enact such policies without infringing upon the First Amendment associational rights of fraternal organizations.[89] The case did not reach the equal protection question.

Specifically, in *Chi Iota Colony of Alpha Epsilon Pi Fraternity v. City University of New York*,[90] the Jewish Fraternity of North America sued a

---

85. Hogan, 458 U.S. at 729–30; Virginia, 518 U.S. at 550.

86. *Id.*

87. *See e.g.*, Danielle L. Schwartz, Comment, *Discrimination on Campus: A Critical Examination of Single-Sex College Social Organizations*, 75 CALIF. L. REV. 2117, 2161 (1987) (arguing "equal protection challenges should prevail against [college social organizations] affiliated with public colleges and universities" because the important governmental interest in preserving freedom of association is not justified by "fixed notions concerning the roles and abilities of males and females" which undergird recognition of single-sex student groups); *but see* Nancy S. Horton, *Traditional Single-Sex Fraternities on College Campuses: Will They Survive In the 1990s?* 18 J.C. & U.L. 419 (1992) (arguing that the First Amendment expressive associational interests of fraternal organizations should permit those organizations to remain single sex).

88. Schwartz, *supra* note 87, at 2161.

89. *See* Chi Iota Colony of Alpha Epsilon Pi Fraternity v. City University of New York, 502 F.3d 136 (2d Cir. 2007).

90. *Id.*

state university in Staten Island claiming that the university's denial of official recognition to single-sex student organizations violated the First Amendment intimate-association rights of its student members. The fraternity limited its membership to Jewish men with the goal of furthering "the traditional values of men's college social fraternities ..., community service, and the expression of Jewish culture."[91] In 2007, the United States Court of Appeals for the Second Circuit reversed the lower court's preliminary injunction enjoying the policy, and remanded for further proceedings.[92] While the case focused only on the claimed associational interests of fraternity members, the court's reasoning could be relevant to equal protection challenges too because the Court found that the policy was justified by important governmental interests.[93]

Specifically, the Court recognized that a university's "interests in applying its non-discrimination policy are substantial" and that "[t]here is undoubtedly a compelling interest in eradicating discrimination based on gender" and ensuring "that all its students have equal access to [university] resources."[94] Conversely, the court concluded that the fraternity's claimed associational interests in achieving a single-sex fraternity were "relatively weak."[95] In the end, the court concluded that the school's "non-discrimination policy impose[d] no great burden on the plaintiffs' enjoyment of those interests; the policy serves several important state interests; and the policy is well tailored to effectuate those interests."[96] But as addressed next, other university efforts to eliminate single-sex student groups have had a rockier path.

---

91. *Id.* at 140.
92. *Id.* at 148–49.
93. *Id.* at 148.
94. *Id.*
95. *Id.* at 149.
96. *Id.*

b. Harvard's Failed Effort to Eliminate Single-Sex Social Groups

In 2018, students and fraternal organizations marshalled equal protections arguments to challenge a similar gender nondiscrimination policy at Harvard University.[97] Federal law bars discrimination by private universities like Harvard that receive federal funds.[98] The policy at issue barred students who participated in any single-sex social club from holding leadership positions in on-campus student organizations, captaining athletic teams, or competing for any prestigious fellowships that require institutional endorsement.[99] Because Harvard's fraternities have not operated as officially sanctioned student groups since the 1980s,[100] Harvard could not impose a nondiscrimination policy upon the groups directly and instead sought to influence their single-sex membership policies by penalizing the students who join them.

Individual students, sororities, and fraternities challenged the nondiscrimination policy as unlawful sex-based discrimination under Title IX.[101] In response, the university claimed its policy aimed to eradicate gender-based harm: the problem of sexual assaults in fraternities.[102] But the challengers argued that the law effectively eliminated "nearly all of Harvard's all women's social clubs" including sororities, and that the pol-

---

97. *See* Engelmayer & Xie, *supra* note 75.

98. Title VI of the Civil Rights Act of 1964, 42 U.S.C. § 2000d (banning discrimination based upon race, color, national origin); Title IX of the Education Amendments Act of 1972, 20 U.S.C.A. §§ 1681 et seq. (barring discrimination based upon sex by any educational institution receiving federal funds). The First Circuit, where the case arose, evaluates gender discrimination under Title IX by reference to the nondiscrimination requirements of Title VII, a statute that governs covered employers. Kappa Alpha Theta Fraternity, Inc. v. Harvard Univ., 397 F. Supp. 3d 97, 106–07 (D. Mass. 2019).

99. *See* Complaint, Kappa Alpha Theta Fraternity, Inc., et al. v. Harvard Univ., 1:18-cv-12485 ¶ 2 (Dec. 12, 2018), https://drive.google.com/file/d/1vBLCAIeWKc_uqaFqLqyAw01Y3oYGSe4m/view.

100. Allison Battey, *Final clubs provide controversial social outlet*, YALE DAILY NEWS, Apr. 5, 2006, at 1, 4 (noting that Harvard social clubs "became completely disassociated from the university in 1984").

101. *Complaint, supra* note 99 at ¶ 2 (The Complaint alleged that "Harvard's Sanctions Policy intentionally and improperly discriminates on the basis of sex in violation of Title IX and the U.S. Constitution's Equal Protection Clause, as applicable to Harvard through the Massachusetts Civil Rights Act." *Id.* at ¶ 12).

102. *Id.* at ¶ 1.

icy furthered gender-based stereotypes, including that men are likely to engage in sexual assault.[103]

The United States District Court for the District of Massachusetts rejected Harvard's motion to dismiss the gender-based discrimination claims, concluding that the plaintiffs stated a plausible claim under Title IX.[104] The court noted that Harvard's policy endorsed the assumption that all-male clubs cause sexual violence and bigotry on Harvard's campus, a view based on stereotypes about how men and women act.[105] It likewise rejected the claim that the policy was free of bias because it applied evenhandedly to men and women.[106] Notwithstanding that the policy "purportedly had a greater impact upon all-female organizations than upon all-male organizations" the court concluded that this did "not mean that the Policy was not originally motivated by bias against all-male social organizations."[107] The court cited the plaintiffs' allegations that "various Harvard committees and administrators have made disparaging comments about all-male 'final clubs', indicating that such organizations promote sexual violence, misogyny, and bigotry."[108]

Following that decision and the Supreme Court's decision in *Bostock v. Clayton County*[109] in 2020, Harvard withdrew its policy. Harvard President Lawrence S. Bacow explained in a statement that although the decision in *Bostock* concerned the rights of LGBTQ people to be free of discrimination in the workplace,[110] the Court's interpretation of sex discrimination could have significant implications for Harvard's policy in

---

103. *Id.*
104. Kappa Alpha Theta, 397 F. Supp. 3d at 108.
105. *Id.*
106. *Id.* at 109.
107. *Id.*
108. *Id.* ("While the alleged bias is not against men generally, it is a bias against a certain subset of men and the Court must accept plaintiff's factual allegations as true for purposes of a motion to dismiss.").
109. 140 S.Ct. 1731 (2020) (addressing Title VII of the Civil Rights Act of 1964).
110. Valerie Strauss, *Harvard Rescinds Policy Against Fraternities, Sororities and Other Single-Gender Organizations*, Wash. Post, Jun. 30, 2020, https://www.washingtonpost.com/education/2020/06/30/harvard-rescinds-policy-against-fraternities-sororities-other-single-gender-organizations; Declan J. Knieriem & Ema R. Schumer, *Harvard Drops Social Group Sanctions Following Supreme Court Sex Discrimination Decision*, Harvard Crimson, Jun. 30, 2020, https://www.thecrimson.com/article/2020/6/30/harvard-ends-social-group-sanctions.

addition to the district court's reasoning.[111] Bacow acknowledged that the district court accepted "'the plaintiffs' legal theory that the policy, although adopted to counteract discrimination based on sex, is itself an instance of discrimination based on sex[.]'"[112]

The district court's reasoning regarding gender-based bias and discrimination may be influential in the event of further lawsuits challenging university policies banning single-sex fraternal organizations whether by public or private universities. As legal scholar Linda C. Mc-Claim put it, the case "squarely raise[d] the issue of whether [single-sex] spaces continue to be necessary and empowering or are an anachronism in the twenty-first century."[113]

The above decisional law suggests a somewhat unclear picture regarding the ability of colleges and universities to require fraternal organizations to follow polices of gender nondiscrimination. While there are strong precedents supporting universities' efforts to regulate officially recognized student social organizations by requiring them to abide by school nondiscrimination policies, whether schools may bar single-sex

---

111. Knieriem & Schumer, *supra* note 110.

112. *Id.* (quoting email of Harvard President Lawrence S. Bacow).

113. Linda C. McClain, *"'Male Chauvinism' Is Under Attack from All Sides at Present": Roberts v. United States Jaycees, Sex Discrimination, and the First Amendment*, 87 FORDHAM L. REV. 2385, 2416 (2019). In contrast to the Harvard litigation, a lawsuit by three Yale University students in 2019 claimed that the university engaged in gender-based discrimination by failing to discourage students from joining single-sex clubs and turning a "blind eye" to fraternities as facilitators of alcohol abuse, sexual harassment, and sexual assault. Anemona Hartocollis, *Three Women Sue Yale, Saying Fraternity Scene Is Enabling Harassment*, N.Y. TIMES (Feb. 12, 2019), https://www.nytimes.com/2019/02/12/us/yale-fraternities.html; Complaint, McNeil et. al v. Yale University, et al, Case 3:19-cv-00209 (Feb. 12, 2019), https://www.classaction.org/media/mcneil-et-al-v-yale-university-et-al.pdf. The complaint also claimed that all-male fraternities deny women and nonbinary people access to social networks that are necessary for employment and career advancement. *Id.* Because the Yale Lawsuit implicates the university's responsibility for the actions of private fraternal organizations it raised different questions than the Harvard discrimination suit but was ultimately unsuccessful. A district court rejected most of the plaintiffs' gender-based discrimination claims finding that they were not cognizable under Title IX, which exempts "the membership practices of a social fraternity or social sorority." Evan Gerstmann, *Understanding the Dueling Lawsuits against Yale and Harvard Over Fraternities and Sororities*, FORBES, Feb. 19, 2019, https://www.forbes.com/sites/evangerstmann/2019/02/19/understanding-the-dueling-lawsuits-against-yale-and-harvard-over-fraternities-and-sororities/?sh=708b5db83516.

fraternal organizations without engaging in sex discrimination itself raises more complicated questions.

Whether other courts will follow the district court in the Harvard lawsuit in future legal disputes and allow gender bias challenges to such policies to go forward will likely depend upon the sex-specific impacts of such policies and the reasons for the universities' efforts to move away from the long history of same-sex fraternal organizations. The fact that Title IX specifically exempts single-sex fraternal organizations from the requirements of the statute will prove significant.

If challenged under equal protection, public colleges and universities will have to show an exceedingly persuasive justification for their elimination of single-sex student organizations, which could be difficult for universities to meet given the long history and arguable salutary purposes of single-sex fraternal organizations, as reflected in Title IX's exemption. The Harvard litigation is a testament to the more searching inquiry courts may employ when assessing university justifications for enacting policies alleged to discriminate on "the basis of sex." Where heightened scrutiny applies courts will not defer to any stated rationales that *might* justify the state's decision. Rather, the actual reasons justifying the law will be scrutinized including an assessment of whether those justifications rely upon gender-based stereotypes.

V. When Do the Activities of Fraternal Organizations Constitute State Action Implicating the Requirements of Equal Protection?

Sororities' and fraternities' relationships with the host universities where they are located inevitably give rise to questions of whether the private organizations' conduct implicates state action triggering the Fourteenth Amendment.[114] As noted above, generally, private actors are not constrained by the Constitution's guarantee of equal protection. But

---

114. *See* Danielle Hernandez, *Entwinement: Why Sororities and Fraternities Should Be Subject to the Constitution*, 6 Emory Corp. Governance & Accountability Rev. Perspectives 1043 (2019); Mary E. Phelan, Nonprofit Organizations: Law and

where there is a symbiotic relationship between the state and the private entity with requisite "interdependence" then the discriminatory acts of the fraternal organization might be charged to the state entities and implicate the requirements of equal protection.[115] Notably, however, the Court has held that mere regulation of the private organization or receipt of a benefit or service from the State is not, in of itself, sufficient to constitute state action and subject the private actor to the restraints of the Fourteenth Amendment.[116]

Still, the possibility that a court might find fraternal organization' actives to constitute the state action gives rise to a host of thorny issues for state colleges and universities with respect to fraternal organizations' membership practices and conduct. This could mean equal protection challenges to single-sex membership policies,[117] challenges to practices that restrict trans members from joining fraternal organizations, or the possibility of additional lawsuits seeking to hold state universities responsible for sexual violence alleged to occur within the spaces and culture of fraternities.[118] Given ongoing attention to the problem of sexual violence on campuses and specifically to the role of fraternal organizations in the problem,[119] universities could also very well face further litigation challenging sexual violence on campus as sex discrimination that violates equal protection.

TAXATION, § 23:10 n.3 (2d ed.), Westlaw (database updated May 2023) ("For sororities and fraternities affiliated with a state educational institution, there is a question whether state action is involved so that the equal protection provision of the Fourteenth Amendment may prohibit discrimination based on race or religion.").

115. *Moose Lodge*, 407 U.S. at 172.

116. *Id.*; Jackson v. Metropolitan Edison Co., 419 U.S. 345 (1974).

117. *See, e.g.*, the discussion of *McNeil v. Yale University, supra* note 113.

118. Stevie V. Tran, Note, *Embracing Our Values: Title IX, The "Single-Sex Exemption," and Fraternities' Inclusion of Transgender Members*, 41 HOFSTRA L. REV. 503 (2012); Jacob Wickliffe, *Civil Rights—Answering the "Million Dollar" Question: The Meaning of "Sex" for the Purposes of Title IX, Title VII, and the Equal Protection Clause, and Its Impact on Transgender Students' Membership in Fraternal Organizations*, 42 ARKANSAS L. REV. 327 (2020); CHRISTINE SCHERER, COMMENT, RUSHING TO GET RID OF GREEK LIFE AND SOCIAL CLUBS: THE IMPACT OF BOSTOCK ON SINGLE-SEX COLLEGE ORGANIZATIONS, 71 CASE W. RES. L. REV. 1165, 1190 (2021) (citing McNeil v. Yale Univ., 436 F. Supp. 3d 489, 499, 510 (D. Conn. 2020)).

119. Laurel A. Mazar & Anne Kirkner, *Fraternities and Campus Sexual Violence: Risk, Protection, and Prevention*, 3 VIOLENCE & GENDER 132, 132–35 (2016).

How such lawsuits may fare will depend to a large degree on whether courts view the role of universities in recognizing, regulating, and partially supporting fraternal organizations as sufficient interdependence or entwinement such that a public university's actions are implicated in the practices of the otherwise private organization. The exposure of private universities that receive federal funds to some of these antidiscrimination challenges is likely less significant given the express exemption for single-sex fraternal organizations under Title IX.

Many state universities have grown "increasingly interdependent with fraternities."[120] Universities provide housing and financial savings to the fraternal organizations, which clearly benefit these private entities, while the colleges may benefit from generous fraternal alumni donations and greater interest in the university from prospective students attracted by the promises of fraternal social life.[121] All of these factors could come to bear, and may be institution specific, in assessing interdependence theories for imposing the requirements of equal protection to private fraternal organizations under the state action doctrine.

VI. Conclusion

Unless a fraternal organization can show a violation of a First Amendment interest or discrimination based on sex or another protected characteristic, the Equal Protection Clause is not a robust source of protection when fraternal organizations claim unfair treatment. But the Equal Protection Clause may constrain those same organizations from engaging in discrimination if they are affiliated with state colleges or universities and their relationship is substantial enough to be deemed symbiotic and interdependent. As debates about inclusivity and single-sex institutions continue, fraternity and sorority membership practices are likely to give rise to further challenges in this area and equal protection law involving fraternal organizations is likely to further develop.

---

120. Gregory S. Parks & Sabrina Parisi, *White Boy Wasted: Race, Sex, and Alcohol Use In Fraternity Hazing*, 34 WIS. J.L. GENDER & SOC'Y 1, 3 (2019).

121. *Id.*

CHAPTER 13

Fair Housing Issues for Fraternities and Sororities

Jade A. Craig

At the start of every school year, many colleges and universities welcome thousands of students, both bright-eyed young people fresh out of high school and students who have gone through the travails of the first year and have found the courage and sheer will to come back to complete their educations. While many students move into dormitories and some live in homes and apartments off campus, some students start the school year by moving into the house for their fraternity or sorority. One of the perks of making it through the gauntlet of "rush" and the membership process is the privilege of living in the chapter's residence. The fraternity or sorority house can serve as a center of the organization's life, providing an unforgettable bonding experience for its members and often drawing back alumni who remember their days living in or coming to the house well. The parties and social events with which most people associate Greek life often overshadow the fact that, indeed, people live there. The fact that student members depend on the house for shelter attaches the space to a host of civil rights protections that anyone interested in supporting or regulating Greek-letter organizations must bear in mind.

The increase in diversity among the student bodies at colleges and universities across the United States has shaped the context in which students live during their college years, both on and off campus. Since the rise of the modern Civil Rights Movement, Congress as well as state and local legislatures have enacted sweeping civil rights legislation that protects the rights of individuals who were once excluded from the mainstream (largely straight white male) college experience, ranging from women and people of color to LGBTQ+ students and students with disabilities. The residence of a local fraternity or sorority chapter has become the location at which many of these rights—and the potential to undermine or violate them—converge. This chapter examines various statutes, cases, and policy issues that are at the intersection of housing and civil rights law in the context of fraternity and sorority chapters. The Fair Housing Act of 1968 (FHA) serves as the leading civil rights law which targets discrimination in the rental and sale of housing. The FHA prohibits discrimination in housing because of race, color, national origin, religion, sex, familial status, and disability. A host of other civil rights protections, however, overlay the FHA to provide additional grounds for civil rights compliance and liability related to these core protected groups.

The relationship between fraternities and sororities and fair housing law starts with a chapter's house and issues among the members. This site, however, is only a starting point. It is helpful to imagine the issues that implicate Greek organizations, starting in the house and spreading outward in concentric circles, in a ripple effect. As one considers the broader context in which fraternity and sorority houses exist, new issues and policy questions emerge not only for national fraternity organizations and their local chapters, but also for universities and the communities where the houses are located.

This review of fair housing law starts with the center of the ripples, with the house as a rock that falls into a pond. It begins with the house itself, namely the rights of fraternity and sorority members who live in the house. Within the context of fraternity and sorority houses, claims of discrimination against students with disabilities are among the most common fair housing issues that organizations face from their members. These claims often arise in response to no-pet policies, which affect students who live with emotional support animals, as well as issues of accessibility for fraternity and sorority members with physical disabilities. These claims also implicate protections under the Americans with Disabilities Act (ADA). This chapter discusses the relationship between the two statutes and compliance with each. The single-sex nature of fraternities and sororities requires heightened awareness of gender stereotypes and respect for LGBTQ+ members to protect their rights under state, federal, and local fair housing laws. The chapter also examines the process of expelling members in fraternity and sorority houses and managing the risk of claims that the organization expelled the member for an impermissible reason, which can cover any protected class.

Local land use law forms the next ring of the circle, as the house becomes subject to zoning ordinances and local regulations. These rules literally affect the ground on which the organization's house sits. The FHA also reaches to discriminatory zoning and land use policies enacted by local governments, many of which can directly affect fraternities and sororities. One of the most consistent trends that emerges, however, is the extent to which local governments or local regulations often exhibit a bias that treats sorority houses differently than fraternity houses. This issue raises concerns around sex discrimination in favor of women and against men and exposes important long-held gender stereotypes that shape local decision making.

Finally, the broader society forms the outermost ring of this review of fair housing law with respect to fraternities and sororities. Taking a bird's-eye view raises the question of how Greek organizations acquire and maintain houses in the first place. From the Great Depression through the 1970s, discriminatory federal housing policies favored whites and disadvantaged people of color, specifically African Americans. These policies affected the ability of all-white fraternities and sororities to obtain access to credit and mortgages to purchase homes. These policies, along with America's racial wealth gap, play a role in explaining why many historically Black fraternities and sororities do not have permanent residences on or near the campuses of the colleges their members attend. Many universities have become open to financing and purchasing fraternity and sorority houses and integrating them into the university's housing stock. Likewise, the private real estate market continues to explore ways to finance or lease fraternity and sorority houses for profit. The opportunity that these trends may present for historically Black Greek organizations raises questions about whether they may run into the potential for racial discrimination in pursuing any one of these options and the relief available to them as a result.

I. The Fair Housing Act in the Fraternity and Sorority House

In 1968, Congress passed the federal Fair Housing Act of 1968, at Title VIII of the Civil Rights Act. Congress provided that the purpose of the FHA is to "provide, within constitutional limitations, for fair housing throughout the United States."[1] The FHA makes it unlawful to discriminate against any person in the terms, conditions, or privileges of sale or rental of a dwelling, or in the provision of services or facilities in connection therewith, because of race, color, religion, sex, or national origin.[2] The Fair Housing Amendments Act extended the FHA's protections to persons with disabilities and families with children, effective March 12, 1989.[3] The FHA also protects persons from interference with their fair housing rights by third parties. Under the Act, it is "unlawful to coerce, intimidate, threaten, or interfere with any person in the exercise or enjoyment of, or on account of his having exercised or enjoyed, or on account of his having aided or encouraged any other person in the exercise or enjoyment of, any right granted or protected" under the Act.[4]

The text of the FHA prohibits discrimination in the occupancy, sale, or rental of a "dwelling."[5] A "dwelling" is defined as a building or structure that will serve as a "residence" for a family or single person.[6] The statute does not define "residence."[7] HUD has further defined the term "dwelling" and included university-provided housing such as "dormitory rooms" as an example.[8] A federal court has also relied on HUD's

---

1. 42 U.S.C. § 3601.

2. 42 U.S.C. § 3604(b)

3. H.R. 1158 - 100th Congress (1987–1988): Fair Housing Amendments Act of 1988, H.R. 1158, 100th Cong. (1988), https://www.congress.gov/bill/100th-congress/house-bill/1158.

4. 42 U.S.C. § 3617.

5. 42 U.S.C. § 3604.

6. 42 U.S.C. § 3602(b).

7. *See* 42 U.S.C. §§ 3601–3609.

8. *See* 24 C.F.R. § 100.201(2021) ("Dwelling unit means a single unit of residence for a family or one or more persons. Examples of dwelling units include ... other types of dwellings in which sleeping accommodations are provided but toileting or cooking facilities are shared by occupants of more than one room or portion of the dwelling, rooms in which people sleep. Examples of the latter include *dormitory rooms*....") (emphasis added). *But see* 24 LAURA ROTHSTEIN, ANIMAL L. 13 (2018).(noting that, despite HUD's

definition and an analysis of the statute to conclude that a university's "student housing facilities are clearly 'dwellings' within the meaning of the FHA."[9] Many other federal courts have also assumed that the FHA applies to university housing without any further analysis of the issue.[10] A federal court has reached a similar conclusion in the context of Greek housing. In *Entine v. Lissner*, the plaintiff, a sorority member with a disability, filed suit alleging violations of the ADA, Section 504 of the Rehabilitation Act, and the FHA.[11] The court granted a preliminary injunction based on its finding that she was likely to prevail on her ADA claim and, as a result, she would succeed on her other claims, including her FHA claim, because it was a "less demanding statute[]."[12]

The FHA "makes little effort to define the scope of proper defendants."[13] The substantive provisions of the Act "simply declare certain housing practices to be unlawful without specifying who may be held responsible for these practices."[14] Given the breadth of the Act's reach, organizations must be mindful that not only can the organization be liable under the FHA, liability may also extend to officers, directors, and resident leaders who make decisions. The FHA provides for vicarious liability and the case law treats a claim of housing discrimination as a

---

regulation, "this issue has never been definitively decided by the courts. The HUD guidance is not a federal regulation that has gone through notice and comment, so it is not absolutely settled that all university housing is covered.")

9. United States v. Univ. of Neb. at Kearney, 940 F. Supp. 2d 974, 983 (D. Neb. 2013)

10. *See e.g.*, Fialka-Feldman v. Oakland Univ. Bd. of Tr., 678 F. Supp. 2d 576, 587–88 (E.D. Mich. 2009) (assuming that the FHA applied to university-provided housing but denying the plaintiff's claim because the university provided reasons other than the plaintiff's disability to justify rejecting his application for rental housing); Kuchmas v. Towson Univ., 553 F. Supp. 2d 556, 561–63 (D. Md. 2008) (determining that the statute of limitations on the plaintiff's claim had not run, without questioning whether the FHA applied to university housing).

11. *See* Entine v. Lissner, No. 2:17-CV-946, 2017 WL 5507619, at *5 (S.D. Ohio Nov. 17, 2017). The FHA provides an exception for "private clubs." See 42 U.S.C. 3607(a). Under the terms of the statute, however, and the ways in which courts have interpreted the term, it is unlikely that the traditional college fraternity or sorority would be considered a "private club." Stephen Clowney, Do Fraternities Violate the Fair Housing Act? An Empirical Study of Segregation in the Greek Organizations, 41 YALE L. & POL'Y REV. 152, 206-09 (2023).

12. *Id.* at *9 n.7.

13. ROBERT G. SCHWEMM, WHO MAY BE LIABLE UNDER THE FAIR HOUSING ACT—INTRODUCTION, HOUSING DISCRIMINATION LAW AND LITIGATION § 12B:1 (2022).

14. *Id.* (footnote omitted).

tort action to which traditional agency principles apply.[15] Vicarious liability can result from an actual or an apparent agency relationship. "Actual agency exists when the agent and the principal agree to have the former act on the latter's behalf and subject to the latter's control."[16] Under HUD's fair housing regulations, an agent "includes any person authorized to perform an action on behalf of another person regarding any matter related to the sale or rental of dwellings."[17] Liability, however, does not extend up to officers and directors. In 2003, the Supreme Court rejected a claim against an individual president of a real estate firm whose salesman had violated the FHA, holding that "in the absence of special circumstances it is the corporation, not its owner or officer, who is the principal or employer, and thus subject to vicarious liability for torts committed by the employees or agents."[18]

While there are some reasonable restrictions on who may be held liable, the general rule is that "one who commits one of the acts proscribed by the statute's substantive provisions is liable to suit, unless he is covered by one of the exemptions[.]"[19] The most relevant exemption is the private club exemption. As discussed below, however, it is doubtful that a traditional Greek-letter organization affiliated with a college or university is covered under the exemption.

---

15. *See* Meyer v. Holley, 537 U.S. 280, 285 (2003); ROBERT G. SCHWEMM, WHO MAY BE LIABLE UNDER THE FAIR HOUSING ACT—INTRODUCTION, HOUSING DISCRIMINATION LAW AND LITIGATION § 12B:1 (2022).

16. ROBERT G. SCHWEMM, WHO MAY BE LIABLE UNDER THE FAIR HOUSING ACT—INTRODUCTION, HOUSING DISCRIMINATION LAW AND LITIGATION § 12B:1 (2022) (citing cases).

17. *See* 24 C.F.R. § 100.20 (1996) (referring to brokers and agents dealing with matters "including offers, solicitations or contracts and the administration of matters regarding such offers, solicitations or contracts or any residential real estate-related transactions").

18. Meyer v. Holley, 537 U.S. 280, 286 (2003).

19. ROBERT G. SCHWEMM, WHO MAY BE LIABLE UNDER THE FAIR HOUSING ACT—INTRODUCTION, HOUSING DISCRIMINATION LAW AND LITIGATION § 12B:1 (2022) (footnote omitted).

a. Fair Housing Act's Private Club Exemption

The Fair Housing Act does not prohibit a "private club not in fact open to the public, which as an incident to its primary purpose or purposes provides lodgings which it owns or operates for other than a commercial purpose, from limiting the rental or occupancy of such lodgings to its members or from giving preference to its members."[20] While this exemption has not encountered much litigation, one commentator suggests that it "appears to be intended to cover temporary rooming facilities of social organizations such as university clubs."[21] The extent to which the exemption "might apply to these programs may depend on whether the university owns and operates the housing or whether it is entirely separate from any involvement of the university."[22] In the case of fraternities and sororities, it should be noted that this exemption may not generally apply because housing affiliated with a college or university is not considered "temporary" or "transient."[23] Section 3607(a) also specifically refers to "lodgings" instead of "dwellings" to limit the private club exemption to temporary accommodations—not the semester-long or yearlong stay common for most Greek house residents.[24] Additionally, this defense is limited to fraternities and applies to individuals who are *not* members of the Greek-letter organization seeking to reside in the chapter's house. The members themselves who reside in the house are still covered under the FHA's protected classes.

b. Claims of Discrimination by Members Residing on Organization Houses

While the FHA is probably the most comprehensive of the civil right statutes that apply to the context of Greek housing, it is only one of several that must be considered to understand the panoply of protections

---

20. 42 U.S.C. § 3607(a).

21. Robert Schwemm, Exempted dwellings and other defenses—§3607(a), Housing Discrimination Law and Litigation § 9:5 (2022).

22. *24* Laura Rothstein, Animal L. 13 (2018).

23. *See* United States v. Univ. of Neb. at Kearney, 940 F. Supp. 2d 974, 977–78 (D. Neb. 2013).

24. *See e.g.*, United States v. Columbus Country Club, 915 F.2d 877, 884–85 (3d Cir. 1990); Robert Schwemm, Exempted dwellings and other defenses—§3607(a), Housing Discrimination Law and Litigation § 9:5 (2022).

available to students residing in fraternity and sorority houses. The hook with most of these statutes is the Greek-letter organization's affiliation with a college or university. The colleges and universities with which sororities and fraternities are affiliated generally must recognize them in order for them to operate.[25] For example, interfraternity and Panhellenic councils supervise their activities, and the catalogues and brochures that universities provide to prospective and current students often include descriptions of the Greek-letter organizations.[26] A university has the power to withdraw recognition of existing Greek-letter organizations absent compliance with strict requirements or refuse recognition of new fraternities and sororities unless they complete an extensive screening process.[27] In this way, colleges and universities control the conduct and reach of fraternities and sororities.[28] While these rules seek to protect the welfare of students, they also can control the supply and demand in both recruitment for Greek-letter organizations and in student housing.[29]

The ownership of Greek houses differs across campuses. Some universities own and regulate the houses.[30] At others, a fraternity or sorority's national organization, a private corporation, or a local landlord may own or regulate the house.[31] Despite the different ownership structures of the homes, the relationship between the university and the organization generally functions as the hook that makes the law attach to the conduct related to fraternity and sorority houses.

With respect to relations with actual members residing in chapter houses, the most relevant federal statutes are the FHA, the ADA, Section

---

25. *See e.g.*, 3 MARILYN E. PHELAN, NONPROFIT ORGANIZATIONS: LAW AND TAXATION §23:11 n.7 (2d ed.).

26. *See e.g.*, 3 MARILYN E. PHELAN, NONPROFIT ORGANIZATIONS: LAW AND TAXATION §23:11 n.7 (2d ed.).; Jared S. Sunshine, *The Fraternity As Franchise: A Conceptual Framework*, 42 J.C. & U.L. 375, 405 (2016) ("[U]niversities usually delegate recognition of new chapters to a quasi-official school-controlled council of existing fraternities.") (footnote omitted).

27. *See Id.* (footnotes omitted).

28. *See* Gregory F. Hauser, *Social Fraternities at Public Institutions of Higher Education: Their Rights Under the First and Fourteenth Amendments*, 19 J.L. & Educ. 433, 435–38 (1990) ("A critical tool for the institutions has been the power to 'recognize' a chapter.").

29. Jared S. Sunshine, *The Fraternity As Franchise: A Conceptual Framework*, 42 J.C. & U.L. 375, 405 (2016) (footnotes omitted).

30. *See e.g.*, Rebecca J. Huss, *Canines on Campus: Companion Animals at Postsecondary Educational Institutions*, 77 Mo. L. Rev. 417, 457 (2012) (footnotes omitted).

31. *See e.g., Id.*

504, and Title IX of the Education Amendments of 1972 (Title IX). These laws also often have state law counterparts that may apply. This section introduces these statutes generally and discusses the context in which challenges most often arise: the rights of students with disabilities, the rights of LGBTQ+ students, and residents' rights during the process of discipline or expulsion from the residence.

c. Disability Rights

The FHA, the ADA, and Section 504 all prohibit discrimination on the basis of disability. While the FHA has the broadest mandate and application among these three, they each apply in the context of Greek-letter organizations, and to colleges and universities more broadly in important ways. The ADA broadly protects the rights of individuals with disabilities in various areas of American life, including in access to state and local government services and places of public accommodation.[32] Title II of the ADA applies to the services, activities, and programs of state and local governments. Title III prohibits discrimination due to disability in the activities of places of public accommodation, namely businesses that are generally open to the public, including private colleges and universities.[33] Section 504 of the Rehabilitation Act of 1973 provides that "[n]o otherwise qualified individual with a disability in the United States ... shall, solely by reason of her or his disability, be excluded from the participation in, be denied the benefits of, or be subjected to discrimination under any program or activity receiving Federal financial assistance[.]"[34] Title II and Title III both extend to Section 504. The ADA also extends the prohibition on discrimination established by Section 504 to all activities of state and local governments even if they do not receive federal financial assistance.[35]

---

32. 42 U.S.C. § 12204 *et seq.*; Nondiscrimination on the Basis of Disability in State and Local Government Services, 75 Fed. Reg. 56164, 56164 (Sept. 15, 2010).

33. *Id.* (citing 42 U.S.C. § 12182); *see also* 42 U.S.C. § 12101(b)(2) & 28 C.F.R. § 36.104.

34. 29 U.S.C. § 794; *see also Se. Cmty. Coll. v. Davis*, 442 U.S. 397, 400 (1979) (holding that professional schools may impose physical qualifications for admission to their clinical programs).

35. Nondiscrimination on the Basis of Disability in State and Local Government Services, 75 Fed. Reg. 56164, 56164 (Sept. 15, 2010) (citing 42 U.S.C. § 12131).

With respect to the rights of students with disabilities, the most common that face fraternity and sorority residences include (1) the use of service animals and emotional support animals and (2) physical access to the residence. Policies governing service and emotional support animals normally fall under Title II of the ADA while physical access issues fall under Title III of the ADA. Both issues, however, implicate Section 504.[36]

1. SERVICE ANIMALS

ADA regulations issued by the U.S. Department of Justice (DOJ) require covered entities to "make reasonable modifications in policies, practices, or procedures when the modifications are necessary to avoid discrimination on the basis of disability" unless it can show that the modification will "fundamentally alter the nature of the service, program, or activity."[37] They also specifically require these same modifications to "permit the use of a service animal by an individual with a disability."[38] The ADA, however, is unique from the FHA in that it limits the definition of a "service animal" to a dog or miniature horse with specific training.[39] Under the ADA, no other type of animal may be considered a service animal.[40] Specifically, under both Titles II and III, a service animal includes "any dog that is individually trained to do work or perform tasks for the benefit of an individual with a disability, including a physical, sensory, psychiatric, intellectual, or other mental disability."[41]

---

36. The reach of Section 504 is particularly broad in this field. As one commentator has suggested: "Today, virtually all higher education institutions are prohibited from discriminating against disabled individuals by both the Rehabilitation Act and the ADA because they receive federal funds through a variety of grants and loans that pay for research and instructional costs. If colleges and universities accept any federal money, all of their operations are subject to Section 504 dictates.", 147 ROBERT C. CLOUD, ED. LAW REP. 391 (2000).

37. 28 C.F.R. § 35.130(b)(7).

38. 28 C.F.R. § 35.136(a).

39. Prior to the U.S. Department of Justice's change in the regulations on March 15, 2011, federal regulations defined a "service animal" under the ADA by the animal's function rather than its species. See Darian B. Taylor, LL.M., *Service Animals Under Americans with Disabilities Act, 42 U.S.C.A. §§ 12101 et seq.*, 53 A.L.R. Fed. 3d art. 1 (2020).

40. See 28 C.F.R. § 36.104 ("Other species of animals, whether wild or domestic, trained or untrained, are not service animals for the purposes of this definition" of "service animal.").

41. 28 C.F.R. § 35.104 (2011) & 28 C.F.R. § 36.104.

Regulated entities must also make the same concessions to "permit the use of a miniature horse by an individual with a disability if the miniature horse has been individually trained to do work or perform tasks for the benefit of the individual with a disability."[42] Miniature horses, however, are subject to more restrictions than dogs.[43]

A service animal must perform work or tasks that directly relate to the individual's disability.[44] DOJ regulations list examples of services that a protected service animal may perform, but does not limit the covered tasks to these services:

- assisting individuals who are blind or have low vision with navigation and other tasks,
- alerting individuals who are deaf or hard of hearing to the presence of people or sounds,
- providing nonviolent protection or rescue work,
- pulling a wheelchair,
- assisting an individual during a seizure,
- alerting individuals to the presence of allergens, retrieving items such as medicine or the telephone,
- providing physical support and assistance with balance and stability to individuals with mobility disabilities, and
- helping persons with psychiatric and neurological disabilities by preventing or interrupting impulsive or destructive behaviors.[45]

---

42. 28 C.F.R. § 35.136(i)(1) & 28 C.F.R. § 36.302(c)(9)(i).

43. *See* 28 C.F.R. § 35.136(b) (providing that dog who serves as a service animal may be removed if "(1) [t]he animal is out of control and the animal's handler does not take effective action to control it; or (2) [t]he animal is not housebroken"); *cf. id.* at 35.136(i) & 28 C.F.R. § 36.302(c)(9)(ii) (providing that a public entity may evaluate whether it can make reasonable modifications to allow the mini-horse to enter the facility by considering both the handler's control over the horse and whether it is housebroken as well as "[t]he type, size, and weight of the miniature horse and whether the facility can accommodate these features" and whether its "presence in a specific facility compromises legitimate safety requirements that are necessary for safe operation").

44. 28 C.F.R. § 36.104.

45. 28 C.F.R. § 36.104.

The fact that an animal's presence may deter crime does not on its own render it a "service animal."[46] Neither does its status as an emotional support animal.[47]

2. EMOTIONAL SUPPORT ANIMALS

The ADA does not include emotional support animals within the definition of service animal or extend it the same rights.[48] The FHA and Section 504, however, do protect students' rights to keep emotional support animals in campus residences.[49] Emotional support animals (ESAs) have become even more important as the number of college students who struggle with mental and physical health challenges increases.[50] A 2015 study indicates that one-third of college students have some type of emotional disorder, such as anxiety or depression.[51] The use of ESAs has also risen among students with mental health issues and studies have found that these animals significantly improve students' moods, stress, and anxiety levels.[52]

The difference between coverage for ESAs starts with the definitions. The FHA defines the term "assistance" to include both service animals *and* "other animals that do work, perform tasks, provide assistance, and/or provide therapeutic emotional support for individuals with disabilities."[53] Any animal outside of this definition is a "pet" and may be treated

---

46. 28 C.F.R. § 36.104.

47. *See* 28 C.F.R. § 36.104.

48. *See* 28 C.F.R. § 36.104 (providing that an animal's role in providing "emotional support, well-being, comfort, or companionship" is not protected under the ADA).

49. *See* U.S. Dep't of Hous. & Urb. Dev., FHEO Notice 2020-01(Jan. 28, 2020), at 1 & n.3, https://www.hud.gov/sites/dfiles/PA/documents/HUDAsstAnimalNC1-28-2020.pdf; *see also* 34 C.F.R. §§ 104.41 & 104.45.

50. *See* 394 Whitney Kristen Dedmon-woods et al., Ed. Law Rep. 1, 2 (2021) (citing 11 Daphne C. Watkins et al., Qualitative social work 319 (2011) (2011); Center for Collegiate Mental Health, 2017 Annual Report, https://sites.psu.edu/ccmh/files/2018/01/2017_CCMH_Report-1r3iri4.pdf).

51. *See* 394 Whitney Kristen Dedmon-woods et al., Ed. Law Rep. 1, 2 (2021) (citing 191 Maria Sarmento, Procedia-Social & Behav. Sci. 12 (2015), https://www.sciencedirect.com/science/article/pii/S1877042815028669?via%3Dihub).

52. *See* 394 Whitney Kristen Dedmon-woods et al., Ed. Law Rep. 1, 2 (2021).

53. U.S. Dep't of Hous. & Urb. Dev., FHEO Notice 2020-01(Jan. 28, 2020), at 3, https://www.hud.gov/sites/dfiles/PA/documents/HUDAsstAnimalNC1-28-2020.pdf.

as such under the Greek-letter organization's rules and policies.[54] Under the FHA, a "reasonable accommodation is a change, exception, or adjustment to a rule, policy, practice, or service that may be necessary for a person with a disability to have equal opportunity to use and enjoy a dwelling, including public and common use spaces."[55]

3. ADDRESSING REQUESTS FOR ACCOMMODATIONS

ADA regulations allow covered housing providers to ask only two questions of someone seeking to enter with a dog or miniature horse: whether an animal is required because of a disability and what task(s) the animal has been trained to perform, and only when the answers to those questions are not "readily apparent."[56] Covered entities may not require the animal to demonstrate a task or inquire about the nature of the person's disability.[57] The ADA does not require the owner or handler to provide documentation or register the service animal. Thus, purported registration systems like a "Holographic Service Dog ID Card" or an "Official Service Dog Registry" are not required proofs of a person's entitlement to use a service animal under the law.[58]

Under the FHA, the student must request an accommodation to reside with their ESA. The request does not have to use the term "reasonable accommodation." It can also be oral and the requestor does not have to put the request in writing, although HUD's 2020 Guidance Notice suggests that "persons making a request are encouraged to do so in order to avoid miscommunication."[59] A college, university, or Greek housing provider may ask for documentation to support the student's right to keep the ESA, but they are not allowed to seek information regarding the student's diagnosis.[60] These housing providers may use some discretion

---

54. *Id.*

55. *Id.* at 7.

56. *See* 28 C.F.R. § 36.302(c)(6); *see also* Sande Buhai, *Preventing the Abuse of Service Animal Regulations*, 19 N.Y.U. J. Legis. & Pub. Pol'y 771, 772–73 (2016).

57. 28 C.F.R. § 35.136(f).

58. *See* Sande Buhai, *Preventing the Abuse of Service Animal Regulations*, 19 N.Y.U. J. Legis. & Pub. Pol'y 771, 773 (2016).

59. U.S. DEP'T OF HOUS. & URB. DEV., FHEO NOTICE 2020-01 (Jan. 28, 2020), at 7, https://www.hud.gov/sites/dfiles/PA/documents/HUDAsstAnimalNC1-28-2020.pdf.

60. *Id.* at 9, 14 & 16.

regarding the review of Internet-based sources to purportedly establish a student's right to an ESA under the FHA. For example, HUD's 2020 Guidance notes that "[s]ome websites sell certificates, registrations, and licensing documents for assistance animals to anyone who answers certain questions or participates in a short interview and pays a fee."[61]

HUD takes the position that the housing provider has a right to request "reliable documentation" and that these kinds of documents are generally not sufficient to establish "a non-observable disability or disability-related need for an assistance animal."[62] On the other hand, a student may rely on a "legitimate, licensed health care professional" who delivers services remotely, including via the Internet.[63] HUD also provides as an example of a reliable form of documentation a note from the person's healthcare professional who has personal knowledge of the individual.[64] This form of documentation may be preferable, however, given that a professional whom a student meets online purely to assess their need for an ESA may not have the requisite personal knowledge to make the required link between their disability and the need for the animal.

The documentation can be general as to the student's condition. The housing provider is not entitled to know the specific details of the student's disability. The information should, however, be specific as to the assistance or therapeutic emotional support provided by the animal. In short, the documentation must show a "relationship or connection between the disability and the need for the assistance animal[,]" particularly "where the disability is non-observable, and/or the animal provides therapeutic emotional support."[65] In some states, a student who fraudulently misrepresents that they are qualified to use a service animal or that a particular animal that they use is a trained service animal

---

61. *Id.* at 11.

62. *Id.*

63. *Id.* These kinds of mental health services agencies, however, even though they may be licensed, are "questionable from a professional standards perspective and inconsistent with psychological ethics and forensic standards and the law," according to an article from the American Psychological Association. *See* 47 JEFFREY N. YOUNGGREN ET AL., PROF. PSYCH. 255, 257 (2016).

64. U.S. DEP'T OF HOUS. & URB. DEV., FHEO NOTICE 2020-01(Jan. 28, 2020), at 11, https://www.hud.gov/sites/dfiles/PA/documents/HUDAsstAnimalNC1-28-2020.pdf.

65. *Id.* at 12.

may be subject to criminal or civil penalties.[66] A student's fraudulent misrepresentation may also serve as grounds to terminate a rental agreement.[67]

If the student has a qualifying disability and the ESA represents a reasonable accommodation, the housing provider may then consider if the animal is appropriate to keep in campus housing. Under the FHA and Section 504, the animal does not have to be specially trained and it does not have to be a dog or a miniature horse. This issue becomes important as students rely on a diverse array of animals to serve as ESAs.[68]

While there is no blanket restriction on the types of animals a student can keep, the student's burden to demonstrate a need for the particular animal increases as the animal becomes more unusual. According to HUD guidance, the housing provider should permit animals "commonly kept in households" outside of certain exceptions. Specifically, HUD states that the accommodation should normally be granted if "the

---

66. Multiple states and U.S. territories provide that a misrepresentation of an entitlement to a service animal, ESA, or both constitutes a misdemeanor or may render the individual liable for a fine. *See* Sande Buhai, *Preventing the Abuse of Service Animal Regulations*, 19 N.Y.U. J. Legis. & Pub. Pol'y 771, 791 (2016) (citing at least fifteen states); *see also, e.g.*, FLA. STAT. § 413.08(9) (2020) ("A person who knowingly and willfully misrepresents herself or himself, through conduct or verbal or written notice, as using a service animal and being qualified to use a service animal or as a trainer of a service animal commits a misdemeanor of the second degree" and must perform community service, preferably for an organization that serves people with disabilities); FLA. STAT. § 817.265 (2020) (providing that misrepresenting oneself as needing an ESA or providing false information or written documentation of need for an ESA is misdemeanor); UTAH CODE ANN. § 62A-5b-106(2) (West 2019); TENN. CODE ANN. § 39-16-304 (2023); IOWA CODE ANN. § 216C.11(3) (West 2019); 68 PA. STAT. ANN. § 405.5(a) (West 2018); GUAM CODE ANN. § 34406(b); WYO. STAT. ANN. § 35-13-203(b) (2023); MINN. STAT. ANN. § 609.833(2) & (3) (West 2018); *see also* ARIZ. REV. STAT. ANN. § 11-1024(K) (2018) (providing civil penalty up to $250 for each misrepresentation); ALA CODE. § 24-8A-4(a) (2018) (individual may be subject to fine or misdemeanor for first offense). Colorado, however, recently repealed its laws criminalizing misrepresentations related to service and assistance animals and now provides for expungements of the records of persons who were previously convicted of the crime. *See* 2022 Colo. Legis. Serv. Ch. 276 (S.B. 22-099) (enacting COLO. STAT. § 24-72-706, providing for expungements, and repealing COLO. STAT. §§ 18-13-107.3(1) & 18-13-107.7(1)).

67. *See e.g.*, TENN. CODE ANN. § 66-7-111(f)(1); TENN. CODE ANN. § 66-28-406(f)(1).

68. *See* Ilana Linder, *Emotional Support Bunny Case Has Settled*, FRATERNAL LAW NEWSLETTER (Jan. 2020), https://fraternallaw.com/newsletter2/emotional-support-bunny-case-has-settled#:~:text=Alpha%20Omicron%20Pi%20Fraternity%20(%E2%80%-9CAOPi,filed%20against%20the%20two%20entities.

animal is a dog, cat, small bird, rabbit, hamster, gerbil, other rodent, fish, turtle, or other small, domesticated animal that is traditionally kept in the home for pleasure rather than for commercial purposes.... For purposes of this assessment, reptiles (other than turtles), barnyard animals, monkeys, kangaroos, and other non-domesticated animals are not considered common household animals."[69] With respect to household animals, a college, university, or Greek housing provider cannot place a blanket ban on specific kinds of animals, such as certain dog breeds or limits based on an animal's size.[70]

According to HUD, the FHA also does not ban unusual animals outright. Instead, HUD advises that in the case of a non-household animal, the individual has a "substantial burden of demonstrating a disability-related therapeutic need for the specific animal or the specific type of animal" and should "submit documentation from a healthcare professional confirming the need for this animal." With respect to any animal, qualifying or not, a college, university, or Greek housing provider can refuse to allow the student to keep the requested animal if it "poses a direct threat that cannot be eliminated or reduced to an acceptable level through actions the individual takes to maintain or control the animal (e.g., keeping the animal in a secure location)."[71]

The presence of service or assistance animals may raise concerns regarding an organization's premises liability insurance. On one hand, individuals with disabilities are entitled to reasonable accommodations or modifications of policies "when the modifications are necessary to avoid discrimination on the basis of disability, unless the public entity can demonstrate that making the modifications would fundamentally alter the nature of the service, program, or activity" or "impose an undue financial and administrative burden on the housing provider[.]"[72] If the source of that burden is an insurance carrier, however, the calculus changes. HUD has issued guidance which provides that an insurance

---

69. U.S. DEP'T OF HOUS. & URB. DEV., FHEO NOTICE 2020-01(Jan. 28, 2020), at 12, https://www.hud.gov/sites/dfiles/PA/documents/HUDAsstAnimalNC1-28-2020.pdf.

70. *Id.* at 14.

71. *Id.*

72. *See* Crowder v. Kitagawa, 81 F.3d 1480, 1485 (9th Cir. 1996) (quoting 28 C.F.R. § 35.130(b)(7)); Warren v. Delvista Towers Condo. Ass'n, Inc., 49 F. Supp. 3d 1082, 1086 (S.D. Fla. 2014) (citing Schwarz v. City of Treasure Island, 544 F.3d 1201, 1220 (11th Cir. 2008)).

carrier has placed an undue financial and administrative burden on a housing provider if the carrier would "cancel, substantially increase the costs of the insurance policy, or adversely change the policy terms because of the presence of a certain breed of animal or a certain animal."[73] The organization would need to "verify[] such a claim with the insurance company directly and consider[] whether comparable insurance, without the restriction, is available on the market."[74] For the insurance carrier, the practice may violate federal laws prohibiting discrimination based upon disability.[75]

In short, a Greek housing provider may not maintain a blanket "no pets" policy that does not provide an exception for students with disabilities who require service animals or ESAs. Instead, as one commentator suggests," the organization should engage in a "proactive, interactive process between the stakeholders as well as training for those making accommodations."[76] House managers should provide a process by which students can request an accommodation and have that accommodation reviewed based on the limitations outlined above. The organization should maintain a policy that outlines key items, including (1) steps for updating the accommodation, (2) animal identification, (3) owner conduct, (4) owner responsibilities, (5) housing policies, (6) allowed spaces, (7) animal care during an emergency event, (8) removal of an emotional

---

73. U.S. Dep't of Hous. & Urb. Dev., *Insurance Policy Restrictions As A Defense for Refusals to Make A Reasonable Accommodation* (June 12, 2006), https://www.mvfairhousing.com/pdfs/2006-06-12%20HUD%20memo%20on%20insurance%20policy%20restrictions%20related%20to%20reasonable%20accommodations.PDF.

74. *Id.*

75. U.S. Dep't of Hous. & Urb. Dev., *Insurance Policy Restrictions As A Defense for Refusals to Make A Reasonable Accommodation* (June 12, 2006), https://www.mvfairhousing.com/pdfs/2006-06-12%20HUD%20memo%20on%20insurance%20policy%20restrictions%20related%20to%20reasonable%20accommodations.PDF; *see also Wai v. Allstate Ins. Co.*, 75 F. Supp. 2d 1 (D.D.C. 1999) (holding that refusing to provide standard property insurance at ordinary rates to landlords who rent their homes to disabled persons "makes unavailable or denies a dwelling" in violation of the Fair Housing Act); *N.A.A.C.P. v. Am. Fam. Mut. Ins. Co.*, 978 F.2d 287, 297 (7th Cir. 1992) (refusing to issue insurance on equal terms to individuals in predominantly minority neighborhood constitutes race discrimination and "makes housing unavailable" under the FHA).

76. 24 Ani B. Satz, Animals as Living Accommodations, Animal L. 1, 9 (2018) (citing *24* Laura Rothstein, Animal L. 13 (2018).

support animal, and (9) any additional relevant policies that an institution may have in place.[77]

4. CONFLICTS AMONG MEMBERS REGARDING SERVICE/ASSISTANCE ANIMALS

In some cases, students will inevitably run into conflict over the presence of a service or emotional support animal. As a policy matter, a student's housemates, suitemates, or roommates should be informed of the request and there should be a process by which these individuals can object to the request.[78] These objections may sometimes involve a claim that the student's accommodation conflicts with a health issue of another housemate. For example, in *Entine v. Lissner*,[79] a member of the Chi Omega sorority's chapter at Ohio State University required the services of an emotional support animal to cope with several diagnosed mental disorders and panic attacks. Entine sued the university's ADA coordinator when the university required her to move out of the sorority house or live there without Cory, her King Charles Cavalier spaniel, because Cory allegedly exacerbated the symptoms of another member who had been diagnosed with Crohn's disease.[80] For the university, the issue presented "a thorny and unmapped legal issue," namely, how it "should reconcile the needs of two disabled students whose reasonable accommodations are (allegedly) fundamentally at odds."[81] While it may at first appear like a crisis, the "direct threat" exception in ADA regulations contemplates this issue.

A Greek housing provider must permit the use of a service animal unless it "would pose a direct threat to the health and safety of others[.]"[82] Under the regulation, a covered entity "must make an individualized assessment, based on reasonable judgment that relies on current

---

77. 394 WHITNEY KRISTEN DEDMON-WOODS ET AL., ED. LAW REP. 1, 11 (2021) (providing recommendations for policy provisions).

78. *Id.* at 10.

79. No. 2:17-CV-946, 2017 WL 5507619 (S.D. Ohio Nov. 17, 2017).

80. Entine v. Lissner, No. 2:17-CV-946, 2017 WL 5507619, at *5 (S.D. Ohio Nov. 17, 2017).

81. Entine v. Lissner, No. 2:17-CV-946, 2017 WL 5507619, at *1 (S.D. Ohio Nov. 17, 2017).

82. *See* 28 C.F.R. § 35.139; *see also Entine v. Lissner*, No. 2:17-CV-946, 2017 WL 5507619, at *1 (S.D. Ohio Nov. 17, 2017).

medical knowledge or on the best available objective evidence, to ascertain: the nature, duration, and severity of the risk; the probability that the potential injury will actually occur; and whether reasonable modifications of policies, practices, or procedures or the provision of auxiliary aids or services will mitigate the risk."[83] This direct threat analysis may involve the collection and review of medical evidence to determine if the student who has raised an objection can establish that the service animal has actually caused harm, such as an increase in the objecting student's own medical conditions.[84] For example, the DOJ has provided specific guidance which indicates that "[a]llergies and fear of dogs are not valid reasons for denying access or refusing service to people using service animals."[85] When an individual is allergic to dog dander and must use the same space as the person who uses the service animal, "both should be accommodated by assigning them, if possible, to different locations within the room or different rooms in the facility."[86] The housing provider must explore other alternatives short of removing the service animal. The process is not "disability neutral" and requires proof of a close nexus between the service animal and the harm suffered by the objecting resident that cannot be mitigated any other way.[87]

5. PHYSICAL ACCESS FOR STUDENTS WITH DISABILITIES

Students with physical disabilities also have the right to accommodations that allow them physical access to places of public accommodation and residences. These requirements may include constructing wheelchair ramps and making reasonable modifications like installing grab bars and handrails. While the physical access to the residential space falls under the FHA, fraternities and sororities may also be subject to

---

83. 28 C.F.R. § 35.139(b).

84. *See* Entine v. Lissner, No. 2:17-CV-946, 2017 WL 5507619, at *8 (S.D. Ohio Nov. 17, 2017) (finding that direct threat analysis failed to establish an exception to the service animal requirement where "none of the evidence shows that it was Cory that caused Goldman's [the objecting sorority house resident] increased Crohn's symptoms").

85. U.S. Dep't of Justice, *ADA Requirements: Service Animals* (last updated Feb. 24, 2020), https://www.ada.gov/service_animals_2010.htm.

86. *Id.*

87. *See* Entine v. Lissner, No. 2:17-CV-946, 2017 WL 5507619, at *9–*10 (S.D. Ohio Nov. 17, 2017).

Title III's requirements if they host social events open to the public, including the university population.[88] Greek organizations are generally implicated under the ADA and Section 504 as part of their relationship to the higher education institution with which they are affiliated.[89] For example, a fraternity or sorority cannot "lawfully deny a disabled student a reasonable accommodation that would permit him or her to live in its dormitories. Indeed, the DOJ has consistently taken the position that all aspects of a school's student activities and of the educational experience (including, for example, research activities and fraternity housing) are covered by Title III of the ADA."[90]

Guidance from the DOJ in 1994 specifically addressed the application of physical access requirements to fraternities and sororities. University-owned or operated houses must meet ADA new construction standards.[91] For example, in a case involving the University of Toledo, the university planned to build a $7.4 million apartment complex for fraternities and sororities without elevators. After a lawsuit brought by a disability rights organization, the university entered a settlement in which it agreed to redesign the facility, providing platform lifts to provide access to persons with disabilities.[92]

If the house is privately owned and will not become owned or operated by the university for the foreseeable future, the house may fall within the ADA's private club exemption. Whether a particular facility is a private club requires a case-by-case analysis. Some of the relevant factors include the degree to which the establishment is open to non-

---

88. *See* U.S. Dep't of Justice, *Americans with Disabilities Act Technical Assistance Manual* § III-1.2000; see also 28 C.F.R. pt. 36, app. B at 665 col. 2, 666 col. 1 (2002) ("A facility can be a residential dwelling under the FHA and still fall in whole or in part under at least one of the 12 categories of places of public accommodation.").

89. Letter from Deval L. Patrick, Assistant Attorney General, Civil Rights Division, U.S. Dep't of Justice to Sen. Trent Lott, Doc. #129 (May 2, 1994), https://www.justice.gov/sites/default/files/crt/legacy/2010/12/15/cltr129.txt ("[u]niversities are places of public accommodation" and university-owned Greek houses must comply with ADA standards like other university facilities).

90. *Regents of Mercersburg Coll. v. Republic Franklin Ins. Co.*, 458 F.3d 159, 167 (3d Cir. 2006).

91. Letter from Deval L. Patrick, Assistant Attorney General, Civil Rights Division, U.S. Dep't of Justice to Sen. Trent Lott, Doc. #129 (May 2, 1994), https://www.justice.gov/sites/default/files/crt/legacy/2010/12/15/cltr129.txt.

92. *See Ability Ctr. v. Univ. of Toledo*, No 3:89-CV-7561 (N.D. Ohio, settled Nov. 1989).

members, the breadth of club's advertising for members, whether it charges substantial membership fees, and the degree to which it receives public funding, among others.[93] This exemption is hard to prove, however, where the Greek organization hosts events at the house and opens the house to the general public—beyond the members and their personal guests.[94] If it does, the organization must make public areas of the house accessible during those events.[95] "The more often such public events occur, the higher the obligation to make the publicly used areas accessible."[96] For example, if a Greek organization hosts an event once every several years, a temporary wheelchair ramp may be sufficient. If it hosts several events during the course of a year, it may be obligated to build a permanent ramp.[97]

These requirements, however, pose challenges for organizations with older residences, some of which have historic landmark designations.[98] These homes generally were not designed with accessibility features like elevators and are difficult to retrofit. These issues, however, must be taken into account when building renovations take place. The ADA requires covered entities to alter facilities and remove barriers where these changes are "readily achievable."[99] The ADA defines readily achievable as "easily accomplishable and able to be carried out without

---

93. Letter from Deval L. Patrick, Assistant Attorney General, Civil Rights Division, U.S. Dep't of Justice, to Sen. Trent Lott, Doc. #129 (May 2, 1994), https://www.justice.gov/sites/default/files/crt/legacy/2010/12/15/cltr129.txt (listing these and other relevant factors).

94. Letter from Deval L. Patrick, Assistant Attorney General, Civil Rights Division, U.S. Dep't of Justice, to Sen. Trent Lott, Doc. #129 (May 2, 1994), https://www.justice.gov/sites/default/files/crt/legacy/2010/12/15/cltr129.txt.

95. *Id.*

96. *Id.*

97. *Id.*

98. *See e.g.*, U.S. Nat'l Park Service, Nat'l Register of Hist. Places Registration Form (Jan. 28, 2004), https://npgallery.nps.gov/GetAsset/0281da5a-35ee-40b0-bb21-321b64271b95/ (entering Alpha Tau Omega Fraternity House in Reno, Nevada on National Register of Historic Places); Jessica Fargen, *UNL's greek houses make National Register of Historic Places list*, THE DAILY NEBRASKAN (June 16, 2006), https://www.dailynebraskan.com/unls-greek-houses-make-national-register-of-historic-places-list/article_caaef81c-5829-5136-83b7-82508dc7646a.html (announcing that thirty-five buildings on Greek Row at the University of Nebraska Lincoln were entered on the National Register of Historic Places).

99. *See* 28 C.F.R. § 36.304 & 36.405 (regarding historic places).

much difficulty or expense."[100] The organization should consider several factors, including the "costs of the project, the resources of the facility and entity, and the nature of the entity and its operations."[101] For places designated as historic landmarks under federal, state, or local law, the organization must provide "alternative methods of access" in a way that "will not threaten or destroy the historic significance of the building or the facility."[102] Owners of these residences may be required to modify their accessibility features to ensure they comply with the ADA and its accessibility standards.

d. LGBTQ+ Residents

As an initial matter, it must be noted that fraternities and sororities have a great deal of control under federal law of their membership practices. Where organizations discriminate in membership decisions, there are important institutional barriers to challenging discrimination in their membership policies. Title IX of the Education Amendments of 1972 explicitly exempts fraternities and sororities from its provisions, which is core to "[t]he legal foundation on which fraternities exist today."[103] The Civil Rights Act of 1964 also specifically does not allow the U.S. Commission on Civil Rights "to inquire into or investigate any membership practices or internal operations of any fraternal organization, any college or university fraternity or sorority, any private club, or any religious organization."[104] Thus, the issues of fair housing arise with

---

100. 42 U.S.C. § 12181(9).

101. *See* Molski v. Foley Ests. Vineyard & Winery, LLC, 531 F.3d 1043, 1047 n.2 (9th Cir. 2008) (citing 42 U.S.C. § 12181(9)).

102. 28 C.F.R. § 36.405(a).

103. Stevie V. Tran, *Embracing Our Values: Title IX, the "Single-Sex Exemption," and Fraternities' Inclusion of Transgender Members*, 41 Hofstra L. Rev. 503, 523 (2012); 20 U.S.C. § 1681(a)(6) ("[Title IX] shall not apply to membership practices of a social fraternity or social sorority which is exempt from taxation under section 501(a) of title 26, the active membership of which consists primarily of students in attendance at an institution of higher education....") (internal citation omitted).

104. Pub. L. No. 88-352, § 504(a), 78 Stat. 241 (1964) (codified as amended in 42 U.S.C. § 1975a(b)). The U.S. Commission on Civil Rights is an "independent, bipartisan, fact-finding federal agency" whose mission is "to inform the development of national civil rights policy and enhance enforcement of federal civil rights laws ... through objective and comprehensive investigation, research, and analysis on issues of fundamental

respect to protections afforded to LGBTQ+ members of an organization that live in the chapter house.

The FHA does not specifically identify individuals who are gay, lesbian, bisexual, transgender, or queer (LGBTQ+) as a protected class. There is a growing trend, however, to interpret civil rights protections against discrimination on the basis of sex to include sexual orientation and gender identity, particularly in the wake of the U.S. Supreme Court's decision in *Bostock v. Clayton County*,[105] where the Court reached this conclusion in the context of employment discrimination under Title VII of the Civil Rights Act of 1964. Even before *Bostock*, courts had interpreted discrimination against a person because their dress or behavior does not match the stereotypes associated with their gender as sex discrimination.[106] In the context of transgender students, this challenge may also come up where a member joins the organization with a particular gender identity and then transitions to a different gender identity. For example, in *Schroer v. Billington*,[107] a district court held that treating an individual differently "after being advised that she planned to change her anatomical sex by undergoing sex reassignment surgery was literally discrimination 'because of ... sex.'" Indeed, the court made an analogy to an individual who was fired for deciding to convert from Christianity to Judaism, which it called a "clear case" of religious discrimination.[108]

Several federal courts have followed suit in recognizing that discrimination against LGBTQ+ people constitutes discrimination on the basis of sex under the FHA.[109] HUD has implemented an executive order that

---

concern to the federal government and the public." U.S. Comm'n on Civ. Rts., *Our Mission*, https://www.usccr.gov/about/mission (last visited June 28, 2022).

105. 140 S. Ct. 1731 (2020).

106. *See* Price Waterhouse v. Hopkins, 490 U.S. 228 (1989), *superseded by statute on other grounds*, Civil Rights Act of 1991, Pub. L. No. 102-166, 105 Stat. 1074, §107; *Barnes v. City of Cincinnati*, 401 F.3d 729, 733–35 & 737 (6th Cir. 2005) & *Smith v. City of Salem*, 378 F.3d 566, 568 (6th Cir. 2004) (protecting gender-nonconforming men against employment discrimination where they allegedly did not act "masculine enough").

107. 577 F. Supp. 2d 293 (D.D.C. 2008).

108. *Id.* at 306–08.

109. *See* Wetzel v. Glen St. Andrew Living Community, *LLC*, 901 F.3d 856, 862 (7th Cir. 2018) (upholding lesbian's harassment claim as being covered by the FHA's ban of sex discrimination); Kummerow v. OHAWCHA.org, No. 21-CV-635-WMC, 2022 WL 873599, at *4 (W.D. Wis. Mar. 24, 2022) (presuming that an LGBT plaintiff's Fair Housing Act claim fell within the prohibition against sex discrimination) (citing *Wetzel*).

follows this interpretation.[110] Many states and municipalities have also adopted anti-discrimination laws in housing and public accommodations, some of which specifically protect the LGBTQ+ community.[111] Thus, the principle protecting LGBT people under the FHA is becoming increasingly ensconced in the law.

These protections extend to LGBTQ+ members of fraternities and sororities who reside in the chapter's residence under the FHA. They may also extend to these students by virtue of Title IX. Title IX of the Education Amendments Act of 1972 prohibits discrimination based on sex in education programs or activities that receive federal financial assistance.[112] It provides that students shall not be "excluded from participation in, be denied the benefits of, or be subjected to discrimination under any education program or activity" on the basis of sex.[113] While Title IX largely insulates fraternities and sororities from challenges to their single-sex status, it does apply to the *universities* that host Greek organizations. Traditionally, courts have considered Title IX in the context of athletics, employment discrimination, and sexual harassment.[114] Fraternities, however, enjoy "a great deal of latitude" in determining whether they will include LGBTQ+ members because of this exemption. Title IX also protects the university from liability for recognizing frater-

---

110. U.S. Dep't of Hous. & Urban Dev., *Implementation of Executive Order 13988 on the Enforcement of the Fair Housing Act* (Feb. 11, 2021), https://www.hud.gov/sites/dfiles/PA/documents/HUD_Memo_EO13988.pdf. (interpreting the FHA's prohibition on sex discrimination to include discrimination because of sexual orientation). It should be noted that at least one higher education institution has challenged the application of the order against it. In April 2021, the School of the Ozarks, a private Christian university, filed suit against the Biden Administration, arguing that the requirement to accept LGBTQ+ students in housing violated its free speech and free exercise rights under federal law. *See* Sch. of the Ozarks, Inc. v. Biden, No. 6:21-03089-CV-RK, 2021 WL 2301938 (W.D. Mo. June 4, 2021). The district court rejected its request for a preliminary injunction against the order and the case remained on appeal as of July 2022.

111. *See* 2 SEXUAL ORIENTATION AND THE LAW, ESTABLISHING SUBSTANTIVE BASIS FOR CLAIM § 11:15 (2020) (noting that "[t]wenty-one states, the District of Columbia, and more than [one hundred] municipalities have enacted LGBT inclusive non-discrimination laws and offer protections against housing discrimination").

112. U.S. Dep't of Educ., *Title IX and Sex Discrimination* (last modified Aug. 20, 2021), https://www2.ed.gov/about/offices/list/ocr/docs/tix_dis.html.

113. *See* 20 U.S.C. § 1681(a).

114. *See* Stevie V. Tran, *Embracing Our Values: Title IX, the "Single-Sex Exemption," and Fraternities' Inclusion of Transgender Members*, 41 Hofstra L. Rev. 503, 524 & n.177 (2012).

nities that remain single sex. To retain federal funding, the university may only recognize social fraternities that have an "active membership of which consists primarily of students in attendance at an institution of higher education."[115]

The university, however, may become liable for sex discrimination against a current member where the fraternity or sorority expels a member from its residence, leaving them without housing, but the individual remains a member of the organization. For example, a fraternity member may tolerate a transgender member, but may not want to live with the person in the residence. As a result, the issue does not implicate the "membership practices" of the organization which are exempt under Title IX. Instead, it may constitute eviction from housing, just as if the university itself had evicted the student from a dormitory based on a protected status.

The broader challenge, however, are some barriers to entry that face LGBTQ+ college students in becoming members of Greek organizations. Dating back to the 1980s and 1990s, the media has issued reports of homophobia involving fraternities and sororities.[116] As colleges and universities have become more diverse, they have become more inclusive of LGBTQ+ students, including transgender students. Fraternities and sororities have been described as the "last frontier" for transgender inclusion on college campuses.[117] From a legal standpoint, the law does not prohibit or interfere with an organization's decision to include transgender members and the inclusion of transgender members does not endanger a group's single-sex status or its First Amendment rights of

---

115. 20 U.S.C. § 1681(a)(6); *see also* Stevie V. Tran, *Embracing Our Values: Title IX, the "Single-Sex Exemption," and Fraternities' Inclusion of Transgender Members*, 41 Hofstra L. Rev. 503, 526 (2012).

116. *See e.g.*, Evan G.S. Siegel, *Closing the Campus Gates to Free Expression: The Regulation of Offensive Speech at Colleges and Universities*, 39 Emory L.J. 1351, 1400 (1990); *Ouster of Gay Pledge Troubles UVm*, BOSTON GLOBE, Mar. 11, 1990, at 77 (University of Vermont fraternity reportedly rejected a gay student, which led to an uproar on campus); Reid, *Region's Gay and Lesbian Students Discuss Bias, Violence, Activism*, BOSTON GLOBE, Feb. 18, 1990, at 31 (describing anti-homosexual violence on college campuses in the Northeast); *Group Disciplined for Harassing Lesbian Sorority*, N.Y. TIMES Feb. 11, 1990, at 52, col. 5 (sexual harassment and threats directed at lesbian sorority members at the University of California at Los Angeles).

117. *See* Stevie V. Tran, *Embracing Our Values: Title IX, the "Single-Sex Exemption," and Fraternities' Inclusion of Transgender Members*, 41 Hofstra L. Rev. 503, 505 (2012) (citation omitted).

intimate association that may exclude the opposite sex.[118] An organization should make the requirements for transgender people to become members and to maintain their membership status as alumni consistent with the organization's purposes, values, and creeds.[119]

e. Risks of Discrimination in the Expulsion of Members

A decision to expel a member from the Greek organization's residence is arguably the moment at which the fraternity or sorority is most at risk of facing a claim of housing discrimination from the member targeted for eviction. The FHA prohibits discrimination on the basis of a protected status. A member cannot be expelled from a fraternity or sorority house because of their race, color, national origin, religion, disability, or sex. Familial status is less likely to arise unless the case involves pregnancy or children under the age of eighteen, but familial status is also a protected status under the Act.[120] Given that cases of overt discrimination are increasingly rare in the post-civil-rights-era climate, it is more likely that a claim of discrimination may come from the question of whether bias informs the policies or rules which the organization may accuse someone of violating.[121] For example, the no-pet policies described above that do not allow for a reasonable accommodation for a member with a disability may violate that member's fair housing rights. Prohibiting the cooking of certain kinds of dishes that are associated with the culture of a foreign country may constitute discrimination based on national origin.[122] Enforcing house rules or assigning house

---

118. *See Id.* at 538–40. (describing several policies adopted by national bodies of fraternities and sororities on the admission of transgender members and refining the definition of "male" to include individuals who were "self-identified" as male or who were "male identified at the time of induction").

119. *See Id.* at 528–29 (2012).

120. 42 U.S.C. §§ 3602(k) & 3604.

121. The Fair Housing Act prohibits discrimination in the "terms, conditions, or privileges of ... rental of a dwelling, or in the provision of services or facilities in connection" with the rental. *See* 42 U.S.C. § 3604(b).

122. For example, plaintiffs have filed complaints alleging discrimination or retaliation related to alleged adverse actions taken against them related to their identity and odors associated with cooking South Asian or African dishes. *See e.g., Clark v. Oakhill Condominiums Ass'n, Inc.*, No. 3:08-CV-283RM, 2008 WL 4280370, at *8 (N.D. Ind. Sept. 15, 2008); HUD v. Ramapo Towers Owners Corp., HUDALJ 02- 94- 0486- 8 & HUDALJ 02- 95- 0008- 8 (1996); Sandy Hill Apts. v. Kudawoo, No. CIV. 05-2327(PAM-

privileges differently against a non-white member as opposed to a white member may amount to racial discrimination. The claims become more salient, however, if there is additional evidence of discrimination.[123] That search for additional evidence, of course, can involve extensive, time-consuming litigation to prove – a circumstance that an organization would certainly want to avoid. As a result, the organization must take a comprehensive review of its rules to consider whether they do raise concerns about whether they treat members differently or could have a disparate negative impact on members based on a protected status.[124]

The organization must develop due process requirements prior to removing a member from housing. As an initial matter, the organization must have rules which the members know well. It is critical that the organization's process for expulsion demonstrates the clear violation of a chapter rule of which all of the members have ample notice.[125] Generally, courts will accept the content of a private organization's rules, as long as they are reasonably related to the organization's purpose. Likewise, the court normally will not second-guess the expulsion of a member unless the organization has failed to provide due process. In those instances, the court may order a new hearing that affords due process.

JSM), 2006 WL 2974305, at *1 (D. Minn. Oct. 16, 2006). The cases failed, however, because there was a lack of a causal nexus between the statements, standing alone, and the adverse action.

123. An example of a case where evidence of additional discrimination may be stronger is *HUD v. Lovejoy*, in which current and prospective tenants in an apartment complex in Washington filed a complaint with HUD for discrimination based on national origin, race, and familial status. The charging document filed by the DOJ asserted that the property manager not only stated that "[p]eople from India live on dirt floors and cook over an open flame" and that she did not want to smell the cooking of Black and Indian families. She also refused to show these families certain units with new carpet and appliances, claiming that they would ruin them based on these stereotypes. The district court entered a consent order resolving the case. *See United States v. Summerhill Place*, No. 2:10-cv-01150-JLR (W.D. Wash. Mar. 8, 2011), docket no. 20, https://www.justice.gov/sites/default/files/crt/legacy/2011/03/21/summerhillsettle.pdf.

124. The Fair Housing Act prohibits both disparate treatment and policies that have a disparate impact on members of a protected class. According to the Supreme Court, "[r]ecognition of disparate-impact liability under the FHA also plays a role in uncovering discriminatory intent: It permits plaintiffs to counteract unconscious prejudices and disguised animus that escape easy classification as disparate treatment." *Texas Dep't of Hous. & Cmty. Affs. v. Inclusive Cmtys. Project, Inc.*, 576 U.S. 519, 540 (2015).

125. *See* Robert E. Manley, *Time to Throw Out A Member?*, Fraternal Law Newsletter, Jan. 1998, https://fraternallaw.com/newsletter2/time-to-throw-out-a-member.

There are several relevant elements to incorporate into an organization's due process procedures:

1. The accused must be given clear notice (preferably in writing) of the rule violation of which the member has been accused.
2. The member must be given notice of a time and place of a hearing.
3. At the hearing, the decision maker(s) must be fair and impartial.
4. At the hearing, the accused must be able to be present when the accuser is testifying about the alleged infraction.
5. The accused must be able to cross-examine the accuser.
6. The accused must be able to confront any witnesses presented against the accused.
7. The accused must be free to testify in self-defense.
8. The accused must be free to present witnesses for the defense.
9. The accused must be free to make any reasonable argument as to why the accused is not guilty.[126]
10. The accused should receive a clear determination of wrongdoing (again, preferably in writing) that provides a basis for the findings and a clear opportunity to appeal within a reasonable timeframe.[127]

Certain elements of these procedures can be challenging to implement within an organization of close friends and associates. For example, it can be uncomfortable for someone to accuse a fraternity or sorority member of misconduct publicly. Allowing anonymous accusations, however, can take away an accused's right to face the accuser and respond to the allegations directly. Special changes, however, may need to be made in cases of extreme alleged misconduct, such as sexual harassment or assault. For example, the accused and accuser may obtain the services of a third-party representative, free of charge to each person,

---

126. *See Id.*

127. These elements are adapted from the author and Robert Manley of the law firm of Manley and Burke, which specializes in representing Greek-letter organizations. *See Id.*

who cross-examines both the accused and the accuser on behalf of the other party.[128] The decision-maker should not be the individual charged with receiving the complaint or who handled counseling procedures related to the dispute.[129] Dual roles of the judges can deny the accused the right to a fair and impartial judge.[130] It should, however, be a member of the organization or an individual within the organization (e.g., either at the chapter or national level) given that Title IX prohibits a university's interference with "membership practices" of a social fraternity or sorority and this decision involves the adjudication of a dispute between members regarding the violation of specific internal organization rules. An appeals procedure that follows this determination is important because it allows for a decision to be reviewed at a higher level, preferably by individuals more removed from the facts on the ground, like the regional or national organization. It can provide a cooling-off period in case the chapter decided to expel a member in a period of group anger. It also can allow the organization to resolve disputes internally without litigation, as it is unlikely that a court would accept jurisdiction over the case when the parties have not exhausted their internal grievance procedure.[131]

Implementing rules that are sensitive to individual rights and adhering to due process requirements overall can reduce the likelihood that an organization will make a decision that violates members' fair housing rights.

---

128. Regulations under Title IX can serve as a helpful guidepost in developing due process procedures, particularly as they are tailored to adjudicating disputes around sensitive allegations in the post-secondary education context. Title IX requires that a party's advisor conduct questioning of the accused and relevant witnesses rather than the party himself or herself. *See* 34 C.F.R. § 106.45(b)(6)(i); *Questions and Answers on the Title IX Regulations on Sexual Harassment*, U.S. Dep't of Educ., at 21 (updated June 28, 2022), https://www2.ed.gov/about/offices/list/ocr/docs/202107-qa-titleix.pdf.

129. Similarly, taking a cue from Title IX procedures, the decisionmaker in that context is neither the Title IX coordinator or the investigator on the case. 34 C.F.R. § 106.45(b)(7)(i).

130. Robert E. Manley, *Time to Throw Out A Member?*, Fraternal Law Newsletter, Jan. 1998, https://fraternallaw.com/newsletter2/time-to-throw-out-a-member.

131. *Id.*

II. Local Government Land Use Regulation

Under land use and zoning law, fraternity and sorority houses present fundamental challenges of classification, namely whether to regulate them as residences or otherwise. They have residential characteristics, but the occupants are generally unrelated. They require some features that are not common to single or two-family homes, including parking lots and multiple reserved parking spaces. These features are more often associated with multi-family properties such as apartment buildings or commercial properties, like hotels and rooming houses. They also have some more commercial or atypical residential aspects, including their regular use for communal social events. While this volume covers the law surrounding this conundrum in a separate chapter, these issues raise fair housing concerns to the extent local governments regulate fraternity houses differently than sorority houses. These kinds of regulations may constitute discrimination on the basis of sex. This disparity normally favors women in sorority houses and disadvantages men in fraternity houses.

a. Application of the Fair Housing Act

While one normally associates the FHA with regulating cases of housing discrimination against individuals, it also has a robust application in the context of land use and zoning law.[132] Fair housing law has addressed sex discrimination in local law in a variety of contexts, ranging from chronic nuisance ordinances that penalize women who require an inordinate amount of police protection as victims of domestic violence to sex stereotyping against men in the banning of single-room occupancy housing.[133] The bias and gender stereotyping in the regula-

---

132. Indeed, to set the record straight, HUD and the DOJ have issued joint guidance detailing the ways in which the Fair Housing Act applies to local land use and zoning policies. JOINT STATEMENT OF U.S. DEP'T. OF HOUSING & URB. DEV. & U.S. DEP'T OF JUSTICE, STATE AND LOCAL LAND USE LAWS AND PRACTICES AND THE APPLICATION OF THE FAIR HOUSING ACT (Nov. 10, 2016) https://www.justice.gov/opa/file/912366/download#:~:text=The%20Fair%20Housing%20Act%20thus,because%20of%20a%20protected%20characteristic.

133. *See* Noah M. Kazis, *Fair Housing for A Non-Sexist City*, 134 Harv. L. Rev. 1683 (2021) (describing various contexts in which the fair housing law framework may apply to challenge sex discrimination in local government policy).

tion of fraternity and sorority houses, however, has received less attention. The differences in the application of land use regulations runs throughout the case law in which plaintiffs challenge the location of houses for Greek-letter organizations.

b. Bias and Gender Stereotyping in the Regulation of Fraternity and Sorority Residences

Many cities prohibit the presence of fraternity or sorority houses in residential areas or restrict them to particular districts. As early as 1931, a state supreme court ruled that "[a] Greek letter fraternity violates a zoning ordinance when it occupies and uses in an exclusive, residential district a residence as a chapter house."[134] There are several cases, however, in which courts have provided exceptions for sororities, but not fraternities, dating back to the 1920s. In *City of Syracuse v. Snow*,[135] the city planning commission passed an ordinance that would prohibit residences in a zone where a sorority maintained its chapter house.[136] The court reasoned that the regulation was unreasonable because Syracuse University could only house fewer than 15% of the women enrolled.[137] During the early days of coeducation, male students outnumbered female students by more than two to one.[138] The court expressed concern that the women who did not live on campus had to live in boarding houses, which were "very difficult to supervise" and that the "sorority plan of settlement" was "much to be preferred."[139] It characterized the sorority house as a place in which the women "live in common together, under the supervision of a chaperon" and "study and perform their duties in living rooms together," living a life that made it a "college family," if not a traditional one.[140] It rejected the city's characterization of the sorority as carrying on "business, trade[] or industry" that the city could regulate, citing previous decisions involving a home for girls and a "la-

---

134. City of Lincoln v. Logan-Jones, 235 N.W. 583, 584 (Neb. 1931).
135. 205 N.Y.S. 785, 785 (N.Y. Sup. Ct. 1924).
136. Id.
137. Id.
138. Id.
139. Id.
140. Id.

dies orphan society."[141] The cases generally portray life in a sorority house as very quiet and sedate, one that the court deems worthy and consistent with its view of a "family" for zoning purposes.

Similar undercurrents of gender stereotyping surface in the context of property tax exemptions. In 1914, the Kansas Supreme Court held that Kappa Kappa Gamma, a "society ... of young women" that used a residence as a "literary hall and dormitory" may qualify for a tax exemption, even if some students at the university are not able to gain admission to the society.[142] In a case dealing with men in a fraternity, the result was the opposite. A New York court denied a fraternity house tax-exempt status, despite the fact that it was "organized exclusively for moral or mental improvement, or for educational, scientific, or literary purposes[.]" A state law provided that the real property of a corporation used exclusively for carrying out one or more of these purposes was exempt from taxation.[143] The court found, however, that a college fraternity chapter house, used chiefly as a place of abode for the members of the fraternity, is not used "exclusively" for any of the purposes mentioned in the statute, though the fraternity was organized for such purposes, and is not exempt.[144]

Some zoning ordinances that specifically restrict fraternity houses from residential districts do not similarly explicitly refer to sorority houses.[145] In one case, the city had a specific residential district for fraternities, designated "R-F."[146] Courts also often single out fraternity houses as examples of nuisances with no reference to sorority houses. For example, in *Village of Belle Terre v. Boraas*,[147] the U.S. Supreme Court

---

141. *Id.* (citing City of Rochester v. Rochester Girl's Home, 194 N.Y.S. 236 (N.Y. Sup. Ct. 1922); Easterbrook v. Hebrew Ladies Orphan Society, 82 A. 561 (Conn. 1912)).

142. Kappa Kappa Gamma House Ass'n v. Pearcy, 142 P. 294 (Kan. 1914).

143. People ex rel. Delta Kappa Epsilon Soc. of Hamilton Coll. v. Lawler, 74 A.D. 553, 556 (N.Y. App. Div. 1902), *aff'd*, 71 N.E. 1136 (1904).

144. People ex rel. Delta Kappa Epsilon Soc. of Hamilton Coll. v. Lawler, 74 A.D. 553 (N.Y. App. Div. 1902), *aff'd*, 71 N.E. 1136 (1904).

145. *See* Verland C.L.A., Inc. v. Zoning Hearing Bd. of Twp. of Moon, 556 A.2d 4, 5 (Pa. 1989) (defining "family" permitted to occupy residential zone to mean "[o]ne or more persons occupying a premises and living as a single housekeeping unit, as distinguished from a group occupying a boarding house, lodging house, club, fraternity or hotel").

146. Boothroyd v. Zoning Bd. of Appeals of Amherst, 868 N.E.2d 83, 85 n.6 (Mass. 2007).

147. 416 U.S. 1 (1974).

specifically singles out fraternity houses as facilities that "present urban problems" that local governments have the authority to restrict from residential areas.[148] According to the court, "fraternity houses and the like" cause "[m]ore people occupy a given space; more cars rather continuously pass by; more cars are parked; noise travels with crowds."[149]

The arguments against the presence of fraternity houses often amount to gender stereotyping against men. Many of these conflicts show up in the coded language focusing on the differing social activities of fraternities as opposed to sororities. For example, in 1949, the Supreme Court of Georgia held that the operation of a residence as a fraternity house violated a restrictive covenant in a deed that prohibited the use of the property for any purpose other than as a "residence."[150] The court focused on the activities that took place at the fraternity house and its features, suggesting that these activities were inconsistent with the use of the home as a "residence" within the terms of the deed restrictions. According to the court, the defendant fraternity used the "college fraternity house as a gathering place for its members wherein the members hold fraternity meetings, stage initiations into the fraternity, hold dances, rush parties, and other forms of entertainment, and where there is located on the first floor a store room, numerous radios, a soft-drink vending machine, and where other items of merchandise are offered for sale to those present in the house from time to time." Outside, there was a "large neon sign" lit up while "the occupants engaged in dancing and other activities."[151] The residential use of the house, however, was not necessarily the basis for enforcing the restrictive covenant. The court noted that it had held "that the identical restrictive covenant here involved was not violated by the operation of a boarding

---

148. *Id.* at 9.

149. *Id.* These fears are long-standing, as a state high court heard, but rejected a similar argument that a building that once served as a fraternity house should not be allowed to continue as a nonconforming use under a local ordinance where a planning engineer testified that "a fraternity house is 'detrimental to single family use by reason of increased noise and traffic hazard, the possible increased fire hazard and general production of conditions which are not compatible to single family incumbency." State ex rel. Morehouse v. Hunt, 291 N.W. 745, 748 (Wis. 1940).

150. Mu Chapter Bldg. Fund v. Henry, 51 S.E.2d 841, 841 (Ga. 1949).

151. *Id.*

house[.]"[152] The court drew a distinction between an all-male residence and another case in which a married woman operated a house with nineteen residents, presumably some of whom were women or families with children.[153]

The same tendency to regard houses for men differently than those for women continues into the present. In the early 2000s, Oklahoma's highest court considered whether a fraternity could continue to operate as a nonconforming use in a building that previously served as a boarding house for retired women.[154] The city characterized the fraternity chapter house as a "private club" rather than a boarding house, capitulating to neighbors' objections that the house would create noise, congestion, and problems that the women's boarding house did not create. On appeal, the court ruled that the uses were substantially similar, despite the evidence which showed that the fraternity would have more social gatherings and generate more noise. As the court explained, "a mere increase in volume, intensity, or frequency of a nonconforming use is generally recognized as insufficient to invalidate it."[155]

The gender stereotyping of houses for fraternities and sororities dates back to the early 20th century, when society held different expectations for the social lives of men as opposed to women. Similar stereotypes, however, have not completely gone away and work their way into the reasoning used to justify decisions about the housing and property rights of all-male residences versus all-female residences. Fraternities and sororities are uniquely susceptible to this particular fair housing challenge.

---

152. *Id.* at 843 (1949) (citing John Hancock Mut. Life Ins. Co. v. Davis, 160 S.E. 393 (Ga. 1931)).

153. Mu Chapter Bldg. Fund v. Henry, 51 S.E.2d 841, 843 (1949); *cf.* John Hancock Mut. Life Ins. Co. v. Davis, 160 S.E. 393, 393–94 (Ga. 1931)) (Beck, P.J., dissenting).

154. Triangle Fraternity v. City of Norman ex rel. Norman Board of Adjustment, 63 P.3d 1 (Okla. 2002), *reh'g denied* (Feb. 3, 2003).

155. *Id.* at 7.

III. Housing Policy in Acquiring and Maintaining Organization Residences

The question of fair housing rights for Greek-letter organizations implicates the issue of how fraternities and sororities acquire houses in the first place. This story predates the Fair Housing Act and the civil rights protections the nation relies on today. From the Great Depression through the 1970s, discriminatory federal housing policies favored whites and disadvantaged people of color, specifically African Americans. These policies affected the ability of all-white fraternities and sororities to obtain access to credit and mortgages to purchase homes. These policies, along with America's racial wealth gap, play a role in explaining why many historically Black fraternities and sororities do not have permanent residences on or near the campuses of the colleges their members attend. Many universities have become open to financing and purchasing fraternity and sorority houses and integrating them into the university's housing stock. Likewise, the private real estate market continues to explore ways to finance or lease fraternity and sorority houses for profit. The opportunity that these trends may present for historically Black Greek organizations raises questions about whether they may run into the potential for racial discrimination in pursuing any one of these options and the relief available to them as a result.

a. Hate Crimes Against Fraternity and Sorority Residences

Fraternities and sororities have their own history of racial discrimination and exclusion, consistent with the history of racism in the broader American society. For example, in the early 2010s, several organizations challenged an amendment to the Michigan state constitution that prohibited affirmative action in public education, employment, and contracting.[156] In their dissent, Justices Sonia Sotomayor and Ruth Bader Ginsburg detailed the history of racial discrimination in Michigan state universities that racial minorities had fought to overcome for decades. They noted that "[t]he housing and extracurricular policies at these in-

---

156. *Schuette v. Coal. to Defend Affirmative Action, Integration & Immigrant Rts. & Fight for Equal. By Any Means Necessary (BAMN)*, 572 U.S. 291 (2014).

stitutions also perpetuated open segregation," including the fact that "some fraternities and sororities excluded Black students from membership."[157] Many historically white universities did not allow Black students to live on campus into the 1940s and 1950s.[158] The early Black fraternities and sororities also served to meet a practical problem. For the organizations started at predominately white colleges, students were often allowed to study at the school, but not permitted to live on campus. Greek-letter organizations provided a place for students to live together.[159]

Black Greek-letter organizations (BGLOs) have historically faced intense opposition to developing houses on or near college campuses. For example, members of Alpha Kappa Alpha sorority's (AKA) chapter at the University of Alabama reported overcoming serious "obstacles and racism" to secure a house on sorority row in January 1986.[160] At that time, the president of Chi Omega, one of the University of Alabama's historically white sororities, sent a memo to six sororities to examine how AKA receiving a house would "disrupt the lives of the members of these sororities."[161] Two months later, the school's newspaper and the Associated Press reported on March 29, 1986, that a wooden cross was burned on the house's front lawn.[162] Security saw two people at the site and questioned them before they were released.[163]

---

157. *Id.* at 382 (2014) (Sotomayor & Ginsburg, JJ., dissenting). Students report that this phenomenon apparently continues today. *See e.g.*, Allie Grasgreen, *It's Not Just Alabama*, INSIDE HIGHER ED (Sept. 19, 2013), https://www.insidehighered.com/news/2013/09/19/segregated-sororities-not-limited-alabama-experts-say (noting that "[t]he University of Alabama has faced a barrage of criticism over the past several days, after its student newspaper published an account of black students being denied membership into white sororities because of their race").

158. *See* Dara Stack, *Making a home: Black Greek life on campus*, THE DAILY ILLINI (Jan. 19, 2022), https://dailyillini.com/life_and_culture-stories/2022/01/19/making-a-home-black-greek-life-on-campus/ ("Up until 1945, Black students at the University were not permitted to live on campus.").

159. *See* PAULA GIDDINGS, IN SEARCH OF SISTERHOOD: DELTA SIGMA THETA AND THE CHALLENGE OF THE BLACK SORORITY MOVEMENT (1988).

160. Joseph King & Javon Williams, *'Sometimes it's like we're not there': Black students reflect on exclusion in Greek community*, THE CRIMSON WHITE (Dec. 3, 2020), https://cw.ua.edu/69998/news/sometimes-its-like-were-not-there-black-students-reflect-on-exclusion-in-greek-community/.

161. *Id.*
162. *Id.*
163. *Id.*

On the night of August 4, 1988, the Phi Beta Sigma fraternity house at the University of Mississippi went up in flames. The house burned down before any of the brothers could move in. The house sat on a lot situated between two historically white fraternities on the university's famed fraternity row.[164] Fire officials found an "accelerant" in an upstairs closet of the house and determined that arson was the cause of the fire—an act that many suspected was racially motivated.[165] Just two months later, in a show of resilience, chapter members moved into a newly renovated house, making it the first BGLO with a house on campus and the first Black fraternity on Fraternity Row. Shortly thereafter, the chapter obtained a loan for its full purchase.[166] Due to financial difficulties, however, the fraternity could not repair the house after it suffered damage from an uprooted tree in 2005 and the land again became vacant.[167]

The hostility to BGLOs with residences remains a challenge today for some organizations. For example, in 2020, there were 40 Greek homes at the University of Alabama. Only two of them belonged to a historically Black Greek-letter organization.[168] Alpha Kappa Alpha members at the University of Alabama recounted an incident in which a member called campus police after someone banged on the sorority house's door saying, "We see you b---, open the door."[169] The campus police reportedly responded that it was probably a prank and refused to look at security camera footage to identify the harasser. The women also reported that white students in other Greek organizations asked questions like "Why [is] you guys' house so small?" and "Are you all a

---

164. *See* Mckenzie Richmond, *NPHC Greek houses absent on Fraternity and Sorority Row*, THE DAILY MISSISSIPPIAN (Oct. 11, 2018), https://thedmonline.com/black-fraternity-houses/.

165. *Id.*

166. Eta Beta Chapter of the Phi Beta Sigma Fraternity, Inc., *About Ole Miss Sigmas*, https://www.olemisssigmas.com/about (last visited June 27, 2022).

167. *See* Eta Beta Chapter of the Phi Beta Sigma Fraternity, Inc., *About Ole Miss Sigmas*, https://www.olemisssigmas.com/about (last visited June 27, 2022); Mckenzie Richmond, *NPHC Greek houses absent on Fraternity and Sorority Row*, THE DAILY MISSISSIPPIAN (Oct. 11, 2018), https://thedmonline.com/black-fraternity-houses/.

168. Joseph King & Javon Williams, *'Sometimes it's like we're not there': Black students reflect on exclusion in Greek community*, THE CRIMSON WHITE (Dec. 3, 2020), https://cw.ua.edu/69998/news/sometimes-its-like-were-not-there-black-students-reflect-on-exclusion-in-greek-community/.

169. *Id.*

scrapbooking club?"[170] In 2018, the school's newspaper published a graphic insert of all of the houses on sorority row. The only sorority not mentioned in the graphic was Alpha Kappa Alpha. Ironically, the graphic was in pink and green—the national sorority's official colors.[171] Historically Black colleges are also not immune to these kinds of attacks. In April 2022, the plots belonging to four historically Black fraternities and sororities at Howard University—one of the nation's oldest historically Black universities—in Washington, DC, were all vandalized with graffiti.[172]

The federal Fair Housing Act specifically allows for both civil remedies and criminal sanctions against an individual for the use or attempted use of force to injure, intimidate, or interfere with another due to the victim's protected class status.[173] These crimes range from cross burnings and arson to vandalism and written and oral threats.[174] Thus, fraternity and sorority members and organizations that face this kind of harassment are not left without recourse, if these rights are protected to the fullest extent of the law.

---

170. *Id.*

171. *Id.*

172. Lauren Lumpkin, *After its property was defaced, a sorority came together to rebuild*, Wash. Post (Apr. 16, 2022 at 8:00 a.m. EDT), https://www.washingtonpost.com/education/2022/04/16/howard-university-greek-organizations-vandalism/. These incidents took place in the context of multiple bomb threats at historically Black colleges around the nation and growing tensions between Howard University and residents in the gentrifying neighborhood surrounding the school. *See id.*; Tara Bahrampour, *Students say dog walkers on Howard campus are desecrating hallowed ground*, Wash. Post (Apr. 19, 2019 at 7:25 p.m. EDT), https://www.washingtonpost.com/local/social-issues/students-say-dog-walkers-on-howard-campus-are-desecrating-hallowed-ground/2019/04/19/2c136732-62ca-11e9-9ff2-abc984dc9eec_story.html.

173. *See* 42 U.S.C. § 3631; *see also* 24 C.F.R. § 100.400. Several other federal criminal statutes may apply as well. *Hate Crimes—Fair Housing Month*, U.S. Dep't. of Justice https://www.justice.gov/hatecrimes/spotlight/april-fair housing-month#:~:text=The%20FHA%20also%20has%20criminal,April%20is%20Fair%20Housing%20Month.

174. *Criminal Interference with Fair Housing Rights*, U.S. Dep't. of Justice (updated Jan. 13, 2022), https://www.justice.gov/crt/criminal-interference-fair housing-rights.

b. Disparities in Access to Greek Houses

At many predominantly white institutions, traditional Black Greek-letter organizations either do not have houses or a small number of them have their own residences.[175] The lack of a fraternity house can place Black Greek-letter organizations at a disadvantage because they lack a common place to meet and share meals like other historically white Greek organizations.[176] The disparity in housing ownership for historically Black fraternities and sororities comes down to a cascading set of socioeconomic factors that converge to affect these organizations. One of the common explanations for the disparity in the ownership of houses for historically Black fraternities and sororities is that they have smaller chapter sizes, particularly at predominantly white universities. For example, in 2015, fraternities that belong to the Interfraternity Council (the historically white fraternity association) at the University of Georgia (UGA) had an average chapter size of 90 members and sororities in UGA's Panhellenic Council (the historically white sorority association) had an average chapter size of 247 members. By contrast, the National Pan-Hellenic Council (NPHC), the historically Black fraternity and sorority association, at UGA had an average chapter size of sixteen members. The Multicultural Greek Council had an average of nineteen members.[177] These organizations have smaller chapters at predominantly white universities in part because of disproportionately lower enrollment numbers for Black students at predominantly white institutions. In many public universities, African American student enrollment does

---

175. Joseph King & Javon Williams, *'Sometimes it's like we're not there': Black students reflect on exclusion in Greek community*, THE CRIMSON WHITE (Dec. 3, 2020), https://cw.ua.edu/69998/news/sometimes-its-like-were-not-there-Black-students-reflect-on-exclusion-in-greek-community/ (noting that, in 2020, there were 40 Greek homes at the University of Alabama, and that only two of them belonged to a historically Black Greek-letter organization).

176. See Mckenzie Richmond, *NPHC Greek houses absent on Fraternity and Sorority Row*, THE DAILY MISSISSIPPIAN (Oct. 11, 2018), https://thedmonline.com/Black-fraternity-houses/.

177. Mariana Viera, *Disparity in Greek housing due to chapter sizes, funding*, THE RED & BLACK (updated Jan 8, 2015), https://www.redandBlack.com/uganews/greeklife/disparity-in-greek-housing-due-to-chapter-sizes-funding/article_de0e0c86-cfdf-11e3-b16a-0017a43b2370.html.

not reach parity with the state's population of Black residents, which is not the same for their white counterparts.[178]

Chapter dues and fees as well as help from a national organization often provides funding for Greek housing. However, a disproportionate number of African American and Latino college students come from lower-income households.[179] The amount of student loan debt that African American students carry is almost double the amount than that of white students.[180] A 2021 poll commissioned by LendEDU, a survey of 500 college students with student loan debt who were also members of Greek-letter organizations indicated that 54.8% of students admit to using student loan funds to pay fraternity or sorority dues.[181] As a result, students of color often have less disposable income to cover higher chapter dues and fees, which would be necessary to finance the building of a fraternity or sorority house.

c. University Financing of Greek Residences

The overwhelming majority of Greek houses sit on land owned by the college or university with which they are affiliated.[182] Public universities have become intimately involved in the governance of the sororities and fraternities. Almost all large universities have a professionally staffed Office of Greek Life that supports and guides the Greek organizations.

---

178. *See Does Black Representation in Public Colleges & Universities Mirror the State's Black Population?*, THE EDUCATION TRUST (Mar. 6, 2019), https://edtrust.org/press-release/does-Black-representation-in-public-colleges-universities-mirror-the-states-Black-population/.

179. Morgan Taylor & Jonathan M. Turk, *Race and Ethnicity in Higher Education: A Look at Low-Income Undergraduates*, AM. COUNCIL ON HIGHER ED. (2019), available at https://www.equityinhighered.org/resources/ideas-and-insights/race-and-ethnicity-in-higher-education-a-look-at-low-income-undergraduates/

180. Andre M. Perry et al., *Report: Student loans, the racial wealth divide, and why we need full student debt cancellation*, BROOKINGS INSTITUTION (June 23, 2021), https://www.brookings.edu/research/student-loans-the-racial-wealth-divide-and-why-we-need-full-student-debt-cancellation/.

181. Mike Brown, *Student Loan Money for Greek Life Dues? 55% of "Greek" Student Borrowers Admit to Doing So*, LENDEDU(Apr. 26, 2021), https://lendedu.com/blog/student-loan-money-for-greek-life-dues/.

182. *See* Robert Manley & Timothy M. Burke, *Greek Houses on University Land*, FRATERNAL L. NEWSLETTER, at 1 (Jan. 2004), https://fraternallaw.com/wp-content/uploads/2018/12/087-January-2004.pdf.

More importantly, the overwhelming majority of Greek houses sit on land owned by the university. In some states, the university constructs, owns, and operates the Greek houses. In other jurisdictions, the college rents land to the national Greek organizations.[183] Across the country, thousands of undergraduates currently live in fraternity and sorority houses, saving universities "untold millions of dollars in the construction and maintenance of campus-owned and -controlled dormitories."[184]

Universities, however, have become willing to finance the development of fraternity and sorority residences. For example, in August 2008, the Board of Governors of the State University System of Florida passed a resolution authorizing the University of Central Florida Finance Corporation to issue taxable debt to finance the purchase and renovation of two former fraternity houses on the university's main campus.[185] The university submitted a proposal to incorporate the houses into its Housing and Residence Life System. The university projected the purchase, renovation, and furnishing of the house for an estimated $3.8 million. The debt service payments, however, would be funded from revenues generated from the operation of the fraternity houses. The Board noted that, while Florida's state universities had not been involved in the financing of fraternity houses, the practice was "more common" in other states.[186]

This institutional support for Greek housing has not historically reached BGLOs, a key constituency of the fraternity and sorority community. This divergence in support for access to Greek housing for historically non-white organizations raises legal and policy questions as to whether universities may be subsidizing all-white housing communities when it comes to Greek row on or near their campuses.

It is possible, however, to develop innovative approaches to meeting this need. For example, in October 2019, Vanderbilt University completed construction of its National Pan-Hellenic Council (NPHC)

---

183. *See* Stephen Clowney, *Sororities As Confederate Monuments*, 108 Ky. L.J. 617, 619 (2020) (footnote omitted).

184. Caitlin Flanagan, *The Dark Power of Fraternities*, ATLANTIC (Sept. 9, 2019, 2:00 PM), https://www.theatlantic.com/magazine/archive/2014/03/the-dark-power-of-fraternities/357580/.

185. *See* Proposed Board Action, Bd. of Governors, State Univ. Sys. of Fla., Aug. 7, 2008, https://www.flbog.edu/wp-content/uploads/0009_0156_1434_063-FAC-UCF-Greek-Housing-Agenda-Item_Draft.pdf.

186. *Id.*

House. The residence hall will house all of the fraternities and sororities in the NPHC. Thus, the smaller chapters can have their own residence on Greek row in a single building.[187] While an individual residence for each chapter would be ideal, the shared residence hall represents a potential compromise for giving these organizations the benefits of joint living that historically white Greek-letter organizations have enjoyed.

Discrimination in the terms and conditions of university decisions regarding the financing of Greek housing—for example, where the university refuses to make financing available to a historically Black fraternity or sorority, but makes it available for a similarly situated, predominately white Greek organization—may give rise to claims of discrimination. In these scenarios, historically minority Greek organizations may be able to bring claims against the university under the Fair Housing Act based on the provision that prohibits "mak[ing] housing unavailable" on the basis of race. There may be other grounds for claims, including race discrimination in violation of Title VI of the Civil Rights Act, where the university receives federal financial assistance.

This issue also implicates disparities in financing of Greek housing for fraternities and not sororities. Students and officials at several universities have raised concern that fraternities are more likely to have chapter houses than sororities at their colleges.[188] One of the common reasons given for the disparity is a pernicious urban legend that a sorority house may be considered a "brothel" under local laws criminalizing prostitution.[189] There is, however, no record of local laws that impose a per se ban on sorority houses or a record of actions enforcing any anti-prostitution

---

187. *Vanderbilt celebrates grand opening of new National Pan-Hellenic Council House*, MyVU News (Oct. 21, 2019, 1:09 PM), https://news.vanderbilt.edu/2019/10/21/vanderbilt-celebrates-grand-opening-of-new-national-pan-hellenic-council-house/.

188. *See e.g.*, Gracine Wilson et al., *The lack of sorority houses at AU*, AU Live (Feb. 20, 2020), https://au-live.com/8920/opinion/the-lack-of-sorority-houses-at-au/ (discussing "the lack of sorority houses at [Ashland University]"); Christina Berberian, *Inequality in the Greek system*, The Poly Post (Sept. 25, 2018), https://thepolypost.com/news/2018/09/25/inequality-in-the-greek-system/ (Greek life official noting that while the college did not sponsor or regulate off-campus houses, the phenomenon of many sororities not having houses "once started as the stigma where boys are allowed to have houses but girls are not. It was a double standard in that sense").

189. *See e.g.*, Peter Jacobs, It's A Myth That Sorority Houses Would Be Brothels If They Had Alcohol, Business Insider (Jan. 21, 2015, 3:08 PM), https://www.businessinsider.com/its-a-myth-that-sorority-houses-would-be-brothels-if-they-had-alcohol-2015-1 (discussing myth); *Sexism in University Housing Rule*, Opinion—The Uni-

laws against sorority houses just by virtue of their existence. The prevalence of this myth carries a history of sexism that university policies governing Greek housing should seek to avoid. Indeed, university funding decisions that favor fraternity houses over sorority houses may constitute discrimination on the basis of sex in violation of Title IX and potentially the Fair Housing Act.

d. The Private Real Estate Market for Greek Housing

The financing of Greek housing has also become big business. Access to financing for Greek-letter organizations, however, implicates the racial wealth gap in America when it comes to the construction or maintenance of houses for historically minority fraternities and sororities. Most Greek-letter organizations operate as nonprofit corporations.[190] Generally, nonprofit organizations often face difficulties in getting access to credit.[191] Studies also consistently report that minority-owned corporations disproportionately face barriers in access to credit. For example, a Federal Reserve study reported that, while Black-owned businesses were more likely to apply for bank financing, lenders fully funded less than half of their applications. The study also found that Black-owned businesses were two times as likely to be turned down for loans as white business owners.[192] As a result, they have difficulty expanding their operations or pursuing new objectives. It is difficult to imagine that these challenges are any different for a minority fraternity or sorority organization.

Real estate agents often invite investors to "buy a sorority house and get an absolute net lease, meaning all you do is collect a rent check. The

---

VERSITY NEWS (Feb. 8, 2012), https://unewsonline.com/2012/02/sexism-in-university-housing-rule/ (noting students' familiarity with myth).

190. Indeed, the Internal Revenue Code provides fraternities and sororities tax-exempt status as social clubs. *See* 26 U.S.C. § 501(c)(7).

191. *See* Press Release, *Federal Reserve Board modifies Main Street Lending Program to provide greater access to credit for nonprofit organizations such as educational institutions, hospitals, and social service organizations*, FED. RESERVE SYS. BD. OF GOVERNORS (July 17, 2020), https://www.federalreserve.gov/newsevents/pressreleases/monetary20200717a.htm (changing rules to expand access to credit for nonprofit organizations).

192. Local Initiatives Support Corporation, *Expanding Black Business Credit Initiative Closes $29M for the Black Vision Fund*, LISC (Mar. 17, 2022), https://www.lisc.org/our-stories/story/expanding-Black-business-credit-initiative-closes-29m-Black-vision-fund/ (citing study).

tenant covers all expenses for operating the property."[193] The same invitation to finance is not necessarily the same for fraternity houses. It may be that investors think a sorority house is a safer investment because of certain gender stereotypes, namely that women are socialized to maintain a home in good condition and that members of a sorority may have less rowdy social events at their residence than men. Just as these kinds of stereotypes may influence local land use decisions involving fraternity houses, they often make lenders averse to financing the purchase of fraternity houses.[194]

The Fair Housing Act applies to any housing transaction, including applications for credit and financing of housing purchases. The Equal Credit Opportunity Act (ECOA) of 1974, however, also provides an additional basis for relief in this context. ECOA prohibits creditors from discriminating against applicants in any credit transaction on the basis of race, color, religion, national origin, and sex, among other grounds. ECOA also applies to business credit applications.[195] It is important that Greek-letter organizations be vigilant in protecting their rights to access to credit to the extent impermissible discrimination poses a barrier to funding. These issues, however, also involve long-term systemic challenges and disparities in access to wealth that plague the broader housing market. Thus, organizations seeking to expand their residential options must focus on both their fair housing rights and shoring up their access to capital long term.

---

193. *Invest in Sorority or Fraternity Houses? Yep, you can*, YELLOW TAIL REALTY ADVISORS (June 22, 2019), https://yellowtailrealtyadvisors.com/invest-in-sorority-or-fraternity-houses-yep-you-can/.

194. *See, e.g.*, Emily Martin, *RMA [Risk Management Association] LinkedIn Discussion Focuses on Lending to Fraternities*, THE RMA JOURNAL (Oct. 2012), https://cms.rmau.org/uploadedFiles/Credit_Risk/Library/RMA_Journal/Credit_Risk_Management/RMA%20LinkedIn%20Discussion%20Focuses%20on%20Lending%20to%20Fraternities.pdf (quoting a risk management professional who observed that "[e]very credit officer at a bank worries that if they finance a fraternity it's going to turn out like Animal House. They worry that they'll lose money, respect, and damage the reputation of their bank by being involved").

195. *See* 15 U.S.C. § 1691 et seq.; 12 C.F.R. pt. 202.

IV. Conclusion

Fraternity and sorority chapter houses operate in a world with civil rights protections that touch the individual members living in their residences and their relationship to the broader society. Multiple civil laws, most notably the federal Fair Housing Act and its state and local counterparts and Title IX, protect some Greek organization members most at risk for discrimination, including students with disabilities and LGBTQ+ students. They touch on everyday living arrangements, ranging from no-pet policies that may ban the use of emotional support animals to behavior that holds members from marginalized groups to different standards in the house, despite the organization's broader commitment to camaraderie and deep emotional bonds between all of the members. It is critical that chapters and universities that interface with Greek organizations adopt policies and procedures that take these rights into account.

In the broader society, the public views fraternities and sororities differently, even in spite of statements of equality before the law. This chapter has examined some underlying biases against fraternities dating back decades that may still factor into land use decision-making of which anyone supporting Greek organizations should be aware. In the same way, however, the world's perspective on the backgrounds of an organization's members and alumni can affect their ability to build a house in which they create community in the same way as more privileged Greek counterparts. The history of discrimination and violence, particularly against African Americans, has placed Black Greek-letter organizations literally under fire and made it harder for them to make their mark on an institution with a residence. Greek organizations that face this kind of hostility have rights to civil relief and to pursue criminal prosecution under the Fair Housing Act and other laws that can empower their growth and success.

As colleges and universities take a greater role in financing and owning Greek housing, it is critical that policymakers address historic inequalities and pursue equity in their development projects. Alternatives to large residences, including dedicated living areas for smaller fraternities and sororities, can overcome the tendency to focus on large Greek organization chapters to the exclusion of smaller ones. This is particularly important since the majority of historically minority Greek chapters at predominately white institutions tend to be smaller. In this way, colleges can avoid running afoul of federal laws banning race and sex discrimination in their Greek housing programs. Finally, as organizations go it alone on the private market, they may face discriminatory barriers in access to credit to support their growth. This process brings in an additional set of protections.

PART FOUR:
BROADER ISSUES

CHAPTER 14

Antitrust and Consumer Protection Law

Susan Navarro Smelcer

I. Introduction

Antitrust and consumer protection are not areas of law traditionally associated with fraternal organizations. But issues arising from these laws touch aspects of fraternal organizations' interactions with colleges and universities that restrict fraternal organizations' activities.

Over the past 30 years, some fraternal organizations (both national organizations and local chapters) have fought to retain ownership of their houses in the face of intense pressure from universities to sell. Increasingly space-strapped universities have sought to both narrow the scope of Greek life on campus and expand their footprint to provide additional university housing and enhanced student-life offerings. Some universities have sought to purchase fraternity and sorority houses as a way to accomplish both goals.

Antitrust concerns may arise when a university pairs this desire to purchase Greek-owned properties with policies that require all students to live in university housing or threaten to withdraw university recognition from an intransigent chapter. In response, some fraternal organizations have claimed that universities violate federal antitrust law by seeking to establish or by maintaining a monopoly in the local market for student housing. While this argument has been rejected by a federal district court, the matter of antitrust liability for universities in this area is far from settled.

Antitrust concerns may also arise from other university actions, such as restricting a fraternal organization's ability to supply social services, recruit new members, or continue to exist as a recognized campus organization. Universities have traditionally possessed a great deal of latitude in recognizing campus organizations and structuring their activities—but this does not mean that universities could not incur liability, given the gatekeeping function they hold over student life. Under some conditions, this gatekeeping function may be sufficient to maintain a claim for antitrust liability—although such theories have not yet been tested through litigation.[1]

More recently, fraternal organizations have advanced novel arguments under state unfair trade practice (UTP) laws to resist university policies that affect the organization or operation of Greek life. UTP claims litigated to date involve students' reliance on a university's allegedly false representations about the availability of Greek housing. Limited litigation of these claims, like fraternal organizations' antitrust claims, have been unsuccessful in state courts. But UTP laws vary from state to state, and such claims may be available (and successful) in the future.

This chapter is organized as follows:

1. Introduction to antitrust law, emphasizing the uniformity of antitrust laws across the country and the importance of geographic and product definition in the success of a claim
2. Discussion of the cases to date proposing antitrust liability for real estate disputes, focusing on the *Hamilton College* case (1995–2002) and the more recent *Delta Kappa Epsilon Alumni Corp. v. Colgate University* (2007) decision. This section will pay special attention to the importance of market definition in determining the ultimate success of the fraternal organization's claims.

---

1. Mark D. Bauer, *Small Liberal Arts Colleges, Fraternities, and Antitrust: Rethinking Hamilton College*, 53 CATHOLIC UNIV. L. REV. 347, 365 (2004) ("Other courts have held that the Sherman Act may regulate a wide array of other college activities, such as intercollegiate sports.").

3. Overview of state consumer protection and UTP laws, emphasizing common requirements across states and emphasizing the diversity of coverage of such laws across the country
4. Recent attempts by fraternal organizations to allege violations of state consumer protection and UTP laws, with a focus on *Kent Literary Club of Wesleyan University v. Wesleyan University* (2021)

II. Antitrust Law and the University

Antitrust law comprises federal and state statutes and judicial decisions that govern unfair methods of competition in the United States. Antitrust's statutory history derives from the late 1880s, when large "trusts" (or conglomerations of businesses in the same industry) exercised massive social, political, and economic power over large swaths of American life.[2]

The founding document of American antitrust law is popularly known as the Sherman Act. The bulk of federal antitrust law is derived from two short sections in the Sherman Act, codified as 15 U.S.C. §§ 1–2.[3] These sections reflect the codification of certain existing common law terms and are enforced at both the federal and state levels, through en-

---

2. In most other nations, these types of laws are referred to as "competition law."

3. The Sherman Act is not the only source of antitrust law, but it is the most important. Most notably, the Clayton Act of 1914 (codified at 15 U.S.C. §§ 12–27) extends the Sherman Act by prohibiting (1) price discrimination against competitors (§§ 13–13a), (2) sales conditional on an exclusive dealing agreement (§ 14); (3) mergers and acquisitions of stock of another company where the effect "may be substantially to lessen competition" (§ 18); and (4) interlocking directorates and officers of two or more firms such that "the elimination of competition by agreement between them would constitute a violation of any of the antitrust laws" (§ 19). Additional types of price discrimination are prohibited under the Robinson-Patman Act of 1936. *See* Fed. Trade Comm'n, *Price Discrimination: Robinson-Patman Violations*, Guide to Antitrust Laws, https://www.ftc.gov/advice-guidance/competition-guidance/guide-antitrust-laws/price-discrimination-robinson-patman-violations (last visited Nov. 22, 2022). Section 5 of the Federal Trade Commission Act authorizes the FTC to enforce the Sherman and Clayton Acts in tandem with the DOJ. Fed. Trade Comm'n, Policy Statement Regarding the Scope of Unfair Methods of Competition Under Section 5 of the Federal Trade Commission Act Commission File No. P221202 (Nov. 10, 2022), https://www.ftc.gov/system/files/ftc_gov/pdf/P221202Section5PolicyStatement.pdf.

forcement actions by the US Department of Justice (DOJ), the Federal Trade Commission (FTC), and state agencies and authorities.[4]

Section 1 of the Sherman Act prohibits collaboration between competitors or between a supplier or a distributor that results in the "unreasonable" restraint of trade.[5] Agreements between competitors in the same market are "horizontal" agreements; agreements between firms at different levels of the supply chain are "vertical."[6] Some types of conduct, such as agreements between competitors to fix prices, allocate customers, or apportion geographic or product markets,[7] are presumptively or per se illegal.

Courts and agencies evaluate the competitive effects of other types of collaborative conduct, such as horizontal refusals to deal with a competitor or vertical agreements to set minimum retail prices, under the burden-shifting *rule of reason* analysis. *Rule of reason* analysis (and its vari-

---

4. STEPHANIE W. KANWIT, *The Federal Trade Commission Act as a consumer protection law*, in FEDERAL TRADE COMMISSION § 4:1, Westlaw (database updated Oct. 2022). The FTC's power to prohibit "unfair methods of competition" refers to its ability to prosecute economic actors for behavior that harms the free market. In practice, the scope and contours of the FTC's antitrust enforcement mirrors Sherman Act enforcement by the DOJ. *See* FED. TRADE COMM'N, GUIDE TO ANTITRUST LAWS, https://www.ftc.gov/advice-guidance/competition-guidance/guide-antitrust-laws (last visited Feb. 20, 2023) (discussing the FTC Bureau of Competition's summary of and guidance regarding its antitrust enforcement authority).

5. *E.g.*, Texaco, Inc. v. Dagher, 547 U.S. 1, 1–2 (2006) (noting that the Court "has not taken a literal approach to [the Sherman Act's] language" and that this Court has instead recognized that "Congress intended to outlaw only *unreasonable* restraints" (citing State Oil Co. v. Khan, 522 U.S. 3, 10 (1997))).The full text of Section 1 declares, "Every contract, combination in the form of trust or otherwise, or conspiracy, in restraint of trade or commerce among the several States, or with foreign nations, is declared to be illegal. Every person who shall make any contract or engage in any combination or conspiracy hereby declared to be illegal shall be deemed guilty of a felony, and, on conviction thereof, shall be punished by fine not exceeding $100,000,000 if a corporation or, if any person, $1,000,000, or by imprisonment not exceeding 10 years, or by both said punishments, in the discretion of the court." 15 U.S.C. § 1.

6. For example, an agreement between two competing bar prep companies is considered to be horizontal, because the two companies compete against each other at the same level of the supply chain and provide the same service. *See, e.g.*, Palmer v. BRG of Ga., Inc., 498 U.S. 46 (1990). Agreements between a distributor of women's accessories and the retail stores that sell those accessories are considered to be vertical. *See, e.g.*, Leegin Creative Leather Products, Inc. v. PSKS, Inc., 551 U.S. 877 (2007).

7. *E.g.*, United States v. Sealy Co., 388 U.S. 350 (1967) (finding that an arrangement to allocate territories among trademark licensees were "part of an 'aggregation of trade restraints' including unlawful price fixing and policing").

ants) assesses whether the anticompetitive effects of the agreement at issue outweigh the procompetitive benefits. As the Court explained in *National Society of Professional Engineers v. United States*, the factfinder's inquiry determines only whether the conduct at issue "is one that promotes competition or one that suppresses competition."[8]

Section 2, on the other hand, is concerned with monopolization by a single actor (i.e., unilateral conduct) and attempts by multiple firms to coordinate or collaborate with the goal of monopolizing a market (i.e., multilateral conduct).[9] This is where the Sherman Act's guidance ends, however. The Supreme Court filled out Section 2's prohibition on monopolization in *United States v. Grinnell Corp.* by defining the act of monopolization as having two distinct elements: "(1) the possession of monopoly power in the relevant market and (2) the willful acquisition or maintenance of that power as distinguished from growth or development as a consequence of a superior product, business acumen, or historic accident."[10]

The theoretical definition of monopoly power is intuitive. Monopolists possess the ability to shape the competitive landscape. But conducting the factual determination necessary to establish whether a defendant has monopoly power is more challenging. Monopoly power itself has no clear definition other than "the power to control prices or exclude competition" in a relevant product or geographic market.[11] Courts have traditionally viewed the ability to control prices and exclude competition as "so intimately intertwined that ... [i]t is inconceivable that price could be controlled without power over competition or vice versa."[12]

Analytically, market power is most commonly defined as market share of a particular geographic or product market.[13] A defendant or

---

8. 435 U.S. 679, 691 (1978).

9. 15 U.S.C. § 2 ("Every person who shall monopolize, or attempt to monopolize, or combine or conspire with any other person or persons, to monopolize any part of the trade or commerce among the several States, or with foreign nations, shall be deemed guilty of a felony.")

10. 384 U.S. 563, 570–71 (1966).

11. United States v. E.I. duPont de Nemours & Co., 351 U.S. 377, 391 (1956).

12. *Id.* at 392.

13. *See* Spectrum Sports, Inc. v. McQuillan, 506 U.S. 447, 459 (1993) ("[D]emonstrating the dangerous probability of monopolization in an attempt case also requires inquiry into the relevant product and geographic market and the defendant's economic power in that market.").

group of defendants with a large market share provides circumstantial evidence of "sufficient leverage to influence marketwide output."[14] Geographic markets comprise well-defined areas where the anticompetitive conduct occurring. A geographic market may be as small as a 30-mile radius,[15] the entire United States,[16] or even the world.[17]

A product market encompasses all goods or services that are reasonable substitutes for each other.[18] Products in the same market are those that consumers can (and do) use for the same purpose.[19] Courts draw these boundaries "by examining such practical indicia as industry or public recognition of the submarket as a separate economic entity, the product's peculiar characteristics and uses, unique production facilities, distinct customers, distinct prices, sensitivity to price changes, and specialized vendors."[20] In an early and influential case filed by the DOJ to enjoin a merger between shoe manufacturers, for example, the Supreme Court found that men's, women's, and children's shoes all constituted different markets. The Court reasoned that "[t]hese product lines are recognized by the public; each line is manufactured in separate plants; each has characteristics peculiar to itself rendering it generally noncompetitive with the others; and each is, of course, directed toward a distinct class of customers."[21]

---

14. Rebel Oil Co., Inc. v. A. Richfield Co., 51 F.3d 1421, 1437 (9th Cir. 1995).

15. *E.g.*, Gordon v. Lewistown Hosp., 272 F. Supp. 2d 393, 433 (M.D. Pa. 2003), *aff'd*, 423 F.3d 184 (3d Cir. 2005).

16. *E.g.*, U.S. v. Continental Can Co., 378 U.S. 441, 447 (1964).

17. *E.g.*, Epic Games v. Apple, Inc., 559 F. Supp. 3d 898, 1027 (N.D. Cal. 2021) ("Having found the relevant product market to be that of mobile gaming transactions, the Court finds the area of effective competition in the geographic market to be global, with the exception of China.").

18. Brown Shoe Co. v. U.S., 370 U.S. 294, 325 (1962) ("The outer boundaries of a product market are determined by the reasonable interchangeability of use or the cross-elasticity of demand between the product itself and substitutes for it."). *See also* U.S. v. Microsoft Corp., 253 F.3d 34, 51–52 (D.C. Cir. 2001) ("Because the ability of consumers to turn to other suppliers restrains a firm from raising prices above the competitive level, ... the relevant market must include all products reasonably interchangeable by consumers for the same purposes.") (citing Rothery Storage & Van Co. v. Atlas Van Lines, Inc., 792 F.2d 210, 218 (D.C. Cir. 1986) and U.S. v. E.I. du Pont de Nemours & Co., 351 U.S. 377, 395 (1961)) (internal quotations omitted).

19. U.S. v. Anthem, Inc., 236 F. Supp. 3d 171, 194 (D.D.C. 2017).

20. Brown Shoe Co. v. U.S., 370 U.S. 294, 325 (1962).

21. *Id.* at 326.

Product markets may also encompass "clusters" or "bundles" of goods or services.[22] So-called "cluster" markets combine multiple single-product markets that "share competitive conditions."[23] Consider the Sixth Circuit's analysis of cluster markets in *Promedica Health System, Inc. v. Fed. Trad Comm'n*.[24] In this case, the FTC sought to enjoin a merger of two hospital systems in Lucas County, Ohio.[25] The FTC argued—and the Sixth Circuit accepted—that the appropriate product market was defined as a "clustered" market for primary and secondary inpatient services.[26] Notably, obstetric (OB) services were excluded from this definition. The court reasoned that the competitive conditions for OB-related services were dissimilar from primary and secondary care services.[27] As a result, the court was required to analyze the competitive impact of the merger on OB services separately.[28]

Bundle markets, on the other hand, are markets where the combination of goods or services for sale constitute a unique product.[29] Supermarkets provide the canonical example. Consumers use supermarkets

---

22. U.S. v. Grinnell Corp., 384 U.S. 563 (1966) (holding the "cluster of services" comprising central station protection services constituted the relevant product market when evaluating § 1 and § 2 claims against four central station protection service providers specializing in different types of protection services, such as fire, burglary, etc.).

23. Kevin Hahm & Loren K. Smith, *Clarifying Bundle Markets and Distinguishing Them From Cluster Markets*, ANTITRUST SOURCE 1, 1 (Feb. 2021), https://www.brattle.com/wp-content/uploads/2021/06/21761_clarifying_bundle_markets_and_distinguishing_them_from_cluster_markets.pdf.

24. Promedica Health System, Inc. v. Fed. Trade Comm'n, 749 F.3d 559 (6th Cir. 2014).

25. *Id.* at 561.

26. Primary medical services are defined as "[t]he most basic" inpatient services, including "hernia surgeries, radiology services, and most kinds of inpatient obstetrical (OB) services." Secondary services require more specialized equipment and personnel; these include bariatric surgery and hip replacements. *Id.*

27. *Id.* at 566.

28. *Id.* at 568 ("The relevant markets, for purposes of analyzing the merger's competitive effects, are what the Commission says they are: (1) a cluster market of primary (but not OB) and secondary inpatient services . . . , and (2) a separate market for OB services.").

29. *See* Hahm & Smith, *supra* note 23, at 3 ("Unlike cluster markets, which aggregate a number of individual relevant markets, a bundle market is the collection of products or services that comprise the relevant market where customers value suppliers offering a package of goods and benefit from the 'one-stop' shopping experience.").

as a "one-stop" destination for multiple items and base decisions on "the price of the basket of goods."[30]

In some cases, a plaintiff may be able to supplement (or supplant) product and market definitions by producing direct evidence that the defendant or defendants was able to "profitably raise prices substantially above the competitive level."[31] Direct evidence is the most compelling indicator of monopoly power.[32] But such evidence is rarely created or is difficult to produce.[33]

At first glance, antitrust law—a body of law governing commercial relationships and focused on maintaining the free market for the benefit of consumers—would seem to have little relevance to universities. Most universities are nonprofit organizations,[34] and many are creatures of the state.[35]

But courts have increasingly recognized that even nonprofit organizations, including private universities, can operate in profit-seeking

---

30. *Id.*

31. U.S. v. Microsoft Corp., 253 F.3d 34, 51 (D.C. Cir. 2001).

32. *See* Fed. Trade Comm'n v. Ind. Fed'n of Dentists, 476 U.S. 447, 460–61 (1986) (citations omitted) ("Since the purpose of the inquiries into market definition and market power is to determine whether an arrangement has the potential for genuine adverse effects on competition, 'proof of actual detrimental effects ... obviate the need for an inquiry into market power....'"); *see also* Andrew I. Gavil, *Copperweld 2000: The Vanishing Gap Between Sections 1 and 2 of the Sherman Act*, 68 ANTITRUST L.J. 87, 89 (2000) ("[T]he Court has demonstrated a pronounced interest in according greater weight to direct evidence of market power, such as actual exclusion, higher prices, or lower output, than to circumstantial evidence of market power in the form of market shares calculated within defined relevant markets.").

33. *E.g.*, William H. Page, *Direct Evidence of a Sherman Act Agreement*, 83 ANTITRUST L.J. 347, 348 n.11 (2020) (citing cases).

34. *See* Daniel C. Levy, *For-profit versus Nonprofit Private Higher Education*, 54 INT'L HIGHER EDUC. 12, 12 (2009), https://doi.org/10.6017/ihe.2009.54.8414; *see also* NATIONAL CENTER FOR EDUCATION STATISTICS, *Digest of Education Statistics, Table 317.10* (2021), https://nces.ed.gov/programs/digest/d21/tables/dt21_317.10.asp (indicating that for-profit educational institutions comprised only 704 (17.9%) of the 3,931 total degree-granting postsecondary institutions).

35. The National Center for Education Statistics recorded a total of 3,931 degree-granting institutions of higher education in 2021. Of these, 1,587 (40.4%) are public and 2,344 (59.6%) are private. National Center for Education Statistics, *supra* note 34.

ways[36] or engage in activities that have "commercial objectives."[37] These commercial activities are most obvious when the university operates businesses, such as campus bookstores, in direct competition with for-profit businesses. For example, in *Sunshine Books, Ltd. v. Temple University*, the Third Circuit concluded that Temple University could be held liable under antitrust laws when its bookstore sold textbooks below cost during a one-week-long "manager's special."[38]

Universities can also engage in commerce in less obvious ways. For example, in *United States v. Brown University*, the Third Circuit determined that universities' competition over financial aid packages is inherently commercial.[39] This particular case concerned an agreement between several Ivy League universities to "distribute financial aid exclusively on the basis of need and to collectively determine the amount of financial assistance commonly admitted students would be awarded."[40] The Third Circuit agreed with the DOJ that the universities' plan to coordinate financial aid "implicate[d] trade or commerce," concluding that "the payment of tuition in return for educational services constitutes commerce."[41]

Note that both of the above-mentioned cases involved private universities. Similar behaviors by state schools are more likely to be deemed "state actions" and exempt from antitrust liability on the basis of sovereign immunity.

---

36. Goldfarb v. Va. State Bar, 421 U.S. 773, 791 (1975) ("The fact that the State Bar is a state agency for some limited purposes does not create an antitrust shield that allows it to foster anticompetitive practices for the benefit of its members."). United States v. Brown Univ., 5 F.3d 658, 666 (3d Cir. 1993) (explaining that "[c]ourts classify a transaction as commercial or noncommercial based on the nature of the conduct in light of the totality of surrounding circumstances").

37. Donnelly v. Bos. Coll., 558 F.2d 634 (1st Cir. 1977) (citing Marjorie Webster Junior Coll. v. Middle States Ass'n of Colls. and Secondary Schs., 432 F.2d 650 (D.C. Cir. 1970) (distinguishing the accreditation process from commercial activities)). For a more in-depth discussion of each of the cases discussed in this section, see Jared S. Sunshine, *Antitrust Precedent & Anti-Fraternity Sentiment: Revisiting Hamilton College*, 39 CAMPBELL L. REV. 59 (2017).

38. 697 F.2d 90, 91 (3d Cir. 1982).

39. 5 F.3d 658 (3d Cir. 1993).

40. *Id.* at 661.

41. *Id.* at 666.

The Supreme Court first promulgated rules governing state-action antitrust immunity in *Parker v. Brown*.[42] In *Parker*, the Court considered whether a California state law regulating the "harvesting and marketing" of the state's 1940 raisin crop violated the Sherman Act.[43] The Court concluded that the "Sherman Act makes no mention of the state ... and gives no hint that it was intended to restrain state action or official action directed by a state."[44]

Contrast *Sunshine Books* with *Cowboy Book v. Board of Regents for Agricultural & Mechanical Colleges ex rel. Oklahoma State University of Agriculture and Applied Science*.[45] Like the Temple University bookstore, Oklahoma State University (OSU) subsidized textbook purchases at its bookstore by extending credit to students. But the district court in *Cowboy Book* found that, unlike Temple, OSU was immune from antitrust liability. OSU's Board of Regents, while not a state agency, was a "constitutionally created department of the state government ... given broad and express powers under Oklahoma states."[46] Given this, the district court concluded that "the act of extending credit to students in this case could be construed as an act of sovereignty" by the state of Oklahoma.[47]

Other university-affiliated groups or businesses not expressly empowered through the state constitution or statutes may also be immune from antitrust liability under so-called *Parker* immunity. But such immunity is not automatically granted, as the district court explained in *Cowboy Book*. Rather, a state-created entity or a private party may receive *Parker* immunity if they are accountable to the state in a meaningful way. In particular, the challenged competitive restraint must both be "'clearly articulated and affirmatively expressed by state policy'" and "'actively supervised' by the state itself."[48]

---

42. Parker v. Brown, 317 U.S. 341 (1943).

43. *Id.* at 345, 350–51.

44. *Id.* at 351.

45. 728 F. Supp. 1518 (W.D. Okla. 1989).

46. *Id.* at 1522–23 (citing Title 70 O.S. § 3412(o) in part, which stated that the Board is hereby "expressly granted every power necessary or convenient to make institutions under its jurisdiction effective for the purposes for which they were created and are maintained and operated").

47. *Id.* at 1522.

48. Cal. Retail Liquor Dealers Ass'n v. Midcal Aluminum, Inc., 445 U.S. 97 (1980) (citation omitted) (discussing City of Lafayette v. La. Power & Light Co., 435 U.S. 389 (1978)). More recent Supreme Court cases have held that substate governmental entities

The first prong requires that the policy in question be "clearly articulated and affirmatively expressed."[49] This means that the state must express something more than neutrality about a particular action of a substate unit.[50] Rather, the state must make a specific grant of power to a subunit or a private party. But the state need not be explicit that the policy will produce an anticompetitive effect. Rather, the anticompetitive effect need only be a "'foreseeable result' of what the State authorized."[51]

Anticompetitive behavior flowing from state policy must also meet the second prong: active supervision by the state.[52] Municipalities that administer an anticompetitive policy satisfy this prong by definition.[53] But the Court has required state-created regulatory boards[54] and state universities[55] to demonstrate "that state officials have and exercise power to review particular anticompetitive acts of private parties and disapprove those that fail to accord with state policy."[56] This ensures that any state-affiliated body controlled by active market participants remains accountable to the state.[57]

Antitrust immunity for state-adjacent or state-authorized actors—including state universities—is not a foregone conclusion under this two-pronged test. Consider the case of *Seaman v. Duke Universi-*

---

need not meet the "active supervision" prong for *Parker* immunity to attach. F.T.C. v. Phoebe Putney Health Sys., 568 U.S. 216, 226–27 (2013) ("This rule preserves to the States their freedom to use their municipalities to administer state regulatory policies free of the inhibitions of federal antitrust laws without at the same time permitting purely parochial interests to disrupt the Nation's free-market goals." (citing *La. Power & Light*, 435 U.S. at 415–16 (internal quotations and ellipses omitted)).

49. Cmty. Commc'ns Co., Inc. v. City of Boulder, 455 U.S. 40, 51 (1982).

50. *Id.* at 56 (holding that a neutral grant of "home-rule" to cities within a state does not meet the Court's requirement that the policies enacted by a local government be "clearly articulated and affirmatively expressed" by the state).

51. *Phoebe Putney Health Sys.*, 568 U.S. at 227 (citing Town of Hallie v. City of Eau Claire, 471 U.S. 34, 42 (1985)).

52. *Midcal Aluminum*, 445 U.S. at 105.

53. Town of Hallie v. City of Eau Claire, 471 U.S. 34, 46 (1985) ("We now conclude that the active state supervision requirement should not be imposed in cases in which the actor is a municipality.").

54. *E.g.*, N.C. State Bd. of Dental Exam'rs v. F.T.C., 574 U.S. 494 (2015).

55. *Cowboy Book*, 728 F. Supp. at 1522.

56. *N.C. State Bd. of Dental Examiners*, 574 U.S. at 507 (citing Patrick v. Burget, 486 U.S. 94, 101 (1988)).

57. *Id.* at 509–510.

ty.[58] In this case, the US District Court for the Middle District of North Carolina rejected an argument that the University of North Carolina (UNC) should automatically be granted immunity for a noncompete agreement with Duke University. This agreement between UNC and Duke eliminated competition between the two schools for faculty and suppressed faculty salaries.[59] The district court found that UNC's "status as a constitutionally established entity is not enough to entitle it and its employees to *ipso facto* state action immunity from antitrust liability" under *Parker*.[60]

Courts appear more likely to grant *Parker* immunity for state schools when the policy at issue directly affects students. In *Cowboy Book*, for example, the district court also concluded that—even if OSU were not a constitutionally created entity with broad powers—the university's decision to subsidize textbooks was both clearly articulated state policy by an entity actively supervised by the state. In particular, the court observed that the bookstore's policy of extending credit "reflect[ed] a *clearly articulated* state policy to displace competition in student affairs."[61] Moreover, the state "actively supervised" OSU through the statutory scheme in place to audit university finances.[62]

---

58. Seaman v. Duke Univ., No. 1:15-CV-462, 2016 WL 1043473 (M.D.N.C. Feb. 12, 2016).
59. *Id.* at *2.
60. *Id.* at *1.
61. *Cowboy Book*, 728 F. Supp. at 1523 (emphasis added).
62. *Id.* at 1522.

III. Fraternities' Use of Antitrust Claims Against Universities

Private parties have rarely pursued antitrust claims against universities. The most well-known of these was filed by four fraternities against Hamilton College in 1997.[63] Hamilton College is a small, private college in Clinton, New York.[64] The college's first fraternities were founded in 1837.[65] They began providing room and board to students in the 1880s.[66] The fraternity houses at issue in this case—described by one commentator as "sprawling mansions"—were constructed in 1920.[67] Originally an all-male institution, fraternities played a "central role" among Hamilton's student body.[68] But Greek affiliation among Hamilton's students has waned over time. In 1960, almost 90% of Hamilton students belonged to a fraternity.[69] This number shrank to roughly 68% in 1978 when Hamilton began admitting women after merging with Kirkland College.[70] By the mid-1990s, Greek membership declined to approximately 20%.[71]

Hamilton College had long required only freshmen to live on campus.[72] This arrangement permitted Greek organizations to house members—an arrangement that began to raise concerns that "private societ-

---

63. Hamilton College is the most thoroughly examined case in this area. *See* Bauer, *supra* note 1 (describing roots of and long-standing relationship between small liberal arts colleges and fraternities and providing an analysis of the Hamilton College case); Sunshine, *supra* note 37 (providing an overview of "Greek-Gown" relations and relevant antitrust actions against universities with a focus on Hamilton College).

64. Hamilton Chapter of Alpha Delta Phi, Inc. v. Hamilton Coll., 128 F.3d 59 (2d Cir. 1997).

65. Bauer, *supra* note 1, at 369.

66. *Id.*

67. *Id.* (citing Karen W. Arenson, *Trust Suit Reinstates Against College's Curbs on Fraternities*, N.Y. TIMES, Oct. 29, 1997, at B11).

68. Karen W. Arenson, *Trust Suit Reinstates Against College's Curbs on Fraternities*, N.Y. TIMES, Oct. 29, 1997, at B11, available at https://www.nytimes.com/1997/10/29/nyregion/trust-suit-reinstated-against-college-s-curbs-on-fraternities.html.

69. Bauer, *supra* note 1, at 368.

70. Arenson, *supra* note 68.

71. Bauer, *supra* note 1, at 368.

72. Hamilton Chapter of Alpha Delta Phi, Inc. v. Hamilton Coll., No. 95-CV-0926, 1996 WL 172652, at *2 (N.D.N.Y. Apr. 12, 1996), *rev'd*, 128 F.3d 59 (2d Cir. 1997); Bauer, *supra* note 1, at 369.

ies hurt Hamilton's academic reputation."[73] Following a study of residential student life in 1992, the board of trustees determined that "a connection existed between fraternity-dominated social life and Hamilton's inability to attract the most qualified students, many of whom were female."[74] Hamilton College addressed this concern by changing its residency policy to require all sophomores to live on campus beginning with the 1993–94 school year.[75]

Hamilton's trustees created a special Committee on Residential Life to comprehensively review policies around the college's residential life in 1994.[76] The committee articulated several objectives, including "ensur[ing] greater integration of academic and residential life to better promote the college's educational mission."[77]

Ultimately, the committee recommended that "[a]ll students ... live in College housing, and all residential spaces will be available to all students."[78] The college adopted this recommendation for the 1996–97 school year, requiring all students—even those living in sanctioned Greek houses—to live on campus and purchase a campus meal plan.[79] In an affidavit, one trustee admitted that the change was prompted by "an excess number of dormitory beds because of poor management."[80]

Hamilton College faced a different dilemma: it now had too few beds to house all students.[81] Unoccupied fraternity houses provided a solution. When fraternities objected, one Hamilton College trustee told Delta Kappa Epsilon (DKE) alumni, "Gentlemen, this is a done deal....

---

73. *Hamilton Coll.*, 1996 WL 172652, at *2 (citing Compl. ¶ 21).

74. *Id.* (citing Second Kantrowitz Aff. Ex. B, at 4).

75. Bauer, *supra* note 1, at 370.

76. HAMILTON COLLEGE, A REPORT ON THE INSTITUTIONAL SELF-STUDY OF HAMILTON COLLEGE PREPARED FOR THE COMMISSION ON HIGHER EDUCATION OF THE MIDDLE STATES ASSOCIATION OF COLLEGES AND SECONDARY SCHOOLS 144 (October 2000), https://my.hamilton.edu/college/institutional_research/selfstudy2001part1.pdf [hereinafter *Self-Study Report*].

77. *Hamilton Coll.*, 1996 WL 172652, at *2.

78. *Self-Study Report*, *supra* note 76, at 145.

79. *Id.*; Hamilton Chapter of Alpha Delta Phi, Inc. v. Hamilton Coll., 106 F. Supp. 2d 406, 407 (N.D.N.Y 2000).

80. Bauer, *supra* note 1, at 370 (citing Aff. Of Francis O'Brien, Former Trustee of Hamilton Coll. at ¶¶ 26–36, *Hamilton Coll.*, 128 F.3d 59 (No. 96-7599)).

81. *Hamilton Coll.*, 1996 WL 172652 (noting that, between 1986 and 1996, "there were between 200 and 250 more Hamilton students than the college itself could house").

The College simply isn't going to allow the place to be used by the fraternity unless it's under Hamilton's control."[82]

Four fraternities sued Hamilton College in the US District Court for the Northern District of New York.[83] They sought to enjoin Hamilton from putting its new residential policies into effect. The fraternities argued that Hamilton College was monopolizing the market for "residential services" in Clinton, New York—a violation of the Sherman Act § 2.[84]

The district court was faced with a difficult question: did the college's housing policy involve "trade or commerce" such that Hamilton's residential housing policy fell within the ambit of Sherman Act? Or was Hamilton's housing policy merely "an incidental restraint of trade" and not sufficiently commercial "to warrant application of the antitrust laws"?[85]

The fraternities argued that the college's residential policy was clearly commercial and intended to raise revenues by "(1) forcing all Hamilton students to purchase residential services from Hamilton; (2) allowing Hamilton to raise its prices for such services; and (3) attempting to purchase the fraternity houses at below-market prices."[86]

The district court disagreed. Initially, the court held that Hamilton's residential policy was not, as the fraternities argued, "a pretext designed to obfuscate [the] purely commercial purpose."[87] Rather, the court held that the conduct at issue affected "the actual or potential day-to-day lives of the students" and "intimately related to academic life."[88] In the court's view, the academic character of the policy removed the challenged conduct from the required "trade or commerce" and granted Hamilton's motion to dismiss.

---

82. Bauer, *supra* note 1, at 371 (citing Aff. Of Donald E. Burns, Alumni President, Hamilton Chapter of Delta Kappa Epsilon, *Hamilton Coll.*, 128 F.3d 59 (No. 96-7599)).

83. *Hamilton Coll.*, 1996 WL 172652.

84. *Hamilton Coll.*, 106 F. Supp. 2d at 407.

85. Hamilton Chapter of Alpha Delta Phi, Inc. v. Hamilton Coll., 128 F.3d 59, 64 (2d Cir. 1997) (citing Marjorie Webster Junior Coll., Inc. v. Middle States Association of Colls. & Secondary Schs., Inc., 432 F.2d 650, 654 (D.C. Cir. 1970), *cert. denied*, 400 U.S. 965 (1970)).

86. *Hamilton Coll.*, 128 F.3d at 66.

87. *Id.*

88. *Hamilton Coll.*, 1996 WL 172652, at *4.

On appeal, the Second Circuit rejected the district court's reasoning.[89] The district court had treated the nexus between the challenged conduct and interstate commerce as a jurisdictional requirement.[90] But the Second Circuit explained that "the inquiry into whether the impact of the challenged activity is merely incidental to a noncommercial purpose, or is distinctly noncommercial in character, is a question that goes to the substantive reach of the Sherman Act, not to the jurisdiction of the court."[91]

In particular, the Second Circuit held that the district court should not have relied on Hamilton College's (contested) claim that "[its] decision regarding residential services concerns education rather than commercial gain."[92] But the court also rejected the fraternities' contention that "anything a college or university does to enhance its reputation is, as a matter of law, commercial activity subject to antitrust scrutiny."[93] Rather, the court acknowledged that colleges and universities "engage in a wide spectrum of conduct, ranging from the distinctly noncommercial to the purely proprietary."[94] The Second Circuit reversed the district court's decision, permitting the fraternities to move forward with their claims.

On remand, Hamilton College filed a motion for summary judgment. It argued that the fraternities had inappropriately defined the relevant product and geographic market. Recall that the fraternity plaintiffs had alleged that Hamilton College was attempting to monopolize "the market for residential services for students matriculating at Hamilton College" in Clinton, NY. The college, on the other hand, argued the relevant market to be "'the market in which Hamilton College competes: the market for highly selective colleges.'"[95]

---

89. *Hamilton Coll.*, 128 F.3d at 59. Note that the fraternities appealed after the district court granted a motion to dismiss. The circuit court faulted the district court's failure to accept all of the plaintiff's allegations—in particular, the plaintiff's allegations as to the nature of the restriction—as true. *Id.*

90. *Id.* at 66.

91. *Id.*

92. *Id.* (citing Hamilton Chapter of Alpha Delta Phi, Inc. v. Hamilton Coll., No. Civ.A. 95-CV-0926, 1996 WL 172652, at *6 (N.D.N.Y. Apr. 12, 1996).

93. *Id.* at 65.

94. *Id.*

95. Hamilton Chapter of Alpha Delta Phi, Inc. v. Hamilton Coll., 106 F. Supp. 2d 406, 410 (N.D.N.Y. 2000) (citation omitted).

Note how the difference in market definitions shifts the nature of the case. The plaintiffs define a relatively small market comprising a single good (residential services) to a narrow population (Hamilton students) in a small geographic area (Clinton, NY). Hamilton College necessarily holds a monopoly in this narrow market. But the college's definition is much broader. Hamilton College argues that the market comprises a cluster of goods—"academic services, health services, financial aid and residential services, as well as qualities such as size and location"—to a broad population (prospective college students) across a large geographic area (the entire nation).[96] Even the plaintiffs' expert conceded that Hamilton College did not have market share in this broader market.[97]

The district court sided with Hamilton College. The true choice for students, declared the court, occurred when selecting among competing colleges. And the plaintiffs had failed to account for how a raise in residential housing prices at Hamilton College would affect Hamilton's ability to compete for top-flight students.[98] In particular, the college argued that competition with other liberal arts colleges would prohibit Hamilton from raising prices for residential services above a competitive level. In other words, Hamilton College would be unable to act as a monopolist of residential services because competition among "reasonably interchangeable" colleges prevented Hamilton from raising its prices.

The court ultimately granted Hamilton College's motion for summary judgment. It found that the plaintiffs' definition of the market was "artificially narrow" and "defined essentially in terms of the practice of which [the plaintiffs] complain"—that is, the market was based on contract and not market forces.[99] As a result, the court concluded that the fraternities' proposed market definition was "incorrect as a matter of law."[100] All four fraternities eventually sold their houses to Hamilton College.[101]

---

96. *Id.* at 412.
97. *Id.* at 410.
98. *Id.* at 413.
99. *Id.*
100. *Id.*
101. Three of the four original fraternity plaintiffs sold their houses to Hamilton College after winning at the Second Circuit due to mounting legal fees. The final fraternity plaintiff, Sigma Phi, sold its house to Hamilton after the Northern District of New York granted summary judgment. Bauer, *supra* note 1, at 375; Mike Debraggio, *Hamilton*

This case—like many antitrust cases—hinged on the product and market definition. Hamilton College posed no monopolization risk in a national (or even regional) geographic market for services provided by liberal arts colleges. This definition may be appropriate when thinking about the choices made by students making an initial decision to matriculate.

But the court failed to consider the difficulties faced by matriculated students, who had already invested time and money attending Hamilton College. Course credits may not fully transfer, financial aid may not be available, and students may have otherwise invested time and energy into developing relationships with professors and other students that would be difficult to replicate.[102] In other words, transferring to another school would entail "transaction costs" that students making an initial enrollment choice do not face.

Some have argued that this case is best analyzed as an attempt to monopolize a secondary market: students choose Hamilton College and are then forced to choose Hamilton's residential services. This situation is similar to the circumstances in *Eastman Kodak v. Image Technical Services*.[103] Kodak sold copier machines, copier parts, and offered its customers repair services. Customers could also have their copiers repaired by independent services organizations (ISOs). ISOs depended on the availability of Kodak copier parts to compete with Kodak for repairs, and many customers preferred ISOs' higher-quality service. Kodak began refusing to sell copier parts for use in the secondary market, pushing out ISOs.

A group of ISOs sued. They argued that Kodak was violating § 1 by attempting to *tie* the Kodak repair services to the sale of Kodak parts. Plaintiffs also alleged that Kodak was attempting to monopolize repair services for Kodak copiers in violation of § 2. The plaintiffs' arguments require conceptualizing the service and parts market as *separate* markets. The relevant consumers are, by definition, owners of Kodak copiers. Kodak rejected this distinction, however. It argued that parts and service necessarily comprised a unified market.

---

and Sigma Phi Agree to Terms, HAMILTON COLLEGE (Feb. 14, 2003), https://www.hamilton.edu/news/story/hamilton-and-sigma-phi-agree-to-terms.

102. Bauer, *supra* note 1, at 381.

103. 504 U.S. 451 (1992).

The Supreme Court found Kodak's proposed market definition wanting. Service and parts are two separate markets because the record indicated that "there [was] sufficient consumer demand so that it is efficient for a firm to provide service separately from parts."[104]

The Court also rejected Kodak's argument that "a single brand of a product or service can never be a relevant market under the Sherman Act." Rather, the Court found:

> The relevant market for antitrust purposes is determined by the choices available to Kodak equipment owners. Because service and parts for Kodak equipment are not interchangeable with other manufacturers' service and parts, the relevant market from the Kodak equipment owner's perspective is composed only of those companies that service Kodak machines.[105]

The Court's ruling in *Eastman Kodak* suggests that the Northern District of New York should have disentangled the clustered product market definition offered by Hamilton College to comprise two distinct markets: the primary market for selecting undergraduate education and a separate secondary market for student residential services. Like service and parts, educational services and residential services appear to comprise two distinct markets, as historically there was "sufficient consumer demand so that it [was] efficient for a [fraternity] to provide [residential] services separately from [educational services]."[106] This would mean that the relevant consumer class, like Kodak copier owners, would not be all potential students but only those actually enrolled at Hamilton. Under this analysis, Hamilton College would have been much less likely to prevail.

---

104. *Id.* at 462.
105. *Id.* at 481–82 (citations omitted).
106. *Id.* at 462.

IV. Overview of Consumer Protection and Unfair Trade Practices Laws

Consumer protection and unfair trade practices laws can also provide fraternities with avenues to challenge university actions. Such laws are often referred to as "Unfair and Deceptive Acts and Practices" (UDAP) statutes.[107]

Fraternal organizations may find state consumer protection and UDAP laws more useful when facing a challenge to their charter or another negative action by a university. Section 5 of the Federal Trade Commission Act (FTC Act) provides the FTC with broad power to proscribe consumer harms across industries. But its reach is limited by the FTC's somewhat narrow interpretation of expansive statutory language and Congress's failure to include a private right of action (PROA) for enforcement in the FTC Act.[108]

State UDAP law, often called "Little FTC Acts," may provide a PROA, depending on the state. The standards adopted to prove a state UDAP claim also vary from state to state and are linked to court and agency interpretations of Section 5 of the FTC Act. Some states have adopted an older, but more expansive interpretation of what it means for a practice or act to be "unfair" or "deceptive." Others mirror the FTC's much narrower current interpretation.

---

107. CAROLYN L. CARTER, NATIONAL CONSUMER LAW CENTER, CONSUMER PROTECTION IN THE STATES: A 50-STATE REPORT ON UNFAIR AND DECEPTIVE ACTS AND PRACTICES STATUTES (2009), https://filearchive.nclc.org/car_sales/UDAP_Report_Feb 09.pdf.

108. 15 U.S.C. §45(b).

a. Limiting "Unfair" and "Deceptive" Practices Under FTC Act, Section 5

At the federal level, Section 5 of the FTC Act invests the FTC with the power to regulate and prosecute "persons, partnerships, or corporations"[109] from engaging in "unfair or deceptive practices."[110] Phrases like "unfair" and "deceptive" lack specificity by design. The flexibility in these terms allows the FTC to adapt to new business practices or behaviors—much like the ambiguous language in the Sherman Act.[111]

The FTC has defined "deceptive" acts as ones in which there is a material "representation, omission or practice that is likely to mislead [a reasonable] consumer."[112] The commission assesses what is "reasonable" from the viewpoint of a reasonable consumer within the target audience. This means evaluating whether the deceptive act would likely mislead a typical consumer who is reasonably well informed and acting reasonably under the circumstances.[113] The misrepresentation must also be material. In other words, it must be likely to affect the consumer's decision to purchase or use the product or service. Finally, the FTC often looks at the overall "net impression" created by an advertisement or marketing practice to determine if it is deceptive.[114]

---

109. 15 U.S.C. §45(a)(2). The statute excludes the following parties from the FTC's purview: "banks, savings and loan institutions described in [15 U.S.C. 57(a)(f)(4);] common carriers subject to the Acts to regulate commerce[;] air carriers and foreign air carriers subject to part A of subtitle VII of Title 49[;] and persons, partnerships, or corporations ... subject to the Packers and Stockyards Act." *Id.*

110. 15 U.S.C. §45(a)(1).

111. *See* Fed. Trade Comm'n v. Gratz, 253 U.S. 421, 430 (1920) (Brandeis, J., dissenting) (noting the intended flexibility in the term "unfair" in the phrase "unfair methods of competition"); Fresh Grown Preserve Corp. v. Fed. Trade Comm'n, 125 F.2d 917, 919 (1942) (citation omitted) (stating that the addition of the phrase "'unfair or deceptive acts or practices in commerce' ... enlarged instead of lessened the scope of the jurisdiction of the Commission").

112. *See* Statement by James C. Miller, Chairman of the Fed. Trade Comm'n, *FTC Policy Statement on Deception* (Oct. 14, 1983), https://www.ftc.gov/system/files/documents/public_statements/410531/831014deceptionstmt.pdf.

113. Miller, *supra* note 112, at 1.

114. Fed. Trade Comm'n, Enforcement Policy Statement on Deceptively Formatted Advertisements (Dec. 22, 2015), https://www.ftc.gov/system/files/documents/public_statements/896923/151222deceptiveenforcement.pdf.

"Unfair" acts are less well defined.[115] In general, unfair acts "impede consumers' ability to make informed choices."[116] The FTC's standard for determining "unfair" acts has narrowed since the FTC promulgated its first standard in 1964.

This earlier rule, called the Cigarette Rule, was first articulated in conjunction with an FTC rule regulating the labeling and packaging of cigarettes.[117] The Commission recognized that "[n]o enumeration of examples can define the outer limits of the Commission's authority to proscribe unfair acts or practices."[118] Rather, the Commission's goal was to "enforce a sense of basic fairness in business conduct."[119] But it provided three factors which, if present, would "surely violate Section 5 even if there is no specific precedent for proscribing it."[120] These factors asked:

> (1) whether the practice, without necessarily having been previously considered unlawful, offends public policy as it has been established by statutes, the common law, or otherwise—whether, in other words, it is within at least the penumbra of some common law, statutory, or other established concept of fairness; (2) whether it is immoral, unethical, oppressive, or unscrupulous; (3) whether it causes substantial injury to consumers (or competitors or other businessmen).[121]

---

115. David L. Belt, *The Standard for Determining 'Unfair Acts or Practices' Under State Unfair Trade Practices Acts*, 80 CONN. BAR J. 247, 249 ("As one commentator has noted with respect to section 5(a)(1) of the FTC Act, "given this broad mandate, it is not surprising that vagueness of definition and uncertainty of application have marked the FTC law of unfair trade practices.") (citing DEE PRIDGEN, CONSUMER PROTECTION AND THE LAW § 9.1 at 663 (2006)).

116. J. Howard Beales, Former Director at the Bureau of Consumer Protection of the Fed. Trade Comm'n, *The FTC's Use of Unfairness Authority: Its Rise, Fall, and Resurrection*, (May 30, 2003), https://www.ftc.gov/news-events/news/speeches/ftcs-use-unfairness-authority-its-rise-fall-resurrection (detailing how the FTC's unfairness doctrine has changed over time).

117. Belt, *supra* note 115, at 256–57.

118. Statement of Basis and Purpose of Trade Regulation Rule 408, Unfair or Deceptive Advertising and Labeling of Cigarettes in Relation to the Health Hazards of Smoking, 29 Fed. Reg. 8325, 8355 (1964) [hereinafter *FTC Cigarette Rule*].

119. *Id.*
120. *Id.*
121. *Id.*

The FTC's statement of the Cigarette Rule indicated that all three factors were sufficient, but failed to clarify which (if any) were necessary, or sufficient, standing alone.

The Supreme Court adopted the Cigarette Rule in *FTC v. Sperry & Hutchison Co.* in 1972.[122] It gave Section 5 a capacious reading and affirmed the FTC's standalone Section 5 authority to prohibit "unfair and deceptive acts and practices" beyond the enforcement of antitrust law. Under this interpretation, the FTC could prevent and prosecute acts contrary to public policy, as well as unethical, immoral, oppressive, or unscrupulous acts, that harmed a variety of parties.[123]

The *Sperry & Hutchinson* decision represents the apex of the FTC's standalone Section 5 authority. Between 1972 and 1980, the FTC applied the rule broadly. In particular, the FTC clarified that a practice need not meet all criteria to be considered unfair. Rather, "a practice may be unfair because of the degree to which it meets one of the criteria or because to a lesser extent it meets all three."[124]

This broad interpretation raised congressional ire. In 1980, the FTC issued a revised statement of its unfairness policy in response to a congressional inquiry.[125] This new interpretation presented a balancing analysis. It defined an unfair practice as having three components: the act (1) injures consumers, (2) violates public policy, (3) is ethical or unscrupulous.[126]

"Unjustified consumer injury" is the most important element of the analysis and sufficient to constitute an unfairness finding.[127] But this injury is only legally cognizable if it is "substantial, ... not outweighed by any countervailing benefits to consumers or competition that the practice produces; and ... must be an injury that consumers themselves could not reasonably have avoided."[128]

---

122. 405 U.S. 233 (1972).

123. *Id.* at 243; *see also* Belt, *supra* note115, at 258–59.

124. Belt, *supra* note115, at 261–62.

125. Fed. Trade Comm'n, Policy Statement on Unfairness, (Dec. 17, 1980), https://www.ftc.gov/legal-library/browse/ftc-policy-statement-unfairness [hereinafter *1980 Unfairness Statement*].

126. *Id.*

127. *Id.*

128. *Id.*

Consumer injury is also necessary to the analysis. Unethical or unscrupulous conduct or conduct otherwise against public policy—absent consumer injury—does not the meet the legal requirements for a stand-alone Section 5 violation under the FTC's updated interpretation.

Congress codified the bulk of this policy statement in 1994.[129] In particular, Congress limited the FTC's ability to restrict "unfair" conduct to those acts or practices that are "likely to cause substantial injury which is not reasonably avoidable by consumers and not outweighed by countervailing benefits to customers or competition."[130] The statute further clarified that, while the FTC could consider evidence that the conduct was against public policy, "[s]uch public policy considerations may not serve as a primary basis for such [a] determination."[131]

Section 5 regulates commercial transactions, and a variety of consumer-oriented acts supplement the FTC's Section 5 authority.[132] Universities' commercial transactions can generate liability under this patchwork of federal consumer protection law—even in areas that seem closely intertwined with the school's educational mission, such as residential services.

Most relevant here, the FTC has prosecuted a variety of deceptive advertising and marketing practices involving false, misleading, or unsubstantiated claims from for-profit universities. In 2016, for example, the FTC sued DeVry University in the US District Court for the Central District of California pursuant to its Section 5 authority.[133] The FTC claimed that DeVry misrepresented both the employment rates of and income earned by DeVry graduates.[134] Ultimately, DeVry settled these charges and agreed to pay "$49.4 million in cash to be distributed to

---

129. The Federal Trade Commission Act Amendments of 1994, Pub. L. No. 103-312, 108 Stat. 1691 (1994).

130. 15 U.S.C. § 45(n).

131. *Id.*

132. Fed. Trade Comm'n, *Legal Library: Statutes*, https://www.ftc.gov/legal-library/browse/statutes (last visited Aug. 5, 2023) ("The Commission has enforcement or administrative responsibilities under more than 70 laws.").

133. Compl. for Permanent Injunction and Equitable Relief at ¶ 1, Fed. Trade Comm'n v. DeVry Education Group, Inc., No. CV-16-00579-MWF-SSx (C.D. Cal. May 9, 2016).

134. *Id.* at ¶¶ 16–18 (alleging that DeVry falsely represented that "obtaining a degree from [DeVry] is highly likely to result in obtaining a desirable job soon after graduating—a well-paying, career-oriented job in the student's chosen field of study").

qualifying students who were harmed by the deceptive ads, as well as $50.6 million in debt relief."[135]

b. Limiting "Unfair" and "Deceptive" Practices Under State UDAP Laws

Every state (and the District of Columbia) has adopted some type of consumer protection law.[136] These state UDAP laws may provide broad protections for consumers and permit private enforcement. Others may not.[137] Like the FTC Act, all state consumer protection acts provide for *public* enforcement. But some state consumer protection acts also provide for a PROA. These acts supplement federal authority and may provide an attractive alternative for litigants due to "the relatively low standards predicated for determining liability" in some states.[138]

State UDAP laws generally require the plaintiff to demonstrate that the defendant engaged in an unfair or deceptive practice that caused the plaintiff some tangible harm.[139] But the standard required to find a violation varies from state to state. Some states, such as Connecticut and Massachusetts, have adopted and retained the FTC's original Cigarette

---

135. FED. TRADE COMM'N, *Press Release: DeVry University Agrees to $100 Million Settlement with FTC* (Dec. 15, 2016), https://www.ftc.gov/news-events/news/press-releases/2016/12/devry-university-agrees-100-million-settlement-ftc.

136. CARTER, *supra* note 107, at 5.

137. *Id.*; Jack E. Karns, State Regulation of Deceptive Trade Practices Under "Little FTC Acts": Should Federal Standards Control?, 94 DICK. L. REV. 373, 373 (1990).

138. *Id.* at 374.

139. *See, e.g.*, Anoush Cab, Inc. v. Uber Tech., Inc., 8 F.4th 1, 15 (1st Cir. 2021) ("A successful [Massachusetts unfair and deceptive trade practice statutory] claim thus has three elements: (1) the defendant engaged in an unfair method of competition or committed an unfair deceptive act or practice; (2) a loss of money or property was suffered; and (3) the defendant's unfair or deceptive method, act or practice caused the loss suffered."); Hangman Ridge Training Stables, Inc. v. Safeco Title Ins., Co., 719 P.2d 531 (Wash. 1986) ("We hold that to prevail in a private CPA action ... a plaintiff must establish five distinct elements: (1) unfair or deceptive act or practice; (2) occurring in trade or commerce; (3) public interest impact; (4) injury to plaintiff in his or her business or property; (5) causation."); Westgate Resorts, Ltd. V. Sussman, 387 F. Supp. 3d 1318, 1363 (M.D. Fla. 2019) ("[FDUTPA claims have] three elements: (1) a deceptive act or unfair practice; (2) causation; and (3) actual damages.") (internal quotations omitted)).

Rule for determining whether conduct is "unfair."[140] As the First Circuit observed, the "consumer friendly" standard of unfairness "goes far beyond the scope of the common law action for fraud and deceit."[141]

Other states, such as Florida, adopted verbatim the FTC's modern interpretation of unfairness.[142] Still others, such as Arizona and Virginia, have enacted more narrow laws that fail to provide a general ban on "unfair" or "unconscionable" conduct.[143]

States' Little FTC Acts may be attractive alternatives to more traditional common law theories of commercial harm—for example, negligent misrepresentation, promissory estoppel, and tortious interference, to name a few—due to statutory provisions allowing more extensive recovery. Plaintiffs may be able to recover not only compensatory damages, but (in some cases) treble damages, punitive damages, and/or attorney fees and costs, depending on the state. For example, the Massachusetts unfair and deceptive trade practices statute allows plaintiffs to recover double or treble damages if the conduct is both a violation of the statute *and* "willful or knowing."[144]

---

140. Kent Literary Club of Wesleyan Univ. v. Wesleyan Univ., 257 A.3d 874, 900–01 (Conn. 2021) (interpreting the Conn. Unfair Trade Practices Act); Katz v. Belveron Real Estate Partners, LLC, 28 F. 4th 300, 313 (1st Cir. 2022) (interpreting the Mass. Consumer Protection Act).

141. *Kent Literary Club*, 257 A.3d at 900 (describing the Cigarette Rule as "consumer friendly"); *Katz*, 28 F.4th at 313 (describing the relative breadth of the rule).

142. Parziale v. HP, Inc., 445 F. Supp. 3d 435, 445 (N.D. Cal. 2020) (interpreting the Florida Deceptive and Unfair Trade Practices Act).

143. CARTER, *supra* note 107, at 12.

144. Baker v. Goldman, Sachs & Co., 771 F.3d 37, 52 n.9 (1st Cir. 2014).

V. Recent Attempts by Fraternal Organizations to Allege Violations of State Consumer Protection and UTP Laws

Fraternities and sororities may be able to rely on state consumer protection or unfair competition laws when challenging university actions. One recent (and successful) example of this can be found in *Kent Literary Club of Wesleyan University at Middletown v. Wesleyan University*.[145] In this case, a fraternity and a student sued Wesleyan University under the Connecticut Unfair Trade Practices Act (CUTPA) for promissory estoppel, negligent misrepresentation, tortious interference with business expectancies, and other violations of CUTPA, after Wesleyan University suspended the fraternity from housing upperclassmen students.

Like *Hamilton College*, the dispute in this case arose from Wesleyan College's changes to its residential housing policies. Wesleyan University required all undergraduate students to live in university-approved housing.[146] Upperclassmen were permitted to live in approved Greek housing, including the DKE House. DKE permitted only male members to live in its house, which was owned by an alumni group, the Kent Literary Club (KLC).[147]

DKE's and KLC's relationship with Wesleyan was governed by a "Greek Organizations Standards Agreement." This contract, among other rights and responsibilities, permitted termination of the agreement by either party "for any reason upon thirty days' notice."[148] It also required that DKE be bound by the same university rules and policies as any other Greek organization—policies that Wesleyan was "permitted to amend or modify at any time."[149] The university was required to enforce the agreement equitably among the Greek organizations, with the caveat that nonenforcement of any provision was "not to be con-

---

145. No. MMX-CV-15-6013185-S, 2017 WL 2453237, at *2 (Conn. Super. Ct. Apr. 26, 2017).

146. *Id.* at *1.

147. *Id.*

148. Kent Literary Club of Wesleyan Univ. v. Wesleyan Univ., 257 A.3d 874, 880 (Conn. 2021).

149. *Id.*

strued as a waiver with respect to any subsequent breaches" of the standards agreement.[150]

Wesleyan announced in September 2014 that it would require all residential fraternities to become coeducational by 2017.[151] This announcement came in response to multiple allegations of sexual assaults occurring at other fraternity houses—assaults that resulted in more than one lawsuit against Wesleyan University.[152] DKE and KLC objected to the mandate, arguing that their national charter did not allow women members.[153] The university clarified that the fraternities need only coeducate the houses themselves—not membership in the fraternity as an organization. Each fraternity was required to submit a coeducation plan by January 5, 2015.[154]

DKE and KLC met this deadline—but with reservations and a response described by a KLC representative prior to submission as "the preliminary and half-baked status of our current thinking."[155] Wesleyan communicated that the DKE/KLC plan was "sufficient as a starting point" but required additional information to remain an approved housing option for the 2015–16 school year. Wesleyan required DKE and KLC to confirm by February 6, 2016, the following information:

> (1) the name of the sorority that the fraternity would partner with in coeducating DKE House; (2) residential policies, use of facilities, rule and administrative proceedings; (3) conversion of three rooms for female occupancy in the 2015–2016 academic year, with those residents allowed to have full and equal access to common areas; and (4) continued efforts to coeducate DKE House within three years.[156]

---

150. *Id.*

151. *Kent Literary Club*, 2017 WL 2453237, at *1.

152. Charles D. Ray & Matthew A. Weiner, *Supreme Deliberations: The Legal Fallout of Coeducating a Fraternity*, CONN. LAWYER 34 (July/Aug. 2021), https://www.ctbar.org/docs/default-source/publications/connecticut-lawyer/ctl-vol-31/6-julyaug-2021/ctl-julyaug-21---supreme-deliberations.pdf.

153. Kent Literary Club of Wesleyan Univ. v. Wesleyan Univ., No. MMXCV156013185S, 2015 WL 3974538, at *2 (Conn. Super. June 2, 2015).

154. *Id.* ("On December 4, 2014, [the University] clearly stated in an email to DKE representatives '[w]e are seeking meaningful coeducation of the residence as a condition of continuing in program housing. We are not requiring coeducation of DKE as an organization.'").

155. *Id.* (internal quotations omitted).

156. *Kent Literary Club*, 2017 WL 2453237, at *2.

DKE and KLC interpreted the university's request that DKE/KLC name a partner sorority as a "new requirement" and asked that the university withdraw the request. Wesleyan limited the scope of the request to "the name of the sorority that DKE intend[ed] to partner with and [the] steps [DKE/KLC] envision[ed] taking in developing the partnership," as well as DKE/KLC's timeline. In response, a KLC representative communicated that DKE/KLC could not "commit, at [that] point in time, to fully co-educate" the DKE house within three years.[157]

Wesleyan terminated DKE's Standards Agreement effective June 18, 2015.[158] The university concluded that the fraternity's response failed to "provide reasonable detail" as to how DKE/KLC would fully coeducate the house and "effectively [ran] out of time to resolve these critical issues" in the current housing cycle.[159]

DKE and KLC subsequently filed suit against Wesleyan in February 2015.[160] The plaintiffs alleged that Wesleyan's actions throughout their negotiations violated CUTPA[161] and constituted negligent misrepresentation and tortious interference with KLC's business expectations. In addition, DKE and KLC alleged that Wesleyan made assurances as to the continued operation of the DKE house and, as a result, were subject to promissory estoppel.[162]

Note that plaintiffs did not allege that Wesleyan had violated the Standards Agreement. Wesleyan was entitled to change the terms of the Standards Agreement at its discretion and terminate the agreement for any reason with 30 days' notice.

The issue in the case boils down to whether Wesleyan acted in bad faith during the negotiations between the fraternity and the university such that its behavior was separately tortious.[163] In particular, plaintiffs alleged tortious conduct on three grounds. First, DKE/KLC argued that

---

157. *Kent Literary Club*, 2015 WL 3974538, at *9 (internal quotations omitted).

158. Tim Burke & Manley Burke, *DKE Wins Right to Return to its House at Wesleyan and its Attorney's Fees*, FRATERNAL L. NEWSLETTER (Jan. 2018), https://fraternallaw.com/newsletter2/dke-wins-right-to-return-to-its-house-at-wesleyan-and-its-attorneys-fees.

159. *Kent Literary Club*, 2015 WL 3974538, at *4.

160. Hannah Docter-Loeb & Sara McCrea, *Connecticut Supreme Court Reverses Prior Decision on DKE House Lawsuit*, WESLEYAN ARGUS (Mar. 11, 2021), http://wesleyanargus.com/2021/03/11/connecticut-supreme-court-reverses-prior-decision-on-dke-house-lawsuit/.

161. CUTPA is codified at Conn. Gen. Stat. § 42-110a et seq.

162. *Kent Literary Club*, 257 A.3d 874, 879 (Conn. 2021).

163. Ray & Weiner, *supra* note 152.

Wesleyan had falsely guaranteed that coeducating the residential (as opposed to the organizational level) was sufficient to retain housing status.

Second, DKE/KLC argued that Wesleyan had deceived DKE/KLC by promising that the university would allow DKE to coeducate its house over three years. Instead, Wesleyan revoked DKE's participation in the university's residential housing program within the first six months after DKE/KLC submitted their initial coeducation plan.

Finally, DKE/KLC claimed that Wesleyan reneged on a promise to *future* Wesleyan students that they could live at the DKE House.[164] In other words, DKE/KLC alleged that Wesleyan "never intended to allow them to coeducate solely at the residential level and that, in fact, his coeducation requirement was merely a pretext to sever ties with DKE and to force [KLC] to sell the centrally located DKE House to the university."[165]

Despite the different causes of action—negligent misrepresentation, promissory estoppel, tortious interference, and CUTPA violations—all share a common theme. Each claims a deviation from good faith negotiations surrounding DKE's continued participation in Wesleyan's housing program.

The fraternity experienced some initial success in the trial court. After denying the defendant's motion for summary judgment, DKE and KLC received $386,000 in damages following a successful jury trial.[166] The plaintiffs also sought attorney fees and costs, as well as punitive damages under the CUTPA, in a post-verdict motion for equitable relief. The Court granted the plaintiffs' motion with respect to fees and costs, ordering Wesleyan to pay the plaintiffs an additional $411,363.44.[167]

Wesleyan appealed the jury's decision and requested transfer to the Connecticut Supreme Court.[168] The Court took issue with the trial court's jury instructions with respect to the legal implications of the Standards Agreement, but it found support for plaintiffs' claim that Wesleyan's bad faith behavior violated the CUTPA.

---

164. *Id.*

165. *Kent Literary Club*, 257 A.3d at 881.

166. Burke & Burke, *supra* note 158.

167. *Id.*

168. Erin Hussey, *DKE Lawsuit Against the University Reaches Connecticut Supreme Court*, WESLEYAN ARGUS (Jan. 31, 2019), http://wesleyanargus.com/2019/01/31/dke-lawsuit-against-the-university-reaches-connecticut-supreme-court/.

The CUTPA prohibits parties from engaging in "unfair methods of competition and unfair or deceptive acts or practices in the conduct of any trade or commerce."[169] Connecticut's courts have adopted and consistently applied the FTC's Cigarette Rule:[170] determines a practice to be "unfair" if it (1) "offends public policy as it has been established by statutes, common law, or otherwise"; (2) "is immoral, unethical, oppressive or unscrupulous"; or (3) "causes substantial injury to consumers...."[171] Plaintiffs need not demonstrate that the injury be "unjustified" as required by the modern FTC unfairness standard.[172] In other words, under Connecticut's application of the Cigarette Rule, CUTPA does not require plaintiffs to show that the injury "is not outweighed by countervailing benefits to consumers or competition, and consumers themselves could not reasonably have avoided it."[173]

The Connecticut Supreme Court recognized that the parties' enforceable rights arise from the Standards Agreement—an agreement that left the plaintiffs with little recourse.[174] Wesleyan was certainly within its rights to terminate the agreement with little notice and change the terms of the agreement at its discretion. As the Court explained, "When a party acts consistently with its rights under a contract, its conduct cannot violate CUTPA."[175]

But the Court recognized that a CUTPA violation can arise when a defendant "has acted in bad faith with respect to the contract."[176] Here, the Court determined that the plaintiffs had provided sufficient for a jury to have to have found Wesleyan liable for those bad faith negotia-

---

169. *Kent Literary Society*, 257 A.3d at 889 (citing Conn. Gen. Stat. § 42-110b(a)); *see, e.g.*, Abrahams v. Young & Rubicam, Inc., 240 Conn. 300, 306–307, 692 A.2d 709 (1997) (requiring the plaintiff to demonstrate that the plaintiff "(1) engaged in unfair methods of competition or unfair or deceptive acts or practices (2) in the conduct of any trade or commerce, (3) resulting in (4) an ascertainable loss of money or property, real or personal, by the plaintiff.").

170. *Id.* at 900.

171. In re Cablevision Consumer Litigation, 864 F. Supp. 2d 258 (Mar. 28, 2012).

172. *Kent Literary Club*, 257 A.3d at 899–900.

173. *Id.* at 900.

174. *Id.* at 883–84.

175. *Id.* at 886.

176. *Id.* at 889 (citing Levitz, Lyons & Kesselman v. Reardon Law Firm, P.C., No. 3:04cv00870 (JBA), 2005 WL 8166987, at *5 (D. Conn. Mar. 31, 2005)).

tions.[177] At trial, the plaintiffs presented evidence that Wesleyan had told the plaintiffs that coeducating the fraternity (as opposed to just the house) was sufficient to remain in the residential housing program.[178] Several witnesses also testified "not only that Wesleyan would work with the plaintiffs to accomplish the residential coeducation of the DKE House, but also that the deadline to fully coeducate the house could be extended ... as long as the plaintiffs continued to make substantial progress toward that goal."[179] This testimony was further supported by several emails between Wesleyan officials and the plaintiffs.[180]

The plaintiffs additionally presented evidence that Wesleyan officials were motivated by personal dislike and never intended to allow DKE to remain in the residential housing program. For example, the plaintiffs submitted evidence that the two Wesleyan officials involved in the coeducation process had expressed that "'eliminating Greek organizations would be ideal.'"[181] Additional evidence demonstrated Wesleyan officials' antipathy toward DKE specifically and the university's desire to purchase the DKE House.[182]

The Court concluded that the plaintiffs had produced sufficient—although not overwhelming—evidence for the jury to find Wesleyan liable for all counts. The case, however, was remanded for a new trial due to errors in jury instructions regarding both the role of the Greek Organizations Standards Agreement in cabining liability and the appropriate methods of calculating damages.[183] DKE and KLC ultimately settled with the university.[184]

Note how the relatively more expansive rule benefits the plaintiffs in this case. Under the FTC's modern standard, the plaintiffs would have needed to demonstrate that the "substantial injury" they experienced

---

177. *Id.* at 896.

178. *Id.*

179. *Id.*

180. *Id.* (discussing Nov. 2014 and Jan. 2015 emails where Wesleyan representatives offered assurances they were committed to helping DKE retain its programming status through the 2015–16 academic year).

181. *Id.* at 897 (referencing an Apr. 2014 meeting).

182. *Id.*

183. *Id.* at 880.

184. Jem Shim, *University Reaches Settlement with Delta Kappa Epsilon in Seven-Year Lawsuit*, The Wesleyan Argus (Apr. 28, 2022), http://wesleyanargus.com/2022/04/28/university-reaches-settlement-with-delta-kappa-epsilon-in-seven-year-lawsuit/.

was not outweighed by countervailing benefits to consumers and that the plaintiffs could not have reasonably avoided it. This more stringent standard would have permitted the university to demonstrate the benefits of removing DKE from the residential housing policy—perhaps by providing evidence of better integration of academic and residential life or increasing equity and safety on campus.[185]

This case illustrates how consumer protection laws may present an avenue for Greek organizations to challenge university decision-making, but only when the university acts in bad faith outside of the four corners of the relevant Standards Agreement. Within the agreement itself, DKE and KLC had no recourse. Moreover, relief may be limited depending on the state in which the conduct occurred. States adopting the modern FTC unfairness standard may find themselves less likely to prevail in the face of countervailing educational and social benefits claimed by the university.

VI. Conclusion

Antitrust and consumer protection laws, though not traditionally associated with fraternal organizations, have become increasingly relevant in disputes between universities and these organizations, particularly regarding the ownership of fraternity and sorority houses. Universities' attempts to purchase Greek-owned properties and implement policies affecting the operation of Greek life on campus have led to antitrust and state unfair trade practices claims. Although the limited litigation of these claims has been unsuccessful so far, the matter of antitrust liability for universities remains unsettled, and future UTP claims could potentially succeed, given the variation in state laws.

---

185. Each of these were goals of Hamilton College's decision to end Greek organizations' participation in the College's residential life program. *Self-Study Report, supra* note 76, at 144–159.

CHAPTER 15

Employment Law Issues for Fraternities and Sororities

Ann C. Juliano

As fraternal organizations face increasing pressures with hazing and insurance issues, one could excuse them for failing to focus on some basic legal issues facing every organization. But ultimately, fraternal organizations are employers, and thus face the same myriad issues faced by any employer. Employment law includes federal law, state law, and, in some cases, local law. Fraternal organizations must be aware of the scope of employment decisions and policies that must be addressed.

This chapter begins with a discussion of the basics of employment law—the concept of employment at will and the emerging definitions of "employee." The chapter next turns to a high-level overview of the federal laws governing employers. Although a complete discussion of all state laws is beyond the scope of this chapter, this overview will familiarize fraternities and sororities with the general issues so they may avoid unforeseen legal issues. Topics summarized include immigration laws, antidiscrimination laws, workplace safety, workers' compensation, wage and hour laws, and unemployment insurance. This chapter will then turn to specific issues of interest to fraternal organizations.

I. The Basics

a. Employment at Will

Before diving into specifics, a few threshold premises should be understood. First, unless an exception applies, the law defaults to a model which seeks to allow employers to run their workplaces as they see fit. This default rule is known as "employment at will." The (almost cliché) description of employment at will is that an employer may fire an employee for a good reason, a bad reason, or no reason at all (just not a prohibited reason). Conversely, an employee may quit for a good reason, a bad reason, or no reason.

Numerous exceptions apply to "employment at will." For example, an employer needing "cause" to fire is a restriction on employment at will. Particularly relevant to fraternal/sorority organizations are restrictions listed in employment contracts, collective bargaining agreements, or employee handbooks and manuals. Each of these restrictions limit an organization's ability to fire employees "at will." For example, an employment manual stating that employees will not be terminated without "good cause" limits the ability to fire employees. Further, even if the reasons for termination are not listed, employers may restrict themselves by implementing mandatory procedures prior to termination. This could include a system of escalating discipline, a mandatory probationary period, or automatic hearings.

Apart from the above self-imposed restrictions, employers' decisions concerning employees are restricted by state and federal law. These restrictions are primarily found in statutes. However, some restrictions arise under contract and tort law. As mentioned above, provisions in an employee handbook may create an implied contract and thereby restrict an employer's ability to terminate employees. Additionally, employees may bring claims for wrongful discharge. Most jurisdictions recognize a claim for discharge in violation of public policy. Typically, the policy must be expressed clearly in a legislative or constitutional provision. Restrictions in federal statutes are discussed in the section below.

b. Definition of Employee

Many statutory protections apply only if an individual is considered an employee, thus, an understanding of the legal definition of "employee" is essential to fraternal organizations. This issue is intertwined with the relationship between the national organization and the individual chapters. Is the house director employed by the National or a separate national house corporation or a local house corporation? Other individuals who may fall in either category could include a cook and maintenance workers at a local chapter house.

Often, this is not a difficult question. In most cases, the workers at the national headquarters will be considered employees. If there is a contract with a house director, the employment status will be explicitly determined in that document. However, if it is vague, the employer must make a determination of employment status in order to meet the obligations under federal and state statutes. Complicating matters are the many legal factors that impact whether one may be considered an "employee."

Most often, the question is a distinction between "employee" and "independent contractor." Several tests have been developed by the courts. The first test is known as the "control test," which arose from respondeat superior cases (where a party injured by an employee on the job wants to sue the employer to recover greater damages). Relying on the law of agency, courts turned to the "master-servant" relationship test for guidance. This is also referred to as the common law test. There are several versions of this multifactor test,[1] but the focus remains on the ability of one party to direct the particulars of the job. In other words, the court considers not just what the job is (development, for example) but the amount of control the business exercises over the person in completing the job, versus how much control the employee exercises in completing their work. Therefore, one way to view the "control" is to examine the level and amount of supervision of the employer over the worker.

In the leading Supreme Court case on this question, *Nationwide Mutual Insurance Co. v. Darden*, the Court stated that the main consideration is the hiring party's right to control the manner and means by which the product is accomplished, and set forth several factors to review in applying the control test:

> the skill required; the source of the instrumentalities and tools; the location of the work; the duration of the relationship between the parties; whether the hiring party has the right to assign additional projects to the hired party; the extent of the hired party's discretion over when and how long to work; the

---

1. *See e.g.*, RESTATEMENT (SECOND) OF AGENCY § 220.

method of payment; the hired party's role in hiring and paying assistants; whether the work is part of the regular business of the hiring party; whether the hiring party is in business; the provision of employee benefits; and the tax treatment of the hired party.[2]

A second test examines whether the worker is economically dependent on the employer or if the worker is in business for himself. The test uses a totality of the circumstances approach, which is more flexible than the control test. The central question is whether the worker is able to set out on her own or if she must rely on the employer.

Courts have developed additional factors for the economic realities test:

> 1) the degree of the alleged employer's right to control the manner in which the work is to be performed; 2) the alleged employee's opportunity for profit or loss depending upon his managerial skill; 3) the alleged employee's investment in equipment or materials required for his task, or his employment of helpers; 4) whether the service rendered requires a special skill; 5) the degree of permanence of the working relationship; 6) whether the service rendered is an integral part of the alleged employer's business.[3]

Recently, states have legislated in this area.[4] Typically, this legislation creates a presumption that workers are employees, unless the employer is able to prove three things: (1)the business is unable to control or direct what the worker does, either by contract or in actual practice; (2) the worker performs tasks outside of the entity's usual business; and (3) the worker is engaged in an independently established trade. This is known as the "ABC test." If it is not clear under an employment agreement or one of the tests above, fraternal organizations should check the state law to see if the ABC test has been adopted.

---

2. Nationwide Mut. Ins. Co. v. Darden, 503 U.S. 318, 323–324 (1992) (citing Community for Creative Non-Violence v. Reid, 490 U.S. 730, 751–752 (1989)).

3. Donovan v. DialAmerica MKTG., Inc., 757 F.2d 1376, 1382 (3d Cir. 1985).

4. *See e.g.*, CAL. LAB. CODE § 2750.3; MASS. GEN. LAWS. ch. 149, § 149B(a).

II. Overview of Federal Antidiscrimination Laws

This section provides a high-level overview of a variety of federal employment laws. The goal is to provide fraternal organizations with a broad outline of federal employment laws so that they may be aware of the issues to consider when acting as an employer.

a. Immigration

Considering the beginning of the hiring process, fraternal organizations must be aware of the immigration laws as they relate to hiring. The Immigration Reform and Control Act of 1986 prohibits undocumented workers from working in the United States.[5] Employers with four or more employees may not discriminate against any individual, other than an unauthorized alien, with respect to hiring or discharge on the basis of national origin or citizenship.[6] Most likely, an individual house corporation will not have four or more employees, but most national headquarters will. Fraternal organizations are easily able to meet their obligations by completing a Form I-9 for each employee, which involves examining the documentation offered by the employee to verify that the documents reasonably appear to be genuine and do relate to the employee who is offering the documents.

b. Discrimination

Turning to the federal laws most at issue in hiring, employers must not violate the provisions of the federal antidiscrimination in employment statutes. There are three primary statutes: Title VII of the Civil Rights Act of 1964 (Title VII);[7] the Age Discrimination in Employment Act of 1967 (ADEA),[8] and the Americans with Disabilities Act of 1990 (ADA).[9] Title VII prohibits actions taken "because of" race, color, reli-

---

5. 8 U.S.C. § 1324a *et seq.*
6. 8 U.S.C. § 1324b *et seq.*
7. 42 U.S.C. § 2000e.
8. 29 U.S.C. § 621 *et seq.*
9. 42 U.S.C. § 12101 *et seq.*

gion, national origin, and sex.[10] Under the category of "sex," the Supreme Court recently made clear that sexual orientation and gender identity are covered.[11] Further, Congress amended the statute to prohibit discrimination on the basis of pregnancy. The age discrimination statute prohibits actions taken "because of" age against someone who is at least 40 years old. Finally, the ADA prohibits actions taken against a qualified individual with a disability.

These statutes apply to hiring, firing, compensation, terms, conditions, or privilege of employment.[12] In some instances, an employer may be liable for the impact of neutral employment criteria.[13] For example, if an employer requires all employees possess a valid driver's license, there could be an impact on individuals with disabilities. If an employer requires employees to have played collegiate football, that will have an impact on female applicants. Such neutral criteria are valid if the employer can prove they are job related and consistent with business necessity.[14]

Additional actions prohibited by the statutes include harassment and retaliation. Each statute has been interpreted to prohibit allowing or creating a hostile work environment because of membership in a protected class.[15] In other words, if an employee is being harassed because of their age (or any of the other protected classes), that could be a violation of the statute.[16] The harassment doesn't have to relate to a tangible job ac-

---

10. Another federal statute, Section 1981 of the Civil Rights Act of 1866, 42 U.S.C. § 1981, prohibits race discrimination in the "mak[ing] and enforce[ement] of contracts." The Supreme Court has held that § 1981 applies to nongovernmental employers and applies to employment contracts. Note that the statute only prohibits discrimination because of race.

11. Bostock v. Clayton County, 140 S. Ct. 1731 590 U.S. ___ (2020).

12. 42 U.S.C. § 2000e-2(a)(1).

13. 42 U.S.C. § 2000e-2(k)(1)(A)(i).

14. Id.

15. Meritor v. Vinson, 477 U.S. 57 (1986).

16. There are other elements to a hostile environment claim. The behavior at issue must be because of the employee's membership in a protected class, the behavior must be sufficiently severe or pervasive to alter the conditions of employment from both an objective and a subjective perspective, and the employer must be found liable for its actions. Harris v. Forklift Systems, Inc., 510 U.S. 17 (1993). The employer's liability will turn on the organizational status of the harasser and looks to whether the employer had notice of the actions, the employer's efforts to prevent or correct the behavior, and the actions of the employee to avoid harm and provide the employer with notice. Burlington Indus. v. Ellerth, 524 U.S. 742 (1998).

tion (in other words, being demoted or fired). If the work environment is altered because of the employee's race or religion or any of the other protected classes, then there is a violation. Further, employers will be liable if a supervisor conditions tangible employment benefits on acquiescence to sexual demands. This is known as quid pro quo harassment. As for retaliation, if an employee engages in activity to oppose an action that is unlawful under these statutes and the employer takes an adverse action against him, then the employer has engaged in prohibited retaliation.[17] In addition, if an employer testifies or participates in a hearing concerning unlawful activity and the employer acts against her, that is also unlawful retaliation.[18]

Fraternal organizations should be aware of obligations to provide reasonable accommodations for employees on specific matters. First, under Title VII, employers must provide reasonable accommodations for the religious practices and observances of their employees. The employer must do so unless there is an undue hardship.[19] Refusing to hire someone because he will need an accommodation is a violation of Title VII, as is refusing to provide an accommodation to a current employee.[20] If an employee requests an accommodation for a sincerely held religious belief, the employer must either make a reasonable accommodation or show that it cannot provide a reasonable accommodation because of an undue hardship.

Providing a reasonable accommodation means that the employer must provide some manner of change in the workplace to allow the employee to engage in his religious practice. Examples include an exception from the "no caps" rule for an employee who wears a headscarf, or allowing an employee to take breaks at a certain time to engage in prayer.

To meet this obligation, an employer does not need to select the reasonable accommodation suggested by the employee. In addition, the employer does not have to prove that the accommodation suggested by the employee would create an undue hardship. If the accommodation offered allows the employee to engage in her observance or practice,

---

17. 42 U.S.C. § 2000e-3.
18. *Id.*
19. 42 U.S.C. § 2000e-1(j).
20. EEOC v. Abercrombie & Fitch, 575 U.S. 768 (2015).

then the employer has met its obligation.[21] An employer needs to prove undue hardship only if it is going to argue that it cannot provide any reasonable accommodation. The Supreme Court has defined "undue hardship" as substantial increased costs.[22]

Turning to the ADA, fraternal organizations should be aware that the Act protects three categories of employees. Specifically, it covers individuals with a present disability, which means an individual with a physical or mental impairment that substantially limits a major life activity.[23] A plaintiff might also have a record of such an impairment or be regarded as having such an impairment.[24] If an employer does not hire an individual because it believes that person has an impairment (even if the person does not have an impairment), the employer has violated the ADA. To receive coverage under the ADA, an individual must be qualified. The ADA defines "qualified" as "an individual who, with or without reasonable accommodations, can perform the essential functions" of the job.[25] If a function is not "essential," and the individual cannot perform it, then he remains qualified.

Further, the ADA requires employers to make reasonable accommodations for employees and applicants with known physical or mental impairments.[26] Reasonable accommodations include making the building accessible by providing elevators, ramps, etc. The statute specifically considers job restructuring, part-time or modified work schedules, and reassignment to a vacant position as reasonable accommodations.[27] Further, the provision for aides, readers, and interpreters are also reasonable accommodations. An employer is not obligated to provide a reasonable accommodation if it would amount to an undue hardship. The statutory definition of undue hardship is an accommodation requiring significant difficulty or expense.[28] This is a stricter standard to meet than the standard under religious accommodations. However, whether something

---

21. Ansonia Bd. of Educ. v. Philbrook, 479 U.S. 60, 69 (1986).
22. Groff v. DeJoy, 600 U.S. 447 (2023).
23. 42 U.S.C. § 12102(1)(a).
24. 42 U.S.C. § 12102(1)(b)–(c).
25. 42 U.S.C. § 12111(8).
26. 42 U.S.C. § 12111(9).
27. Id.
28. 42 U.S.C. § 12111(10)(A).

amounts to an undue hardship is also dependent on the size and financial resources of the workplace.

There are a few other statutes to keep in mind related to antidiscrimination laws. First, the Equal Pay Act is another statute that covers compensation in the workplace.[29] The EPA is an amendment to the Fair Labor Standards Act (FLSA), which regulates wages and hours. It covers only *wages* and only prohibits discrimination based on sex.[30] Because the EPA is part of the FLSA, it covers those employers who qualify as an "enterprise engaged in commerce or in the production of goods for commerce," defined as those engaged in interstate commerce or production of goods for interstate commerce and generating over $500,000 in revenue.[31] Because fraternal organizations are nonprofit organizations, the enterprise definition will most likely not apply. However, employees engaged in interstate commerce or in the production of goods for interstate commerce are also covered. For example, this could be an employee who prepares the alumni magazine to send across the country. The EPA prohibits the employer from paying wages to employees at a rate less than the rate paid to employees "of the opposite sex" for "equal work."[32] The statute goes on to define "equal work" as "the performance of which requires equal skill, effort, and responsibility, and which are performed under similar working conditions."[33]

The Family and Medical Leave Act of 1993 (FMLA)[34] applies to employers with 50 or more employees and requires that employers provide up to 12 weeks of unpaid leave for the birth or adoption of a child or for a serious health condition of the employee, a spouse, parent, or child. Only employees who have worked for at least 12 months for the employer for a minimum of 1,250 hours in the past year are eligible.[35] When foreseeable, the employee is required to give notice to the employer of the need for the leave.[36] Further, employers are required to reinstate em-

---

29. 29 U.S.C. § 206(d)(1).
30. Technically it covers the "rate" of pay which means the statute covers wages but also bonuses, vacation pay, etc.
31. 29 U.S.C. § 203(s)(1).
32. 29 U.S.C. § 206(d)(1).
33. *Id.*
34. 29 U.S.C. §§ 2601–2659.
35. *Id.* at § 2611.
36. *Id.* at § 2612.

ployees returning from FMLA leave to the same or an equivalent position after the leave.[37]

Another statute employers should be aware of is the Genetic Information Non-Discrimination Act of 2008 (GINA).[38] Under this statute, employers with 15 or more employees are forbidden from discriminating based on genetic information and from seeking to obtain an employee's or an employee's family member's genetic information. Genetic information includes family medical history, information about the genetic tests of an employee or family member, and use of genetic services by an employee or family member. There are a few limited exceptions in GINA. Most relevant to fraternal organizations is the ability to request information to comply with certification requirements under the FMLA.

Finally, fraternal organizations may not discriminate against service members (including National Guard members), applicants to uniformed services, and veterans because of their military service.[39] The United Services Employment and Reemployment Rights Act of 1994 applies to all employers and requires employers to reinstate service members after military service subject to certain requirements, including that the length of absence from the workplace does not exceed five years.

III. Terms and Conditions of Employment

Many of the antidiscrimination laws discussed above impact the terms and conditions of employment. However, there are four other major employment law issues that must be addressed: wage and hour laws, workplace safety issues, worker's compensation, and unemployment compensation.

---

37. Id. at § 2614
38. 42 U.S.C. Ch. 21F.
39. 38 U.S.C. §§ 4301–4335.

a. Wages and Hours

Wage and hour issues are some of the trickiest issues for fraternal organizations as employers. The FLSA[40] requires covered employers to pay at least minimum wage to employees and to pay time and a half for any hours worked over 40 hours/week. This statute only applies to those workers who qualify as "employees." Second, the statute applies only to "enterprise" employers or employees engaged in commerce. As discussed above in the section on the EPA, most fraternal organizations, as nonprofits, will not fall within the "employer as enterprise" definition of employer. However, an individual worker engaged in commerce will be covered. Recall that the test for "engaged in commerce" is very broad. An employee who works at a location that produces goods that cross state lines will be considered engaged in commerce even if that employee is not involved in producing the goods. Finally, the FLSA has many exemptions for certain categories of workers, including administrative and professional. These exemptions applied to fraternal organizations will be discussed in greater detail below.

The FLSA requires employers to pay at least the federal minimum wage, which is currently $7.25 per hour, for non-tipped employees. However, many states have their own minimum wage laws which require a higher wage. Fraternal organizations must meet the higher wage required. The issue of paying overtime for hours worked in excess of 40 hours per week is also a difficult issue for fraternal organizations and is discussed below.

b. Workplace Safety

Although fraternal organizations may not prioritize workplace safety, federal law imposes obligations on them as employers. The federal Occupational Safety and Health Act (OSHA) applies to all "persons engaged in business affecting commerce who have employees."[41] Overall, employers must meet the "general duty clause" and keep the workplace free from recognized hazards that are likely to cause death or serious physical harm. Although OSHA has many more specific requirements

---

40. 29 U.S.C. § 202(a).
41. 29 U.S.C. §§ 651, 652(5).

for other types of industries, national headquarters must provide drinking water, access to bathrooms, and a comfortable temperature (this does not automatically require air conditioning). Safe entrances and exits must also be provided. For chapter house environments, fraternal organizations must meet the standards for cooking spaces for food workers and safe living spaces for house directors.

c. Worker's Compensation

Every state has a worker's compensation program. Through these programs, workers who are injured while in the scope of employment are entitled to certain resources, including compensation. This entitlement provides certainty to injured workers who do not need to go through the filing of a suit and waiting to see if they will be compensated. As a tradeoff, injured workers are not able to bring a claim for tort damages and the worker's compensation benefits are the sole remedy available to injured workers. Although there may be differences in specifics between states, there are some generalities. First, worker's compensation benefits are paid by the employer to the injured worker. Second, the compensation is less than the full amount of lost wages (often set at half of the employee's wages). Third, the injury must "arise out of and in the course of employment." Injuries that occur due to intentional employee misconduct are usually excluded from coverage. However, injuries that occur during an employer-sponsored recreational activity may be covered. For example, an injury that occurs during the summer softball league could very well be a compensable injury.

d. Unemployment Compensation

Unemployment benefits are provided through a joint federal/state program. The Federal Unemployment Compensation Act[42] imposes a tax on payroll which is reduced to a very low rate if the employer is covered by a state unemployment compensation law. Fraternal organizations will almost always meet the definition of employer covered by the

---

42. 42 U.S.C. §§ 501–504.

Act.[43] Thus, fraternal organizations, most likely, will need to look to state law to determine the specifics of eligibility for unemployment benefits. Keep in mind that these benefits are available only to those workers who are classified as employees. Further, to be eligible for benefits, an employee must have earned a minimum amount of wages in a covered job during the period prior to becoming unemployed. Next, the employee must currently be unemployed but able and available for work. Generally, this means that the former employee is seeking work.

Employees who voluntarily quit their jobs are not entitled to unemployment benefits. In some states, employees who quit with "good cause" remain eligible for unemployment benefits. Employees who are fired for misconduct are generally not eligible for benefits as well. Keep in mind that having good cause to fire an employee does not mean the employee engaged in misconduct. For example, an employer who consistently errs in keeping development records in order could be fired for good cause but would not have engaged in misconduct.

IV. A Few Thoughts on Other State Law Issues

Although a state-by-state analysis is beyond the scope of this chapter, fraternal organizations should be aware that state law may also impose requirements on employers. For example, some state antidiscrimination laws apply to employers with far fewer employees than the federal antidiscrimination law.[44] State laws may also contain additional protected classes not covered by federal law, such as having natural hair or familial status. State laws may also cover workers not covered by federal law. For example, New York state law protects volunteers from sexual harassment even though they are not "employees."[45] Finally, state laws have expanded in recent years to prohibit employers from seeking certain information

---

43. Employers must pay the unemployment tax if (1) they pay wages to employees totaling $1,500, or more, in any quarter of a calendar year; or (2) they had at least one employee during any day of a week during 20 weeks in a calendar year.

44. For example, Pennsylvania's law applies to employers with 4 or more employees. 43 P.S. § 954(b).

45. N.Y. Lab. Law § 201-g.

during the hiring phase such as any criminal background questions (known as "ban the box") or specific background questions (such as convictions over seven years old). Finally, some states and localities have banned asking applicants for their prior salary information in efforts to close the gender wage gap. Fraternal organizations need to check information provided by the state Equal Employment office to make sure they have the relevant, up to date information.

V. Fraternal-Organization-Specific Issues

a. Hiring High-Level Employees

Usually, hiring employees will not be a difficult process. However, it is vital that fraternal organizations pay careful attention when hiring high-level executives or executive directors. The single most important aspect to consider is the amount of compensation. To maintain nonprofit status, fraternal organizations' activities must remain directed toward the exempt purposes. Further, activities must not serve the private interests, or private benefit, of an individual or organization. This is known as the rule against private inurement or benefit and its interpretation often focuses on the compensation paid to employees, specifically, board members, officers, directors, and high-level employees of the organization.[46] If these high-level individuals benefit from overly high compensation, the fraternal organization could face penalties and possibly lose its tax-exempt status.[47] Further, if the fraternal organization is organized as a 501(c)(3) or 501(c)(4), the high-level individuals themselves could be subject to penalties.

When reviewing the compensation offered to a highly compensated individual at a fraternal organization, the touchstone is "reasonable." The total compensation package offered, including income,[48] bonuses,[49] and

---

46. Internal Revenue Service, *How to Lose Your 501(c)(3) Tax-exempt Status (without really trying)*, https://www.irs.gov/pub/irs-tege/How%20to%20Lose%20Your%20Tax%20Exempt%20Status.pdf.

47. Id.

48. Income includes housing allowances, retirement accounts, insurance premiums, and any memberships that benefit the employee.

49. Nonprofits must be very careful when offering bonuses, particularly those based on incentives, as these are closely scrutinized to ensure the compensation remains "reasonable" and not "excessive."

other benefits (such as health insurance, paid leave, reimbursement for continuing education or professional development) must be at or below fair market value. Thus, the nonprofit must know the market rate when setting compensation. The fraternal organization should look to "comparable" organizations when determining the market rate. The comparables should be other nonprofits located in the same or similar area, with a comparable mission of the organization, and a similar budget. Fortunately, many state and national nonprofit associations collect this information and produce reports that allow other nonprofits to make the necessary comparisons.[50]

To increase the likelihood that the compensation structure will be found to meet the "reasonable" standard, fraternal organizations should document the efforts taken to review comparable salary and benefit information, inform the board of directors of the way the compensation amount was determined, and obtain the board's approval of the compensation. Further, these steps should be followed every time a compensation decision is made. For example, if the employment agreement with the executive director allows for annual bonuses, the amount of the bonus should be discussed and approved by the entire board of directors each year.

Although the amount of compensation is the most important factor for hiring the executive director, there are a few other terms organizations should include in any employment agreement. First, the agreement should explicitly state whether the individuals are employees or independent contractors. Second, the agreement should have a term of employment stated. Often agreements for executives will state an initial term and then include the possibility for renewal. The agreement should clearly state the options following the end of the term of employment, including whether the agreement will be renewed and how that renewal will take place. If the agreement requires notice from either party, the fraternal organization should take care to make sure the procedural requirements are met. Finally, the agreement should state how and for what reasons the agreement might be terminated. This is discussed in greater detail below.

---

50. Some of these reports are available for free to members and others must be purchased. The leading national reports are published by GuideStar, The Nonprofit Times, and Columbia Books.

b. Wage and Hour Issues

One of the biggest employment issues facing fraternal organizations involves wage and hour claims. As stated above, under the FLSA, employees are entitled to overtime if they work more than 40 hours per week. This is determined on a week-to-week basis. In other words, if an employee works 30 hours one week and 50 hours the next week, this does not balance out to 40 hours. Rather, for the 50-hour week, the employee will be entitled to 10 hours of overtime. Thus, the key question is determining the "hours worked."

Before a more detailed discussion of the standards for determining what time counts as "hours worked," fraternal organizations should start with a few threshold questions. First, does our organization fall within the FLSA? Recall that the FLSA applies to "enterprise employers." Because this definition requires over $500,000 in earned revenue, many nonprofits will not fall within this definition. Donations, membership fees, dues, and contributions are not counted as revenue earned. Only income-producing activities, such as sales from a gift shop, will be counted as revenue producing. However, the "enterprise" category is only one way for a fraternal organization to have obligations under the FLSA. Individual employees could also trigger those obligations. Thus, organizations should next ask whether any of their employees fall within coverage under the FLSA. Independent contractors do not fall within FLSA coverage and neither do volunteers. Employees individually engaged in interstate commerce or in the production of goods for interstate commerce, or in any closely related process or occupation directly essential to such production do fall within the coverage. Recall from above that the "engaged in commerce" test is very broad. A national organization reaching out to alumni across the country will most likely have employees engaged in interstate commerce. In other words, a fraternal organization may not be considered an "enterprise employer" but may have obligations under the FLSA to specific employees.

The next question to consider is whether any of the covered employees are exempt from FLSA coverage. Organizations often wish to categorize employees as exempt, but this determination should not be made lightly. Miscategorization of employees can result in large penalties for the employer. High-level employees at the national headquarters will often be exempt under the "professional" category and because they receive a salary above the minimum. Determinations of exemptions are extremely fact specific and must meet a three-part test. First, the employee must be paid on a salary basis. This means that the employee must be paid the same amount each week regardless of the hours worked or the product produced. Second, the employee must earn a salary above the regulatory minimum, currently $684/week. In other words, if the employee earns fewer than $684/week (assuming a 52-week work year, $35,568/year), that employee cannot be exempt and will receive the protections of the statute. Finally, the employee's position must meet the "duties" requirements of one of the exemptions. Most relevant to national headquarters would be the administrative or executive exemptions. In short, to fall within the executive exemption, the employee's primary duty must be managing the organization, a customarily recognized department or subdivision of the enterprise, and the employee must manage at least two people. To meet the administrative exemption, the employee's primary duty must be the performance of office or nonmanual work directly related to the management or general business operations of the employer or the employer's customers and must include the exercise of discretion and independent judgment with respect to matters of significance.[51] When in doubt, it is advisable to treat employees as nonexempt and provide at least the relevant minimum wage and restrict working hours to 40 hours/week.

The positions of house directors and chapter consultants cause the most issues under the FLSA. Because house directors often live in the chapter house and because chapter visitors are traveling from house to house,[52] it is often difficult to keep track of when these individuals are working and when they are not. Additionally, some house directors are allowed to stay in the house during the summer or school breaks. If they take on official responsibilities during this time, such time will need to be compensated. However, it is vital that fraternal organizations establish set expectations for working and nonworking hours as well as create a detailed system for recordkeeping. Further, it should be clear which entity is the employer—the chapter, the local chapter housing corpora-

---

51. Exemption for Administrative Employees Under the Fair Labor Standards Act (FLSA), US Department of Labor (Revised Sept. 2019) https://www.dol.gov/agencies/whd/fact-sheets/17c-overtime-administrative.

52. Not every fraternal organization treats its Chapter Visitors as employees. Some are classified as volunteers who live at the house they are visiting and receive free room and board. These workers would be considered volunteers and not subject to FLSA.

tion, or the national headquarters. Ideally, there is only one employer to limit the exposure of the other related entities.

Fraternal organizations should create a weekly schedule for these types of employees with 40 hours (or fewer) worked. There should be a clear system for keeping track of those hours worked and a previously agreed-upon system for requesting and approving additional hours to be worked. Organizations should make clear that any time worked will be compensated. The importance of recordkeeping is not simply to limit overtime expenses but also to ensure compliance with the FLSA, which requires detailed recordkeeping with records to be kept for three years.

c. Worker's Compensation

Worker's compensation issues arise most frequently for employees employed by house corporations or chapter houses (although such claims could arise for any employee at the national headquarters). Recall from the discussion above that eligibility for worker's compensation depends upon state law. In most cases, a worker must be classified as an employee to be eligible for worker's compensation and may only be compensated for injuries suffered in the course of employment. Due to the all-encompassing nature of the house director duties, there is a wide exposure for worker's compensation. For example, if a house director is injured on the way to pick up supplies for the chapter house, she may be entitled to worker's compensation as one court held.[53] Another case involved a back injury by an employee hired as a cook and housekeeper.[54] She was injured while attempting to lift a box of books at the fraternity house and received benefits under the worker's compensation program.[55]

Many state laws have exclusion for "domestic service" and, in some cases, define domestic service as "services of a household nature in or about a private home, local college club, or local chapter of a college fraternity or sorority, performed by individuals such as cooks, maids, ... handymen, [and] gardeners ..."[56] Applying the state of Minnesota's cor-

---

53. Kaplan v. Alpha Epsilon Phi Sorority, 42 N.W.2d 342, 345 (Minn. 1950).

54. Schmitt v. Alpha Delta Phi Fraternity House, 307 N.Y.S.2d 780 (N.Y. App. Div. 1970).

55. Id.

56. OCGA §34-8-33. See also F.S. §443.03(5)(g) 2, F.S.A., ("(g) The term 'employment' shall not include: 2. Domestic service in a private home, local college club, or local chapter of a college fraternity or sorority;").

ollary to this provision, an individual who came once a week to clean a chapter house and was injured while cleaning was determined not to be entitled to worker's compensation.[57]

Chapter houses should check the state law to see if independent contractors are covered under the worker's compensation program. If they are, houses should consider hiring only those contractors with their own worker's compensation insurance. Otherwise, houses face exposure to pay compensation for every worker as an independent contractor. This could include handymen, bartenders, caterers, and others if hired directly by the chapter house (as opposed to a catering company or an event-planning service).

d. Terminating the Employment Relationship

When the employment agreement is created, fraternal organizations should also contemplate the end of the employment relationship. As stated at the beginning of this chapter, most employees are employees at will and may be fired without cause (unless the employer has restricted itself in some way) if no statutes are violated. However, for those employees with a contract, the employer should include the manner and method by which the employment may be terminated and by which party.

For example, the agreement may state the employee has the power to terminate the agreement early. If this term is included, the organization should include requirements for notice. In other words, must the employee provide two-weeks' notice or two months? The details will be dependent on the organization's understanding of the time required to secure a replacement and the ability of the organization to function without someone in the position at issue. The agreement may also include the circumstances under which the organization may terminate the agreement early. Basically, the two options are with cause and for no cause provided. The ability to terminate the agreement without the need to provide cause is more expedient for the organization because there is no need to gather documentation to make the cause determination. Regardless of the decision of whether to include a "no cause" provision, fraternal organizations should include the ability to terminate for cause and should define what constitutes cause.

---

57. Fingerson v. Alpha Tau Chapter of Zeta Tau Alpha Sorority, 267 N.W. 212 (Minn. 1936).

For every possible outcome of the employment agreement, the agreement should delineate the next steps. For example, is the employee entitled to compensation if the agreement is terminated early? Typically, termination for cause would not involve the payment of any severance pay but an early termination for no cause given would, even if the employee is the party who decides to terminate the agreement. More important than the ultimate decision of whether to provide severance pay is for the agreement to explicitly state the terms. Which terms to include in the agreement are a matter for each organization to determine as it balances the need to attract top employees with the need to protect itself.

Employers who terminate an agreement early for no cause given should consider asking the employee to sign a release of claims in exchange for the provision of severance pay (if not required by the agreement). If the employee is over 40 years of age, the fraternal organization must follow the requirements of the Age Discrimination in Employment Act. Any waiver of ADEA claims must be "knowing and voluntary." This requires the waiver to be written in language that is clearly understood, specifically refer to rights under the ADEA, inform the employee that she should consult an attorney, provide 21 days to consider the release, and provide seven days to revoke the agreement.[58]

e. Employment Issues and COVID-19

In the last few years, employers have faced a host of novel issues as the COVID-19 pandemic continually created new questions of the rights of employers and employees. What may have come as a shock to many employees is that the starting point for many of these questions is not whether the employer is allowed to take certain actions, but instead, one should ask, "is there anything preventing the employer from doing that?" To determine that, an employer should consider federal, state, and local laws.

When the pandemic started, some employers began to cancel vacation time and to require employees not to travel out of state. (Remember the days of quarantines for out-of-state travel). In some cities, employers prohibited employees from commuting on public transportation. Absent a collective bargaining agreement, provision in an employee hand-

---

58. 29 U.S.C. §626(f)(1).

book, or terms in an individual contract, there is no "entitlement" to vacation time. Therefore, an employer may cancel an employee's vacation. Some state laws prohibit an employer from taking action for an employee's conduct that is otherwise lawful.[59]

However, at this point, the interaction of employment law and COVID-19 centers on mask and vaccine mandates. The Supreme Court struck down the Biden administration's attempt to create an Emergency Temporary Standard to require certain employers adopt a vaccine or test requirement for their workplaces.[60] However, that opinion has no bearing on the actions of a private employer. Fraternal organizations may require employees to be vaccinated, may require employees to wear masks in the workplace, and may require employees to provide information concerning their vaccination status.[61] They may do so because there is no law preventing them from doing so, with one caveat—they must provide reasonable accommodations to employees' religious practices and disabilities. Employers need not simply agree to an employee's request for an exception from any workplace rules but may ask for documentation to support the claim of disability status and may request more information concerning an employee's sincere religious belief.

VI. Conclusion

Hopefully, this chapter has provided fraternal organizations with an overview of the issues that must be considered when operating as employers. The sheer number of laws and subject areas can be a bit daunting. But it is important to keep in mind, as repeated throughout this chapter, that organizations must consult their state and local laws to de-

---

59. CAL. LAB. CODE § 96(k) (protecting "lawful conduct occurring during nonworking hours away from the employer's premises"); COLO. REV. STAT. §24-34-402.5 (protecting " any lawful activity off the premises of the employer during nonworking hours"); N.Y. LAB. CODE § 201-d (protecting "an individual's legal recreational activities outside work hours, off of the employer's premises and without use of the employer's equipment or other property"); N.D. ST § 14-02.4-03 (protecting "lawful activity off the employer's premises during nonworking hours which is not in direct conflict with the essential business-related interests of the employer").

60. Nat'l Fed. Indep. Bus. v. Dep't of Lab., 142 S.Ct. 661 (2022).

61. Despite the many videos posted on social media, this is not a violation of HIPAA. HIPAA does not apply to employers requesting information from employees.

termine if there are additional obligations on employers. Finally, simply because the law allows an employer to take certain actions or treat employees in a particular fashion does not mean that you must. Employers are always able to take steps to create inclusive, welcoming, supportive workplaces to help employees thrive and grow.

CHAPTER 16

Intellectual Property Rights

Ashley R. Dobbs

Intellectual property rights (IP), including patents, trademarks, copyrights, rights of publicity, and trade secrets, can be a huge source of revenue for any organization. Unfortunately, national fraternities and sororities (collectively, "fraternal organizations") have not always adequately protected their intellectual property, nor capitalized on royalties associated with the licensing of their intellectual property.

This chapter will primarily focus on trademark issues, as the specific area of intellectual property that is most applicable to fraternities and sororities, and the need for fraternities and sororities to be diligent about the enforcement of their trademark rights, or else lose their ability to recover for trademark infringement.

This chapter will also analyze the extent to which trademark protection extends to a national fraternal organization's use of its Greek letters, the potential for the enforcement of trademark protection to ward off liability resulting from the actions of others not associated with a fraternal organization or its local chapters, and the best practices that fraternal organizations can follow to better protect their intellectual property. This chapter will end with considerations and strategies to avoid incurring potential liabilities related to the intellectual property of others.

I. Introduction to Intellectual Property

Intellectual property law creates and protects intangible rights arising primarily from creations of the minds of inventors, writers, graphic designers, painters, makers, and other creators. They are rights related to intangible property that cannot be touched or felt, unlike personal property or real property. Over time, this area of the law has expanded to include other kinds of intangible property rights that don't neatly fit into other ownership rights of personal and real property, such as rights of privacy and publicity. Intellectual property rights are generally identified as:

- patent,
- trade secret,
- publicity/privacy rights,
- copyright, and
- trademark.

The types of intellectual property rights most relevant for fraternities and sororities, from both an income and liability perspective, are trademark and privacy/publicity rights. However, it is also important to understand the different types of IP laws and how they differ in what they protect. While there is some overlap between the categories, each category focuses on a different type of right and expression. Section I of this chapter provides an overview of patent, trade secret, publicity, and copyright law; Section II focuses exclusively on trademark law, the most pertinent IP rights for fraternal organizations.

a. Patent

In the United States, patent law is exclusively governed by federal law, arising from the power granted by the US Constitution[1] and implemented by the US Patent and Trademark Office (USPTO)[2] and the federal courts.[3] Subject to the statutory requirements for the particular type

---

1. U.S. CONST. art. I, § 8.
2. 35 U.S.C. § 1.
3. 35 U.S.C. § 141; 25 U.S.C. §§ 2701–2721.

of invention, a US patent provides inventors a time-limited, exclusive right in an invention.

The right granted to the patent holders is one "to exclude others from making, using, offering for sale, or selling" or importing the invention which is the subject of the patent.[4] Note, patents are geographically specific, so an invention must be protected in each country where you want to be able to assert your rights.

There are three types of patents recognized under US law: utility, design, and plant.

Utility patents are what we usually think of as inventions: machines and tools, or chemicals. It broadly includes any implementation of a new, non-obvious, and useful "process, machine, manufacture, or composition of matter, or any new and useful improvement thereof."[5] For example, Coca-Cola invented a glass-front, refrigerated vending machine for dispensing drink containers and successfully obtained a utility patent for it.

On the other hand, design patents protect new, original, and ornamental designs for an article of manufacture.[6] Design patents can protect the appearance of functional items, such as jewelry. The patent will protect either the surface ornamentation on the item, the shape or configuration of the item, or both. Note that a design patent only protects these ornamental aspects, and not the product's functionality or usefulness.[7] For example, in 1915, the USPTO granted a patent in the design of the curvy glass bottle used for Coca-Cola.[8] Earlier, in 1914, the USPTO granted a patent in the design of a Delta Theta Phi fraternity pin.[9]

Finally, plant patents protect the rights of anyone who invents or discovers and asexually reproduces any distinct and new variety of plant.

---

4. 35 U.S.C. § 271.
5. 35 U.S.C. §§ 101–105.
6. 35 U.S.C. § 171.
7. Auto. Body Parts Ass'n v. Ford Glob. Techs., LLC, 930 F.3d 1314, 1318 (Fed. Cir. 2019).
8. U.S. Patent No. 48,160.
9. U.S. Patent No. 45,238.

1. LIMITATIONS TO PATENTS

Note, however, while the statute itself is intentionally broad, the Supreme Court narrowed the field of what is patentable, eliminating patents for "laws of nature, physical phenomena, and abstract ideas."[10] However, that doesn't mean the application of such an idea in developing an invention is necessarily unpatentable. The courts will engage in a two-part analysis: is the patent claim "directed to" a law of nature, physical phenomenon, or abstract idea?[11] If so, then does the patent claim contain an "inventive concept," rather than "well-understood, routine, conventional activities previously known to the industry?"[12]

A patent application requires a detailed description of the implementation of the process or implementation of the idea, including technical drawings and instructions. So in many cases, an inventor or company may instead choose to protect their process or method or recipe using trade secrets. For example, Coca-Cola holds utility patents in any number of formulas, such as "Oral sweetener compositions and methods," but they have never sought a patent in the legendary secret formula for "original Coke," because it would require disclosing the actual recipe.

All in all, it is best to consult a patent attorney early in the process to determine whether an idea or invention is patentable, and if so, how best to protect it.

b. Trade Secret

1. DEFINITIONS

Trade secrets—economically valuable secrets such as formulas or processes—can be indefinitely protected from misuse and misappropriation by commercial competitors both through tort law and by statute. All states but New York and the District of Columbia have adopted a form of the Uniform Trade Secret Act, which defines a trade secret as:

> ... information, including a formula, pattern, compilation, program, device, method, technique, or process that:

---

10. Diamond v. Diehr, 450 U.S. 175, 185 (1981).
11. Alice Corp. v. CLS Bank Int'l, 573 U.S. 208, 217 (2014).
12. *Id.* at 221, 225.

- Derives independent economic value, actual or potential, from not being generally known to, and not being readily ascertainable by proper means by, other persons who can obtain economic value from its disclosure or use; and
- Is the subject of efforts that are reasonable under the circumstances to maintain its secrecy.[13]

In addition, a private cause of action for trade secret misappropriation under federal law was created, with the passage of the Defend Trade Secrets Act of 2016 (amending the Economic Espionage Act).[14] This act allows for private civil actions in federal court to seek to protect and enforce trade secrets impacting interstate or international commerce, as well as government enforcement for criminal actions (i.e., theft, conspiracy). This act supplements, but does not supersede state law rights of action.[15]

2. ACQUIRING RIGHTS

There is no formal method for acquiring or securing one's rights in a trade secret; rather, any purported trade secret can only be protected by the methods an entity uses to protect and maintain the secrecy and to prevent unauthorized disclosure. The enforcement of these rights will typically arise through civil action in court, usually in seeking an injunction to prevent an action that would result in disclosure.[16] Success in such an action, aside from meeting the jurisdiction's injunctive relief standards, will depend on proving the existence of a trade secret and demonstrating the "reasonable efforts" to protect such secret(s).

3. EXAMPLES

So, referring back to the Coca-Cola example, the company has been able to establish a unique following of loyal customers who distinctly

---

13. Unif. Trade Secrets Act § 1(4) (Unif. L. Comm'n 1985).
14. 18 U.S.C. § 1831.
15. 18 U.S.C. § 1838.
16. *Cf.* United States v. Williams, 526 F.3d 1312, 1316 (11th Cir. 2008) (codefendants Joya Williams convicted and sentenced to 96-month sentence, and Ibrahim Dimson to 60-month sentence, for conspiracy to commit theft of trade secrets from Coca-Cola, under 18 U.S.C. section 1838(a)).

prefer the flavor of their soda to other "cola," and exhibit extraordinary brand loyalty on the basis of that flavor. Because no other company can exactly replicate the unique taste, the secrecy of the formula provides an economic value and advantage to Coca-Cola, vis-a-vis its competitors. A company wishing to divert some of those loyal customers by replicating the formula could not figure out the formula easily, but could benefit from the disclosure and use of the formula. So that demonstrates an existence of information that could potentially be subject to trade secret protection.

The next requirement is that the owner of the trade secret take "reasonable" efforts "under the circumstances" to maintain secrecy. The determination of what is "reasonable" is the subject of much case law, but generally speaking, such tools as nondisclosure agreements, password protections, locked safes, and "need to know" access to details, have all been considered reasonable measures. There are legends about the lengths Coca-Cola goes to to protect the formula, which far exceed "reasonable." Which is understandable, given their investment in the brand and the potential for another 100+ years of trade secret protection.

For example, while a fraternal organization may hold certain things to be "secrets" to be maintained by its membership, not all such things would necessarily qualify as a "trade secret." Initiation rites may be zealously guarded, but they do not necessarily confer an economic advantage to the organization, such that they would be protectable trade secrets. Membership and alumni information, on the other hand, might be protectable by trade secrets, if it consists of more than simply names and contact information, took some effort by the organization to compile, and otherwise meets the jurisdiction's requirements for protection. For example, some state statutes explicitly include "customer lists" in their definition of trade secrets.[17] Others have recognized under common law that a corporation's customer lists may be recognized as a trade secret.[18] And at least one court recognized that a company's list of fraternity and sorority members would be considered a trade secret, as a customer list.[19] It remains to be seen whether a membership organization's roster would be provided the same degree of protection, but it stands to reason that if it otherwise met the criteria, it would be so entitled.

---

17. *See e.g.*, CONN. GEN. STAT. ANN. § 35-51 (West, Westlaw through 2022 Reg. Sess.).
18. *See e.g.*, Poller v. BioScrip, Inc., 974 F. Supp. 2d 204, 216 (S.D.N.Y. 2013).
19. Sethscot Collection, Inc. v. Drbul, 669 So. 2d 1076, 1078 (Fla. Dist. Ct. App. 1996).

c. Copyright

1. DEFINITIONS

Copyright law protects *original,* creative expression by humans, *fixed* in a *tangible* medium (i.e., song, art, novel, photo).[20] It protects the original *way* an idea is expressed, not the idea itself. It includes artistic, literary, dramatic, or musical works presented in a tangible medium, such as a book, other written work, drawing, photograph, movie, or software.

Fixed means the work has been captured in a "sufficiently permanent [medium] ... to permit it to be perceived, reproduced, or otherwise communicated for a period of more than transitory duration."[21] This means that works that are not fixed (improv, unrecorded performances) may be protected under common law or state statute, but not under the federal copyright act.[22]

The owner of a copyright has a bundle of exclusive rights which allows him or her to control how his or her work is used. These rights include the right to copy, distribute, perform the work, and to make *derivative works.* This protection is given to works to prevent unauthorized copying.

Copyrights have a fixed term. For works created on or after January 1, 1978, the term generally is 70 years after the author's death or, for works made for hire, pseudonymous, and anonymous works, the shorter of 120 years from creation or 95 years from publication.

2. WHAT IS NOT PROTECTED BY COPYRIGHT?

Copyright does not protect things that are considered facts, not original, or not fixed in a tangible medium. Some explicit exclusions include: ideas or processes; names, short phrases, titles or slogans; fonts; formulas, lists of ingredients or contents, recipes; and functional aspects of three-dimensional objects (i.e., furniture).[23]

---

20. 17 U.S.C. § 102.
21. 17 U.S.C. § 101.
22. H.R. Rep. No. 94-1476, at 52 (1976).
23. *See* U.S. Copyright Off., Circular No. 33, Works Not Protected by Copyright 1–5 (2021), https://www.copyright.gov/circs/circ33.pdf; U.S. Copyright Office, Compendium of U.S. Copyright Office Practices § 313.3 (3d ed. 2021).

In addition, there are some kinds of copying of otherwise protected works that are permitted, under the concept of *fair use*. Fair use attempts to balance creators' interests in benefitting from their creative labors, with the freedom of expression valued under US laws.[24] Under this affirmative defense to infringement, certain types of copying for purposes such as criticism, commentary, news reporting, teaching, scholarship, or research, are not considered infringement.[25] The courts will weigh the "fair use" factors included in the statute[26] in a very fact-specific inquiry, on a case-by-case basis. There is no black and white formula for determining how much copying or taking of a work is too much for fair use, so it is important to have a very good understanding of the law before relying on a fair-use defense, rather than seeking permission (or "license") to use a copyrighted work.

3. ACQUIRING RIGHTS

Copyrights vest automatically in the creator of a work (referred to as an "author" in the statute, for all forms of work), as soon as a work is committed to paper, film, a computer disk, or some other tangible form, subject to the "work for hire" exception below. Registration with the US Copyright Office, under authority of the federal Copyright Act, provides certain benefits and is required for bringing suit in federal court. But registration is not required for ownership to attach.

The *work for hire* exception means that copyrights vest in the creator unless they (1) are an employee and create something within the scope of their work, or (2) are an independent contractor, where (i) there is a

---

24. *U.S. Copyright Office Fair Use Index*, U.S. COPYRIGHT OFF., https://www.copyright.gov/fair-use/ (last updated Aug. 2022).

25. 17 U.S.C. § 107.

26. The Copyright Act identifies four factors to consider when determining fair use, including:
> (1) [T]he purpose and character of the use, including whether such use is of a commercial nature or is for nonprofit educational purposes;
> (2) the nature of the copyrighted work;
> (3) the amount and substantiality of the portion used in relation to the copyrighted work as a whole; and
> (4) the effect of the use upon the potential market for or value of the copyrighted work.

17 U.S.C. § 107.

signed, written agreement explicitly ordering or commissioning the work and identifying it as "work for hire," (ii) the agreement was signed before the work was created, and (iii) the work falls within one of the specific categories of "work for hire" (a contribution to a collective work, part of a motion picture or other audiovisual work, translation, supplementary work [i.e., forward, editorial notes, etc.], compilation, instructional text, test, answer material for a test, or atlas).[27]

If you want to acquire the rights in something that a nonemployee created for you, and it does not fall under the *work for hire* provisions above, then you must have a written assignment agreement which outlines the scope of the rights being transferred to you. Absent a written agreement, if there is a later dispute, it will be interpreted that the creator maintains ownership of the copyrights, having granted you a limited, nonexclusive right to use the material as you have.

4. BENEFITS OF FEDERAL REGISTRATION

Again, while federal registration is not required for ownership of copyrights, registration (or refusal) is necessary to enforce those rights in court and helps establish one's claim to a copyright.[28] There are also other benefits of federal registration. While you can register a copyright any time within its life, you are eligible to recover attorneys' fees and statutory damages in an infringement suit, only if you register prior to infringement or within three months after the *publication*[29] of the work.[30]

Registration also enables you to work with the US Customs and Border Protection for protection against the importation of infringing cop-

---

27. 17 U.S.C. § 101.

28. COMPENDIUM (THIRD) § 202 (citing 17 U.S.C. § 411(a)); *e.g.*, Fourth Est. Pub. Benefit Corp. v. Wall-Street.com, LLC, 139 S. Ct. 881 (2019) (adopting the "registration rule" in holding that, subject to a few narrow statutory exceptions, federal registration or refusal is required before filing an infringement suit).

29. The Copyright Act defines "publication" as "the distribution of copies or phonorecords of a work to the public by sale or other transfer of ownership, or by rental, lease, or lending," as well as "[t]he offering to distribute copies or phonorecords to a group of persons for purposes of further distribution, public performance, or public display...." 17 U.S.C. § 101. Publication does not include "[a] public performance or display of a work." *Id.*

30. 17 U.S.C. §§ 412, 504–505.

ies of materials.[31] In addition, copyright registration is ultimately necessary for enforcing online infringement "takedown" requests, on websites which allow posting of user-generated content (i.e., YouTube, Instagram, Pinterest). The Digital Millennium Copyright Act (DMCA) safe-harbor provisions require that such websites must honor the takedown request of any copyright owner claiming their rights have been infringed by a post to the site.[32] In return, if the original poster disputes the takedown request, either based on an allegation of a right to use the material, or fair use, the website must honor that request and the material goes back up.[33] The alleged copyright holder then has only 14 days to institute an infringement lawsuit in order to have the material taken down, without having to start the whole process all over again.[34] While any party can file a takedown request simply on their assertion of copyright ownership in materials, having a registration is necessary for actually filing suit.[35]

5. EXAMPLES

Again, Coca-Cola's advertising provides examples of many types of copyrightable materials. One of their 20th-century campaigns included a series of "artistic" calendars, trays, posters, and bookmarks, with fine art portraits of models holding the products.[36] Even absent the commercial use, these paintings were protected by copyright, since they were (1) original, (2) creative, and (3) fixed in a tangible medium.

Similarly, a fraternal organization might have numerous items or symbols they might want to protect via copyright, such as any original art or drawings of crests, flags, emblems, or logos;[37] written works such as books, newsletters, pamphlets, blog posts or other web articles; or official organization-commissioned photographs or films.

---

31. COMPENDIUM (THIRD) §§ 202, 623.2; *see* 17 U.S.C. § 602.

32. 17 U.S.C. § 512(c).

33. 17 U.S.C. § 512(g).

34. 17 U.S.C. § 512(g)(2)(C).

35. 17 U.S.C. § 512(c)(3); *see supra* note 27 and accompanying text.

36. *See* COCA-COLA CO., 125 YEARS OF SHARING HAPPINESS 6, 10 (2011), https://www.coca-colacompany.com/content/dam/journey/us/en/our-company/history/coca-cola-a-short-history-125-years-booklet.pdf.

37. *See* below, as to how logos and crests might also be protected under trademark law.

d. Right of Publicity/Right of Privacy

Right of publicity is the right of an individual to control the commercial use of his or her identity, which includes an image, voice, signature, or anything else that can be associated exclusively with a particular individual. Contrast this with the right of privacy, which is generally the "right to be left alone," but could also be construed as the right of an individual to prevent the use of their image or likeness in certain ways. In the United States, each of these is governed by state laws. The legal elements and scope of protection for each of these varies from state to state. Issues can arise when images or names of individuals are used in a commercial context to promote goods, services, or events, in a way that either usurps their right to publicity (student athletes, celebrities) or invades their right to publicity (individuals caught in private moments or placed in a false light) (see Section IV for further discussion of potential issues for fraternal organizations).[38]

e. Trademark

The next type of intellectual property protects "brands," or trademarks. A trademark identifies the *source* and *quality* of goods and services and must be *distinctive* enough to allow consumers to distinguish competitors from one another in the marketplace.[39] Trademark rights were initially protected under common law in state courts, and a body of law has evolved defining these terms. Congress passed federal laws beginning in the 1800s, which established enhanced protections for federally registered trademarks, with procedures and enforcement administered by the USPTO and the federal courts. The federal statutes initially codified, but did not supersede, common law trademark rights. Federal law continued to evolve, building on and adding to state and common law, with the Lanham Act in 1946, as amended. Trademark law has many specific terms of art (identified in italics below), which will be defined and explained throughout the sections which follow. As trade-

---

[38]. 2 J. Thomas McCarthy & Roger E. Schechter, The Rights of Publicity and Privacy §§ 7:1–7:3 (2d ed. 2022) (discussing infringing uses of personal identity in a commercial setting).

[39]. 15 U.S.C. § 1127; 3 J. Thomas McCarthy, McCarthy on Trademarks and Unfair Competition ("McCarthy") § 3:1 (5th ed. 2022).

mark is one of the areas of IP most likely to arise as both an opportunity and an issue of protection for fraternal organizations, the next section will expand on this area of the law.

II. Trademarks— Common Law and Federal Law

The goal of trademark law, whether at state or federal level, is to both protect (1) consumers from counterfeits and knockoffs and (2) businesses from unfair competition. For example, Coca-Cola brand loyalists want to be able to tell they are picking up a product that has the particular characteristics, taste, and quality they have come to expect from a particular maker of soda pop, and not accidentally buy a product that has a brand or other marking that is *confusingly similar* to their favorite brand. Similarly, someone who prefers a different taste (not "lesser," but different quality) would want to be able to distinguish their preferred cola (R.C., Pepsi) from Coca-Cola. In addition to protecting consumers, signaling product quality, and protecting businesses' investment in building goodwill, trademarks allow businesses like Coca-Cola to benefit from the investment they have made in marketing and advertising, without another company free riding on the goodwill they've established by passing off an inferior product.

Companies can use *distinctive* words, symbols, combined words and designs, product packaging (also known as *trade dress*), colors, smells, and even sounds to identify their products and services and distinguish them from others in the marketplace. While some people distinguish trademarks for services as "service marks," it is appropriate to refer to all these types of brand identification as "trademarks" or "marks."

Many times, a company may choose to use and protect multiple trademarks for its various lines of products, as well as components of each of its trademarks. For example, Coca-Cola maintains federal trademark registrations for Coca-Cola, Coke, the combination of the "dynamic ribbon" that appears below the stylized script of its word mark, and for the shape of its original glass bottle, in the form of product packaging, or trade dress.[40]

Similarly, fraternal organizations, to the extent that they have distinctive marks, whether names, logos, crests, slogans, or particular color combinations,[41] used in connection with the sale of either goods (i.e., logo'd apparel or jewelry), the provision of services (i.e., fundraising for philanthropic events),[42] or in providing a *collective mark* (as a membership organization), may be entitled to enforceable trademark rights.

a. US Trademark Rights Are Initially Acquired Under Common Law by the First to Use the Mark in Commerce

Common law trademark rights accrue upon a company's first use of a *distinctive* mark in connection with the sale of particular goods or services in the marketplace, that *is not confusingly similar* to an existing mark, and continue (1) as long as the company continues to use the mark and (2) the mark owner does not lose rights in the mark, either through uncontrolled licensing (referred to as *naked licensing*) or because the mark becomes a generic term for the goods or services (i.e., aspirin, escalator). At common law, these exclusive rights are limited to (1) the geographic area in which the first user can prove their use, (2) any area where they would be reasonably expected to expand, and (3) the area where they can demonstrate brand recognition by consumers. This geographic scope can be expanded through registration with a state office, or with the federal government agency (USPTO), or in a specific country or region.

---

40. This is also an example of the overlap between design patents and trade dress trademarks.

41. In addition to the standard trademark infringement cases cited in this chapter, at least one court found that "distinctive two-color combination and founding year of each plaintiff organization" could potentially be protectable unregistered trademarks or trade dress. Alpha Kappa Alpha Sorority Inc. v. Converse Inc., 175 F. App'x 672, 674, 679 (5th Cir. 2006) (Fraternal organizations successfully alleged unregistered trade dress and trademarks, sufficient to support a complaint).

42. For example, Gamma Phi Beta's trademark MOONBALL (U.S. Reg. No. 4,979,765) is used in connection with events raising funds for their philanthropic partner. *Our Signature Philanthropy Event: Moonball*, Gamma Phi Beta, https://www.gammaphi-beta.org/Philanthropy/About-Our-Philanthropy (last visited July 11, 2023).

In the US, the first person or entity to *use* a trademark in connection with the sale of goods or services has *priority* and is entitled to stop others from using any trademark that is the same or *confusingly similar*, when used in connection with the same, similar, or related goods or services. In limited cases, certain marks deemed by a court to have become *famous*, may have even broader rights in unrelated areas of goods and/or services.

1. USE CAN BE THROUGH AUTHORIZED LICENSES

The "use" of a mark in commerce may validly arise through the licensed use by others. For example, a company may contract with a manufacturer to produce goods on its behalf, and provide a limited license to the manufacturer to "use" the mark to imprint it on the goods itself, or labels or tags of such goods. Federal law encapsulates what was recognized by the majority at common law:[43] as long as such use is "controlled" by the trademark owner, "with respect to the nature and quality of the goods or services," then such use will be considered use by the trademark owner.[44] However, if a trademark owner does not impose quality controls or other limitations on the use of its mark ("naked licensing"), it risks losing all rights to control (or prevent infringement) of its mark.[45] See Section III below for additional information regarding licensing.

---

43. 3 McCarthy, *supra* note 37, § 18:54 ("[T]rademark and service mark licensing is permitted under state law following the same rules and conditions as under federal law." (citing Restatement (Third) of Unfair Competition § 33 cmt. a (Am. L. Inst. 1995); Giersch v. Scripps Networks, Inc., 90 U.S.P.Q.2d (BL) 1020, 1024 (T.T.A.B. 2009))).

44. 15 U.S.C. § 1055 ("If first use of a mark by a person is controlled by the registrant or applicant for registration of the mark with respect to the nature and quality of the goods or services, such first use shall inure to the benefit of the registrant or applicant, as the case may be.").

45. Haymaker Sports, Inc. v. Turian, 581 F.2d 257, 261 (C.C.P.A. 1978) ("Uncontrolled licensing of a mark results in abandonment of the mark by the licensor.... [T]here is no evidence that they exercised any quality control.").

b. A Mark Must Be Both *Distinctive and Not Likely to Cause Confusion with Other Marks in the Marketplace*

Marks serve to distinguish between one company's products or services and another's, so they must be both (1) *distinctive* (as in, not a generic name for the goods), and (2) *not confusingly similar* to another mark for the same or similar goods. The more distinctive the mark, the greater its level of legal protectability. Under trademark law, therefore, marks exist on a spectrum of distinctiveness, from the undistinguishable, unprotectable "generic" name on the one end, to the other end of the spectrum: highly distinctive, made-up, "fanciful" words.

1. DISTINCTIVENESS

A word, symbol, etc. must either be *inherently distinctive* or have *acquired distinctiveness* in order to function as a trademark. The levels of distinctiveness, ranked in terms of strength and legal protectability, are described by courts as follows:

> *Generic Terms* consist of the common name of the goods or services to which they are applied. They can never function as a trademark and are not capable of acquiring secondary meaning when used in their generic sense. (Examples: computer for selling computers, auto for selling automobiles.) This is because your competitors must also use these words to describe their competing goods or services, so it would be unfair to grant a sort-of monopoly on the use of those words to one party.

> *Descriptive Marks* describe either the goods or services or a characteristic or quality thereof. (Example: AMERICAN AIRLINES for airline services.) Included in this group are (1) laudatory words that attribute superiority to the goods (e.g., GOLD MEDAL and SUPREME), (2) geographic terms, and (3) surnames. Descriptive marks are NOT inherently distinctive. Again, if the words in the marks are useful for describing the product or service, it may be unfair to grant exclusive rights to one party.

If a company can show that through their marketing/advertising time, expenditures, and efforts,[46] consumers have come to associate the descriptive word with the particular company as a source of goods or services, as opposed to the word's everyday association with the general type of goods or services, a court or the USPTO may find that an otherwise descriptive mark (or portion of a mark) has *acquired distinctiveness* (or *secondary meaning*), and is therefore distinctive in the marketplace (and a protectable trademark).

> *Suggestive Marks* suggest, rather than describe, the goods or services or some characteristic thereof. The consumer must use imagination to understand the connection. (Examples: COPPERTONE for suntan oil; NETFLIX for streaming movies.) Although suggestive marks are more easily understood by consumers and easier to promote than arbitrary or fanciful marks, suggestive marks are still considered *inherently distinctive*; that is, they are per se protectible as trademarks.
>
> *Arbitrary Marks* use existing words but have no meaning in relation to the goods or services. (Examples: APPLE for computers; TIDE for detergent.) Arbitrary marks are *inherently distinctive*. They can be easier to protect but can be more expensive to promote and advertise, since you need to invest in advertising to create the connection between your unusual use of a word and the services or goods provided.
>
> *Fanciful Marks* are created from words that are coined or made up and that have no meaning in relation to the goods or services with which they are used. (Examples: HÄAGEN-DAZS for ice cream; GOOGLE for internet search services.) Fanciful marks are the strongest of all marks and are entitled to the most protection, as they are considered "inherently distinctive." However, similar to arbitrary marks, they require an investment in educational marketing and brand

---

46. 3 McCarthy, *supra* note 39, § 15:30 (discussing circumstantial evidence of secondary meaning, including advertising). "Factors such as amount and manner of advertising, volume of sales, and length and manner of use may serve as circumstantial evidence relevant to the issue of secondary meaning."; *see, e.g.*, Converse, Inc. v. Int'l Trade Comm'n Sketchers U.S.A., Inc., 909 F.3d 1110, 1120 (Fed. Cir. 2018).

awareness campaigns. Owners of fanciful marks for new products must also be careful that their mark does not become the verb or noun describing their service or good, by providing and using a generic name where appropriate. (Examples: KLEENEX brand tissue, XEROX brand copiers, VELCRO brand fasteners.)

To further illustrate the differences between the level of distinctiveness, if you were to use the purported mark APPLES, ETC. for selling apples, the mark would be considered generic, as used in connection with those goods. However, if you were providing a retail fruit stand, APPLES, ETC. would arguably be descriptive of a key component of your services. On the other hand, if you were selling computers in connection with the same mark, that would be considered "arbitrary."

In selecting a mark, companies frequently select a word that describes a characteristic of the goods or services, thinking that helps their target market of consumers know who they are and what they do. Counterintuitively, the more descriptive the mark, the less protection it provides; this means that other parties may be free to use descriptive words to advertise competitive products. (Examples: SINGAPORE AIRLINES vs. UNITED AIRLINES.) Conversely, the less descriptive the mark, the greater the chance of exclusive protection for the mark.

2. NO LIKELIHOOD OF CONFUSION WITH AN EXISTING MARK USED WITH SIMILAR GOODS/SERVICES

Assuming that the distinctiveness hurdle is overcome, the next consideration is whether there is a prior trademark which would bar the use of the proposed mark, because it would be *likely to cause confusion* among the consuming public. This is a fact-based inquiry, and is the basis of determining whether a junior mark infringes on a prior, senior mark.

"Likelihood of confusion" is the test of trademark infringement, at common law, state, and federal, and is also used by the USPTO to determine whether a mark may be granted registration. Each jurisdiction has developed its own touchstone case by which a court makes this multi-factor analysis;[47] but they all bear similarity to the *DuPont* factors used

---

47. All courts analyzing a claim of infringement, based on both federal and state law, apply a likelihood of confusion test. 3 MCCARTHY, *supra* note 39, § 23:1.50 (collecting

by the USPTO and the Federal Circuit, which consider (among other things) the similarity of the marks themselves, the relatedness of the goods or services, the comparative trade channels and buyers, the fame of either mark, any evidence of actual confusion (or lack thereof), and "any other established fact probative of the effect of use."[48] While a court may consider all the factors, even the difference in just one of the DuPont factors can be dispositive.[49]

It's important to note that it is not a question of whether the marks or goods/services are identical, but if they are close enough to cause confusion among the relevant consumers in the marketplace. It is a subjective, fact-specific inquiry and it is difficult to always predict an outcome; but some principles have developed, informed by precedential decisions both at the Trademark Trial and Appeal Board (TTAB) and Federal Circuit, but other jurisdictions as well. The analysis and study of these decisions can (and do) fill a multivolume treatise,[50] but a high-level consideration can be guided by the following, and can allow a practitioner to at least identify potential areas for further inquiry.

In any analysis, the initial comparison begins with these two elements: the marks themselves and the goods/services. For example, on one end of the spectrum, if the marks themselves are the same, and the goods or services are competitive with one another, then usually there is

---

state law tests). At the federal level, each jurisdiction has also developed its own version of the list of likelihood of confusion factors, and a practitioner is advised to use the appropriate test for the forum: (1) the First Circuit uses eight *Pignon* factors; (2) the Second Circuit uses eight *Polaroid* factors; (3) the Third Circuit uses ten Lapp factors; (4) the Fourth Circuit uses seven *Pizzeria Uno* factors, but sometimes uses other lists of factors; (5) the Fifth Circuit uses eight factors, referred to as the "digits of confusion" test; (6) the Sixth Circuit uses eight *Frisch* factors; (7) the Seventh Circuit uses seven *Helene Curtis* factors; (8) the Eighth Circuit uses eight *SquirtCo* factors; (9) the Ninth Circuit uses eight *Sleekcraft* factors; (10) the Tenth Circuit uses six "King of the Mountain" factors; (11) the Eleventh Circuit uses seven *Frehling* factors; (12) the District of Columbia Circuit uses multifactor lists from other circuits, but has not yet settled on any particular list of factors; and (13) the Federal Circuit uses thirteen *DuPont* factors. Id. § 24:31–24:43.

48. *In re* E. I. duPont de Nemours & Co., 476 F.2d 1357, 1361 (C.C.P.A. 1973).

49. *See* Kellogg Co. v. Pack'em Enters., Inc., 951 F.2d 330, 332 (Fed. Cir. 1991) ("The first *duPont* factor simply outweighs all of the others which might be pertinent to this case.").

50. *See e.g.*, 1 ANNE GILSON LALONDE, GILSON ON TRADEMARKS (Matthew Bender, 2022); LOUIS ALTMAN & MALLA POLLACK, CALLMAN ON UNFAIR COMPETITION, TRADEMARKS & MONOPOLIES (4th ed. 2022); 3 MCCARTHY, *supra* note 37.

going to be a finding of likelihood of confusion: the consumers will likely be confused as to whether these goods/services come from the same company.

On the other hand, even if the marks are the exactly the same, but the goods/services are completely unrelated and not competitive, then the marks can coexist (subject to the exception of *famous* marks under federal law, discussed below). Even if a mark shares similar elements and is used with similar goods/services, where the overall commercial impression is different, the marks can coexist.[51]

However, issues may arise when the marks are the same (or very similar) and the goods/services are somehow "related," even if not competitive. In considering whether the goods or services of the parties are "related," the consideration is whether buyers are likely to believe that the goods/services come from the same source, or are somehow connected with or sponsored by the same company. So, for example, the Ninth Circuit considered that BLACK & WHITE was used on a wide variety of goods (medicines, cosmetics, coffee, candy, bags, fountain pens, sheet music, hoof-rot remedy, cornmeal, flour, soap, pencils, ginger ale, cotton prints, canned goods, and tobacco) without infringing on the senior owner's rights in the trademark BLACK & WHITE for Scotch whiskey; however, there was trademark infringement caused by the defendant's unauthorized use of the mark BLACK & WHITE on beer, because the use was "related" and the kind of confusion in such a case would be a confusion of sponsorship, affiliation or connection.[52]

Even where the USPTO or a court may find that two marks present a likelihood of confusion, a settlement or agreement between the parties can better resolve the issue. Aside from laying out the 13-factor analysis for assessing likelihood of confusion, the *DuPont* case was also noteworthy in that it held that the USPTO should defer to any coexistence or cooperation agreement between the parties, and allow registration to proceed if the parties themselves agreed that there was no likelihood of confusion. The court reasoned that since the two commercial parties were driven by their profit interests, and it would be counter to those

---

51. Omega Sa (Omega Ag) (Omega Ltd.) v. Alpha Phi Omega, 118 U.S.P.Q.2d (BL) 1289 (T.T.A.B. 2016) (holding fraternity's crest, containing the word "omega" and used in connection with jewelry, not confusingly similar to watchmaker's allegedly famous OMEGA mark).

52. Fleischmann Distilling Corp. v. Maier Brewing Co., 314 F.2d 149 (9th Cir. 1963).

interests to allow there to be marketplace confusion, then it stood to reason that they were better positioned than the USPTO's examining attorney, to determine whether two marks could exist side by side without consumer confusion.

c. Federal Law Expands upon These Rights

1. EXPANDED GEOGRAPHIC RIGHTS TO THE ENTIRE US (AND TERRITORIES)

In addition to common law rights, you can acquire enhanced rights in a trademark by being the first to register it with the USPTO. Federal law does not create the trademark rights one acquires through common law, but it can provide additional benefits.[53] For example, common law rights are limited in geographic scope, but federal registration grants rights throughout the United States. A few relevant examples of statute-created rights follow.

2. COLLECTIVE MARKS

Collective membership marks (recognized in the 1946 passage of the Lanham Act) are just like other trademarks, except they are controlled by organizations who permit their members to use the mark to indicate membership.[54] Many fraternal organizations' primary use of their trademarks falls under this type of trademark, rather than the traditional trademark use in connection with the offering for sale of other services or with the licensing for use on jewelry and other logo'd merchandise.

For collective membership marks, the owner of the mark must exercise control over the use of the mark; and, because the sole purpose of a membership mark is to indicate membership, use of the mark is by its members.[55] When applying for federal protection of a collective membership mark, the owner must explain how it controls and restricts the

---

53. *See* Turner v. HMH Publishing Co., 380 F.2d 224, 228 (5th Cir.) (citation omitted), *cert. denied,* 389 U.S. 1006 (1967) ("[R]egistration of a trademark confers only procedural advantages and does not enlarge the registrant's rights, for ownership of the trademark rests on adoption and use, not on registration."

54. 15 U.S.C. §§ 1127, 1054.

55. 37 C.F.R. § 2.44(a)(4)(i)(C) (2021).

use of its mark by and to members. In most instances, a simple statement that the applicant's bylaws or other written provisions specify the manner of control, is sufficient.[56] It is important to note that the organization itself owns the registration and the rights attendant in the mark, not the individual members or chapters of the organization.[57] Aside from this difference, collective membership mark registrations are treated the same as other trademark registrations.[58]

3. INTENT TO USE APPLICATIONS

While common law trademark rights are based on the first person to actually use the mark in commerce, federal law allows an application to be filed based on an "intent to use" a mark in interstate commerce. However, the applicant must provide evidence of actual use in interstate commerce within 36 months of a provisional approval of any such application. The mark still must be distinctive, and meet all the statutory and regulatory requirements. Assuming such an application meets all necessary requirements, it grants the applicant a constructive date of first use, based on the application date.

In a sense, the applicant is placing "dibs" on a mark, and will be able to block any later-filed applications or uses of the proposed mark on the same or similar goods/services. This right, however, is limited by any actual use of the mark by others which precedes the application date. Where this happens, the prior, nonregistered user, is entitled to exclusive rights to the mark in the geographic area where they can prove first use.

---

56. *Trademark Manual of Examining Procedures* ("TMEP") § 1303.01(a)(i)(A) (July 2022 ed. 2022), https://tmep.uspto.gov/RDMS/TMEP/current (last visited Dec. 1, 2022).

57. Sigma Chi Fraternity v. Sethscot Collection, No. 98-CV-2102, 2000 WL 34414961, at *6 (S.D. Fla. Apr. 7, 2000), *aff'd*, 48 F. App'x 739 (11th Cir. 2002).

58. In some cases, alleged trademark infringers have tried to defend their actions by claiming that fraternal organizations with collective membership marks may not produce and sell goods that have the marks. This is a misunderstanding of the law. "In short, the prohibition does not apply to collective marks; pursuant to the language of 15 U.S.C. § 1054, a collective mark receives the same protection as a trademark." Alpha Tau Omega Fraternity, Inc. v. Pure Country, Inc., 2004 WL 3391781, at *5 (S.D. Ind. Oct. 26, 2004). Collective membership mark owners are explicitly permitted to use "the same mark as a membership mark by members and, also, as a trademark or a service mark by the parent organization." TMEP § 1304.03; 15 U.S.C. § 1054.

The later applicant can be granted exclusive rights to use the mark everywhere else.[59]

"Intent to use" applications are particularly useful as an organization is considering expanding or establishing licensing and merchandising efforts in various product lines. The initial filing of such an application is quite straightforward, and can be maintained up to three years, if an organization has the wherewithal to pay extension fees every six months.

4. "FAMOUS" MARKS — EXPANSIVE PROTECTION BUT HIGH BAR TO PROVE

i. Expanded Protection

While registered trademarks are usually entitled to protection from use of confusingly similar with the same, similar, or related goods, a "famous" mark may be entitled to expanded protection beyond the usual scope of the specific goods and services in its trademark application.[60] A mark may only be determined to be "famous" upon the finding of a court, after examining the evidence presented by the owner of the mark (see below).[61] After a mark has been deemed to have become "famous," the owner may enjoin someone who uses a mark or trade name, where the latter might "dilute" the value of the famous mark, either by "blurring"[62] or "tarnishment."[63] The concept of dilution is subtly different from likelihood of confusion; as the prohibition in the latter case is to protect consumers, while the former is to protect the owners of "famous" marks.[64]

ii. Pleading and Evidentiary Requirements

While in the past, trademark litigants frequently threw in a "dilution" claim like spaghetti (to see if it would stick), revisions to the statute in 2006 were made to underscore Congress's intent that it be considered a

---

59. Dawn Donut Co. v. Hart's Food Stores, Inc., 267 F.2d 358 (2d Cir. 1959).
60. 15 U.S.C. § 1125(c)(1).
61. 15 U.S.C. § 1125(c)(2)(A).
62. 15 U.S.C. § 1125(c)(2)(B).
63. 15 U.S.C. § 1125(c)(2)(C).
64. *See* Moseley v. V Secret Catalogue, Inc., 537 U.S. 418, 431 (2003) ("Confusion leads to immediate injury, while dilution is an infection, which if allowed to spread, will inevitably destroy the advertising value of the mark." (citing H.R.Rep. No. 104-374, at 3 (1995))).

rare and "extraordinary remedy."[65] A mark is "famous" if "it is widely recognized by the general consuming public of the United States as a designation of source of the goods or services of the mark's owner," based on a court's determination, after considering "all relevant factors," including:

> (i) The duration, extent, and geographic reach of advertising and publicity of the mark, whether advertised or publicized by the owner or third parties;
> (ii) The amount, volume, and geographic extent of sales of goods or services offered under the mark; and
> (iii) The extent of actual recognition of the mark.[66]

Typically, this requires the trademark owner to provide extensive evidence of its sales and marketing expenditures and efforts, as well as the testimony of an expert witness and/or customer focus group research studies, as to the extent of actual recognition of the mark. As several fraternal organizations have found, conclusory statements as to the year of use or numbers of members will be insufficient.[67] Additionally, such a claim of fame can only be successful against an alleged infringer who

---

65. 4 MCCARTHY, *supra* note 39, § 24:104.

66. 15 U.S.C. § 1125(c)(2)(A); *see, e.g.,* Coach Services, Inc. v. Triumph Learning LLC, 668 F.3d 1356, 1373 (Fed. Cir. 2012) (Holding COACH was not famous for handbags and leather goods: "[A] famous mark is one that has become a 'household name.'").

67. Theta Chi Fraternity, Inc. v. Leland Stanford Junior University, 212 F. Supp. 3d 816, 828–829, (N.D. Cal. 2016) ("Because plaintiff has not made more than conclusory allegations of fame, plaintiff's dilution claims are dismissed."); Alpha Tau Omega Fraternity, Inc. v. Pure Country, Inc., No. IP 01-1054-C-B/F, 2004 WL 3391781, at *12 (S.D. Ind. Oct. 26, 2004) ("Plaintiffs represent that they are among the most well known of the fraternities and sororities on college campuses in the United States. However, other than their unchallenged assertion that many are large and over 100 years old, little evidence has been adduced that would establish their trademarks' fame."); *Sigma Chi*, 2000 WL 34414961 (Sigma Chi marks not sufficiently famous to warrant protection despite allegations that they were "the second largest collegiate social fraternal group," with "226 undergraduate chapters, ... approximately 120 alumni chapters (more than any other Greek social organization), approximately 196,000 alumni members, and approximately 12,000 undergraduate members."); *cf.* Abraham v. Alpha Chi Omega, 781 F. Supp. 2d 396, 430 (N.D. Tex. 2011) (applying the Texas "anti-dilution" statute which does not require a showing of "fame", but simply a "distinctive" mark, in holding fraternal organizations' marks were diluted by unlicensed use of marks).

commences their acts after the mark has acquired fame.[68] Nonetheless, one fraternal organization has succeeded in acquiring such a designation on default judgment ruling, with a bare bones recitation of facts in support of its claim to fame.[69] However, it should be noted that making dilution claims unsupported by evidence does not come without risk. Given the expense required to both prove and refute such a claim in court, if one party is required to reimburse the others' attorneys' fees (particularly if the claims were unsupported or implausible), it might increase the cost significantly.[70]

d. Benefits and Limits of Federal Trademark Registration

Again, while federal registration is not required for trademark ownership or protection (as compared to copyrights), it does provide several distinct advantages. First, as stated above, when granted, a registration gives the trademark owner nationwide protection (subject to the prior marks discussed above), beyond the geographic limitations of common law rights.[71] A registered trademark has these for five years, which can be renewed for further fixed periods, if the mark is still in "bona fide" use in the marketplace. After five years, a mark can become "incontestable," which grants further advantages in any infringement action or defense to the validity of the mark.[72]

The USPTO also maintains a database of registered and applied-for marks, which protects the trademark from being registered by others

---

68. Omega Sa (Omega Ag) (Omega Ltd.) v. Alpha Phi Omega, 118 U.S.P.Q.2d 1289 (T.T.A.B. 2016).

69. Omega Psi Phi Fraternity, Inc. v. Edden, No. 11-CV-80479, 2012 WL 13018589, at *4 (S.D. Fla. Oct. 30, 2012) ("Plaintiff is an internationally recognized fraternity established in 1911. It has nine registered trademarks, two of which are incontestable: "OMEGA PSI PHI FRATERNITY" and the Omega Psi Phi crest. Its merchandise is offered for sale throughout the United States, and it enforces its trademark rights through license agreements with vendors. Therefore, in light of the above factors, the Court finds Plaintiff's marks are famous.")

70. Off Lease Only, Inc. v. Lakeland Motors, LLC, 846 F. App'x 772, 776 (11th Cir. 2021) (upholding district court's award to the prevailing defendant of attorney fees, costs and prejudgment interest, including $29,287.50 for an expert witness to rebut plaintiff's unsupported dilution claim).

71. 15 U.S.C. § 1072.

72. 15 U.S.C. § 1065.

without permission and helps you prevent others from using a trademark that is similar to yours with related goods or services.[73]

Registration also confers the right to use the ® (registration symbol), which gives nationwide constructive notice of the valid trademark registration, to defeat "innocent infringement" claims and help in the calculations of any actual damages claims.

Further, a federal registration is prima facie evidence of the validity of the mark and of related facts pertinent to the registration, which can simplify and streamline enforcement actions against any infringers, thereby reducing and/or eliminating litigation costs,[74] and can allow a trademark owner to potentially recover treble damages, attorneys' fees, and other remedies.[75]

However, note that the trademark owner bears the burden of enforcing its trademark rights against any potential infringers. This can mean monitoring the marketplace, the internet, and the USPTO's publications announcing pending trademark registrations. Further, a trademark owner must (1) use its mark properly as a trademark (avoiding "genericide"); (2) maintain proper control and quality through appropriate licensing agreements; (3) use the mark with the goods/services continuously in interstate commerce; (4) maintain the proper renewals and maintenance filing fees; and (5) take consistent, reasonable efforts to thwart any infringement.

e. USPTO Application Process

1. USE-BASED AND INTENT-TO-USE APPLICATIONS

In order to apply for federal registration, a trademark owner must submit an application that complies with the USPTO's regulations, using their online system.[76] These applications are subject to review and approval by the USPTO, and are subject to refusal on a number of grounds.[77] Applications may be submitted either after a trademark

---

73. *Trademark Electronic Search System (TESS)*, USPTO, http://tess2.uspto.gov/ (last updated Nov. 29, 2022).
74. 15 U.S.C. § 1115.
75. 15 U.S.C. § 1117.
76. TMEP § 301.01.
77. 15 U.S.C. § 1052.

owner has already used their mark in interstate commerce (a "use-based" application), or in anticipation of such use, where the applicant has a "bona fide intent" to use the mark in interstate commerce.

2. EVIDENCE OF USE

Among other details, each type of application requires an identification of the specific mark (including a JPG if it is a logo or design mark), a description of the goods or services with which the mark is being used, and the correct filing fee(s). For "use-based" applications, the dates when the mark was first used in interstate commerce and actual evidence of how the mark is being used in connection with the advertising and/or sale of the goods or services must also be provided with the initial application. For intent-to-use applications, this evidence must be provided within six months of the USPTO's provisional approval of the application, together with an additional filing fee. Applicants may request up to 5 six-month extensions of time to provide this evidence, upon the payment of the extension fee and submitting the appropriate form.

3. INTERNATIONAL CLASSES AND FILING FEES

The universe of potential goods and services has been sorted into "international classes," based on international treaties. This allows for consistency in treatment between countries where applicants file multiple trademark applications.[78] For example, all clothing items fall under International Class 025, while jewelry is classified under International Class 014. Collective membership marks fall under 200 and services such as education or mentoring fall under 041. All filing fees (applications, extensions, renewals) are assessed per mark, per international class. So for example, if a trademark owner wanted to file an application for his or her word mark (i.e., ALPHA OMEGA) and for a design mark (i.e., a logo with a graphic element), for both the collective membership (IC 200) and the licensing of jewelry items (IC014), he or she would need to pay four application fees.

---

78. *WIPO International Nice Classifications*, WORLD INTELL. PROP. ORG., https://www.wipo.int/classifications/nice/en/ (last visited Dec. 1, 2022).

4. SUBSTANTIVE REVIEW

Once an application has been submitted to the USPTO and has met the minimum requirements, it will be assigned to an examining attorney who will conduct a substantive review of the application. In addition to considering whether the mark is distinctive and can function as a trademark, the examining attorney will also search the USPTO's database of registrations and applications to ensure that the applied-for mark is not confusingly similar to any existing or pending registrations, and does not run afoul of any other statutory bars. If they find no reason to reject the application, it will proceed to publication. The mark is then "published for opposition" in the Trademark Official Gazette, which is made available to the public. Anyone who believes they will be harmed by the registration of the mark has 30 days from the publication date to officially register his or her objection, using the methods provided for by the USPTO. If no objection is filed, a registration certificate will be issued in due course (or a "Notice of Allowance" for intent-to-use applications).

5. RECONSIDERATION/APPEAL

If the examining attorney objects to the application for any reason, he or she will issue a letter called an "Office Action" to the applicant, detailing the reasons for the objection and any options the applicant has for curing the objection. Applicants have a set period of time to respond to any objections, either by complying with the actions recommended or providing legal arguments to overcome such objections. If no response is submitted by the applicant, or if the examining attorney is unpersuaded, a "final office action" will be issued, with another response period permitted. At the end of this period, any office action will be made final. If the applicant fails to respond, the application is considered abandoned. If the applicant disagrees with the examining attorney's decision, he or she may also file a "request for reconsideration" to the examining attorney and/or file an *ex parte* appeal of the decision to TTAB. Appeals from decisions of the TTAB then proceed to the Federal Circuit.

6. IMPACT OF FINAL REJECTION

Note, however, an applicant who receives an objection or whose application is rejected is not prohibited from using his or her trademark, and it does not necessarily mean that the mark is not entitled to trademark protection; rather, they may continue to use their mark and rely upon their common law rights. They simply would not be entitled to the protections of federal registration.

f. Trademark Licensing

As stated above, trademark owners can effectuate "use" of their mark in commerce through the licensed use by others, as long as such use is controlled and the trademark owner imposed quality controls and/or other limits on the use.[79] Licensing without these controls or limitations is referred to as "naked licensing," which can result in the loss of some or all rights in the licensed mark,[80] as the mark no longer represents the quality of products or services originally associated with the mark.[81]

As to how much control and limitations are sufficient to avoid losing rights due to naked licensing, "no over-arching rule can be found in the reported decisions, which appear inconsistent and difficult to reconcile."[82] While a trademark owner cannot impose the same degree of quality control on the production of products under license, as it might if it controlled the manufacture or delivery of services, it is still expected to exercise a reasonable degree of control, and the party who would allege naked licensing must meet a high burden of proof.[83] Some courts, including the Seventh Circuit, have adopted the position of the Restatement (Third) of Unfair Competition, "which advocates a flexible approach but allows licensors to rely at least somewhat on the reputation and expertise of licensees."[84] Typically, licensing agreements will grant the licensor the right to control quality, which must also be exercised in some way.[85]

For example, in the *Sigma Chi v. Sethcott* case, there was no question that the national Sigma Chi organization had established sufficient con-

---

79. 15 U.S.C. § 1055.
80. 3 McCarthy, *supra* note 39, § 18:48.
81. Freecycle Sunnyvale v. Freecycle Network, 626 F.3d 509, 512 (9th Cir. 2010).
82. 3 McCarthy, *supra* note 39, § 18:55.
83. Moore Bus. Forms, Inc. v. Ryu, 960 F.2d 486, 489 (5th Cir. 1992).
84. TMT N. Am., Inc. v. Magic Touch GmbH, 124 F.3d 876, 886 (7th Cir. 1997); Restatement (Third) of Unfair Competition § 33 cmt. c (Am. L. Inst. 1995).
85. *Dawn Donut*, 267 F.2d at 368.

trols (even though a local member circumvented all policies): they established a "licensing committee" to review all licensees to ensure that products bearing the Sigma Chi name or insignia "d[id] not portray the Fraternity in a negative light or [were not] otherwise contrary to the ideals of the Fraternity (i.e., that they [did] not glorify alcohol or illegal substance use or [were not] sexist or demeaning to women, minorities, etc.)."[86] Under the revised licensing program, any products utilizing Sigma Chi's marks had to be approved by the licensing committee and would be subject to a license agreement.[87] The quality controls in place involved obtaining samples of the products, assigning a headquarters staff person assigned to supervise the quality of the fraternity's merchandise chapters, and "require[d] the vendors to submit to the Licensing Committee on an annual basis a sample of the products offered, to ensure that the vendor's quality ha[d]n't decreased."[88] Chapters that wished to use an unlicensed vendor had to get approval from the licensing committee, have the vendor sign a license agreement, and submit a sample product for approval.

In addition to the high burden of proof placed upon those who would allege naked licensing, in the *Alpha Tau Omega* case, the court held "the doctrine of licensee estoppel preempts any challenge to the validity of a trademark which would be inconsistent with the terms of the license."[89] Even without this doctrine, the court found the national organization's efforts sufficient to avoid a claim: one organization had a catalogue of approved, licensed merchandise, and "both national organizations ha[d] policies regarding the need to purchase items with their crests, emblems or other marks from licensed or approved vendors and that those policies were conveyed to officers of the local chapters."[90]

Members and chapters are not licensees and may not sublicense trademark use absent authority from the national organization. While there are similarities between the use of a "collective membership" mark by its members, and with licensees' use of a mark with the owner's permission, they are not the same. As with a license for a mark used in

---

86. *Sigma Chi*, 2000 WL 34414961, at *2.
87. *Id.* at *3.
88. *Id.*
89. *Alpha Tau Omega*, 2004 WL 3391781, at *10.
90. *Id.* at *11.

connection with goods or services, a collective membership mark owner must also control and limit the use of its marks to members, using the methods described in its application to the USPTO. However, the right of a member to use the mark does not also equate to the right to sublicense.[91] Even if members were considered licensees of the national organization trademark owner, trademark licenses are generally not assignable in the absence of an explicit provision authorizing assignment in the licensing agreement.[92]

III. Best Practices for Fraternal Organizations—Trademark

Given the many years that fraternal organizations have put into building their heritage and reputations, it is understandable that they might simply want to make sure that their symbols are used appropriately. But there are other reasons a fraternal organization might want to take steps to protect these potential trademarks: generating potential revenue from the sale of licensed products carrying the organization's marks, preventing a vendor from free riding on the organization's reputation by selling unauthorized logo'd merchandise, and/or protecting the organization's reputation by preventing misuse by third parties, whether through use on substandard goods/services, or by suspended or disbanded former chapters and/or alumni.

There are historical reasons why fraternal organizations are relatively late to the party in protecting, enforcing, and monetizing the intellectual property rights. They might have done so in their names, insignias and other unique identifiers.[93] But, even before the passage of the Lanham Act, courts recognized that fraternal organizations and benevolent soci-

---

91. *Id.* at *7 ("While it is undisputed that members of Sigma Chi have a license to use the registered marks, that license is limited—members can only acquire merchandise bearing those marks from licensed vendors.").

92. *In re* XMH Corp., 647 F.3d 690, 696 (7th Cir. 2011).

93. *See e.g.*, Jared S. Sunshine, *The Purloined Greek Letters: Twenty-First Century Developments in the Enforcement of Intellectual Property Rights in Fraternity and Sorority Marks*, 37 QUINNIPIAC L. REV. 679 (2019); Phi Delta Theta Fraternity v. J.A. Buchroeder & Co., 251 F. Supp. 968 (W.D. Mo. 1966); Jared S. Sunshine, *Antitrust Precedent & Anti-Fraternity Sentiment: Revisiting Hamilton College*, 39 CAMPBELL L. REV. 59 (2017).

eties were entitled to be free from unfair competition in the use of their names, despite the noncommercial nature of their enterprises.[94] And, in the case of today's fraternal organizations, the old adage about the futility of closing the barn door after the horse has already escaped does NOT apply.[95] Fraternal organizations can still take effective legal action to protect their intellectual property and stop current and future misappropriation. The first step is to identify what intellectual property rights your organization has that it wants to protect (e.g. trademarks, copyright), and then to consider what, if any, licensing or revenue strategies you might want to pursue with regards to these properties.

There are brand licensing agencies who work with companies to develop these strategies, and existing organizations that specialize in working with fraternal organizations and schools.[96] In developing and implementing any such strategy, an organization will want to consider the best practices which follow.

a. Trademark Registration and Maintenance

Typically, when a business is considering adopting a trademark to use (or has recently done so), they will first conduct a clearance search to determine whether there are any existing trademarks (whether federally or state-registered, or at common law), which may present a hurdle to the proposed mark's adoption. In the case of long-established fraternal organizations seeking to register their marks for the first time, such a clearance search might identify the risks that may present themselves and help an organization both plan for the expense of overcoming po-

---

94. "[I]t is well established that a benevolent, fraternal, or social organization will be protected in the use of its name by injunction restraining another organization from using the same or another name so similar as to be misleading." Grand Lodge, I.B. & P.O.O.E. of World v. Grand Lodge, I.B. & P.O.O.E. of World, 50 F.2d 860, 862 (4th Cir. 1931).

95. Abraham v. Alpha Chi Omega, 708 F.3d 614, 627–28 (5th Cir. 2013) (holding that while claim of laches might bar fraternal organization trademark owner from recovering monetary damages for actions prior to notice to alleged infringer, trademark owner was still entitled to enjoin further infringement and to recover damages for infringement after notice of objection to unlicensed use).

96. *Licensing Information*, GREEKLICENSING, https://greeklicensing.com/licensing/info (last visited Nov. 29, 2022).

tential hurdles and/or tailoring their IP protection and licensing strategies accordingly.

If the organization has not already registered its marks with the USPTO, initial steps might include identifying all those things that the organization uses in a trademark fashion, and then prioritizing the importance of protecting them, as weighed against the organization's budget for both initial applications and long-term maintenance fees. Examples include word mark(s) (i.e., ALPHA OMEGA), design marks (logo versions of word mark, crests, other graphic elements), nicknames, slogans, etc. The initial steps would likely involve applying for the word and design marks as a collective membership mark, followed by any immediate licensing categories in the works.

In addition to the initial registration fees (which are calculated per mark, per international class), once each mark is registered, regular maintenance filings and fees will need to be made at five- and 10-year intervals for each registration, per international class.[97] The following is a Best Practices Checklist:

- What are our trademarks? (Name, nickname, crests, emblems, logos, etc.)
- Are they registered for our membership organization?
- Do we have active licensing programs? (Jewelry, clothing, license plate covers, etc.)
- When are our maintenance and renewal filings due?
- Have we been using the marks continuously in interstate commerce, as trademarks? Can we show evidence of that?
- If not, how can we implement such use (and capture evidence) before the next renewal deadline?

b. Control and Enforcement of Rights Required

A trademark owner bears the burden of protecting and enforcing its rights, both through its own organization's use of its marks, as well as by preventing misuse by others. Fraternal organizations need to be vigilant that their own members and chapters are using the trademark correctly

---

97. *Keeping your registration alive,* USPTO, https://www.uspto.gov/trademarks/maintain/keeping-your-registration-alive (last visited Dec. 2, 2022).

and are not engaging in any use that could potentially impair the trademark's reputation through misuse or kill it outright through "naked" licensing. This is particularly true for collective mark owners, where the primary use of the mark is through its membership.

1. COLLECTIVE MEMBERSHIP — INTERNAL CONTROLS

Organizations typically use their constitutions, bylaws, or other affiliate agreements to identify the standards that their chapters must maintain in order to continue their affiliation with the national organization and to retain rights to hold themselves out under the same name. Nonetheless, some chapters and alumni may persist in using a national organization's name and other identifying information despite a suspension, disaffiliation, or revocation. Among other mechanisms available to national organizations, trademark infringement actions can sometimes be an effective tool to limit unauthorized use by rogue chapters, members, or alums. These actions can be taken whether the national organization has a federal registration, or is simply relying upon its common law rights; however, as can be seen in the *Kappa Sigma* case below, having federal registrations can simplify and streamline any litigation, with the courts recognizing the prima facie validity of the trademarks.

For example, national fraternity Kappa Sigma sued an erstwhile local chapter at Dartmouth College in Hanover, New Hampshire, for its continued use of Kappa Sigma Gamma after voluntarily disaffiliating from the national organization in 1980, after the chapter had failed to keep up with its obligations and dues to the national chapter.[98] The local organization, despite its representations to the national organization to the contrary, proceeded over the next six years to solicit alumni members for contributions, while still referring to itself as "Kappa Sigs" and/or "Kappa Sigma Gamma."[99]

The national organization tried, unsuccessfully, during that time to end the local entity's actions and eventually brought suit in 1986 to enjoin the local chapter from holding itself out as "Kappa Sigs" or "Kappa

---

98. Kappa Sigma Fraternity v. Kappa Sigma Gamma Fraternity, 654 F. Supp. 1095, 1097 (D.N.H.), *modified in part, rev'd in part on reconsideration by* 659 F. Supp. 117 (D.N.H. 1987).

99. Kappa Sigma, 654 F. Supp. at 1097.

Sigma Gamma," relying upon its five active US trademark registrations.[100] The national chapter prevailed in a summary judgment motion regarding its claims of trademark and service mark infringement, false designation of membership, and misrepresentation pursuant to the Lanham Act, with the court relying on the validity and incontestability of the federal registrations, the clear likelihood of confusion with the junior use,[101] and the presumption of harm.[102] The court ultimately concluded that the local chapter intentionally and deliberately chose the name Kappa Sigma Gamma so as to capitalize on its prior affiliation with Kappa Sigma.[103] In doing so, it rejected the local organization's suggestion that "laches" was an appropriate defense, both because the requested relief was injunctive, not monetary, and because "the evidence before the Court is replete with instances of plaintiffs' attempting to effect a rapprochement during the five-year period between disaffiliation and the filing of this suit."[104]

In granting injunctive relief, the infringing local chapter was required to immediately[105] stop using any and all Kappa-Sigma-registered marks; to stop holding itself out as "Kappa Sigma" or "Kappa Sigs" or other such similar derivatives that represent it as a member of Kappa Sigma; and to remove all public listings in telephone directories, maps, etc., using Kappa Sigma or other related designations (i.e., "K Sigs"), and any other name which includes the Greek letters "kappa" or "sigma" as a portion of its corporate or business name.[106]

---

100. *Id.*
101. *Id.* at 1100.
102. *Id.* at 1103.
103. *Id.* at 1098.
104. *Id.* at 1102.
105. The amount of time allowed as to publications only was extended and the imposition of attorneys' fee was rescinded, upon reconsideration. Kappa Sigma Fraternity v. Kappa Sigma Gamma Fraternity, 659 F. Supp. 117, 118 (D.N.H. 1987). The court had originally granted the national organization's attorneys' fees and costs, but reversed upon reconsideration, in light of recent decisions interpreting the statute awarding attorneys' fees in "extraordinary cases" and based on the finding that "the name Kappa Sigma Gamma was intentionally chosen to benefit from Kappa Sigma's reputation, but that the evidence does not support a finding of an intent to deceive the alumni or the new pledges as to the fraternity's continued affiliation with the national fraternity." *Id.* at 119.
106. *Kappa Sigma*, 654 F. Supp. at 1103.

In a similar situation, in 1992, a local chapter at Northwestern University in Evanston, Illinois had notified the national Alpha Delta Phi organization that it was withdrawing to become a local fraternity; however it appears to have continued using the national organization's name.[107] In 1993, the national fraternity sued the disassociated local chapter for federal trademark infringement and related state claims, including interference with business relations, recovery of property, and misappropriation of trade secrets, relying upon its common law[108] trademark rights.[109] Later that year, the parties participated in a settlement conference, which resulted in neither party admitting liability or infringement; nonetheless, the parties agreed that the local chapter would stop public use of the Alpha Delta Phi name within one month and private and administrative use of the name within three months.[110]

The litigation continued, as the local chapter (now referred to as "Chi Delta Chi") had filed counterclaims against the national organization, until the national chapter successfully moved to have the case dismissed for mootness.[111] In doing so, the court rejected the local chapter's counterclaims and attempts to block the national chapter from using its name in the Northwestern University area at any time in the future, as an impermissible request for prospective relief.[112]

i. Limitations of This Approach

The national chapter of Theta Chi fraternity declared its local chapter at Leland Stanford Junior University inactive around 1988, due to lack of membership and improper conduct by residents in 1988.[113] Over 30 years later, the national organization discovered that the alumni organi-

---

107. Alpha Delta Phi Int'l, Inc. v. Chi Delta Chi, No. 93 C 2012, 1995 WL 32622, at *1 (N.D. Ill. Jan. 26, 1995).

108. The national organization filed a federal trademark application for its collective membership mark in 2015, relying upon use dating back to 1832. ALPHA DELTA PHI, Registration No. 4,944,988.

109. *Alpha Delta Phi*, 1995 WL 32622, at *1.

110. Oct. 27, 1993 Minute Order (Docket Entry #41), Alpha Delta Phi Int'l, Inc. v. Chi Delta Chi, No. 93 C 2012, 1995 WL 32622 (N.D. Ill. Jan 26, 1995) (No. 1:93-CV-02012).

111. Alpha Delta Phi, 1995 WL 32622, at *1.

112. Alpha Delta Phi, 1995 WL 32622, at *3.

113. Complaint at ¶ 57, Theta Chi Fraternity, Inc. v. Leland Stanford Junior Univ., 212 F. Supp. 3d 816, 824–25 (N.D. Cal. 2016) (No. 5:16CV01336).

zation inhabiting the house was still using explicit references to their THETA CHI marks, and took steps at that time to rein it in and limit use by the disaffiliated group, trying to engage the university in the process. Frustrated in its attempts, the national fraternity filed suit against the alumni association in 2012 and reached a settlement agreement in 2013, where the alumni association agreed to stop using both the THETA CHI marks and the CHI THETA CHI marks, as well as to wind up and dissolve the entity.[114]

In 2015, the national organization discovered violations of the terms of the settlement agreement, including promotions of events that they felt brought the national organization's name into disrepute. In 2016, they again filed suit, seeking enforcement of the settlement agreement's terms, alleging infringement and dilution of its two federally registered marks, and bringing the university into the fray. Unfortunately for the plaintiff, in the likelihood of confusion analysis, the court focused on the lack of direct competition with the university (not considering the potential confusion arising from sponsorship or affiliation).[115]

The court suggested the delay of over 20 years before the national organization made a complaint (among other factors), undermined any complaint of potential or actual confusion.[116] The court also rejected their dilution claims and completely shot down the national organization's claim to fame, noting that the fraternity had left the area in 1988 due to lack of membership, so they were not even locally famous, much less having shown any evidence of a "a high level of actual recognition among the consuming public[.]"[117] (It is also possible that this summary dismissal of likelihood of confusion was impacted by the court's impatience in the plaintiff's claiming dilution in a conclusory way.)

ii. Best Practices Checklist

Presuming a fraternal organization has taken the initial steps of registering and protecting its trademark, it may also want to consider the following:

---

114. Theta Chi Fraternity, Inc. v. Alumni Ass'n of Chi Theta Chi House, 112-cv-235099 (Oct. 31, 2012).

115. Theta Chi Fraternity, Inc. v. Leland Stanford Junior Univ., 212 F. Supp. 3d 816, 824–25 (N.D. Cal. 2016).

116. *Id.* at 825.

117. *Id.* at 828–29.

- Do we have a written policy regarding how our trademarks and name are permitted to be used by chapters and members? Have we covered: letterhead, business cards, websites, social media, advertisements and fliers?
- Have we considered developing comprehensive "brand guideline" books which are distributed to any members or chapters who wish to use the organization's marks and other marketing collateral? (Such guidelines usually include approved, high-quality images of logos, as well as specific standards of use, and explicit approval mechanisms for various uses.)
- Have we clearly outlined an approval policy that chapters and individual members must follow for any uses outside the pre-approved use in our policy?
- Have we conducted training sessions or webinars on a periodic basis for new chapters and members, to educate them on how to use the IP appropriately and how to comply with the organization's rules about use?
- Have we uniformly enforced these guidelines and policies with all chapters and members?
- Do we need to conduct any audits or remedial enforcement?
- Does our commercial general liability policy include advertising liability protection?[118] How does the policy define "advertising"? Is it broad enough to cover our organization's activities and any potential claims?

2. THIRD PARTY LICENSING — INTERNAL AND EXTERNAL CONTROLS

As national fraternal organizations have increasingly been active in protecting and monetizing their interests in their marks in licensed products, a growing body of law has evolved, which helps support them in stopping unlicensed users and infringers, as seen in the cases cited in Section II(f) above. The primary hurdles that the fraternal organizations have had to overcome were past practices of nonenforcement against

---

118. First State Ins. Co. v. Alpha Delta Phi Fraternity, No. 1-94-1050, 1995 WL 901452, at *8 (Ill. App. Ct. Nov. 3, 1995).

third-party vendors and/or loose enforcement or control over the actions of its chapters and members, who engaged with nonapproved vendors for licensed products. These present themselves in defenses and/or counterclaims that the trademark owners have lost their rights either through "naked licensing" or failure to enforce their rights over the years ("laches"). Each of these can be overcome, as illustrated by the cases discussed above; however, fraternal organizations would be advised to learn from the mistakes of the past and the best practices of the successful plaintiffs, in the licensing and quality control practices going forward (see checklists below).

3. LICENSING INTERNAL CONTROLS — BEST PRACTICES CHECKLIST

In working with your chapters and members, consider:

- Do we have written policies regarding the need to purchase items with our symbols, crests, emblems, or other marks from licensed or approved vendors?
- Do they include instructions about how chapters and individual members can seek approval for use of the marks on additional licensed products?
- Have our policies been conveyed to officers of the local chapters? Are they aware of the national organization's licensing program and efforts at quality control?
- Should we consider providing a catalogue containing approved products for purchase?
- Are there additional ways we can ensure local chapters do not use unlicensed local vendors to obtain "swag" for special occasions and events?[119]

---

119. The courts recognize that many times national organization have limitations in implementing their policies, but good faith efforts are given due credit: "We acknowledge from this deposition testimony, buttressed as well by our own common sense, that the Greek organizations do not have total and complete control over the use of their insignias nationwide. However, we are not convinced that the manner in which local chapters seek out custom made souvenirs or favors for particular events amounts to an uncontrolled grant of a license or violates the core principles of trademark law." *Alpha Tau Omega*, 2004 WL 3391781, at *11.

- Have we considered designating a staff member whose sole responsibility is to protect the organization's intellectual property, monitor its appropriate use, and pursue violators?[120]

4. LICENSING — EXTERNAL CONTROLS — BEST PRACTICES CHECKLIST

In addition to making sure its entire organization, chapters, and members are aware of and adhering to its licensing protocols, fraternal organizations need to make sure that they implement the necessary quality controls and protections with their external licensees, as well as ensure they are diligently enforcing the terms of its agreements and shutting down violators in a timely fashion. Some fraternal organizations work with a licensing organization, such as the group of fraternal organizations who brought suit for trademark infringement in 2004 against Pure Country Inc., a maker of logo'd afghans and other soft goods.[121] It is worth noting that in this case, all but one of the fraternal organizations had registered incontestable marks, which the court found established their protectable interest and met the first prong of the infringement test (is there a protectable interest?).[122] The Best Practices Checklist is as follows:

- Do we have comprehensive, written agreements with all third-party vendors producing licensed products?
- Do those agreements (among other necessary terms):
  - Explicitly identify the mark, symbol, or words permitted to be used and any limitations on use (such as in particular colors or combinations), including any applicable USPTO registration or application serial numbers;
  - Explicitly identify what products and/or services are permitted by the license, limit the license to these products/

---

120. *See e.g.*, Delta Sigma Theta Sorority, Inc. v. Allen Professional Graphics Group, LLC, 212 F. Supp. 3d 116, 120 (D.D.C. 2014) (Fraternal organization granted preliminary injunction against terminated licensee, on basis of trademark infringement claim. "This Court has repeatedly recognized that trademark infringement and unfair competition are offenses that, by their very nature, cause irreparable injury.").

121. *Alpha Tau Omega*, 2004 WL 3391781, at *1.

122. *Id.* at *4.

- services, and require any expansion to be subject to written agreement;
- Identify whether the license is limited to a specific geographic territory (for example, if chapters in different areas may use different licensees and avoid controlling the market);
- Identify which uses (i.e., manufacture, sale, promotion) are permitted by the license;
- Explicitly identify any uses which are prohibited (e.g., online advertising) or limitations on the use or sale of licensed products (e.g., to verified members of the fraternal organization), or other guidelines (e.g., "Vendor Code of Conduct");[123]
- Provide detailed instructions on appropriate trademark notices to be used;
- Clearly identify any payment terms, including upfront fees, royalties, or other payments;
- Include a right to inspect and supervise the production facilities and the right to inspect samples of designs and samples of any merchandise prior to its sale or distribution, to ensure the vendor's products meet the fraternal organization's quality standards;
- Address indemnification arising from any product liability claims (and insurance to cover any such claims);
- Require the licensee to acknowledge the organization's ownership of the licensed mark, its validity, that all use of the trademark(s) inures to the organization's benefit, and expressly include a "no-challenge" clause;
- Address notice, cooperation, indemnification, and litigation costs arising from any third party infringement; and
- Identify the term and renewal of the license?[124]

---

123. Complaint at ¶ 22, *Delta Sigma Theta*, 212 F. Supp. 3d 116 (No. 1:14CV01403) ("[L]icensed vendor shall confine its sales of merchandise bearing Delta's Marks to Delta members and Delta-approved events; ... that the licensed vendor must put in place safeguards designed to protect against unauthorized sales of merchandise bearing Delta's Marks, including sales to non-members....").

124. The absence of a specific term may mean the license is terminable at will. *See* A.T.N., Inc. v. McAirlaid's Vliesstoffe GmbH & Co., K.G., 557 F.3d 483 (7th Cir. 2009).

- Have we done a comprehensive audit to identify any unlicensed use of the organization's marks on products and contacted each vendor?
- Do we have an ongoing procedure for continuing to monitor the marketplace for violations?

In the event you discover licensing violations, differing approaches may be warranted from soft invitations to license and collaborate, as initially employed in the *Alpha Tau Omega* case, to strongly worded "cease and desist" letters as a prelude to litigation. Active "policing" of your marks is necessary to protect your rights in the future. If you fail to do so, then an infringer may be successful in a laches or naked licensing claim.

IV. Avoiding IP Liability by Members and Chapters

While a fraternal organization works to protect and benefit from its trademarks, copyrights, and other IP, it must also be diligent that it is not exposing itself to liability through infringement of other parties' intellectual property.

a. Trademark Infringement of Third Parties

As discussed previously, a fraternal organization can protect its distinctive names, logos, crests, slogans, particular color combinations, etc. as trademarks, which prevents others from using these symbols to sell goods or services in a way that would be misleading or confusing to the public. On the other hand, it is important that an organization ensure its members or chapters are not improperly using the trademarks of other parties.

1. TRADEMARK INFRINGEMENT DEFINED

Owners of federally registered trademarks may bring a federal civil action for trademark infringement against anyone using their registered mark or a similar mark in a manner likely to cause consumer confusion.[125] More specifically, trademark infringement is "the unauthorized use of a trademark or service mark on or in connection with goods and/or services in a manner that is likely to cause confusion, deception, or mistake about the source of the goods and/or services."[126]

2. BURDEN OF PROOF

In order to prevail in a trademark infringement case for a mark registered with the USPTO, a trademark owner has the burden of proof that the other party used the mark at issue without the owner's permission, in commerce in connection with the advertising or sale of goods or services, where such use is likely to "cause confusion, or to cause mistake or to deceive."[127]

3. DEFENSES

A defendant in such a case has several potential avenues to counter such a claim, rebutting each of the factors raised by the plaintiff by arguing that there is no likelihood of confusion, or that the defendant's use was not "in commerce," for example. The defendant could also challenge the validity or enforceability of the trademark itself, dispute any damages claims, and raise equitable defenses. There are also affirmative defenses, such as laches, and other defenses that essentially boil down to claiming that the use was not in a trademark fashion, so is not actionable. While "fair use" is generally a copyright defense, courts have adopted a version for trademarks, which include the so-called "descriptive fair use", "nominative fair use," parody, and/or the right of free speech.[128]

(i) **Descriptive fair use** occurs when the mark allegedly being infringed is actually a descriptive term and is being used by the other party in its descriptive connotation, not as an indicator of origin or as a brand/logo. For example, a court found that the candy manufacturer's trademark for Swee-

---

125. 15 U.S.C. § 1114(1).

126. *About Trademark Infringement*, USPTO (June 8, 2018, 2:03 PM), https://www.uspto.gov/page/about-trademark-infringement; 15 U.S.C. §§1114, 1116–1118.

127. Boston Prof'l Hockey Ass'n, Inc. v. Dallas Cap & Emblem Mfg., Inc., 510 F.2d 1004, 1009–10 (5th Cir.), *cert. denied*, 423 U.S. 868 (1975).

128. 6 MCCARTHY, *supra* note 39, § 31:1; 15 U.S.C.A. § 1115.

TARTS® was not infringed by Ocean Spray®'s use of the term "sweet-tart" descriptively for a juice drink that was both sweet and tart, observing, "Both sweet and tart are words of description in ordinary English, quite unlike words such as 'Exxon' or 'Kodak,'"[129] and given that, there was no evidence supporting consumer confusion.

(ii) **Nominative fair use** refers to a situation when one company refers to another's trademark in promoting or describing its own goods or services. For example, when one company uses its competitor's mark in comparative advertising, or in a listing of the brands carried in a retail store. There is a difference of opinion between circuits as to whether it is an actual affirmative defense or simply a defense to likelihood of confusion;[130] however, the components of the analysis articulated by the Third Circuit are generally used by the courts:

1. Is the use of plaintiff's mark necessary to describe (1) plaintiff's product or service and (2) defendant's product or service?

2. Is only so much of the plaintiff's mark used as is necessary to describe plaintiff's products or services?

3. Does the defendant's conduct or language reflect the true and accurate relationship between plaintiff and defendant's products or services?[131]

In essence, this defense asserts that the putative infringer is entitled to talk about the trademark owner's products or services, by using the registered trademark, as long as they are not trying to compete for the same consumers or confusing those consumers.[132]

---

129. Sunmark, Inc. v. Ocean Spray Cranberries, Inc., 64 F.3d 1055, 1058 (7th Cir. 1995); *see also* KP Permanent Make-Up, Inc. v. Lasting Impression I, Inc., 543 U.S. 111, 122–23 (2004) (registrant gets an exclusive right not in the original, descriptive sense of words in a descriptive mark, but only in the secondary one associated with the markholder's goods).

130. *See* discussion in 6 MCCARTHY, *supra* note 39, § 31:156.50; *see, e.g.*, Rosetta Stone Ltd. v. Google, Inc., 676 F.3d 144, 155, 102 U.S.P.Q.2d 1473 (4th Cir. 2012) (Google's use of the ROSETTA STONE mark as a keyword for advertising was "nominative.").

131. Century 21 Real Est. Corp. v. Lendingtree, Inc., 425 F.3d 211, 228 (3d Cir. 2005).

132. 6 MCCARTHY, *supra* note 39, § 31:156.50.

(iii) **Parody** can be a defense where the unauthorized use of the trademark does not cause confusion or improperly suggest endorsement. Parody almost always is a successful defense for creative or expressive works (i.e., magazine, TV show).[133] Almost all courts attempt to balance free speech rights with trademark law's policy of preventing consumer confusion by using the "Rogers" test,[134] from a 1989 case involving the actress Ginger Rogers' objection to Italian filmmaker Federico Fellini's use of her name in the title (she lost). The two-part balancing test asks whether "the public interest in avoiding consumer confusion outweighs the public interest in free expression," and will only prohibit the use of the trademark if it has "no artistic relevance to the underlying work whatsoever" or, even if there IS artistic relevance, if its use "explicitly misleads as to the source or the content of the work."[135]

However, a parody defense is less likely to succeed when the trademark is used to sell another's products in competition with the trademark owner.[136] And the outcome is uncertain with products which are arguably both expressive and for commercial use, as in the case of t-shirts.[137] In many of these cases, the use of parodies of famous marks has been considered not infringing, such as the use of "Chewy Vuiton" dog toys parodying Louis Vuitton's luxury brand mark.[138] However, the question of whether a commercial use of a trademark parody is protected creative expression or crosses the line into improper use of another's trade-

---

133. 6 MCCARTHY, *supra* note 39, § 31:154.

134. 6 MCCARTHY, *supra* note 39, § 31:144.50

135. Rogers v. Grimaldi, 875 F.2d 994, 999, (2d Cir. 1989).

136. *See e.g.*, Harley Davidson, Inc. v. Grottanelli, 164 F.3d 806, 812–13 (2d Cir. 1999) (Defendant's use of plaintiff's mark was not parody, since it made "no comment on Harley's mark; it simply use[d] it somewhat humorously to promote [its] own product and services, which is not a permitted trademark parody use" and was essentially trademark use for a competing services, since Harley-Davidson offered motorcycle repair services and defendant used the logo to promote his repair and parts business.)

137. *See e.g.*, Nike, Inc. v. Just Did It Enters., 6 F.3d 1225, 1232 (7th Cir. 1993).

138. Louis Vuitton Malletier S.A. v. Haute Diggity Dog, LLC, 507 F.3d 252 (4th Cir.2007).

mark, is far from settled, as illustrated by the ongoing dispute between VIP Products LLC, maker of dog toys that parody Jack Daniel's trade dress, and Jack Daniel's Properties Inc.[139]

The inquiry in all these cases is fact-specific, subjective, and as the leading commentator on trademark law has observed, "because of judicial discomfort over the commercial nature of the accused use as a brand and a perception of free riding, outcomes are uncertain and litigation is enormously expensive."[140]

4. APPLICATION TO FRATERNAL ORGANIZATIONS

Many of the prior cases in this chapter discussed straightforward examples of trademark infringement, where a party was using the exact same mark as the trademark-owning fraternal organization for the same goods/services in what amounted to counterfeiting or unauthorized, unlicensed product sales. In the *Sigma Chi* case, where a product manufacturer produced items with the fraternal organization's trademarks without approval and despite explicit requests to cease and desist, the plaintiff was able to show that the infringer did not have permission AND the use was "confusingly similar."[141] The *Kappa Sigma* case, where the disaffiliated chapter continued to use the organization's trademarks without authorization, demonstrated how infringement liability can also arise when use of a third party's trademark mistakenly leads the consumer to believe there is some sponsorship or affiliation between the trademark owner and the unauthorized user.[142]

Assuming a fraternal organization is not in a dispute with another organization about the use of the same or similar marks for their organizations, **confusion as to sponsorship or affiliation** is one way in which chapters may stumble into trademark infringement territory. The other

---

139. VIP Products LLC v. Jack Daniel's Properties, Inc., 953 F.3d 1170, 1175 (9th Cir. 2020), later proceedings 2022 WL 1654040 (9th Cir. 2022) *cert. granted* 143 S. Ct. 476 (2022).

140. 6 McCarthy § 31:154, citing Dogan & Lemley, Parody as Brand, 105 Trademark Rptr 1177, 1204 (2015).

141. *See e.g., Sigma Chi*, 2000 WL 34414961 at *7–8.

142. *See e.g., Kappa Sigma*, 654 F. Supp. at 1097.

likely arenas where risk could arise is by use of others' trademarks by chapters promoting events and/or "joke" t-shirts. For example, a local chapter may decide to host and promote a "Super Bowl Party" or "March Madness Dance," not realizing that these are federally registered trademarks which are zealously enforced by the NFL and the National Collegiate Athletic Association (NCAA), perhaps beyond the protection to which they are legally entitled.[143] For example, a car dealership promoted sales by using the phrase "Markdown Madness" in advertisements (and for which it sought a federal trademark registration). The NCAA both attempted to block the registration at the USPTO, contending it infringed on its MARCH MADNESS trademark for the spring basketball tournament, and sued the dealership in federal court.[144] Before the court could rule in the final round of the two-year battle, and determine whether there was any likelihood of confusion between the marks, or whether any of the other defenses raised were valid, the parties reached a confidential settlement.[145]

5. BEST PRACTICES

Fraternal organizations can best avoid wading into the uncertain, subjective thicket of trademark infringement defenses and risking the expense of defending against trademark infringement by educating their chapters and members how to avoid infringing others' trademarks.

  a. Don't use others' trademarks to promote events.
  b. Don't put a third party's trademarks on apparel, cups, websites, or anything, even if it's a parody.
  c. Get permission from the trademark owner if you must use it, such as when you are conducting a cosponsored event.

---

143. In addition to the frequent actions against counterfeit licensed merchandise, the NFL has even threatened to sue a church for advertising a "Super Bowl" party. Michelle Kaminsky, *Super Bowl Legal Blitz: Inside The NFL's Legendary Trademark Defense*, FORBES (Jan. 30, 2018, 6:20 AM), https://www.forbes.com/sites/michellefabio/2018/01/30/inside-the-nfls-legendary-trademark-defense/?sh=31e88f6d3293.

144. National Collegiate Athletic Association v. Ken Grody Management Inc., 8:18-cv-00153 (C.D. Cal. June 26, 2018). *See also National Collegiate Athletic Associations v. Kizzang LLC*, No. 1:17-cv-00712-JMS-MPB (S.D. Ind. May 17, 2018) (Game developer allegedly infringed on NCAA's marks).

145. Bill Donahue, *NCAA Sues Over 'Markdown Madness' As Tourney Nears*, LAW360 (Jan. 29, 2018, 5:03 PM), https://www.law360.com/articles/1006558.

d. Consult the fraternal organization's lawyer if the use appears to be descriptive or nontrademark use, including parody.

b. Copyright Infringement of Third Parties

Fraternal organizations should also take care that their chapters and members are not incurring liability by infringing on other's copyrights when promoting its organization and events, and creating their own content.

1. COPYRIGHT INFRINGEMENT DEFINED

If you use someone else's copyrighted work without permission, whether it is to reproduce, distribute, perform, publicly display, or create a "derivative work," that is copyright infringement.[146] Unlike plagiarism, copyright infringement cannot be avoided through attribution; it requires permission.

2. BURDEN OF PROOF

In order to prevail in a copyright infringement case, a plaintiff must prove (1) ownership of a valid copyright, and that there was (2) unauthorized copying of the (3) original elements of the work in question.[147]

Registration of a copyright with the US Copyright Office is a precondition to bring suit in federal court for copyright infringement,[148] and the registration certificate can serve as proof of the ownership of a valid copyright. "Original" in copyright law means (1) that "the work was independently created by the author (as opposed to copied from other works)," and (2) that it possesses "at least some minimal degree of creativity."[149]

To prove unauthorized copying, the copyright holder must show both that there was (1) factual copying of the original work in question ("that defendant knew of the protected work, had access to it, and used it as

---

146. 17 U.S.C. § 501.
147. Feist Publications v. Rural Telephone Service Co., 499 U.S. 340 (1991).
148. Fourth Est. Pub. Benefit Corp. v. Wall-Street.com, LLC, 139 S. Ct. 881, 886 (2019).
149. *Feist*, 499 U.S. at 345.

model, template, inspiration or part to produce its own rival work") and (2) that the two works are "substantially similar."[150] Factual copying may be demonstrated either by direct evidence, or inferred by "demonstrating that the defendant had access to the copyrighted work and that there are probative similarities between the allegedly infringing work and the copyrighted work."[151] "Substantial similarity," which leads to a conclusion of infringement or misappropriation, is a question of fact, and the exact analysis and phrase of this misappropriation depends on the circuit.[152] For example, the Fifth Circuit requires that a "a side-by-side comparison must be made between the original and the copy to determine whether a layman would view the two works as 'substantially similar.'"[153]

3. DEFENSES

A defendant can fend off a copyright infringement case in many ways, including asserting that the work at issue is not copyrightable material at all, or that they had no access to the original work, and the allegedly infringing work was independently created. As discussed previously in Section 1, one common defense to copyright infringement is "fair use." Again, as explained previously, a fair use defense is a subjective analysis made by weighing the four factors described above.[154] Such a defense is more likely to succeed if a defendant can demonstrate a noncommercial or educational use of the copyright, that the entire (or the most important part of the) work was not used, and that the complained-of use wasn't in competition with or didn't replace the intended market for the work at issue. The types of uses that are generally considered "fair use" are parody, news reporting, scholarly or educational use, or criticism.

---

150. 4 Melville B. Nimmer & David Nimmer, Nimmer on Copyright § 13D.02 (Matthew Bender, Rev. Ed., 2022).

151. Compulife Software, Inc. v. Newman, 959 F.3d 1288, 1301 (11th Cir. 2020).

152. 4 Nimmer on Copyright § 13D.02 (2022); *see e.g.*, Tanksley v. Daniels, 902 F.3d 165, 171 (3d Cir. 2018) ("[S]ubstantial similarity 'is usually an extremely close question of fact,' which is why even 'summary judgment has traditionally been disfavored in copyright litigation.'").

153. Bridgmon v. Array Sys. Corp., 325 F.3d 572, 576–77 (5th Cir. 2003).

154. 17 U.S.C. § 107.

4. BEST PRACTICES

Defending copyright infringement claims can be unpredictable and expensive. Fraternal organizations would be advised to avoid liability and risk in this arena by again educating their chapters and members how to avoid infringing on others' copyrights.

    a. Ask for permission and get a license before you use someone else's creative work. Attribution is not enough without permission.
    b. Just because an image or photograph or written work is on the internet does NOT mean it is "public domain" or free to use without permission.
    c. Do not assume something is "fair use"; ask for a legal consultation.

V. Conclusion

By following the best practices above and employing a comprehensive strategy of brand protection and chapter education, a national fraternal organization can ensure that its "brand" is protected, fund its mission through careful product licensing, and avoid unnecessary liability from marketing and social activities by its member chapters.

CHAPTER 17

Property and Zoning Law

Shelley Ross Saxer

In property and land-use matters, fraternities and sororities ("fraternal organizations") interact with local zoning officials, neighbors, universities, and the courts. For much of the 20th century, land-use concerns of fraternal organizations focused on zoning provisions that governed the definition of "family," which sought to limit a variety of group-home uses from single-family districts. In *Village of Belle Terre v. Boraas*,[1] the US Supreme Court upheld such restrictions against civil rights challenges. The Court wrote, "[t]he regimes of boarding houses, fraternity houses, and the like present urban problems. More people occupy a given space; " more cars rather continuously pass by; more cars are parked; noise travels with crowds. A quiet place where yards are wide, people few, and motor vehicles restricted are legitimate guidelines in a land-use project addressed to family needs."[2] While there are still zoning issues with the definition of single-family or residential use, most cities now regulate fraternal organizations through "institutional" zoning districts in areas near university campuses.

---

1. 416 U.S. 1, 9 (1974).
2. *Id.*

I. Zoning

a. Single-Family Residential

Zoning litigation involving fraternal organizations in the 20th century illustrates the attempts to classify a fraternity as a single-family use. In *Pettis v. Alpha Alpha Chapter of Phi Beta Pi*,[3] the Nebraska Supreme Court relied on *Village of Euclid v. Ambler Realty*[4] to support the validity of the zoning ordinance under the police power.[5] The court determined that "a company of approximately 20 or 30 unrelated young fraternity men" did not fall within the meaning of family as required in the "A" residence district.[6] Instead, the zoning ordinance expressly confined fraternities to the "B" residence district.[7] Thus, the city of Omaha did not allow the fraternal organization to use the property it had purchased in the "A" district.[8] Conversely, the court in *City of Syracuse v. Snow* held that a sorority recognized by Syracuse University belonged in the class A residential district as a "family" use.[9] Policy concerns appeared to influence these opposing court decisions.

In Nebraska, the court was concerned about the negative impacts of fraternity life on the neighbors, while the Syracuse decision focused on the positive impact of Syracuse University on the city's growth and pros-

---

3. 213 N.W. 835, 839 (Neb. 1927).

4. 272 U.S. 365 (1926).

5. 213 N.W. at 839.

6. 213 N.W. at 837–38 (noting that "it is a matter of common knowledge and well established that groups of students are for the most part exuberant, boisterous, and hilarious, and that they do not ordinarily keep regular hours and are addicted to the use and abuse of vibrant and sonorous musical instruments").

7. *Id.* at 837.

8. *Id.* (recognizing that using this property in the "A" district for a fraternity house would depreciate the property value of surrounding homes and would likely interfere with the neighbors' use and enjoyment of their properties).

9. 205 N.Y.S. 785, 789 (Sup. Ct. 1924) (stating that "[a] college sorority is a family, a college family, perhaps, but nevertheless its membership not only live together, and cook together, but are bound together by fraternal ties; ties that, in many instances, are more binding and enduring then those of kinship"). But see City of Schenectady v. Alumni Ass'n of Union Chapter Delta Chi Fraternity, 168 N.Y.S.2d 754, 755 (App. Div. 1957) (declining to follow City of Syracuse v. Snow as authority for finding that a group of twenty-three students constitute a 'single family' and holding that a fraternity was not a single-family residence as required for location in the 'A' zone).

perity and the need for supervised college housing.[10] Similarly, the Indiana appellate court in *Kappa Inc. v. City of Terre Haute* recognized "that in the field of higher education, fraternities and sororities have become and are an integral part of college and university life for many students."[11] The court noted that many successful men and women "have brought renown and prestige to the respective fraternities and sororities," but, nevertheless, confirmed that a fraternity was not a family use and must instead locate in the business district as allowed by the city ordinance, not in the residential district.[12]

Zoning ordinances typically define uses such as "single-family residential," "multifamily residential," "dwelling unit," "household," "boarding house," "rooming house," and "fraternity or sorority house." Undefined or ambiguous terms "must be construed reasonably with regard to both the objects sought to be obtained and to the general structure of the ordinance as a whole."[13] In *Adams v. Town of Brunswick*, neighbors argued that property owners seeking to lease a house divided into two apartments violated the Brunswick zoning ordinance because the use would be a prohibited boarding house.[14] The court agreed with the town that the use qualified as an allowable two-household dwelling for rental to eleven Bowdoin College students and that the ordinance definitions did not "limit either 'households' or 'dwelling units' to families."[15] The neighbors argued that because the definition of boarding house "ends with the sentence, 'Includes a college fraternity or sorority,'" any occupation by students would constitute a "boarding house."[16] The court noted that a fraternity is different from the occupancy of two groups of tenants who by chance are students in that "[a] fraternity has a lasting purpose independent of its current residents—students are admitted to and expelled from it, they may quit, drop out of school or graduate, but the

---

10. *See* Snow, 205 N.Y.S. at 788–89.

11. 226 N.E.2d 907, 912 (Ind. Ct. App. 1967) (noting that the fraternity should consider a petition for variance or an application to rezone).

12. *Id.*

13. Adams v. Town of Brunswick, 987 A.2d 502, 507 (Me. 2010) "(quoting Davis v. SBA Towers II, 979 A.2d 216, 219 (Me. 2009)..

14. *Id.* at 504.

15. *Id.*

16. *Id.* at 509.

fraternity remains."[17] Even so, the zoning ordinance allows the owners to lease two apartments to two groups of students because the ordinance does not distinguish between a dwelling unit and a boarding house based on the types of individuals who occupy the premises.[18]

In *Nanos v. Town of Mansfield*, a Connecticut court enjoined the town's enforcement of its ordinance precluding a "Fraternity/Sorority House" from using a single-family residence as a fraternity house.[19] The court held that the zoning regulation defining a "Fraternity/Sorority House" was unconstitutionally vague because the plaintiff proved that a person of ordinary intelligence would not be able to determine what activities the regulations prohibited.[20] The court illustrated this difficulty by noting "a party in a house rented by four members of the rugby, baseball, basketball, or football teams would not violate [the regulation, but] ... if those four tenants also belonged to a fraternity, the party would be in violation of the regulation."[21] In addition, the court applied a rational basis standard and held that the regulation violated equal protection because "[t]here is no rational basis for distinguishing between four unrelated tenants who belong to fraternities or sororities and four unrelated tenants who do not belong to 'Greek letter' organizations."[22]

In addition to establishing zoning regulations excluding fraternal organizations from single-family residential zones, municipalities have retained the ability to exclude fraternity or sorority houses from multi-family residential zones. In *City of Long Beach v. California Lambda Chapter of Sigma Alpha Epsilon Fraternity*, the city permitted fraternity and sorority houses in an apartment house district, but only with the grant of a special permit; otherwise they could locate in a business district.[23] The court observed that the city council was aware of the fact that "[t]he 'rush parties,' the dances, the rallies and other manifestations of

---

17. *Id.*
18. *Id.* at 510.
19. 1994 WL 504117 at *1 (Conn. Super. Ct. 1994).
20. *Id.* at *7–*8. ("Any building or portion of a building used for accommodating a fraternity or sorority for the purpose of lodging, dining, entertaining, or assembly.").
21. *Id.* at *8.
22. *Id.* at *10.
23. 63 Cal.Rptr. 419, 421 (Ct. App. 1967).

the collegiate sprit are present in a fraternity house and frequently absent in a boarding house, a lodging house or an apartment."[24]

Municipalities have also attempted to control the externalities of college life by more stringently regulating activities within homes housing such occupants. For example, in *Delta ETA Corp. v. City Council of City of Newark*, the city council of Newark, Delaware, eventually approved a developer's application to subdivide three existing houses in a zone "intended for garden apartments, boarding houses, rooming houses, lodging houses, private dormitories or fraternity houses."[25] This approval came after the city council denied the subdivision application in 2002, but imposed several conditions the developer asserted were unreasonable.[26] With the court's "strong encouragement," the litigants were able to resolve all of the conditions except for one: "If the property is leased to or operated as a fraternity and/or sorority, that the sale, distribution, or consumption of alcoholic beverages shall not be permitted anywhere on the premises."[27] The developer objected to this remaining condition as an unreasonable restriction on the "lawful consumption of alcohol, in the privacy of one's home" since it is likely there will be tenants over the age of 21 who choose to consume alcohol.[28] The Delaware court was sympathetic to the city's "concerns of excessive alcohol consumption" in a population of mostly college students, but determined that the city's restriction on the legal consumption of alcohol exceeded the regulatory authority delegated to it by the state legislature.[29]

b. Historic Landmarks and Districts

Another mechanism for zoning with fraternal organizations in mind is historic district zoning. For example, some municipalities may designate an older fraternity or sorority house as historic or as part of an historic district.[30] In *Coalition for Non-Profit Student Housing v. City of*

---

24. *Id.* at 423–424.
25. 2005 WL 1654581, at *1 (Del. Super. Ct. 2005).
26. *Id.*
27. *Id.*
28. *Id.* at *2.
29. *Id.* at *3.
30. *See e.g.*, Adams v. Town of Brunswick, 987 A.2d 502, 504 (Me. 2010) (noting that property owners received a certificate of appropriateness to provide new windows for a

Minneapolis, the city designated certain fraternity and sorority houses owned by the coalition as part of a University of Minnesota Fraternity Row Historic District.[31] Reviewing the city's historical preservation-designation proceedings as quasi-judicial, the court required that the zoning decision not be unreasonable, arbitrary, or capricious.[32] After an extensive review of the city's historic designation process, the court determined that the historic designation was not arbitrary or capricious because "the city based its decision on a 182-page report, transcripts from various meetings, supplemental reports, and presentations from the opposing sides."[33]

The court also found that the noncontiguous nature of the historic district did not make it arbitrary and that the zoning ordinance did not treat similarly situated properties differently within the study parameters for designation.[34] The coalition's argument that the designation criteria in the regulations were unconstitutionally vague, that the city failed to assess the regulatory and economic impact on the proposed property, and that the designation process violated the property owner's due-process rights, were unsuccessful.[35] The court held that the city's criteria "are widely used and accepted, and are not unconstitutionally vague;" the historic-designation process does not require the city to consider financial and regulatory burdens on proposed property in the abstract and the property owners received procedural due process through proper notifications and public hearings.[36]

c. Institutional Zoning

Institutional zoning may have solved the *Village of Belle Terre* problem, but the terms of such "institutional" zoning on fraternal organizations has opened a new line of controversies. The city's "institutional" use typically requires the fraternal organization to be in good standing with the university. If the fraternal organization loses that good standing

---

fraternity house in the historic district).
31. 2004 WL 2220950, at *1–2 (Minn. Ct. App. 2004).
32. *Id.* at *4.
33. *Id.* at *5.
34. *Id.* at *5–6.
35. *Id.* at *7.
36. *Id.*

with the university, the loss in status may violate the city's zoning code and result in fines and abatement proceedings, potentially terminating the fraternity or sorority use pursuant to the city's zoning ordinance. A loss of good standing or disapproval by a university often arises in the context of university administrative proceedings. In such proceedings, federal law may protect the privacy of a proceeding and the adjudication receives only minimal due process protections.

Without a university's sanction or recognition of the fraternal organization, the city will not permit the fraternity or sorority to remain in the institutional zone. For example, in *City of Bloomington Bd. of Zoning Appeals v. UJ-Eighty Corp.*,[37] the city's zoning ordinance permitted fraternal organizations in the "institutional" zone, but required Indiana University to sanction or recognize the fraternity.[38] The trial court held that this language was an improper delegation of legislative authority to the university, but the Indiana Supreme Court later rejected that argument.[39] The court found that Bloomington did not delegate any authority to Indiana University to define "fraternity" and "sorority," as the university already possessed that power.[40] Instead, the city ordinance defined this land use based on its relationship with the university.[41] Therefore, the corporation that owned the fraternity house was subject to Bloomington's citation for a zoning violation when the university revoked its recognition and approval of the fraternity before the end of the lease, precluding any subsequent occupancy.[42]

Similarly, in *New Hampshire Alpha of SAE Tr. v. Town of Hanover*,[43] the town's zoning ordinance permitted student residences, such as fraternal organizations, in "institutional" zones but only by special exception.[44] The code defined a "Student Residence" as a "building designed for and occupied by students and operated in conjunction with another institutional use."[45] Dartmouth College revoked a fraternal organiza-

---

37. 163 N.E.3d 264 (Ind. 2021), *cert. denied*, 142 S. Ct. 232 (2021).
38. *Id.* at 265.
39. *Id.*
40. *Id.* at 267.
41. *Id.* at 268.
42. *Id.* at 265.
43. 207 A.3d 219, 220–221(N.H. 2019).
44. *Id.*
45. *Id.*

tion's official recognition by the university after learning of the suspension of the national charter of the Dartmouth chapter.[46] That, in turn, caused the zoning administrator to find the fraternal organization violated the local city ordinance and continued operation subject to daily fines.[47] Relying on its earlier decision in *Dartmouth Corp. of Alpha Delta v. Town of Hanover*, the New Hampshire Supreme Court recognized that in *Alpha Delta*, the word "conjunction" indicated that the property use "'must have some union, association or combination with the College.'"[48] However, in this case, derecognition of the fraternity by the college does not necessarily mean that the property is not being used in conjunction with another institutional use in the district—it "is merely one factor to be considered by the ZBA."[49] Thus, there is no delegation of the Zoning Board of Appeals (ZBA) authority to the college because the ZBA, not the college, determines whether the property use is in conjunction with an institutional use.[50]

Institutional zoning ordinances may also attempt to tie the fraternity or sorority house's physical location to the associated institution. For example, in *Phi Kappa Iota Fraternity v. Salt Lake City*, the city required that fraternity or sorority houses in a residential zone be located within 600 feet of the institution to which they are incident.[51] The fraternity house at issue in this case was just outside the 600-foot boundary and was subject to criminal prosecution if it continued to use the property it

---

46. *Id.*

47. *Id.*

48. *Id.* at 223 (quoting Dartmouth Corp. of Alpha Delta v. Town of Hanover, 159 A.3d 359, 368 (N.H. 2017)).

49. *Id.*

50. *Id.* at 224. *See also* Schweizer v. Board of Adjustment, No. 06A-08-007, 2009 WL 597630 at *3 (Del. Super. Ct. March 4, 2009) (explaining that when the University of Delaware suspended the fraternity, it was not an unconstitutional delegation by the city of its legislative powers as the University did not make a zoning decision, and that not only a zoning decision could have zoning consequences.). *But see* 425 Prop. Ass'n of Alpha Chi Rho, Inc. v. State Coll. Borough Zoning Hearing Bd., 223 A.3d 300, 313 n.9 (Pa. Commw. Ct. 2019) (noting that because the court decided that using the property as a fraternity house was a lawful nonconforming use, "it is unnecessary to address whether the Zoning Ordinance is substantively invalid due to impermissibly delegating regulatory and decision-making powers to Penn State," but concluding that if it were to address this issue, "we would conclude that the Borough has unconstitutionally delegated its authority to determine the existence of a 'Fraternity House' under the Zoning Code.").

51. 212 P.2d 177, 178–179 (1949).

had recently purchased as a fraternity.[52] The fraternity and one of the neighbors who lived within the 600-foot boundary challenged the ordinance as unconstitutional.[53] The court affirmed that the city's selected method of concentrating fraternities and sororities rather than dispersing them to a wider area was "not unreasonably discriminatory, arbitrary or capricious" as a way to address traffic congestion.[54] These zoning cases show how the courts give great deference to local legislative action designed to deal with the noise, congested traffic, and other inconveniences incident to a university, including frequent gatherings and boisterous conduct of fraternal organizations in residential neighborhoods.[55]

d. Variances and Special-Use Permits

Successful zoning regimes provide flexibility to deal with unanticipated issues at the time of zoning implementation. Variances may offer a remedy for a zoning ordinance that uniquely harms an individual landowner by precluding their ability to obtain a reasonable return on investment through no fault of their own. A use variance allows a landowner to make a different use of their property than what the zoning ordinance permits. An area variance, dealing with bulk and height requirements, permits a landowner to build with minor adjustments to height or setbacks because of hardship unique to them so long as the variance does not harm the neighbors.[56] The purpose of a variance is to provide an avenue for relief in situations where applying a zoning ordinance will impose practical difficulties or unnecessary hardships in unique and individual cases.[57]

To obtain an area variance, some courts require an applicant to show that they have satisfied the "practical difficulties" test as follows:

---

52. *Id.* at 179.
53. *Id.* at 177.
54. *Id.* at 179.
55. *Id.* at 179–180.
56. *See e.g.*, Chico Corp. v. Delaware-Muncie Bd. of Zoning Appeals, 466 N.E.2d 472 (Ind. Ct. App. 1984) (evidence of fraternities causing special problems relating to the public health, safety, morals, or general welfare justified the area performance standards that must be met regarding acreage and setback limitations).
57. 75 Am. Jur. 3d *Proof of Facts* § 13 (updated 2022).

(1) Whether compliance with the strict letter of the restrictions governing area, set backs, frontage, height, bulk, or density would unreasonably prevent the owner from using the property for a permitted purpose or would render conformity with such restrictions unnecessarily burdensome; (2) whether a grant of the variance applied for would do substantial justice to the applicant as well as to other property owners in the district, or whether a lesser relaxation than that applied for would give substantial relief to the owner of the property involved and be more consistent with justice to other property owners: and (3) whether relief can be granted in such a fashion that the spirit of the ordinance will be observed and public safety and welfare secured.[58]

In *Alumni Control Board, Alpha Psi Chapter, Delta Sigma Phi Fraternity, Inc. v. City of Lincoln*, the Nebraska Supreme Court applied the practical difficulties test to find that the board of zoning appeals' denial of a fraternity application for an area variance was not unreasonable, arbitrary or illegal.[59] The fraternity sought an area variance to build a four-story fraternity house measuring 30 by 60 feet, although the existing building code allowed a maximum of 28 by 48.6 feet.[60] The court noted that in most cases involving area variances, there is a substandard lot.[61] However, here the fraternity's lot is not substandard, but a code-compliant building could house only 36 men given the city zoning code and the University of Nebraska housing code requirements.[62] Even though the fraternity argued it would be economically undesirable to house fewer than 48 men, the court found no evidence that the fraternity faced practical difficulties unique to their lot as the code and economic factors applied equally to other fraternities in the same zoning district.[63]

---

58. See e.g., Alumni Control Bd. Alpha Psi Chapter Delta Sigma Phi Fraternity, Inc. v. City of Lincoln, 137 N.W.2d 800, 802–803 (Neb. 1965) (citing 2 RATHKOPF, THE LAW OF ZONING AND PLANNING 45-28 (3d ed.)).

59. *Id.* at 803.
60. *Id.* at 801.
61. *Id.* at 802.
62. *Id.* at 801.
63. *Id.* at 802–803.

A use variance is typically associated with "unnecessary hardship," while an area variance is concerned with "practical difficulty."[64] An area variance does not relate to a change of use, but a use variance "permits a use other than that prescribed by the zoning ordinance in a particular district."[65] In *Cassidy v. Triebel*, the local chapter of Gamma Phi Beta Corporation purchased property from a husband and wife to use as a sorority house.[66] The sellers and the sorority sought a use variance to maintain the property as a one-family dwelling for the sorority members, which the board of appeals denied.[67] The home under contract for sale was located in the "B" two-family district, but the city only permitted sororities and fraternities in the "C" or "D" apartment districts.[68] The "B" district excluded sororities and fraternities, but the sorority argued that it would occupy the premises as a single housekeeping unit or family.[69] Nevertheless, the court determined that the city validly established restrictions on use in its zoning ordinance and it acted reasonably in denying the variance.[70]

In *In re Jennings' Estate*, the trustees of the estate planned to lease the premises to the Rho Chapter of Phi Kappa Fraternity and applied to Pittsburgh's board of adjustment for a variance to use the property as a multiple dwelling instead of a one-family dwelling.[71] The Supreme Court of Pennsylvania relied upon *Village of Euclid v. Ambler Realty Co.* to support Pittsburgh's authority to restrict residences in a district to single-family dwellings.[72] The *Jennings* court upheld the board of adjustment's denial of a variance based on evidence from neighboring property owners that occupying the property as a fraternity house would decrease the value of their properties and make the community less desirable for residential use.[73] Although the court recognized that the

---

64. *Id.* at 802.

65. *Id.*

66. 85 N.E.2d 461, 462–463 (Ill. App. Ct. 1948).

67. *Id.* at 463–464.

68. *Id.* at 465.

69. *Id.* at 465.

70. *Id.* at 466–467.

71. 198 A. 621, 621 (Pa. 1938).

72. *Id.* at 623 (citing Village of Euclid v. Ambler Realty Co., 272 U.S. 365 (1926) for support, among other decisions).

73. *Id.* at 622–23.

one-family residential classification of the estate's property was a serious hardship on the estate, there was "no practical difficulty in limiting residences in this district to one family dwellings."[74] The court affirmed the board of adjustment's decision after carefully reviewing the evidence and finding no "manifest and flagrant abuse of discretion" by the board that would require reversal.[75]

A municipality may grant a use variance but condition its authorization on the landowner's adherence to specific conditions. In *Township of Franklin v. New Jersey Chinese Community Center*,[76] the township's board of adjustment granted the landowner a use variance, allowing it to operate a cultural and educational center with the understanding that it would only use the space for indoor activities and that the landowner would not rent it out.[77] The variance was subject to limitations that there would be no outdoor activities and that any special events would be held inside the cafeteria.[78] The center rented out its property to a fraternity to use for a barbeque where the police stopped a fight in the parking lot where 200 to 300 people were gathered.[79] The court upheld the township's citation for violating a zoning permit by conducting a prohibited use—an outside barbeque.[80]

A special exception or conditional use permit allows a landowner to use their property as permitted in their zone, but the zoning officials must review and approve their request with any conditions necessary to mitigate adverse impacts on their neighbors. Sometimes, it can be difficult to determine whether a variance or a special exception is in order. For example, in *Mullen v. Zoning Hearing Board of the City of Lock Haven*, the Pennsylvania court needed to determine whether the city should have considered the fraternity's application for a special exception as a variance application instead.[81] The court concluded that the city should have treated the application for a special exception to use the property as a boarding house as a variance application for a fraternity house in-

---

74. *Id.* at 623.
75. *Id.* at 622.
76. 2013 WL 4504091, at *1 (N.J. Super. Ct. App. Div. 2013).
77. *Id.*
78. *Id.*
79. *Id.* at *2.
80. *Id.*
81. 35 Pa. D. & C.3d 542, 543 (Pa. Com. Pl. 1984).

stead.[82] In *Mullen*, the city's zoning ordinance distinguished between boarding houses and fraternity houses and permitted boarding houses as a special exception in a low-density residential district.[83] Because the city only permitted fraternity houses as special exceptions in residential high-density and public institutional areas, "the only way that property within [a low density residential district] could be used as a fraternity house would be by the granting of a variance."[84]

When a municipality's legislative branch allows a particular use as a permitted use within a zoning district upon application for a special exception or conditional use permit, the permit cannot be denied on the basis that the use is incompatible so long as its impact on the neighborhood does not exceed what was originally contemplated by the legislature. For example, in *Franklin and Marshall College (F&M College) v. Zoning Hearing Board of City of Lancaster*, the college applied for a special exception to convert a single-family dwelling it owns into a boarding house and then lease it to a fraternity.[85] The zoning hearing board rejected the application because there were already other fraternities on the block and adding another one was "not compatible with adjacent and other properties in the district."[86] On appeal from the denial, the *F&M College* court first determined that the proposed parking facility met the minimum off-street parking space requirements.[87] Second, the college sought a variance to allow the structure to extend three feet rather than five feet from the property line, which the board denied.[88] The court agreed with the board that the college would need to amend its plan before receiving a special exception.[89] Third, although neighbors feared the additional parking issues and noise in the neighborhood, the city had legislated that fraternities were a permitted use in this zoning

---

82. *Id.*

83. *Id.* at 544.

84. *Id.* at 544–45 (understanding how such an error was made but remanding to the zoning hearing board for a rehearing as to a variance application for use as a fraternity house).

85. 371 A.2d 557, 558–559 (Pa. Commw. Ct. 1977).

86. *Id.* at 559.

87. *Id.*

88. *Id.*

89. *Id.* at 560.

district.⁹⁰ Therefore, the neighbors would need "to show that the impact of the proposed fraternity house on the public interest would be 'greater than that normally to be expected from such cases.'"⁹¹ While the court appreciated the neighbors' protestations about the potential impact on the peace and quiet of their neighborhood, there was no evidence in the record showing that the proposed use would have "'any substantial effect on the health, welfare and safety of the community.'"⁹² Therefore, the *F&M College* court ordered that the zoning hearing board grant a special exception to the college once it amended its plan to meet the five-foot side yard requirement.⁹³

The court in *Tempo Holding Co. v. Oxford City Council* reviewed a similar denial of a special use to allow a fraternity to locate in a commercial district.⁹⁴ The zoning ordinance at issue permitted residences in a commercial district as an "additional use" so long as the proposed use met certain enumerated standards.⁹⁵ Tempo applied for an additional-use permit to use its property located in a commercial district as a fraternity or sorority house.⁹⁶ Tempo's property was within two blocks of multiple-unit student housing and other fraternity and sorority houses, but these nearby properties were in a residential district, which specifically permitted such uses.⁹⁷ Neighbors opposed Tempo's proposed use, alleging that it would interfere with a nearby funeral home and would change the character of the neighborhood.⁹⁸ After the city denied the permit, the trial court found that Tempo had complied with the standards required by the zoning code and that the denial was an arbitrary exclusion of fraternity and sorority uses.⁹⁹ The appellate court concluded that the trial court's finding "was supported by a preponderance of reliable, probative, and substantial evidence" requiring that a permit be issued.¹⁰⁰

---

90. *Id.*
91. *Id.*
92. *Id.* (quoting the lower court decision).
93. *Id.*
94. 603 N.E.2d 414, 415 (Ohio Ct. App. 1992).
95. *Id.*
96. *Id.*
97. *Id.*
98. *Id.* at 416.
99. *Id.* at 418.
100. *Id.* at 419.

Conversely, in *Brooks v. Fisher*, the City of Martin's Board of Zoning Appeals denied Tennessee landowners' request for a permit to lease their property for use as a fraternity house by Phi Kappa Tau Fraternity.[101] The city's zoning ordinance provided that fraternities, as well as other specified uses, are permitted as a matter of right in a residential district so long as they are approved by the Board of Zoning Appeals and comply with any permit conditions necessary to protect the character of the district.[102] In that case, the board denied the permit after neighbors testified that the fraternity's occupation of the property had been noisy, unruly, and generally incompatible with the community.[103] The court concluded that the zoning ordinance grants an "absolute right to use this property for a fraternity house" if it complies with reasonable conditions imposed by the board.[104] Thus, the board cannot consider "the testimony of the neighbors concerning the activities of plaintiffs' present tenants in the property" in deciding whether to grant the permit.[105] The court held that the board acted arbitrarily and capriciously in denying the permit and remanded the case so that the board could "prescribe any reasonable conditions and requirements for obtaining the permit requested."[106]

When a fraternity house is using premises permitted under a special-use permit, a city should also permit proposed accessory uses to the primary use as a special use unless there is evidence that such a use "will impair the character, welfare, convenience, and property values of the neighborhood in question."[107] In *City of Baltimore v. Poe*, Phi Sigma Delta Alumni Association, John Hopkins University Chapter, Inc., applied to the city for a permit to use property located in a residential district for a fraternity house.[108] A lower court reversed the city's grant of the permit, finding that the fraternity house was a business activity, excluded from the residential zone because it provided room and board and was a "[c]lub, the chief activity of which is a service customarily

---

101. Brooks v. Fisher, 705 S.W.2d 135, 135–36 (Tenn. Ct. App. 1985).
102. *Id.* at 136.
103. *Id.*
104. *Id.* at 138.
105. *Id.* at 137–38.
106. *Id.* at 138.
107. Grand Chapter of Phi Sigma Kappa v. Grosberg, 291 N.Y.S.2d 608 (N.Y. App. Div. 1968).
108. 168 A.2d 193, 193–194 (Md. 1961).

carried on as a business."[109] The appellate court agreed with the city and the fraternity that a fraternity house provides room and board for a small proportion its members, which is only an incidental part of its program.[110] Because the chief activities of a fraternity house are social and educational for all members, rooming facilities are an accessory use and do not make the house a business activity excluded by the zoning ordinance.[111] The court affirmed the city's grant of a permit for the fraternity house.[112]

Variances and special exceptions differ in structure, as described above, but litigants may sometimes confuse the terminology. Although courts will generally "treat the case for what it is, regardless of what the parties call their respective positions," the applicant for a variance or special exception must present the required evidence for the issuance of the appropriate permit.[113] In 1958, the Phi Lambda Theta fraternity associated with Bucknell University purchased a new fraternity house and applied for a certificate of occupancy.[114] The board of adjustment granted the certificate, but "protesting neighbors appealed to the Court of Common Pleas, which reversed the Board and revoked the certificate."[115] Upon review of the ordinance describing permitted uses in a residential district, the court determined "that the Fraternity may exist as a multiple dwelling under subsection A, and as a fraternity house, without the need of a special exception, under sub-section H."[116] Therefore, the court determined that neither a variance nor a special exception was required for a certificate of occupancy.[117] Because zoning ordinances "impose restrictions on the free use of property and are in derogation of the common law," a court must strictly construe such restrictions.[118] Subsection H defined a permitted use in a residential district as "Club, fraternity house,

---

109. *Id.* at 195.
110. *Id.* at 196.
111. *Id.*
112. *Id.* at 197.
113. Application of Phi Lambda Theta House Assn., 161 A.2d 144, 145 (Pa. 1960) (citing Root v. City of Erie Zoning Bd., 118 A.2d 297 (Pa. Super. Ct. 1955)).
114. *Id.* at 144–145.
115. *Id.* at 145.
116. *Id.*
117. *Id.*
118. *Id.* at 146.

or lodge when authorized as a special exception."[119] Without the existence of a comma after "lodge," the court construed subsection H, as written "Club. Fraternity house. Lodge, when authorized as a special exception," and concluded that the fraternity did not need a special exception.[120] This case serves as a reminder that ordinances restricting the use of land are subject to strict construction and that such construction may provide relief to a fraternal organization dealing with zoning regulations.

e. Nonconforming Uses

A municipality may permit a use that existed before it adopted a zoning ordinance or after it amended a zoning ordinance to exclude the existing use. Officials may permit a nonconforming use to remain until the use changes, is abandoned, or the ordinance specifies amortization after specific events or a set timeline. A change in ownership does not destroy the preexisting nonconforming use so long as the property is used substantially the same way as the nonconforming use.[121] However, in some situations involving a fraternity or sorority house, a discontinuance of a nonconforming use, even for a short time, may terminate the nonconforming use.[122] For example, in *Schweizer v. Board of Adjustment of City of Newark*, the University of Delaware suspended the Pi Kappa Alpha (PIKE) fraternity for violating the university's rules of conduct.[123] The city evicted the PIKE fraternity members and advised the property owner that it could no longer use the property as a fraternity or sorority house because the nonconforming use terminated.[124] The owners leased the premises to another fraternity within a year of learning of PIKE's suspension and argued that the Newark Code allows a revival of a nonconforming use within a year of discontinuance.[125] However, the applicable zoning ordinance provided that when a university suspends a fra-

---

119. *Id.* at 145.
120. *Id.* at 146.
121. Triangle Fraternity v. City of Normal ex rel. Norman Bd. Of Adjustment, 63 P.3d 1, 8 (Okla. 2002).
122. Schweizer v. Bd. Of Adjustment, No. 07A-08-007, 2009 WL 597630, at *4 (Del. Super. Ct. March 4, 2009).
123. *Id.* at *3.
124. *Id.* at *1.
125. *Id.* at *4.

ternity, the nonconforming use of the property expires immediately.[126] Thus, subsequently leasing to another fraternity within a year of discontinuance did not preserve the nonconforming use.[127]

In *Triangle Fraternity v. City of Norman, ex rel. Norman Bd. of Adjustment*, the Supreme Court of Oklahoma held that a fraternity's proposed "use as a residential building for persons who are not members of the same family" was substantially the same as the preexisting use, thus the existing nonconforming use continued to the fraternity.[128] The property was a fraternity or sorority house between 1930 and 1958, and from 1958 to 2000, it was a retirement home for women, owned by a church.[129] The fraternity house and retirement home both met the definition of a boarding house under the zoning code and the city required that fraternities and sororities obtain a boarding house permit.[130] The court determined that a fraternity house would not significantly change the character of the neighborhood because:

> [t]he only real difference in the fraternity's proposed use and the Church's prior use of the property is the age of the occupants coupled with an increase in the volume, intensity, and frequency of social gatherings. However, a mere increase in volume, intensity, or frequency of a nonconforming use is generally recognized as insufficient to invalidate it.[131]

Similarly, the court in *State ex rel. Fraze v. Peve* found that the board of adjustment had substantial evidence to conclude that the conversion of a nonconforming rooming house into a nonconforming fraternity house did not terminate the nonconforming use.[132] A zoning ordinance in the city of Maryville, Missouri, allowed "one non-conforming use [to be changed] to another so long as two conditions are met: first, that the second non-conforming use be 'of the same degree of non-conformity' as the first; and, second that no 'structural alterations' be made in the

---

126. *Id.*
127. *Id.*
128. 63 P.3d 1, 7–8 (Okla., 2002).
129. *Id.* at 7.
130. *Id.*
131. *Id.*
132. 614 S.W.3d 23, 24 (Mo. Ct. App. 1981).

structure in connection with the change of use."¹³³ The parties in this case agreed that because both a rooming house and a fraternity house have the same classification under the Maryville zoning ordinance, they are "'of the same degree of non-conformity.'"¹³⁴ However, neighborhood residents alleged that the alterations made to the house were structural in character.¹³⁵ The court affirmed the trial court and board of adjustment conclusion that under the Maryville zoning ordinance, "[n]one of the described alterations constituted a 'structural alteration.'"¹³⁶

Zoning policy is against indefinitely extending nonconforming uses because the public goal is to eliminate such uses so that eventually the zoning districts will contain only conforming uses.¹³⁷ Extending or increasing an existing nonconforming use will allow local authorities to discontinue the nonconformity as "[t]he public effort is not to extend a nonconforming use but rather to permit it to exist as long as necessary and then to require conformity in the future."¹³⁸ Contrary to the court's finding in *Triangle Fraternity* that using property as a fraternity was not an extension of a nonconforming use, the court in *Coleman v. City of Walla Walla* held that using property as a fraternity house "would constitute an extension of an existing non-conforming use in violation of the zoning regulations."¹³⁹ In *Triangle Fraternity*, the existing nonconforming use was a retirement home for women; while in *Coleman*, the existing nonconforming use was a rooming house.¹⁴⁰ Even though these two decisions may appear incongruous, each determination as to whether a nonconforming use has changed significantly to justify its termination depends on the facts of the case and the court's view of zoning policies.¹⁴¹

---

133. *Id.* at 24.

134. *Id.*

135. *Id.* at 24–25.

136. *Id.* at 25.

137. Coleman v. City of Walla Walla, 266 P.2d 1034, 1035–36 (Wash. 1954).

138. *Id.* at 1036.

139. *Id.* at 1037.

140. *Compare* Triangle Fraternity v. City of Norman, 63 P.3d 1, 3 (Okla., 2002), *with* Coleman, 266 P.2d 1034, 1035–1036 (Wash. 1954).

141. *See e.g.*, 425 Prop. Ass'n of Alpha Chi Rho, Inc. v. State Coll. Borough Zoning Hearing Bd., 223 A.3d 300, 313 (Pa. Commw. Ct. 2019) (holding that property used as a fraternity house before the adoption of a zoning ordinance restricting the definition of "Fraternity House" was a lawful nonconforming use that could be continued even though

When a nonconforming use is abandoned, it may no longer be able to continue operating. In *Sigma Gamma Fraternity, Inc. v. Barilla*, the City of Oswego Zoning Board of Appeals (ZBA) determined that the fraternity "abandoned the prior nonconforming use of its property as a fraternity house."[142] The court held that this finding was consistent with the terms of the ordinance and substantial evidence supported the ZBA's conclusion that the abandonment was voluntary.[143] However, the mere cessation of a nonconforming use does not destroy the right to continue or resume the use so long as the use is not abandoned.[144] In *State ex rel. Morehouse v. Hunt*, the Supreme Court of Wisconsin determined that the owner of a property did not abandon the nonconforming use, where the property was originally used as a fraternity before and after a zoning ordinance was enacted that restricted the area to single-family residences.[145] Instead, by temporarily using it as a residence until it could lease or sell the building as a fraternity house, the owner had a right to continue the nonconforming use.[146]

f. Eminent Domain and Takings

The Fifth Amendment to the US Constitution provides in part, "nor shall private property be taken for a public use without just compensation."[147] When the government condemns private property under the Fifth Amendment, there must be a public purpose to promote the general health, safety, morals, and welfare of the community.[148] The defini-

---

Penn State withdrew recognition of Alpha Chi Rho as a fraternity); *329 Prospect Avenue Corp. v. State Coll. Borough Zoning Hearing Bd.*, No. 1635 C.D. 2018, 2019 WL 6770148, at *2 (Pa. Commw. Ct. Dec. 12, 2019) (relying on *425 Prop. Ass'n of Alpha Chi Rho, Inc.* in concluding that the use of the property as a fraternity was a lawful nonconforming use that could continue after Penn State withdrew its recognition of Sigma Alpha Mu because the zoning ordinance restricting fraternity use based on its relationship with the university was implemented in 2010, well after the house received a special exception in 1989).

142. 810 N.Y.S.2d 698, 698 (App. Div. 2006).
143. *Id.*
144. State ex. rel. Morehouse v. Hunt, 291 N.W. 745, 750 (Wis. 1940).
145. *Id.* at 749.
146. *Id.* at 750 (concluding that a lapse for a year was a reasonable time to resume the nonconforming use).
147. U.S. CONST. amend. V.
148. *Id.*

tion of what constitutes a public purpose is broad and is entitled to great deference by the courts.[149] In *Sigma Tau Gamma Fraternity House Corp. v. City of Menomonie*, the city attempted to condemn the fraternity's property under Wisconsin's Tax Increment Law.[150] In 1978, the city adopted a resolution to take the property necessary "for the purpose of elimination of blighted and slum areas within the City of Menomonie."[151] The Supreme Court of Wisconsin determined that the Tax Increment Law did not authorize the city to condemn the fraternity's property by eminent domain.[152] Although the court found that the law was constitutionally valid, "the law was intended only as a financing vehicle for projects, not as a new and independent authorization for further urban redevelopment projects."[153] While the city has a right to eliminate blight by condemning land, it must exercise this power under the statute that authorizes condemnation for such a purpose.[154]

Landowners may also demand compensation by bringing an inverse condemnation claim when the government regulation restricts their property so severely that they no longer have a private property interest remaining.[155] Some states also have a "damagings clause" in their constitutions, which requires the government to pay just compensation when a public action damages private property. For example, in *Mayor of Athens v. Gamma Delta Chapter House Corp.*, the court explained that the Georgia Constitution provides that "private property shall not be taken *or damaged* for public purposes without just and adequate compensation being first paid."[156] In this case, the sorority had been using a strip of land for a roadway as its sole means of access to its property for

---

149. Kelo v. City of New London, 545 U.S. 469 (2005).
150. 288 N.W.2d 85, 86 (Wis. 1980).
151. *Id.* at 87.
152. *Id.* at 88.
153. *Id.*
154. *Id.* at 89.
155. Pa. Coal v. Mahon, 260 U.S. 393, 415–16 (1922) ("[W]hile property may be regulated to certain extent, if regulation goes too far, it will be recognized as a taking."); *see e.g.*, Lucas v. S.C. Coastal Council, 505 U.S. 1003 (1992); Penn Cent. Transp. Co, v. City of New York, 438 U.S. 104 (1978); Horne v. Dep't of Agric., 476 U.S. 350 (2015); Cedar Point Nursery v. Hassid, 141 S. Ct. 2063 (2021) for additional examples of private property being restricted due to regulatory action.
156. 70 S.E.2d 621, 623 (Ga. Ct. App. 1952).

twelve years.[157] The city destroyed this easement of access when it "excavated, graded and constructed a street and sidewalk ... leaving a 17-foot bank, which is too steep to permit the building of a driveway into the [sorority's] premises."[158] Therefore, the city's actions in developing a street destroyed the ingress and egress to the sorority's property, entitling the sorority to a judgment for the market value impairment.[159]

g. State Preemption

State or federal law may also preempt local ordinances that conflict with the sovereign law. One Oregon municipality attempted to restrict the consumption of alcohol on premises occupied by a fraternity via a zoning ordinance that established a strict liability crime for any person who permitted or hosted a juvenile party on their premises where a minor consumed or possessed alcohol.[160] The court in *City of Corvallis v. Pi Kappa Phi* held that the city's "hosting" ordinance was unconstitutional, even though Corvallis was a home rule city.[161] Viewing the city ordinance as criminalizing conduct, the court analyzed the preemption challenge according to any conflicts between the ordinance and state law under Oregon's Liquor Control Act.[162] It declared that "[a]n ordinance that criminalizes conduct conflicts with a state statute if it 'either prohibits conduct that the statute permits ... or permits conduct that the statute prohibits."[163] The *Corvallis* court extensively analyzed both the city ordinance and the state statute, finding that the state statute preempted the ordinance because the ordinance created a strict liability crime whereas the state legislature made a "deliberate choice not to punish property owners" when the property owner is not culpable.[164]

---

157. *Id.* at 622.
158. *Id.* at 622.
159. *Id.* at 624.
160. City of Corvallis v. Pi Kappa Phi, 428 P.3d 905, 906 (Or. Ct. App. 2018).
161. *Id.* at 907.
162. *Id.* at 909.
163. *Id.* at 908 (quoting State v. Krueger, 144 P.3d 1007, 1008 (Or. Ct. App. 2006)).
164. *Id.* at 912.

II. Neighbors and Private Land-Use Controls

a. Restrictive Covenants

Restrictive covenants are private contractual agreements regarding the use of land. These promises restrict the use of land in conflict with the policy that law favors the free alienability of property such that the court will strictly construe restrictive covenants against the party trying to enforce the promise. In *Smith v. Lambda Alpha Epsilon Fraternity Inc.*, single-family homeowners sought to enjoin the use of neighboring property as a fraternity based on a restrictive covenant restricting the properties to residential purposes with no two-family houses or flats allowed.[165] The court held that the covenant limited the use to "residential purposes" and although a college fraternity is not a "single family," it is a residence and because the intent of the covenant was unclear, a trial was required to resolve the issue.[166]

In *Mu Chapter Bldg. Fund v. Henry*, the trial court determined whether a fraternity house would violate a covenant requiring "that the premises 'shall not be used otherwise than for residence purpose.'"[167] The Supreme Court of Georgia affirmed the trial court decision and held that a fraternity house is distinguishable from a boarding house and its operation would violate the restrictive covenant.[168] The court had previously interpreted an identical restrictive covenant to allow the operation of a boarding house.[169] However, here the activities of a fraternity house "when engaged in by exuberant and hilarious young people, might reasonably be said to constitute a decided disturbance to the peace and quiet of a sedate and elderly group of peaceful citizens in a strictly residential neighborhood" and thus violate a restrictive covenant designed to pursue such peace and quiet.[170] Similarly, the Supreme Court of Michigan in *Seeley v. Phi Sigma Delta House Corporation* held that a restrictive covenant with the purpose "to maintain the quiet, the privacy, and family character of a residential district," limited land use to "one single

---

165. 224 N.Y.T.S.2d 878, 879 (Sup. Ct. 1961).
166. *Id.* at 880 (denying the neighbors a temporary injunction).
167. 51 S.E.2d 841, 843–44 (Ga. 1949).
168. *Id.* at 844.
169. *Id.* at 843.
170. *Id.*

private dwelling house."[171] Concluding that a court cannot use definitions from housing codes and zoning ordinances to construe a restrictive covenant, the court determined that the restriction "means one house, for a single family, living in a private state, and prohibits a college fraternity."[172]

b. Nuisance

The law of nuisance prevents the substantial and unreasonable, non-trespassory interference with a neighbor's use and enjoyment of their property. It is a property tort, which provides a remedy in the form of an injunction or damages, sometimes referred to as "judicial zoning." Unlike public controls of land use through zoning and housing codes, which are proactive in nature to prevent conflicting land uses, nuisance provides a reactive response to a neighbor's interference with nearby properties.

In *Edmunds v. Sigma Chapter of Alpha Kappa*, the trial court determined that the use of rural property for fraternity social events was a nuisance justifying injunctive relief and the appellate court affirmed.[173] The local chapter at Central Missouri State University formed a non-profit corporation to buy property and make it available for student use.[174] Adjacent neighbors, the Edmunds, sued the corporation, alleging nuisance from the fraternity social events and seeking injunctive relief.[175] The court decision included an extensive discussion of the offending activities such as noise from parties until 3:00 a.m. or 4:00 a.m., vehicles on the property with "music blaring" and "tires spinning," large crowds with yelling and chanting, gun target practice, parties of 600 or 700 people, and trash littering on adjacent properties.[176]

After determining that the use of the fraternity property constituted a nuisance, the trial court directed the corporation to abate the nuisance with specific instructions as to activities prohibited on the property, such as restricting weapon discharges, limiting the maximum number

---

171. 222 N.W. 180, 182 (Mich. 1928).
172. *Id.*
173. 87 S.W.3d 21, 23 (Mo. Ct. App. 2002).
174. *Id.* at 23.
175. *Id.* at 23–24.
176. *Id.* at 24–25.

of people allowed on the property, and designating a contact person for violations.[177] The corporation appealed, contending that the trial court lacked jurisdiction because it failed to join the local chapter of the fraternity as a necessary party.[178] However, based on the privity between the local chapter and the corporation, the court determined that the members of the local chapter were *not* indispensable parties.[179] The corporation also argued that the trial court's restrictions were not a proper balancing of the equities between the parties and that the court should have considered the fraternity's occupation of the premises before the Edmunds purchased their property.[180] The appellate court agreed that the priority of occupation is a factor in determining reasonableness of the owner's use of land, but there was no evidence that the trial court failed to consider this factor when it concluded that the corporation's use of the property was a nuisance.[181] Finally, the court reviewed the trial court's remedy as to scope and breadth and concluded that the trial court acted within its discretion in fashioning the various requirements.[182]

c. Other Neighborhood Challenges

Neighbors may also challenge the construction or expansion of student housing as violating environmental statutes, such as when the construction or expansion of existing housing allegedly causes significant environmental impacts. In *Elmwood Neighborhood Ass'n v. City of Davis*, a neighborhood association alleged that the city violated the California Environmental Quality Act (CEQA) when it concluded that a project to expand student housing for the Cal Aggie Christian Association (CA) did not create a significant impact on the environment and issued a mitigated negative declaration.[183] The court affirmed the trial court's denial of the neighbors' petition for writ of mandate, finding that there was no substantial evidence that this infill project along Russell Boulevard, re-

---

177. *Id.* at 25–26.
178. *Id.* at 26.
179. *Id.* at 28.
180. *Id.* at 29.
181. *Id.* at 29.
182. *Id.* at 30.
183. No. C052006, 2007 WL 2471050, at *3 (Cal. Ct. App. 2007).

ferred to as "fraternity row," would create significant adverse impacts to the physical environment.[184]

III. Property Issues Within the Fraternal Organization and the College or University

The relationship among local chapters, national and international fraternal organizations, and the colleges or universities to which they are connected, may create confusion over property ownership and the incidents of property ownership in real estate transactions. In *Gamma Eta Chapter of Pi Kappa Alpha v. Helvey*,[185] a nonprofit housing corporation attempted to compel the local chapter of an international fraternity to submit to arbitration after the local chapter sued the housing corporation.[186] The local chapter alleged that the housing corporation, which leased the fraternity house from a landlord and then subleased it to undergraduate students at the University of Southern California (USC), "grossly inflated expenses and overcharged the chapter by more than $106,000," and committed acts constituting "constructive fraud, breach of fiduciary duty, unjust enrichment, negligent misrepresentation, and [other claims]."[187]

Each member of the USC fraternity signed an individual lease with the housing corporation, which acted as the local chapter's agent in negotiating with landlords for lease terms and pricing.[188] These individual leases between the housing corporation and the students did not contain an arbitration provision and there was no contract between the housing corporation and the local chapter as a whole.[189] Nevertheless, the student members of the local chapter were required to sign an agreement, which described the relationship between the local chapter and the interna-

---

184. *Id.* at *1.
185. 258 Cal. Rptr. 3d 260 (Ct. App. 2020).
186. *Id.* at 262.
187. *Id.* at 262–264.
188. *Id.* at 263.
189. *Id.*

tional fraternity.[190] This agreement provided as a condition of membership, stating that the student member agreed to arbitrate any disputes between the member, the chapter, the fraternity, or any person *affiliated* with the fraternity.[191] The international fraternity recognized the housing corporation as affiliated with the fraternity and directed the local chapter to "immediately withdraw its lawsuit and seek to resolve this dispute first by mediation, and if not successful, then by binding arbitration."[192] The *Helvy* court found that the local chapter was subordinate to the international fraternity and could not disregard the authority of the instruction to mediate or arbitrate.[193] Thus, because both the international fraternity and the housing corporation demanded arbitration, the court reversed the trial court decision denying the motion to compel arbitration and remanded for the trial court to compel the local chapter to arbitrate with the housing corporation.[194]

When a college or university terminates its relationship with a fraternity or sorority, the membership's lease of the fraternal house may be in jeopardy. The Supreme Court of Maine in *Chi Realty Corporation v. Colby College*[195] held that the college did not breach its agreement for the lease of a house to Zeta Psi Fraternity when its trustees decided to dispossess all fraternities from houses on campus.[196] The agreement provided that the college would recognize the realty corporation's property rights if the fraternity no longer had a chapter at Colby.[197] The court held that the fraternity did not need to breach its obligations to the college to maintain academic and social standards in order for the agreement between the college and the realty corporation to terminate. It was sufficient that the decision of the college to change its housing policy and withdraw recognition of all fraternities resulted in the termination of its agreement with the realty corporation when Zeta Psi Fraternity ceased to have a chapter at Colby College.[198]

---

190. *Id.*
191. *Id.*
192. *Id.* at 267.
193. *Id.*
194. *Id.* at 262, 269.
195. 513 A.2d 866 (Me. 1986).
196. *Id.* at 867.
197. *Id.* at 868.
198. *Id.*

The title to real property used as a fraternity or sorority house may be at issue when local or national fraternal organizations terminate or merge their corporate identities. For example, in *Pi Lambda Phi Fraternity, Inc. v. Seneca Beta Corp.* the appellate court affirmed the trial court's denial of summary judgment, finding that there were clear issues of fact that needed to be resolved at trial.[199] First, there was an issue to whether the alleged merger of Beta Sigma Tau Fraternity into Pi Lambda Phi Fraternity was intended to include the real property owned by Beta Sigma Tau.[200] Second was the issue of the interpretation of Seneca Beta Corporation's certificate of incorporation as to its operation of the premises as a boarding or rooming house after the Hobart College Chapter of Beta Sigma Tau Fraternity was no longer an active fraternity.[201] Finally, the court needed to determine "whether the chapter of Beta Sigma Tau at Hobart College ceased to function as an active fraternity and if so, whether the parent Beta Sigma Tau Fraternity was not then functioning as an active national fraternity."[202] For a convoluted, quiet title action involving a local fraternity chapter, a national chapter, and purchasers at a foreclosure sale, see *Sigma Tau Gamma Fraternity Delta Chapter v. Citizens Building and Loan Ass'n.*[203]

A college or university may also attempt to require property owners to sell fraternity or sorority houses to the institution when housing programs change. Colgate University unanimously adopted a new residential program requiring most students to live in university-owned housing beginning in the 2005–06 academic year.[204] To implement this new program, the university required all fraternities and sororities, whose affiliates owned their houses, to transfer ownership of their houses by the end of 2004.[205] The university agreed to negotiate the purchase price for these chapter houses, but indicated it would withdraw recognition from any fraternity that refused to sell the house to the university.[206] The

---

199. 388 N.Y.S.2d 802, 804 (App. Div. 1976).
200. *Id.*
201. *Id.*
202. *Id.*
203. 67 P.2d 582 (Kan. 1937).
204. Delta Kappa Epsilon Alumni Corp v. Colgate Univ., No. 2005-1762, 2006 WL 568314, at *1 (N.Y. Sup. Ct. 2006).
205. *Id.*
206. *Id.* at *2.

Delta Kappa Epsilon (DKE) fraternity refused to sell and sought declaratory and injunctive relief to prevent Colgate from withdrawing its recognition.[207] The court severely limited its judicial review of an educational institution's academic and administrative decisions to whether the institution's action was arbitrary and irrational and if it acted in good faith.[208] It found that the statute of limitations barred the action and that Colgate did not act in bad faith or arbitrarily or capriciously when it implemented a new residential education program that required the university to own the student housing property.[209]

IV. Conclusion

Zoning plays a vital role in allowing local governments to regulate land uses in their area. Fraternities and sororities present a unique opportunity for creative regulation, and courts differ in their approaches to dealing with these organizations and their desire for housing. Ultimately, municipalities have the power to regulate these organizations as long as the regulation is not arbitrary or capricious. The structure of fraternal organizations can present challenges to local governments in determining ownership, but precedent provides avenues of solutions for problems created by complex ownership dynamics.

Although issues remain in determining the definition of "single-family" and "residential" uses, municipalities' use of institutional zoning has provided potential solutions to these zoning problems by connecting the fraternal organization with the local university or college for regulation assistance. Recognizing that institutional zoning depends on this connection, the loss of good standing or recognition by the university or college could change zoning allowances for fraternal organizations. Fraternal organizations illustrate the challenges associated with land-use planning as well as the solutions embedded in planning and exceptions for nontraditional land uses. Using variances, conditional use and special permits, and nonconforming use exceptions, fraternal organizations

---

207. *Id.*
208. *Id.*
209. *Id.* at *3–4.

have found success via the institution of land-use planning and the availability of judicial review of local land-use decisions.

Index

#

15 U.S.C. §45 (Section 5 of the Federal Trade Commission Act), 335, 352, 353, 356
15 U.S.C. §§ 1-2, 334–337, 340, 342, 347, 348, 351, 353
18 U.S.C. §241, 237
42 U.S.C. §1983, 237
42 U.S.C. §1985, 237
501(c) entities
   501(c)(2), 65, 85, 86, 89
   501(c)(3), 65, 66, 67, 70, 71, 73, 80, 81, 82, 83, 84, 85, 86, 90, 380
   501(c)(4), 65, 89, 90, 380
   501(c)(7), 54, 57, 65, 66, 67, 68, 69, 70, 71, 73, 75, 76, 77, 80, 82, 83, 88, 89, 327

A

ABC test, 370
Actual agency, 207, 211, 290
Actual authority, 120, 253
Administrative searches, 257
Adverse selection, 206
African American, 94, 114, 117, 118, 124, 126, 236, 287, 311, 319–324, 326, 327, 329, 396, 407
Age Discrimination in Employment Act of 1967, 371, 386
Agency relationship, 119, 120, 172, 173, 187, 207, 210–212, 216, 217, 222, 290
Agent, 10, 94, 119, 120, 166, 290, 464
Alcohol, 37, 49, 60, 93, 100, 118, 119, 121, 133, 141, 146, 148, 155–157, 160, 162, 167, 168, 169–179, 181, 184–191, 193–195, 200, 201, 204, 209, 212, 213, 217, 218, 220, 254, 270–273, 280, 283, 326, 417, 443, 460
American Association of University Professors, 228
Americans With Disabilities Act, 6, 286, 289, 292–294, 296, 297, 302–306, 371, 372, 374
Andrea Dworkin, 229
Antitrust liability, 334, 341, 342, 344, 365
Apparent agency, 290
Apparent authority, 120, 174, 207, 252, 253
Arbitrary marks, 404
Arbitration agreement, 114, 116, 127, 134
Area variance, 447–449
Assistance animals, 298–300, 302
Assumption of duty, 186

B

Berkeley Free Speech Movement, 229
Black fraternities and sororities, 114, 117, 287, 319–321, 323, 325, 329
Board of directors, 10, 21, 26, 55–59, 62, 83, 89, 94, 99, 108, 381
Bull Connor, 229
Bundle markets, 339
Business Judgment Rule, 37, 39, 41, 43, 50
Bylaws, 57–63, 127, 173, 186, 409, 421

C

Catharine Mackinnon, 229
Censorship , 230, 236
Chief legal officer, 12, 13
Cigarette Rule, 354, 355, 357, 358, 363
Civil liability, 39, 93, 107, 110, 119, 120, 168, 174, 207, 209
Civil Rights, 51, 123, 144, 149–151, 229, 237, 239, 242, 261, 262, 278, 279, 282, 285, 286, 288, 304–307, 319, 326, 329, 371, 372, 439
Civil Rights Movement, 229, 285, 286
Clery Act, 150
Cluster markets, 339
Common household animals , 300
Community caretaker exception, 258, 259
Compliance, 4, 5, 7–10, 12, 13, 22–24, 26, 34–36, 40, 42, 45, 48–50, 52, 61, 93, 95–104, 106–110, 204, 286, 287, 292, 384, 448
Compliance program, 7, 35, 48, 95, 96, 99–103, 109
Conditional use permit , 450, 451
Confusion as to sponsorship or affiliation , 433
Consent exception, 245, 246, 248, 252–254, 256
Consumer class, 351
Consumer injury, 355, 356
Content-based restriction , 239
Control test, 369, 370

Copyright , 390, 395–398, 419, 430, 435–437
Corporate criminality, 38, 39, 45, 47, 49
Corporate governance, 3, 12, 39, 41, 53, 54, 58, 59, 63, 99, 100, 103, 105, 107
Criminal liability, 39, 44, 48, 93–96, 101, 103, 109, 220
Critical Race Theory, 229
Custodial liability, 215, 216

D

Dear Colleague Letter, 149–151
Defend Trade Secrets Act of 2016, 393
Deferred rush policy, 271
Deliberate indifference, 41, 153, 154, 273
Department of Education , 146, 149–152, 154, 231
Derivative litigation, 107
Descriptive fair use, 430
Descriptive marks, 403
Digital Millennium Copyright Act, 398
Disability, 293, 295, 296, 300, 372
Disciplinary sanctions, 274
Disparate negative impact, 311
Distinctive mark , 401, 403, 411, 415
Domestic service, 384
Dormant Chapter Houses, 88
Dormitory rooms, 288, 289
Due-process clause, 250, 251
Dupont factors, 405, 406
Duty of care, 40, 97, 98, 134
Duty of loyalty, 40
Duty of obedience, 40, 95, 97, 98, 100, 109
Duty of oversight, vi, xx, 37, 39, 41, 42, 43, 45, 47, 49, 50, 51, 52
Dwelling, 162, 180, 181, 183, 216, 285, 286, 288, 293, 294, 308–310, 315–318, 325, 326, 328, 329, 360, 440, 442, 445, 458, 461

INDEX

E

Emotional support animals, 296, 299, 301
Employee, 22, 26, 102, 103, 109, 367–373, 375–380, 382–387, 396
Employment at will, 367, 368
Enterprise employer, 377, 382
Equal Credit Opportunity Act of 1974, 328
Equal Pay Act, 375, 377
Equal protection violations, 262
Ethics, 4–6, 12, 13, 24–28, 36, 355
Exceedingly persuasive justification, 265, 275, 281
Exigent circumstances, 254, 255

F

Fair Housing Act of 1968, 286–294, 296–301, 303, 304, 307, 308, 310, 311, 314
Fair Labor Standards Act, 375, 377, 382–384
Fair use, 396, 398, 430, 431, 436, 437
Family and Medical Leave Act of 1993, 375, 376
Fanciful marks, 404, 405
Federal Arbitration Act, 123, 136
Federal funding, 149, 241, 261, 262, 273, 309
Federal Trade Commission, 6, 335, 336, 339, 352–358, 363–365
Fiduciary, 102
Financing, 4, 17, 287, 319, 324–329, 459
Foreseeability, 157–163, 165, 178, 179, 191, 192
Fraternal organization, 35, 53, 54, 57–60, 62, 65, 71, 73, 81, 88, 93, 99, 113, 114, 116–121, 125, 126, 142–144, 145–149, 152–155, 161, 162, 167, 168, 169, 170, 176, 179, 182–185, 192, 197–203, 205, 209, 214, 215, 217, 218, 223, 227, 231, 233, 236, 238–243, 245, 246, 253, 256, 260, 262, 263, 266–283, 285–287, 289, 291–293, 303, 304, 306, 308–310, 312, 315–329, 334, 345–349, 352, 359, 360, 364, 365, 367, 389, 390, 411, 426, 439–442, 447–449, 451, 453, 456, 465–467
Fraternity and sorority housing, 245, 246, 248, 249, 251–255, 258, 259, 289, 291, 292, 297, 300–302, 304, 305, 321, 323–327, 329, 330, 334, 346, 359
Fraternity foundation, 56, 73, 83
Fraternity/Sorority House, 61, 83, 87, 133, 155, 156, 162, 165, 166, 177, 180, 182–184, 186, 189–191, 207, 219, 222, 254, 255, 269, 305, 316–318, 321, 323, 384, 440–443, 445, 446, 448–459, 461, 464
Freedom of association, 277
Freedom of speech, 227, 229, 230, 232, 242, 432
Fundamental right, 265

G

Gender-based stereotypes, 276, 278, 279, 281
Generic terms, 403
Genetic Information Non-Discrimination Act of 2008, 376
Geographic market, 337, 338, 348, 350
George Wallace, 229
Good faith immunity, 232, 233, 237
Governance structure, 40, 58, 62
Governing documents, 57, 126

H

Harvard ban on single-sex organizations, 278–281
Hate speech, 20, 71, 164, 167, 213, 223, 230, 234, 236, 239, 240, 309
Hazing, 36, 37, 49–51, 93–95, 100, 103, 110, 111, 113, 114, 116–123, 133, 134, 141, 142, 148, 164, 167, 176, 200, 201, 204, 205, 207, 209, 211–213, 217–223, 262, 268, 270–273, 283, 367

Heightened protection, 263
Higher Education Act, 230, 231, 241
Historical preservation-designation, 444
Housing corporation, 53, 55, 56, 61, 88, 181, 383, 464, 465
HUD's 2020 Guidance Notice, 297

I

Immigration Reform and Control Act of 1986, 371
Immunity, 43, 232, 233, 237, 238, 341–344
Important governmental purpose, 275
In-house counsel, 3–13, 15–24, 28, 29, 31–36
In-house legal department, 5, 8–10, 12, 13, 15–24, 29–32, 35
In loco parentis, 185, 197, 216, 248, 250, 255, 258
Independent contractor, 369, 385, 396
Initiation, 99, 113, 117, 119, 120, 133, 134, 173, 175, 176, 207, 394
Institutional zoning, 445
Insurance, 29–32, 36, 61, 78, 121, 148, 197–206, 208–210, 212–214, 219, 222, 223, 300, 301, 367, 369, 380, 381, 385, 428
Intellectual property, 389, 390, 399, 400, 411, 419, 420, 425, 429
Intent-to-use, 413–415
Interdependence, 237, 261–263, 281–283, 342, 344
Interfraternity and Panhellenic councils, 292
Internal Revenue Code, 65–68, 70–76, 80, 81, 83–85, 88, 89

J

John T. Casteen III, 271
Judicial zoning, 189, 314, 462, 463

K

Karen Haynes, 232

L

Land-use law, 287, 316, 441, 446, 454, 462
Landowner liability, 161, 162, 164–167, 187, 300
Lanham Act, 399, 408, 418, 422
Legally effective consent, 256
Lester Maddox, 229
LGBTQ+, 32, 274, 279, 282, 307, 308, 372
Liability insurance, 31, 198, 202, 203, 205, 206, 214, 218, 222, 223
Litigation, 5, 7, 9, 13, 14, 28, 30, 31, 34, 35, 59, 76, 94, 97, 103–110, 113–116, 119–121, 124, 125, 127, 198–200, 205, 207, 209, 238, 242, 245, 246, 271, 272, 280–282, 289–291, 311, 313, 334, 363, 365, 413, 421, 423, 428, 429, 433, 436, 440
Little FTC Acts, 352, 357

M

Master-servant relationship test, 369
Microaggressions, 232
Minority, 7, 319, 417
Monitoring obligation, 98, 99, 106
Moral hazard, 197, 210, 212–214
Multifamily residential zones, 442
Multi-unit dwellings, 249, 285, 304, 314, 325, 443

N

Nathaniel Hiers, 232
Nazi, 229
Negligence, 37, 42, 114, 122, 133, 146, 155, 157, 161, 164–166, 170, 172, 176, 177, 181, 185, 186, 190, 191, 199, 208, 211, 218–220
Nominative fair use, 430, 431
Non-conformity, 317, 318, 446, 455–458, 467
Nondiscrimination policy, 274, 278
Nonrecognition, 275

O

Occupational Safety and Health Act, 377
Official recognition, 160, 161, 227, 238, 241, 268–271, 275, 277, 445, 446
On behalf of a government entity, 252
Outside counsel, 6, 7, 9, 11–15, 21, 27, 32, 33, 35

P

Parker immunity, 342, 344
Parody, 430–436
Patent, 390–392
Plain Meaning Rule, 203
Practical difficulties test, 447, 448
Privacy/publicity rights, 390
Private actor, 252
Private club, 70, 262, 289–291, 304, 306, 318
Private dispute resolution, 114, 115
Private right of action, 352, 357
Probable cause, 247, 257
Product markets, 336, 338, 339
Property Tax Exemption, 66, 86–88

Q

Quid pro quo harassment, 373

R

Rational basis review, 264
Readily achievable, 305
Reasonable accommodation, 297, 299, 301, 304, 310, 373, 374
Reasonable expectation of privacy, 247, 249, 256
Recruiting, 271, 272, 282
Residential purposes, 461
Respondeat superior, 120, 181, 192, 207, 369
Restatement (Third) of Unfair Competition, 402, 416
Restrictive covenants, 461
Risk management plan, 100, 203, 204

S

Scrutiny, 37, 44, 47, 126, 144, 239, 265, 266, 273, 281, 348
Section 3607(a), 291
Section 5 of the FTC Act, 352, 353
Section 504 of the Rehabilitation Act, 289, 293
Service animal, 294–299, 302, 303
Set aside, 71–73, 79
Sex discrimination, 149, 273, 279–282, 287, 307–309, 314, 330
Sexual assaults, 37, 49, 100, 145–168, 198, 199, 201, 204, 209, 210, 216, 220, 222, 223, 279, 280, 282
Single family, 439–442, 449, 451, 458, 461, 467
Single-sex student groups, 35, 37, 39, 49, 51, 52, 53, 54, 57–60, 62, 65–67, 70–74, 78, 80, 81, 83, 86, 88–91, 93, 99, 113, 114, 116–121, 125, 126, 142–144, 145–148, 152–155, 161, 162, 167, 168, 169, 170, 176, 179, 182–185, 192, 197–203, 205, 207, 209, 210, 213, 214, 217, 218, 223, 227, 231, 236, 238–241, 246, 256, 261–263, 265–283, 285–287, 289, 291, 292, 303, 304, 306, 308–310, 315–329, 333–335, 345–349, 352, 359, 360, 365, 367, 368, 370, 371, 373–385, 387, 389, 390, 399–401, 408, 409, 411, 418–420, 425–427, 433–435, 437, 439–445, 447–449, 451, 453, 456, 464–467
Social club, 54, 57, 69–71, 74, 75, 275, 278, 282, 327
Social host, 169, 170, 174, 177–180, 183, 184, 188, 189, 193, 303, 304
Sorority governance, 54, 58
Special exception, 445, 450–452, 454, 455, 457
Special relationship, 155, 156, 169, 186, 192, 193, 200, 211, 216
Speech codes, 230, 234

Standard of Review, 263
State Action, 237, 261–263, 281–283, 342, 344
Substantial assistance, 175, 178, 179, 184
Substantially similar, 436
Suggestive marks, 404
Suspect class, 265

T

Tax exemption, 66–68, 70, 81, 86–88, 91, 316
Tax-deductible donation, 66, 80
Tenure , 228, 238, 241
Title II of the ADA, 293, 294
Title III of the ADA, 293, 294, 303, 304
Title IX of the Education Amendments of 1972, 147, 149–154, 167, 168, 229, 231, 242, 272, 273, 278–283, 293, 306, 308, 309, 313, 327, 329
Title VI of the Civil Rights Act, 278, 326
Title VII of the Civil Rights Act of 1964, 6, 229, 242, 278, 279, 282, 307, 353, 371, 373
Tort liability, 157, 198, 199, 208, 211
Totality of the circumstances test, 163, 252
Trade dress , 400, 401, 433
Trade secret, 390, 392–394
Trademark, 61, 351, 394, 400, 401, 404, 405, 419, 425, 430, 432, 433, 437

U

Unbridled discretion , 233
Unconscionability, 115, 116, 128–131, 134–144, 358
Undue hardship, 373–375
Unfair and Deceptive Acts and Practices, 352, 357
Unfair trade practice, 334, 335, 359, 365

Uniform Trade Secret Act, 392
United Services Employment and Reemployment Rights Act of 1994, 376
University-student relationship, 255
US Constitution, 123, 278, 390, 458
 Fifth Amendment, 458
 First Amendment, 227, 228, 229, 230, 232, 233, 234, 236, 239, 240, 263, 265, 266, 267, 269, 274, 275, 276, 277, 280, 283, 309
 Fourteenth Amendment (Equal Protection Clause), 228, 256, 261, 262, 263, 264, 268, 272, 273, 278, 281, 282, 283, 292
 Fourth Amendment, 245, 246, 247, 248, 249, 251, 252, 254, 255, 256, 258, 259
US Copyright Office, 396, 435
US Customs and Border Protection, 397
US Department of Justice, 6, 38, 44–48, 51, 294, 295, 303, 304, 311, 314, 335, 336, 338, 341
US Patent and Trademark Office, 390, 391, 399, 401, 404–409, 412–415, 418, 420, 427, 430, 434
Use variance, 447–450
Use-based, 413, 414

V

Variances, 447, 448, 454, 467
Vicarious liability, 7, 166, 167, 186, 187, 215, 217, 289, 290
Voluntary consent, 252–254
Voting rights, 63, 105

W

Warrant , 247, 248, 251, 255–260, 347, 411
Warrantless search, 254–256, 259
Work for hire , 396, 397
Worker's compensation, 376, 378, 384, 385

Y
Yates Memo, 38, 39, 45–49, 51

Z
Zoning regulations, 287, 316, 441, 446, 454, 462
Zoning violation, 445